Behavioral Intervention for Young Children with Autism

A Manual for Parents and Professionals

Behavioral Intervention for Young Children with Autism

A Manual for Parents and Professionals

Edited by

Catherine Maurice

Coeditors

Gina Green, Ph.D.
Director of Research
New England Center for Autism

Stephen C. Luce, Ph.D.
Vice President of Program Operations
Bancroft, Inc.

pro·ed
8700 Shoal Creek Boulevard
Austin, Texas 78757-6897

pro·ed

Library of Congress Cataloging-in-Publication Data

Behavioral intervention for young children with autism : a manual for
    parents and professionals / edited by Catherine Maurice : co
    -editors. Gina Green, Stephen C. Luce.
        p.   cm.
    Includes bibliographical references and index.
    ISBN 0-89079-683-1 (alk. paper)
    1. Autistic children—Rehabilitation.   2. Behavior modification.
    3. Behavior therapy for children.   I. Maurice, Catherine.
    II. Green, Gina.   III. Luce, Stephen C.
RJ509.A9B3427   1996
618.92′898206—dc20   95-26290
                                                             CIP

This book is designed in Cheltenham Book and Syntax.

Production Manager: Alan Grimes
Production Coordinator: Karen Swain
Managing Editor: Tracy Sergo
Art Director: Thomas Barkley
Reprints Buyer: Alicia Woods
Editor: Cindy Hass/Carlisle Publishers Services
Editorial Assistant: Claudette Landry
Editorial Assistant: Martin Wilson

Printed in the United States of America

    4   5   6   7   8   9   10   00   99   98   97

Contents

CHAPTER 4

Are Other Treatments Effective? • 45
Tristram Smith

Part 3
What to Teach

CHAPTER 5

Selecting Teaching Programs • 63
Bridget Ann Taylor and Kelly Ann McDonough

Part 4
How to Teach

CHAPTER 6

Teaching New Skills to Young Children with Autism • 181
Stephen R. Anderson, Marie Taras, and Barbara O'Malley Cannon

CHAPTER 7
Behavioral Analysis and Assessment: The Cornerstone to Effectiveness • 195
Raymond G. Romanczyk

Part 5
Who Should Teach?

CHAPTER 8
Identifying Qualified Professionals in Behavior Analysis • 221
Gerald L. Shook and Judith E. Favell

CHAPTER 9
Recruiting, Selecting, and Training Teaching Assistants • 231
Jack Scott

CHAPTER 10
The UCLA Young Autism Model of Service Delivery • 241
O. Ivar Lovaas

Part 6
Practical Support: Organizing and Funding

CHAPTER 11
Community-based Early Intervention for Children with Autism • 251
Ronald C. Huff

CHAPTER 12
Funding the Behavioral Program: Legal Strategies for Parents • 267
Mark Williamson

Part 7
Working with a Speech-Language Pathologist

CHAPTER 13
Incorporating Speech-Language Therapy into an Applied Behavior Analysis Program • 297
Robin Parker

CHAPTER 14
Strategies for Promoting Language Acquisition in Children with Autism • 307
Margery Rappaport

Part 8
Working with the Schools

Part 9
From the Front Lines: Parents' Questions, Parents' Voices

CHAPTER 18
In Search of Michael • 359
Margaret Harris

CHAPTER 19
Rebecca's Story • 365
Elizabeth Harrington

CHAPTER 20
Brandon's Journey • 373
Cyndy Kleinfield-Hayes

CHAPTER 21
Peter's Story • 377
Elizabeth Braxton

Preface

Until recently, autism has been considered by many as a hopeless, incurable, and absolute condition. Now, however, research suggests that intensive behavioral intervention, begun when a child is between 2 and 5 years old, can have a significant and lasting positive impact. This intervention leads to improvement in virtually all children, and in some cases it leads to complete eradication of any sign of the disorder. While behavioral intervention is also the treatment of choice for older children and adults with autism, research shows that its potential for dramatic improvement is greatest with young children. It is that positive research that inspires and focuses this book.

What is autism? For some time autism has been considered a pervasive developmental disability. It is presumed to be a biological disorder of brain development, not an emotional disorder that results from parental behavior or family dysfunction. Exactly what causes the abnormal brain development is not known at this time—in part because autism has not yet been reliably detected by brain scans or other medical tests. At present, autism is diagnosed by direct observations of a child's behavior. It is estimated to affect 5–15 of every 10,000 children born worldwide, regardless of race, culture, parental characteristics, or family socioeconomic status. Boys are affected about three to four times more often than girls (Rapin, 1991; Schreibman, 1988).

The label *autism* is applied when a qualified professional (usually a licensed psychologist or a physician) determines that before the age of 3 years, a child displays a number of marked deficits and excesses in several behavioral domains: communication, symbolic or imaginative activities (such as play), reciprocal social interaction, and interests and activities. Within each of these areas, any of several abnormalities may be observed. Communication impairments, for example, may include no useful vocal or nonvocal communication, speech that is repetitive or nonsensical, or well-developed speech that is not used socially (e.g., to engage in normal conversation). Development of play behavior may be severely delayed. If it develops at all, it usually lacks spontaneity, variety, and social components. In fact, all social interactions are often impaired to the point that the individual seems largely uninterested in and unresponsive to other people. The range of interests and activities may be very restricted. Often, a few stereotyped patterns of behavior are repeated over and over. Other problems that are not unique to autism but often accompany it include attentional problems; abnormally high- or low-activity levels; disruptive behavior (e.g., tantrums, shrieking); destructive behavior toward property, others, or self; abnormal responses to sensory stimuli; seizures; and apparent insensitivity to physical dangers and pain. Many children with autism also have great difficulty learning. A small percentage score in the normal range on tests of cognitive abilities, but 75%–80% function in the mild to severe range of mental retardation (Rapin, 1991).

A diagnosis of autism should be based on extensive direct observation of the child and comprehensive interviews with family members and other caregivers. A number of behavioral checklists can help differentiate autism from other childhood disorders (e.g., mental retardation without autism, specific language disorders, schizophrenia), and some standardized assessments can help define the extent of developmental delay or deviation. However, all psychological, educational, and language tests are subject to problems of reliability in identifying autism (American Psychiatric Association, 1994; Rapin, 1991; Rutter & Schopler, 1987). Moreover, the wide range of behaviors associated with autism and the individuality of each child's behavioral profile make a *typical* case somewhat difficult to define. In other words, the presence or absence of single behaviors cannot definitively rule out or confirm autism, although cliches, caricatures, and overgeneralizations about autism abound. To give but one example of such an overgeneralization, public perception seems to be that all autistic children rock their bodies back and forth. One possible result of this perception might be that a mother and father may have concerns about their child, but delay seeking a diagnosis because they have read that autistic children rock, and their child does not happen to rock.

To further complicate these difficulties, many pediatricians, to whom parents first turn when they suspect a problem in their child, tend to not recognize the early symptoms of the disorder. Many parents of autistic children report to us that their pediatrician told them to "Wait and see. He'll grow out of it."

When a diagnosis is finally made, it is usually made by one or several specialists, as noted above. It is not unusual, however, for different professionals to label the disorder differently, as in the case where one professional says "autism," the next says "pervasive developmental disorder with autistic features," and the next says "pervasive developmental disorder, not otherwise specified." While some of these labels may make parents feel better, no hard evidence exists that any of these different labels should be taken any less seriously than the term *autistic.* There seems to be an understandable tendency for many parents and professionals to want to avoid, at all costs, the word autistic. A parent may say, for instance, "Dr. X says my child is not autistic, she only has autistic tendencies," or "she only has pervasive developmental disorder." However, if the parent is encouraged to then make therapeutic decisions based on the impression that the child's condition is very mild or transient, those decisions may not be optimal for the child.

Taken together, it is obvious that all of these diagnostic difficulties can (and often do) lead to problems of delay, denial, confusion, or psychological turmoil for parents. Unfortunately the question of how to diagnose and label a child is only one of many controversial topics in the field of autism research and treatment. Another is the optimal age for such a diagnosis, and the optimal age to begin treatment. Some professionals refuse to confer a diagnosis until the child is 3 or 4 or even 5, at which point they may finally label him or her "autistic." Meanwhile, 1, 2, or 3 years may have passed, years in which the child could have been engaged in a structured, intensive treatment program.

If parents receive several vague, placating, or conflicting opinions from different diagnosticians, but continue to have grave concerns over a child's development, they might consider beginning a program of early intervention anyway. This may be preferable to waiting for everyone to agree on the diagnosis and losing valuable time in the process.

It is our hope that this manual will offer some assistance to parents, and to the professionals who aid them, in the challenging task of making science-based treatment decisions, and procuring effective early intervention for children with autism.

–The Editors

REFERENCES

American Psychiatric Association. (1994). *Diagnostic and statistical manual* (4th ed.). Washington, DC: Author.

Rapin, I. (1991). Autistic children: Diagnosis and clinical features. Supplement to *Pediatrics, 87,* 751–760.

Rutter, M., & Schopler, F. (1987). Autism and pervasive developmental disorders: Concepts and diagnostic issues. *Journal of Autism and Developmental Disorders, 17,* 158–186.

Schreibman, L. (1988). *Autism.* Newbury Park, CA: Sage.

PART ONE

Introduction

CHAPTER ONE

Why This Manual?

Catherine Maurice

The phone rings. "Hello?" The caller might be the mother of a child newly diagnosed with autism. Sometimes she is nervous, almost breathless with anxiety. She has many questions—questions that I have heard over and over again.

"I want to get my little boy into behavioral therapy. How do I start? Where can I find trained help?"

"How can I pay for this therapy? How much does it cost?"

"My little girl is 6 years old. Is it too late to start a behavioral program?"

"My daughter is only 2. I'm worried about such an intensive level of therapy."

"My son does smile and look at me. Will behavioral therapy destroy his spirit?"

"I want to do a behavioral program, but I want to combine it with occupational therapy (or speech therapy or vitamin therapy, etc.). Can I combine several different approaches?"

I could go on and on. Over the past 2 years, the questions are always the same, and they are all urgent.

Parents call because I wrote a book about our own family's struggle with autism (Maurice, 1993). Two of our children, first our daughter and then our younger son, had been diagnosed with the condition, both around the age of 2. In the beginning, I had the good fortune to hear about an article describing the remarkable results obtained by Dr. O. Ivar Lovaas, of the University of California at Los Angeles (Chance, 1987). Dr. Lovaas, we learned, had achieved unprecedented results for young children with autism by treating them in an intensive behavioral program that typically entailed up to 40 hours a week of individualized instruction.

From the article, I formed a very hazy understanding of the approach Dr. Lovaas had employed with the children. I understood it to be a form of "behavior modification," and at the time, that term conveyed to me a mechanistic, forceful method of training dogs and seals and even rodents—nothing to which any loving parent would ever subject a *child*. I was encouraged by Dr. Lovaas's positive results, but dismayed by any thought of using behavior modification on my 2-year-old.

I was disabused of these prejudices and preconceptions when, out of sheer desperation, I agreed to let a young woman named Bridget Taylor show me what this type of teaching entailed, for a strictly controlled trial period in my home ("No aversives! This is my house!"). Bridget was able to demonstrate, in a very short time, how effective an approach based on the principles of Applied Behavior Analysis can be for children with autism. Under her tutelage, my daughter not only began to learn how to communicate, but started to make eye contact, to pay attention to us and to the world around her. I remember the day that I first began to believe I had been wrong about behavioral intervention. It was the day that my Anne-Marie walked to the door on Bridget's arrival, looked up into her eyes, and smiled.

Thank God I was able to trust my daughter's smiling eyes, and not my own preconceptions about this type of intervention. Under the guidance of Bridget and several other therapists, we were able to bring first our daughter and then later our son to health (Perry, Cohen, & DeCarlo, 1995).

But our experience left me frustrated, indeed appalled, by the continuing ignorance about behavioral intervention on the part of various "autism experts," many of whom had not kept abreast of the professional literature. I decided to write about my family's experience. In June 1993, my book was published, and then the stream of letters and phone calls began.

I knew from reading these letters and listening to these phone calls, and from my own experience, that parents (and other people who care about our children) had a vital need for credible information. When we are faced with a diagnosis of autism, we need to know how to sift through various recommendations, how to discriminate and judge among our options. We need factual information, preferably science-based and time-tested. We don't need everyone's opinion; we need objective data with the highest possible degree of reliability. We need guidance that is truly well-founded and objectively validated.

I knew that I could offer parents some understanding, for I had seen that our experience with diagnosis, sorrow, fear, miracle cures, inflated promises, false expertise, and uncertainty was not unique. Indeed, many of the letters I received included very similar remarks: "You have written our story. . . . You could have been describing what we went through. . . . I couldn't believe how similar our experience was to yours." It seemed that the pain and frustration that our family had known was shared by many families.

All parents who receive word that there is something wrong with their child experience fear and grief, but a diagnosis of autism seems commonly to produce an overwhelming degree of devastation and confusion. This is due, in part, to widespread hopelessness and ignorance about the condition. To begin with, most of us have virtually had to hound our pediatricians with our concerns. The pediatrician typically denies or underplays the problem until the child's condition deteriorates to the point where a pediatric neurologist, a psychologist, or a psychiatrist will finally confirm the validity of our fears.

Faced with a diagnosis of autism, which specialists often tell us is irremediable, many of us feel instantly alienated, instantly alone. We have to grieve alone, because usually our friends and families, although often loving and wanting to understand, do not have a clue as to what we're talking about, or they tend to have the same reaction as the pediatrician, minimizing the problem or castigating us as "overprotective" parents.

Why such widespread denial on the part of pediatricians, relatives, and often parents? I don't know. Maybe it has to do with the rarity of the condition, or with the subtle nature of autism's onset in early childhood, or with how normal most children with autism look. Maybe it has to do with the fact that until very recently, autism was considered to entail, in virtually every instance, both a devastating prognosis and lifelong permanence.

In any case, once we have received and managed to believe the diagnosis, we are then bombarded with contradictory advice and everyone's pet theory about causation and treatment. Despite strong evidence to the contrary, numerous members of the medical, psychological, and special education professions still see autism as an emotional disorder, caused by some psychological trauma, to be treated appropriately only by gentle understanding of the child and resigned coping on the part of the parents. Support groups and seminars on stress management abound. People who have had no success in actually treating autism spend their time counseling parents, focusing not on what the parents can do for their child, but on how the parents might "change their attitude" toward the condition. Parents are often told that it is not only advisable, but morally imperative to accept their child the way he is. Anything other than

such acceptance is looked upon as a manifestation of a lack of love. Twenty-five years of witnessing the ineffectiveness of this approach still has not dissuaded its advocates.

We who refuse to accept these hand-holding programs thus quickly learn that we have to become overnight experts, doing our own research, evaluating treatment modalities, and finding our own programs or therapists.

Parents thus career from crisis to crisis. Extraordinary demands are placed on our spiritual, emotional, physical, and financial resources. We must fight on many different fronts while tending to our other children, earning a living, putting meals on the table, and trying not to cry too much in front of people.

And yet, beyond understanding some of what other parents were going through, I could not give them the concrete guidance they sought. Dr. Bernard Rimland, director of the Autism Research Institute in San Diego, had suggested that I write out my responses to some of the most frequent questions and make them available to parents. But I had worked with only two children and seen a few dozen more; I could not assume that such a limited experience would qualify me to know what to do with anyone else's child. I had only the most cursory knowledge of the research literature; I was not trained in scientific research or psychology. The questions parents were asking me were too important to believe that my common sense, my maternal instinct, or my parental perspective could adequately handle them.

Furthermore, I had no desire to join the ranks of people who did present themselves as experts in autism based on their limited personal experience. Of course we who have "been there," whether as parents of people with autism or as individuals diagnosed with autism, have every right to speak or write of our own experiences. But we are not automatically qualified, thereby, to make public pronouncements about causes or treatments, unless we can point to credible scientific research in support of our statements. If I recover from cancer, or if I am the parent of a child who has recovered from cancer, does that entitle me to lecture people, based on my experience alone, on the "best" treatment for cancer? Does that entitle me to sell my services as a cancer-care provider? If I have an M.A., a Ph.D., or an M.D. after my name, does that enable me to claim any particular expertise in autism? Not if the M.A. is in sociology, or the Ph.D. is in Chinese folklore, or the medical degree has never included any study of the current scientific research in autism.

Over the past few years, I have been growing more and more alarmed at the number of people who do make such statements outside of their area of expertise, and equally alarmed at the extraordinary faith with which parents, many educators and therapists, and members of the media automatically accept those pronouncements.

I had seen the damage wrought by this lack of discrimination and judgment in the world of autism. The history of autism has been dominated by self-appointed authorities who decided, without testing their theories in any controlled fashion, that they understood the genesis of or the optimal treatment for this disorder. Such false authority has taken many forms: Bruno Bettelheim, who had concluded that bad mothers cause autism, reigned unchecked for decades, the strength of his influence resting not on rigorous testing of his psychogenic theory, but on the self-perpetuating, self-reinforcing expertise granted to him by parents and professionals alike. Today, there are still many such authorities whose strength rests on nothing more than their popular following, their longevity in the field, or the emotional seductiveness of their theories and therapies.

But look at the role that we parents play in supporting and endorsing such false expertise. Who keeps the authority figures in authority? Why do we continue to support worthless treatments and self-proclaimed experts in the face of little or no real progress in our children? How did play therapy come to be one of the most often recommended treatment options for so many children with autism (in spite of an apparently complete lack of evidence validating its effectiveness), if not in part through our collusion? Who keeps buying into the latest fad, pouring hundreds of thousands of dollars into therapies that have virtually no published, peer-reviewed, credible support? The history of autism is a history of, as someone once put it, "failed treatments and fads," including everything from psychoanalysis of the child, to psychoanalysis of the mother, to "rage reduction," to "patterning," to "total acceptance," to "maternal rebonding," and so on. Sadly enough, however, we parents have supported every one of those failed treatments, those fads, and the authority figures who promoted them.

I think I understand, at least in part, why we keep doing so. When my daughter was diagnosed, I didn't know what the scientific literature said, and the people to whom I initially turned for guidance didn't either. My frantic call to the Autism Society of America yielded an outdated list of reading material that included a book called *Autism: Nightmare Without End.* They also sent a list of the symptoms of autism and a newsletter containing an endless stream of personal opinions written by parents, anecdote after anecdote about untested treatment options, and columns written by people with no apparent scientific credentials.

There was no mention of behavioral intervention, nor any mention of any professional journal that supported behavioral intervention. My pediatrician did not know what to do. Several of the professionals to whom I initially spoke had nothing better to recommend than some counseling for me—"to help you cope with the stress." I was advised by one special education teacher to "take some time for you—maybe get a manicure?" And I found rampant distortion of and denigration of behavioral intervention—by people who had no idea of what such intervention entailed.

In this wasteland of nonhelp, I was open to anyone who would tell me *what to do.* And I was willing to trust anyone who would preach something other than coping. Moreover, all my powers of reason and objectivity were crumbling before the fact that I was losing my child. I was as vulnerable as any parent out there to anyone who would breathe the word *cure,* anyone who would whisper the command "Trust me, and all will be well."

In my case, I believed that holding therapy was my magic bullet. It was championed by people who seemed to have stellar credentials—Nobel prizewinners, no less. (Never mind that their field of study was birds: I was willing to overlook such minor details.) It was based on a theoretical model of biological imprinting that seemed at least somewhat plausible to me. At the time, I thought I could distinguish mumbo-jumbo from good scientific research. Actually, I was fairly ignorant of what constituted truly sound methodology, objective data, and controlled research. Most significantly, however, I needed to believe what my saviors were telling me. I was generally aware of some of holding therapy's flawed premises and dubious proofs, but the strength of my own desire for a cure produced a "willing suspension of disbelief," to borrow a phrase from the literary world.

Since then, I have watched thousands of desperate parents flock to each new "breakthrough" treatment—from swimming with dolphins, to various forms of "insight/bonding/accepting" therapy, to brushing/rocking/stroking therapy, to a new one called "drum therapy," or "rhythmic entrainment," to the scandal of Facilitated Communication, discredited by every single controlled, objective test to which it has been subjected, yet still promising to instantly unlock communication in people with autism. I have heard "consultants" (what's a consultant?) lecture parents on some ill-defined but pervasive cliché called "sensory overload" in autistic people; optometrists hawking $500 glasses to cure the symptoms of autism; speech therapists making unsupported claims about the curative powers of "auditory retraining"; nutritionists confidently describing the powers of special diets to heal the "brain pathology" of autism (neurologists should be very glad to hear of how many therapists and parents have confidently identified the brain pathology of autism, something the neurologists have been attempting to do for decades); and New Age gurus telling us that all we have to do is accept the child for who he is, and then he will choose to come out of his autism when he is ready. But one of the scariest things I ever heard in the autism world was a parent, at a large conference in Westchester County, New York, angrily and personally attacking a professional who dared even to raise questions about the scientific foundations of these increasingly outrageous claims. "I am deeply offended!" she shouted at the professional. "You do us a disservice!" In the audience, I thought, "No, she is doing us all a service, after 4 decades of charlatanism, quackery, and nonsense."

There is almost no limit to what we can be persuaded to believe when our despair, or our hurt, or our fear is combined with a promise of healing and hope. The appeal to the emotions seems far more powerful than the appeal to reason, and there is no dearth of people willing to play to those emotions and eager to adopt that authority role. And parents, just as I did, continue to believe in anyone who can give them comfort, anyone who will give them hope, putting the blinders on when it comes to scrutinizing the credentials of these messiahs, the empirical support for their theories, or the rationality of their statements. One eminent authority in the autism world has asserted that people with autism communicate via extrasensory perception. What's next? Moon-dust elixir for autism?

What I had to learn about autism was that there are no gurus, no magic bullets. What I learned was that reason and scientific research—cumulative, painstaking, collegial work on the part of many people—has produced the most beneficial results for people with autism. We don't have a universal cure for autism, but we have an approach that is creating a new future for many people with autism and producing full recovery for some. Today, behavior analysis and its applications have evolved, through countless research projects and controlled studies, into a highly complex and refined corpus of knowledge. I learned that this field is not the province of one or two superstars, but is populated by thousands of researchers and practitioners—people who have dedicated their careers to advancing and refining our knowledge of how children with autism learn, and our understanding of the most effective ways of teaching them. Above all, I learned that we parents, no matter how much we long for a panacea, must allow ourselves to be guided by something other than our own panicky need for instant answers. We must allow ourselves to be guided by our God-given *reason,* our gift of *logic,* as well as our hope and our prayers and our faith.

Unfortunately, in the quest for rational, authoritative information, the situation for parents still remains highly compromised by the indiscriminate, anything-goes attitude of many individuals and established organizations that are supposed to be helping and guiding us. We should look very skeptically at any publication that advises us to, as one mother paraphrased it, "Throw everything against the wall and see what sticks." We might do well to look critically at any organization whose publications endorse, advertise, or otherwise even tacitly support every one of those dubious choices and latest miracle cures, while apparently remaining ignorant of what is appearing in the professional, science-based literature. The harm that is caused by such a politically correct, let's-not-offend-anyone attitude is incalculable. Money, energy, opportunities, and precious time go down the drain when parents are encouraged to pursue anything and everything, whether or not it is backed by reliable evidence.

Much of this indiscriminate attitude is dressed up in an appealing message about the necessity of remaining open-minded to different treatments. Of course we should remain open to all promising avenues of research and treatment, but there is a difference between a promising area of inquiry and the myriad treatments that continue to be endorsed in spite of weak or absent supportive data. If that history of "failed treatments and fads" has taught us anything, it is that we either turn to interventions whose credibility rests on something other than opinion, anecdote, or emotional need, or we will repeat this history *ad infinitum.* The fact that "each child is different," so often preached by the supporters of dubious therapies, is no justification for letting our children be used as guinea pigs for every new breakthrough that hits the autism world.

In short, it had become apparent to me and to several researchers and psychologists with whom I was discussing these issues, that the autism world continued to be dominated by an astonishing amount of misinformation, false expertise, and ferocious ideological warfare. It was equally apparent, given the growing research findings about the value of early intervention, that there was a critical need for parents to gain access to science-based, accurate information about such intervention. I believed that we had enough books and articles about coping with the emotional turmoil of autism, and we had nowhere near enough books addressing the issue of effective early intervention for autism and current research findings.

In early 1994, I began to search for the people willing and able to contribute to such a book. Fortunately, I have come to know and trust some researchers and practicing psychologists who believe in good science, not in the superiority of their own insights or in the "try anything" approach. I turned to Dr. Stephen Luce, vice president of program operations at Bancroft, Inc., a large rehabilitative facility in southern New Jersey, for help in organizing an outreach manual and in contacting key people who could help us out.

Together, we sketched out the backbone of our manual, delineating the major chapter divisions quickly. Our basic strategy was to put ourselves in the shoes of parents, and ask ourselves the key questions that parents ask when they are trying to procure effective treatment for their newly diagnosed child.

I also called Cyndy Kleinfield-Hayes, a parent and strong advocate for children with autism, to ask if she wanted to participate. Not only did she contribute a chapter, she also furnished critical organizational support in the earliest phases of the project, and provided valuable insights from her perspective as a mother still involved in active home programming for her son.

One key decision that Stephen and I made early on, was to concentrate our efforts on the young population. Not that we hold the needs of adolescents or adults to be any less urgent. This is an area of grave concern, and the paucity of quality services for this population remains critical. However, we knew that this manual would become unmanageably broad and diluted if we tried to focus on too many questions and address too many issues. We needed to carve out one discrete area—early behavioral intervention for young children with autism—and try to do as good a job as possible on that already very complex topic.

After we had our basic outline, Steve and I invited a core group of people, whose work we knew, to join the project and contribute a response to some of our questions. We also asked them to suggest others who might want to contribute.

The criteria for inclusion as a contributor were few, but fairly specific. We needed people who were well versed in the field of study called Applied Behavior Analysis. We were seeking people with either significant research experience in this field, or significant clinical experience, and preferably both. We needed people who believed in the value of objective data and results, as opposed to "received wisdom" of any sort. We needed people who understood the importance of a science-based approach to autism treatment, an approach that welcomed professional scrutiny, peer review, objective validation, and the test of time. We needed people with compassion, who understood that the best assistance they could offer parents was not only understanding and empathy, but concrete information, specific guidelines, and empirical knowledge, the fruit of their experience and study.

At an initial meeting to launch our project in May 1994, we identified and articulated the basic premise that all of us supported and that informs this manual: that Applied Behavior Analysis has been proved, through extensive research over the past half-century, to be the most effective intervention we have for treating people with autism or pervasive developmental disorder. (See Chapter 3 for an overview of this research.)

Another significant point of agreement among us is that, to my knowledge, no contributor thinks of Applied Behavior Analysis as a cure for autism. The term *cure* implies a universality or uniformity of effect that this treatment does not provide. Although several of us have seen children who have recovered normal functioning after behavioral treatment, we have also seen many children who retain some degree of impairment, handicap, or abnormal functioning, even after intensive behavioral intervention. Rate of learning varies under this approach. I, and other parents and professionals who are involved in the field of autism, increasingly believe that the word *autism* is analogous to the word *cancer*. There is one name for many different forms and degrees of severity of the disorder. Some forms are more responsive to treatment than others.

In fact, in my experience in the autism world, it is not the proponents of behavioral intervention who throw around the word *cure;* rather, it is their critics who use the word when they want to contend that the behaviorists are making false promises. From what I have seen, the researchers and clinicians who have been achieving the most exciting results in autism are those who avoid such overly dramatic words and phrases as *cure,* or *breakthrough,* or *emergence of a hidden child.*

Aside from identifying these broad areas of agreement, neither I nor Steve Luce told people what to write or which topic we wanted them to treat. We sent them the list of topics and asked them to select one. (If they had all selected the same topic, we would have had to negotiate, but that did not happen.) Nor did we aim for group agreement on all subjects treated. We wanted contributors to speak for themselves, representing their clinical or research experience, while still remaining faithful to the most current, most data-based, and most generally accepted principles of Applied Behavior Analysis. If there were differences of opinion with respect to particular techniques or procedures, however, we were prepared to include them. Such differences would allow readers to see that the application of behavior analysis varies from practitioner to practitioner and that, within the general principles of this discipline, what works for one child might not work as well for another. Moreover, many technical aspects of the discipline are still under study, and there is not enough hard data yet to make definitive or absolute statements about particular issues. Two examples that come to mind are the best means of shaping eye contact, and the optimum number of hours per week that a child should be in therapy. Readers will notice that different contributors to this manual may have different opinions on these and other topics, for the simple reason that not enough research has been done to make definitive statements on these issues.

Once the project was launched, it gained momentum quickly, and we were fortunate to win the enthusiastic support of many highly respected researchers, experienced behavior analysts, and skilled therapists. Dr. Luce had agreed to be a coeditor, along with Dr. Gina Green, director of research at the New England Center for Autism. Both, in addition to working in academic and administrative positions, had published extensively, and currently serve on the editorial boards of several scientific journals. Their agreement to coedit the manual made me confident that our work would be subjected to rigorous standards of professional scrutiny.

What *is* Applied Behavior Analysis? In the simplest possible terms (*my* terms, as a mother who learned the approach and applied it to the teaching of her own children), Applied Behavior Analysis involves the breakdown of all skills into small, discrete tasks, taught in a highly structured and hierarchical manner. Central to the successful application of this method is the art of differential reinforcement. That is, the therapist, parent, or caregiver learns how to systematically reward or reinforce desired behaviors, and ignore, redirect, or discourage inappropriate behaviors. Also central to any well-run behavioral program is the therapist's close monitoring of what is working and what is not working. Data on all the child's learning are recorded regularly, and the therapist adjusts the teaching programs and protocol with respect to what the data indicate about the child's progress.

Everything, from learning not to scream and throw tantrums to learning to sleep through the night, to play appropriately with toys, to use communicative language, and to learning age-appropriate social interaction, along with many other skills, can be successfully "shaped," or taught, through this methodology. (I say *can be* taught. Not all children learn at the same rate or with the same degree of suc-

cess as others. The vast majority of children do make progress, but there remains great variability in the long-term outcome for different children. Rate of learning may depend on the inherent potential of the child, on the skill of the teacher, or on other as-yet-unidentified factors.)

Needless to say, a therapist must be keenly aware of an individual child's learning style as well as the latest research on curricula and methodology. The field of Applied Behavior Analysis is evolving constantly, and it is highly probable that some of the material presented in this handbook will soon become dated.

Is autism then "a problem of behavior" as one critic of Applied Behavior Analysis scornfully asked? Obviously, no rational person would consider autism to be a manifestation of poor manners or uncivil behavior. Most researchers, clinicians, and parents now accept the increasing evidence that autism is a neurobiological disorder, and most would like to see a lot more research (that is, a lot more credible research) done on brain functioning in autism. But some of us who espouse this method tend to believe that early structured behavioral intervention may indeed have some rerouting or restructuring effect on a developing nervous system. Moreover, until someone identifies the exact brain pathology operative in autism, all we can usually observe are the external behaviors of people with autism. Those of us who have seen the effectiveness of Applied Behavior Analysis believe that many of those behaviors, ranging from rudimentary self-care tasks to complex skills such as interactive social language, can become permanent parts of a child's repertoire if they are broken down into components that the child can handle, taught well enough, learned early enough, and practiced consistently enough. If one can train the body to run the mile in under four minutes, if one can train the fingers to play a Chopin polonaise, perhaps one can train the developing brain to repair, or compensate for, some circuitry that has begun to go awry.

Perhaps a more direct way to express the effectiveness of behavioral intervention for autism is to say that it seems to help children learn how to learn. (I believe it was Dr. Ivar Lovaas who first used this phrase. I took it up in my book because I found it such an apt description of what Applied Behavior Analysis seems to *do* for children.) With my own children, I found I could use this method to break down learning for them in a way that they could handle, and then fade back and allow them to take over the learning as soon as they were ready. They seemed, at their worst, to be largely indifferent to and unaware of events and phenomena around them. They certainly did not respond to much of what went on in the environment. But instead of allowing them to sit in a corner and engage in meaningless, repetitive, solitary activity, we began to learn how to help them focus on us, on our words, and on the world around them. We learned, for instance, how to break down language, both receptive and expressive language, into tiny components, and we learned how to actively teach those components to them. Using the methods of prompting, shaping, modeling, and reinforcing that Bridget demonstrated for us, we saw that our children could start assimilating information, and assimilating more and more information as time went on. After a while, we saw that we could begin to progressively fade back on the structure and intensity of the teaching, as they began to take over more and more of the learning themselves. Like other children, they began to spontaneously pick up more and more from the environment, until they were finally learning, without support, from a normal school and home environment.

I hope that readers have gathered by now that behavioral therapy has little to do with merely correcting behavior. It entails a comprehensive program for teaching skills across all domains, from the linguistic, to the cognitive, to the social, to the mundane tasks of getting dressed, brushing one's teeth, and so on. Part of the misinformation that assaults parents consists of the confident assertion by educators, social workers, and others that behavioral therapy is for managing behavior, while special education is for handling academics or language acquisition. Unfortunately, however, many special education programs in this country seem to amount to little more than custodial care for children with autism.

Again, the rate of progress varies under a behavioral approach. On the more positive side, I know of several children who attained normalcy in 2 or 3 years, attend regular classes in regular schools, and have friends. Moreover—and more significantly than my anecdotal information—several data-based reports have appeared indicating that intensive early behavioral intervention can result in hitherto unprecedented outcomes for children with autism and pervasive developmental disorder. Among the most significant of these studies is the 1985 paper by researchers at the Princeton Child Development Institute, who reported that between 40% and 60% (over a certain time interval) of children who had begun treatment with them before reaching the age of 5 improved to the point where they could be enrolled in public schools (Fenske, Zalenski, Krantz, & McClannahan, 1985). Subsequently, in 1987, Dr. Ivar Lovaas of UCLA reported that nine of nineteen children who received intensive early behavioral intervention in his treatment program attained normal cognitive and intellectual functioning, and were able to be mainstreamed and to complete first grade with normal peers (Lovaas, 1987). A follow-up report on these best-outcome children, published in the *American Journal on Mental Retardation,* revealed that they had maintained their gains; as young adults, they were apparently indistinguishable from normal peers (McEachin, Smith, & Lovaas, 1993). (Again, see Chapter 3 for an overview and discussion of these and other studies.)

Clearly, Applied Behavior Analysis is not a panacea. Anyone who looks objectively at these studies will understand that even under the very best, most professionally run programs, the majority of children still do not make it to normalcy, recovery, or unsupported inclusion in normal schools. In the few years that I have been involved with autism, I myself have become acquainted with children whose progress has been relatively slow. Steady, but slow. They never stop learning, but it is likely that they will need some form of structured intervention for many years in order to maximize their potential and help them live more fulfilling lives.

Thus, the "perfect" treatment—one that will provide the possibility of a normal life for all children and their families—has yet to be developed. To date, however, scientific research shows that Applied Behavior Analysis has consistently achieved the most significant results for children with autism.

Unfortunately, it is currently very difficult for parents or interested professionals to gain immediate access to the most effective forms of this treatment. At the present time, parents must wait 6 to 9 months to procure even a 2-day workshop from one of the few reputable behavioral programs in this country. The waiting time for actual admission into one of these programs stretches from 1 year to never. The supply of quality services cannot meet the current demand. Trained, qualified professionals who know how to administer this type of treatment are extremely hard to find. There is tremendous interest on the part of parents, professionals, and educators in this therapy, but there is a gap between the professional behavioral community's ability to train new people and the need that exists right now. Moreover, in many communities, it is hard for behavioral therapists to procure endorsement or support from agencies set up to provide services to autistic children, and this too contributes to the scarcity of people willing to devote their careers to this field.

This situation means, among other things, that the field is ripe for abuse, in the sense that a few individuals, knowing the desperation of parents, are beginning to charge exorbitant fees, thereby effectively denying this therapy to all but the wealthy or the very resourceful. Another type of potential abuse looms in the proliferation of untrained "therapists" who don't really know what they're doing, but charge parents for their services anyway.

Knowing the need, we decided to compile as much concrete information as we could for parents and other interested people, in a book which would, when published, be immediately available to anyone. But nothing is simple. Even in the formative stages of the book, I was aware of the potential and actual arguments against it. It is, according to some critics, "irresponsible" and "dangerous" to put this information into "laymen's" hands. Only trained professionals know how to do this, are qualified to do this. No one should encourage *parents* to do this kind of work with autistic children!

Setting aside the time-worn authoritarianism and paternalism inherent in a few of these objections, parts of this argument are valid. There is danger that a few parents or therapists will take our information too literally, attempt to apply it too rigidly to a child. There is danger of misinterpretation of or overadherence to our sample flowcharts and curricula. There may be misunderstanding of the principles of reinforcement and clinical timing. There is no "recipe" for Applied Behavior Analysis. Each child's educational programming will be different from another's. These children may all have autism or pervasive developmental disorder, but they are nonetheless individuals, with varying manifestations of the disorder and varying degrees of severity. Each child brings his or her unique personality into the picture, and we cannot hope to approximate the type of help that a child could receive from a trained person paying attention to his or her specific needs.

This said, however, it is also true that all information about autism has to be adapted to individual children. All concrete recommendations, whether given in a book, a handout, a workshop session, or a school program, must be tested, tried, and modified according to the child's response. In fact, it is the very nature of Applied Behavior Analysis that procedures be individually tailored to each child. Everyone works by trial and error in a behavioral program, taking information and adapting it according to a child's changing needs. In the current state of affairs, some people are fortunate to have access to more information than others, so their trials and errors can be better-informed than others. I see no compelling reason to deny parents information because some might misunderstand it, or apply it imperfectly. I see no kindness in "protecting" parents by keeping them ignorant.

Consider this analogy: A woman's time to give birth has arrived. She is far from any civilized place, where she could be hospitalized and receive all the latest in professional expertise and state-of-the-art delivery care. Two people are arguing over what to do for her.

The first says "I will help her delivery because I have this manual here that gives me a rough idea of how to do this."

The second says "You can't deliver babies. You don't have a medical degree! She should be in a hospital!"

The first responds "Either someone helps her—now—or we will lose both mother and baby."

Women don't choose to give birth at inopportune times in remote places. Parents don't choose to be locked out of the few good programs that treat autistic children. It just happens. I envision this outreach manual as an emergency first-aid kit, a stopgap measure. Time is a crucial factor here. A growing body of evidence supports the value of *early* behavioral intervention for the best outcome. People cannot, and will not, wait years for the behavioral community to slowly respond to their needs—they are fighting for their children.

Obviously, the ideal solution would be for every child, immediately upon diagnosis, to obtain placement in a well-supervised, well-staffed, intensive behavioral program, whether at home or at school. The ideal solution would be to have one very experienced person supervising highly competent therapists, all of whom would have had some research and clinical training at a reputable university, school, or clinic.

Dozens—indeed, hundreds—of people are organizing and working hard, right now, to achieve such an ideal solution. Many of them are parents of newly diagnosed children, who are not only working for their own children, but are passionately concerned about other people's children as well. These parents have seen the effectiveness of Applied Behavior Analysis, and will not be satisfied until all children have the opportunity to benefit from this treatment.

But grassroots movements take time, and the qualified and caring professionals cannot keep pace with the demands being placed on them. No contributor to this manual would ever claim that this book could *replace* a qualified person or a quality program. We simply hope that it will help people who are struggling now, often without professional guidance, to learn more about early behavioral intervention for autism.

To complicate matters, the very words *quality, quality control,* and *qualified* are themselves the subject of controversy and discussion. Many of us would like to see some form of certification or licensing of applied behavior analysts, some standardization of what *trained* or *qualified* means, at a national level. Unfortunately, capitalizing on the surge of interest in Applied Behavior Analysis for autistic children, a few people are beginning to make exaggerated claims about their level of expertise in this field. Many of us long for some agreed-upon standards that could guide parents in their search for professional assistance. It's bad enough that we don't have enough trained people to go around. The situation becomes even more serious when there are no national criteria and procedures for determining who is competent to deliver behavioral services. Drs. Gerald Shook, Judith Favell, and Jack Scott have written chapters for this manual on these important issues.

No contributor has written on an unimportant issue. Our manual is already very long, and yet there is no chapter I would eliminate. I have already mentioned several of our contributors, and before closing this introductory chapter I want to express my profound gratitude to all the others. Stephen Anderson, Barbara O'Malley Cannon, and Marie Taras have written on "Teaching New Skills to Children with Autism," an overview of some crucial strategies and techniques employed in the field. Andrew Bondy's chapter is designed to assist those who want to advocate for more effective public school education for their children. Elizabeth Braxton, Cyndy Kleinfield-Hayes, Elizabeth Harrington, and Margaret Harris have all contributed chapters on how autism has affected their children. Gina Green lends credibility to the overused term "empowerment," by providing readers with the conceptual guidelines they need to make their own discriminations and judgements about the host of "options" purported to be effective for autism. In a second chapter, she offers a much-needed overview of what research studies can and cannot presently tell us about early behavioral intervention for autism. Kathleen Dyer and Steve Luce address many of the most common questions that parents ask, and their concerns about behavioral intervention. Ron Huff describes the efforts of a group of Sacramento-based parents to organize and procure funding for their children's behavioral program. Susan Johnson, Linda Meyer, and Bridget Taylor spell out, in very helpful detail, a supported inclusion model utilized at the Alpine Learning Group for progressively integrating a child into a mainstream classroom. Ivar Lovaas shares many valuable observations on staffing and training issues, observations gleaned from a lifetime of study devoted to effective intervention for children with autism. Bridget Taylor and Kelly McDonough

have submitted a gold mine of teaching programs, programs that will surely inspire many more creative ideas in those who read and use them. Robin Parker and Margery Rappaport encourage a dialogue between the disciplines of Applied Behavior Analysis and Speech-Language Pathology, and in so doing, provide parents and therapists with many concrete strategies for facilitating language. Ray Romanczyk elucidates some of the most important components of any effective behavioral program: the different means of analyzing and assessing behavior. Mark Williamson has donated his legal expertise to make the battle for funding easier for other families. And finally, Tristram Smith has furnished readers with a powerful, courageous, and solidly rational assessment of several alternative therapies for autism.

Still, our manual could have been 10 times as long, and we would not have covered everything that needs to be explained and exemplified when discussing early intensive behavioral intervention for children with autism. The topic itself is so important that as the time came to send the manuscript to PRO-ED, I found myself dragging my feet, not pressing quite as hard to get the drafts of chapters back from contributors. The need to get the work out quickly competed with the need to make sure that the work was good, that is, as professional and careful as we could possibly make it. As our publication date draws near now, I am hyperconscious of the manual's imperfections.

However, whenever I wake up at night worrying about all that we could have said and didn't, all that we should have covered but did not have the space for, I take comfort in two thoughts. First, the manual must have some merit, because I had the privilege of working with many of the parents and professionals whose intelligence, compassion, reason, and dedication I admire most in the autism community today. Second, for the mothers and fathers who are currently seeking help for a beloved child, it is better to offer some concrete assistance, however inadequate or incomplete, than to willingly allow their pleas to be met with yet more blame, indifference, misinformation, or silence.

AUTHOR NOTE

I would like to offer special thanks to Gina Green, not only for coediting this manual, but for all that she has taught me about science, pseudoscience, and intellectual courage; to Steve Luce, our other coeditor, for giving so constantly of his time and encouragement, and for supporting this project well before anyone else joined it; to Cyndy Kleinfield-Hayes and another friend, Evelyne Estey, for doing all the groundwork of researching and contacting potential publishers; and to my husband, for the practical, psychological, and spiritual support he has offered me throughout this endeavor.

Catherine Maurice
East Hampton, New York
July 1995

REFERENCES

Chance, P. (1987, December). Saving Grace. *Psychology Today,* 42–44.

Fenske, E. C., Zalenski, S., Krantz, P. J., & McClannahan, L. E. (1985). Age at intervention and treatment outcome for autistic children in a comprehensive intervention program. *Analysis and Intervention in Developmental Disabilities, 5,* 49–58.

Lovaas, O. I. (1987). Behavioral treatment and normal educational and intellectual functioning in young autistic children. *Journal of Consulting and Clinical Psychology, 55,* 3–9.

Maurice, C. (1993). *Let me hear your voice: A family's triumph over autism.* New York: Knopf.

McEachin, J. J., Smith, T., & Lovaas, O. I. (1993). Long-term outcome for children with autism who received early intensive behavioral treatment. *American Journal on Mental Retardation, 4,* 359–372.

Perry, R., Cohen, I., & DeCarlo, R. (1995). Case study: Deterioration, autism, and recovery in two siblings. *Journal of the American Academy of Child and Adolescent Psychiatry, 34,* 232–237.

PART TWO

Choosing an Effective Treatment

CHAPTER TWO

Evaluating Claims about Treatments for Autism

Gina Green

Sometime shortly after a young child is diagnosed with autism or pervasive developmental disorder, the quest for help begins. Families typically feel an understandable urgency to get treatment for the child as soon as possible. When they seek information about available treatments, they often get a long and perplexing list that includes education, Auditory Integration Training, various drugs, vitamins and other "natural" substances, imitation therapy (Options), Facilitated Communication, Sensory Integration Therapy, music therapy, Gentle Teaching, special diets of various kinds, Applied Behavior Analysis, patterning, deep pressure therapy, dolphin therapy, rhythmic entrainment (drum therapy), and more. Some treatments are said to produce miraculous results overnight (or even faster), with relatively little effort or expense. Some are reported to benefit most, if not all, people with autism. For many such claims, a moment's careful reflection may be all it takes to assess the odds that they could be true and to realize that the odds are slim to none.

It's rarely that easy, however, for a host of reasons. First, virtually everyone who works to better understand and serve people with autism wishes ardently for breakthroughs. We all want a cure for this puzzling disorder; short of that, we want at least to enable people with autism to live the most full and happy lives possible. But this is a two-edged sword. The same factors that make dedicated and enthusiastic parents, advocates, teachers, and researchers can produce a special kind of vulnerability, a tendency to accept claims about treatments without scrutinizing the basis for those claims as closely as we should. Additionally, when the exact cause of a condition is not known and the prognosis is not especially good, new treatments are invented (or old ones are recycled) with astonishing frequency. Reports about quick fixes, miracle cures, and breakthrough treatments have proliferated since autism was first labeled over 50 years ago. They have never been more prevalent—or confusing—than they are today.

Unfortunately, as the number and variety of therapies has increased, it seems that professionals are less and less inclined to provide families with strong, data-based advice to help them make informed choices among the various therapies. The prevailing view seems to be, "Since we don't know the cause of autism, we don't know what might or might not work. So we might as well try everything, including the implausible and even the outlandish. What have we got to lose?" Arguments like these seem reasonable on their face and can be very appealing to someone who feels that doing something—*anything*—is better than doing nothing. But this hit-or-miss approach is no more likely to lead to positive, lasting outcomes for any individual with autism than it is to produce solid, reliable advances in knowledge about the disorder in general. In fact, it can lead to harm, or at the very least, perpetuation of the current situation: an ever-changing kaleidoscope of therapies, most with little or no sound evidence to support their effectiveness, many with potential or known harmful side effects (for a review, see Chapter 4).

Finally, perhaps as a function of the perplexing nature of autism and the severity of its impact, debates about causes and treatments tend to provoke intense emotional responses. The search for information and help is thus influenced at least as much by ideologies, personal beliefs, and social movements as by logic and objective data.

SCIENCE, PSEUDOSCIENCE, AND ANTISCIENCE

For purposes of this chapter, approaches to answering fundamental questions about how and why the world works, including questions about the nature of autistic behavior and what might be done about it, can be grouped into three broad categories: science, pseudoscience, and antiscience. Science relies on direct, objective observation and measurement of phenomena, systematic arrangements of events, procedures to rule out alternative explanations for what is observed, and repeated demonstrations (called replications) by individuals working independently of one another. Descriptions and examples of these and other features of scientific method, as they relate to treatments for autism, make up most of this chapter. Pseudoscience treats phenomena that do not have the hallmarks of scientific methods or evidence as if they were scientific. Beliefs that are not based on objective facts are "dressed up" to superficially resemble science. For example, by the use of selected scientific jargon or endorsements by people with scientific credentials. Antiscience is the outright rejection of the time-tested methods of science as a means of producing valid and useful knowledge. In the extreme antiscientific view, there are no objective facts. Pseudoscience and antiscience are not new by any means; both are widespread in modern Western culture. They are the basis for lucrative industries ranging from astrology to certain psychotherapy practices to medical quackery (Jacobson, Mulick, & Schwartz, 1995; Pendergrast, 1994; Randi, 1982; Shermer, 1994; Stanovich, 1992; Wolfensberger, 1994).

Many therapies that are currently being promoted for autism are pseudoscientific or antiscientific. They are said to produce high success rates very rapidly with a wide range of disorders. Little training or expertise is required to administer them; belief and faith, on the other hand, are essential. Other proven treatments for autism are said to be unnecessary, inferior, or harmful, but no objective evidence is provided to back up those assertions. In fact, little or no objective evidence is offered in support of claims about the therapies—only testimonials, anecdotes, and personal stories (more on these later). Catchy, emotionally appealing slogans are used in marketing the therapies and associated products. Claims of effectiveness, as well as the "theories" underlying the therapies, often contradict immense bodies of empirical knowledge as well as common sense, which are instantly discounted and discarded in favor of anecdotal evidence about the new therapy. New evidence from objective scientific research is also rejected if it does not reinforce the promoters' claims about the therapies. Promoters of some therapies for autism are working outside their areas of expertise. They do not conduct rigorous objective evaluations, often maintaining that the therapy's effects are real but so fragile that they are destroyed by the mere suggestion of critical scrutiny, or that the effects cannot be measured by standard methods, or that practitioners and parents should not wait for careful research to be completed. Researchers who do use rigorous methods to study the therapies and produce evidence contrary to promoters' claims, along with others who voice honest skepticism, are labeled narrow-minded, out of date, resistant to new ideas, and intent on persecuting the promoters. Coincidentally, promoters often benefit financially and otherwise from adoption of the therapies.

To complicate matters even further, some of these therapies *appear* to work: the child might seem to be better while in the therapy, or for a short time after. Very often the family and those who administer the therapy feel good simply because they are doing something. If the therapy also seems to help the child—whether in actuality, or simply in the perception of hopeful families and therapists—a behavioral trap is set: Using the therapy is reinforced powerfully, making its continued use likely even when objective evidence shows that the child is not actually improving, or that other treatments are more effective. Escaping traps like these can be extremely difficult. When caregivers and professionals get caught in them, the child is denied the benefits of validated treatments.

Scientists are certainly not immune to the seductions of fame and fortune, nor to errors of judgment, nor even full-blown delusions. Arguably, scientists are among the more suggestible among us. The scientific method is not fail-safe, but it has built-in checks and balances in its emphasis on objective data, independent replication, and critical peer review of research reports (Cromer, 1993; Shermer, 1994; Stanovich, 1992; Wolfensberger, 1994). Unfortunately, many of the elements of science are omitted from (or worse, declared irrelevant to) the evaluation and promotion of many therapies for autism, so the self-correcting mechanisms of science have no opportunity to rein in unsubstantiated claims. The situation in autism treatment is largely the opposite of disciplined science. The "anything goes" approach that many adopt, an over-reliance on personal accounts and testimonials, and the desperation that characterizes many family members and service providers combine to produce the perfect breeding ground for pseudoscience and antiscience (Stanovich, 1992; Wolfensberger, 1994). It's no wonder that the history of autism treatment is replete with fad therapies and frauds, repeated cycles of false hopes raised and dashed, millions of dollars wasted, and thousands of children deprived of effective or potentially effective treatment.

WHY THIS CHAPTER?

Even the most experienced, highly trained professional can find it difficult to sort through the claims and evidence about treatments for autism. For families who may know little or nothing about autism at the moment someone applies that label to their young child, the task can seem overwhelming. The problem is compounded by an urgent desire for treatment *now.* It would be nice if there were some simple way to determine which treatments were likely to have some real benefits, which were not likely to be effective but probably wouldn't do much harm, and which held hidden dangers. Unfortunately there are no simple tests or rules. Many therapies that appear benign or even highly beneficial at first blush, prove harmful on close examination or when used for an extended period of time. There are, however, some features that distinguish plausible claims from the implausible, relatively unambiguous evidence from suggestive but inconclusive reports, and treatments that have been subjected to rigorous scientific scrutiny from pseudoscientific treatments and social movements.

This chapter attempts to provide some guidance through the maze of autism treatments. (The terms *treatment, therapy,* and *intervention* are used interchangeably here to refer to anything that is done to or with a child that may change the child's behavior and/or biology, both broadly defined.) It suggests a number of questions to ask about treatment claims, and some decision rules for evaluating answers to those questions. All aim to produce an answer to one overriding question: Is there convincing evidence from sound scientific research that the treatment is effective? The main premise of this chapter is that treatment effects must be verified through systematic, experimental research using objective measurement procedures and controls to rule out alternative explanations for apparent effects. Identifying treatments that are supported by sound scientific evidence entails gathering and weighing different kinds of evidence, the methods by which the evidence was gathered, and the qualifications of those who study, promote, and implement the treatment. Each of those topics is addressed in this chapter, with reference to additional sources of information. One source that I drew from liberally and recommend highly is *How to Think Straight about Psychology* by Keith E. Stanovich (1992, 3rd edition), published by HarperCollins. (This book could well be titled simply *How to Think Straight.*) Another is Tristram Smith's chapter in this book.

A related premise of this chapter is that for every child with autism, every waking moment is precious. The vast majority of the child's time and other resources ought to be invested in treatments that have been shown, through scientific research, to produce the most lasting beneficial effects on the broadest range of behavioral deficits and excesses that constitute autism. Every moment the child spends in thera-

pies that are minimally effective, ineffective, unproven, or likely to be harmful is a moment that he or she could have spent participating in treatment that has a known probability of success in the hands of a competent therapist or teacher. When the child is very young, those may be moments that are lost forever. It appears that there is a relatively narrow "window of opportunity" for young autistic children during which the most effective available treatment—Applied Behavior Analysis—can mean the difference for many between lifelong severe disability and some approximation to normal functioning (Anderson, Avery, DiPietro, Edwards, & Christian, 1987; Fenske, Zalenski, Krantz, & McClannahan, 1985; Harris, Handleman, Gordon, Kristoff, & Fuentes, 1991; Lovaas, 1987; Maurice, 1993; McEachin, Smith, & Lovaas, 1993; Perry, Cohen, & DeCarlo, 1995; Smith, 1993).

To underscore the importance of subjecting claims about autism treatments to rigorous scrutiny, imagine that you are making a decision about a drug or surgical procedure that someone recommends for your child. Before accepting the recommendation, you owe it to your child to ask, "Just what is this treatment? Exactly what is it supposed to do? Who will administer the treatment, and how can I be sure they are qualified to do so? How will its effects on my child be evaluated, and by whom? What is the likelihood that the treatment will actually help? How has that likelihood been determined? If the treatment has proven effective, how long do the effects last? What are the risks of short- and long-term negative side effects? How have they been determined? What safeguards are in place if my child experiences negative side effects? Is this the most effective treatment available? How was that determined? Is there another treatment that is similarly effective but has fewer negative side effects? What is the cost of the treatment? What will happen if we do nothing?"

The guidelines suggested here should be applicable to almost any treatment modality, therapy, program, or therapist. In fact, I urge readers to use them to evaluate every bit of information they obtain about treatments for autism, including information presented in this book.

TYPES OF EVIDENCE

When someone says, "This treatment can help your child with autism," the first and most important questions to ask are, *"How do you know that? What exactly is the basis for your claim?"* The task is to sort the wheat from the chaff—to find out just what the evidence is, then to decide if it is solid enough to support the claims, and if you can feel confident and safe in subjecting your child to the treatment. Several different kinds of evidence may be offered in support of treatment claims. They vary along several dimensions. The "end points" of some of the most important dimensions are described next, with examples to help you make the relevant discriminations.

Speculation vs. Demonstration

A distinction that is extremely important but not always obvious is the difference between pure speculation about a treatment and actual, documented demonstrations that the treatment works. Given the number and variety of therapies that are said to help children with autism, the rate at which new ones come along, and the resources required to do careful research, it stands to reason that at any point in time there will be many therapies that have not been subjected to comprehensive evaluation, and some that have never been tested rigorously.

Many people to whom parents turn for help with their autistic child recommend treatments just because they *think* the treatments might be helpful. Some of those people can be very persuasive by virtue of their personal repertoires, professional titles ("doctor" is especially impressive to many people), or both. For example, consider the following: "We know from medical research that the brain is pliable, especially in children, and that it can change physically in response to sensory input. So I highly recommend Sensory Integration Therapy for your young autistic child, because the people who promote it say that it improves the way the brain organizes sensory input, and I believe that's possible." Statements like these have the ring of authority (e.g., "medical research") and seem plausible. Spoken by someone with "M.D." after his or her name (e.g., a neurologist or pediatrician) to a parent or teacher who desperately wants a treatment that will fix a child's brain, such statements can have a tremendous impact. No matter who utters them, statements like these should *always* be questioned and investigated thoroughly before resources are invested in the treatment. To follow through with the example, at this writing there have been no published, scientifically sound demonstrations that Sensory Integration Therapy actually produces measurable changes in autistic brains. In fact, methodologically sound studies have failed to document any specific, positive, lasting changes in brain function or behavior that could be attributed with confidence to Sensory Integration Therapy (more on this later, and in Chapter 4).

Subjective vs. Objective Evidence

Subjective evidence is information based on someone's personal perspective. Because people are imperfect and variable in their abilities to observe, remember, and report events, subjective reports are inherently biased and inconsistent. *A large number of subjective reports that seem to describe the same events are no more unbiased or reliable than one,* especially when the reports come from people who are predisposed (by strong suggestions, common wishes, or common profits) to produce similar reports. Put simply, people see what they want to see, and are extraordinarily easy to fool (Randi, 1982; Sagan, 1993; Shermer, 1994; Stanovich, 1992). These are facts of human behavior that apply to parents of children with autism, promoters of treatments, and scientists alike. Well-trained scientific researchers, intensely aware of these facts of human behavior, know that the evidence they should question most stringently is their own subjective impression. Good scientists take special precautions to minimize the influence of natural human biases on the evidence they obtain and the conclusions they draw. That is, they use procedures to ensure that evidence is obtained by objective means.

Perfect objectivity is unattainable in any enterprise involving humans, but there are a number of ways to approximate it. One is to define the phenomena of interest—for example, a treatment procedure and the behavior and/or biology of a child with autism that the treatment is supposed to change—in terms of observable, measurable events. Then anyone who can understand the definitions and carry out the measurement procedures can determine whether or not the phenomena occur, how much or how often, when, and under what conditions. (A crucial assumption, of course, is that those who develop the definitions and measurement procedures have specific expertise in the topic under study.) In short, operational definitions and measurements make phenomena accessible to public evaluation, verification, and replication, which are not possible when events are described in terms of individual perceptions or intuitions. Operational definitions allow debates about conflicting claims to be resolved on the basis of something other than personal beliefs and dogma (Christensen, 1985; Green, 1994b; Shermer, 1994; Stanovich, 1992).

Another step toward objectivity is accomplished by minimizing human bias in the measurement process. Accurate, reliable measurement is essential for evaluating whether a treatment does what it is expected to do. The most objective measurement is done by instruments or machines, which is standard practice in the measurement of biological variables, but often not feasible for measuring many behavioral variables. For instance, if a dietary treatment is claimed to change the biochemistry of a child with autism, that claim can be evaluated in part by using instruments to measure certain substances in blood samples taken before, during, and after treatment. (Of course, humans still have to read the instruments and interpret the results, so a prudent evaluation will also include procedures to control for likely biases on their part—to be discussed shortly.) It would be more difficult, though not impossible, to use machines to evaluate claims that the dietary treatment also changes the child's behavior (e.g., attending, activity level, learning rate, social interactions). Instead, evaluations of behavior change may rest entirely on direct observations of the child by other people.

Given the natural tendency of people to bring their own biases to everything they observe, how can direct observational data be collected and measured with any degree of objectivity? Behavioral scientists routinely employ a number of practices to increase the objectivity of evidence about treatment effects:

1. *Operational definitions, mentioned above, are a must.* The behavior of interest is defined in observable terms, as specifically as possible.

2. *Measurement procedures are also specified clearly.*

3. *Individuals who are not involved in delivering the treatment are trained to observe and record the level of the behavior (e.g., how often it occurs, at what intensity, for how long, in what proportion of opportunities, under what circumstances) according to the operational definitions and measurement procedures.* Usually two or more trained observers conduct observations at the same time, but independently of each other, (i.e., they do not talk about or look at each other's recordings). At the end of each observation, their recordings are compared, and the degree to which their observations match is calculated. Data are considered accurate and reliable only when the observations of two or more independent observers match both the operational definitions and each other's observations to a high degree (Christensen, 1985; Kazdin, 1982; Page & Iwata, 1986; Stanovich, 1992).

4. *To the greatest extent feasible, those who deliver the treatment and record and analyze the data are kept unaware of the investigator's hunches (hypotheses) as to what she expects to find.* If possible, participants are also kept unaware that they are receiving treatment. Alternatively, participants may be told that the treatment is in effect when it is not. Procedures like these are referred to as "blind" controls for bias. In drug research, for example, double-blind procedures are stan-

dard: Participants are sometimes given the active drug, sometimes an inactive placebo, but neither they nor the people who give them the substances are informed as to which one is in effect at any given time. In general, if the participants' behavior changes simply because they believe they are receiving treatment, the change will be observed when they are receiving the placebo. In fact, the strong tendency for people to report that they feel better when they think they're receiving treatment is called the "placebo effect." When participants unknowingly receive the active drug and an effect is seen that is over and above the effect found in the placebo condition, the effect can usually be attributed to the treatment with reasonable confidence (Christensen, 1985; Stanovich, 1992).

5. *Multiple measures of the effects of treatment can be obtained (e.g., direct observations by trained observers, plus standardized tests administered by others, plus parental ratings of behavior).* If they produce similar findings, it is likely that the effects are real and do not simply reflect the bias of a single observer or set of observers.

Examples of Subjective Evidence

Biographies, autobiographies, and other personal accounts (e.g., describing how an individual experiences autism and what he or she finds helpful) fall in the category of subjective evidence. So do testimonials, anecdotes, rumors, and uncorroborated self-reports. Even the personal observations and opinions of experienced clinicians and scientists are no more than subjective impressions unless they are verified, measured objectively, and repeated by others. A good deal of case study evidence is subjective (although case studies can yield relatively objective evidence, if they include operational definitions, quantitative measurement, controls for observer bias, and other features; Kazdin, 1982).

Facilitated Communication is a classic example of a procedure that is claimed to be extraordinarily effective for individuals with autism and other disabilities. Many are said to reveal literacy and other skills they do not demonstrate by any other means when a normally capable person ("facilitator") touches their hand or arm to assist them in pointing to letters or words (e.g., Biklen, 1990, 1992, 1993; Crossley, 1992). To date, virtually all of the evidence backing that claim is subjective: personal accounts, anecdotes, and testimonials, mostly from people who are invested emotionally (and in some cases, financially) in proving the claim. Numerous evaluations using objective measurement procedures show that the vast majority of "facilitated" communications come from facilitators, not people with disabilities (e.g., American Psychological Association, 1994; Cummins & Prior, 1992; Felce, 1994; Green, 1993, 1994a, 1994b; Green & Shane, 1994; Hudson, in press; Jacobson et al., 1994; Jacobson et al., 1995; Smith & Belcher, 1994; also see Chapter 4).

Examples of Objective Evidence

As mentioned earlier, data produced by instruments or machines (e.g., X rays, various medical laboratory tests, computer-managed tasks or tests) are relatively objective, assuming that the instruments are working properly and that the humans who read and interpret the data are well trained and monitored. Results of standardized measures like intelligence and achievement tests can also be relatively objective if the people who administer, score, and interpret the results adhere strictly to prescribed procedures and rules, which are usually developed through rigorous research. Likewise, evidence obtained through any of a wide range of direct observational methods can be relatively objective if it meets the criteria described earlier.

Objective, scientific evidence about treatment effectiveness makes up much of the research literature in Applied Behavior Analysis. Many examples relevant to treatments for autism can be found in a number of scientific professional journals—*Journal of Applied Behavior Analysis; Research in Developmental Disabilities; Behavior Modification; Journal of Autism and Developmental Disorders; Journal of Behavioral Education; Education and Treatment in Mental Retardation and Developmental Disabilities;* and the *American Journal on Mental Retardation,* to name a few. Several illustrations can be found in studies of the effectiveness of early behavioral intervention for autism. For example, to minimize one important source of bias, children were diagnosed by qualified professionals other than those delivering the treatment. Treatment effects were measured with standardized IQ, language, and other tests as well as direct observational methods (e.g., Anderson et al., 1987; Birnbrauer & Leach, 1993; Fenske et al., 1985; Harris et al., 1991; Lovaas, 1987; McEachin et al., 1993). At least one study also asked parents to report their impressions about how treatment of their children impacted on their own stress levels (Birnbrauer & Leach, 1993). In follow-up evaluations of autistic children who received early intensive treatment, Lovaas and his colleagues kept evaluators "blind" as to children's histories, that is, their diagnoses and what kind of treatment they had received (Lovaas, 1987; McEachin et al., 1993).

Indirect vs. Direct Measures

One way to evaluate the effects of a treatment is to ask the person receiving the treatment to report what happened. Another is to ask those around the person receiving treatment to report their perceptions. In addition to being subjective, these types of measures (especially the latter) are indirect. The alternative is to measure the effects of treatment by observing directly what happens to those receiving the treatment. Of course, procedures like those described previously should be used to make direct measures as objective as possible. For example, consider a treatment that is supposed to alter the way someone's brain works. The effects of the treatment could be evaluated indirectly by asking the individual whether he thinks his brain functions differently after treatment than before, or by asking his family and friends to make that same judgment. Alternatively, a direct measure of brain function before and after treatment could be obtained with a technique such as functional magnetic resonance imaging (MRI), which provides a picture of what the brain actually does. For treatments that are intended to change the behavior of a child with autism (e.g., attending, communicating, interacting with others, playing), indirect measures include caregiver reports in various forms (e.g., surveys, questionnaires, interviews, and the like); direct measures include real-time observations of the child's behavior, preferably by trained observers using objective behavioral definitions and specific measurement procedures.

Indirect measures of treatment effects are important data in and of themselves, and should be part of all comprehensive evaluations. They do not, however, constitute complete, accurate, or conclusive evidence about treatment effects. Direct measures are necessary.

Noncomparative vs. Comparative Information

Evidence offered to support claims about a treatment should also be scrutinized for the quality and type of comparisons it implies or makes possible. The all-important question, "What is the most effective treatment available for my child's condition?" implies the need to know how each treatment compares with no specific treatment and with many other treatments. Parental reports such as, "My child's behavior is much better now that he's had Therapy X" *suggest* comparison, but their value for drawing any general conclusions is extremely limited, no matter how many such reports there are or how strong the conviction with which they are delivered. The same applies to reports from clinicians that are based solely on informal observations.

Anecdotal evidence (like the kinds of parental and clinical reports mentioned above) has limited usefulness. In addition to the problems inherent in all subjective reports, each such report represents an isolated event: the observation, experience, or perception of one person, unmeasured and unverified by any impartial outside party. Additionally, it is easy to generate testimonials in support of almost any treatment. Naturally, *almost anyone who invests time, money, and hope in a treatment will tend to report that the treatment is helpful.* Indeed, *all* of the treatments that are claimed to be effective for autism have their fans, many eager to testify to the effectiveness of their favorite(s). Reliance on anecdotal reports and testimonials to evaluate treatments for autism, however, has many serious shortcomings. For one, it would lead to the conclusion that all of the various therapies for children with autism are equally effective. Common sense suggests that this is probably not true. Overdependence on anecdotal evidence also helps perpetuate false explanations and ineffective treatment approaches, and holds back real progress toward understanding autism and developing effective treatments for it. In short, anecdotal reports and testimonials lack the comparative information that is logically necessary to support a conclusion that a treatment is effective or that one treatment is better than another (Green, 1994b; Stanovich, 1992).

On the other hand, personal reports and clinical observations can identify variables that might be worthy of further investigation. They often spawn systematic, objective research that yields important information, even if it shows only that there was no substance to the anecdotal reports. Sometimes informal observations about treatment effects are borne out by scientific research, resulting in new facts and improved treatment methods with broad applicability. That happens only as a result of many careful comparisons using objective measurement procedures like those described previously. It is not sufficient, however, merely to compare a child's condition after some months of Therapy Z with his condition before that therapy began. The apparent change could be caused by any of several events or variables. One of the most potent alternatives that must be ruled out in evaluating treatments is the placebo effect: The child might seem better after exposure to the therapy simply because those making the evaluation expect him to be. Other possible explanations for the apparent change are that time has passed and the child has matured physically, learned from things that have been happening in his life in addition to Therapy Z, or benefited from the extra attention that came with the therapy (Campbell & Stanley, 1963; Huck, Cormier, & Bounds, 1974; Kazdin, 1982; Stanovich, 1992).

The goal of scientific research—whether it addresses a basic question, such as how one type of learning occurs, or a practical question like whether a particular method is effective for teaching a child with autism to communicate—is to sift through the possible explanations for the phenomenon to find the variable or variables that actually cause it. This requires observing and measuring the phenomenon under different conditions, and comparing the results. At the very least, comparisons must be constructed so that some of the potential explanations can be ruled out, and others can be confirmed. Over the course of many systematic comparisons (i.e., tests of the potential explanations), one explanation usually emerges as the best (Campbell & Stanley, 1963; Huck et al., 1974; Kazdin, 1982). Again, anecdotes and testimonials simply do not provide enough information to allow false explanations to be ruled out (Green, 1994b; Sagan, 1993; Stanovich, 1992). This leads to a related distinction between types of research and the evidence they produce.

Descriptive (Uncontrolled) vs. Experimental (Controlled) Research

Research comes in many varieties. All good research starts with careful observation and description of the phenomena of interest under natural conditions. This is necessary to get an accurate picture of the dimensions of the phenomena, and the other events or variables that tend to occur with them. When behavior is the topic of interest—for example, a child's vocalizing—it is essential to see and describe its current level and forms, and events that precede and follow occurrences of the behavior. The conscientious observer might watch a child and record vocalizations occurring under various conditions: different times of day, settings (e.g., school, home, car or bus), social situations (e.g., alone, with adults, with other children), and activities (e.g., free play, teaching sessions, peer interactions). The observer would take detailed notes about the ambient conditions and what happened before and after each vocalization by the child. She might also observe or interview other important people in the child's life, such as caregivers, siblings, and peers.

Obviously this kind of observation and description can provide rich and interesting information. A great deal of research (e.g., qualitative research, currently popular in education) is purely descriptive, painting comprehensive and detailed pictures of phenomena and the contexts in which they occur, often organizing the details in ways that can serve a host of purposes. Careful observation and description are essential for generating questions or hypotheses about the phenomenon: Is the child more likely to vocalize in the presence of adults or other children? Do the child's vocalizations change when an adult imitates what the child has vocalized? How do the vocalizations vary in form, volume, and inflection in different situations? Simple observation and description alone cannot provide conclusive answers to questions like these, because none of the several possible explanations for variations in the child's vocalizations can be ruled out. To do that, it is necessary to arrange observations so that possible explanations can be tested systematically—that is, to conduct *controlled* observations. Instead of simply observing what happens to the behavior of interest under conditions where all of the events that might affect it are free to vary, the scientist often selects one event that is likely to affect the behavior and explicitly arranges for it to be present and absent, while measuring carefully to see if the behavior changes. All other factors are held constant. In research jargon, the behavior under study is called the *dependent variable,* and each event that can potentially affect the behavior (e.g., a treatment or teaching procedure) is called an *independent variable.* (Campbell & Stanley, 1963; Christensen, 1985; Huck et al., 1974; Kazdin, 1982; Sidman, 1960; Stanovich, 1992.)

Suppose a researcher wants to test the possibility that having an adult imitate a child's vocalizations (the independent variable) will increase the child's rate of vocalizing (the dependent variable). The researcher might measure rates of vocalizing during several observation sessions with an adult present who does nothing when the child vocalizes, then during several sessions when the adult imitates every vocalization the child makes. Preferably, both of those conditions should be repeated at least once more each. Other factors that might influence the child's vocalizing are kept the same throughout all observations, for example, the setting, the adult, the time of day, the length of the observation sessions, the number of sessions in each condition or phase, and so on. If the child's vocalization rate is higher when the adult imitates the child than when he does not, and that difference holds when the conditions are repeated, we could have some confidence that the independent variable—the adult imitating the child's vocalizations—and not some other event caused increases in the child's rate of vocalizing.

Before the researcher could be confident that adult imitation was a generally effective intervention for increasing vocalization rates in children with autism, however, the experiment just described would have to be repeated with other children, other adults, other settings, and so on. It would also be important to do additional controlled comparisons to rule out or

confirm other plausible explanations. For instance, the observed increase in vocalizations might have been due to the fact that the adult interacted with the child each time the child vocalized, rather than to the adult's imitative responses *per se.* To test the specific effects of the adult's imitative responses, an adult imitation condition could be compared with a condition in which the adult interacted with the child and vocalized something other than what the child had just vocalized. Still other controlled comparisons would be needed, of course, to justify the conclusion that adult imitation was more effective than any other intervention for increasing child vocalizations.

The complexities and intricacies of experimental control are well beyond the scope and purpose of this chapter. Suffice it to say that all controlled comparisons are not created equal. How well experimental control is achieved in any given experiment is a function of many factors. When alternative explanations (also called *extraneous variables*) are well controlled, an experiment is said to be *internally valid.* That is just another way of saying that we can be reasonably confident that the observed effects were due to the independent variable(s) manipulated in the experiment. If important extraneous variables are not well-controlled, then it is possible that they (or some other unidentified events), and not the independent variable, were responsible for the effect. For these reasons, it is always risky to take the reported results and conclusions of any study at face value without scrutinizing the research methods (Campbell & Stanley, 1963; Christensen, 1985; Huck et al., 1974; Kazdin, 1982; Sidman, 1960).

While it is easiest to achieve the necessary control in artificial situations like laboratories, it is entirely possible to do controlled experiments in naturalistic settings. It's just trickier. Experiments are done in everyday settings all the time, whether or not they are identified as such. For instance, every time a parent tries a new strategy to get a child with autism to sample a food the child has been refusing, the parent is doing an experiment of sorts. Add some objective measurement, systematic comparisons, and a few other wrinkles, and you have a formal experiment. Behavior Analysis treatment with a young child with autism actually can be seen as a series (perhaps a multitude) of little experiments, in which the effects of various independent variables (teaching strategies) on various dependent variables (responses by the child) are evaluated systematically. Cumulatively, they can provide invaluable objective evidence about the efficacy of the entire treatment "package" for that particular child. Such evidence accumulated across many children can be powerful indeed (Barlow & Hersen, 1984; Kazdin, 1982; Sidman, 1960).

There is also the matter of *external validity,* or generalizability, which refers to the confidence with which the results of an experiment can be applied to people and situations other than those involved in the experiment. Of course, this is a very important issue in treatment research; it's one of the main reasons for doing treatment research. If an experiment is not internally valid, however—if we can't be reasonably sure that the treatment (and not something else) produced the observed effects—then there is nothing to generalize (Campbell & Stanley, 1963).

Many factors determine the external validity of an experiment. In general, it is enhanced to the extent that the participants, settings, and other aspects of the experiment resemble those to which we wish to apply its results (Barlow & Hersen, 1984; Campbell & Stanley, 1963; Christensen, 1985; Kazdin, 1982). This brings up another set of questions that would be prudent to ask anyone who suggests a treatment for your child: Has the treatment been evaluated by several independent investigators with a reasonable number of children with autism? How were their diagnoses determined? What were the children's characteristics and histories? Were they representative of children with autism in general? With what proportion of children studied was the treatment effective? Did the effects last? Did they carry over to situations outside the study? What negative side effects were observed? Were there any positive side effects? What were the competencies of the people who delivered the treatment in the research studies? Am I likely to be able to find people with the necessary expertise to provide this treatment to my child?

Facilitated Communication

Three currently popular therapies for autism illustrate three different points along the continua described in the preceding sections. For example, claims that Facilitated Communication (FC) is a remarkably effective intervention for many people with autism have been backed up mainly with anecdotal evidence, as noted earlier. The only published research that seems to support the claims about FC consists of a few qualitative studies describing astonishing communications that *appeared* to be produced by people with autism with the physical assistance of facilitators. These studies did not define the treatment or its supposed effects specifically, measured nothing, provided no specific information about the participants, and employed few controls for observer or researcher bias. Most important, they included no controls for the very plausible alternative explanation that the facilitators were doing the spelling. Yet the authors of these reports concluded that FC was effective for dra-

matically improving the communication and cognitive skills of people with disabilities (e.g., Biklen, 1990, 1992, 1993; Biklen et al., 1991; Biklen & Schubert, 1991; Sabin & Donnellan, 1993). Dozens of investigators from around the world, however, have found that when they implemented simple controls for the possibility that facilitators were doing the spelling (e.g., by preventing facilitators from knowing what communications were expected, or simply by having facilitators look away from the spelling device), very few articulate or accurate responses were spelled. Well-controlled studies so far have found no evidence that FC is an effective and reliable intervention (Cummins & Prior, 1992; Felce, 1994; Green, 1993, 1994a, 1994b; Green & Shane, 1994; Hudson, in press; Jacobson et al., 1994; Jacobson et al., 1995; Smith & Belcher, 1994).

Sensory Integration Therapy

Sensory Integration Therapy is said to be effective for improving the sensory processing capabilities of the brain. That is inferred from observing improvements in a number of areas in people with autism, mental retardation, cerebral palsy, and other disabilities: eye contact, learning, self-injurious behavior, stereotypic responses, hyperactivity, communication, motor skills, and others. Although it has been promoted for at least 25 years and is widely used, Sensory Integration Therapy has been the subject of relatively little rigorous research. Typically, Sensory Integration Therapy in one or more of its various forms is delivered in one-to-one sessions over extended periods of time. It involves activities that many children (and adults, for that matter) might find enjoyable (e.g., swinging, rocking, massage). Observation that a child *likes* an activity, however, is not by itself evidence that the activity is producing significant, lasting changes in the child's brain and/or behavior, or any short-term benefits other than momentary pleasure. For a sound conclusion that this therapy alone was responsible for any apparent changes in the child, the changes would first need to be documented over time by objective methods. It would also be necessary to conduct controlled experiments to rule out several plausible alternatives to the possibility that Sensory Integration Therapy *per se* produced the changes: placebo effects; maturation; the potential reinforcing effects of sensory stimulation, motor activities, and adult attention; escape from demands; and others. Most studies reporting that Sensory Integration Therapy is effective lack the necessary controls to permit any alternative explanations to be ruled out. Many lack operational definitions of the critical variables as well as objective measurement procedures and controls for observer bias. Well-controlled studies found that Sensory Integration Therapy was ineffective or no more effective than other treatments (Arendt, MacLean, & Baumeister, 1988; Lindscheid & Valvano, 1987; Shore, 1994). One study found that it increased, rather than decreased, self-injurious behavior in one subject (Mason & Iwata, 1990).

Applied Behavior Analysis

Studies of the effectiveness of Applied Behavior Analysis for young autistic children have employed a variety of objective assessment and control procedures. All of the published studies had children diagnosed by professionals other than those delivering treatment or conducting the study, employed operational definitions of variables, provided specific information about the participants, and used objective procedures to measure treatment effects (in some, both standardized tests and direct observational measures). Some kept the professionals who recorded the treatment outcome measures blind to the children's diagnoses and histories (Birnbrauer & Leach, 1993; Lovaas, 1987; McEachin et al., 1993). Comparisons of the behavior of young children with autism were made both before and after treatment and with children who began treatment after the age of 5 (Fenske et al., 1985), with normally developing children (e.g., Harris et al., 1991; McEachin et al., 1993), with comparable autistic children who did not participate in behavior analytic treatment (Birnbrauer & Leach, 1993), and with comparable autistic children who received less intensive behavior analytic treatment and a variety of other therapies (Lovaas, 1987). Much research remains to be done to replicate these studies, and to determine precisely why some children show dramatic improvements while others make modest or few gains. Direct comparisons with other specific treatments are also needed. For these and other reasons, generalizations from the existing research should be made cautiously. On the other hand, these studies were sufficiently well-controlled to allow some important alternative explanations for the documented effects to be ruled out (e.g., maturation, placebo effects, more typical education, and other therapies).

Statistical vs. Clinical (or Educational) Significance

This distinction is a little different than those discussed so far. A good deal of scientific treatment research uses group research designs and statistical tests to determine if a treatment is more effective than one treatment or some other treatment. For example, one group of participants might receive the treatment of interest (and be labeled the "treatment" or "experimental" group), and another comparable group might receive no specific treatment or some other treatment (the "control" or "comparison" group). Generally speaking, the same measures (e.g., one or more behavioral tests or observational ratings) are administered to all participants in both groups before and after (and sometimes during) the period of time in which the experimental group receives treatment. Individual scores are summed and averaged to yield a statistic called the *mean.* A statistical index of overall variability in scores (the *standard deviation*) is usually calculated also, along with other statistics appropriate to the research question and design. The statistics for the experimental group are compared mathematically with those of the control group to determine the probability that the measured difference(s) between the groups could have occurred by chance. If that probability is very low, then the difference is said to be "statistically significant." Assuming that the experimental group's mean score was the higher, the treatment is then said to be more effective than no treatment or another treatment, whichever the case may be.

Group and statistical comparisons are important and necessary for determining if one treatment approach is better than another for producing an outcome with a group of individuals in general—for example, to answer "actuarial" questions like, "Is Program A better than Program B, on average, for developing prereading skills in kindergartners?" They have some serious limitations, however, when it comes to making decisions about individuals. For one thing, group mean scores may not accurately reflect the actual effects of treatment on any individual in the group. Means can be inflated or deflated by single high or low scores respectively, especially if the sample (group) size is relatively small. Mean scores and statistical comparisons actually "wash out" or obscure individual differences. Indeed, reports of group design studies often include no information whatsoever about individual participants, such as how many individuals in each group improved, stayed the same, or got worse over the course of the study, how much each individual was affected by the treatment, and the characteristics of those who responded positively, negatively, and not at all to the treatment. In short, it can be very difficult to tell from reports of group design studies how closely any participant resembled an individual with whom one is concerned, and how likely it is that the treatment will have a desirable effect on that individual. Similarly, statistical differences among group averages on some measure(s) of treatment effectiveness may not reflect treatment effects that had practical significance for many (or any) individuals who received the treatment. For example, statistically significant differences can be obtained when many in the treatment group improve a little while many in the control group improve less or not at all; or when a few in the treatment group improve a lot while many in the control group improve a little, or a few get worse; or any of several other combinations. In other words, statistically significant group differences may not indicate that a treatment produced clinically or educationally significant benefits for most of those who received it.

Many behavior analysts use single-subject, rather than group, research designs. They focus on measuring the level(s) of an individual's behavior(s) on several occasions when a particular treatment is not in effect (often called the *baseline*), implementing treatment over a period of time while measurement continues, and evaluating how much the treatment affects behavior by looking at graphed representations of all measurements. This process is typically repeated (replicated) with the same participant, if practical, or with other participants, or in other settings. Variability in behavior is generally considered interesting and important, rather than something to be reduced or eliminated mathematically. Individual characteristics that may be relevant to treatment effectiveness are also considered important, as are details about how the treatment was delivered to each individual and under what conditions. Behavior analysts sometimes use statistics, and often study the behavior of groups and aggregate data from a number of single-subject experiments to broaden the base from which generalizations about treatment effects may be drawn. In general, however, treatment research in Applied Behavior Analysis is much less concerned with statistically significant differences between group average measures than with differences that are functionally important to the individual in her everyday life.

SUMMARY

In examining claims about any treatment for autism, the goal should be to discover the quality of the evidence that supports the claims. The more objective and rigorous the methods by which evidence is produced, the less ambiguous it is, and the more confidence one can feel about basing important decisions on it. The range of evidence that might be offered to back up treatment claims is represented in Figure 2.1, with some descriptors to help identify specific types of evidence and methods used to produce them.

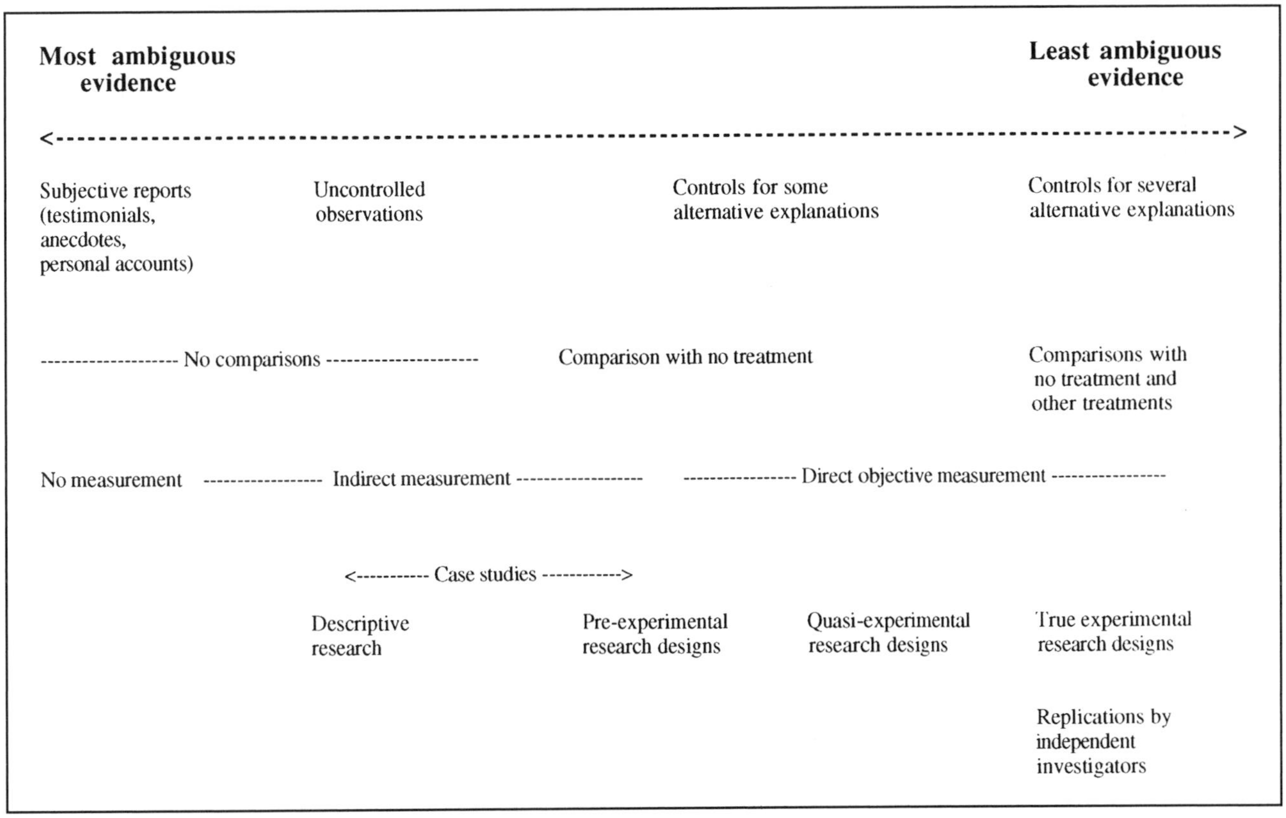

Figure 2.1. Types of evidence about treatment effects.

Personal accounts, testimonials, and anecdotal reports can be intriguing. They may suggest interesting questions that should be explored further. They are virtually worthless, however, for evaluating treatment effectiveness or producing substantive knowledge (Campbell & Stanley, 1963; Shermer, 1994; Stanovich, 1992). In addition, compelling personal stories have many pitfalls. Their vividness tends to overshadow less ambiguous information, provoke emotional responses, and distract us from more rational, objective evaluation (Stanovich, 1992). Subjective reports about treatment effects should be treated with extreme caution, regardless of their source(s), unless they are corroborated with solid objective data. This is not to say that the personal experiences of people who receive treatments, their families, and others around them are unimportant. The importance of including such information in the overall evaluation of any treatment has long been recognized by most disciplines involved in treatment research, including Applied Behavior Analysis (e.g., see Birnbrauer & Leach, 1993; Fuqua & Schwade, 1986; McClannahan & Krantz, 1993; Meyer & Evans, 1993). Subjective reports and uncontrolled observations alone, however, are inadequate for determining whether a treatment works. Controlled experiments using objective measurement procedures are necessary (Campbell & Stanley, 1963; Green, 1994b; Green & Shane, 1994; Meyer & Evans, 1993). The more remarkable the claims about a treatment, and the more profound their implications, the more rigorously the treatment should be evaluated (Wolfensberger, 1994).

RECOMMENDATIONS

What then is the most prudent course for a family to follow in deciding whether to try Therapy X, Y, or Z for their child with autism? Several recommendations follow from the premises presented at the beginning of this chapter:

- First, ask those who claim that the treatment might help, "How do you know that?" along with the follow-up questions suggested throughout this chapter.

- If it sounds to good to be true, it probably is. Be very skeptical about all astonishing claims.

- Beware of those offering nothing more than testimonials, especially if they stand to gain financially from sales of the therapy or its accoutrements.

- Seek published scientific research articles about the treatment and critical reviews of research written by qualified professionals.

- If you can, ask someone who is skilled in reading and interpreting research reports for help.

- Evaluate the evidence you obtain against the criteria described in this chapter.

- If a treatment is new, or the evidence about it is highly ambiguous, steer clear of the treatment. If there have been only a few "preliminary" or "pilot" studies, remain very cautious until more data are available.

- If a number of published studies seem to show that a treatment is effective, scrutinize them very carefully. Were they published in respected, peer-reviewed scientific journals? What are the backgrounds and qualifications of the investigators? How were treatment effects measured? How sound are the controls for likely alternative explanations? What benefits and risks have been well documented?

- Regardless of the current status of scientific evidence about a treatment, if it is going to be used with your child you have the right and the obligation to find out specifically what the treatment is, exactly what it is supposed to do for your child, the competencies of those who will deliver and evaluate the treatment, the risks and benefits, and the costs (in money, time, and emotional energy).

- Demand objective evaluation of the effects of every treatment used on your child.

All this does not necessarily imply that new treatments should not be explored, merely that you should view them with healthy skepticism and caution until they have been evaluated by objective methods. Any treatment that has beneficial effects will stand up to rigorous scientific scrutiny, and all children with autism deserve treatment by methods that have the most sound objective evidence behind them. That is where the vast majority of resources should be invested. This is not to say that you should avoid other therapies completely; some might be helpful adjuncts to the main treatment approach. Here too, caution is advised. Take care that adjunct therapies do not counter the intended effects of the main treatment, or carry harmful side effects, including the temptation to take the child's time away from the most potentially effective treatment to invest it in therapies that give the illusion of quicker results, or mainly benefit someone other than the child.

Suppose we are considering treatments for a child with some disorder other than autism, say a curable type of cancer, and that a number of different treatments are available for this cancer, some of which have little or no objective evidence supporting them. Scientific research has shown that the most effective treatment currently available for this cancer returns about 50% of children to normal or near-normal health, but it requires that the child spend most of her waking hours receiving the treatment. It must be administered by specially trained individuals who know how to evaluate its effects precisely. For most of us, the decision would not be very difficult in this case: We would choose the treatment with demonstrated effectiveness. While the child is undergoing treatment, would it be wise to attend to related health issues like making sure that she is receiving good nutrition, and controlling *bona fide* allergies, infections, and sources of discomfort as best we can? Of course. Might we also arrange for the child to have as many enjoyable experiences as possible, such as affectionate physical contact, play activities, contact with peers, sensory experiences, interactions with animals, or listening to music? Sure. But if any of these adjunct therapies jeopardized the chances for the main treatment to work, even if only by taking time away from it, would we subject the child to the adjunct therapy? Hopefully not. The issues in choosing treatments for autism are much the same.

WHICH PATH: SCIENCE OR PSEUDOSCIENCE/ANTISCIENCE?

Paradoxically, in an age when the array of therapies for autism may be at its largest and most perplexing, the main choice for parents—indeed, for the field of autism research and treatment as a whole—seems more clear than ever. It is a choice between pseudoscience/antiscience and science. Pseudoscience and antiscience have not produced any real progress in understanding and treating autism. Science has. Many questions about autism have not yet been answered, and never will be unless parents and professionals choose the path that is more likely to lead to real long-term solutions for children, individually and collectively. The choice is clear.

ACKNOWLEDGMENTS

Support for the development of this chapter was provided by The New England Center for Autism, Inc. and by National Institute of Child Health and Human Development research grant HD27703 to the E. K. Shriver Center for Mental Retardation. I am grateful to Catherine Maurice for the opportunity to contribute to this project, and for wisdom and convictions shared; and to Vincent Strully, Jr., Executive Director, and the staff, students, and families of The New England Center for Autism for their invaluable help.

REFERENCES

American Psychological Association (1994, August). *Resolution on Facilitated Communication.* Washington, DC: Author.

Anderson, S. R., Avery, D. L., DiPietro, E. K., Edwards, G. L., & Christian, W. P. (1987). Intensive home-based early intervention with autistic children. *Education and Treatment of Children, 10,* 352–366.

Arendt, R. E., MacLean, W. E., Jr., & Baumeister, A. A. (1988). Critique of sensory integration therapy and its application in mental retardation. *American Journal on Mental Retardation, 92,* 401–411.

Barlow, D. H., & Hersen, M. (1984). *Single case experimental designs* (2nd ed.). New York: Pergamon.

Biklen, D. (1990). Communication unbound: Autism and praxis. *Harvard Educational Review, 60,* 291–315.

Biklen, D. (1992, January). Typing to talk: Facilitated Communication. *American Journal of Speech and Language Pathology,* pp. 15–17.

Biklen, D. (1993). *Communication unbound: How Facilitated Communication is challenging traditional views of autism & ability-disability.* New York: Teachers College Press.

Biklen, D., Morton, M. W., Saha, S. N., Duncan, J., Gold, D., Hardardottir, M., Karna, E., O'Connor, S., & Rao, S. (1991). "I AMN OT A UTISTIVC ON THJE TYP" ("I'm not autistic on the typewriter"). *Disability, Handicap, & Society, 6,* 161–179.

Biklen, D., & Schubert, A. (1991). New words: The communication of students with autism. *Remedial and Special Education, 12,* 46–57.

Birnbrauer, J. S., & Leach, D. J. (1993). The Murdoch early intervention program after 2 years. *Behaviour Change, 10,* 63–74.

Campbell, D. T., & Stanley, J. C. (1963). *Experimental and quasi-experimental designs for research.* Chicago: Rand McNally.

Christensen, L. (1985). *Experimental methodology* (3rd ed.). Boston: Allyn & Bacon.

Cromer, A. (1993). Pathological science: An update. *Skeptical Inquirer, 17,* 400–407.

Crossley, R. (1992). Getting the words out: Case studies in Facilitated Communication training. *Topics in Language Disorders, 12,* 46–59.

Cummins, R. A., & Prior, M. P. (1992). Autism and assisted communication: A response to Biklen. *Harvard Educational Review, 62,* 228–241.

Felce, D. (1994). Facilitated Communication: Results from a number of recently published evaluations. *British Journal of Learning Disabilities, 22,* 122–126.

Fenske, E. C., Zalenski, S., Krantz, P. J., & McClannahan, L. E. (1985). Age at intervention and treatment outcome for autistic children in a comprehensive intervention program. *Analysis and Intervention in Developmental Disabilities, 5,* 49–58.

Fuqua, R. W., & Schwade, J. (1986). Social validation of applied behavioral research: A selective review and critique. In A. Poling & R. W. Fuqua (Eds.), *Research methods in applied behavior analysis* (pp. 265–292). New York: Plenum.

Green, G. (1993). Response to "What is the balance of proof for or against Facilitated Communication? *AAMR News & Notes, 6*(3), 5.

Green, G. (1994a). Facilitated Communication: Mental miracle or sleight of hand? *Skeptic, 2,* 68–76.

Green, G. (1994b). The quality of the evidence. In H. C. Shane (Ed.), *Facilitated Communication: The clinical and social phenomenon* (pp. 157–225). San Diego: Singular Press.

Green, G., & Shane, H. C. (1994). Science, reason, and Facilitated Communication. *Journal of the Association for Persons with Severe Handicaps, 19,* 151–172.

Harris, S. L., Handleman, J. S., Gordon, R., Kristoff, B., & Fuentes, F. (1991). Changes in cognitive and language functioning of preschool children with autism. *Journal of Autism and Developmental Disorders, 21,* 281–290.

Huck, S. W., Cormier, W. H., & Bounds, W. G. (1974). *Reading statistics and research.* New York: Harper & Row.

Hudson, A. (In press). Disability and Facilitated Communication: A critique. In T. H. Ollendick & R. J. Prinz (Eds.), *Advances in clinical child psychology* (Vol. 17). New York: Plenum.

Jacobson, J. W., Eberlin, M., Mulick, J. A., Schwartz, A. A., Szempruch, J., & Wheeler, D.L. (1994). Autism and Facilitated Communication: Future directions. In J. L. Matson (Ed.), *Autism in children and adults: Etiology, assessment, and intervention* (pp. 59–83). Pacific Grove, CA: Brooks/Cole.

Jacobson, J. W., Mulick, J. A., & Schwartz, A. A. (1995). A history of Facilitated Communication: Science, pseudoscience, and antiscience. *American Psychologist, 50,* 750–765

Kazdin, A. E. (1982). *Single-case research designs.* New York: Oxford University Press.

Lindscheid, T. R., & Valvano, J. (1987). Neurodevelopmental treatment and behavioral methodology. In J. A. Mulick & R. F. Antonak (Eds.), *Transitions in mental retardation, Vol. 2: Issues in therapeutic interventions* (pp. 189–210). Norwood, NJ: Ablex.

Lovaas, O. I. (1987). Behavioral treatment and normal educational and intellectual functioning in young autistic children. *Journal of Consulting and Clinical Psychology, 55,* 3–9.

Mason, S. A., & Iwata, B. A. (1990). Artifactual effects of sensory-integrative therapy on self-injurious behavior. *Journal of Applied Behavior Analysis, 23,* 361–370.

Maurice, C. (1993). *Let me hear your voice.* New York: Knopf.

McClannahan, L. E., & Krantz, P. J. (1993). On systems analysis in autism intervention programs. *Journal of Applied Behavior Analysis, 26,* 589–596.

McEachin, J. J., Smith, T., & Lovaas, O. I. (1993). Long-term outcome for children with autism who received early intensive behavioral treatment. *American Journal on Mental Retardation, 4,* 359–372.

Meyer, L. H., & Evans, I. M. (1993). Science and practice in behavioral intervention: Meaningful outcomes, research validity, and usable knowledge. *Journal of the Association for the Severely Handicapped, 18,* 224–234.

Page, T. J., & Iwata, B. A. (1986). Interobserver agreement: History, theory, and current methods. In A. Poling & R. W. Fuqua (Eds.), *Research methods in applied behavior analysis* (pp. 99–126). New York: Plenum.

Pendergrast, M. (1994). *Victims of memory.* Hinesburg, VT: Upper Access Books.

Perry, R., Cohen, I., & DeCarlo, R. (1995). Case study: Deterioration, autism, and recovery in two siblings. *Journal of the American Academy of Child and Adolescent Psychiatry, 34,* 232–237.

Poling, A., & Fuqua, R. W. (1986). *Research methods in applied behavior analysis.* New York: Plenum.

Randi, J. (1982). *Flim-flam!* Buffalo, New York: Prometheus Books.

Sabin, L. A., & Donnellan, A. M. (1993). A qualitative study of the process of Facilitated Communication. *Journal of the Association for the Severely Handicapped, 18,* 200–211.

Sagan, C. (1993, March 7). What's really going on? *Parade Magazine,* pp. 4–7.

Shermer, M. (1994). How thinking goes wrong. *Skeptic, 2,* 42–49.

Shore, B. A. (1994). Sensory-integrative therapy. *Self-Injury Abstracts and Reviews, 3,* 1–7.

Sidman, M. (1960). *Tactics of scientific research.* New York: Basic Books.

Smith, M. D., & Belcher, R. G. (1994). Facilitated Communication and autism: Separating fact from fiction. *Journal of Vocational Rehabilitation, 4,* 66–74.

Smith, T. (1993). Autism. In T. R. Giles (Ed.), *Handbook of Effective Psychotherapy* (pp. 107–133). New York: Plenum.

Stanovich, K. E. (1992). *How to think straight about psychology* (3rd ed.). New York: HarperCollins.

Wolfensberger, W. (1994). The Facilitated Communication "craze" as an instance of pathological science: The cold fusion of human services. In H. C. Shane (Ed.), *Facilitated Communication: The clinical and social phenomenon* (pp. 57–122). San Diego: Singular Press.

CHAPTER THREE

Early Behavioral Intervention for Autism

What Does Research Tell Us?

Gina Green

Autism. For most of the half-century that label has been in use, many have understood it as a life sentence for the individuals to whom it has been applied. Most were expected to have serious and permanent deficits in communication, play, relating to others, and learning. A very small proportion of people with autism (less than 5%) might be expected to achieve independent functioning as adults, but even within this tiny group many retain at least some autistic characteristics. Historically, most people with autism have required extensive treatment and supports throughout their lives (Rapin, 1991; Rimland, 1994; Rutter, 1970; Rutter & Schopler, 1987; Szatmari et al., 1989). Today the mainstream position is that autism is a "severely incapacitating lifelong developmental disability." It is considered treatable; indeed, a wide variety of treatments, therapies, and techniques are claimed to help (or even cure) people with autism, and new ones are invented regularly (Autism Society of America, 1995).

Until recently, however, none of those treatments has offered any solid, realistic basis for changing the view that autism is a permanent disability. Several studies have now shown that one treatment approach—early, intensive instruction using the methods of Applied Behavior Analysis—can result in dramatic improvements for children with autism: successful integration in regular schools for many, *completely normal functioning* for some (Anderson, Avery, DiPietro, Edwards, & Christian, 1987; Birnbrauer & Leach, 1993; Fenske, Zalenski, Krantz, McClannahan, 1985; Harris, Handleman, Gordon, Kristoff, & Fuentes, 1991; Lovaas, 1987; Maurice, 1993; McEachin, Smith, & Lovaas, 1993; Perry, Cohen, & DeCarlo, 1995; Sheinkopf & Siegel, in press). In fact, there is abundant scientific evidence that Applied Behavior Analysis methods (also called *behavioral intervention* or *behavioral treatment*) can produce comprehensive and lasting improvements in many important skill areas for most people with autism,

regardless of their age. No other treatment for autism offers comparable evidence of effectiveness (Lovaas & Smith, 1989; Schreibman, 1988; Schreibman, Charlop, & Milstein, 1993; Smith, 1993; see also Chapters 2 and 4 in this manual).

Despite the evidence, families with young autistic children are often told incorrectly that all treatments are equally effective or, even more inaccurately, that behavioral intervention is ineffective or harmful. They are likely to be encouraged to try whatever fad treatment is currently in vogue, or to mix and match among the many options on the market. Families who are fortunate or diligent enough to discover the one approach with scientifically proven effectiveness often express the need for a single, fairly concise summary of research on early behavioral intervention for autism. This chapter attempts to address that need. Its purposes are to (a) provide a brief overview of Applied Behavior Analysis principles and methods as they apply to teaching young children with autism; (b) review studies of early behavioral intervention for autism that have been published in the peer-reviewed professional literature; and (c) summarize what research tells us about early behavioral intervention for autism, as well as questions that remain to be answered by further research.

THE INTERVENTION OF CHOICE: APPLIED BEHAVIOR ANALYSIS

Applied Behavior Analysis employs methods based on scientific principles of behavior to build socially useful repertoires and reduce problematic ones (Cooper, Heron, & Heward, 1989). The behavior analytic view is that autism is a syndrome of behavioral deficits and excesses that have a neurological basis, but are nonetheless amenable to change in response to specific, carefully programmed, constructive interactions with the environment. Extensive research has shown that children with autism do not learn readily from typical environments, but many can learn a great deal given appropriate instruction (e.g., Harris & Handleman, 1994; Koegel & Koegel, 1995; Lovaas & Smith, 1989; Schreibman, 1988; Schreibman et al., 1993).

Behavior analytic treatment for autism focuses on teaching small, measurable units of behavior systematically. Every skill the child with autism does not demonstrate—from relatively simple responses like looking at others, to complex acts like spontaneous communication and social interaction—is broken down into small steps. Each step is taught (often in one-to-one teaching situations, to begin with) by presenting a specific cue or instruction. Sometimes a prompt is added (such as gentle physical guidance) to get the child started. (A word of caution: Prompts of all kinds should be used sparingly and faded quickly to avoid making the child dependent on them.) Appropriate responses are followed by consequences that have been found to function effectively as reinforcers—that is, when those consequences have consistently followed the child's response, it has been shown that the response was likely to occur again. A high-priority goal is to make learning fun for the child. Another is to teach the child how to discriminate among many different stimuli: his name from other spoken words; colors, shapes, letters, numbers, and the like from one another; appropriate from inappropriate behavior. Problematic responses (such as tantrums, stereotypies, self-injury, withdrawal) are explicitly not reinforced, which often requires systematic analyses to determine exactly what events function as reinforcers for those responses. Preferably, the child is guided to engage in appropriate responses that are incompatible with the problem responses.

Teaching trials are repeated many times, initially in rapid succession, until the child performs a response readily, without adult-delivered prompts. The child's responses are recorded and evaluated according to specific, objective definitions and criteria. Those data are graphed to provide pictures of the child's progress, enabling the teacher or parent to adjust the teaching procedures whenever the data show that the child is not making the desired gains. The timing and pacing of teaching sessions, practice opportunities, and consequence delivery are determined precisely for each child and each skill. In this way, instruction can be highly personalized and tailored to each child's learning style and pace.

To maximize the child's success, emerging skills are also practiced and reinforced in many less structured situations. With some children, certain skills can be taught entirely in relatively unstructured situations from the outset. Such "incidental" or "naturalistic" practice opportunities have to be arranged carefully, however, to ensure that they occur frequently, and that consequences are provided consistently. Ideally, there is a gradual progression from one-to-one to small group to large group instruction. Simple responses are built systematically into complex and fluid combinations of typical, age-appropriate responses. The overall emphasis is on teaching the child how to learn from the normal environment, and how to act on that environment in ways that will consistently produce positive outcomes for the child, her family, and others (Harris & Handleman, 1994; Koegel & Koegel, 1995; Lovaas et al., 1981; Lovaas & Smith, 1989; Schreibman et al., 1993; and Chapters 6 and 7 in this book).

The effective and ethical use of Applied Behavior Analysis methods requires special training, which interested parents should seek. Like any treatment procedures, these can be misused, inadvertently or intentionally. It is particularly important to have competent, well-trained behavior analysts guiding and supervising behavioral treatment for autistic children for several reasons. Research has shown that stereotypic, disruptive, and destructive responses are often provoked by specific (but not always obvious) events, and maintained by sensory stimulation, attention from others, the termination of events like requests or demands, or combinations of these (Green & Cuvo, 1993; Lovaas & Smith, 1989; Repp & Singh, 1990; Taylor & Carr, 1992, 1994). Individuals who mean well but are unaware of this research and its implications, and unskilled in the necessary assessment and behavior-change procedures, may interact with the child in ways that actually make problem behavior worse (Eikeseth & Lovaas, 1992; Meinhold & Mulick, 1990; Taylor & Carr, 1992, 1994; Vyse & Mulick, 1988). For example, providing an autistic child with attention, sensory stimulation, or the opportunity to escape from demands following instances of self-injury may very well *increase* the rate of occurrence of self-injury (e.g., Lovaas & Simmons, 1969; Mason & Iwata, 1990; and see Chapter 6).

Additionally, procedures that are intended to reduce inappropriate responses, such as time out from positive reinforcement, are easy to misuse and abuse. Unless they are administered carefully, with supervision and monitoring by well-trained professionals, such procedures can jeopardize the child's fundamental rights and worsen rather than improve behavior (e.g., Green, 1990; Repp & Singh, 1990). One of the keys to producing lasting treatment gains in children with autism is consistency. Caregivers who do not know the events that can trigger or maintain problem behavior are often inconsistent in their interactions with autistic children. They may unintentionally provide a child with mixed messages, impeding rather than fostering the development of adaptive skills, and strengthening rather than decreasing problematic responses. Further, if behavior-change procedures are not carried out consistently across settings, people, and time, any gains the child makes are likely to be lost. Happily, research shows that many parents learn to be consistent, effective behavior-change agents for their children, and can play a vital role in their treatment (Koegel & Koegel, 1995; Lovaas, 1987; McEachin et al., 1993; Schreibman, 1988).

The discipline of Applied Behavior Analysis is based on more than 50 years of scientific research and evolves continually as new evidence emerges. Ideally, behavioral intervention for autistic children should be guided by ongoing, competent professional analysis of previous and current research findings in behavior analysis, as well as related areas (Green, 1990; VanHouten et al., 1988).

EARLY BEHAVIORAL INTERVENTION: RESEARCH FINDINGS

Applied Behavior Analysis techniques have proven effective for improving a wide range of skills in children and adults with autism. So far, however, only a few studies have evaluated the effectiveness of many behavioral techniques combined into a comprehensive, intensive program for preschool-age children with autism. Those that have been published in peer-reviewed research journals are described in the following sections. Research on home-based early intervention is presented first, followed by research on school- or center-based early intervention.

The studies included here evaluated the effects of comprehensive behavioral programming on the overall functioning of children with autism or pervasive developmental disorder (PDD). That is, the investigators measured effects on children's intellectual functioning, language, social interaction, adaptive (or self-care) skills, play, and maladaptive behavior. Some investigators used global measures that encompassed several of those skill domains (e.g., standardized, objective intelligence [IQ] tests, developmental scales, adaptive behavior scales, or enrollment in schools for typically developing children); others used several specific measures.

Studies showing that behavioral intervention can produce large improvements in specific and important areas like peer interactions and classroom behavior

(e.g., Strain, Hoyson, & Jamieson, 1985), imitation (e.g., Young, Krantz, McClannahan, & Poulson, 1994), self-care (e.g., Pierce & Schreibman, 1994), and various language skills (e.g., Taylor & Harris, 1995) were not included in this chapter simply because there are too many of them. Also, reports about program effectiveness that have appeared in sources other than peer-reviewed research journals (e.g., Strain & Cordisco, 1994, and others in Harris & Handleman, 1994) were not included.

Home-based Behavioral Intervention

The UCLA Young Autism Project

The most thorough studies of home-based behavioral intervention for young children with autism have been conducted by Ivar Lovaas and colleagues at the University of California–Los Angeles (UCLA). The first was reported by Lovaas in 1987. An intensive-treatment experimental group of 19 children with autism reportedly received 40 hours a week of one-to-one behavioral treatment from trained therapists (mostly UCLA students). A comparable group of children received fewer than 10 hours a week of one-to-one behavioral treatment with UCLA-trained therapists (the minimal-treatment control group). A second control group of 21 comparable children was treated in programs other than the UCLA project. All children received a diagnosis of autism from qualified professionals not associated with the study, and started treatment before the age of 4 years. The three groups of children had similar measured developmental levels, language and play skills, and rates of stereotypic behavior when treatment began. All participated in treatment for at least 2 years.

The children in the intensive-treatment group received one-to-one teaching at home, at school, and in the community (when appropriate). Instruction focused on increasing language, attending, imitation, social behavior, appropriate independent play, cooperative peer play, and self-care skills, as well as decreasing aggressive, stereotypic, and ritualistic behavior and tantrums. After the first 2 years, it was determined that children who were able to benefit from regular school placement received behavioral treatment for 10 hours or fewer each week while they completed regular kindergarten, and minimal consultation from trained therapists while they completed first grade. Children who did not gain enough skills to function successfully in regular classrooms continued to receive 40-hour-a-week treatment for up to 6 years. Children in the minimal-treatment control group received a variety of other interventions in addition to 10 hours a week of behavioral intervention; the second control group also received various other interventions (but not intensive behavioral treatment).

All children were reevaluated between the ages of 6 and 7 years by examiners who did not know which group they were in. Their educational placements were also verified. These follow-up measures revealed striking differences between the experimental group and both control groups. Of the 19 children in the intensive-treatment group, nine (47%) successfully completed regular first grade and obtained average or above-average scores on IQ tests (94–120; 100 is average). This was an average gain of 37 IQ points over the course of treatment, and a gain of 31 points more than the minimal-treatment group, on average. Eight children (42%) successfully completed first grade in classes for language-delayed or learning-disabled children, and had IQ scores that were, on average, in the mild range of mental retardation. They had made substantial improvements in most other areas (communication, adaptive behavior) but not enough to enable them to participate fully in regular classrooms. The remaining two children were placed in classes for autistic/mentally retarded children and had IQ scores in the profoundly mentally retarded range. In contrast, only one child from the two control groups completed regular first grade successfully and achieved an IQ score in the average range. Eighteen (45%) were in classes for children with language and learning disabilities, and 21 (53%) were in classes for autistic/mentally retarded children. Their IQ scores remained unchanged from the beginning of treatment, which is consistent with other follow-up studies of children with autism who have received typical educational services (Freeman et al., 1991; Rutter, 1970; Schreibman, 1988; also see Chapter 4).

The nine children in the original (Lovaas, 1987) intensive-treatment group who had achieved normal functioning by the end of first grade, participated in a long-term follow-up study (McEachin et al., 1993). These children were reevaluated when they were 13 years old, on average. They were compared with children from the minimal-treatment control group from the 1987 study. Examiners who were not familiar with the children's histories administered intelligence tests, adaptive behavior scales, and a personality inventory to those from the intensive-treatment group, as well as age-matched children whose development had always been typical. Similar evaluations were conducted with children from the control groups. Educational placements were also evaluated. Results indicated that the effects of the intensive behavioral treatment persisted: Eight of the nine formerly autistic children continued to succeed in regular classrooms. One was in a special education class, but an-

other child from the original experimental group who had not completed regular first grade successfully had later moved into regular classes and was enrolled in junior college at the time of the follow-up study. Thus the proportion of intensively treated children who attained normal functioning in school remained 47% (9 of 19). Similarly, IQ score gains these children had shown at the end of first grade were maintained, and scores remained on average 30 points higher than those of the control group. Scores on adaptive behavior and personality measures were also significantly higher than those of the control group, whose school placements (all in special education classes) had also remained unchanged. In fact, "blind" examiners could not distinguish the formerly autistic children who received early intensive behavioral intervention from typically developing children of the same age on measures of cognitive, academic, social, or adaptive skills.

The groundbreaking research by Lovaas and his colleagues raises several intriguing possibilities. First, it suggests that intensive teaching that requires young children with autism to engage actively with their physical and social environments and provides them with consistent, differential consequences can result in completely normal functioning for many. Contrary to what some critics have said, behavioral intervention does not necessarily result in children who merely "act normal" in rote fashion. If that were the case, the children who achieved the best outcomes would not have demonstrated sufficiently flexible behavior to be judged normal by teachers and examiners who did not know their histories. Indeed, there is no solid evidence that behavioral intervention makes autism worse or makes children robot-like—but these misconceptions persist. Second, the studies suggest that intensive behavioral intervention produces substantially better outcomes than other available treatments for young children with autism. Children in the control groups, who received a variety of other interventions, generally did not fare nearly as well as children in the intensive behavioral treatment group over the same period of time. Third, the studies suggest that young children with autism must be involved in behavioral intervention for a large number of hours every week over an extended period of time to have the best chance for optimal outcomes. Normal functioning was achieved only by children who received intensive behavioral treatment for 40 hours a week, 50 weeks a year, for at least 2 years. Those who received behavioral treatment for only 10 hours a week or not at all, with one exception, did not show much improvement.

As with most studies, those reported by Lovaas and his colleagues do not by themselves provide conclusive answers to all questions about early intervention for autism. They raise several important issues; some have been addressed by other published studies discussed in this chapter, some are the focus of ongoing research, and still others remain to be answered in future studies. Among the more burning questions are these: Exactly how did the majority of children in the intensive treatment group differ from the 47% "best-outcome" minority before treatment, and in their responsiveness to particular components of treatment? This leads to a broader question: Which children are likely to respond best to intensive behavioral intervention? Are there characteristics (e.g., degree of developmental delay or disorder, level and course of language development, learning style, etc.) that can be assessed before treatment begins, or early in treatment, to determine if a child is going to be more or less responsive? For example, other research has shown that the development of useful language by the age of five is associated with more positive outcomes for children with autism. Also, despite its limitations, IQ score is a relatively good predictor of later academic and overall adjustment (Rapin, 1991; Rutter & Schopler, 1987; Schreibman, 1988). Consistent with those findings, most of the best-outcome children from the 1987 study learned to imitate adult speech by the end of 3 months of intensive treatment, although many had little or no useful vocal speech when they entered treatment (ASA, 1994). The best-outcome children also had somewhat higher IQ scores before treatment than those in the intensive-treatment group who did not achieve normal functioning (Lovaas & Smith, 1988). Otherwise, the reports published by Lovaas and colleagues provided little information about individual children that might have revealed exactly how those who responded dramatically to intensive behavioral intervention differed from those who did not.

Other questions have to do with the nature of the intervention. Many different individuals served as therapists in the Lovaas (1987) study, most of them college students and parents. It is very likely that the manner and skill with which they delivered the intervention varied, which may account in part for the variability with which the children apparently responded. The published articles reported only general information about how the therapists were trained and what they did, and no direct measures of how well or how consistently the therapists performed over the course of treatment, exactly how much treatment was provided by parents vs. other therapists, and so on. Of course, authors usually have to omit some details from published research reports because of space limitations imposed by journals. Accordingly, Lovaas and his coauthors referred readers of their journal articles to *The ME Book* (Lovaas et al., 1981) for details about

treatment procedures. That begs the question of how well therapists actually carried out the procedures as intended, however. In addition, since *The ME Book* was published a number of years ago, it does not include the many new teaching techniques and refinements that have resulted from research conducted in the meantime by the UCLA Young Autism Project as well as many other behavior analysts.

Answers to these and other questions are very important not only to other researchers, but also to families, advocates, service providers, policymakers, and others concerned with providing effective treatment to young children with autism at a time when resources are becoming ever more scarce. More careful, rigorous studies like those conducted by Lovaas and his colleagues will be needed to obtain credible, reliable answers (see Chapters 2 and 4).

The studies reported by Lovaas and his colleagues suggest that early, intensive, home-based behavioral intervention provides the best opportunity for a sizable proportion of children with autism to have normal lives. Those studies would have relatively limited value, however, if they could not be repeated (replicated) by other, independent practitioners, families, and researchers (Foxx, 1993). Fortunately there have been several efforts to replicate them, at least in part, and others are in progress at this writing.

The May Institute Study

In a study conducted in Massachusetts, 14 youngsters with autism (average age: 43 months) received 15–25 hours per week of intensive behavioral teaching from trained teachers and parents in their homes (Anderson et al., 1987). Their overall mental age (MA), adaptive behavior, and language development were measured with standardized tests administered by professionals not directly associated with the project. Parents and teachers also recorded data every day on each child's progress toward instructional goals as well as levels of maladaptive behavior. Additionally, project staff used a standardized measure (the Uniform Performance Assessment System, or UPAS) to assess each child's progression through normal developmental sequences in several skill domains. These measures were taken before treatment and after one year of treatment. For seven children who completed a second year of treatment, assessments were repeated at the end of the second year.

After one year of treatment, MA and social-age scores increased to some degree (ranging from 2 to 23 months) for 12 of 13 children tested. Nine of the eleven children with whom language tests were repeated after one year of treatment made gains of 3–18 months. Similar improvements were revealed by the UPAS, but gains in communication skills were smaller than gains in other skill areas (e.g., social and self-help). Children who received a second year of intensive behavioral treatment continued to improve in most areas at about the same rates as they had in the first year. Improvements were significant as measured by statistical tests comparing average group scores on standardized tests completed before treatment with those readministered after one year of treatment. For eight of the thirteen children, rates of learning in the first year of treatment were also found to be accelerated relative to normal development; this was true for all children who continued in treatment for another year. All children progressed on their individual instructional objectives, mastering 20 objectives in the first year, on average. None, however, were integrated full time in regular classrooms at the time the study ended, although 31% were integrated at least 2 hours a week (Anderson et al., 1987).

As Anderson and his coauthors were careful to point out, their study differed from the study by Lovaas (1987) in a number of ways. Any of several characteristics of the children and the treatment might account for the less favorable outcomes obtained by Anderson and colleagues. The children were nearly a year older, on average, and there was a larger difference (by an average of 6 months) between their chronological ages and measured mental ages when treatment started. They participated in treatment about half as many hours per week as the children in the Lovaas (1987) intensive treatment group (an average of 20 hours per week vs. 40 hours or more per week), over a shorter total duration (1–2 years vs. 2–6 years). No physically aversive procedures were used by Anderson et al. (1987), whereas reprimands and thigh slaps were provided as consequences for aggression, noncompliance, and other maladaptive responses by some children in the Lovaas (1987) study. Additionally, there was no control group of comparable children who received another type of intervention, or no particular intervention, for direct comparison with behavioral intervention.

On the other hand, Anderson et al. (1987) obtained detailed data on all children before they began treatment (baseline) and throughout the course of treatment. Baseline data showed that none of the children were making appreciable progress in the preschool programs in which they were participating. For each child, appropriate responding increased and maladaptive behavior decreased when and only when behavioral intervention began. That is, behavioral intervention was compared directly with no particular intervention (i.e., typical education) for each child, and replicated across children and behaviors. Such

within-subject comparisons and replications, or single-subject experiments, can provide powerful evidence of treatment effectiveness (Barlow & Hersen, 1984; Kazdin, 1982; also see Chapter 2). In addition they can document specific changes in behavior that may be too small to be detected by broad measures like standardized tests, but are nonetheless very meaningful and important to the individual child and those around her. Finally, unlike Lovaas (1987), Anderson and colleagues evaluated the skills of the parent therapists, providing some evidence that the treatment procedures were carried out with relative consistency and skill across all participating children.

The Murdoch Early Intervention Program

Another evaluation of intensive, home-based behavioral intervention for autism was conducted by behavior analysts at Murdoch University in Western Australia (Birnbrauer & Leach, 1993). Nine young children with autism or PDD (average age: 39 months) received an average of 18.72 hours per week of one-to-one instruction from trained parents and volunteers (college students, other family members, friends) supervised by individuals with advanced training in Applied Behavior Analysis. A control group of five similar children did not receive behavioral treatment. Standardized assessments of intellectual functioning (IQ), language development, and adaptive behavior were administered to all children before and at the end of a 2-year treatment period by examiners who were not associated with the program. Direct observations, parent interviews, and a personality inventory were used to evaluate the severity of each child's autistic behavior before and after treatment. Additionally, samples of each child's play, instruction-following, imitation skills, and maladaptive behavior were videotaped before, during, and at the end of the treatment period, and scored by "blind" independent raters. For children in the treatment group, performance data and details about individual programs were recorded during every teaching session. Finally, parents completed a stress index twice a year.

At the end of the 2-year treatment period, four of the nine children in the treatment group had made substantial gains as measured by IQ, language, and adaptive behavior tests. They achieved IQ scores of at least 80 (89–103), whereas before treatment the independent examiners had judged them untestable. Language and adaptive behavior test scores also improved considerably, but not as much as IQ, so that measured performances in those areas were still below chronological-age levels. The communication, play, instruction-following, social, self-help, and tantrum behavior of these four children had also improved considerably as measured by direct observational assessments and the personality inventory. Stereotypic response levels were essentially the same as before treatment, however. Four of the other five children in the treatment group made moderate improvements, while one made only minimal gains. In contrast, one of five children in the control group made substantial improvements in adaptive behavior and language, but not in intellectual functioning, over the 2-year period. That child had the most advanced skills and least severe autistic characteristics of all the children when the study began. One other child in the control group made moderate improvements, but three made few or minimal gains on any measures.

Scores on the stress index were high for parents of children in both groups when treatment started. By the end of 2 years, scores for parents of children in the behavioral treatment group had improved (i.e., their reported stress levels had decreased) by an overall average of 12.8 points, in comparison to an overall improvement of 1.8 points for parents of children in the control group.

The Birnbrauer and Leach (1993) study had many features in common with the Lovaas (1987) study. Children in the treatment group were slightly older and had slightly lower adaptive behavior and intelligence scores before treatment than those in the Lovaas study, but they were otherwise very similar. Outcomes were similar as well, in that just under half of the children in both studies made substantial improvements in 2 years of treatment; however, the best-outcome children in this study were not shown to achieve completely normal functioning as did those in the UCLA studies, although they seemed to be moving in that direction at the end of 2 years. The major difference between the studies was that the Australian children received considerably fewer hours a week of treatment than those in the UCLA intensive-treatment group were said to receive, and less than the 30 hours the investigators sought.

The quality of treatment delivered in the two studies may have differed as well. Like Anderson et al. (1987) but unlike Lovaas (1987), Birnbrauer and Leach used no physically aversive consequences in treatment. Additionally, their volunteer therapists received most of their training on the job, while the college student therapists in Lovaas' study reportedly had prior and ongoing academic as well as practical training in behavioral principles and procedures. It is impossible to determine how treatment differed in the two studies, however, because neither measured the competencies of therapists or the extent to which they adhered to treatment protocols (see Birnbrauer & Leach, 1993, p. 72).

The UC—San Francisco Study

Recently the effects of intensive, home-based behavioral intervention on young children with autism were evaluated by researchers at the Pervasive Developmental Disorders (PDD) Clinic, Langley Porter Psychiatric Institute, University of California at San Francisco (Sheinkopf and Siegel, in press). This clinic was conducting a long-term study of young autistic children who had received initial diagnostic evaluations at the clinic. On follow-up evaluations, the researchers happened to notice that a number of children were reported to have received intensive, home-based behavioral intervention. They designated 11 of those children to constitute a treatment group. Each was paired with a child from the larger study who did not receive behavioral intervention. Pairs of children were matched for chronological age (which averaged just under 3 years), mental age (MA; just under 2 years, on average), diagnosis (10 pairs, autism; 1 pair, PDD), and the interval between their initial and follow-up evaluations. Each child's intellectual ability (mental age and/or IQ) was estimated with standardized tests on initial and follow-up evaluations at the clinic. Additionally, the severity of their autistic symptoms was rated on a scale from zero (symptom not present) to three (severe), and a diagnosis was established by consensus of at least three clinic staff.

The researchers were not involved in deciding which children received behavioral treatment or in providing treatment. They were "blind" to group membership when they compared the measures of the children's status before and after treatment. This effectively ruled out the possibility of biased selection of children for the behavioral treatment group, a criticism that some have made about the Lovaas (1987) study (e.g., see Schopler, Short, & Mesibov, 1989; Lovaas et al., 1989).

Information about interventions in which children participated was obtained through phone interviews with parents. From these reports it appeared that children in the treatment group received an average of just under 20 hours a week of one-to-one, in-home instruction with behavioral methods (range: 9.43–38.75 hours per week) for periods ranging from 7 to 24 months. Trainers were mostly paraprofessionals (college students, relatives, friends) recruited by parents, who reportedly were assisted in training and supervision by one of three master's-degreed "behavior therapists" working in the San Francisco area. Children in the treatment group also attended school an average of a little more than 6 hours per week. None of the children in the control group received intensive behavioral intervention, according to parental reports, but they attended school an average of 10.7 hours per week. All children in both groups were placed in special education classes initially.

Statistical comparisons of averaged test results indicated that, as a group, the children who received intensive behavioral treatment had significantly higher MA and IQ estimates after treatment than matched children in the control group (recall that these scores were very similar for both groups initially). Examination of individual IQ test data reveals some interesting patterns. All 10 children in the behavioral treatment group for whom follow-up data were available improved on IQ measures, most of them by substantial amounts. In the control group, six children improved by small to moderate amounts, four had lower scores, and one stayed the same. After treatment, six of the ten children in the behavioral treatment group achieved IQ scores of at least 90. However, three of them had scores near 90 before treatment began; all three of those children had higher scores after treatment (about 95, 100, and 115). Three of the eleven control group children had IQ estimates of 90 or above after the treatment interval, but two of those had scored around 90 before treatment. When the IQ data for matched pairs of children are compared, it appears that for seven pairs the child receiving behavioral treatment improved more than his matched partner over the same time period. Within those pairs, the IQ scores of three control group children decreased from initial assessments, while two remained the same and two increased slightly. For two other pairs, treatment and control group children made roughly equivalent IQ gains. In one case the control group child's IQ increased more than that of the matched child receiving behavioral intervention, and for one pair no follow-up data were available for the treatment group child.

The authors reported that the number of autistic symptoms did not differ significantly for the two groups of children either before or after treatment, but the symptoms of the children in the treatment group were rated as significantly less severe after treatment (Sheinkopf & Siegel, in press).

Results of this study add to the evidence that intensive behavioral intervention increases the intellectual functioning (as measured by standardized, objective tests) of many young autistic children. Behavioral intervention also appears to be more effective than other interventions in that regard, or at least the typical interventions that are available to autistic preschoolers. In this study, the "blind" assignment of children to groups and evaluations by professionals who were not associated with treatment, together with the matching procedures employed, lend credence to these conclusions. Unfortunately no measures of adaptive behavior, language, social skills, or

educational performance were obtained, so there is no basis for judging whether any children attained normal or near-normal functioning in those important domains, nor for evaluating how specific characteristics of the children (e.g., language skills, learning styles) were related to outcomes.

More important, the only information about the nature of the behavioral treatment provided to children in the Sheinkopf and Siegel study was obtained indirectly through parental reports. These included general information, such as how long treatment was provided and by how many therapists, but nothing specific about the training or competencies of the therapists or precisely what they did. No information was provided about the level of involvement of the master's-level behavior therapists in training and supervising those working directly with the children, nor how much of the direct intervention was provided by parents vs. paraprofessionals. The studies summarized earlier all had at least one doctoral-level psychologist or behavior analyst providing overall supervision for treatment implementation and evaluation; that did not appear to be the case here. Further, there is not enough information in the report to determine whether the amount of behavioral treatment (in number of hours per week and total number of weeks) related to individual outcomes, although the authors did report that the IQs of children who received an average of about 30 hours a week of behavioral treatment generally improved more than the IQs of those who received about 20 hours a week. (Readers should note, however, that this author reviewed a prepublication version of the Sheinkopf and Siegel report, cited here with the investigators' permission. More details may be included in the version that is revised for publication.)

The Maurice Children

The effectiveness of early intensive behavioral intervention for two siblings with autism was documented in a book written by their mother (Maurice, 1993), as well as a case study published in a professional journal (Perry et al., 1995). The two children were each diagnosed with autism at about the age of 2 years by independent professionals who did not know about each other's evaluations. Intensive treatment was provided by master's-degreed behavior analysts and the children's mother, along with a speech-language pathologist. Formal, one-to-one teaching sessions were conducted for 10–35 hours per week, but incidental and informal instruction provided by the parents outside of those sessions meant that the children participated in intervention during most of their waking moments. The first child, a girl, made rapid progress within the first year of treatment, at which point her younger brother was diagnosed and started an intensive behavioral program. He too responded well to behavioral intervention. Intensive treatment continued for both children for about 2 years, and was reduced gradually as they began to attend regular preschools. By the ages of 39 and 53 months respectively, they no longer met criteria for the diagnosis of autism, and behavioral treatment was discontinued.

Both children successfully completed regular kindergarten, and have gone on to do very well in typical classrooms where teachers who do not know their histories evaluate them as academically advanced and socially well-adjusted. Three of the professionals who diagnosed the children evaluated their progress (on a standardized test of adaptive behavior as well as their impressions from direct observations) at intervals of 6–9 months until behavioral treatment was discontinued. At that point these professionals, who were not involved in providing treatment to the children, reported that both were fully recovered from autism (Perry et al., 1995).

While they were not formal experiments, the case studies of these two children include several features that make them credible: documentation of little or no progress before treatment (baseline); objective measurement of treatment effects repeated over extended periods of time; intensive behavioral treatment introduced systematically across many behaviors, producing relatively rapid and dramatic improvements each time; and verification of diagnoses, pretreatment (baseline) measures, and outcomes by several independent observers (Kazdin, 1982).

School- or Center-based Behavioral Intervention

The effectiveness of educational programs using the methods of Applied Behavior Analysis with preschool and school-age children with autism has been documented in countless articles published in scientific journals like the *Journal of Applied Behavior Analysis, Research in Developmental Disabilities, Journal of Autism and Developmental Disorders, Behavior Modification,* and others. Many have been reviewed and compiled in books. Several respected preschool programs were described in considerable detail in a recent book edited by Harris and Handleman (1994). Only a couple of programs, however, have documented broad effects of comprehensive, intensive behavioral programming provided in a school or center in reports published in peer-reviewed research journals.

The first study of this kind was conducted by staff of the Princeton Child Development Institute (PCDI), a private nonprofit program that provides educational and other services to children with autism and their families on a thoroughgoing Applied Behavior Analysis model. Outcomes for nine children who enrolled at PCDI before the age of 60 months (Group 1) were compared with outcomes for nine comparable children who enrolled after the age of 60 months (Group 2). All were diagnosed by agencies outside PCDI, and were enrolled in the program for 24 months or more. Behavioral intervention was delivered primarily in the PCDI school program for about 27.5 hours per week, 11 months a year, by a number of teachers and therapists trained in Applied Behavior Analysis. Most children lived with their families, and their parents were trained to implement behavioral procedures at home. One child in Group 1 and four children in Group 2 lived in PCDI-run community group homes, where professional staff also provided behavioral intervention.

Treatment outcomes were defined as positive (the child lived at home and was enrolled full-time in a regular school) or not (the child remained in treatment). It is important to note that children began to make transitions from PCDI to regular school programs only when objective, direct observational data showed that they had language, social, self-care and leisure skills, and control of problem behaviors that were sufficient for them to benefit from placement in regular classrooms (McClannahan & Krantz, 1994). Transitions were accomplished gradually while the children's progress was measured by PCDI staff, and were completed when data showed that skills had generalized to the regular school setting. Results of the study showed that six of nine children who enrolled at PCDI before the age of 60 months (i.e., 67%) achieved positive outcomes, compared to just one of the nine children who enrolled after the age of 60 months (Fenske et al., 1985).

This study had a number of limitations: It did not employ an experimental research design; there were no direct measures of specific outcomes (e.g., language development, maladaptive behavior, self-help skills, social skills, intellectual functioning); and the published report did not include any detailed information about the intervention, or measures of treatment integrity. Nor was any information about individual children included in the report. However, PCDI researchers have a long and distinguished record of scientific research on behavioral teaching procedures for children and youth with autism, staff training, parent training, and program evaluation (e.g., Krantz, Zalenski, Hall, Fenkse, & McClannahan, 1981; McClannahan & Krantz, 1993; McClannahan, Krantz, & McGee, 1982). The study by Fenske et al. (1985) provides important evidence about the relation between age of entry into a high-quality, school-based behavioral program and outcomes for children with autism.

Another study was conducted by researchers at the Douglass Developmental Center, Rutgers University (Harris et al., 1991). This center provides preschool education using methods of Applied Behavior Analysis for children with autism in a segregated classroom as well as a classroom in which children with autism are integrated with typically developing peers (Handleman & Harris, 1994). The study evaluated changes in intellectual functioning and language development in children with autism over the course of about a year's participation in the center's program, in comparison with their same-age, typically developing peers. Diagnoses of autism were made by outside agencies and confirmed by a clinical psychologist at the center. Typically developing children were drawn from the center's integrated preschool and day care center.

A standardized IQ test (the Stanford-Binet IV) was administered to nine preschoolers with autism when they were 50 months old, on average, and to nine typically developing preschoolers (average age: 45 months). The same test was given again 10–11 months later (posttest). On the first test administration (pretest), the average IQ score for the children with autism was 67.5; the average for the typical youngsters was 114.11. On posttesting, the children with autism achieved an average IQ score of 86.33 (an average gain of 18.78 points), while the average for the typical children did not change significantly. Scores of seven of the nine children with autism improved by at least 10 points.

A different group of 16 preschoolers with autism and a sample of 12 typically developing peers were pre- and posttested on the Preschool Language Scale at intervals of 9–10 months. Scores for both groups increased by about eight points, which was statistically significant, but scores of the children with autism were well below those of their typical peers on both pre- and posttests.

As the authors noted, the children with autism were relatively advanced when this study began. Their average IQ score was nearly 70, their average age was more than 4 years, and their autistic characteristics were rated mild to moderate. Nonetheless, the gains they made in intellectual functioning over a period of just under one year were substantially greater than the negligible changes that have been documented in other research with 4-year-olds with autism, and exceeded those of their normal peers. It is not known whether the improvements maintained because no long-term data were reported. Unfortunately the study included no measures of other important skills like social interaction, play, self-help skills, and maladaptive behavior, which do not necessarily improve with increases in IQ scores, so the impact of behavioral intervention on the children's overall functioning can-

not be determined. In addition, no specific information was provided about the nature or intensity of the intervention, and there were no comparisons involving preschoolers with autism who received no treatment or some other type of intervention. Thus it is not clear whether the improved intellectual functioning demonstrated by seven of nine children with autism was the direct result of their participation in a behavioral preschool program, but it seems likely given the other research reviewed above and in Chapter 4.

SUMMARY AND IMPLICATIONS

The body of research on early behavioral intervention for autism is quite small, and many important questions remain to be answered. Taken together, however, the studies just reviewed provide reasonably strong evidence about a number of issues. Those are summarized next, along with their implications and questions that need to be addressed in future research.

Effectiveness

There is little doubt that early intervention based on the principles and practices of Applied Behavior Analysis can produce large, comprehensive, lasting, and meaningful improvements in many important domains for a large proportion of children with autism. For some, those improvements can amount to achievement of completely normal intellectual, social, academic, communicative, and adaptive functioning. In fact, a large majority of young children with autism benefit from early behavioral intervention. Most show substantial improvements in many adaptive, useful skill areas and reductions in problematic behaviors. Only a small proportion (about 10% of those studied so far) have been found to make few or no improvements despite intensive efforts (e.g., Anderson et al., 1987; Birnbrauer & Leach, 1993; Lovaas, 1987; McEachin et al., 1993; Sheinkopf & Siegel, in press).

The best documented positive effect is improved intellectual functioning as measured by standardized IQ tests or developmental scales. Virtually every study reviewed here found this effect. Again, the majority of children studied made at least some gains in IQ scores over the course of 1–6 years of behavioral treatment; slightly fewer than half made large gains (from levels indicative of moderate to severe mental retardation to levels in the normal range, in many cases), and a small percentage made few or no gains (Anderson et al., 1987; Birnbrauer & Leach,

1993; Harris et al., 1991; Lovaas, 1987; Sheinkopf & Siegel, in press). Improvements in language, social skills, play, self-help, and problematic behavior (e.g., tantrums, stereotypic and ritualistic responding, withdrawal, self-injury, aggression) were found to be somewhat less widespread and robust than IQ changes, although that may be a function of characteristics of the children or the treatment provided in different studies, or other variables (e.g., Anderson et al., 1987; Birnbrauer & Leach, 1993). Clearly, large and meaningful improvements in all domains were attained by some children who ultimately became indistinguishable from their peers on every dimension (Maurice, 1993; McEachin et al., 1993; Perry et al., 1995).

Successful integration in regular schools is another positive effect that is well supported by data. Many children with autism who received at least 2 years of intensive behavioral intervention starting at an early age went on to participate in classrooms for typical children of the same age, some with no or relatively little ongoing special support (Fenske et al., 1985; Harris et al., 1991; Maurice, 1993; Lovaas, 1987; McEachin et al., 1993; Perry et al., 1995; Sheinkopf & Siegel, in press). It is important to emphasize that the researchers represented in this chapter, for the most part, had extensive objective data showing that the skills of children with autism actually persisted or continued to improve when they were placed in regular classrooms, which happened only *after* there was clear evidence that the children had developed the skills necessary to succeed in those settings (see Chapter 16). This approach differs considerably from the "total inclusion" social movement that would have all children with autism (and other disabilities) placed immediately and permanently in regular classrooms regardless of their beginning or ongoing skill development, and without regard to objective evidence of effectiveness (e.g., Biklen, 1992; Stainback & Stainback, 1992).

There is strong evidence that behavioral intervention is more effective for young children with autism than no intervention, and more effective than typical early education services and assorted other therapies. This inference is based on the results of studies reviewed here that compared early behavioral intervention to no treatment or typical education (i.e., control groups or individual pretreatment baselines); a large body of research comparing the effectiveness of behavioral intervention to other procedures for changing specific behaviors of young children with autism (e.g., social skills, communication, and maladaptive responses); and the lack of strong scientific support for almost every other specific therapy for autism (Anderson et al., 1987; Birnbrauer & Leach, 1993; Harris et al., 1991; Lovaas, 1987; Maurice, 1993;

McEachin et al., 1993; Sheinkopf & Siegel, in press; also see Schreibman, 1988; Smith, 1993; and Chapters 2 and 4 in this book).

To this author's knowledge, however, no studies have directly compared comprehensive, intensive behavioral intervention with intervention based on another orientation (e.g., play therapy, sensory integration, a child-centered developmental model) provided to comparable children for a comparable amount of time. There are some hints that early educational efforts that are not explicitly behavior-analytic can produce some improvements in children with autism who participate in them for many hours a week over an extended time (e.g., Rogers & Lewis, 1989). In addition, some of the studies reviewed here found that an occasional control group child who participated in other interventions improved substantially (e.g., Birnbrauer & Leach, 1993; Lovaas, 1987; Sheinkopf & Siegel, in press). Few details about those children were reported, but some of them appeared to be relatively advanced prior to intervention (Birnbrauer & Leach, 1993; Sheinkopf & Siegel, in press). Further, the other interventions have not been well-specified nor evaluated in scientifically rigorous studies to date. The limited objective evidence available so far suggests that other interventions do not produce improvements as large as those that have been shown to result from behavioral intervention (Lovaas, 1987; Sheinkopf & Siegel, in press; also see Smith, 1993).

Age for Optimal Effectiveness

The optimal age to begin intensive behavioral intervention is before the age of 5. So far, the best outcomes have been reported for children who started treatment at age 2 or 3 (Birnbrauer & Leach, 1993; Lovaas, 1987; Maurice, 1993; McEachin et al., 1993; Perry et al., 1995; Sheinkopf & Siegel, in press). At present there seems to be no compelling reason to delay intervention as soon as autistic behavior is verified and the child has sufficient motor skills to carry out simple actions. It remains to be seen, however, whether very young children (i.e., 2 years or younger) will tolerate and benefit from teaching sessions that are as lengthy and structured as those commonly used with children ages 3 and older; that is, there may prove to be an interaction between the child's age or developmental level and treatment intensity, however, the latter is defined.

There may be an optimal period during which the young, developing brain is very modifiable. In some children with autism the repeated, active interaction with the physical and social environment that is ensured by intensive behavioral intervention may modify their neural circuitry, correcting it before the neurobiological correlates of autistic behavior become relatively permanent (Lovaas & Smith, 1989; McEachin et al., 1993; Niemann, in press; Perry et al., 1995; Smith, 1993). At this point in time, of course, these are merely plausible speculations that remain to be investigated in scientific studies.

The Nature of the Intervention

Behavioral intervention is a "package" treatment with many elements and dimensions. The studies reviewed in this chapter represent some of the first attempts to evaluate the whole package, applied in a comprehensive, intensive, and sustained way, with young children. Families, researchers, practitioners, service providers, policymakers, and others naturally have many questions about the nature of the treatment: What are the essential components? Exactly how is it done? Who can deliver the intervention effectively? What does *intensive* mean, in practical terms? How intensive does intervention have to be to have the desired effects? How long should it continue? Unfortunately, most studies published so far include very little specific information about how behavioral intervention was provided to the children studied, so many of the foregoing questions need to be addressed in future research. Some points that can be inferred from existing research, with varying degrees of confidence, are summarized next.

Components

Applied Behavior Analysis comprises many assessment and behavior-change procedures. They are all derived from scientifically established principles of behavior. Many procedures, singly and in certain combinations, have been validated repeatedly in scientific studies, but new techniques and combinations are constantly being developed and evaluated. The only published, comprehensive package of procedures and skill sequences for teaching young children with autism is *The ME Book* (Lovaas et al., 1981). As mentioned earlier, the version that is currently available does not incorporate techniques and strategies that have been developed since its publication. Most of the published research reports reviewed earlier did not describe specifically which of the many components of behavioral intervention were employed in the studies. That was partly out of necessity, not only because of space limitations in professional journals but because the very nature of Applied Behavior Analysis is that it is highly individualized. Behavior-change procedures and progressions are tailored to each child's current levels of functioning and projected future needs. It would be helpful nonetheless to know more about specific aspects of the intervention provided to participants in treatment evaluation studies like the ones reviewed here.

One component of behavioral intervention for young children with autism that has been addressed to some extent in the formal studies is the use of aversive consequences to reduce levels of inappropriate responding. Lovaas (1987) reported that sharp verbal reprimands and light thigh slaps appeared to be necessary to effect meaningful reductions in problem behavior for some children. Both the Anderson et al. (1987) and Birnbrauer and Leach (1993) studies opted not to employ aversive physical stimulation. In general their approach did not produce outcomes as impressive as those of Lovaas (1987), which may have been due to the exclusion of aversive treatment components or to any of several other differences. Children in both of those studies received fewer hours of treatment per week than reported in the Lovaas (1987) study; children in the Anderson et al. (1987) study were older; and therapists in the Birnbrauer and Leach (1993) study may have had less extensive training. On the other hand, physical aversives were not part of the intervention for the Maurice children, both of whom achieved normal functioning (Maurice, 1993; Perry et al., 1995). In short, it is not possible to draw any strong conclusions from the available evidence as to whether aversive components add to or detract from the effectiveness of early behavioral intervention.

Intensity

This may be one of the most important dimensions of behavioral intervention; surprisingly, it has not been well defined. Researchers have described intensity only in terms of the number of hours that children were reported to be receiving treatment. Those reports appear to have been largely anecdotal; no measures of actual time children were engaged in treatment, verified by independent observers, have been provided to date. Nor was information provided on other important dimensions of treatment intensity, such as proportions of time spent on discrete-trial drills vs. incidental teaching opportunities, or the amount and type of programming provided by parents vs. other therapists.

Much more specific, reliable information about treatment intensity is needed, for many reasons. For one, it is very difficult to draw comparisons across studies when we do not know how they differed on this important treatment variable. Then there is the question of cost-effectiveness, which is vitally important to families and advocates who are trying to procure funding for behavioral intervention, and to families, insurance companies, service providers, and policymakers who must make difficult decisions about resource allocation (time and labor, as well as money). Obviously the intensity of treatment must be well specified if valid and useful cost-effectiveness formulas are to be developed. Further, common sense as well as empirical facts about behavior suggest that it is not the number of hours allocated for intervention that is important, but rather what is *done* during that time. A very skilled therapist or parent could probably accomplish more with a child in 10 hours than a less-skilled individual could do given 30 hours with the same child. The crucial aspect of treatment intensity will probably prove to be something like rate of learning opportunities (e.g., number of programmed arrangements of specific antecedents, responses, and consequences presented for the child per minute).

A further qualification is that, to date, there is very little evidence from sound research about the relative effectiveness of behavioral intervention at different degrees of intensity. Lovaas (1987) reported that about 40 hours per week was considerably more effective than about 10 hours per week. Sheinkopf and Siegel (in press) inferred that about 30 hours a week produced greater IQ gains in children than an average of around 20 hours per week, but they determined treatment intensity from indirect, unverified reports and did not relate degrees of improvement to weekly or total hours of treatment specifically. The children who achieved positive outcomes in the study by Fenske et al. (1985) received at least 27.5 hours per week of intensive behavioral intervention as preschoolers in the Princeton Child Development Institute's programs, but no comparisons were made with children who spent less time per week in intervention. Studies in which children received an average of about 20–25 hours of treatment weekly (Anderson et al., 1987; Birnbrauer & Leach, 1993) found somewhat more modest effects than those reported to result from 40 hours per week (Lovaas, 1987). As noted above, however, those studies also differed from Lovaas' study in other ways. The research designs employed have not made it possible to separate the effects of treatment intensity clearly from the effects of other variables in any studies published to date.

Given these limitations, inferences about optimal treatment intensity should be made cautiously. The only conclusion supported by the data at this point in time is that the best outcomes have been reported for children who participated in behavioral intervention for at least 30 hours per week.

Duration

Most of the questions and limitations just noted for treatment intensity also apply to treatment duration, or the total treatment period (months, years) that is likely to produce the best outcomes. Almost no comparative information is available from the published research. Not surprisingly, Anderson et al. (1987) found that youngsters who made good progress in 1 year of treatment made even more over a second year, but they did not compare the progress of children who had 2 years of treatment with that of children who terminated behavioral intervention after 1 year. Most of the best-outcome children in the initial Lovaas (1987) study achieved normal functioning after 2 years of intensive (40 hours per week, 50 weeks per year) behavioral intervention, but one child eventually did so after 6 years (McEachin et al., 1993). The retrospective study by Sheinkopf and Siegel (in press) included children who participated in behavioral intervention for periods ranging from 7 months to nearly 2 years. The data were not presented in such a way, however, that a relation between time in treatment and outcomes could be inferred. Further, it is likely that treatment effectiveness will prove to be the product of an interaction between treatment intensity and duration, therapist competencies, and child characteristics. Until those variables are defined specifically and studied rigorously, the question of optimal treatment duration cannot be answered conclusively. Again, the only safe conclusion at this point seems to be that the best outcomes have been reported for children who participated in intensive behavioral intervention for at least 2 consecutive years, if not longer (Anderson et al., 1987; Birnbrauer & Leach, 1993; Fenske et al., 1985; Maurice, 1993; Perry et al., 1995; Lovaas, 1987; McEachin et al., 1993; Sheinkopf & Siegel, in press).

Quality

Still another dimension of behavioral intervention is the quality with which it is delivered. Arguably, quality might encompass variables like intensity and duration, but for purposes of this discussion it is defined as the extent to which those providing treatment do so in accordance with empirically validated best-practice standards as well as legal and ethical guidelines. This is another issue in early behavioral intervention for autism on which objective evidence is sorely lacking; its importance is self-evident. With the exception of Anderson et al.'s measures of parents' skills, none of the studies published to date have provided any data about the competencies of therapists, teachers, or trainers, or objectively verified information about what they actually did during intervention sessions. As Birnbrauer and Leach (1993) argued, measurement of treatment quality and integrity should be a high-priority topic for future research.

Setting

The bulk of the research reviewed here dealt with early behavioral intervention that was largely home based, usually leading (when successful) to a combination of home-, community-, and school-based intervention. No direct comparisons of home- vs. school-based behavioral intervention for young children with autism have been published, to this author's knowledge. Given the well-documented effectiveness of school-, center-, and community-based programs for people with disabilities that use the methods of Applied Behavior Analysis, there is every reason to think that skilled parents, teachers, and therapists can provide effective behavioral intervention for young children in various settings. It is not the place but the quality with which treatment is delivered that is likely to play the greater role in producing good results. A couple of qualifications are in order, however: (a) Given the deficits in attending, observing, understanding spoken language, following instructions, and sustaining engagement in constructive activities that typify many young children with autism, initial instruction should take place in settings that are quiet and as free of distractions as possible; and (b) treatment must be extended to settings other than the primary one to produce lasting, generalized effects.

On the other hand, it makes good behavioral sense to teach children with autism in contexts that are as similar as possible to those in which their same-age peers live and learn. Since most very young children spend a good deal of their time at home, and learning how to function effectively within the family is one of the most important lessons of early life, it makes sense to provide behavioral intervention to very young children with autism in their homes, at least initially. Additionally, parental involvement in treatment may be a crucial component of effective behavioral intervention for young children with autism, and that may be enlisted more readily when treatment takes place in the home (Lovaas, 1987). Not all families, however, are able to take on an intensive home-based program, so it would seem best if a range of options were available, including school-based programs. Additionally,

it is entirely possible and very desirable to involve parents as active partners in treatment delivered primarily by a school or center; indeed, virtually every behavioral preschool program does so (Harris & Handleman, 1994).

Conclusion

While many questions remain to be answered by sound scientific studies, the results of research conducted so far have several implications for making decisions about treatment for young children with autism:

1. *The intervention of choice is intensive instruction using the methods of Applied Behavior Analysis. Intensive* means that carefully planned learning opportunities are provided and reinforced at a high rate by trained teachers and therapists (including parents), under conditions that maximize the probability that the child will benefit from instruction, throughout most of every day, for a minimum of 2 years. It seems best to aim for at least 30 hours of intervention per week to begin with. That much time may not be necessary for every child, but if the intervention is delivered competently, the child is not likely to be harmed from participating for 30 hours or more a week, and is very likely to benefit substantially. After a while, if data show that the child does just as well with fewer hours, then the amount of time could be reduced.

2. *Intervention should begin before the child reaches the age of 5.*

3. *To be effective, Applied Behavior Analysis treatment must be delivered by individuals with extensive training in the methods, ideally under the ongoing supervision of professionals who have advanced training and experience in Applied Behavior Analysis principles and methods.*

4. *The cost of providing intensive behavioral treatment for a young child with autism is minimal considering the gains that can be achieved.* After about 2 years of intensive intervention, research would predict substantial cost reductions for most children, significantly lower or no continuing special expenditures for many. In contrast, the cost of lifelong specialized services to accommodate a severe disability—the likely outcome for most children with autism who do not receive early intensive behavioral intervention—runs into the millions of dollars for each individual (Birnbrauer & Leach, 1993; Lovaas, 1987). Autism is a low-incidence disorder, so the up-front investment in intensive behavioral intervention for any agency serving young autistic chil-

dren is likely to be relatively low, and the payoffs potentially monumental. For children with autism and their families, the benefits could be priceless.

ACKNOWLEDGMENTS

Development of this chapter was supported by National Institute of Mental Health Grant MH5 0237-02 to the E. K. Shriver Center and The New England Center for Autism. A previous version was prepared to assist families who were seeking funding for behavioral programs, and was distributed as a working paper by The New England Center for Autism. I am grateful to Steve Luce, Catherine Maurice, and Tristram Smith for their helpful comments on a draft of this chapter, to Jennifer McIntire for her assistance in gathering background materials, to B. F. Skinner for giving us a science of behavior, and to the children, family members, teachers, therapists, and researchers whose achievements make that science live.

REFERENCES

American Psychiatric Association. (1994). *Diagnostic and statistical manual* (4th ed). Washington, DC: American Psychiatric Association.

Anderson, S. R., Avery, D. L., DiPietro, E. K., Edwards, G. L., & Christian, W. P. (1987). Intensive home-based early intervention with autistic children. *Education and Treatment of Children, 10,* 352–366.

Autism Society of America [ASA]. (1994). Interview with Ivar Lovaas. *Advocate, 26*(1), 13–15.

Autism Society of America [ASA]. (1995). *Advocate, 27*(1), 3.

Barlow, D., & Hersen, M. (1984). *Single case experimental designs.* New York: Pergamon.

Biklen, D. (1992). *Schooling without labels.* Philadelphia: Temple University Press.

Birnbrauer, J. S., & Leach, D. J. (1993). The Murdoch early intervention program after 2 years. *Behaviour Change, 10,* 63–74.

Cooper, J. O., Heron, T., & Heward, W. (1989). *Applied Behavior Analysis.* Columbus, OH: Merrill.

Eikeseth, S., & Lovaas, O. I. (1992). The autistic label and its potentially detrimental effect on the child's treatment. *Journal of Behavior Therapy and Experimental Psychiatry, 23,* 151–157.

Fenske, E. C., Zalenski, S., Krantz, P. J., & McClannahan, L. E. (1985). Age at intervention and treatment outcome for autistic children in a comprehensive intervention program. *Analysis and Intervention in Developmental Disabilities, 5,* 49–58.

Foxx, R. M. (1993). Sapid effects awaiting independent replication. *American Journal on Mental Retardation, 97,* 375–376.

Freeman, B. J., Rahbar, B., Ritvo, E. R., Bice, T. L., Yokota, A., & Ritvo, R. (1991). The stability of cognitive and behavioral parameters in autism: A 12-year prospective study. *Journal of the American Academy of Child and Adolescent Psychiatry, 30,* 479–482.

Green, G. (1990). Least restrictive use of reductive procedures: Guidelines and competencies. In A. C. Repp and N. N. Singh (Eds.), *Perspectives on the use of nonaversive and aversive interventions for persons with developmental disabilities* (pp. 479–493). DeKalb, IL: Sycamore Press.

Green, G., & Cuvo, A. J. (1993). Mental retardation: Behavioral treatment. In V. B. VanHasselt and M. Hersen (Eds.), *Handbook of behavior therapy and pharmacotherapy for children: A comparative analysis* (pp. 105–128). Needham Heights, MA: Allyn & Bacon.

Handleman, J. S., & Harris, S. L. (1994). The Douglass Developmental Disabilities Center. In S. L. Harris and J. Handleman (Eds.), *Preschool education programs for children with autism* (pp. 71–86). Austin, TX: PRO-ED.

Harris, S. L., & Handleman, J. S. (1994). *Preschool education programs for children with autism.* Austin, TX: PRO-ED.

Harris, S. L., Handleman, J. S., Gordon, R., Kristoff, B., & Fuentes, F. (1991). Changes in cognitive and language functioning of preschool children with autism. *Journal of Autism and Developmental Disorders, 21,* 281–290.

Kazdin, A. E. (1982). *Single-case research designs.* New York: Oxford University Press.

Koegel, R. L., & Koegel, L. K. (1995). *Teaching children with autism.* Baltimore: Paul H. Brookes.

Krantz, P. J., Zalenski, S., Hall, L. J., Fenske, E. C., & McClannahan, L. E. (1981). Teaching complex language to autistic children. *Analysis and Intervention in Developmental Disabilities, 1,* 259–297.

Lovaas, O. I., Ackerman, A., Alexander, D., Firestone, P., Perkins, M., Young, D. B., Carr, E. G., & Newsom, C. (1981). *Teaching developmentally disabled children: The ME book.* Austin, TX: PRO-ED.

Lovaas, O. I. (1987). Behavioral treatment and normal educational and intellectual functioning in young autistic children. *Journal of Consulting and Clinical Psychology, 55,* 3–9.

Lovaas, O. I., & Simmons, J. Q. (1969). Manipulation of self-destruction in three retarded children. *Journal of Applied Behavior Analysis, 2,* 143–157.

Lovaas, O. I., & Smith, T. (1988). Intensive behavioral treatment for young autistic children. In B. B. Lahey & A. E. Kazdin (Eds.), *Advances in clinical child psychology* (Vol. 11, 285–324). New York: Plenum.

Lovaas, O. I., & Smith, T. (1989). A comprehensive behavioral theory of autistic children: Paradigm for research and treatment. *Journal of Behavior Therapy and Experimental Psychiatry, 20,* 17–29.

Lovaas, O. I., & Smith, T., & McEachin, J. J. (1989). Clarifying comments on the Young Autism Study. *Journal of Consulting and Clinical Psychology, 57,* 165–167.

Mason, S. A., & Iwata, B. A. (1990). Artifactual effects of sensory-integrative therapy on self-injurious behavior. *Journal of Applied Behavior Analysis, 23,* 361–370.

Maurice, C. (1993). *Let me hear your voice.* New York: Knopf.

McClannahan, L. E., & Krantz, P. J. (1993). On systems analysis in autism intervention programs. *Journal of Applied Behavior Analysis, 26,* 589–596.

McClannahan, L. E., & Krantz, P. J. (1994). The Princeton Child Development Institute. In S. L. Harris & J. S. Handleman (Eds.), *Preschool education programs for children with autism* (pp. 107–126). Austin, TX: PRO-ED.

McClannahan, L. E., Krantz, P. J., & McGee, G. G. (1982). Parents as therapists for autistic children: A model for effective parent training. *Analysis and Intervention in Developmental Disabilities, 2,* 223–252.

McEachin, J. J., Smith, T., & Lovaas, O. I. (1993). Long-term outcome for children with autism who received early intensive behavioral treatment. *American Journal on Mental Retardation, 4,* 359–372.

Meinhold, P. M., & Mulick, J. A. (1990). Counter-habilitative contingencies in institutions for people with mental retardation: Ecological and regulatory influences. *Mental Retardation, 28,* 67–73.

Niemann, G. W. (in press). The neurodevelopment of autism: Recent advances. In P. Vostanis (Ed.), *Advances in assessment and management of autism.* London: Association for Child Psychology and Psychiatry.

Perry, R., Cohen, I., & DeCarlo, R. (1995). Case study: Deterioration, autism, and recovery in two siblings. *Journal of the American Academy of Child and Adolescent Psychiatry, 34,* 232–237.

Pierce, K. L., & Schreibman, L. (1994). Teaching daily living skills to children with autism in unsupervised settings through pictorial self-management. *Journal of Applied Behavior Analysis, 27,* 471–481.

Rapin, I. (1991). Autistic children: Diagnosis and clinical features. *Supplement to Pediatrics, 87,* 751–760.

Repp, A. C., & Singh, N. N. (1990). *Perspectives on the use of nonaversive and aversive interventions for persons with developmental disabilities.* DeKalb, IL: Sycamore Press.

Rimland, B. (1994). Recovery from autism is possible. *Autism Research Review International, 8,* 3.

Rogers, S. J., & Lewis, H. (1989). An effective day treatment model for young children with pervasive developmental disorders. *Journal of the American Academy of Child and Adolescent Psychiatry, 28,* 207–214.

Rutter, M. (1970). Autistic children: Infancy to adulthood. *Seminars in Psychiatry, 2,* 435–450.

Rutter, M., & Schopler, E. (1987). Autism and pervasive developmental disorders: Concepts and diagnostic issues. *Journal of Autism and Developmental Disorders, 17,* 159–186.

Schopler, E., Short, A., & Mesibov, G. (1989). Relation of behavioral treatment to "normal functioning": Comment on Lovaas. *Journal of Consulting and Clinical Psychology, 57,* 162–164.

Schreibman, L. (1988). *Autism.* Newbury Park, CA: Sage.

Schreibman, L., Charlop, M. H., & Milstein, J. P. (1993). Autism: Behavioral treatment. In V. P. VanHasselt & M. Hersen (Eds.), *Handbook of behavior therapy and pharmacotherapy for children: A comparative analysis* (pp. 149–170). Needham Heights, MA: Allyn & Bacon.

Sheinkopf, S., & Siegel, B. (in press). Home-based behavioral treatment for young autistic children. *Journal of Autism and Developmental Disorders.*

Smith, T. (1993). Autism. In T. R. Giles (Ed.), *Handbook of effective psychotherapy* (pp. 107–133). New York: Plenum.

Stainback, S., & Stainback, W. (1992). Schools as inclusive communities. In W. Stainback & S. Stainback (Eds.), *Controversial issues confronting special education* (pp. 29–43). Boston: Allyn & Bacon.

Strain, P. S., & Cordisco, L. K. (1994). LEAP Preschool. In S. L. Harris & J. S. Handleman (Eds.), *Preschool education programs for children with autism* (pp. 225–244). Austin, TX: PRO-ED.

Strain, P. S., Hoyson, M., & Jamieson, B. (1985). Normally developing preschoolers as intervention agents for autistic-like children: Effects on class deportment and social interaction. *Journal of the Division for Early Childhood, 9,* 105–115.

Szatmari, P., Bartolucci, G., Bremner, R., Bond, S., & Rich, S. (1989). A follow-up study of high-functioning autistic children. *Journal of Autism and Developmental Disorders, 19,* 213–225.

Taylor, B. A., & Harris, S. L. (1995). Teaching children with autism to seek information: Acquisition of novel information and generalization of responding. *Journal of Applied Behavior Analysis, 28,* 3–14.

Taylor, J. C., & Carr, E. G. (1992). Severe problem behaviors related to social interaction. *Behavior Modification, 16,* 305–335.

Taylor, J. C., & Carr, E. G. (1994). Severe problem behaviors of children with developmental disabilities: Reciprocal social influences. In T. Thompson & D. B. Gray (Eds.), *Destructive behavior in developmental disabilities* (pp. 274–289). Thousand Oaks, CA: Sage.

VanHouten, R., Axelrod, S., Bailey, J. S., Favell, J. E., Foxx, R. M., Iwata, B. A., & Lovaas, O. I. (1988). The right to effective behavioral treatment. *Journal of Applied Behavior Analysis, 21,* 381–384.

Vyse, S. A., & Mulick, J. A. (1988). Ecobehavioral assessment of a special education classroom: Teacher-student behavioral covariation. *Journal of the Multi-handicapped Person, 1,* 201–216.

Young, J. M., Krantz, P. J., McClannahan, L. E., & Poulson, C. L. (1994). Generalized imitation and response-class formation in children with autism. *Journal of Applied Behavior Analysis, 27,* 685–697.

CHAPTER FOUR

Are Other Treatments Effective?

Tristram Smith

Chapter 3 amply documented that behavioral treatment helps many children with autism. But what about other interventions? What options besides behavioral treatment are available, and which, if any, are effective? Should any be implemented in addition to, or instead of, behavioral treatment? Should any be avoided?

Anyone who consults professionals or reads about children with autism soon discovers that treatment choices for these children are many and varied. Dozens of interventions exist, and new ones are being proposed all the time. To complicate matters further, these interventions often attract heated controversy. A particular intervention may be heralded as a breakthrough by some, yet derided as an atrocity or a hoax by others.

Faced with so many choices and so much controversy, some parents may hesitate to enroll their children in any intervention program, for fear of selecting the wrong treatment and thereby causing irreparable harm. By hesitating, however, they risk losing valuable time. At the opposite end of the spectrum, some parents may feel obliged to try everything they possibly can, for fear of overlooking an intervention that might help their children. However, this too entails risks; for example, it may drain time, energy, and resources from the most effective interventions or expose children to questionable treatments.

A better strategy, in the author's judgment, is to pick interventions whose effectiveness has been established in multiple scientific studies published in professional journals, while steering clear of the rest. As discussed in Chapter 2, scientific studies are designed to yield the most careful, reliable evaluation possible of whether an intervention really works. Other sources of information, such as subjective opinions expressed by parents or professionals, also may (and often do) provide accurate information. Unfortunately, however, these sources are frequently incorrect, as this chapter will show. There are many possible reasons for this. For example, parents or professionals may report that a treatment worked, even though it did not, because this is what they want to believe or because they neglected to consider im-

provements that would have occurred regardless of treatment as the children grew older and more mature. Scientific studies are aimed at minimizing such problems. To obtain impartial ratings of children's behavior, investigators may employ observers who do not know the purpose of the study or the history of the children who participate. Investigators may also compare measurements of treatment effects taken by two or more independent observers in order to assess whether the observers agree on what they see. Additionally, they may contrast treated children with similar children who did not receive treatment, as a test of whether treated children achieve more favorable outcomes than they would have without treatment. Admittedly, mistakes do occur in scientific studies (as in any other human endeavor), but the safeguards in such studies make mistakes substantially less frequent than those in other sources. Hence, scientific studies are generally the most trustworthy form of evidence.

The present chapter reviews scientific studies on interventions other than behavioral treatment. Nonbehavioral special education classes, which are the main service-providers for most children with autism are discussed first, followed by descriptions of individual therapies, which often supplement classroom instruction. Three kinds of individual therapies, each having several variants, are considered: (a) speech and language therapies, (b) sensory-motor therapies, and (c) psychotherapies. Finally, biological interventions, such as medications and special diets, are examined. The chapter concludes with a summary and recommendations.

SPECIAL EDUCATION

While many special education programs employ some behavioral procedures, only a small minority can be classified as behavior analytic, as described in the preceding chapter. This section outlines prominent non-behavior-analytic programs.

Project TEACCH

Project TEACCH, a statewide program in North Carolina founded by Eric Schopler (Schopler & Olley, 1982) and currently directed by Gary Mesibov, has been the most influential special education agency serving children with autism. Schopler, Mesibov, and their associates occasionally draw upon behavioral procedures to teach self-care skills and manage disruptive behavior, but they reject many other aspects of behavioral treatment, particularly procedures for teaching language (Schopler, Reichler, & Lansing, 1980). They contend that children are unlikely to use skills acquired from such procedures in everyday settings, and they assert that teaching methods derived from personal experience are more likely to produce satisfactory results. They have outlined the methods they have developed in treatment manuals (Schopler, Reichler, & Lansing, 1980; Schopler, Lansing, & Waters, 1983), though they have not performed scientific studies on any of these methods.

In contrast to behavioral treatment, Project TEACCH is aimed primarily at designing sheltered settings that help children make use of the skills they already possess, rather than at helping children to enter more "normal" or "typical" settings (C. Lord & Schopler, 1994). Most children with autism in TEACCH are assigned to classrooms that include other children with developmental disabilities. The teachers, most of whom are licensed in special education, set up workstations for each child in the classroom. The children work alone at their workstations, often separated by dividers from the rest of the class, and perform tasks selected by their teachers. These tasks are individually chosen for each child but tend to be repetitive, visual-motor activities such as sorting objects by color or folding letters into envelopes. Cues are provided to help children carry out tasks independently (e. g., baskets of various colors for color sorting or pictures displaying the various stages of folding a letter). Children often perform several different tasks at one sitting by following a schedule displayed in front of them that commonly uses a series of pictures. They may also use pictures to communicate with others. Parents frequently receive instruction in the use of workstations, picture schedules, and picture communication in the home.

Only one study has evaluated the effectiveness of Project TEACCH classrooms (Schopler, Mesibov, & Baker, 1982). The participants in this study were 657 past and present students in Project TEACCH. Fifty-one percent had been diagnosed with autism; the remainder suffered from other unspecified communication handicaps. The participants ranged in age from 2 to 26 years old. One group of participants had received only a diagnostic evaluation; a second group had received an evaluation and parent training; a third group had had an evaluation and placement in a TEACCH classroom; and the fourth group had participated in an evaluation, parent training, and classroom. The investigators supplied no information on the number of participants in each group or the procedure for assigning participants to groups. To evaluate the services that participants received, parent questionnaires were mailed to participants' homes. Of these questionnaires, 348 (53%) were returned. The majority of respondents indicated that Project TEACCH had been very helpful. Those having the most contact with the agency gave the highest ratings. Staff members concurred that Project TEACCH was effective on ratings that they assigned to a subset of 108 students. The procedure for selecting these students was not specified. Lastly, the adolescents and adults with autism, in the study, were found to have an institutionalization rate of 7%. That figure was considerably lower than the rates of 39% to 74% recorded in studies of individuals with autism in the 1960s.

Unfortunately, this study contains a number of very serious weaknesses. The participants were extremely heterogeneous (as noted above, almost half were not autistic; also, some were toddlers, and others were adults). The procedure for assigning participants to groups was not described. There was much missing data. It was not clear whether parent and staff ratings were anonymous; if not, respondents may have felt pressure to give favorable ratings. Even if the ratings were anonymous, they may have overestimated children's progress because they came from parents and staff (who, understandably, would be eager to see improvements, whether they actually occurred or not), rather than from independent evaluators. Finally, though Schopler and colleagues (1982) were correct in asserting that the adolescents and adults in their study had a much lower institutionalization rate than did individuals in studies conducted in the 1960s, they were not justified in interpreting this finding as proof of the efficacy of TEACCH. The lower institutionalization rate may have been due to changes in government policy. During the late 1960s and 1970s, governments in the United States and elsewhere closed down or sharply decreased the size of institutions, with the result that by 1980 the number of individuals in institutions was only a small fraction of what it had been before. Hence, the institutionalization rate reported by Schopler and colleagues is about what one would expect, whether or not individuals had participated in TEACCH.

With its emphasis on making use of skills that children already possess, Project TEACCH may offer a congenial situation for children, allowing them to perform activities they enjoy and to experience mastery while doing so. TEACCH also may be congenial for teachers and parents, supplying methods for keeping children independently and usefully occupied. Thus, despite all the problems in this study, the high levels of satisfaction reported by parents and staff may be an accurate reflection of how they felt about TEACCH. Still, it remains unclear how much children with autism actually learn from workstations and other unstudied instructional devices used by TEACCH, as no research has addressed this question. Also of concern is the possibility that some children miss the opportunity to become more like typically developing children and enter less restrictive settings, as these goals receive relatively little attention in TEACCH. To address such concerns, scientifically sound evaluations of TEACCH are essential.

Other Public School Classes

Special education classes outside Project TEACCH vary widely. However, in the author's experience, most classes share with TEACCH the occasional use of a few behavioral procedures, an emphasis on structured schedules, and an orientation toward helping children function in sheltered settings rather than toward enabling them to function more like typically developing children. Only one scientific study has evaluated such classes. Bartak and Rutter (1973; Rutter & Bartak, 1973) compared three classes for children with autism (average age, 8.5 years): Unit A contained eight students and provided psychotherapy (see the section on psychotherapies later in this chapter); Unit B had 18 students who received individualized interventions, with some students engaging in structured activities and others spending most of their time in free play; Unit C emphasized teaching academic skills to its 24 students in a carefully planned, structured manner. Children were assessed while in the classroom and at a follow-up approximately 4 years later. In the classroom, Unit C children engaged in more constructive activities and fewer ritualistic behaviors, such as flapping their hands in front of their eyes, than Unit B children, who in turn surpassed Unit A children on these measures. At follow-up, Unit C children also showed superior educational attainment. However, all children remained severely delayed in these areas, IQ scores did not change, and parental reports revealed no difference between the units in how the children behaved at home. Hence, Unit C outperformed the other two units, but its advantage was limited and may have been confined to the school setting. Moreover, at the beginning of the study, Unit C children were functioning at a substantially higher level than children in the other units: Unit C had an average IQ of 66, compared to 48 for Unit A and 52 for Unit B. Thus, the initial discrepancy between groups, rather than the classroom environment, may account for the superior outcome of Unit C. The investigators attempted to rule out this possibility, but, according to statisticians, no satisfactory procedure exists for doing so (F. M. Lord, 1967). In sum, this study has many noteworthy features (e.g., comparison groups, detailed assessments, long-term follow-ups). Consequently, it is often cited as evidence that children with autism can benefit from structured classrooms such as the one in Unit C. However, it is more accurate to regard the results as inconclusive.

Some investigators have argued that children with autism improve when they enter school, but the existing evidence does not support this contention. Children appear to continue developing at about the same rate before and after entering school (Freeman, Ritvo, Needleman, & Yokota, 1985; C. Lord & Schopler, 1989). A related argument is that the current generation of children with autism is functioning better than previous generations, when many children with autism were excluded from school. Supporters of this argument contend that a higher percentage of children with autism speak communicatively now than in the past. However, evidence for such a trend is sketchy at best. Furthermore, even if the trend were to be confirmed, two reasons for skepticism about the role of schools would remain. First, the diagnosis of autism is given to a much wider range of children now than in the past (Szatmari, 1992) and hence may include a higher percentage of speaking children. Second, children may participate in other interventions such as behavioral treatment, and these interventions, rather than schools, could be responsible for any gains in speech that may have occurred.

The Higashi School

One alternative to special education classes in the public schools is the Higashi School (Roland, McGee, Risley, & Rimland, 1988), which is based in Japan and runs a large program in Boston. The Higashi School shares two features with behavioral treatment, though it was developed independently: (a) the use of prompts and prompt-fading procedures to teach new skills and (b) the reduction of behavior problems by ignoring them and practicing appropriate, alternative behaviors. However, other important behavioral procedures, such as the use of discrete trials, are not emphasized, nor is language training. The curriculum focuses on academic skills, fine arts, and physical education.

Rimland (1987a) sent questionnaires to 27 non-Japanese parents whose children with autism were enrolled in the Higashi School in Japan. Nineteen parents responded, and all reported that the school had been very helpful, surpassing other services their children had previously received. These results are open to question because the respondents formed a select group that may not have been representative of all the participants in the Higashi Program. Moreover, as noted in Chapter 2 and at the outset of this chapter, parent evaluations should be interpreted cautiously because there is a natural tendency to want to believe that interventions were helpful, even if they actually were not. Additionally, some aspects of the curriculum seem highly questionable. For example, though children with autism certainly should have opportunities to draw, listen to music, and so forth, it is doubtful that instruction in the fine arts should have a higher priority than instruction in language, social skills, and self-care (as seems to be the case in the Higashi School). Nevertheless, the results reported by Rimland (1987a) suggest that further evaluations of the Higashi School may be warranted.

Full Inclusion

Some schools avoid placing children with autism in special education classes at all and have adopted a policy called *full inclusion*. In such schools, children with autism attend regular classes with typically developing children. Sometimes, other children with disabilities are also in the class. Often (perhaps usually), the child with autism is accompanied by an aide. Studies indicate that inclusion with average children can be helpful when children with autism already have some ability to interact appropriately with the teacher and with the other students. However, it does not appear helpful otherwise (e.g., Myles, Simpson, Ormsbee, & Erickson, 1993; Strain, 1983). That is, if children with autism already have some basic skills, placement in a regular class helps them use these skills in a group (rather than only one-to-one) and with other children (rather than only adults). But if they do not have such skills, they are unlikely to acquire them in a regular classroom, where there tend to be numerous distractions, high requirements to cooperate with instructions, and few opportunities for receiving individualized assistance without disturbing the rest of the class.

Summary

Even though special education classes are the main service-providers for children with autism, little scientific evidence exists to show that such classes are helpful (except when they rely on behavior-analytic teaching methods, as reviewed in the preceding chapter). The classes may provide a congenial setting for children with autism, but they seem less likely than behavior-analytic programs to enable them to become more like typically developing children.

SPEECH AND LANGUAGE THERAPIES

Behavior analysts have developed numerous scientifically validated procedures to teach children with autism to communicate through vocal speech (Lovaas, 1977). Some children with autism progress very rapidly with such instruction (cf. Lovaas, 1987); others, however, progress much more slowly. For children in the latter group, behavior analysts have devised alternative strategies, such as teaching sign language or communication through pictures (e.g., Carr, 1979).

Despite the success of behavior-analytic approaches to teaching children with autism to communicate, licensed speech and language therapists seldom use such approaches (Snyder & Lindstedt, 1985), though notable exceptions exist (as discussed elsewhere in this book). Nonbehavioral speech and language therapists have developed many different treatments, most of which are aimed at stimulating children's natural interest and ability in learning language (Snyder & Lindstedt, 1985). The treatments customarily take place in one-to-one sessions held from ½ to 3 hours per week. The evidence on the outcomes achieved by such treatments can be succinctly stated: To the author's knowledge, no scientific studies have evaluated whether any form of speech and language therapy, other than behavior analysis, helps children with autism.

Children with autism seem to require many hours a week of instruction in order to achieve significant gains in language (Lovaas & Smith, 1989). For example, of the 40 hours per week of instruction provided by Lovaas (1987), language instruction was the single largest component, accounting for more than half the hours. Studies with less language instruction have yielded much smaller gains in language than those reported by Lovaas. Therefore, by itself, speech and language therapy is probably not intensive enough to be very effective. However, it may augment other interventions by identifying areas that need remediation or offering strategies for promoting the use of language skills in everyday settings (see Chapters 13 and 14).

SENSORY-MOTOR THERAPIES

One of the oldest and most popular notions about children with delays, including those diagnosed with autism, is that they have difficulty processing sensory input from the environment and/or translating such input into effective action. In this view, children may be overaroused or underaroused by normal levels of sensory input. Consequently, according to theorists, such children have difficulty perceiving and responding to environmental events. Moreover, they try to moderate their arousal levels by engaging in ritualistic behaviors such as rocking their bodies back and forth. Since about 1,800 numerous sensory-motor therapies have been proposed in an effort to alleviate these hypothesized deficits. At one time or another, many of the most influential figures in the history of special education have advocated such therapies: Itard, Seguin, Montessori, Frostig, Delacato, and others. These educators have believed that, by getting to the root of children's learning difficulties, the therapies could cure developmental disabilities (Spitz, 1986).

Consistent with sensory-motor theories, children with autism engage in many ritualistic behaviors, and they often respond in unexpected ways to environmental events. For example, they may be so unresponsive when their names are called that others wonder if they are deaf, yet they may cringe when they hear other seemingly innocuous sounds such as a ringing telephone. Nevertheless, no one knows whether these behaviors are in fact due to nonoptimal arousal and, if so, what physiological problems cause the nonoptimal arousal (Arendt, MacLean, & Baumeister, 1988). Because of this fundamental gap in sensory-motor theories, investigators have had no systematic way to develop treatments that might improve arousal levels, relying instead on speculation. Not surprisingly, therefore, evaluations of such therapies often have been disappointing (see Kavale & Mattson, 1983).

Sensory Integration Therapy

One sensory-motor treatment for children with autism is Sensory Integration Therapy (Ayres, 1972, 1979), which is typically administered by licensed occupational therapists, either in the public schools or in the private sector. In Sensory Integration Therapy, therapists stimulate children's skin and vestibular system. This stimulation consists of activities such as swinging in a hammock suspended from the ceiling, spinning in circles on specially constructed chairs, brushing parts of children's bodies, and engaging in physical activities that require balance (Ayres, 1972).

Though a number of informal case reports and poorly designed studies have indicated that Sensory Integration Training may be helpful for children with autism, scientifically sound research has not confirmed this finding. In the only controlled study on children with autism that has appeared in a scientific journal, Reilly, Nelson, and Bundy (1983) compared Sensory Integration Therapy to table-top activities such as coloring and completing puzzles. Eighteen children with autism, averaging 8 years of age, were observed for an hour of Sensory Integration Therapy and an hour of table-top activities. Reilly and colleagues reported that, during table-top activities, children spoke more appropriately than they did during Sensory Integration Therapy. Hence, they concluded that tabletop activities may be more productive. However, this study was limited in two ways. First, all of the observations took place while children were in treatment sessions; hence, they did not indicate whether either Sensory Integration Therapy or table-top activities affected children's behavior in their everyday lives. Second, the treatments were extremely short (one hour each).

Several investigations have evaluated Sensory Integration Therapy for children with other developmental disabilities (reviewed by Shore, 1994). The results of these investigations have generally been consistent with those reported by Reilly and colleagues (1983): Children who receive Sensory Integration Therapy do not show increased motor development (Jenkins, Fewell, & Harris, 1983; Huff & Harris, 1983), decreased self-injury (Dura, Mulick, & Hammer, 1988; Mason & Iwata, 1990), reduced ritualistic behaviors (Iwasaki & Holm, 1989), or other benefits (Densom, Nuthall, Bushnell, & Horn, 1989). In an intensive analysis of three children, Mason and Iwata (1990) reported that Sensory Integration Therapy was less effective than behavioral treatment in reducing self-injury. In fact, for one of the three children, the therapy appeared to increase (rather than decrease) the rate of this behavior. Thus, studies on Sensory Integration Therapy are sparse, but they have consistently yielded adverse findings.

Though Sensory Integration Therapy does not appear to enhance language, control disruptive behaviors, or otherwise reduce autistic behaviors, it may offer enjoyable and healthy, physical activity. Such activity is as important for children with autism as it is for typically developing children. However, forms of activity other than Sensory Integration Therapy, such as playing table-top games (Reilly et al., 1983) or climbing on playground equipment, may be just as enjoyable and healthy, and may not require the involvement of a professional.

Auditory Integration Training

Another sensory-motor therapy, Auditory Integration Training (Rimland & Edelson, 1995), was developed by a physician (Guy Berard) and is currently offered by a variety of professionals and nonprofessionals who have completed a workshop on this treatment. The treatment begins with an audiogram (observations by the therapist) to determine the frequencies at which a child's hearing appears to be too sensitive. Subsequently, the child spends 10 hours listening to music played through a device that filters out the frequencies identified by the audiogram. The child wears headphones while listening to the music. Usually, the 10 hours of treatment are spread out over 2 weeks, and children often discontinue other educational or therapeutic activities during this period.

Advocates of Auditory Integration Training speculate that hypersensitive hearing causes aggression, hinders children from interacting with others, and impairs their ability to attend to instructional situations. Therefore, they anticipate that, by reducing hypersensitivity, the training will yield widespread improvements in children's behavior (Stehli, 1991). Though there is no scientific evidence to support the view that hypersensitivity is responsible for other problems displayed by children with autism (and hence no reason to expect that Auditory Integration Training would produce widespread improvements, even if it did reduce hypersensitivity), the treatment attracted a great deal of attention in the early 1990s.

Rimland and Edelson (1995) conducted the first evaluation of Auditory Integration Training. Eighteen individuals with autism, aged 4–21 years, were matched into pairs based on age, sex, history of ear infections, and severity of problems with hypersensitive hearing, as reported by parents. One individual in each pair, selected at random, received Auditory Integration Training, and the other received a placebo treatment. The placebo treatment, unlike Auditory Integration Training, did not filter out sound frequencies from the music, but the situation was otherwise identical. During the study, the individuals with autism, their families, and therapists were not informed whether the individuals were receiving treatment or placebo. One individual dropped out before completion of the study.

Rimland and Edelson (1995) reported that, at the follow-up evaluation, individuals in the treatment group had improved more than individuals in the placebo group on parent-report measures of behavior problems and comprehension of speech. However, this result may not have been the result of Auditory Integration Training. Rather, they may have been due to preexisting differences that arose between the groups despite the investigators' attempts to match them: the treatment group started off with more severe problems, as reported by parents, and hence may have had more room to improve. Another significant problem was that, following treatment, the groups did not differ on how sensitive they were to sounds, as measured by audiograms. Because sound sensitivity was the main target

of treatment, the failure to find a difference on this variable raises the possibility that, despite favorable parental reports, the treatment actually may have had no effect on the children. A final problem was that the measure of hypersensitive hearing, the audiogram, has not been shown to be a valid assessment procedure.

A second study (Rimland & Edelson, 1994) surveyed 445 parents whose children with autism had undergone this treatment and found that most parents considered the treatment to have been beneficial. However, as already noted, such parent reports should be viewed cautiously. This is true even when, as in Rimland and Edelson's study, the investigators obtain reports from large numbers of parents. Also, the study did not address questions left unresolved by the earlier study (whether Auditory Integration Training is more helpful than placebo, and whether the audiogram is a valid measure). Thus, it remains unclear whether Auditory Integration Training helps children with autism.

Interest in Auditory Integration Training has stemmed primarily from a report that the treatment cured one child with autism (Stehli, 1991). Detailed histories of individual children, such as the one by Stehli, are often fascinating to read and may serve a useful purpose in bringing a treatment to the attention of a wide audience. By themselves, however, such histories prove little, especially when (as was true of Stehli's report) there was no independent, objective verification of the child's diagnosis, her level of functioning prior to treatment, and her progress in treatment. Even when such verification exists, it is still crucial to evaluate the effects of the treatment with other children. Professionals and parents should seek evidence from scientific studies that a treatment is consistently helpful for many children before they implement or endorse it.

Further studies may or may not show that Auditory Integration Training is beneficial. If they do, experience suggests that the gains are likely to be much more circumscribed than those reported by Stehli, for the following reason. Auditory Integration Training focuses on one specific problem, hypersensitive hearing. Many other treatments also focus on one specific problem. Research has shown that such treatments may eliminate the problem they address, but they do not bring about widespread changes (Lovaas & Smith, 1989). For example, language instruction may increase the vocabulary of children with autism, but it does not increase the frequency of such children's social interactions. Therefore, therapists need to teach social interactions as well as language. Similarly, then, one may anticipate that, if Auditory Integration Training proves helpful, it would reduce hypersensitive hearing and problems closely related to it (e.g., irritability in response to certain sounds), but would not enhance language, social skills, play with toys, and so forth.

Facilitated Communication

Facilitated Communication (Biklen, 1993) derives from the hypothesis that children and adults with autism or other developmental disabilities have a motor deficit that prevents them from expressing themselves even though they possess a sophisticated understanding of spoken and written language. To overcome this conjectured problem, trained facilitators (professionals or nonprofessionals who have completed a workshop on the treatment) hold people's hands, wrists, or arms to help them spell messages on a keyboard or a board with printed letters. This intervention has attracted extensive publicity because of reports that it produces sudden, dramatic increases in appropriate language displayed by people with autism and other disorders. According to these reports, when people who were previously thought to have no communicative language participated in Facilitated Communication, they began to compose poetry, divulge personal thoughts and feelings, excel at advanced schoolwork, and display many other complex language skills.

Unfortunately, the reality has proved to be quite different (see Shane, 1994, for a series of articles on this topic). Following the publicity given to Facilitated Communication, hundreds of children and adults with a variety of disabilities have been evaluated in scientific studies, yet not one has been found to benefit from Facilitated Communication. Rather, all the complex statements that were attributed to these people turned out to have been authored by their facilitators. Investigators discovered this problem by setting up situations in which the facilitators sometimes were kept from knowing what was to be spelled, or what information their partner was receiving. For example, in some evaluations, the facilitators and children were simultaneously asked questions that the other could not see or hear. Sometimes the questions were the same for both the facilitators and the children; sometimes they were different. When the questions were the same, the answers were often correct; when they were different, most answers were responses to the facilitator's questions, not the child's. Thus, the facilitators must have been the ones doing the spelling. Investigators have tried many other procedures to see what happened when the facilitator did not know what answer was expected, or when the facilitator could not see the spelling device and therefore did not know what answer was being given. Over and over again, when investigators have used careful methods, the results have been the same: "facilitated" messages have not come from people with disabilities.

Facilitated Communication not only fails to unlock hidden language skills, it also may cause serious problems. For example, under the illusion that a child possesses complex language skills, parents or professionals may stop treatments aimed at enhancing such skills. Also, because children may spend a great deal of time in Facilitated Communication, they may cut back on their use of other forms of communication and lose previously mastered skills due to lack of practice. Families may be harmed, too. Parents often become upset when they discover that they were deceived about their child's language. They also may encounter problems because advocates of Facilitated Communication believe that many children with autism have been sexually molested. One well-known investigator estimated that 25% of typically developing children are victims of molestation and that the incidence of molestation in children with autism is "more than four times" this figure! Though such mathematical gaffes are amusing, the real-life effects are not: Accusations of molestation often have arisen from Facilitated Communication, and many of these accusations have been directed at parents. Such accusations almost always prove to be utterly unfounded, as would be expected given the fact that the child did not author them. Even so, some of the accusations have caused children to be taken away from their parents for extended periods of time while investigations were ongoing. Falsely accused families in several countries have spent thousands of dollars defending themselves and have experienced immeasurable trauma.

Perhaps most tragically of all, the problems with Facilitated Communication were foreseeable. The premise of this treatment (that children with autism have deficits in motor skills that prevent vocal and written expression, despite having considerable knowledge of language) is incorrect. Motor skills are a strength for most children with autism, and many can type, write, and draw independently without the help of a facilitator. Many can also speak clearly and fluently, although they may have problems with other aspects of language, such as comprehension, grammar, and abstract concepts.

The debacle of Facilitated Communication offers an especially striking illustration of how observations by parents and professionals may go awry. All available evidence indicates that most individuals involved in the treatment sincerely wished to be helpful and that they genuinely and wholeheartedly believed Facilitated Communication to be effective. Yet their beliefs were found to be totally incorrect. Many facilitators have become distraught upon discovering this fact, and some have even formed support groups to overcome the guilt they experienced (Pitsas, 1993). Regrettably, however, others continue to believe in (and practice) Facilitated Communication. Clearly, such service-providers should be avoided.

PSYCHOTHERAPIES

Psychoanalysis

From the 1940s when autism was first hypothesized to be a distinct disorder, to the 1960s, the standard treatment for children with autism was psychoanalysis. The popularity of psychoanalysis has waned since the 1960s; however, it remains very much in demand, and it is still the dominant treatment in many parts of Europe. The chief proponent of psychoanalysis, Bettelheim (1967), believed that mothers of children with autism are extremely cold individuals who treat their children like specimens in a science laboratory and harbor "murderous impulses" (p. 70) toward them. The children, according to Bettelheim, develop autism as a defense against this horrible situation. They withdraw from the world as much as possible into a solitary (autistic) state.

As described by Bettelheim, psychoanalytic treatment entails separating children with autism from their mothers, preferably for a lengthy stay in a residential program. Once in treatment, the children are granted as much freedom as possible in an atmosphere of warmth and love. Therapists place particular emphasis on displaying warmth and love at times when, according to psychoanalysts, children are withdrawing into an autistic state—for example, when they display ritualistic or aggressive behavior. Therapists also offer interpretations of the behaviors that the children exhibit. While their children are undergoing treatment, the mothers may also enter psychotherapy in order to work on the unconscious conflicts that, in the psychoanalytic view, produced their children's autistic state.

Most investigators have concluded that psychoanalysis is harmful (e.g., Schopler, 1971). Mothers may be devastated when blamed—quite falsely, as numerous studies have shown—for their children's condition (Cantwell & Baker, 1984). Excluding mothers from their children's treatment is probably also a mistake, limiting how much the children are likely to change in everyday settings. An additional problem is that children receive the most love and warmth when they display the most severe problems; this has been shown to reinforce the problems and thereby make them worse (Lovaas & Simmons, 1969). Finally, the treatment allows children to select their own activities, which usually results in their engaging in ritualistic behaviors, or attempting to escape the therapy situation rather than learning anything new. In view of these problems, the continuing use of psychoanalysis as a treatment for autism is dismaying, and, like the experience with Facilitated Communication, it demonstrates how unreliable subjective opinions promoted by some professionals can be.

Other Psychotherapies

Psychoanalytic concepts have strongly influenced other psychotherapies developed by psychiatrists and psychologists. For instance, Greenspan's (1992) play therapy attempts to help children "form a sense of their own personhood—a sense of themselves as intentional, interactional individuals" (p. 5). According to Greenspan, this sense of personhood arises from experiencing emotion-laden relationships with therapists and parents. Humanistic play therapy (Axline, 1965; DesLauriers & Carlson, 1969) emphasizes encouraging children with autism to express their feelings by playing with toys in a setting where they receive unconditional positive regard from therapists. In "holding therapy" (Tinbergen & Tinbergen, 1983; Welch, 1987) therapists view autism as a failure of the mother and child to "bond." To correct this hypothesized problem, the mother forcibly holds the child close to her so as to cause "the autistic defense . . . to crumble" (Welch, 1987, p. 48). "Options" (Kaufman, 1976) offers individualized, loving attention to a child in a residential setting for most of the child's waking hours. "Gentle Teaching" (McGee & Gonzales, 1990) has the goal of showing children with autism that social interactions are rewarding, so that bonding occurs between the children and their therapists. This is accomplished by exhibiting "unconditional and authentic valuing" of children (McGee & Gonzales, 1990). None of these therapies have been evaluated in scientific studies on children with autism, although Gentle Teaching has been found to be nonhelpful for children with other developmental disabilities (Mudford, 1995). Until proven otherwise, it may be assumed that the therapies are at best ineffective and at worst harmful because they share many of the weaknesses associated with psychoanalysis.

Summary

Research is scanty on all nonbehavioral individual treatments for children with autism except Facilitated Communication and psychoanalysis. Investigations have indicated that the latter two treatments are based on erroneous theories and harm children with autism and their families. The remaining treatments (speech and language therapies, Sensory Integration Therapy, and Auditory Integration Training) may offer some benefits, although this has yet to be demonstrated, and the available evidence on one treatment (Sensory Integration Therapy) is not promising. If the treatments are beneficial, they probably do not improve all areas of functioning; rather, improvements are likely to be confined to the few specific behaviors targeted for treatment.

BIOLOGICAL TREATMENTS

Medications

Because autism is biological in origin, researchers have made extensive efforts to find effective medications for children with this diagnosis. Nevertheless, medications currently have only limited use for such children. They may help control disruptive behaviors such as aggression or rituals, but they have little or no effect on other behaviors. The medications, whose effects are best documented, are the major tranquilizers (also called *antipsychotics* or *neuroleptics*), especially nonsedating ones such as haloperidol (Haldol). These medications often produce rapid reductions in the aggression displayed by children with autism as young as 3 years of age (Locascio et al., 1991), but they commonly also produce severe side effects, such as involuntary, disfiguring bodily movements. Hence, most investigators believe that therapists should try behavioral interventions first, especially when working with young children.

A number of small studies indicate that fluoxetine (Prozac), an antidepressant, clomipramine (Anafranil), also an antidepressant, and naltrexone, which blocks the action of opiate receptors in the brain, may suppress self-injury and excessive activity (e.g., Campbell et al., 1990; Gordon, Stale, Nelson, & Rapoport, 1993; Leboyer et al., 1992). However, more extensive research is needed to confirm these findings.

In the 1980s, a flurry of studies evaluated fenfluramine (usually used to suppress appetite), following a report that one child with autism made major gains after taking the medication. The studies indicated that despite the encouraging initial report, fenfluramine is not a useful medication for this population (Campbell, 1989). This outcome confirms that, as discussed in connection with Auditory Integration Training, reports on an individual child are often intriguing but do not offer a sound basis for adopting an intervention.

Many other medications have been studied, but none have been clearly shown to be helpful. One commonly prescribed medication, methylphenidate (Ritalin), appears to have a predominately negative effect, increasing rituals in children with autism (Campbell, 1989).

Diets

Many children with autism have idiosyncratic eating habits. For example, they may be very picky about what they eat, or they may crave large amounts of certain foods. Nevertheless, according to the few studies conducted on this topic (e.g., Shearer, Larson, Neuschwanger, & Gedney, 1982), they manage to consume as many nutrients as typically developing children. Moreover, they meet or exceed the United States Recommended Daily Allowance (RDA) for all essential nutrients except calcium, for which they have been found to consume 92% of the RDA (probably enough to prevent problems; Shearer et al., 1982). Additionally, they appear well-nourished on standard medical tests. Because of these findings, most professionals refrain from intervening in this area, except to expand the range of foods that the children are willing to eat.

A few professionals, however, have suggested that in some cases, the idiosyncratic eating habits of children with autism reflect a serious underlying problem, namely difficulty tolerating certain substances found in foods. They argue that eliminating these substances from children's diets may spare the children much physical discomfort and also improve their behavior (Reiten, 1987). Therefore, they recommend placing children with autism on special diets, so that families can judge whether their particular child seems to benefit. Most of these special diets were originally developed for children with attention deficit hyperactivity disorder (ADHD) and were only later applied to children with autism. The first diet to attract widespread attention was the Feingold Diet, developed by the pediatrician and allergist Ben Feingold (1975). This diet forbids foods that contain preservatives, colorings, or other additives (i.e., almost all prepackaged foods). It also forbids salicylates, which are found naturally in most fruits and in a number of other items such as reduced-calorie sodas. Subsequent authors developed diets that eliminated other substances. For example, Crook (1994) has prescribed a diet that excludes not only additives and salicylates, but also sugar, milk, wheat, eggs, corn, chocolate, and citrus (p. 1902). Other authors have hypothesized that some children should curtail their consumption of yeast and/or soy.

No scientifically sound studies have evaluated whether children with autism really have trouble tolerating these foods or whether any of the diets are helpful to them. The effects of the Feingold Diet and low-sugar diets (but none of the others) have been assessed for children with ADHD and for typically developing children. Regarding the Feingold Diet, reviews have shown that the more scientifically rigorous a study is, the less likely it is to report that the diet is beneficial (e.g., Kavale & Forness, 1983). A similar pattern has emerged in studies of low-sugar diets (e.g., Wolreich et al., 1994). Thus, most investigators are skeptical of these diets.

Plainly, regimens like the Feingold Diet impose a substantial burden on whoever does the shopping and cooking. Eliminating food additives may mean having to prepare foods from scratch. Forbidding milk products does away with a major food group, and restricting the other foods listed earlier also may require radical changes in eating habits. For example, yeast resides in, among other things, most cereals, breads, pastas, and baked items, as well as in condiments (ketchup and mayonnaise) and many medications and vitamins taken in pill or capsule form. Recognizing this problem, the authors of most diet books include recipes (e.g., Feingold, 1975), and they often recommend that families test a particular diet for a short period of time before deciding whether to implement it on a long-term basis. Nevertheless, as previously discussed, families' evaluations are, unfortunately, not always accurate, and incorrect evaluations pose risks. For example, even when recipes are available, shopping and cooking are likely to remain arduous. Moreover, because of their pickiness, children with autism may reject the meals that have been so painstakingly prepared. Other family members may be less than enthusiastic as well. If children reject meals, the diet could reduce the amount of nutrients they consume. Considering these potential problems and the lack of evidence that special diets are helpful, such diets appear to be more trouble than they are worth.

Megavitamins

A few investigators have asserted that some children with autism require much higher doses of certain nutrients than can be obtained from any diet (Rimland, 1987b). According to these investigators, children with autism have a genetic or acquired medical disorder (as yet unspecified) that increases their requirement for specific nutrients. Research based on this hypothesis has centered on (a) vitamin B_6 (pyridoxine), which is a chemical whose primary function is to help digest proteins, (b) magnesium, a mineral that helps build bones, maintain nerve and muscle cells, and enhance the function of many enzymes in the body, or (c) a combination of B_6 and magnesium. High doses of other nutrients also have been recommended but have not been researched.

As of this writing, 15 studies on B_6 and magnesium have appeared in scientific journals. In these studies, doses of B_6 have varied quite a bit, ranging from 30 to 3,000 milligrams per day. However, even doses at the low end of this range are many times higher than the United States RDA, which is between 1 and 2 milligrams per day for most children and adults. Doses of magnesium have generally been between 350 and 500 milligrams per day (the RDA for most people is between 80 to 400 milligrams). In all 15 studies, the investigators have reported that megadoses of B_6 with or without magnesium help a substantial subgroup of children with autism—perhaps 30%–50% of all such children. Most of these studies have contained important methodological safeguards, particularly the use of a "double-blind" procedure (a procedure in which neither the children nor those who observed them knew whether the children were receiving nutritional supplements or placebos). Consequently, Rimland (1987b) has concluded that the benefits of B_6 and magnesium are well established.

However, other investigators, including the researchers who have conducted the largest number of studies on this topic (Martineau, Barthelemy, Garreau, & Lelord, 1988), have been more hesitant, raising concerns about the methodology used in studies of nutritional supplements (see Kleijnen & Knipschild, 1991). For example, a large part of the data supporting the use of high doses of B_6 and magnesium comes from parent or staff reports, which must be interpreted with caution (as emphasized repeatedly in this chapter). When independent observers have supplied the reports on children (Martineau, Barthelemy, Cheliakiner, & Lelord, 1985), no information has been presented on the level of agreement among different observers in their scoring of children's behaviors. Apart from these measurement issues, another concern is that when children stop taking high doses of nutrients, withdrawal symptoms may occur (Gualtieri, Evans, & Patterson, 1987). It is not known whether such symptoms occur following a reduction in B_6 and magnesium intake. However, if they do, the finding that B_6 with magnesium is superior to no treatment may not mean that these nutrients have therapeutic value; instead, it may mean that stopping these nutrients makes children worse (Gualtieri et al., 1987).

Some individuals believe that, even if the scientific case for taking high doses of these nutrients is not clear-cut, there is little risk in taking nutritional supplements. Nutrients are natural and healthy, and one can't have too much of a good thing, the reasoning goes. It is true that nutritional supplements cause fewer problems than many (probably most) prescription medications. However, they are not free of risk. High doses of B_6 (about 200 milligrams per day in adults, presumably less in children, though no one knows how much less) can cause nerve damage, manifested by muscle weakness and numbness (Deutsch & Morrill, 1993). This damage is usually reversible but poses a significant problem while it lasts. High doses of magnesium (higher than those given in studies on children with autism) can cause abnormally slow heartbeat and weakened reflexes (Deutsch & Morrill, 1993). None of these problems have been observed in studies on children with autism (Rimland, 1987b), but other problems have. In one study, negative effects occurred almost as often as positive effects: Lelord and colleagues (1981) reported that, while 15 of 44 children with autism improved when they took B$_6$ and magnesium, another 10 developed problems (nausea, excitability, and more severe autistic behavior; Lelord et al., 1981, p. 223). Though other studies have reported a much lower percentage of children with negative side effects, none has specified what procedures were used to identify such side effects. Thus, additional research on this topic is needed. Also, all of the studies on B$_6$ and magnesium, except a report on one child, have evaluated children over short periods of time, whereas most advocates of nutritional supplements recommend long-term use. Thus, long-term use of B$_6$ and magnesium may cause unforeseen problems.

In sum, it is impressive that all 15 published studies on high doses of B$_6$ and magnesium for children with autism have reported favorable results. However, a number of significant unknowns remain: whether independent observers would see benefits as consistently as parents and staff do; whether withdrawal symptoms occur; what the risk of side effects is; and what the long-term effects might be. Therefore, it may be best to reserve judgment, pending additional research on these topics.

Prevention and Treatment of Infections

A number of investigators suspect that some children with autism have impaired immune systems (see Frith, 1989, pp. 79–80). One sign of impairment is that many of these children get sick frequently. Ear infections are especially common. Also, infections that pose little danger to most children may rage out of control for several days. For example, rubella (German measles) or herpes zoster (chicken pox) may cause high fevers (above 104°F) and attack the brain, as evidenced by seizures, convulsions, headaches, pupil dilation, loss of coordination, and other symptoms. Antibiotics and other medications prescribed in an effort to control these illnesses may suppress the immune system further or create a problem if there was not one already. A few parents have reported that their children appeared to develop normally until they developed an out-of-control infection, after which they suddenly began to display autistic behaviors. Such observations suggest that immune system problems may lead to autism in some children, though this connection is far from firmly established.

Some have speculated that vaccinations may trigger the same tragic effects as out-of-control infections. To the author's knowledge, however, there are no documented cases in which a child received a vaccine, became quite ill in the following week or so (in reaction to the vaccine), and developed autism immediately thereafter. Obviously, if there were such cases, there would be reason to investigate the matter further. Lacking such cases, however, one may suspect that the association between vaccinations and autism is purely coincidental. Most vaccinations in the United States occur prior to 2 years of age, and this also happens to be the time when most parents first notice something amiss in the development of children with autism. Vaccinating children with or without autism remains the clear choice, in the author's judgment.

Another consequence of suppressed immune systems, according to some investigators, is that children with autism get yeast infections that invade the gastrointestinal tract and/or the brain (Crook, 1987). Most physicians react with skepticism to this theory (see the editor's comment following Shaw, 1995). They contend that, while yeast infections in surface areas such as the mouth are fairly common, yeast infections in internal organs are extremely rare in all but the most severely immune-suppressed individuals (e.g., individuals with advanced AIDS). Among those who believe that systemic yeast infections regularly occur in children with autism, estimates of the prevalence of such infections range from 5% to 95% (Shaw, 1995). Thus, the estimates are almost as far apart as possible, revealing that different investigators cannot agree on when a yeast infection is present. In other words, measures of yeast infection appear to be quite unreliable. The treatments for yeast infection consist of modifying the diet (as discussed in the section on that topic) and prescribing oral mycostatin (Nystatin) or fluconazole (Diflucan). No scientifically sound, published studies have shown that these interventions are effective for children with autism. Because of the inability to diagnose yeast infections dependably, the difficulty in adhering to a low-yeast diet, and the side effects associated with the medications (for example, possible liver damage), intervention for systemic yeast infections appears unwise unless the child has an immune-suppressing condition like AIDS in addition to autism. In such a case, a physician specializing in infectious diseases would need to implement the treatment.

Summary

Major tranquilizers reduce disruptive behaviors, but they also may produce serious negative side effects. Therefore, behavioral treatments are preferable in most cases. No other medication has been clearly shown to be beneficial, nor have diets, megavitamins, or treatments of infections. However, several interventions have shown promise, especially Prozac, Anafranil, naltrexone, and high doses of B_6 with magnesium. These interventions merit further research. To varying degrees, all of the interventions discussed in this section entail a risk of negative side effects.

CONCLUSIONS

Nonbehavioral special education classes, individual therapies, and biological interventions (except major tranquilizers) have not been established as effective treatments for children with autism. Some treatments, especially Facilitated Communication and psychoanalysis, are quite harmful and definitely should be avoided. Major tranquilizers offer an alternative to behavioral treatment for managing disruptive behavior, but they can cause major side effects and therefore are a last resort rather than a first-line intervention. Several other biological treatments (Prozac, Anafranil, naltrexone, and B_6 with magnesium) may be effective but require further research.

In short, behavioral treatment has much more scientific support than any other intervention for children with autism. Consequently, if behavioral treatment is available, or if families are in a position to set up their own behavioral treatment program, the best initial course of action may be to concentrate exclusively on carrying out behavioral treatment as well as possible, rather than looking for ways to supplement it with other treatments.

As emphasized throughout this book, substantial individual differences exist in how children with autism respond to behavioral treatment. Some learn very quickly, some much more slowly. Thus, a very difficult question arises: If there are no scientifically proven alternatives to behavioral treatment, what should be done if a child has difficulty with this treatment? There are ways of modifying behavioral treatment to emphasize visual means of communication (for example, sign language or pictures), as discussed in Chapter 15. Also the curriculum can be adjusted by focusing more on self-care and other skills that will promote independence even if a child remains delayed in development. Other investigators have suggested that children's motivation to learn can be increased by replacing discrete trial instruction with less structured interventions, although, at present, the evidence for the efficacy of this approach is sparse (Smith, 1993).

These ways of revising the curriculum are not entirely satisfactory because they do not enable children with autism to catch up to other children in development. Thus, despite the recommendation given above to concentrate on behavioral treatment, it is clear that for children who progress slowly, one may have to consider alternatives. For example, one might supplement behavioral treatment with other interventions, such as medications identified in this chapter as possibly effective. Or one might replace it with an intervention such as TEACCH that focuses on accommodating children's existing strengths rather than on teaching new skills. Unfortunately, no guidelines exist for making such decisions, and parents and service-providers must simply rely on their best judgment as to how to serve a child's needs most effectively.

More generally, it is clear that behavioral treatment does not have all the answers for children with autism. Indeed, while the treatment has achieved considerable success and is continually being improved as new research is conducted (as discussed in the preceding chapter), one may be skeptical that it ever will have all the answers, given the complexity of autism. Thus, research is of prime importance in identifying other interventions that enhance the effectiveness of behavioral treatment, that serve as an alternative to it, or that replace it altogether. Behavioral treatment appears to be the best option currently available, but this may change in the future.

ACKNOWLEDGMENTS

Much of this chapter is adapted, with the publisher's permission, from Smith (1993). I thank Gina Green, Steve Luce, and Catherine Maurice for reviewing previous drafts of this chapter.

REFERENCES

Arendt, R. E., MacLean, W. E., Jr., & Baumeister, A. A. (1988). Critique of Sensory Integration Therapy and its application in mental retardation. *American Journal on Mental Retardation, 92,* 401–411.

Axline, V. M. (1965). *Dibs: In search of self: Personality development in play therapy.* Boston: Houghton Mifflin.

Ayres, A. J. (1972). *Sensory integration and learning disorders.* Los Angeles: Western Psychological Association.

Ayres, A. J. (1979). *Sensory integration and the child.* Los Angeles: Western Psychological Association.

Bartak, L., & Rutter, M. (1973). Special educational treatment of autistic children: A comparative study. I. Design of study and characteristics of units. *Journal of Child Psychology and Psychiatry, 14,* 161–179.

Bettelheim, B. (1967). *The empty fortress.* New York: Free Press.

Biklen, D. (1993). *Communication unbound: How facilitated communication is challenging traditional views of ability/disability.* New York: Teachers College.

Campbell, M. (1989). Pharmacotherapy in autism: An overview. In C. Gillberg (Ed.), *Diagnosis and treatment of autism* (pp. 203–217). New York: Plenum.

Campbell, M., Anderson, L. Y., Small, A. M., Locascio, J. J., Lynch, N. S., & Chorocco, M. C. (1990). Naltrexone in autistic children: A double-blind and placebo controlled study. *Psychopharmacology Bulletin, 26,* 130–135.

Cantwell, D. B., & Baker, L. (1984). Research concerning families of children with autism. In E. Schopler & G. B. Mesibov (Eds.), *The effects of autism on the family* (pp. 43–68). New York: Plenum.

Carr, E. G. (1979). Teaching autistic children to use sign language: Some research issues. *Journal of Autism and Developmental Disorders, 9,* 345–359.

Crook, W. G. (1987). Nutrition, food allergies, and environmental toxins [letter]. *Journal of Learning Disabilities, 20,* 260–261.

Crook, W. G. (1994). Sugar and children's behavior [letter]. *New England Journal of Medicine, 330,* 1901–1902.

Densom, J. F., Nuthall, G. A., Bushnell, J., & Horn, J. (1989). Effectiveness of a sensory integrative therapy for children with perceptual-motor deficits. *Journal of Learning Disabilities, 22,* 221–229.

DesLauriers, A. M., & Carlson, C. F. (1969). *Your child is asleep: Early infantile autism.* Homewood, IL: Dorsey Press.

Deutsch, R. M., & Morrill, J. S. (1993). *Realities of nutrition.* Palo Alto, CA: Bull Publishing.

Dura, J. R., Mulick, J. A., & Hammer, D. (1988). Rapid clinical evaluation of sensory integrative therapy for self-injurious behavior. *Mental Retardation, 26,* 83–87.

Feingold, B. F. (1975). *Why your child is hyperactive.* New York: Random House.

Freeman, B. J., Ritvo, E. R., Needleman, R., & Yokota, A. (1985). The stability of cognitive and linguistic parameters in autism: A 5-year study. *Journal of the American Academy of Child Psychiatry, 24,* 290–311.

Frith, U. (1989). *Autism: Explaining the enigma.* Cambridge, MA: Blackwell.

Gordon, C. T., Stale, R. C., Nelson, J. E., & Rapoport, J. L. (1993). A double-blind comparison of clomipramine, desipramine, and placebo in the treatment of autistic disorder. *Archives of General Psychiatry, 50,* 441–447.

Greenspan, S. I. (1992, October/November). Reconsidering the diagnosis and treatment of very young children with autistic spectrum or pervasive developmental disorder. *Zero to Three, 13,* 1–9.

Gualtieri, T., Evans, R. W., & Patterson, D. R. (1987). The medical treatment of autistic people: Problems and side-effects. In E. Schopler & G. B. Mesibov (Eds.), *Neurobiological issues in autism* (pp. 325–338). New York: Plenum.

Huff, D. M., & Harris, S. R. (1983). Using sensorimotor integrative treatment with mentally retarded adults. *The American Journal of Occupational Therapy, 41,* 227–231.

Iwasaki, K., & Holm, M. B. (1989). Sensory treatment for the reduction of stereotypic behaviors in persons with severe multiple disabilities. *The Occupational Therapy Journal of Research, 9,* 170–183.

Jenkins, J. R., Fewell, R., & Harris, S. R. (1983). Comparison of sensory integrative therapy and motor programming. *American Journal of Mental Deficiency, 88,* 221–224.

Kaufman, B. N. (1976). *Son-rise.* New York: Harper & Row.

Kavale, K. A., & Forness, S. R. (1983). Hyperactivity and diet treatment: A meta-analysis of the Feingold Hypothesis. *Journal of Learning Disabilities, 16,* 324–330.

Kavale, K. A., & Mattson, P. D. (1983). "One jumped off the balance beam": Meta-analysis of perceptual-motor training. *Journal of Learning Disabilities, 16,* 165–173.

Kleijnen, J., & Knipschild, P. (1991). Niacin and Vitamin B_6 in mental functioning: A review of controlled trials in humans. *Biological Psychiatry, 26,* 931–941.

Leboyer, M., Bouvard, M. P., Launey, J., Tabuteau, F., Waller, D., Dugas, M., Kerdelhue, B., Lensing, P., & Panksepp, J. (1992). A double-blind study of naltrexone in infantile autism. *Journal of Autism and Developmental Disorders, 22,* 311–313.

Lelord, G., Muh, J. P., Barthelemy, C., Martineau, J., Garreau, B., & Callaway, E. (1981). Effects of pyridoxine and magnesium on autistic symptoms: Initial observations. *Journal of Autism and Developmental Disorders, 11,* 219–230.

Locascio, J. J., Malone, R. P., Small, A. M., Kafantaris, V., Ernst, M., Lynch, W. S., Overall, J. E., & Campbell, M. (1991). Factors related to haloperidol response and dyskinesias in autistic children. *Psychopharmacology Bulletin, 27,* 483–499.

Lord, C., & Schopler, E. (1989). The role of age at assessment, developmental level, and test in the stability of intelligence scores in young autistic children. *Journal of Autism and Developmental Disorders, 19,* 483–499.

Lord, C., & Schopler, E. (1994). In S. L. Harris & J. S. Handleman (Eds.), *Preschool education programs for children with autism* (pp. 87–106). Austin, TX: PRO-ED.

Lord, F. M. (1967). A paradox in the interpretation of group comparisons. *Psychological Bulletin, 68,* 304–305.

Lovaas, O. I. (1977). *The autistic child: Language development through behavior modification.* New York: Irvington.

Lovaas, O. I. (1987). Behavioral treatment and normal educational and intellectual functioning in young autistic children. *Journal of Consulting and Clinical Psychology, 55,* 3–9.

Lovaas, O. I., & Simmons, J. Q. (1969). Manipulation of self-destruction in three retarded children. *Journal of Applied Behavior Analysis, 2,* 143–157.

Lovaas, O. I., & Smith, T. (1989). A comprehensive behavioral theory of autistic children: Paradigm for research and treatment. *Journal of Behavior Therapy and Experimental Psychiatry, 20,* 17–29.

Martineau, J., Barthelemy, C., Cheliakine, C., & Lelord, G. (1985). Vitamin B$_6$, magnesium and combined B$_6$-Mg: Therapeutic effects in childhood autism. *Biological Psychiatry, 20,* 467–478.

Martineau, J., Barthelemy, C., Garreau, B., & Lelord, G. (1988). Brief report: An open middle-term study of combined vitamin B$_6$-magnesium in a subgroup of autistic children selected on their sensitivity to this treatment. *Journal of Autism and Developmental Disorders, 18,* 435–447.

Mason, S. A., & Iwata, B. A. (1990). Artifactual effects of sensory-integrative therapy on self-injurious behavior. *Journal of Applied Behavior Analysis, 23,* 361–370.

McGee, J. J., & Gonzales, L. (1990). Gentle teaching and the practice of human interdependence: A preliminary group study of 15 persons with severe behavior disorders and their caregivers. In A. C. Repp & N. N. Singh (Eds.), *Perspectives on the use of nonaversive and aversive interventions for people with developmental disabilities* (pp. 215–230). Sycamore, IL: Sycamore Publishing.

Mudford, O. C. (1995). Review of the Gentle Teaching data. *American Journal on Mental Retardation, 99,* 345–355.

Myles, B. S., Simpson, R. L., Ormsbee, K., & Erickson, C. (1993, December). Integrating preschool children with autism with their normally developing peers: Research findings and best practices recommendations. *Focus on Autistic Behavior, 8,* 1–18.

Pitsas, M. (1993). Facilitated Communication [letter]. *Autism Research Review International, 7*(4) 6.

Reilly, C., Nelson, D. L., & Bundy, A. C. (1983). Sensorimotor versus fine motor activities in eliciting vocalizations in autistic children. *The Occupational Therapy Journal of Research, 3,* 199–211.

Reiten, D. J. (1987). Nutrition and developmental disabilities: Issues in chronic care. In E. Schopler & G. B. Mesibov (Eds.), *Neurobiological issues in autism* (pp. 373–388). New York: Plenum.

Reynolds, R. D., & Leklem, J. E. (1980). Recommended methods for Vitamin B$_6$ analysis. In J. E. Leklem & R. D. Reynolds (Eds.), *Methods in Vitamin B$_6$ nutrition: Analysis and status assessment* (pp. 383–387). New York: Plenum.

Rimland, B. (1987a). *Evaluation of the Tokyo Higashi Program for autistic children by parents of the international division students.* Unpublished manuscript.

Rimland, B. (1987b). Megavitamin B$_6$ and magnesium in the treatment of autistic children and adults. In E. Schopler & G. B. Mesibov (Eds.), *Neurobiological issues in autism* (pp. 390–405). New York: Plenum.

Rimland, B., & Edelson, S. M. (1994). The effects of Auditory Integration Training on autism. *American Journal of Speech-Language Pathology, 3,* 16–24.

Rimland, B., & Edelson, S. M. (1995). Auditory integration training in autism: A pilot study. *Journal of Autism and Developmental Disorders, 25,* 61–70.

Roland, C. C., McGee, G. G., Risley, T. R., & Rimland, B. (1988). *Description of the Tokyo Higashi Program for autistic children* (ICBR Publication No. 77). San Diego: Autism Research Institute.

Rutter, M., & Bartak, L. (1973). Special educational treatment of autistic children: A comparative study. II. Follow-up findings and implications for services. *Journal of Child Psychology and Psychiatry, 14,* 241–270.

Schopler, E. (1971). Parents of psychotic children as scapegoats. *Journal of Contemporary Psychotherapy, 4,* 17–22.

Schopler, E., Lansing, M., & Waters, L. (1983). *Individualized assessment and treatment for autistic and developmentally disabled children.* Baltimore, MD: University Park Press.

Schopler, E., Mesibov, G. B., & Baker, A. (1982). Evaluation of treatment for autistic children and their parents. *Journal of the American Academy of Child Psychiatry, 21,* 262–267.

Schopler, E., & Olley, J. G. (1982). Comprehensive educational services for autistic children: The TEACCH model. In C. R. Reynolds & T. B. Gutkin (Eds.), *Handbook of school psychology* (pp. 626–643). New York: Wiley.

Schopler, E., Reichler, R. J., & Lansing, M. (1980). *Individualized assessment and treatment for autistic and developmentally disabled children, Vol. 2: Teaching strategies for parents and professionals.* Austin, TX: PRO-ED.

Shane, H. C. (Ed.). (1994). *Facilitated Communication: The clinical and social phenomenon.* San Diego: Singular.

Shaw, W. (1995, March/April). Pursuing a new idea. *The Advocate* (pp. 12–13).

Shearer, T. R., Larson, K., Neuschwanger, J., & Gedney, B. (1982). Minerals in the hair and nutrient intake of autistic children. *Journal of Autism and Developmental Disabilities, 12,* 25–34.

Shore, B. A. (1994). Sensory-integrative Therapy. *Self-injury Abstracts and Reviews, 3*(1), 1–7.

Smith, T. (1993). Autism. In T. R. Giles (Ed.), *Effective psychotherapies* (pp. 107–133). New York: Plenum.

Snyder, L. S., & Lindstedt, D. E. (1985). Models of child language development. In E. Schopler & G. B. Mesibov (Eds.), *Communication problems in autism* (pp. 17–35). New York: Plenum.

Spitz, H. (1986). *The raising of intelligence.* Englewood, NJ: Lawrence Erlbaum.

Stehli, A. (1991). *The sound of a miracle: A child's triumph over autism.* New York: Doubleday.

Strain, P. S. (1983). Generalization of autistic children's behavior change: Effects of developmentally integrated and segregated settings. *Analysis and Intervention in Developmental Disabilities, 3,* 23–34.

Szatmari, P. (1992). A review of the DSM-III-R criteria for autistic disorder. Special issue: Classification and diagnosis. *Journal of Autism and Developmental Disabilities, 22*, 507–527.

Tinbergen, W., & Tinbergen, E. A. (1983). *Autistic children: New hope for a cure.* London: Allen and Unwin.

Welch, M. G. (1987). Toward prevention of developmental disorders. *Pennsylvania Medicine, 90*, 47–52.

Wolreich, M. L., Lindgren, S. D., Stumbo, P. J., Strunk, L. D., Appelbaum, M. I., & Kiritsby, M. C. (1994). Effects of diets high in sucrose or aspartame on the behavior and cognitive performance of children. *New England Journal of Medicine, 330*, 301–307.

PART THREE

What to Teach

CHAPTER FIVE

Selecting Teaching Programs

Bridget Ann Taylor
Kelly Ann McDonough

As you begin the challenge of setting up a home program, you will need to select meaningful instructional programs for your child. Because no two children have the same strengths and needs, initial program selection must be based on each child's current abilities. Selecting programs for your child will be an ongoing task. Each time your child masters a program, you will need to select another. This chapter will present a framework for choosing teaching programs for your child so that meaningful instruction can proceed.

CONDUCTING A SKILLS ASSESSMENT

The three curriculum guides in this chapter outline skills you may want to teach your child. The objectives are arranged in beginning, intermediate, and advanced guides, but the hierarchy is not rigid. The first step in selecting programs is to assess your child's skills and deficits. The curriculum guides can be used as a framework for an initial assessment. Starting with the *Beginning Curriculum Guide,* determine your child's proficiency in the skills outlined and generate a list of prospective teaching programs. Keep the following questions in mind when assessing your child's skills:

• **Is the skill demonstrated upon your verbal instruction?** Some children will demonstrate responses on their own but not when asked by an adult. For example, you may observe your child labeling objects while playing, but when you hold an object up and ask her to label it, she is not able to do so. When assessing your child's skills be sure that she is able to perform the response when you present the relevant questions or stimuli.

• **Is the skill demonstrated without your assistance?** When assessing a particular skill, determine your child's proficiency without your assistance. For example, if you want to know whether your child can

follow one-step instructions, direct the instruction to him without providing a gesture (e.g., do not point toward his shoes when saying "Get your shoes"). Or, if you want to know if your child can complete simple activities (e.g., puzzles and shape sorters), present the activity and provide a verbal instruction (e.g., "Do the puzzle"), without providing physical guidance.

• **Is the skill demonstrated reliably over time?** Some children are inconsistent in their responses. It is important to establish that a particular skill can be demonstrated on several different occasions. Just because your child performs the response once does not mean that the skill is part of her repertoire. When assessing a skill, provide several opportunities to determine if your child can reliably (e.g., 8 out of 10 opportunities) perform the response.

• **Are all components of the skill demonstrated?** Your child might be able to demonstrate part of a skill but not all. For example, he might be able to identify three body parts or imitate one or two actions. While this is a good start, you'll want to make sure that your child can perform an adequate number of responses within each program. In determining the adequate number of responses within each program, consider the age of your child (e.g., most preschool children can identify 10 or more body parts). When assessing a particular program (e.g., one-step instructions), determine an appropriate number of responses and assess your child's performance across all of them.

• **Is the skill demonstrated with several different people, in several different contexts, with various stimuli?** Sometimes children with autism can perform skills with certain people but not others (e.g., with their mother but not with the baby-sitter), only in specific contexts (e.g., follows the instruction "Get your cup" only in the kitchen when juice is visible), or only with specific stimuli (e.g., labels Thomas The Train but not other toys). When assessing a particular skill, be sure it can be demonstrated with several people in a number of contexts and with various stimuli.

SELECTING PROGRAMS

Once you have assessed your child's skills, you must decide which ones to begin teaching. The following questions are presented to assist you in selecting teaching objectives for your child. Each time you choose a teaching program for your child, ask the following questions:

• **Does your child have the necessary prerequisite skills for this program?** When you choose a teaching program, ask yourself what skills your child may need to perform the response. For example, you may want your child to request in sentences, but she may not be able to repeat words. You may want to teach your child to initiate play interactions with siblings, but she is not able to follow simple instructions. Breaking a skill down into its component parts can help you identify what other skills you may need to teach first.

• **Is this program developmentally/age-appropriate for your child?** Although a normal developmental model of skill acquisition cannot be rigidly applied to children with autism, programs should loosely reflect a sequence of development that would be expected of a typical child. When identifying a skill to teach, ask yourself if another child of similar age could perform the same skill.

• **Will this skill help to reduce problem behaviors?** Choose teaching programs that are likely to have a positive impact on your child's behavior. For example, teaching communicative responses such as pointing and gesturing yes and no may help reduce problem behaviors that serve a communicative function. Additionally, teaching your child to engage in independent play activities may reduce stereotypic behaviors.

• **Will this skill lead to the teaching of other skills?** When choosing skills to teach, identify those that are likely to build on one another. For example, teaching your child to imitate sequenced gross motor actions (e.g., imitating two actions in the correct order) will probably lead you to teach your child to follow two-step verbal instructions.

• **Is this skill likely to generalize?** Because skills are often difficult to generalize for children with autism, choose programs and target responses that your child will have ample opportunity to practice beyond the teaching sessions. For example, you are more likely to ask your child to "Shut the door," "Turn on the light," and to "Get your shoes" throughout the day, as opposed to "Raise arms" and "Stomp your feet." Responses that are associated with naturally occurring positive consequences are more likely to generalize.

• **Will your child acquire this skill within a reasonable time frame?** Although rates of learning vary greatly across children and skills, priority should be given to teaching skills that your child is likely to acquire in a reasonable amount of time. For example, if your child does not speak, he or she will need to learn effective communicative responses. Your child can learn to point to desired items relatively quickly, in comparison to requesting in phrases. Choosing skills that will be acquired in a reasonable time frame will be reinforcing for you, your child, and your teaching staff.

• **Is this an important skill for you and your family?** Choose skills that will have positive implications for your child's participation in family activities. Although matching colors is an important readiness skill, teaching your child to identify family members will have a greater impact on your child's participation in the family.

• **Is this a skill that your child can use throughout the day?** Choose to teach skills that are functional for your child. For example, learning to follow simple instructions, using yes and no, pointing to desired items, and completing play activities are useful for your child and can be incorporated into his day.

GETTING STARTED

When you begin a home program, start with a limited number of skills for the first few weeks. It is better to aim for fast acquisition in a limited number of areas than slow, inconsistent progress in many areas. This will also allow you and your teaching staff to become proficient in the teaching methodology and for your child to get used to the structure of the sessions. Although programming should be individualized for each child, typically, entry-level programming will include an attending program (e.g., responding to name), a receptive language program (e.g., following a one-step instruction), an imitation program (e.g., imitating a gross motor movement), an expressive language program (e.g., pointing to desired items), and a matching task (e.g., matching identical objects). As your child progresses, add additional programs according to his needs.

DESCRIPTIONS OF THE PROGRAMS

The curriculum guides are followed by descriptions of teaching programs for a number of the objectives listed in the guides (not all objectives are outlined in the program sheets). Target responses, prerequisites, materials, prompting strategies, and some helpful hints are provided. To conserve space, many of the receptive and expressive language programs are combined on one sheet. Each program sheet can be copied from the manual and inserted in your child's program book. Many of the programs offer sample target responses, but these are simply to get you started. Teach responses that are relevant to you and your child.

The teaching procedures are generic and may need to be modified for your child. For example, the programs have been written with the assumption that your child will initially require prompting (assistance) to perform the response correctly. Although prompting suggestions are provided, there are many error-correction procedures that could be used when your child responds incorrectly or fails to respond at all. Refer to Chapter 6, "How to Teach," for more specific information about teaching strategies.

Some of the receptive language and matching programs require you to present stimuli such as photographs on a table. The number of stimuli you present will vary according to the current steps of the program. It is recommended, however, when teaching discrimination tasks, to present a minimum of three stimuli to minimize the likelihood that a correct response is due to chance.

As you scan the program sheets, you may see some unfamiliar terms. They are defined briefly here.

1. *Prompts.* Prompts refer to any assistance that is provided to your child so that she will successfully perform a response. Prompts can be verbal ("Get the ball"), physical (taking your child's hand and placing it on the ball), gestural (pointing to the ball), positional (placing the ball closer to your child), or modeled (demonstrating the response for your child to observe and copy). When beginning a teaching program, determine the degree of assistance (prompts) required for your child to demonstrate an errorless performance of a response. Fade (remove) prompts gradually and systematically over teaching sessions, so that your child is able to perform the target response without assistance.

2. *Time-Delay Prompt.* A time-delay prompt is a procedure in which the time between presentation of an instructional stimulus and a prompt is gradually increased. Initially, prompts are provided at the same time as or immediately after the instruction. Over subsequent teaching sessions, the prompt is delayed by gradually increasing the time interval. For example, when teaching a child to answer the question "What's your name?" a prompt (e.g., modeling the correct answer) is provided immediately after the question is presented for the first few trials. When the child responds

reliably to the prompt (e.g., by saying her name after the model prompt on three consecutive trials), a short delay is introduced between the instruction and the prompt. For instance the instructor might say "What's your name?" wait 2 seconds, and then model the response. As long as the child continues to respond correctly, this delay might remain the same for, perhaps, three trials. Then the delay between instruction and prompt would be increased by 2 seconds, to 4 seconds, then to 6 seconds, and so on. The goal is to have the child respond correctly before a prompt is provided.

3. *Differential Reinforcement.* Differential reinforcement refers to reinforcing some responses while not reinforcing others. For example, when you first teach a skill, reinforce responses that occur with some assistance (prompts). Over successive teaching trials, gradually use less and less assistance, and only reinforce responses that occur with reduced assistance rather than responses that require greater assistance. Eventually only reinforce responses that are correct and do not require your assistance.

RESOURCES

A resource section outlining materials for teaching and suggestions for further readings follows the *Advanced Curriculum Guide.* You are encouraged, when possible, to make your own materials (e.g., take photographs of nouns, verbs, emotions, rooms, and scenes from the child's natural environment) and to use these materials to teach multiple programs (e.g., use pictures of actions to teach not only receptive and expressive action verbs but also discrimination of *wh*-questions about a picture). If you are seeking funding for a home program through your local school board, include a list of necessary supplies in your child's Individualized Education Plan to ensure that materials will be provided by your school district. Additional readings and published curricula are included to assist you in teaching programs that are not outlined in this chapter.

ACKNOWLEDGMENTS

Some of the teaching programs presented in this chapter were developed at the Alpine Learning Group, Inc. Others were influenced by programs previously published in works such as *Teaching Developmentally Disabled Children: The ME Book,* by Ivar Lovaas. The authors are grateful to the many children, families, and professionals who have helped with the development of the teaching programs in this chapter.

Beginning Curriculum Guide

Attending Skills

1. Sits in a chair independently
2. Makes eye contact in response to name
3. Makes eye contact when given the instruction "Look at me"
4. Responds to the direction "Hands down"

Imitation Skills

1. Imitates gross motor movements
2. Imitates actions with objects
3. Imitates fine motor movements
4. Imitates oral motor movements

Receptive Language Skills

1. Follows one-step instructions
2. Identifies body parts
3. Identifies objects
4. Identifies pictures
5. Identifies familiar people
6. Follows verb instructions
7. Identifies verbs in pictures
8. Identifies objects in the environment
9. Points to pictures in a book
10. Identifies objects by function
11. Identifies possession
12. Identifies environmental sounds

Expressive Language Skills

1. Points to desired items in response to "What do you want?"
2. Points to desired items spontaneously
3. Imitates sounds and words
4. Labels objects
5. Labels pictures
6. Verbally requests desired items

7. States or gestures yes and no for preferred and nonpreferred items
8. Labels familiar people
9. Makes a choice
10. Reciprocates greetings
11. Answers social questions
12. Labels verbs in pictures, others, and self
13. Labels objects by function
14. Labels possession

Pre-academic Skills

1. Matches
   - Identical objects
   - Identical pictures
   - Objects to pictures
   - Pictures to objects
   - Colors, shapes, letters, numbers
   - Nonidentical objects
   - Objects by association
2. Completes simple activities independently
3. Identifies colors
4. Identifies shapes
5. Identifies letters
6. Identifies numbers
7. Counts by rote to 10
8. Counts objects

Self-help Skills

1. Drinks from a cup
2. Uses fork and spoon when eating
3. Removes shoes
4. Removes socks
5. Removes pants
6. Removes shirt
7. Uses napkin/tissue
8. Is toilet-trained for urination

Intermediate Curriculum Guide

Attending Skills

1. Sustains eye contact for 5 seconds in response to name
2. Makes eye contact in response to name while playing
3. Makes eye contact in response to name from a distance
4. Asks "What?" when name is called

Imitation Skills

1. Imitates gross motor movements from a standing position
2. Imitates sequenced gross motor movements
3. Imitates sequenced actions with objects
4. Imitates actions paired with sounds
5. Imitates block patterns
6. Copies simple drawings

Receptive Language Skills

1. Identifies rooms
2. Identifies emotions
3. Identifies places
4. Follows two-step instructions
5. Gives two objects
6. Retrieves objects out of view
7. Identifies attributes
8. Identifies community helpers
9. Pretends
10. Identifies categories
11. Identifies pronouns
12. Follows directions with prepositions
13. Identifies an object in view when it is described
14. Places sequence cards in order
15. Identifies gender
16. Identifies item that is missing
17. Answers *wh*-questions about objects and pictures
18. Answers yes/no in response to questions about objects and actions
19. Names an object by touch

Expressive Language Skills

1. Imitates two- and three-word phrases
2. Requests desired items in a sentence in response to "What do you want?"
3. Requests desired items spontaneously in a sentence
4. Calls parent from a distance
5. Labels object based on function
6. Labels function of objects
7. Labels and points to body part according to function
8. Labels function of body parts
9. Labels places
10. Labels emotions
11. Labels categories
12. Uses simple sentences
    - It's a . . .
    - I see a . . .
    - I have a . . .
13. Reciprocates information
    - I have . . .
    - I see . . .
    - Social information
14. States "I don't know" when asked to label unknown objects
15. Asks *wh*-questions: "What's that?" and "Where is . . ."
16. Labels prepositions
17. Labels pronouns
18. Answers general knowledge questions
19. Labels gender
20. Describes pictures in a sentence
21. Describes objects in view using attributes
22. Recalls immediate past experience
23. Answers "Where . . .?" questions
24. Names what belongs in rooms
25. Labels function of rooms
26. Labels function of community helpers
27. Answers "When . . .?" questions

(continues)

Intermediate Curriculum Guide (Cont'd)

28. Describes sequence of pictures
29. Delivers a message
30. Role plays with puppets
31. Offers assistance

Pre-academic Skills

1. Matches items from the same category
2. Gives specified quantity of items
3. Matches number to quantity
4. Matches uppercase to lowercase letters
5. Matches identical words
6. Identifies more and less
7. Sequences numbers/letters
8. Completes simple worksheets
9. Copies letters and numbers
10. Identifies written name
11. Draws simple pictures
12. Writes name
13. Pastes/glues
14. Cuts with scissors
15. Colors within a boundary

Self-help Skills

1. Puts on pants
2. Puts on shirt
3. Puts on coat
4. Puts on shoes
5. Puts on socks
6. Washes hands
7. Is toilet-trained for bowel movements
8. Self-initiates for bathroom

Advanced Curriculum Guide

Attending Skills

1. Makes eye contact during conversation
2. Makes eye contact during group instruction

Imitation Skills

1. Imitates complex sequences
2. Imitates peer play
3. Imitates verbal responses of peers

Receptive Language Skills

1. Follows three-step instructions
2. Follows complex instructions from a distance
3. Names a person, place, or thing when it is described
4. Names an object when only part is visible
5. Identifies items that are the same
6. Identifies items that are different
7. Identifies what does not belong based on attribute or category
8. Identifies plural vs. singular
9. Answers *wh*-questions about a short story
10. Answers *wh*-questions about a topic
11. Follows the instructions "Ask . . ." versus "Tell . . ."
12. Finds hidden object given location clues
13. Discriminates when to ask a question and when to reciprocate information

Expressive Language Skills

1. States "I don't know" to unfamiliar questions
2. Labels a category to which an item belongs
3. Names items in a category
4. Retells a story
5. Describes objects not in view with attributes

(continues)

Advanced Curriculum Guide (Cont'd)

6. Recalls past events
7. Describes topics
8. Tells own story
9. Expresses confusion and asks for clarification
10. Labels advanced possessive pronouns
11. Uses correct verb tense
12. Asks a question and retells information
13. Listens to a conversation and answers questions about the conversation
14. Asserts knowledge
15. Answers advanced general knowledge questions
16. Describes how to do something
17. Describes similarities and differences between objects
18. Answers "Which . . .?" questions
19. Asks *wh*-questions when provided with vague information

Abstract Language

1. Answers "Why . . .?" questions
2. Answers "If . . .?" questions
3. Makes logical completions to sentences
4. Describes irregularities in pictures
5. Answers yes/no (factual information)
6. Predicts outcomes
7. Takes another's perspective
8. Provides explanations
9. Excludes an item based on attribute and category
10. Identifies main topic in story and conversation

Academic Skills

1. Defines people, places, and things
2. Completes a pattern
3. Matches written words to objects/objects to written words
4. Reads common words
5. Names letter sounds
6. Names a word beginning with letter sound
7. Names initial, medial, and final consonants

8. Spells simple words
9. States word meaning
10. Identifies simple synonyms
11. Identifies temporal relationships
12. Identifies ordinal numbers
13. Identifies rhyming words
14. Writes simple words from memory
15. Adds single-digit numbers

Social Skills

1. Imitates actions of peer
2. Follows directions from a peer
3. Answers questions from a peer
4. Responds to peer play-initiation statements
5. Plays board game with peer
6. Initiates play statements to peer
7. Reciprocates information to peer
8. Comments to peer during play
9. Asks peer for assistance
10. Offers assistance to peer

School Readiness

1. Waits turn
2. Demonstrates new responses through observation
3. Follows instructions in a group
4. Reciprocates social information in a group
5. Sings nursery rhymes in a group
6. Answers when called on
7. Raises hand to answer question
8. Listens to a story and answers questions about the story
9. Shows and tells

Self-help Skills

1. Brushes teeth
2. Zippers
3. Buttons
4. Snaps

Resources

Noun Cards

1. Photo Cue Cards
   Communication Skill Builders*

2. Photo Nouns (Set One and Set Two)
   Imaginart Communication Products

3. Photo Resource Kit (Nouns)
   PRO-ED

Verb Cards

1. Power Cards: Verb Power (1–3)
   Communication Skill Builders

2. Great Beginnings For Early Language Learning:
   Beginning Verbs
   Communication Skill Builders

3. Photo Action Cards
   Learning Development Aides (LDA)
   ABC School Supply

4. Verbs, Verbs, Verbs
   PRO-ED

Picture Books

1. *My First Word Book*
   Angela Wilkes
   Dorling Kindersley, Inc., 1991

2. *My First Book of Words: 1,000 Words Every
   Child Should Know*
   Lena Shiffman
   Cartwell Learning Bookshelf
   Scholastic, Inc., 1992

3. *The First 1,000 Words and Pictures Book*
   Wishing Well Books
   Joshua Morris Publishing, Inc., 1991

4. *The First Thousand Words: A Picture Book*
   Heather Amery & Stephen Cartwright
   Usborne House, EDC Publishing, 1989

5. *300 First Words*
   Betty Root
   Barron's Educational Series, Inc., 1993

Sequencing

1. Childhood Sequence Photos (Sets 1–3)
   Imaginart Communication Products

2. What Follows Next? 3-Scene Sequence Cards
   Kaplan School Supply

3. Frank Schaffer 4- and 6-Scene Sequencing Cards
   Constructive Play Things

4. Classroom Sequencing Card Library
   Lakeshore

Associations

1. Photo Language Cards
   Association Cards
   Imaginart Communication Products

2. Great Beginnings Associations
   Communication Skill Builders

3. Power Cards Association Power
   Communication Skill Builders

Prepositions

1. Color Cards: Language in Living Color
   Prepositions
   Imaginart Communication Products

2. In, On and Under: A Preposition Lotto Game
   Imaginart Communication Products

3. Great Beginning Prepositions
   Communication Skill Builders

4. Where is it? Spatial Relationship Cards
   ABC School Supply

Adjectives

1. Color Cards: Language in Living Color
   Adjectives
   Imaginart Communication Products

2. Power Cards Opposites Power
   Communication Skill Builders

3. Opposites Matching Game
   ABC School Supply

Emotions

1. Feelings and Faces Game
   Lakeshore

2. Moods and Emotions Poster Pack
   Lakeshore

3. Faces and Feelings/Jeux De Visage
   Constructive Play Things

(continues)

*See pages 72–73 for telephone numbers of all referenced catalogues.

Resources (Cont'd)

Categories/Classification

1. Category Sort
   Imaginart Communication Products
2. Classroom Sorting Materials
   Lakeshore
3. Classification Picture Card Library
   Lakeshore

Verb Tenses

1. Verb Tenses
   Imaginart Communication Products
2. *Syntax Flip Book*—Revised Edition
   PRO-ED

Irregularities

1. "What's Wrong?" Cards (LDA)
   Imaginart Communication Products
2. "What's Funny?" Blackline Masters
   PRO-ED
3. "What's Different?" Cards
   Imaginart Communication Products
4. "150 What's Wrong with this Picture?" Scenes
   Super Duper School Company

Environmental Sounds

1. Living Learning Soundtracks Lotto
   ABC School Supply
2. Photo Sound Lotto (LDA)
   ABC School Supply
3. Hear the World Sound Lotto Game
   Discovery Toys

Matching

1. Photo Object Beginners Lotto
   Lakeshore
2. Memory Match Game
   ABC School Supply
3. First Memory
   ABC School Supply

Games

1. Eight Spin and See Games:
   Lotto Type Game for Visual and Verbal Skills
   Super Duper School Company

2. No Peeking
   Ravensburger
3. Tell a Story
   Ravensburger
4. What's My Name? The Description Game
   Ravensburger
5. Fast Progress (Advanced Language Game)
   Imaginart Communication Products
6. Silly Expressions Board Game
   Discovery Toys
7. First Four Games
   Ravensburger
8. Mystery Garden
   Ravensburger

Wh-Questions

1. See What You're Asking? Games for *Wh*-Questions
   Colleen Murphy
   Communication Skill Builders
2. *Wh*-Programs Who? What? Where? When? Why?
   Patricia J. Collins, Gary W. Cunningham
   PRO-ED
3. Syntax Two: Materials for Teaching *Wh*-Questions
   ECL Publications

Advanced Language

1. *MEER 1, Manual of Exercises for Expressive Reasoning*
   LinguiSystems
2. *MEER 2, Manual of Exercises for Expressive Reasoning*
   LinguiSystems
3. Why?/Because LDA
   ABC School Supply
4. Safety Cards—In and Around the Home
   Imaginart Communication Products
5. SPARC Picture Scenes
   LinguiSystems
6. Think It—Say It: Improving Reasoning and Organization Skills
   Communication Skill Builders

(continues)

Resources (Cont'd)

Academic Curriculums

1. Edmark Reading Curriculum Level 1, 2nd edition
   Edmark Corporation
2. Aims: Pre-Reading Kit
   Continental Press
3. Aims: Mathematics A & B Kits
   Continental Press
4. Special Needs Curriculum: Numbers A–D
   Continental Press
5. Sensible Pencil Handwriting Curriculum
   Ebsco Curriculum Materials

Computer Software

1. First Words
   Laureate
2. First Verbs
   Laureate
3. Micro-LADS
   Laureate
4. First Categories
   Laureate

Miscellaneous

1. Size Sort
   Imaginart Communication Products
2. Our Five Senses
   Imaginart Communication Products
3. IZIT Cards
   PRO-ED
4. Power Cards (Same/Different Power 1: House)
   Communication Skill Builders
5. Color Library: Occupations
   Imaginart Communication Products
6. "Say and Do" K—Worksheets
   Super Duper School Company
7. Dot to Dot and Color by Number Artic
   Worksheets
   Super Duper School Company
8. Deck O' Dough: What's Missing?
   Continental Press
9. Perceptual Activities: Primary
   Academic Therapy
10. ABC Mazes
    Academic Therapy

11. Half-and-Half Design and Color Series
    Academic Therapy
12. Teaching Pictures
    Kaplan
13. Augmentative Communication Products
    Prentke Romich Company
    Mayer-Johnson Company
14. The Best Concept Pictures Ever
    LinguiSystems
15. Brain Quest
    Workman Publishing Company

Catalogs

1. ABC School Supply
   (800) 669-4222
2. Academic Therapy Publications
   (800) 422-7249
3. Communication Skill Builders
   (800) 866-4446
4. Constructive Play Things
   (800) 448-4115
5. Continental Press
   (800) 233-0759
6. Discovery Toys, Inc.
   (800) 426-4777
7. Ebsco Curriculum Materials
   (800) 633-8623
8. ECL Publications
   (602) 246-4163
9. Edmark Corporation
   (800) 362-2890
10. Imaginart Communication Products
    (800) 828-1376
11. Kaplan School Supply
    (800) 334-2014
12. Lakeshore Learning Materials
    (800) 421-5354
13. Laureate Learning Systems, Inc.
    (800) 562-6801
14. LinguiSystems, Inc.
    (800) 776-4332
15. Mayer-Johnson Company
    (619) 550-0084

(continues)

Resources (Cont'd)

16. Oriental Trading Company, Inc.
    (800) 228-2269

17. Paul Brookes Publishing Company
    (410) 337-9580

18. Prentice Hall
    (800) 223-1360

19. Prentke Romich Company
    (800) 262-1984

20. PRO-ED
    (512) 451-3246

21. Research Press
    (217) 352-3273

22. Super Duper School Company
    (800) 277-8737

Books/Journals

1. *Applied Behavior Analysis*
   John O. Cooper, Timothy E. Heron, and
   William L. Heward
   Merrill, 1987

2. *Communication and Language
   Intervention Series*
   Steven F. Warren and Joe Reichle, Eds.
   Paul H. Brookes Publishing, 1990

3. *Focus on Autistic Behavior*
   PRO-ED Journals
   8700 Shoal Creek Blvd.,
   Austin, TX 76758-6897
   (512) 451-3246

4. *The Good Kid Book: How to Solve the Sixteen
   Most Common Behavior Problems*
   Howard Sloane
   Research Press, 1988

5. *The How to Teach Series*
   Vance Hall, Nathan Azrin, Victoria A. Besalel,
   R. Vance Hall, and Marilyn C. Hall
   PRO-ED

6. *Journal of Applied Behavior Analysis*
   Department of Human Development
   University of Kansas
   Lawrence, Kansas 66045
   (913) 843-0008

7. *Journal of Autism and Developmental
   Disabilities*
   Plenum Press
   (212) 620-8000

8. *Let Me Hear Your Voice: A Family's Triumph
   Over Autism*
   Catherine Maurice
   Knopf Publishing Company, 1993

9. *Negotiating the Special Education Maze: A
   Guide for Parents and Teachers*
   Winifred Anderson, Stephen Chitwood and
   Dierdre Hayden
   Woodbine House, 1990

10. *Parents Are Teachers: A Child Management
    Program*
    Wesley C. Becker
    Research Press

11. *Personal Care Skills*
    Project More: Daily Living Skills
    PRO-ED

12. *Steps to Independence: A Skills Training Guide
    for Parents and Teachers of Children with
    Special Needs*, 2nd edition
    Bruce L. Baker and Allen J. Brightman
    Paul Brooks Publishing, 1989

13. *Steps to Independence: Behavior Problems*
    Bruce L. Baker, Allen J. Brightman, Louis J.
    Heifetz, and Diane M. Murphy
    Research Press, 1976

14. *Systematic Instruction of Persons with Severe
    Disabilities*
    Martha Snell
    Prentice Hall, 1993

15. *Teaching Developmentally Disabled Children:
    The ME Book*
    O. Ivar Lovaas
    PRO-ED, 1981

16. *Toilet Training in Less Than a Day*
    Nathan Azrin and Richard Foxx
    Simon and Schuster, 1974

17. *Toilet Training Persons with Developmental
    Disabilities*
    Richard Foxx and Nathan Azrin
    Research Press, 1973

Program	**Makes Eye Contact**

- Program Procedure:

(1) *In Response to Name*—Sit in a chair across from the child. State the child's name and simultaneously prompt eye contact by bringing an edible reinforcer or a small tangible reinforcer to your eye level. When the child makes eye contact with you for 1 second, immediately give reinforcer to the child. Over the teaching sessions, say the child's name and delay your prompt by several seconds to assess if child looks without the prompt. Differentially reinforce responses demonstrated without prompts. Throughout teaching sessions, provide positive reinforcement if child looks at you spontaneously.

(2) *For 5 Seconds*—Repeat procedure in #1 but sustain eye contact for 5 seconds prior to giving the reinforcer to the child. Differentially reinforce responses demonstrated without prompts.

(3) *While Playing*—Give a toy to the child to play with at the table. Sit across from the child and say the child's name. Prompt the child to look at you and reinforce the response. Fade prompts over subsequent teaching trials. Differentially rein-force responses demonstrated with the lowest level of prompting.

(4) *From a Distance*—Repeat procedure in #3 but sit or stand at a distance of 3 feet. State child's name and prompt the child to look at you. Reinforce the response. Fade prompts over subsequent teaching trials. Differentially reinforce responses demonstrated with the lowest level of prompting. Over the teaching sessions, increase the distance between you and the child.

(5) *In Response to "Look at Me."*—Sit in a chair across from the child. State the instruction "Look at me." Use the same prompting and reinforcement procedures as in #1.

- Materials: Edible and tangible reinforcers.

- Suggested Prerequisites: Sits in a chair.

- Prompting Suggestions: Bring reinforcer to eye level for child to track or gently guide child's chin upward to prompt eye contact. Use a time-delay procedure: delay the prompt by 2-second increments across trials.

Instruction	Response		
(1–4) The child's name (5) "Look at me."	**(1–5) Makes eye contact**	**Date Introduced**	**Date Mastered**
1. For 1 second			
2. For 5 seconds			
3. While playing			
4. From a distance			
5. In response to "Look at me."			

▶ *Helpful Hint:* Be sure that your child is looking directly at your eyes and not at the reinforcer.

Program	Imitates Gross Motor Movements

- Program Procedure: Sit in a chair facing the child and establish attending. Present the instruction "Do this" while simultaneously modeling a gross motor movement. Prompt the child to perform the action and reinforce the response. Fade prompts over subsequent trials. Differentially reinforce responses demonstrated with the lowest level of prompting. Eventually, only reinforce correct, unprompted responses.

- Suggested Prerequisites: Sits in a chair.

- Prompting Suggestions: Physically guide the child to perform the response.

Instruction: "Do this."	Response	Date Introduced	Date Mastered
1. Tap table			
2. Clap hands			
3. Wave			
4. Place arms up			
5. Stomp feet			
6. Tap legs			
7. Shake head			
8. Nod head			
9. Turn around			
10. Cover face with hands			
11. Tap shoulders			
12. Jump			
13. Circle arms			
14. Tap stomach			
15. March			
16. Put arms out			
17. Knock			
18. Put hands on waist			
19. Rub hands together			
20. Tap head			

▶ *Helpful Hint:* Some children may learn object-mediated imitation (e.g., ringing a bell, placing a block in a bucket) faster than gross motor movements. After teaching five imitative responses, probe novel ones; the skill may have generalized!

Program — Imitates Actions with Objects

- **Program Procedure:** Place two identical objects on the table. Sit across the table facing the child. Establish attending. Present the instruction "Do this" while simultaneously modeling an action with one of the objects. Prompt child to perform the action with the other object and reinforce the response. Fade prompts over subsequent trials. Differentially reinforce responses demonstrated with the lowest level of prompting. Eventually, only reinforce correct, unprompted responses.

- **Materials:** Objects for the actions.

- **Suggested Prerequisites:** Sits in a chair.

- **Prompting Suggestions:** Physically guide the child to perform the response.

Instruction: "Do this."	Response	Date Introduced	Date Mastered
1. Place block in bucket			
2. Ring bell			
3. Push toy car			
4. Wave flag			
5. Hit drum			
6. Put on hat			
7. Scribble			
8. Wipe mouth			
9. Bang toy hammer			
10. Shake maraca			
11. Feed doll			
12. Hold phone to ear			
13. Drink from cup			
14. Blow horn			
15. Brush hair			
16. Make actions with a doll			
17. Roll Playdoh			
18. Place coin in bank			
19. Kiss doll			
20. Stamp paper			

▶ *Helpful Hint:* Teach play-related imitations that your child might enjoy.

Program	**Imitates Fine Motor Movements**

- Program Procedure: Sit in a chair facing the child and establish attending. State the instruction "Do this" while simultaneously modeling a fine motor movement. Prompt child to perform the movement and reinforce the response. Fade prompts over subsequent trials. Differentially reinforce responses demonstrated with the lowest level of prompting.

- Eventually, only reinforce correct, unprompted responses.

- Suggested Prerequisites: Sits in a chair and imitates gross motor movements.

- Prompting Suggestions: Physically guide child to perform the response.

Instruction: "Do this."	Response	Date Introduced	Date Mastered
1. Clasp hands together			
2. Open and close hands			
3. Tap index fingers			
4. Tap thumbs			
5. Wiggle fingers			
6. Rub hands together			
7. Tap index finger to thumb			
8. Point to body parts			
9. Point index finger to palm			
10. Extend index finger			
11. Place thumbs up			
12. Make a peace sign			

▶ *Helpful Hint:* Keep in mind typical motor development when teaching this program. Many children under age 3 will have difficulty imitating fine motor movements.

Program	Imitates Oral Motor Movements

- **Program Procedure:** Sit in a chair facing the child and establish attending. Present the instruction "Do this" while simultaneously modeling an oral motor movement. Prompt child to perform the movement and reinforce the response. Fade prompts over subsequent trials. Differentially reinforce responses demonstrated with the lowest level of prompting. Eventually, only reinforce correct, unprompted responses.

- **Suggested Prerequisites:** Sits in a chair; makes eye contact; imitates gross and fine motor movements.

- **Prompting Suggestions:** Physically place the child's mouth in the correct position. Use materials that may facilitate responding (e.g., horn or bubbles for blowing, lollipop for sticking tongue out).

Instruction: "Do this."	Response	Date Introduced	Date Mastered
1. Open mouth			
2. Stick out tongue			
3. Put lips together			
4. Tap teeth together			
5. Blow			
6. Smile			
7. Pucker			
8. Kiss			
9. Place tongue to top teeth			
10. Place top teeth over lower lip			

▶ *Helpful Hint:* Assess the goal of this program. If you are introducing it as a prerequisite for verbal imitation, it may be best to pair a sound with the movement from the start. If you're having trouble prompting a movement, try using a mirror. Have the child look at both of your reflections in the mirror when you present the model and then fade the use of the mirror.

Program	Follows One-Step Instructions

- Program Procedure: Sit in a chair facing the child and establish attending. Present the instruction. Prompt the child to perform the response and reinforce. Fade prompts over subsequent trials. Differentially reinforce responses that are demonstrated with the lowest level of prompting. Eventually, only reinforce correct, un-prompted responses.

- Materials: Items needed for the instruction.

- Suggested Prerequisites: For instruction #2, sits in a chair.

- Prompting Suggestions: Physically guide the child to perform the response.

Instruction	Response	Date Introduced	Date Mastered
1. "Sit down."			
2. "Stand up."			
3. "Come here."			
4. "Put hands down."			
5. "Wave bye bye."			
6. "Give me a hug."			
7. "Put arms up."			
8. "Clap your hands."			
9. "Turn around."			
10. "Jump."			
11. "Give me a kiss."			
12. "Throw this away."			
13. "Shut the door."			
14. "Blow a kiss."			
15. "Turn on the light."			
16. "Get a tissue."			
17. "Turn on the music."			
18. "Put on shelf."			
19. "Give me five."			
20. "Stomp your feet."			

▶ *Helpful Hint:* Select instructions that you are likely to ask your child to perform within the context of the day. Choosing instructions that you're likely to use with your child beyond the teaching session will provide natural opportunities for maintenance and generalization.

| Program | Body Parts (Receptive and Expressive) |

- Program Procedure:
  (1) *Identifies Body Parts*—Sit in a chair facing the child. Establish attending and state the instruction "Touch ___ (body part)." Prompt the child to touch correct body part on him/herself and reinforce responses. Fade prompts over subsequent trials and differentially reinforce responses demonstrated with the lowest level of prompting. Eventually, only reinforce correct, unprompted responses.
  (2) *Labels Body Parts*—Sit in a chair facing the child and establish attending. Point to a body part on yourself and say "What is this?" Prompt the child

to name the body part and reinforce the response. Fade prompts over subsequent trials. Differentially reinforce responses demonstrated with the lowest level of prompting. Eventually, only reinforce correct, unprompted responses.

- Suggested Prerequisites:
  (1) Follows five one-step instructions.
  (2) Identifies the body part and labels familiar objects.

- Prompting Suggestions:
  (1) Model the response or physically guide child to perform response.
  (2) Model the correct response.

Instruction	Response		
(1) "Touch ___." (2) "What is this?"	(1) Touches the correct body part (2) Labels body part	Date Introduced	Date Mastered
1. Head			
2. Feet			
3. Stomach			
4. Nose			
5. Mouth			
6. Legs			
7. Eyes			
8. Ears			
9. Hair			
10. Cheeks			
11. Shoulders			
12. Hand			
13. Face			
14. Arm			
15. Fingers			
16. Elbow			
17. Chin			
18. Toes			
19. Thumb			

▶ *Helpful Hint:* Initially choose body parts that are not located within close proximity to one another (e.g., initially, teach discrimination of head and feet rather than nose and eyes).

Program	Objects (Receptive and Expressive)

- Program Procedure:
  (1) *Identifies Objects*—Place object(s) on the table in front of the child. Establish attending and state the instruction "Give me ___ (name of object)." Prompt child to hand you the object and reinforce the response. Fade prompts over subsequent trials. Differentially reinforce responses demonstrated with the lowest level of prompting. Eventually, only reinforce correct, unprompted responses.
  (2) *Labels Objects*—Sit in a chair facing the child. Establish attending and present an object. Say "What is this?" Prompt child to label object and reinforce the response. Fade prompts over subsequent trials.

Differentially reinforce responses demonstrated with the lowest level of prompting. Eventually, only reinforce correct, unprompted responses.

- Materials: Objects.
- Suggested Prerequisites:
  (1) Matches identical objects.
  (2) Follows 15 one-step instructions.
  (3) Imitates sounds and simple words.
- Prompting Suggestions:
  (1) Physically guide child to hand the object to you.
  (2) Model the label.

Instruction (1) "Give me ___." (2) "What is this?"	Response (1) Gives correct object (2) Labels object	Date Introduced	Date Mastered
1.			
2.			
3.			
4.			
5.			
6.			
7.			
8.			
9.			
10.			
11.			
12.			
13.			
14.			

▶ *Helpful Hint:* Choose objects that are relevant to your child. For example, if your child prefers certain toys (e.g., Big Bird or Elmo), use these as the first few objects to teach. The first several objects should sound different (e.g., do not teach "shoe" and "juice" as your first two objects because they sound so similar). If your child has trouble learning receptive labels, try teaching object-related commands (e.g., "Get a tissue" and "Throw the ball"). Gradually move objects closer together and change the instruction to "Give me a tissue" and "Give me the ball."

Program	Pictures (Receptive and Expressive)

- Program Procedure:
  (1) *Identifies Pictures*—Place picture(s) on the table in front of the child. Establish attending and present the instruction "Point to ___ (name of item in picture)." Prompt child to point to the picture and reinforce the response. Fade prompts over subsequent trials. Differentially reinforce responses demonstrated with the lowest level of prompting. Eventually, only reinforce correct, unprompted responses.
  (2) *Labels Pictures*—Sit in a chair facing the child. Establish attending and present a picture for the child to view. Say "What is this?" Prompt child to label the picture and reinforce the response. Fade prompts over subsequent trials. Differentially re-

inforce responses demonstrated with the lowest level of prompting. Eventually, only reinforce correct, unprompted responses.

- Materials: Photographs of objects, and picture cards (see resource list).
- Suggested Prerequisites:
  (1) Matches identical pictures.
  (2) Follows 10–15 one-step instructions and can identify 10–15 objects.
  (3) Labels objects.
- Prompting Suggestions:
  (1) Physically guide child to point to the picture.
  (2) Model the label.

Instruction (1) "Point to ___." (2) "What is this?"	Response (1) Points to correct picture (2) Labels picture	Date Introduced	Date Mastered
1.			
2.			
3.			
4.			
5.			
6.			
7.			
8.			
9.			
10.			
11.			
12.			
13.			
14.			
15.			

▶ *Helpful Hint:* Begin with photographs of objects that your child has learned to identify. Pictures should be visually distinct (e.g., a picture of an apple should be an apple alone, as opposed to an apple on a tree). Photographs of objects that are relevant to your child (e.g., a picture of his or her bed, or a picture of his or her shoe) will assist in promoting generalization.

Program	**Identifies Familiar People**

- Program Procedure:
  (1) *Identification in Pictures*—Place picture(s) on the table in front of the child. Establish attending and state the instruction "Point to ___ (name of person in the picture)." Prompt child to point to the correct picture and reinforce the response. Fade prompts over subsequent trials. Differentially reinforce responses demonstrated with the lowest level of prompting. Eventually, only reinforce correct, unprompted responses.
  (2) *Identification in Person*—With a familiar person in the room, sit in a chair facing the child. Establish attending and state the instruction "Go to ___ (name of familiar person)." Prompt child to walk to familiar person. Reinforce the response. Fade prompts over subsequent trials. Differentially reinforce responses demonstrated with the lowest level of prompting. Eventually, only reinforce correct, unprompted responses.

- Materials: Photographs of familiar people.

- Suggested Prerequisites: Matches identical pictures. Follows 10 one-step instructions and identifies objects in pictures.

- Prompting Suggestions: Physically guide child to perform the response.

Instruction (1) "Point to ___." (2) "Go to ___."	Response (1) Points to correct picture (2) Walks to familiar person	Date Introduced	Date Mastered
1.			
2.			
3.			
4.			
5.			
6.			
7.			
8.			
9.			
10.			

▶ *Helpful Hint:* Before teaching discrimination of two pictures of familiar people, use pictures of objects as distractors. Start with one photo of a person and two photos or pictures of objects. Gradually add more photos of different people. If your child has trouble identifying familiar people in person, try using the photographs as a prompt by holding up the photograph when presenting the instruction "Go to ___."

Program	Verbs (Instructions and Picture Identification)

- Program Procedure:
  (1) *Follows Verb Instructions*—Sit in a chair facing the child. Place necessary materials on a table within the child's reach. Establish attending and state the instruction "Show me ___ (verb)." Prompt child to perform the action and reinforce the response. Fade prompts over subsequent trials. Differentially reinforce responses demonstrated with the lowest level of prompting. Eventually, only reinforce correct, unprompted responses.
  (2) *Identifies Verbs in Pictures*—Place picture on the table in front of the child. Establish attending and state the instruction "Point to ___ (verb)." Prompt child to point to the correct picture and reinforce the response. Fade prompts over subsequent trials. Differentially reinforce responses demonstrated with the lowest level of prompting. Eventually, only reinforce correct, unprompted responses.

- Materials: Objects needed for following the actions and verb card (see resource list).

- Suggested Prerequisites:
  (1) Follows 10 one-step instructions.
  (2) Identifies pictures.

- Prompting Suggestions:
  (1) Model response or physically guide child to perform the action.
  (2) Model the label of the action.

Instruction (1) "Show me ___." (2) "Point to ___."	Response (1) Performs action (2) Points to correct picture	Date Introduced	Date Mastered
1. Standing			
2. Sitting			
3. Clapping			
4. Waving			
5. Eating			
6. Drinking			
7. Turning			
8. Jumping			
9. Hugging			
10. Kissing			
11. Blowing			
12. Sleeping			
13. Knocking			
14. Reading			
15. Drawing			
16. Crying			
17. Brushing			
18. Throwing			
19. Walking			
20. Kicking			

▶ *Helpful Hint:* Start with actions that your child learned as one-step instructions (e.g., teach "show me standing" if he has learned "stand up").

Program	**Environmental Objects (Receptive and Expressive)**

- Program Procedure:
  (1) *Identifies Environmental Object*—Sit in a chair facing the child. Establish attending and present the instruction "Touch the ___ (environmental object)." Prompt child to walk to and touch the object. Reinforce the response. Fade prompts over subsequent trials. Differentially reinforce responses demonstrated with the lowest level of prompting. Eventually, only reinforce correct, unprompted responses.
  (2) *Labels Environmental Object*—Bring child to the environmental object. Establish attending and point to the object. Say "What's this?" Prompt child to label the object. Reinforce the response. Fade prompts over subsequent trials. Differentially reinforce responses demonstrated with the lowest level of prompting. Eventually, only reinforce correct, unprompted responses.

- Suggested Prerequisites:
  (1) Follows one-step instructions and identifies objects.
  (2) Labels objects.

- Prompting Suggestions:
  (1) Physically guide child to perform the response.
  (2) Model the label of the object.

Instruction (1) "Touch the ___." (2) "What's this?"	Response (1) Walks to and touches object (2) Labels object	Date Introduced	Date Mastered
1. Table			
2. Chair			
3. Window			
4. Floor			
5. Wall			
6. Door			
7. Carpet/Rug			
8. Lamp/Light			
9. Stairs/Steps			
10. Shelf			
11. Curtain			
12. Refrigerator			
13. Stove			
14. Sink			
15. Toilet			
16. Bathtub			
17. Bed			
18. Dresser			

▶ *Helpful Hint:* As a prompting technique, begin with your child close to the object and then fade the distance between child and object.

Program	Points to Pictures in a Book

- Program Procedure: Present a page in a picture book to the child. State the instruction "Point to ___ (name of item)." Prompt child to point to correct picture and reinforce the response. Fade prompts over subsequent trials. Differentially reinforce responses demonstrated with the lowest level of prompting. Eventually, only reinforce correct, unprompted responses.

- Materials: Picture books (see resource list).

- Suggested Prerequisites: Identifies objects and pictures.

- Prompting Suggestions: Physically guide a point response. Begin with picture books that have a limited number of items per page.

Instruction: "Point to the ___."	Response: Points to correct picture	Date Introduced	Date Mastered
1.			
2.			
3.			
4.			
5.			
6.			
7.			
8.			
9.			
10.			

▶ *Helpful Hint:* Arrange photos of objects that your child knows in a photo album for him or her to point to. Generalize the skill to less structured, more natural context (e.g., while looking at books before bedtime).

Program	Function of Objects (Receptive and Expressive)

- Program Procedure:
  (1) *Identifies Object by Function*—Place object(s) or picture(s) on the table in front of the child. Establish attending and present the instruction "What do you ___ (function) with?" (e.g., "What do you sweep with?"). Prompt child to point to the correct object or picture. Reinforce the response. Fade prompts over subsequent trials. Differentially reinforce responses demonstrated with the lowest level of prompting. Eventually, only reinforce correct, unprompted responses.
  (2) *Labels Object by Function*—Sit in a chair facing the child. Establish attending. Say "What do you ___ (function) with?" (e.g., "What do you color with?"). Prompt child to label object (e.g., "crayons" or "I color with crayons"). Reinforce the response. Fade prompts over subsequent trials. Differentially reinforce responses demonstrated with the lowest level of prompting. Eventually, only reinforce correct, unprompted responses.

  (3) *Labels Function of Object*—Sit in a chair facing the child and establish attending. Say "What do you do with a ___ (name of object)?" (e.g., "What do you do with a pencil?"). Prompt child to name function of object (e.g., "write" or "I write with a pencil"). Reinforce the response. Fade prompts over subsequent trials. Differentially reinforce responses demonstrated with the lowest level of prompting. Eventually, only reinforce correct, unprompted responses.

- Materials: Objects.

- Suggested Prerequisites:
  (1) Follows one-step instructions; identifies objects; and follows verb instructions.
  (2 & 3) Identifies object by function and labels objects and verbs.

Question	Response		
(1 & 2) "What do you ___ with?" (3) "What do you do with a ___?"	(1) Points to object/picture (2) States name of object (3) States function	Date Introduced	Date Mastered
1. Write with/Pencil			
2. Drink from/Cup			
3. Eat with/Fork			
4. Cut with/Scissors			
5. Read/Book			
6. Sleep in/Bed			
7. Sit on/Chair			
8. Talk on/Phone			
9. Color with/Crayon			
10. Wash with/Soap			
11. Sweep with/Broom			
12. Blow nose with/Tissue			
13. Throw/Ball			
14. Brush hair/Hair brush			

▶ *Helpful Hint:* Only use objects that your child has mastered in the receptive object/picture identification program (i.e., be sure your child can identify a hammer before you teach its function).

Program	Possession (Receptive and Expressive)

- Program Procedure:
  (1) *Identifies Possession*—With a familiar person in view of the child, present the instruction "Touch ___ (person's) ___ (body part or clothing)" (e.g., "Touch Mary's shirt"). Prompt child to touch the correct body part or clothing item and reinforce the response. Fade prompts over subsequent trials. Differentially reinforce responses demonstrated with the lowest level of prompting. Eventually, only reinforce correct, unprompted responses.
  (2) *Labels Possession*—Point to a familiar person's body part or clothing and say "Whose ___ (body part or clothing)?" Prompt child to name the person and the possession (e.g., "Mary's shirt").

Reinforce the response. Fade prompts over subsequent trials. Differentially reinforce responses demonstrated with the lowest level of prompting. Eventually, only reinforce correct, unprompted responses.

- Suggested Prerequisites:
  (1) Identifies body parts or clothing and familiar people (in person).
  (2) Labels body parts or clothing and familiar people.

- Prompting Suggestions:
  (1) Physically guide child to point to correct body part or clothing.
  (2) Model the response.

Instruction	Response	Date Introduced	Date Mastered
(1) "Touch ___ (person's) ___ (body part or clothing)." (2) "Whose ___ (body part or clothing)?"	(1) Touches correct body part or clothing (2) Labels person and body part or clothing		
1.			
2.			
3.			
4.			
5.			
6.			
7.			
8.			
9.			
10.			

▶ *Helpful Hint:* Start with play figures (e.g., "Touch Bert's nose" vs. "Touch Elmo's nose").

| Program | **Identifies Environmental Sounds** |

- Program Procedure:
  (1) *Points to Picture Representing Sound*—Place picture(s) on the table in front of the child. Play sound on cassette player. Ask the question "What do you hear?" Prompt child to point to corresponding picture. Fade prompts over subsequent trials. Differentially reinforce responses demonstrated with the lowest level of prompting. Eventually, only reinforce correct, unprompted responses.
  (2) *Labels Sound*—Play sound on cassette player. Ask the question "What do you hear?" Prompt child to label the sound. Fade prompts over subsequent trials. Differentially reinforce responses demonstrated

with the lowest level of prompting. Eventually, only reinforce correct, unprompted responses.

- Materials: Environmental sounds material (see resource list) and cassette player.

- Suggested Prerequisites:
  (1) Identifies pictures and actions.
  (2) Labels pictures and actions.

- Prompting Suggestions:
  (1) Model the response or physically guide child to point to correct picture.
  (2) Model the correct response.

Question	Response		
(1 & 2) "What do you hear?"	**(1) Points to corresponding picture** **(2) Labels sound**	**Date Introduced**	**Date Mastered**
1. Phone ringing			
2. Clock ticking			
3. Frog			
4. Sneezing			
5. Dog barking			
6. Duck quacking			
7. Baby crying			
8. Cat meowing			
9. Piano playing			
10. Fire engine			
11. Bird chirping			
12. Ball bouncing			
13. Car starting			
14. Water splashing			
15. Pig			
16. Cow mooing			
17. Door bell			
18. Horn blowing			
19. Sipping			
20. Hammer banging			

▶ *Helpful Hint:* Start with sounds that your child may be familiar with. Consider recording sounds heard frequently in your home environment.

Program	Pointing to Desired Items

- Program Procedure:
  (1) *Points to Item in Isolation*—Sit in a chair across from the child. Hold up a preferred item (food or toy). Say "What do you want?" Prompt a point response with child's dominant hand and guide child to touch the item with pointer finger. Immediately give the desired item to the child. Allow child to play with toy or to consume the desired food item. Repeat this procedure and fade prompts over subsequent trials. Differentially reinforce responses demonstrated with the lowest level of prompting. Eventually, only reinforce correct, unprompted responses.
  (2) *Points to Item with Nonpreferred Distracter Present*—Sit in a chair across from the child. Hold up one preferred and one nonpreferred item. Say "What do you want?" Prompt child to point to the preferred item. Immediately give child desired item. Fade prompts over subsequent trials. Differentially reinforce responses demonstrated with the lowest level of prompting. Eventually, only reinforce correct, unprompted responses.
  (3) *Points to Item on Table*—Place one preferred item and one nonpreferred item on the table just beyond child's reach. Say "What you do you want?" Prompt child to point toward desired item. Immediately give child desired item. Fade prompts over subsequent trials. Differentially reinforce responses demonstrated with the lowest level of prompting. Eventually, only reinforce correct, unprompted responses.
  (4) *Points to Item without Verbal Instruction*—Place several preferred items and several nonpreferred items on the table just beyond child's reach. Wait several seconds. If child reaches toward desired item, prompt a point response. Immediately give child desired item. If child does not reach or point spontaneously, entice him or her by sampling an item and then placing the item back on the table or by allowing child access to an item for several seconds and then placing it back on the table. Fade prompts over subsequent trials. Differentially reinforce responses demonstrated with the lowest level of prompting. Eventually, only reinforce correct, unprompted responses.

- Materials: Preferred items (food and toys) and nonpreferred items.

- Suggested Prerequisites: Sits in a chair.

- Prompting Suggestions: Physically guide or model a point response.

Question	Response		
(1–3) "What do you want?"	(1–4) Points to preferred item	Date Introduced	Date Mastered
1. One prepared item			
2. One preferred item and one nonpreferred item			
3. One preferred item and one nonpreferred item on table			
4. Without verbal instruction			

▶ *Helpful Hint:* Make sure items are truly preferred. Change items during teaching session to avoid satiation. Model the label of the desired item when child points to it. When prompting a point, use a consistent prompt that can be systematically faded. Encourage responding in natural contexts!

Program	Requests Desired Items Verbally

- Program Procedure:
  (1) *One-word Request*—Place a preferred and a non-preferred item on the table just beyond child's reach. Say "What do you want?" Prompt child to point to preferred item and to label the item (e.g., "cookie"). Immediately give desired item to the child. Fade prompts over subsequent trials. Differentially reinforce responses demonstrated with the lowest level of prompting. Eventually, only reinforce correct, unprompted responses.
  (2) *Two-word Request*—Place a preferred and a non-preferred item on the table just beyond child's reach. Say "What do you want?" Prompt child to point to preferred item and to verbally request the item (e.g., "I want cookie"). Immediately give desired item to the child. Fade prompts over subsequent trials. Differentially reinforce responses demonstrated with the lowest level of prompting. Eventually, only reinforce correct, unprompted responses.
  (3) *Three-word Request*—Place a preferred and a non-preferred item on the table just beyond child's reach. Say "What do you want?" Prompt child to point to preferred item and to verbally request the item

(e.g., "I want cookie"). Immediately give desired item to the child. Fade prompts over subsequent trials. Differentially reinforce responses demonstrated with the lowest level of prompting. Eventually, only reinforce correct, unprompted responses.
  (4) *Using Adult's Name*—Place a preferred and a non-preferred item on the table just beyond child's reach. Say "What do you want?" Prompt child to point to preferred item and to verbally request the item using your name (e.g., "Mommy, I want cookie"). Immediately give desired item to the child. Fade prompts over subsequent trials. Differentially reinforce responses demonstrated with the lowest level of prompting. Eventually, only reinforce correct, unprompted responses.

- Materials: Preferred and nonpreferred items (toys and food).

- Suggested Prerequisites:
  (1–3) Points to desired items and labels objects.
  (4) Requests in sentences and labels people.

- Prompting Suggestions: Physically guide a point response and model the request phrase.

Question	Response		
(1–4) "What do you want?"	**(1–3) Points and verbally requests** **(4) Uses adult's name**	**Date Introduced**	**Date Mastered**
1. Point + "(label)"			
2. Point + "Want (label)"			
3. Point + "I want (label)"			
4. Point + "(adult's name) I want (label)"			

▶ *Helpful Hint:* Encourage responding in natural contexts. Arrange desired items on a shelf, in the kitchen on the counter, and out of view. Eventually teach your child to approach you, gain your attention (e.g., tap your shoulder), and request in a full sentence. Encourage eye contact when your child is requesting!

Program	Yes/No (Preferred and Nonpreferred)

- Program Procedure:
  (1) *For Nonpreferred Items*—Sit in a chair facing the child. Hold up a nonpreferred item (food or toy) and say "Do you want ___ (name of item)?" Prompt child to shake head no or to say "No." Immediately following the response, remove the nonpreferred item from view and present a reinforcer. Fade prompts over subsequent trials. Differentially reinforce responses demonstrated with the lowest level of prompting. Eventually, only reinforce correct, unprompted responses.
  (2) *For Preferred Items*—Sit in a chair facing the child. Present a preferred item (food or toy) and say "Do you want ___ (name of item)?" Prompt child to nod head yes or to say "Yes." Immediately following the response, give child the preferred item. Fade prompts over subsequent trials. Differentially reinforce responses that are demonstrated with the lowest level of prompting. Eventually, only reinforce correct, unprompted responses.

  (3) *Randomize Yes and No*—Sit in a chair facing the child. Present either a nonpreferred item or a preferred item and say "Do you want ___ (name of item)?" Prompt child to shake head no or to say "No" for the nonpreferred item, or nod head yes or to say "Yes" for preferred items. Following a "No" response, immediately remove the nonpreferred item from view and present a reinforcer. Following a "Yes" response, give child the preferred item. Fade prompts over subsequent trials. Differentially reinforce responses demonstrated with the lowest level of prompting. Eventually, only reinforce correct, unprompted responses.

- Materials: Preferred and nonpreferred food items and objects.

- Suggested Prerequisites: Imitates head shake and head nod or verbally imitates "No" and "Yes."

- Prompting Suggestions: Model a head shake or model "Yes" and "No."

Question	Response		
(1–3) "Do you want ___?"	(1) "No" (2) "Yes" (3) Either "Yes" or "No"	Date Introduced	Date Mastered
1. For nonpreferred			
2. For preferred			
3. Randomize Yes and No			

▶ *Helpful Hint:* Make sure items are truly preferred and nonpreferred. Use "yucky" food items (relish, mustard) that your child does not like as the nonpreferred items.

Program	Labels Familiar People

- Program Procedure:
  (1) *Labels in Picture*—Sit in a chair facing the child. Establish attending. Present a photograph of a familiar person and say "Who is this?" Prompt child to name the person in the picture and reinforce the response. Fade prompts over subsequent trials. Differentially reinforce responses demonstrated with the lowest level of prompting. Eventually, only reinforce correct, unprompted responses.
  (2) *Labels in Person*—With a familiar person in the room, sit in a chair facing the child. Establish at-tending and point to the familiar person. Say "Who is this?" Prompt child to name the person. Reinforce the response. Fade prompts over subsequent trials. Differentially reinforce responses demonstrated with the lowest level of prompting. Eventually, only reinforce correct, unprompted responses.

- Suggested Prerequisites: Identifies familiar people in pictures and in person; labels objects.

- Prompting Suggestions: Model the name of the person.

Question	Response		
"Who is this?" (1) In pictures (2) In person	(1) Names person (2) Names person	Date Introduced	Date Mastered
1.			
2.			
3.			
4.			
5.			
6.			
7.			
8.			
9.			
10.			

▶ *Helpful Hint:* Initially teach familiar people who are distinct looking, such as a parent and a sibling.

Program	**Makes a Choice**

- Program Procedure: Sit in a chair across from the child. Hold two desired items in view of the child. Say "Do you want a ___ or a ___?" Prompt the child to point to the most desired item object and to name the item. Immediately give the chosen item to the child. Fade prompts over subsequent trials. Differentially reinforce responses demonstrated with the lowest level of prompting.

Eventually, only reinforce correct, unprompted responses.

- Suggested Prerequisites: Points to desired items; requests desired items verbally; labels objects.

- Prompting Suggestions: Physically guide the child to point to the desired item and provide a verbal model of the label of the object.

Question: "Do you want a ___ or a ___?"	Response: Points to the desired item and labels item	Date Introduced	Date Mastered
1.			

▶ *Helpful Hint:* To enhance discrimination, start with one highly preferred item and one nonpreferred item. Vary your question (e.g., "Which one do you want?"). If your child is not yet speaking, you can teach the response minus the verbalization (e.g., prompt your child to just point to the desired item). Eventually teach your child to make choices about desired items that are not in view. Be sure to vary the order in which you present your choices to be sure the child is not just choosing the item presented last in the choice (e.g., if you present "Do you want a cookie or an apple?" also present "Do you want an apple or a cookie?").

Program | Social Questions

- Program Procedure: Sit in a chair across from the child. Establish attending and ask a social question. Prompt child to answer the question and reinforce the response. Fade prompts over subsequent trials. Differentially reinforce responses demonstrated with the lowest level of prompting. Eventually, only reinforce correct, unprompted responses.

- Suggested Prerequisites: Follows one-step instructions and imitates words.

- Prompting Suggestions: Use a time-delay prompt. Immediately model the correct response and then delay your model by 2-second increments over subsequent trials.

Example Social Question	Response	Date Introduced	Date Mastered
1. "What's your name?"			
2. "How old are you?"			
3. "How are you today?"			
4. "Where do you live?"			
5. "Who is your sister/ brother?"			
6. "What do you like to play with?"			
7. "What's your father's/ mother's name?"			
8. "What do you like to eat?"			
9. "Where do you go to school?"			
10. "Who is your friend?"			
11. "What's your favorite TV show?"			
12. "What's your address?"			
13. "What's your phone number?"			
14. "What do you like to drink?"			
15. "What's your favorite toy?"			
16. "When's your birthday?"			
17. "What's your teacher's name?"			

▶ *Helpful Hint:* Practice the answers to the questions in verbal imitation first to ensure adequate articulation.

Program — Verbs (Labels in Pictures, Others, and Self)

- Program Procedure:
  (1) *Labels Verbs in Pictures*—Sit in a chair facing the child. Establish attending and present a picture of a person performing an action. Say "What (is/are) (he/she/they) doing?" Prompt child to label the action. Reinforce the response. Fade prompts over subsequent trials. Differentially reinforce responses demonstrated with the lowest level of prompting. Eventually, only reinforce correct, unprompted responses.
  (2) *Labels Verbs in Others*—Sit in a chair across from the child. Establish attending and perform an action. Say "What am I doing?" Prompt child to label the action. Reinforce the response. Fade prompts over subsequent trials. Differentially reinforce responses demonstrated with the lowest level of prompting. Eventually, only reinforce correct, unprompted responses.
  (3) *Labels Verbs in Self*—Prompt child to perform an action (physically guide action or model an action for child to imitate). Say "What are you doing?" Prompt child to label the action. Reinforce the response. Fade prompts over subsequent trials. Differentially reinforce responses demonstrated with the lowest level of prompting. Eventually, only reinforce correct, unprompted responses.

- Materials: Objects needed for the actions and verb cards.

- Suggested Prerequisites: Follows verb instructions and labels pictures.

- Prompting Suggestions: Model the label of the action.

Question (1) "What (is/are) (he/she/they) doing?" (2) "What am I doing?" (3) "What are you doing?"	Response (1–3) Labels action	Date Introduced	Date Mastered
1. Standing			
2. Sitting			
3. Clapping			
4. Waving			
5. Eating			
6. Drinking			
7. Turning			
8. Jumping			
9. Hugging			
10. Kissing			
11. Blowing			
12. Sleeping			
13. Knocking			
14. Reading			
15. Drawing			

▶ *Helpful Hint:* Take photographs of family members performing actions. Be sure to foster generalization by asking your child to label actions in others and himself or herself in natural contexts.

Program | Matches

- Program Procedure: Place item(s) on the table in front of the child. Present an item that corresponds to one of the items to the child and state the instruction "Match." Prompt the child to place the item on top or in front of the corresponding item and reinforce the correct response. Fade prompts over subsequent trials. Differentially reinforce responses demonstrated with the lowest level of prompting. Eventually, only reinforce correct, unprompted responses. Initially, begin with one item present on the table; gradually introduce additional items.

- Materials: Identical objects and pictures, letter cards, colored objects, number cards, and shapes.

- Suggested Prerequisites: Sits in a chair.

- Prompting Suggestions:
  (1) Physically guide the child to perform the response.
  (2) Use a positional prompt by placing the item on the table closer to the child.

Instruction: "Match."	Response: Places item on top or in front of the corresponding item	Date Introduced	Date Mastered
1. Identical objects			
2. Identical pictures			
3. Pictures to objects			
4. Objects to pictures			
5. Colors			
6. Shapes			
7. Letters			
8. Numbers			
9. Nonidentical objects			
10. Associative objects (e.g., pencil to paper)			

▶ *Helpful Hint:* Initially, choose objects that will nest or lie on top of each other (e.g., cup, spoon, or plate). You may want to start with at least three items on the table and vary the positions of the items to enhance discrimination.

Program	Colors (Receptive and Expressive)

- Program Procedure:
  (1) *Identifies Colors*—Place colored material(s) on the table in front of the child. Establish attending and say "Point to ___ (name of color)." Prompt child to point to the correct color and reinforce the response. Fade prompts over subsequent trials. Differentially reinforce responses demonstrated with the lowest level of prompting. Eventually, only reinforce correct, unprompted responses.
  (2) *Labels Colors*—Sit in a chair facing the child. Establish attending and present a colored object. Say "What color is this?" Prompt child to label the color and reinforce the response. Fade prompts over subsequent trials. Differentially reinforce responses demonstrated with the lowest level of prompting. Eventually, only reinforce correct, unprompted responses.

- Materials: Colored paper and colored objects.

- Suggested Prerequisites:
  (1) Identifies pictures.
  (2) Labels objects and pictures.

- Prompting Suggestions:
  (1) Physically guide child to point to correct color. Use positional prompts by placing the colored object that you are asking for closer to the child.
  (2) Model the label of the color.

Instruction	Response		
(1) "Point to ___." (2) "What color is this?"	(1) Points to correct color (2) Labels color	Date Introduced	Date Mastered
1. Blue			
2. Red			
3. Yellow			
4. Green			
5. White			
6. Black			
7. Purple			
8. Orange			
9. Pink			
10. Brown			

▶ *Helpful Hint:* Try incidental teaching techniques to teach expressive colors. Arrange desired items that are different colors in view, but out of reach for your child. When your child requests the item, ask him or her what color the object is before giving it to him or her. For example, place a yellow car, a blue ball, and a green M&M on the table. If your child requests the M&M, hold it up and ask, "What color is it?" Prompt your child to answer and then give him or her the M&M.

| Program | Shapes (Receptive and Expressive) |

- Program Procedure:
  (1) *Identifies Shapes*—Place shape(s) on the table in front of the child. Establish attending and say "Point to ___ (name of shape)." Prompt child to point to the correct shape and reinforce the response. Fade prompts over subsequent trials. Differentially reinforce responses demonstrated with the lowest level of prompting. Eventually, only reinforce correct, unprompted responses.
  (2) *Labels Shapes*—Sit in a chair facing the child. Establish attending and present a shape. Say "What shape is this?" Prompt child to label the shape and reinforce the response. Fade prompts over subsequent trials. Differentially reinforce responses demonstrated with the lowest level of prompting. Eventually, only reinforce correct, unprompted responses.

- Materials: Shapes.

- Suggested Prerequisites:
  (1) Identifies objects and pictures and matches shapes.
  (2) Identifies shapes, labels objects and pictures.

- Prompting Suggestions:
  (1) Physically guide child to point to correct shape. Use positional prompts by placing the shape that you are asking for closer to the child.
  (2) Model the label of the shape.

Instruction (1) "Point to ___." (2) "What shape is this?"	Response (1) Points to correct shape (2) Labels shape	Date Introduced	Date Mastered
1. Circle			
2. Square			
3. Triangle			
4. Rectangle			
5. Diamond			
6. Oval			
7. Star			
8. Heart			

▶ *Helpful Hint:* Begin with three-dimensional shapes that are of the same color and then introduce two-dimensional shapes (e.g., line drawings of shapes). Eventually teach your child to label the shape of objects (e.g., hold up a box and ask "What shape is this?").

Program	Letters (Receptive and Expressive)

- Program Procedure:
  (1) *Identifies Letters*—Place letter(s) on the table in front of the child. Establish attending and say "Point to ___ (name of letter)." Prompt child to point to the correct letter and reinforce the response. Fade prompts over subsequent trials. Differentially reinforce responses demonstrated with the lowest level of prompting. Eventually, only reinforce correct, unprompted responses.
  (2) *Labels Letters*—Sit in a chair facing the child. Establish attending and present a letter. Say "What letter is this?" Prompt child to label the letter and reinforce the response. Fade prompts over subsequent trials. Differentially reinforce responses demonstrated with the lowest level of prompting. Eventually, only reinforce correct, unprompted responses.

- Materials: Letter cards.

- Suggested Prerequisites:
  (1) Identifies pictures.
  (2) Labels pictures.

- Prompting Suggestions:
  (1) Physically guide child to point to correct letter. Use positional prompts by placing the letter that you are asking for closer to the child.
  (2) Model the label of the letter.

Instruction (1) "Point to ___." (2) "What letter is this?"	Response (1) Points to correct letter (2) Labels letter	Date Introduced	Date Mastered
1. A/a			
2. B/b			
3. C/c			
4. D/d			
5. E/e			
6. F/f			
7. G/g			
8. H/h			
9. I/i			
10. J/j			
11. K/k			
12. L/l			
13. M/m			
14. N/n			
15. O/o			
16. P/p			
17. Q/q			
18. R/r			
19. S/s – Z/z			

▶ *Helpful Hint:* If your child has trouble learning letters, try three-dimensional letters (e.g., plastic letter) to enhance discrimination.

Program	**Numbers (Receptive and Expressive)**

- Program Procedure:
  (1) *Identifies Numbers*—Place number(s) on the table in front of the child. Establish attending and say "Point to ___ (number)." Prompt child to point to the correct number and reinforce the response. Fade prompts over subsequent trials. Differentially reinforce responses demonstrated with the lowest level of prompting. Eventually, only reinforce correct, unprompted responses.
  (2) *Labels Numbers*—Sit in a chair facing the child. Establish attending and present a number. Say "What number is this?" Prompt child to label the number and reinforce the response. Fade prompts over subsequent trials. Differentially reinforce responses demonstrated with the lowest level of prompting. Eventually, only reinforce correct, unprompted responses.

- Materials: Number cards.
- Suggested Prerequisites:
  (1) Identifies objects and pictures, and matches numbers.
  (2) Identifies numbers, labels objects and pictures.
- Prompting Suggestions:
  (1) Physically guide child to point to correct number. Use positional prompts by placing the number that you are asking for closer to the child.
  (2) Model the label of the number.

Instruction (1) "Point to ___." (2) "What number is this?"	Response (1) Points to correct number (2) Labels number	Date Introduced	Date Mastered
1.			
2.			
3.			
4.			
5.			
6.			
7.			
8.			
9.			
10.			
11.			
12.			
13.			
14.			
15.			
16.			
17.			
18.			
19–20.			

▶ *Helpful Hint:* It may be time for some new and exciting reinforcers!

© 1996 by PRO-ED, Inc.

Program	Imitating Gross Motor Movements While Standing

- Program Procedure: Stand in front of the child. Establish attending and say "Do this" while simultaneously modeling a gross motor movement. Prompt child to perform the action and reinforce the response. Fade prompts over subsequent trials. Differentially reinforce responses demonstrated with the lowest level of prompting. Eventually, only reinforce correct, unprompted responses.

- Prerequisites: Imitates gross motor movements while seated in the chair.

- Prompting Suggestions:
  (1) Physically guide child to perform the response.

Instruction: "Do this."	Response	Date Introduced	Date Mastered
1. Jump up and down			
2. Turn around			
3. Put arms out			
4. March			
5. Sit on the floor			
6. Bang hands on floor			
7. Knock on door			
8. Crawl			
9. Walk around the chair			
10. Lay down on floor			
11. Put hands on hips			
12. Twist at waist			
13. Touch toes			
14. Run and stop			
15. Lift one foot up			
16. Hop			
17. Fly like an airplane			
18. Crawl under the table			
19. Lift up the chair			
20. Kick a ball			

▶ *Helpful Hint:* Do this program in a "follow-the-leader" format. Have fun with this program and see if you can get your child to play the leader.

Program	**Imitates Sequence (Gross Motor and Actions with Objects)**

- Program Procedure:
  (1) *Gross Motor*—Sit in a chair facing the child and establish attending. Say "Do this" and model two gross motor movements (e.g., clap and then tap your head). Prompt child to perform the two movements in the order they were presented. Reinforce the response. Fade prompts over subsequent trials. Differentially reinforce responses demonstrated with the lowest level of prompting. Eventually, only reinforce correct, unprompted responses.
  (2) *Actions with Objects*—Place two sets of identical objects on the table (e.g., two bells and two flags). Sit across the table facing the child and establish attending. Say "Do this" and model an action with each object. Prompt child to perform the two movements in the order presented. Reinforce the response. Fade prompts over subsequent trials. Differentially reinforce responses demonstrated

with the lowest level of prompting. Eventually, only reinforce correct, unprompted responses.

- Materials: Objects.
- Suggested Prerequisites: Follows one-step instructions; imitates gross motor movements and actions with objects.
- Prompting Suggestions:
  (1) Physically guide child to perform the response.
  (2) Model the second gross motor movement as the child is beginning to perform the first gross motor movement. Gradually model both movements together.
  (3) Say the action as you are demonstrating it. For example, if you model touching your nose and then tapping your head, say "Touch nose," "Touch head" as you model the actions. Gradually begin to fade out the verbal prompts.

Instruction: "Do this."	Response	Date Introduced	Date Mastered
1.			
2.			
3.			
4.			
5.			
6.			
7.			
8.			
9.			
10.			

▶ *Helpful Hint:* Be sure to vary the components of the sequenced gross motor movements (e.g., if you model "Clap hands and touch nose," teach another gross motor sequence with clap hands, such as "Clap hands and wave"). If your child has trouble with sequenced gross motor, try chaining a motor movement and an action with an object (e.g., place a block in a bucket and tap the table). Model functional sequences that are likely to be called for in real life.

Program	Imitates Actions Paired with Sounds

- Program Procedure: Place an assortment of identical objects on the table. Sit across the table facing the child and establish attending. Present the instruction "Do this" and model an action with an object and a verbalization relevant to the action (e.g., push a car and say "Zoom"). Prompt the child to perform the action and the verbalization. Reinforce the response. Fade prompts over subsequent trials. Differentially reinforce responses demonstrated with the lowest level of prompting. Eventually, only reinforce correct, unprompted responses.

- Materials: Objects.

- Suggested Prerequisites: Follows one-step instructions; imitates actions with objects; imitates sounds.

- Prompting Suggestions:
  (1) Physically guide child to perform action.
  (2) Repeat the verbal model as the child is performing the action with the object.

Instruction: "Do this."	Response	Date Introduced	Date Mastered
1. Push car and say "Zoom."			
2. Put play figure down slide and say "Whee."			
3. Bang hammer and say "Bang, bang, bang."			
4. Drink from cup and slurp.			
5. Put phone receiver to ear and say "Hello."			
6. Pick up toy lion and say "Roar."			
7. Bang keys on a toy piano and say "La, la, la."			
8. Make toy frog hop and say "Ribit, ribit."			
9. Move toy snake across the table and say "Sssss."			
10. Pretend to eat a toy sandwich and say "Yummy."			

▶ *Helpful Hint:* Do this program while playing with your child.

Program	Imitates Block Patterns

- Program Procedure: Place an assortment of identical blocks on the table. Sit across the table facing the child and establish attending. Make a block construction with your set of blocks and present the instruction "Build this." Prompt child to build the same construction with his or her set of blocks. Reinforce the response. Fade prompts over subsequent trials. Differentially reinforce responses demonstrated with the lowest level of prompting. Eventually, only reinforce correct, unprompted responses.

- Materials: Objects.

- Suggested Prerequisites: Follows one-step instructions; imitates actions with objects.

- Prompting Suggestions: Physically guide child to build the construction.

Instruction: "Build this."	Response	Date Introduced	Date Mastered
1. Single-block placements			
2. Two-block constructions			
3. Three-block constructions			
4. Four-block constructions			
5. Five-block constructions			

▶ *Helpful Hint:* Begin with one block placement at a time. For example, place five blocks on the table to the right of your child. Present the instruction "Build this." Move one block from your assortment to the middle of the table and prompt your child to pick the correct block from his or her assortment and to place it in front of your block. Repeat this procedure for each block, placing your block in various positions to construct a building. As your child's accuracy improves, repeat this procedure with two blocks and so on. Eventually, teach your child to match your constructions without seeing you make them (e.g., build your construction behind a piece of paper, remove the paper so your child can see the building, and say "Build this").

| **Program** | **Copies Simple Drawings** |

- Program Procedure: Place writing materials (paper and crayons or markers) on the table in front of the child. Present the instruction "Do this," or "Draw a ___," and simultaneously draw a form on the paper (e.g., a circle) for the child to imitate. Prompt child to pick up a writing utensil and to draw the form. Reinforce the response. Fade prompts over subsequent trials. Differentially reinforce responses made with the lowest level of prompting. Eventually, only reinforce correct, unprompted responses.

- Materials: Writing utensil and paper.

- Suggested Prerequisites: Imitates fine motor actions and block patterns; completes fine motor activities such as placing small pegs in a peg board.

- Prompting Suggestions: Physically guide child to perform the response; use visual cues on the paper such as dots that serve as prompts to cue the child where to begin the drawing.

Instruction: "Do this."	Response: Draws correct form	Date Introduced	Date Mastered
1. Vertical line			
2. Horizontal line			
3. Plus sign			
4. Circle			
5. Diagonal line			
6. Straight line letters			
7. Curved letters			
8. Numbers			
9. Shapes			
10. Smile face			
11. Flower			
12. Car			
13. House			
14. Person			
15. Rainbow			

▶ *Helpful Hint:* Have your child practice responses on a child-size easel. If your child does not apply adequate pressure when drawing (e.g., does not push down on the writing utensil, causing the drawing to be too light), try using a different writing utensil such as a colored marker. Make drawing fun!

Program	Rooms (Receptive and Expressive)

- Program Procedure:
  (1) *Locates Rooms*—Sit or stand facing the child. Establish attending. Present the instruction "Go to the ___ (name of room)." Prompt the child to walk into the correct room and reinforce the response. Fade prompts over subsequent trials. Differentially reinforce responses demonstrated with the lowest level of prompting. Eventually, only reinforce correct, unprompted responses.
  (2) *Labels Rooms*—Take child to a room. Establish attending and say "Where are we?" Prompt child to say "In the ___ (name of room)," and reinforce the response. Fade prompts over subsequent trials.

Differentially reinforce responses demonstrated with the lowest level of prompting. Eventually, only reinforce correct, unprompted responses.

- Suggested Prerequisites:
  (1) Follows instructions; identifies pictures and environmental objects.
  (2) Labels objects and environmental objects and locates room.

- Prompting Suggestions:
  (1) Bring child to the room.
  (2) Model the response.

Instruction	Response		
(1) "Go to the ___." (2) "Where are we?"	(1) Walks to correct room (2) States name of room	Date Introduced	Date Mastered
1. Kitchen			
2. Bedroom			
3. Bathroom			
4. Family room			
5. Dining room			
6. Hallway			
7. Garage			
8. (Sibling's) room			
9. Living room			
10. Playroom			

▶ *Helpful Hint:* If your child can repeat words and can label, teach response #2 while you are teaching response #1 (e.g., after you and your child enter the room, present question #2, and then reinforce). Remember to train for generalization by asking your child the question "Where are you?" throughout the day when he or she is in specific rooms. If your child has trouble learning rooms in context, take photographs of the rooms and teach him or her to label them (see the "Places" program).

Program	Emotions (Receptive)

- Program Procedure:
  (1) *Identifies Emotions in Pictures*—Place picture of a person displaying an emotion on the table in front of the child. Establish attending and state the instruction "Point to ___ (emotion)." Prompt child to point to the correct picture and reinforce response. Fade prompts over subsequent trials. Differentially reinforce the responses demonstrated with the lowest level of prompting. Eventually, only reinforce correct, unprompted responses.
  (2) *Displays Emotion*—Sit in a chair facing the child. Establish attending and state the instruction "Show me ___ (emotion)." Prompt child to dis-

play the emotion and reinforce the response. Fade prompts over subsequent trials. Differentially reinforce responses demonstrated with the lowest level of prompting. Eventually, only reinforce correct, unprompted responses.

- Materials: Photographs of people displaying emotions or emotion photo cards (see resource list).

- Suggested Prerequisites: Identifies objects, actions, and familiar people.

- Prompting Suggestions:
  (1) Physically guide child to point to correct picture.
  (2) Model the emotion.

Instruction	Response		
(1) "Point to ___." (2) "Show me ___."	(1) Points to correct picture (2) Displays emotion	Date Introduced	Date Mastered
1. Happy			
2. Sad			
3. Angry			
4. Surprised			
5. Scared			
6. Sleepy			
7. Sick			
8. Tired			
9. Mad			
10. Afraid			

▶ *Helpful Hint:* Take pictures of family members displaying emotions.

| Program | **Places (Receptive and Expressive)** |

- Program Procedure:
  (1) *Identifies Places*—Place picture(s) of place(s) on the table in front of the child. Establish attending and state the instruction "Point to the ___." Prompt child to point to the correct picture and reinforce the response. Fade prompts over subsequent trials. Differentially reinforce responses demonstrated with the lowest level of prompting. Eventually, only reinforce correct, unprompted responses.
  (2) *Labels Places*—Sit in a chair facing the child and establish attending. Present a picture of a place and say "What's this a picture of?" Prompt child to name the place. Fade prompts over subsequent trials. Differentially reinforce responses demonstrated with the lowest level of prompting. Eventually, only reinforce correct, unprompted responses.

- Materials: SPARC Picture Scenes (see resource list) or photographs of places.

- Suggested Prerequisites:
  (1) Identifies pictures, environmental objects, and rooms.
  (2) Labels pictures, environmental objects, and rooms.

- Prompting Suggestions:
  (1) Model the response or physically guide child to point to the picture.
  (2) Model the label of the place.

Instruction	Response		
(1) "Point to ___." (2) "What is this a picture of?"	(1) Points to correct picture (2) Labels place	Date Introduced	Date Mastered
1. Park			
2. Zoo			
3. Library			
4. Beach			
5. Farm			
6. School			
7. Circus			
8. Airport			
9. City			
10. Restaurant			
11. Grocery store			
12. Jungle			
13. Ocean			
14. Hospital			
15. Classroom			
16. Playground			
17. Train station			
18. Birthday party			
19. Museum			
20. Dentist office			

▶ *Helpful Hint:* Take photographs of places that your child frequents.

Program	Follows Two-Step Instructions

- Program Procedure: Sit in a chair facing the child and establish attending. Present a two-step instruction. Prompt child to perform the instructions in the order presented. Reinforce the response. Fade prompts over subsequent trials. Differentially reinforce responses demonstrated with the lowest level of prompting. Eventually, only reinforce correct, unprompted responses.

- Materials: Items needed for the instruction.

- Suggested Prerequisites: Follows one-step instructions; imitates sequenced gross motor movements.

- Prompting Suggestions:
  (1) Physically guide child to perform response or model the response.
  (2) State the second part of the instruction as the child is finishing the first part of the instruction. Gradually begin to state both parts of the instruction together.
  (3) Limit language when presenting the instruction. For example, state " Touch head, touch nose" for "Touch your head and your nose." Gradually begin to add more language as accuracy improves.

Two-step Instruction	Response	Date Introduced	Date Mastered
1.			
2.			
3.			
4.			
5.			
6.			
7.			
8.			
9.			
10.			

▶ *Helpful Hint:* Combine one-step commands already mastered to form two-step commands. Be sure to vary the components of the two-step instruction (e.g., if you teach "Clap your hands and touch your nose," teach another two-step instruction with clap hands, such as "Clap your hands and wave bye-bye"). Teach related two-step instructions that will have relevance for your child (e.g., "Get the ball and make a basket").

Program	Gives Two Objects

- Program Procedure: Place several objects on the table in front of the child. Establish attending and present the instruction "Give me the ___ and the ___" (e.g., "Give me the car and the ball"). Prompt the child to hand you both objects. Reinforce the response. Fade prompts over subsequent trials. Differentially reinforce responses demonstrated with the lowest level of prompting. Eventually, only reinforce correct, unprompted responses.

- Materials: Objects.

- Suggested Prerequisites: Follows two-step instructions and identifies objects.

- Prompting Suggestions: Guide the child to hand you both objects. Say the name of the second object as your child is reaching for the first object. Gradually begin to ask for both objects simultaneously.

Instruction: "Give me ___ and ___."	Response: Hands you both objects	Date Introduced	Date Mastered
1.			

▶ *Helpful Hint:* Prompt your child to retrieve both objects simultaneously using two hands (e.g., one object in one hand, the other in the other hand). If your child has trouble with this program, try limiting the language when you state the instruction (e.g., say "ball, car" rather than "Give me the ball and the car"). Be sure to ask your child to retrieve two objects in natural contexts (e.g., "Get your shoes and your socks").

| Program | **Attributes (Receptive and Expressive)** |

- Program Procedure:
  (1) *Identifies Attribute*—Place on table in front of the child two objects that are similar except for one obvious difference of attribute (e.g., two trucks, one big, one little). Establish attending and state the instruction "Point to the ___ (attribute) ___ (object)" (e.g., "Point to the big truck"). Prompt child to point to the correct object and reinforce the response. Fade prompts over subsequent trials. Differentially reinforce responses demonstrated with the lowest level of prompting. Eventually, only reinforce correct, unprompted responses.
  (2) *Labels Attribute*—Place on table in front of the child two objects that are similar except for one obvious difference of attribute (e.g., two trucks, one big, one little). Establish attending and point to one of the objects. Say "What is this?" Prompt child to

label the object and the attribute (e.g., "It's a big truck"). Fade prompts over subsequent trials. Differentially reinforce responses demonstrated with the lowest level of prompting. Eventually, only reinforce correct, unprompted responses.

- Materials: Objects that differ by attribute and pictures depicting objects that differ by attribute (see resource list).

- Suggested Prerequisites:
  (1) Identifies objects, pictures, familiar people, environmental objects, colors, and emotions.
  (2) Identifies attributes, labels pictures, familiar people, environmental objects, colors, and emotions.

- Prompting Suggestions:
  (1) Physically guide child to point to the picture.
  (2) Model the attribute and the label.

Instruction (1) "Point to the ___ ___." (2) "What is this?"	Response (1) Points to correct attribute (2) Labels object with attribute	Date Introduced	Date Mastered
1. Big/Little			
2. Wet/Dry			
3. Hot/Cold			
4. Clean/Dirty			
5. Tall/Short			
6. Heavy/Light			
7. Empty/Full			
8. Hard/Soft			
9. Young/Old			
10. Old/New			
11. Long/Short			
12. Thick/Thin			
13. Smooth/Rough			
14. Open/Closed			

▶ *Helpful Hint:* At first, drop the label of the object when teaching your child to identify the attribute (e.g., say "Point to big" rather than "Point to the big truck").

Program	Community Helpers (Receptive and Expressive)

- Program Procedure:
  (1) *Identifies Community Helper*—Place picture(s) of community helper(s) on the table in front of the child. Establish attending and state the instruction "Point to ___ (name of community helper)." Prompt child to point to the correct picture. Differentially reinforce responses demonstrated with the lowest level of prompting and fade prompts over subsequent trials. Eventually, only reinforce correct, unprompted responses.
  (2) *Labels Community Helper*—Sit in a chair facing child and establish attending. Present a picture of a community helper and say "Who is this?" Prompt child to label the community helper. Fade prompts over subsequent trials. Differentially re-inforce responses demonstrated with the lowest level of prompting. Eventually, only reinforce correct, unprompted responses.

- Materials: Community helper pictures (see resource list).

- Suggested Prerequisites:
  (1) Identifies pictures, familiar people, environmental objects, and scenes.
  (2) Labels pictures, familiar people, environmental objects, and scenes.

- Prompting Suggestions:
  (1) Model the response or physically guide child to point to the picture.
  (2) Model the label of the community helper.

Instruction	Response	Date Introduced	Date Mastered
(1) "Point to the ___." (2) "Who is this?"	(1) **Points to correct picture** (2) **Labels community helper**		
1. Fireman			
2. Policeman			
3. Mailman			
4. Teacher			
5. Farmer			
6. Garbage man			
7. Barber			
8. Waiter			
9. Bus driver			
10. Pilot			
11. Doctor			
12. Nurse			
13. Truck driver			
14. Dentist			
15. Chef			

▶ *Helpful Hint:* Be sure to point out community helpers to your child when you are out in the community.

Program	Pretends

- Program Procedure: Sit in a chair facing the child and establish attending. Present the instruction "Pretend you're (a) ___ (action, animal, community helper)" (e.g., "Pretend you're drinking"). Prompt child to simulate the action (e.g., for drinking, child brings cupped fist to mouth and makes drinking sound). Reinforce the response. Fade prompts over subsequent trials. Differentially reinforce responses demonstrated with the lowest level of prompting. Eventually, only reinforce correct, unprompted responses.

- Materials: Props needed for pretending to be a community helper (e.g., a fire hat, a doctor's kit).

- Suggested Prerequisites: Follows one-step instructions; imitates actions with object; follows verb instructions; and labels objects. For animals and community helpers, child labels animals and community helpers.

- Prompting Suggestions: Physically guide child to perform response or model the response.

Instruction: "Pretend you're ___."	Response: Child simulates action or pretends to be an animal or community helper	Date Introduced	Date Mastered
1. Drinking			
2. Brushing hair			
3. Washing face			
4. Brushing teeth			
5. Licking ice cream			
6. Driving a car			
7. Sweeping			
8. Putting on a hat			
9. A snake			
10. A lion			
11. A dog			
12. A monkey			
13. A frog			
14. A rabbit			
15. A cat			
16. A bird			
17. A fireman			
18. A doctor			
19. A policeman			
20. A barber			

▶ *Helpful Hint:* This is a fun program to do with siblings and peers!

Program	**Categories (Matches, Identifies, and Labels)**

- Program Procedure:
  (1) *Matches*—Place picture(s) of item(s) belonging to specific categories on the table facing the child. Present a picture of an item from one of the categories and state the instruction "Match." Prompt the child to place the picture in the correct category pile. Reinforce the response. Fade prompts over subsequent trials. Differentially reinforce responses demonstrated with the lowest level of prompting. Eventually, only reinforce correct, unprompted responses.
  (2) *Identifies*—Place pictures of items belonging to specific categories on the table facing the child. Present the instruction "Point to the ___ (category) (e.g., food)." Prompt the child to point to the correct category. Reinforce the response. Fade prompts over subsequent trials. Differentially reinforce responses demonstrated with the lowest level of prompting. Eventually, only reinforce correct, unprompted responses.
  (3) *Labels*—Place piles of categories on the table facing the child. Point to one of the piles and say "What are these?" Prompt the child to label the correct category (e.g., food). Reinforce the response. Fade prompts over subsequent trials. Differentially reinforce responses demonstrated with the lowest level of prompting. Eventually, only reinforce correct, unprompted responses.

- Materials: Category/Classification cards (see resource list).

- Suggested Prerequisites: Labels objects, colors, numbers, letters, shapes, and matches nonidentical objects.

- Prompting Suggestions:
  (1–2) Physically guide child to place card in correct pile.
  (3) Provide a verbal model.

Instruction (1) "Match" (2) "Point to ___." (3) "What are these?"	Response (1) Matches card (2) Points to correct category (3) Labels category	Date Introduced	Date Mastered
1. Food			
2. Clothes			
3. Animals			
4. Toys			
5. Fruit			
6. Tools			
7. Vegetables			
8. Transportation			
9. Instruments			
10. Furniture			
11. Shapes			
12. Letters			
13. Numbers			

▶ *Helpful Hint:* If your child has trouble matching pictures of categories, try using three-dimensional items.

Program	Pronouns (My and Your)

- Program Procedure:
  (1) *Identifies Pronouns*—Sit across from the child. Establish attending and state the instruction "Touch ___ (my/your) ___ (body part or clothing)" (e.g., "Touch my shirt"). Prompt child to touch the correct body part or clothing item and reinforce the response. Fade prompts over subsequent trials. Differentially reinforce responses demonstrated with the lowest level of prompting. Eventually, only reinforce correct, unprompted responses. Teach "your" first, then "my," and then randomize the presentation of "my" and "your."
  (2) *Labels Pronoun*—Sit across from the child. Establish attending and point to either a body part (or clothing) on the child or on you. Say "Whose ___ (body part or clothing)?" Prompt child to name the pronoun and the body part or clothing (e.g., "your shirt"). Reinforce the response. Fade prompts over subsequent trials. Differentially reinforce responses demonstrated with the lowest level of prompting. Eventually, only reinforce correct, unprompted responses. Teach "my" first, then "your," and then randomize the presentation of "my" and "your."

- Suggested Prerequisites:
  (1) Identifies body parts or clothing, familiar people (in person), possession, and follows two-step instructions.
  (2) Labels body parts or clothing, familiar people, and possession.

- Prompting Suggestions:
  (1) Physically guide child to point to correct body part or clothing.
  (2) Model the response.

Instruction (1) "Touch ___." (2) "Whose ___?"	Response (1) Touches correct body part or clothing (2) Labels pronoun	Date Introduced	Date Mastered
1. My			
2. Your			
3. Randomize My and Your			

▶ *Helpful Hint:* Once your child learns to identify pronouns, hold off for a few weeks before teaching your child to label the pronouns. This may help to reduce confusion.

| Program | **Prepositions (Receptive and Expressive)** |

- Program Procedure:
  (1) *Receptive*—Sit in a chair across from the child. Establish attending and hand an object to the child. State the instruction "Put this ___ (preposition) the ___ (location)" (e.g., "Put this on the table"). Prompt the child to place the object in the correct location. Reinforce the response. Fade prompts over subsequent trials. Differentially reinforce responses demonstrated with the lowest level of prompting. Eventually, only reinforce correct, unprompted responses.
  (2) *Expressive*—Place an object in a specific location for the child to view. Say "Where is the ___ (object placed)?" Prompt the child to label the location (e.g., "It's on the table"). Reinforce the response. Fade prompts over subsequent trials. Differentially reinforce responses demonstrated with the lowest level of prompting. Eventually, only reinforce correct, unprompted responses.

- Materials: Objects and picture cards depicting prepositions (see resource list).

- Suggested Prerequisites:
  (1) Follows two-step instructions and identifies environmental objects.
  (2) Labels environmental objects and rooms; repeats phrases.

- Prompting Suggestions: Physically guide child to place object in correct location. Provide a verbal model for response #2.

Instruction	Response	Date Introduced	Date Mastered
(1) "Put this ___ the ___." (2) "Where is the ___?"	(1) Places object in correct location (2) Names location of object		
1. On			
2. In			
3. Under			
4. In front of			
5. Behind			
6. Next to			
7. Between			
8. On top			
9. On the bottom			
10. Beside			

▶ *Helpful Hint:* If your child speaks, teach response #2 while teaching response #1 (e.g., when your child places the object in the location, present the question "Where is the ___?" and then reinforce). Use incidental teaching procedures. For example, place desired items in specific locations. When your child asks for one of the items, ask him or her "Where is the ___ (desired item)?" Prompt your child to label the location and then give the desired item to your child. Teach your child to place himself or herself in specific locations (e.g., "Go under the table"), and ask "Where are you?" Generalize responding to pictures depicting prepositions.

Program	Identifies/Labels Objects When Described (In & Out of View)

- Program Procedure:
  (1) *In View*—Place a group of objects on the table in front of the child. Establish attending and say "I'm thinking of something that's ___ (a description of one of the objects on the table)" (e.g., If an apple is on the table, say "I'm thinking of something that's red, it grows on trees, and you can eat it"). Prompt the child to point to and label the object that you described (e.g., "an apple"). Reinforce the response. Fade prompts over subsequent trials. Differentially reinforce responses demonstrated with the lowest level of prompting. Eventually, only reinforce correct, unprompted responses.
  (2) *Out of View*—Sit in a chair facing the child. Establish attending and say "I'm thinking of something that's ___ (a description of an object)" (e.g., "I'm thinking of something that is round and you can kick it"). Prompt the child to label the object that you described (e.g., "a ball"). Reinforce the response. Fade prompts over subsequent trials. Differentially reinforce responses demonstrated with the lowest level of prompting. Eventually, only reinforce correct, unprompted responses.

- Materials: Objects.

- Suggested Prerequisites:
  (1) In view: labels object, attributes, colors, functions, and categories.
  (2) Out of view: names objects in view when described; describes objects in view using attributes; answers general knowledge questions.

- Prompting Suggestions: Give additional descriptors, point to the object, model the answer, and if not in view, present the object that you are describing.

Instruction	Response		
(1–2) "I'm thinking of something . . ."	(1–2) Labels the object	Date Introduced	Date Mastered
1. Objects in view			
2. Objects not in view			

▶ *Helpful Hint:* Begin with only a few objects in view at a time that are distinct in attributes and functions (e.g., one green item, one yellow item, one that you can eat, one that you can play with). Over time, increase the similarities of the objects (e.g., two red objects, one that you wear and one that you eat). Teach responding to descriptions of places (e.g., "I'm thinking of a place where you can swim and play in the sand," and people; e.g., "I'm thinking of someone who has black hair, she's a girl, she plays with you on Saturdays"). Eventually, teach your child to present you with descriptions, so that you can guess what he or she is thinking about! Vary your instruction (e.g., "Tell me something that's . . ." or "Point to something that . . .").

| Program | **Sequence Cards (Puts in Order and Describes)** |

- Program Procedure:
  (1) *Puts in Order*—Hand the child a set of sequence cards and state the instruction "Put these cards in order." Prompt the child to place the cards on the table from left to right in the correct order. Reinforce the response. Fade prompts over subsequent trials. Differentially reinforce responses demonstrated with the lowest level of prompting. Eventually, only reinforce correct, unprompted responses.
  (2) *Describes Sequence*—Hand the child a set of sequence cards and ask him or her to place the cards in order. Once cards are placed in the correct order on the table, say "Tell me about the pictures." Prompt the child to point to each picture and to describe the sequence of pictures from left to right (e.g., "The girl is pouring juice, she's drinking the juice, and she's putting the cup in the sink"). Reinforce the response. Fade prompts over subsequent trials. Differentially reinforce responses demonstrated with the lowest level of prompting. Eventually, only reinforce correct, unprompted responses.

- Materials: Sequence cards (see resource list).

- Suggested Prerequisites: Describes pictures in full sentences.

- Prompting Suggestions: Guide child to place cards in correct order or model the correct response. Model

Instruction	Response		
(1) "Put the cards in order." (2) "Tell me about the pictures."	(1) Places cards in correct order from left to right (2) Points to and describes each picture from left to right	**Date Introduced**	**Date Mastered**
1. Two-scene sequence			
2. Three-scene sequence			
3. Four-scene sequence			
4. Five-scene sequence			

▶ *Helpful Hint:* If your child speaks, teach response #2 while you are teaching response #1 (e.g., after you prompt your child to place the cards in order, ask him or her to describe each picture). Begin with two-scene sequences and progress to five. Use pictures of events that your child experiences (e.g., climbing up the slide, sitting on the slide, going down the slide). Take photographs of your child engaged in sequential activities and use these to teach the program.

Program	Gender (Receptive and Expressive)

- Program Procedure:
  (1) *Identifies Gender*—Place picture(s) depicting a gender on the table in front of the child (e.g., a picture of a boy, a picture of a girl). Establish attending and state the instruction "Point to ___ (gender)" (e.g., "girl"). Prompt child to point to the correct picture and reinforce the response. Fade prompts over subsequent trials. Differentially reinforce responses demonstrated with the lowest level of prompting. Eventually, only reinforce correct, unprompted responses.
  (2) *Labels Gender*—Sit in a chair facing the child. Establish attending and present a picture depicting a gender. Say "What is this?" Prompt child to label the gender (e.g., "It's a boy"). Reinforce the response. Fade prompts over subsequent trials. Differentially reinforce responses demonstrated with the lowest level of prompting. Eventually, only reinforce correct, unprompted responses.

- Materials: Pictures depicting gender.
- Suggested Prerequisites:
  (1) Identifies pictures and familiar people.
  (2) Identifies gender; labels pictures and familiar people.
- Prompting Suggestions:
  (1) Physically guide child to point to correct picture. Use positional prompts by placing the picture that you are asking for closer to the child.
  (2) Model the label of the gender.

Instruction	Response		
(1) "Point to ___." (2) "What is this?"	(1) Points to correct picture (2) Labels gender	**Date Introduced**	**Date Mastered**
1. Boy			
2. Girl			
3. Man			
4. Woman			
5. Lady			

▶ *Helpful Hint:* Use magazines to find gender pictures. Use pictures that depict gender in a clear, unambiguous way. Eventually teach your child to label the gender of familiar people (e.g., "Is Daddy a woman or a man?" "Are you a boy or a girl?").

| Program | **Answers *Wh*-questions about Objects and Pictures** |

- Program Procedure:
  (1) *With Objects*—Sit in a chair facing the child. Present an object to the child and ask a *wh*-question about the object (see examples below). Prompt the child to answer the question (see examples below). Reinforce the response. Fade prompts over subsequent trials. Differentially reinforce responses demonstrated with the lowest level of prompting. Eventually, only reinforce correct, unprompted responses.
  (2) *With Pictures*—Sit in a chair facing the child. Present a photograph depicting a familiar person performing an action in a specific location (e.g., a picture of daddy cooking in the kitchen). Ask a *wh*-question about the picture (see examples below). Prompt the child to answer the question (see examples below). Reinforce the response. Fade prompts over subsequent trials. Differentially reinforce responses demonstrated with the lowest level of prompting. Eventually, only reinforce correct, unprompted responses. Teach the child to discriminate questions about a single object/picture. Initially, teach the child to discriminate two questions about the object/picture first and then introduce each additional question one at a time.

- Materials: Objects and photographs of familiar people performing actions in specific locations.

- Suggested Prerequisites:
  (1) Objects: labels objects, colors, functions, categories, and locations.
  (2) Pictures: labels familiar people, actions, locations (rooms), and emotions.

- Prompting Suggestions: Model the answer.

Example Questions	Example Responses	Date Introduced	Date Mastered
About objects:			
1. "What's this?"	"It's a banana."		
2. "What color is it?"	"It's yellow."		
3. "What do you do with it?"	"I eat it."		
4. "What's a banana?"	"Fruit."		
1. "What's this?"	"It's a lollipop."		
2. "What color is it?"	"It's red."		
3. "What do you do with it?"	"I lick it."		
4. "How does it taste?"	"It tastes sweet."		
5. "Where do you get one?"	"At the store."		
About pictures:			
1. "Who is this?"	"Mommy."		
2. "What's she doing?"	"She's laughing."		
3. "Where is she?"	"In the T.V. room."		
4. "How does he/she feel?"	"She's happy."		

▶ *Helpful Hint:* If your child has trouble with this program, try presenting the questions in a fixed order and then randomizing the questions over time. Your child does not have to meet all of the suggested prerequisites to begin to discriminate several questions about objects/pictures (e.g., if he or she knows labels and colors, teach discrimination of "What's this?" and "What color is this?").

Program	Yes/No (Objects)

- Program Procedure:
  (1) *For Object* (Yes)—Sit in a chair facing the child. Present an object and say "Is this a ___ (name of object)?" (e.g., "Is this a car?"). Prompt child to say "Yes." Reinforce the response. Fade prompts over subsequent trials. Differentially reinforce responses demonstrated with the lowest level of prompting. Eventually, only reinforce correct, unprompted responses.
  (2) *For Objects* (No)—Sit in a chair facing the child. Present an object and say "Is this a ___ (name of object)?" (e.g., "Is this an apple?"). Prompt child to say "No, it's a (name of another object)" (e.g., "No, it's a car"). Reinforce the response. Fade prompts over subsequent trials. Differentially reinforce responses demonstrated with the lowest level of prompting.

  (3) *Randomize Yes and No*—Sit in a chair facing the child. Present an object and say "Is this a ___ (name of another object)?" or "Is this a ___ (name of object)?" Prompt child to say "Yes" or "No, it's a ___ (name of object)." Reinforce correct responses. Fade prompts over subsequent trials. Differentially reinforce responses demonstrated with the lowest level of prompting. Eventually, only reinforce correct, unprompted responses.

- Materials: Objects.

- Suggested Prerequisites: Answers "Yes"/"No" for preferred and nonpreferred items; labels objects; imitates words; identifies items that are the same and different.

- Prompting Suggestions: Model correct response.

Instruction	Response		
(1) "Is this a ___ (name of object)?" (2) "Is this a ___ (name of another object)?" (3) Randomize 1 and 2.	(1) "Yes" (2) "No, it's a ___ (name of object)." (3) Either "Yes" or "No, it's a ___."	**Date Introduced**	**Date Mastered**
1. Yes			
2. No			
3. Randomize Yes and No			
▶ *Helpful Hint:* Eventually, teach Yes/No responses to questions about actions (e.g., "Is she clapping?") and to general knowledge questions (e.g., "Does it snow in the summer?").			

Program	**Function of Body Parts**

- Program Procedure:
  (1) *Labels Body Part According to Function*—Sit in a chair facing the child and establish attending. Say "What do you ___ (function) with?" Prompt child to point to the correct body part and to name the body part. Reinforce the response. Fade prompts over subsequent trials. Differentially reinforce responses demonstrated with the lowest level of prompting. Eventually, only reinforce correct, unprompted responses.

(2) *Labels Function of Body Parts* —Sit in a chair facing the child. Establish attending. Say "What do you do with your ___ (body part)?" Prompt child to name the function. Differentially reinforce responses demonstrated with the lowest level of prompting.

- Suggested Prerequisites: Identifies and labels body parts; labels objects by function.

- Prompting Suggestions: Model correct response.

Instruction	Response		
(1) "What do you ___ with?" (2) "What do you do with your ___?"	(1) Points to and names body part (2) States function of body part	**Date Introduced**	**Date Mastered**
1. See with/Eyes			
2. Smell with/Nose			
3. Hear with/Ears			
4. Taste with/Mouth			
5. Touch with/Hands			
6. Walk with/Legs			
7. Sneeze with/Nose			
8. Blink with/Eyes			
9. Talk with/Mouth			
10. Kiss with/Lips			

▶ *Helpful Hint:* Have you evaluated your child's reinforcement package lately? It may be time for some new and exciting reinforcers!

Program	Labels Emotions

• Program Procedure:

(1) *Labels Emotions in Pictures*—Sit in a chair facing the child across from you. Establish attending and hold up a picture of a person displaying an emotion. Say "How does ___ (he or she) feel?" Prompt child to label the emotion and reinforce the response. Fade prompts over subsequent trials. Differentially reinforce responses that are demonstrated with the lowest level of prompting. Eventually, only reinforce correct, unprompted responses.

(2) *Labels Emotions in Others*—Sit child in a chair facing you. Establish attending and display an emotion. Say "How do I feel?" Prompt child to label the emotion and reinforce the response. Fade prompts over subsequent trials. Differentially reinforce responses that are demonstrated with the lowest level of prompting. Eventually, only reinforce correct, unprompted responses.

(3) *Labels Emotions in Self*—In specific contexts when child is displaying an emotion (e.g., when child is laughing; when child is crying because he or she is hurt), say "How do you feel?" Prompt child to label the emotion and reinforce the response. Fade prompts over subsequent opportunities. Eventually, only reinforce correct, unprompted responses.

• Materials: Photographs of people displaying emotions or emotion cards (see resource list).

• Suggested Prerequisites: Identifies emotions in pictures; labels objects, actions, and familiar people.

• Prompting Suggestions: Model label of emotion.

Question	Response		
(1) "How does ___ feel?" (2) "How do I feel?" (3) "How do you feel?"	(1–3) Labels correct emotion	Date Introduced	Date Mastered
1. Happy			
2. Sad			
3. Angry			
4. Surprised			
5. Scared			
6. Sleepy			
7. Sick			
8. Tired			
9. Mad			
10. Afraid			

▶ *Helpful Hint:* Use pictures that depict emotions within relevant contexts (e.g., for sad, a picture of a boy crying because he fell off his bike).

| **Program** | **Categories (Labels Category & Names Objects in a Category)** |

- Program Procedure:
  (1) *Labels Category to Which Object Belongs*—Sit in a chair across from the child. Present a picture of an item from a category and ask the child to label the picture (e.g., "What's this?" "A cat"). Say "What's a ___ (label of object)?" (e.g., cat). Prompt child to label the category that the item belongs to (e.g., "an animal"). Reinforce the response. Fade prompts over subsequent trials. Differentially reinforce responses demonstrated with lowest level of prompting. Eventually, only reinforce correct, unprompted responses.
  (2) *Names Objects in a Category*
      (a) In view: Place several category cards on the table facing the child. Say "Name a ___ (category)" (e.g., food). Prompt child to name the item belonging to the category (e.g., "hamburger"). Reinforce the response. Fade prompts over subsequent trials. Differentially reinforce

responses demonstrated with the lowest level of prompting. Eventually, only reinforce correct, unprompted responses.
      (b) Out of view: Sit in a chair across from the child. Establish attending and say "Name a ___ (category)" (e.g., animal). Prompt child to name an item belonging to the category (e.g., "a tiger"). Reinforce the response. Fade prompts over subsequent trials. Differentially reinforce responses demonstrated with lowest level of prompting. Eventually, only reinforce correct, unprompted responses.

- Materials: Category/Classification cards (see resource list).

- Suggested Prerequisites: Labels objects, colors, numbers, letters, shapes; matches categories.

- Prompting Suggestions: Provide a verbal model.

Instruction (1) "What's a ___?" (2a–2b) "Name a ___."	**Response** (1) Labels category (2a–2b) Names item in the category	**Date Introduced**	**Date Mastered**
1. Food			
2. Clothes			
3. Animals			
4. Toys			
5. Fruit			
6. Tools			
7. Vegetables			
8. Transportation			
9. Instruments			
10. Furniture			
11. Shapes			
12. Letters			
13. Numbers			

▶ *Helpful Hint:* Consider teaching matching categories, and program #1 simultaneously (e.g., ask "What's this?" ["a cat"]; "What's a cat?" ["an animal"]; "Good! Match animals").

Program	Uses Simple Sentences

- Program Procedure:

  (1) *It's a*—Sit in a chair across from the child. Present an object for the child to view and say "What is this?" Prompt the child to say "It's a ___ (name of object)." Reinforce the response. Fade prompts over subsequent trials. Differentially reinforce responses demonstrated with the lowest level of prompting.

  (2) *I see a*—Sit in a chair across from the child. Hold up a picture and say "What do you see?" Prompt the child to say "I see a ___ (name of item in the picture)." Reinforce the response. Fade prompts over subsequent trials. Differentially reinforce responses demonstrated with the lowest level of prompting.

  (3) *I have a*—Sit in a chair across from the child. Hand the child an object or have the child choose an object from a basket. Say "What do you have?" Prompt child to say "I have a ___ (name of object)." Reinforce the response. Fade prompts over subsequent trials. Differentially reinforce responses demonstrated with the lowest level of prompting. Eventually, only reinforce correct, unprompted responses.

- Materials: Objects and pictures.

- Suggested Prerequisites: Labels objects and pictures; repeats words.

- Prompting Suggestions: Model the correct response.

Question	Response	Date Introduced	Date Mastered
1. "What is this?"	"It's a ___."		
2. "What do you see?"	"I see a ___."		
3. "What do you have?"	"I have a ___."		

▶ *Helpful Hint:* Question #2, eventually teach your child to label more than one item on a page (e.g., "I see a house, a tree, a car, a ball, and a flower") and generalize responding to picture books.

| **Program** | **Reciprocates Information (I Have . . . I See . . .)** |

- Program Procedure:
  (1) *With Objects*—Sit in a chair facing the child. Hand an object to the child and hold a different object in your hand. Hold up your object and say "I have a ___(name of object that you are holding)." Prompt the child to hold up his or her object and prompt the child to say "I have a ___ (name of object child is holding)." Reinforce the response. Fade prompts over subsequent trials. Differentially reinforce responses demonstrated with the lowest level of prompting. Eventually, only reinforce correct, unprompted responses. Change objects every few trials. Eventually have the child choose his or her own object from a box when reciprocating. Once the child learns to say what he or she is holding, present additional reciprocation statements about the object (see examples below).
  (2) *With Pictures/Books*—Place two pictures on the table for child to view. Point to one of the pictures and say "I see a ___(name of item in the picture)." Prompt child to point to the other picture and to say "I see a ___ (name of item in the picture)." Reinforce the response. Fade prompts over subsequent trials. Differentially reinforce responses demonstrated with the lowest level of prompting. Eventually, only reinforce correct, unprompted responses. Change pictures every few trials. Once child learns to reciprocate one picture, teach responding to pictures in a book (see additional reciprocation statements below).

- Materials: Objects, pictures, and books.
- Suggested Prerequisites: Labels objects; repeats words.
- Prompting Suggestions: Model the reciprocation statement. Use a time-delay procedure by modeling the child's statement immediately after your statement is presented, then fade the presentation of the model by 2-second increments across trials.

Example Statements	Example Responses	Date Introduced	Date Mastered
With objects:			
1. "I have a (duck)."	"I have a (cow)."		
2. "My duck is yellow."	"My cow is white."		
3. "My duck says 'quack.'"	"My cow says 'moo.'"		
4. "My duck lives in a pond."	"My cow lives on a farm."		
With pictures:			
1. "I see a (ball)."	"I see a (flower)."		
2. "I see a (car and a tree)."	"I see a (man and a cake)."		
3. "I see a (red hat)."	"I see a (blue ball)."		
4. "I see a (man walking)."	"I see a (girl swimming)."		
5. "I see a (girl in a car)."	"I see a (boy on the slide)."		

▶ *Helpful Hint:* Train for generalization in natural contexts (e.g., while playing, "I'm playing with a . . . ;" during meals, "I'm eating a . . .").

Program	Reciprocates Social Information

- Program Procedure: Sit in a chair facing the child and establish attending. Present a social statement to the child (e.g., "My name is ___ [your name]"). Prompt the child to reciprocate relevant information about him/herself (e.g., "My name is ___ [child's name]"). Reinforce the response. Fade prompts over subsequent trials. Differentially reinforce responses demonstrated with lowest level of prompting. Eventually, only reinforce correct, unprompted responses.

- Suggested Prerequisites: Answers simple social questions; reciprocates with objects/pictures.

- Prompting Suggestions: Model the reciprocation statement. Use a time-delay procedure by modeling the child's statement immediately after you present your statement, then fade the presentation of the model by 2-second increments across trials.

Example: Social statements	Response: Reciprocates relevant information	Date Introduced	Date Mastered
1. "My name is . . ."			
2. "I am ___ years old."			
3. "I live in . . ."			
4. "I like to play with . . ."			
5. "My brother/sister's name is . . ."			
6. "I like to eat . . ."			
7. "My friend's name is . . ."			
8. "My Mommy/Daddy's name is . . ."			
9. "I like to drink . . ."			
10. "My favorite TV show is . . ."			

▶ *Helpful Hint:* Use the social questions that your child has mastered as reciprocation statements. Eventually, teach your child to reciprocate complex information (e.g., "When I go to the park, I like to . . ." or "I had ___ for lunch"). Teach your child to reciprocate information to peers and in a circle-time activity.

| Program | I Don't Know (Unknown Objects and Questions) |

- Program Procedure:

  (1) *To Unknown Objects*—Sit in a chair across from the child and establish attending. Hold up a known object (one that the child can label), and say "What's this?" (child should label object). Following three trials of asking the child to label known objects, hold up an unknown object (one that the child cannot label) and say "What's this?" Immediately prompt the child to say "I don't know." Reinforce the response. Fade prompts over subsequent trials. Differentially reinforce responses demonstrated with the lowest level of prompting. Eventually, only reinforce correct, unprompted responses. Randomize trials of asking the child to label known and unknown objects. Change objects across teaching sessions.

  (2) *To Unknown Questions*—Sit in a chair across from the child and establish attending. Ask the child a question whose answer he or she knows (e.g., "What's your name?"). (Child should answer the question.) Following three known questions, present a question whose answer the child does not know (e.g., "Who discovered America?"). Immediately prompt the child to say "I don't know." Reinforce the response. Fade prompts over subsequent trials. Differentially reinforce responses emitted with the lowest level of prompting. Eventually, only reinforce correct, unprompted responses. Randomize trials of presenting known and unknown questions.

- Materials: Known and unknown objects.

- Suggested Prerequisites:

  (1) Labels objects; repeats phrases.

  (2) States "I don't know" for unknown objects and answers social questions and simple general knowledge questions.

- Prompting Suggestions: Provide a verbal model of the statement. Use a time-delay procedure by modeling the response immediately following the question, and then fading the presentation of the model by 2-second increments across trials.

Questions	Response	Date Introduced	Date Mastered
(1) "What's this?" (2) Novel questions	(1–2) "I don't know."		
1.			
2.			

▶ *Helpful Hint:* After several successful trials, tell your child the label of the object after each response (e.g., "This is a salt shaker") and the answer to the unknown question.

Program	Asks "What's that?"

- Program Procedure:

  (1) *During an Instructional Task*—Place four pictures that the child can label on the table in front of the child. Establish attending and say "Tell me what you see on the table." Prompt the child (physically guide and provide a verbal model) to point to each picture from left to right and to label each picture (e.g., "cat, ball, tree, apple"). Reinforce the response and fade prompts over subsequent trials. Following several trials of independent responding, remove one of the known pictures and replace it with a picture that the child cannot label. Say "Tell me what you see on the table." Prompt the child (physically guide and provide a verbal model) to point to each picture from left to right and to label each picture (e.g., "cat, ball . . ."). As soon as the child points to the unknown picture, prompt the child to ask "What's that?" Reinforce the response (e.g., "Good asking!") and answer the question (e.g., "It's a vacuum"). Present a new combination of pictures on each trial, each combination consisting of three known pictures and one unknown picture. Change the placement of the unknown picture on each trial. Fade prompts over subsequent trials. Differentially reinforce responses demonstrated with the lowest level of prompting. Eventually, only reinforce correct, unprompted responses.

  (2) *Walking Through the House*—Place an assortment of unknown objects throughout the house. Objects should be placed where they would not ordinarily be found (e.g., a plunger in the bedroom). Take the child for a walk through the house. As soon as you and the child approach an unknown object, prompt the child to point to the object and to ask "What's that?" Reinforce the response (e.g., "Good asking!") and answer the question (e.g., "It's a plunger"). Repeat the above procedure for each approach to an unknown object. Fade prompts over subsequent trials. Differentially reinforce responses demonstrated with the lowest level of prompting. Eventually, only reinforce correct, unprompted responses.

- Materials: Known and unknown pictures and objects.

- Suggested Prerequisites: Labels objects; imitates the question "What's that?"; states "I don't know" for unknown objects and pictures.

- Prompting Suggestions: Provide a verbal model of the question. Use a time-delay procedure by modeling the question immediately after the child points to the unknown picture/object and by fading the presentation of the model by 2-second increments across trials. Present the model in an exaggerated questioning tone of voice.

Instruction	Response	Date Introduced	Date Mastered
(1) "Tell me what you see on the table." (2) Without instruction	(1–2) "What's that?"		
1.			
2.			

▶ *Helpful Hint:* Determine known and unknown objects ahead of time. Promote question asking in natural contexts (e.g., while looking at a book, while on a walk in the park). Use enticing unknown pictures and objects (e.g., colorful toys).

Program	Asks "What's this?"

- Program Procedure: Place an assortment of known and unknown objects in a bag. Hand the bag to the child and say "Tell me what's in the bag." Prompt the child (physically guide and provide a verbal model) to remove each object from the bag, hold it up, and label the object (e.g., "ball, car, Power Ranger"). As soon as the child holds up an unknown object, prompt the child to ask "What's this?" Reinforce the response (e.g., "Good asking!") and answer the question (e.g., "It's a pinwheel"). Fade prompts over subsequent trials. Differentially reinforce responses demonstrated with the lowest level of prompting. Eventually, only reinforce correct, unprompted responses. Change objects every few trials.

- Materials: Known and unknown objects.

- Suggested Prerequisites: Labels objects; imitates the question "What's this?"; states "I don't know" for unknown objects and pictures.

- Prompting Suggestions: Provide a verbal model of the question. Use a time-delay procedure; that is, model the question as soon as the child holds up the unknown object, then fade the presentation of the model by 2-second increments across trials.

Instruction: "Tell me what's in the bag."	Response: Asks "What's this?" when holding up known object	Date Introduced	Date Mastered
1.			

▶ *Helpful Hint:* Determine known and unknown objects ahead of time. Generalize responding to natural contexts (e.g., at dinnertime hand your child an unknown food item and prompt him or her to ask "What's this?"). Use enticing, novel objects (e.g., new, colorful toys). Fade distance between you and child so that he or she walks up to you, displays object, and asks the question.

| **Program** | **Asks "Where is . . . ?"** |

- Program Procedure:
  (1) *When Asked to Retrieve Missing Objects*—Place five objects that the child can identify behind his or her chair (out of view). Show child where the objects are (e.g., turn child toward the group of objects and say "Look, there is a ball, car, book, pencil, and a hat"). Turn child toward you so items are no longer in view of the child. Establish attending and state the instruction "Get the ___ (name of an object present)." Prompt child to retrieve the object and reinforce the response. After three trials of asking the child to retrieve objects that are present, remove one of the items (do not let child see you remove the object). Present the instruction "Get the (name of removed object)." As soon as the child goes behind the chair and begins to look for the object (e.g., looks on floor), prompt the child to ask "Where's the ___ (name of removed object)?" Following the question, say "Here's the ___ (name of removed object)!" Show the object to the child and reinforce the response. Following several trials of asking for objects that are not present, ask for objects that are present. Randomize trials of asking for objects present and objects not present. Fade prompts over subsequent trials. Differentially reinforce responses demonstrated with the lowest level of prompting.

Eventually, only reinforce correct, unprompted responses. Change objects across teaching sessions.
  (2) *During Activities*—Arrange a context where child is expected to complete an activity (e.g., a puzzle or an art project). Prior to engaging the child in the activity, remove one of the objects needed to complete the activity (e.g., remove a puzzle piece, remove the crayons). Prompt child to begin the activity. When child looks for the removed object, prompt him or her to say "Where's the ___ (name of removed object)?" Following the question, say "Here's the ___ (name of removed object)!" Show the object to the child and reinforce the response. Fade prompts over subsequent opportunities. Differentially reinforce responses demonstrated with the lowest level of prompting. Eventually, only reinforce correct, unprompted responses.

- Materials: Objects.

- Suggested Prerequisites: Labels objects; retrieves objects out of view; repeats phrases.

- Prompting Suggestions: Provide a verbal model of the question. Use a time-delay procedure by modeling the question immediately when the child is looking for the object and then fading the presentation of the model by 2-second increments across trials.

Instruction	Response	Date Introduced	Date Mastered
(1) "Get the ___?" (2) Without verbal instruction	(1–2) "Where's the ___?"		
1.			
2.			

▶ *Helpful Hint:* Set up opportunities in natural contexts to generalize responding (e.g., hide child's shoes or coat before it's time to go outside).

| Program | **Pronouns (I and You)** |

- Program Procedure:
  (1) *I*—Prompt the child to perform an action (e.g., physically guide the child to clap his or her hands) and say "What are you doing?" Prompt the child to say what he or she is doing with correct pronoun (e.g., "I am clapping my hands"). Reinforce the response. Fade prompts over subsequent trials. Differentially reinforce responses demonstrated with the lowest level of prompting. Eventually, only reinforce correct, unprompted responses.
  (2) *You*—Sit across from the child. Establish attending and demonstrate an action (e.g., clap your hands). Say "What am I doing?" Prompt child to say what you are doing with the correct pronoun (e.g., "You are clapping your hands"). Reinforce the response. Fade prompts over subsequent trials. Differentially reinforce responses demonstrated with the lowest level of prompting. Eventually, only reinforce correct, unprompted responses.
  (3) *Randomize I and You*—Prompt the child to perform an action (e.g., give the child some juice to drink) and demonstrate an action (e.g., eat a cookie). Say either "What are you doing?" or "What am I doing?" Prompt the child to say what you are doing (e.g., "You are eating a cookie") or to say what he or she is doing (e.g., "I am drinking juice"). Fade prompts over subsequent trials. Differentially reinforce responses demonstrated with the lowest level of prompting. Eventually, only reinforce correct, unprompted responses.

- Suggested Prerequisites: Labels actions, possession, and pronouns (my and your).

- Prompting Suggestions: Model the correct response and use a time-delay procedure.

Question	Response		
(1) "What are you doing?" (2) "What am I doing?" (3) Either 1 or 2	(1) Describes what he or she is doing with correct pronoun "I am . . ." (2) Describes what you are doing with correct pronoun "You are . . ." (3) Either 1 or 2	Date Introduced	Date Mastered
1. I am			
2. You are			
3. Randomize I and You			
▶ *Helpful Hint:* Be sure to ask your child to label pronouns in natural contexts.			

Program	Pronouns (He or She)

- Program Procedure:
  (1) *He or His*—Have a familiar male perform an action in front of the child. Say "What is ___ doing?" (e.g., "What is Billy doing?"). Prompt the child to say what the person is doing with correct pronoun (e.g., "He is clapping his hands"). Reinforce the response. Fade prompts over subsequent trials. Differentially reinforce responses demonstrated with the lowest level of prompting. Eventually, only reinforce correct, unprompted responses.
  (2) *She or Her*—Have a familiar female perform an action in front of the child. Say "What is ___ doing?" (e.g., "What is Mary doing?"). Prompt child to say what the person is doing with the correct pronoun (e.g., "She is clapping her hands"). Reinforce the response. Fade prompts over subsequent trials. Differentially reinforce responses demonstrated with the lowest level of prompting. Eventually, only reinforce correct, unprompted responses.

  (3) *Randomize He and She*—Present either #1 or #2. Prompt the correct response. Reinforce the response. Fade prompts over subsequent trials. Differentially reinforce responses demonstrated with the lowest level of prompting. Eventually, only reinforce correct, unprompted responses.

- Suggested Prerequisites: Labels familiar people, actions, possession, gender, and pronouns (my, your, I, you).

- Prompting Suggestions: Model the correct response and use a time-delay procedure.

Question	Response	Date Introduced	Date Mastered
(1) "What is ___ doing?" (2) "What is ___ doing?" (3) Either 1 or 2	(1) Describes what the person is doing with correct pronoun: "He is . . ." (2) Describes what person is doing with correct pronoun: "She is . . ." (3) Either 1 or 2		
1.			
2.			
3.			

▶ *Helpful Hint:* You can also use pictures of boys, girls, men, and women to teach the responses (e.g., hold up a picture of a man and ask "What is the man doing?").

- Program Procedure: Sit in a chair across from the child and establish attending. Present a question related to a general knowledge topic. Prompt the correct response. Reinforce the response. Fade prompts over subsequent trials. Differentially reinforce responses demonstrated with the lowest level of prompting. Eventually, only reinforce correct, unprompted responses.

- Materials: Materials related to specific topics; Brain Quest (see resource list).

- Suggested Prerequisites: Child has mastered receptive and expressive programs relevant to the topic (e.g., for colors, child labels colors and for community helpers, child labels community helpers).

Suggested General Knowledge Topics and Sample Questions	Sample Responses
Topic: Animals 1. "What does a ___ say?" 2. "What says ___?" 3. "What does a ___ do?" 4. "Where does a ___ live?"	1. Dog/"Woof Woof" 2. Woof Woof/"Dog" 3. Dog/"Bark" 4. Cow/"On a farm"
Topic: Colors 1. "What color is the ___?" 2. "Tell me something that's ___."	1. Sun/"Yellow" 2. Yellow/"Sun"
Topic: Community Helpers 1. "What does a ___ do?" 2. "Who ___?"	1. Fireman/"Puts out fires" 2. Puts out fires/"Fireman"
Topic: Holidays 1. "What holiday comes in ___?" 2. "When is ___?" 3. "What happens on ___?"	1. December/"Christmas" 2. Christmas/"December" 3. Thanksgiving/"We eat turkey."
Topic: Attributes 1. "How does ___ taste?" 2. "Tell me something that tastes ___." 3. "How does ___ feel?" 4. "Tell me something that feels ___." 5. "Tell me something that's ___."	1. Candy/"Sweet" 2. Sour/"Lemon" 3. Snow/"Cold" 4. Soft/"Cotton" 5. Big/"Elephant"
Topic: Seasons 1. "What are the four seasons?" 2. "What season does it ___ in?" 3. "What happens in the ___?" 4. "Tell me something you do in the ___."	1. "Winter, Spring, Summer, Fall" 2. Snow/"Winter" 3. Fall/"Leaves fall off the tree." 4. Summer/"Swim"
Topic: General Preschool 1. "What shines in the sky at night?" 2. "What do chickens lay?" 3. "How many days are in a week?"	1. "The moon" 2. "Eggs" 3. "Seven"

▶ *Helpful Hint:* Initially, use concrete visual materials. For example, use pictures representing holidays when teaching general knowledge questions about holidays.

Program	Describes Pictures in Full Sentences

- Program Procedure: Sit in a chair facing the child. Establish attending and present a picture to the child. State the instruction "Tell me about the picture." Prompt the child to describe the picture in a complete sentence (e.g., "The girl is reading a book"). Reinforce the response. Fade prompts over subsequent trials. Differentially reinforce responses demonstrated with the lowest level of prompting.

- Eventually, only reinforce correct, unprompted responses.
- Materials: Verb cards.
- Suggested Prerequisites: Labels objects, familiar people, actions, gender; repeats phrases.
- Prompting Suggestions: Model the description of the picture.

Instruction: "Tell me about the picture."	Response: Describes picture in full sentence	Date Introduced	Date Mastered
1.			
2.			
3.			
4.			
5.			
6.			
7.			
8.			
9.			
10.			
11.			
12.			
13.			
14.			
15.			

▶ *Helpful Hint:* Take pictures of family members performing actions and teach your child to describe these pictures in full sentences (e.g., "Daddy is cooking a hamburger").

Program	**Describes Objects with Attributes (In View and Out of View)**

- Program Procedure:
  (1) *In View*—Sit in a chair facing the child. Establish attending and present an object to the child. State the instruction "Tell me about this." Prompt the child to label the object and to tell you three things about the object (e.g., "It's a fire truck, it's red and white, it has a ladder, and there's a fireman inside it"). Reinforce the response. Fade prompts over subsequent trials. Differentially reinforce responses demonstrated with the lowest level of prompting. Eventually, only reinforce correct, unprompted responses
  (2) *Out of View*—Sit in a chair facing the child. Establish attending and state the instruction "Tell me about a ___ (name of an object)" (e.g., apple). Prompt the child to describe the object according to attribute, function, and/or category (e.g., "It's red, you can eat it, and it's a fruit"). Reinforce the response. Fade prompts over subsequent trials. Differentially reinforce responses demonstrated with the lowest level of prompting. Eventually, only reinforce correct, unprompted responses.

- Materials: Objects.

- Suggested Prerequisites:
  (1) In view: labels objects, attributes, functions, and categories; repeats phrases.
  (2) Out of view: describes objects in view; labels categories, attributes, and functions; repeats phrases.

- Prompting Suggestions: Model a description of the objects.

Instruction	Response		
(1) "Tell me about this." (2) "Tell me about a ___."	(1) Labels object and tells three things about the object (2) Describes object based on attribute, function, or category	Date Introduced	Date Mastered
1. Objects in view			
2. Objects not in view			

▶ *Helpful Hint:* Shape responses over the teaching sessions (e.g., first teach one descriptor, "It's a red car"; then two, "It's a red car and it has four wheels"; then three, "It's a red car, it has four wheels, and there's a man driving it"). Objects out of view should be those that your child can already describe in view.

Program	Recalls Events (Immediate Past/with a Delay)

- Program Procedure:
  (1) *Immediate Past*—Prompt the child to go to a specific location and to perform an action in the location (e.g., "Go to the bathroom and wash your hands"). Accompany the child to the location. Following the action, return to the teaching room and ask the child several questions about the event (e.g., "Where did you go?" "What did you do there?" "Whom did you see?"). Prompt the child to answer each question (e.g., "To the bathroom," "I washed my hands," "I saw Daddy"). Reinforce each response. Fade prompts over subsequent trials. Differentially reinforce responses demonstrated with the lowest level of prompting. Eventually, only reinforce correct, unprompted responses.
  (2) *With a Delay*—Prompt the child to go to a specific location and to perform an action in the location (e.g., "Let's go to the kitchen and have some cookies and milk"). Return to the teaching room and engage in a play activity (e.g., do a puzzle with the child). After the activity, ask the child questions about the previous activity (e.g., "Where did we go before we did the puzzle?" "What did we do in the kitchen?" "Who was in the kitchen?"). Prompt the child to answer each question (e.g., "We went to the kitchen," "We had cookies and milk," "Sam was in the kitchen"). Reinforce each response. Fade prompts over subsequent trials. Differentially reinforce responses made with the lowest level of prompting. Eventually, only reinforce correct, unprompted responses.

- Suggested Prerequisites:
  (1) Labels rooms, actions, and uses correct tense.
  (2) Recalls events without a delay, retells a story, and describes objects not in view.

- Prompting Suggestions: Model the correct responses.

(1–2) A question about the event	Response	Date Introduced	Date Mastered
	(1–2) Answers the question		
1. No delay			
2. Delay			

▶ *Helpful Hint:* Eventually, drop the verbal prompt of telling your child where he or she is going to go and just physically guide your child to engage in the activity (e.g., lead him or her into the bathroom, guide him or her to wash his or her hands, return to the teaching room and ask a question about the activity). Do fun activities for your child to recall (e.g., run into the bedroom and jump on the bed). Remember to ask your child to recall information in natural contexts throughout the day (e.g., when you get home from the park, ask "Where did we go?" "What did you do at the park?" and "Whom did you see at the park?"). If your child has difficulty with this program, try teaching one recall question at a time (e.g, first teach " Where did you go?" across different events, then "What did you do?" across different events, and then ask both questions, "Where did you go? " and "What did you do?"). Add additional questions as your child's performance improves.

Program | Answers "Where . . .?" Questions

- Program Procedure: Sit in a chair across from the child. Establish attending and ask a "Where . . .?" question (e.g., "Where do you find a refrigerator?"). Prompt child to answer the question (e.g., "in the kitchen"), and reinforce the response. Fade prompts over subsequent trials. Differentially reinforce responses demonstrated with the lowest level of prompting. Eventually, only reinforce correct, unprompted responses.

- Materials: MEER 2 (see resource list).

- Suggested Prerequisites: Labels prepositions, rooms, scenes, and functions of objects.

- Prompting Suggestions: Model the correct response.

Examples: "Where . . .?"	Response	Date Introduced	Date Mastered
1. . . . do you go to sleep?			
2. . . . do you take a bath?			
3. . . . do you cook dinner?			
4. . . . do you live?			
5. . . . do you buy groceries?			
6. . . . do you find a stove?			
7. . . . does Mommy work?			
8. . . . do you play on a slide and swings?			
9. . . . do you go to school?			
10. . . . do you see a lion?			
11. . . . do you go swimming?			
12. . . . do you go when you're sick?			
13. . . . do you get books from?			
14. . . . can you buy hamburgers and french fries?			
15. . . . do you get your hair cut?			

▶ *Helpful Hint:* Use pictures of the locations as prompts.

Program	**Function of Rooms**

- Program Procedure:
  (1) *Labels Room According to Function*—Sit in a chair across from the child. Establish attending and say "What room do you ___ (e.g., sleep) in?" Prompt the child to label the room (e.g., "my bedroom"). Reinforce the response. Fade prompts over subsequent trials. Differentially reinforce responses demonstrated with the lowest level of prompting. Eventually, only reinforce correct, unprompted responses.
  (2) *Labels Function of Rooms*—Sit in a chair across from the child. Establish attending and say "What do you do in the ___ (room)?" (e.g., "What do you do in the kitchen?"). Prompt child to say what he or she does in the room. Reinforce the response. Fade prompts over subsequent trials. Differentially reinforce responses demonstrated with the lowest level of prompting. Eventually, only reinforce correct, unprompted responses.

- Suggested Prerequisites: Labels rooms, function of objects, and actions.

- Prompting Suggestions: Model the correct response.

Question	Response	Date Introduced	Date Mastered
(1) "What room do you ___ in?" (2) "What do you do in the ___?"	(1) Labels room (2) Labels function		
1. Kitchen/Cook			
2. Bedroom/Sleep			
3. Bathroom/Take a bath			
4. Family room/Watch TV			
5. Dining room/Eat dinner			
6. Living room/Watch TV			
7. Playroom/Play with toys			
▶ *Helpful Hint:* Use pictures of rooms as a prompt for response #1.			

Program	Answers "When . . .?" Questions

- Program Procedure: Sit in a chair across from the child. Establish attending and ask a "When . . .?" question (e.g., "When do you go to sleep?"). Prompt child to answer the question (e.g., "at night"), and reinforce the response. Fade prompts over subsequent trials. Differentially reinforce responses demonstrated with the lowest level of prompting. Eventually, only reinforce correct, unprompted responses.

- Suggested Prerequisites: Answers who, where, and why questions.

- Prompting Suggestions: Model the correct response.

Examples: "When . . .?"	Response	Date Introduced	Date Mastered
1. . . . do you go to sleep?			
2. . . . do you take a bath?			
3. . . . do you eat dinner?			
4. . . . do you go to school?			
5. . . . do you wake up?			
6. . . . does it get dark?			
7. . . . does the sun come up?			
8. . . . is Grandma coming?			
9. . . . do you go to the doctor?			
10. . . . is your birthday?			

▶ *Helpful Hint:* Use the MEER 2 book for additional "When. . .?" questions (see resource list).

Program	Delivers a Message

- Program Procedure: Sit in a chair across from the child and establish attending. Present the instruction "Go tell ___ (a person) ___ (a message)" (e.g., "Go tell Mommy that it's time for lunch"). Prompt the child to approach the person, gain his/her attention, and deliver the message (e.g., "Mommy, it's time for lunch"). Reinforce the response. Fade prompts over subsequent trials. Differentially reinforce responses demonstrated with the lowest level of prompting. Eventually, only reinforce correct, unprompted responses.

- Suggested Prerequisites: Repeats phrases; makes requests in sentences; follows two-step instructions; recalls events.

- Prompting Suggestions: Physically guide child to approach the person and model the message for the child to repeat.

Instruction: "Go tell ___ ___."	Response: Child approaches correct person, gains his/her attention, and delivers the message	Date Introduced	Date Mastered
1.			
2.			
3.			
4.			
5.			
6.			
7.			
8.			
9.			
10.			

▶ *Helpful Hint:* Begin with simple request messages (e.g., "Go tell Daddy that you want a cookie"). Gradually increase complexity of messages (e.g., "Go tell Daddy whom you saw at the park"). Make the messages relevant to the context. Encourage eye contact when your child is delivering the message.

| Program | **Role Plays with Puppets** |

- Program Procedure: Sit across from the child on the floor in a play area. Place several puppets of specific characters or animals in front of the child (e.g., a Bert puppet, a frog puppet). Prompt the child to choose a puppet. Place a puppet on your hand and ask the child a question directed at his or her puppet (e.g., "What's your name?"). Prompt the child to answer the question related to his or her puppet (e.g., "Ernie"). Fade prompts over subsequent trials. Differentially reinforce responses demonstrated with the lowest level of prompting. Eventually, only reinforce correct, unprompted responses.

- Materials: Puppets (e.g., Bert, Ernie, animal puppets).

- Suggested Prerequisites: Reciprocates social information and information about object; answers social questions and general knowledge questions.

- Prompting Suggestions: Repeat the question, or provide a verbal model of the correct answer.

A question directed at the puppet	**Response: Correctly answers question related to the puppet**	Date Introduced	Date Mastered
1.			
2.			
3.			

▶ *Helpful Hint:* This program should be taught in a play context with peers. Eventually teach your child to ask your puppet questions! If you do not have puppets, you can do the same program with a play figure (e.g., if you have a Bert doll and an Ernie doll, substitute these for the puppets). Eventually teach reciprocation statements as well as questions.

Program	Same and Different (Receptive)

- Program Procedure:

  (1) *Same*—Place three objects (two that are the same, one different, e.g., two spoons and a ball) on the table in front of the child. Establish attending and say "Which ones are the same?" Prompt the child to hand you the two identical objects. Reinforce the response. Fade prompts over subsequent trials. Differentially reinforce responses demonstrated with the lowest level of prompting. Eventually, only reinforce correct, unprompted responses.

  (2) *Different*—Place three objects (two that are the same, one different, e.g., two spoons and a ball) on the table in front of the child. Establish attending and say "Which one is different?" Prompt the child to hand you the object that is different. Reinforce the response. Fade prompts over subsequent trials. Differentially reinforce responses demonstrated with the lowest level of prompting. Eventually, only reinforce correct, unprompted responses.

  (3) *Randomize Same/Different*—Place three objects (two that are the same, one different, e.g., two spoons and a ball) on the table in front of the child. Establish attending and say either "Which one is different?" or "Which ones are the same?" Prompt the the correct response. Reinforce the response. Fade prompts over subsequent trials. Differentially reinforce responses demonstrated with the lowest level of prompting.

- Materials: Objects.

- Suggested Prerequisites: Matches objects; identifies objects, attributes, colors, and categories.

- Prompting Suggestions: Physically guide child to hand you the correct object(s).

Question	Response		
(1) "Which ones are the same?" (2) "Which one is different?" (3) Either 1 or 2	(1–3) Gives correct object(s)	Date Introduced	Date Mastered
Identical Objects 1. Same 2. Different 3. Randomize Same and Different			
Based on Color 1. Same 2. Different 3. Randomize Same and Different			
Based on Category 1. Same 2. Different 3. Randomize Same and Different			

▶ *Helpful Hint:* Begin with identical objects (e.g., two spoons and a hat), then use ones that are similar based on color (e.g., red ball, red cup, and blue shoe), then use ones based on category (e.g., one apple, one banana, and a cup).

Program	**Identifies What Does Not Belong (Attribute and Category)**

- Program Procedure:
  (1) *Attribute*—Place four objects on the table in front of the child (three that are similar based on attribute and one that is different; e.g., three blue cars and one red car). Say "Which one does not belong?" Prompt the child to point to the correct object and to name the object (e.g., "the red car"). Reinforce the response. Fade prompts over subsequent trials. Differentially reinforce responses demonstrated with the lowest level of prompting. Eventually, only reinforce correct, unprompted responses.
  (2) *Category*—Place four objects on the table in front of the child (three that are similar based on the category they belong to and one that is different; e.g., three fruits and one animal). Say "Which one does not belong?" Prompt the child to point to the correct object and to name the object (e.g, "the dog"). Reinforce the response. Fade prompts over subsequent trials. Differentially reinforce responses demonstrated with the lowest level of prompting. Eventually, only reinforce correct, unprompted responses.

- Materials: Objects in categories and objects similar based on attribute.

- Suggested Prerequisites: Identifies objects that are described; answers "Yes"/"No" in response to questions about objects; identifies objects that are the same and different; labels categories and attributes.

- Prompting Suggestions: Physically guide the child to hand you the correct object and provide a verbal model of the object.

Instruction	Response		
(1–2) "Which one doesn't belong?"	**(1–2) Child points to the correct object and names the object**	**Date Introduced**	**Date Mastered**
1. Attribute			
2. Category			

▶ *Helpful Hint:* Start simply: Place four objects, three identical, one different (e.g., three balls and one cup) on the table. Say "Which one does not belong?" Prompt your child to hand you the cup. Teach your child to express why the object does not belong (e.g., after the child hands you the correct object, say "Good, why doesn't it belong?" Prompt your child to say "Because it's not [a] ___ [e.g., ball]").

Program	Answers *Wh*-questions About a Story

- Program Procedure:

(1) *With Pictures*—Sit in a chair facing the child. Present a picture of someone performing an action in a specific location (e.g., a picture of a sibling swimming at the beach). Tell a simple story about the picture (e.g., "Once upon a time Billy went to the beach and he went swimming"). Ask the child a *wh*-question about the story (e.g., "Who went swimming?", "Where did Billy go?", "What did Billy do at the beach?"). Prompt the child to answer each question (e.g., "Billy," "To the beach," "He went swimming"). Reinforce the response. Fade prompts over subsequent trials. Differentially reinforce responses made with the lowest level of prompting. Eventually, only reinforce correct, unprompted responses.

(2) *Simple Verbal*—Sit in a chair facing the child. Tell a simple story (e.g., "One day, Mommy went to the store and bought some ice cream"). Ask a *wh*-question about the story (e.g., "Who went to the store?", "Where did Mommy go?", "What did Mommy buy at the store?"). Prompt the child to answer each question (e.g., "Mommy," "To the store," "Ice cream"). Reinforce the response. Fade prompts over subsequent trials. Differentially reinforce responses made with the lowest level of prompting. Eventually, only reinforce correct, unprompted responses.

(3) *Simple Story Book*—Sit in a chair facing the child. Read a page from a simple story book and ask a *wh*-question about what was read. Prompt the child to answer the question. Reinforce the response. Fade prompts over subsequent trials. Differentially reinforce responses made with the lowest level of prompting. Eventually, only reinforce correct, unprompted responses.

(4) *Advanced Verbal*—Sit in a chair facing the child. Tell a four-sentence story to the child (e.g., "One day a little boy named Sam went to the park. At the park he found a red ball. He brought the ball home to show his mommy. He played with the ball after dinner and then he went to bed"). Ask a *wh*-question about the story. Prompt the child to answer each question. Reinforce the response. Fade prompts over subsequent trials. Differentially reinforce responses made with the lowest level of prompting.

- Materials: Photographs of familiar people performing actions in specific locations, and story books.

- Suggested Prerequisites: Discriminates *wh*-questions about objects and pictures; recalls events.

- Prompting Suggestions: Model the answer.

(1–4) A *wh*-question about the story	Response	Date Introduced	Date Mastered
	(1–4) Correctly answers the question		
1. With pictures			
2. Simple verbal			
3. Simple story book			
4. Advanced verbal			

▶ *Helpful Hint:* If your child has trouble with this program, try teaching each question separately, then randomizing the questions or reducing the complexity of the story (e.g., "Mommy went to the store." "Who went to the store?").

Program	Answers *Wh*-questions About Topics

- Program Procedure: Sit in a chair across from the child. Establish attending and ask a *wh*-question about a topic (see examples below). Prompt the child to answer the question (see examples below). Reinforce the response. Fade prompts over subsequent trials. Differentially reinforce responses demonstrated with the lowest level of prompting.

Eventually, only reinforce correct, unprompted responses.

- Suggested Prerequisites: Discriminates *wh*-questions about objects and pictures; answers why/because questions, where questions, and when questions.

- Prompting Suggestions: Model the correct response.

Example Topics and Questions	Example Responses	Date Introduced	Date Mastered
1. *Breakfast* "What do you eat for breakfast?" "When do you eat breakfast?" "Why do you eat breakfast?" "Where do you eat breakfast?" "Who makes you breakfast?"	"Pancakes." "In the morning." "Because I'm hungry." "In the kitchen." "Daddy does."		
2. *Taking a bath* "When do you take a bath?" "Who gives you a bath?" "Why do you have to take a bath?" "Where do you take a bath?"	"Before I go to bed." "Mommy does." "To get clean." "In the bathtub."		
3. *School* "Where do you go to school?" "When do you go to school?" "Who do you see at school?" "What do you do at school?" "Why do you go to school?"	"ABC school." "On Mondays." "I see Tommy and Mary." "I play and write letters." "To see my friends and to learn."		

▶ *Helpful Hint:* If your child has trouble with this program, try presenting the questions in a fixed order and randomizing the questions over time.

Program	Follows "Ask . . ." Versus "Tell . . ." Instructions

- Program Procedure:
  (1) *Asks*—With another person in view of the child, present the instruction "Ask ___ (person) ___ (a question)" (e.g., "Ask Billy how old he is"). Prompt the child to approach the person and ask the question (e.g., "Billy, how old are you?"; person should then answer the question). Reinforce the response. Fade prompts over subsequent trials. Differentially reinforce responses demonstrated with the lowest level of prompting. Eventually, only reinforce correct, unprompted responses.
  (2) *Tells*—With another person in view of the child, present the instruction "Tell ___ (person) ___ (information)" (e.g., "Tell Billy how old you are"). Prompt the child to approach the person and tell the information (e.g., "I'm 6 years old"). Reinforce the response. Fade prompts over subsequent trials. Differentially reinforce responses demonstrated with the lowest level of prompting. Eventually, only reinforce correct, unprompted responses.
  (3) *Randomize Ask and Tell*—Present either instruction #1 or instruction #2. Prompt for the correct response. Reinforce the response. Fade prompts over subsequent trials. Differentially reinforce responses demonstrated with the lowest level of prompting. Eventually, only reinforce correct, unprompted responses.

- Suggested Prerequisites: Delivers messages; labels advanced pronouns; answers social questions in full sentences; follows complex instructions from a distance.

- Prompting Suggestions: Physically guide child to approach the person, and model the question or the information for the child to repeat. Use a time-delay procedure.

Instruction	Response	Date Introduced	Date Mastered
(1) "Ask ___ ___." (2) "Tell ___ ___." (3) Either 1 or 2	(1) **Approaches person and asks the correct question** (2) **Approaches person and tells the correct information** (3) **Either 1 or 2**		
1. Ask			
2. Tell			
3. Randomize Ask/Tell			

▶ *Helpful Hint:* Use peers for this program and teach responding related to play activities (e.g., "Ask Billy what he is making," and "Tell Billy what you're making"). Begin with the other person seated next to your child, so you can model the correct response immediately.

Program	Finds a Hidden Object Given Location Clues

- Program Procedure: Place a variety of objects in specific locations around the house (e.g., place a ball in the closet in the bedroom, place child's shoes under the table in the kitchen). Sit in a chair across from the child and establish attending. Present the instruction "Go get the ___ (object). It's ___ (location clues)" (e.g., "It's in the kitchen, under the table"). Prompt the child to retrieve the object. Reinforce the response. Fade prompts over subsequent trials. Differentially reinforce responses demonstrated with the lowest level of prompting. Eventually, only reinforce correct, unprompted responses.

- Suggested Prerequisites: Retrieves objects out of view; identifies rooms; follows directions with prepositions; follows three-step instructions.

- Prompting Suggestions: State one location clue first (e.g., "It's in the kitchen"), then once in the kitchen provide the second clue (e.g., "Under the table"). Gradually provide all the clues simultaneously.

Instruction (1–3) "Go get the ___, it's ___."	Response (1–3) Child finds the object	Date Introduced	Date Mastered
1. One clue (e.g., in the closet)			
2. Two clues (e.g., in the closet, in a brown box)			
3. Three clues (e.g., in the kitchen, under the table, in the red cup)			

▶ *Helpful Hint:* Begin with simple clues in the teaching room (e.g., "Get me the ball. It's under the table"). Gradually increase the complexity of the clues (e.g., "Get me the ball. It's in your room, under your bed, in a red box").

Program	**Discriminates When to Ask/When to Reciprocate**

- **Program Procedure:** Sit in a chair facing the child. Establish attending and present *either* a vague statement to the child (e.g., "I went somewhere to eat last night") *or* a statement for reciprocation (e.g., "I love eating french fries"). Prompt child either to ask a question related to the statement (e.g., "Where did you go?") or to reciprocate information (e.g., "I love eating cookies"). Reinforce the response (if the child asked a question, answer the question [e.g., "I went to the movies"]). Fade prompts over subsequent trials. Differentially reinforce responses made with the lowest level of prompting. Eventually, only reinforce correct, unprompted responses.

- **Suggested Prerequisites:** Reciprocates social information and asks *wh*-questions when provided with vague information.

- **Prompting Suggestions:** Model the question or the statement. Use a time-delay procedure by modeling the response immediately after the vague statement is presented or after the reciprocation statement is presented, and then fading the presentation of the model by 2-second increments across trials.

Examples of Vague Statements and Reciprocation Statements	Examples of Questions and Reciprocal Responses	Date Introduced	Date Mastered
1. Guess what.	"What?"		
2. I went somewhere last night.	"Where did you go?"		
3. I went to the movies. My favorite movie is *The Little Mermaid.*	"My favorite movie is *Pinocchio.*"		
4. I ate something at the movies.	"What did you eat?"		
5. I ate popcorn. I love popcorn!	"I love it too!"		
6. I love it with salt.	"I love it with butter."		
7. I saw someone at the movies.	"Whom did you see?"		
8. I saw Mary. Mary is my best friend.	"Tommy is my best friend."		
9. I'm going to be something really scary for Halloween.	"What are you going to be?"		
10. I'm going to be a ghost.	"I'm going to be a lion."		

▶ *Helpful Hint:* The above are examples. Prompt for responses that are relevant to your child. Present your statements in a natural conversational tone.

| Program | Retells a Story |

- Program Procedure:
  (1) *With Props*—Sit on the floor across from the child and establish attending. Using props (e.g., play figures, toy car, toy slide, and doll house furniture) tell the child a simple story (e.g., "Once upon a time, the girl went to the park. She went down the slide, then she went in the car and drove home"). Present the instruction "Tell me what happened in the story." Prompt the child to retell the story using the props. Reinforce the response. Fade prompts over subsequent trials. Differentially reinforce responses demonstrated with the lowest level of prompting. Eventually, only reinforce correct, unprompted responses.
  (2) *Without Props*—Sit in a chair across from the child. Establish attending and tell the child a simple story (e.g., "Once upon a time there were three bears . . ."). Present the instruction "Tell me what happened in the story." Prompt the child to retell the story. Reinforce the response. Fade prompts over subsequent trials. Differentially reinforce responses demonstrated with the lowest level of prompting. Eventually, only reinforce correct, unprompted responses.

- Materials: Play figures, doll house furniture, toy cars, toy playground equipment (e.g., Little Tykes jungle gym, slide, and swing set).

- Suggested Prerequisites: Imitates complex sequences; describes sequence of pictures; repeats sentences.

- Prompting Suggestions:
  (1) Physically guide child to manipulate the props.
  (2) Model the story for the child to repeat.

Instruction	Response		
(1–2) "Tell me what happened in the story."	(1) Child retells story using props (2) Child retells story	Date Introduced	Date Mastered
1. With props			
2. Without props			

▶ *Helpful Hint:* Begin with simple one-sentence stories and increase the complexity as your child's proficiency improves.

Program	Describes Topics

- Program Procedure: Sit in a chair across from the child and establish attending. Present the instruction "Tell me about ___ (a topic, see examples below)." Prompt the child to describe the topic with three descriptors. Reinforce the response. Fade prompts over subsequent trials. Differentially reinforce responses demonstrated with the lowest level of prompting. Eventually, only reinforce correct, unprompted responses.

- Suggested Prerequisites: Describes objects in view and out of view with attributes; answers general knowledge questions related to the topic; recalls events; repeats phrases.

- Prompting Suggestions: Model the description.

Instruction **"Tell me about ___."** **Suggested topics** **and examples**	Example Responses	Date Introduced	Date Mastered
1. *Holidays* Example: "Tell me about Christmas."	"It's a holiday. It comes in December. Santa comes and brings presents."		
2. *Places* Example: "Tell me about school."	"I go to Elwood school, my teacher's name is Mr. Jones, and I play with Sarah."		
3. *Family* Example: "Tell me about your brother."	"My brother's name is Mark. He is five years old, and he plays Nintendo."		
4. *Special Events* Example: "Tell me about going ice skating."	"I go ice skating with Mommy. We go to the Willow rink. We skate fast."		

▶ *Helpful Hint:* Shape responses over the teaching sessions (e.g., first teach one descriptor, "It's a holiday"; then two, "It's a holiday. It comes in December"; then three, "It's a holiday. It comes in December, and Santa brings me presents").

Program	Tells a Story (with Props)

- Program Procedure:
  (1) *About a Specific Topic*—Sit on the floor across from the child. Place props (e.g., play figures, toy car, toy slide, and doll house furniture) on the floor in front of the child. Present the instruction "Tell me a story about ___ (topic)" (e.g., "Ernie going to the park"). Prompt the child to tell the story using the props (e.g., guide child to manipulate Ernie while modeling "Once upon a time, Ernie got in his car. He drove to the park and he went down the slide. He got in his car and he drove home"). Reinforce the response. Fade prompts over subsequent trials. Differentially reinforce responses demonstrated with the lowest level of prompting. Eventually, only reinforce correct, unprompted responses.
  (2) *No Specific Topic*—Sit on the floor across from the child. Place props (e.g., play figures, toy car, toy slide, and doll house furniture) on the floor in front of the child. Using the props, tell a simple story to the child. Present the instruction "Now it's your turn. Tell me a story." Prompt the child to tell a story using the props (e.g., guide child to manipulate Bert while modeling "Once upon a time, Bert was hungry so he got in his car and drove to McDonald's. He got a hamburger and fries, and then he went home"). Reinforce the response. Fade prompts over subsequent trials. Differentially reinforce responses demonstrated with the lowest level of prompting. Eventually, only reinforce correct, unprompted responses.

- Materials: Play figures, doll house furniture, toy cars, toy playground equipment (e.g., Little Tykes jungle gym, slide, and swing set).

- Suggested Prerequisites: Retells stories; imitates complex sequences; describes sequence of pictures; describes objects in view; repeats sentences.

- Prompting Suggestions:
  (1) Physically guide child to manipulate the props, and model the story for the child to repeat.
  (2) If the child has difficulty creating his or her own story, suggest vague topics (e.g., "You can tell me a story about Ernie"), or start the story by modeling the first sentence and pausing to assess if the child will continue with the story.

Instruction	Response	Date Introduced	Date Mastered
(1) "Tell me a story about ___." (2) "Now it's your turn. Tell me a story."	(1) Child tells story about the topic using the props (2) Child tells story using props		
1. About a topic			
2. No topic			

▶ *Helpful Hint:* This is a good program to do with peers. Sit in a circle and take turns telling stories. For response #2 discourage exact repetitions of your story (e.g., say "Tell a different story" if your child repeats the story you told). Try videotaping simple stories with props and teaching your child to imitate the model presented on the video.

| Program | **Tells a Story (without Props)** |

- Program Procedure:
  (1) *About a Specific Topic*—Sit in a chair across from the child. Establish attending and present the instruction "Tell me a story about ___ (topic)" (e.g., "a scary monster"). Prompt the child to tell a story (e.g., model "Once upon a time, there was a big scary monster. He had red eyes and green teeth"). Reinforce the response. Fade prompts over subsequent trials. Differentially reinforce responses demonstrated with the lowest level of prompting. Eventually, only reinforce correct, unprompted responses.
  (2) *No Specific Topic*—Sit in a chair across from the child. Establish attending and tell the child a simple story. Present the instruction "Now it's your turn, tell me a story." Prompt the child to tell a story. Reinforce the response. Fade prompts over subsequent trials. Differentially reinforce responses demonstrated with the lowest level of prompting. Eventually, only reinforce correct, unprompted responses.

- Suggested Prerequisites: Retells stories; imitates complex sequences; describes sequence of pictures; tells stories with props; describes objects out of view, describes topics; repeats sentences.

- Prompting Suggestions:
  (1) Model the story for the child to repeat.
  (2) If the child has difficulty creating his or her own story, suggest vague topics (e.g., "You can tell me a story about Ernie"), or start the story by modeling the first sentence and pausing to assess if the child will continue with the story.

Instruction	Response		
(1) **"Tell me a story about ___."** (2) **"Now it's your turn, tell me a story."**	(1) **Child tells story about topic.** (2) **Child tells own story.**	**Date Introduced**	**Date Mastered**
1. Specific topic			
2. Without topic			

▶ *Helpful Hint:* Shape storytelling over the teaching sessions (e.g., first reinforce one-sentence stories, then two, and so on). This is a good program to do with siblings and peers.

| Program | **Expresses Confusion and Asks for Clarification** |

- Program Procedure: Sit in a chair across from the child. Establish attending and present a complicated instruction (e.g., ask the child to perform something that you know he or she can't perform, such as "Touch your shin," or state a three-step instruction in a fast manner, or present an instruction with low volume). Prompt the child to express confusion and to ask for clarification (e.g., "I don't understand. Show me how to do that," or "I didn't understand you. Say it again," or "I can't hear you. Say it louder"). Reinforce the response. Fade prompts over subsequent trials. Differentially reinforce responses demonstrated with the lowest level of prompting. Eventually, only reinforce correct, unprompted responses.

- Suggested Prerequisites: States "I don't know" to unfamiliar questions; identifies irregularities in pictures; repeats sentences.

- Prompting Suggestions: Model the correct response.

A Complicated Instruction	Response: Child states that he/she does not understand and asks for clarification	Date Introduced	Date Mastered
1.			
2.			
3.			
4.			
5.			
6.			
7.			
8.			
9.			
10.			
11.			
12.			
13.			
14.			
15.			
16.			
17.			
18.			
19.			
20.			

▶ *Helpful Hint:* Be sure to randomize simple instructions that your child can perform with complicated ones. This will teach your child to discriminate when to ask for clarification and when not to.

Program	**Advanced Possessive Pronouns (I/You)**

- Program Procedure:
  (1) *I/Your/His/Her*—Prompt (physically guide) the child to touch a body part or clothing item on you or on another person. Say "What are you doing?" Prompt the child to say what he or she is doing with the correct pronouns (e.g., "I am touching your head" or "I am touching her shoulder"). Reinforce the response. Fade prompts over subsequent trials. Differentially reinforce responses demonstrated with the lowest level of prompting. Eventually, only reinforce correct, unprompted responses.
  (2) *You/My/His/Her*—Touch a body part or a clothing item on the child or on someone else. Say "What am I doing?" Prompt the child to say what you are doing with the correct pronouns (e.g., "You are touching my shirt" or "You are touching his hat"). Reinforce the response. Fade prompts over subsequent trials. Differentially re-

inforce responses demonstrated with the lowest level of prompting. Eventually, only reinforce correct, unprompted responses.
  (3) *Randomize 1 and 2*—Prompt (physically guide) the child to touch a body part or a clothing item on you or on another person while you are touching a body part or a clothing item on the child or on someone else. Say either question #1 or #2. Prompt the correct response. Reinforce the response. Fade prompts over subsequent trials. Differentially reinforce responses demonstrated with the lowest level of prompting. Eventually, only reinforce correct, unprompted responses.

- Suggested Prerequisites: Labels familiar people, actions, possession, gender, and pronouns (my, your, I, you).

- Prompting Suggestions: Model the correct response and use a time-delay procedure.

Question	Response		
(1) "What are you doing?" (2) "What am I doing?" (3) Either 1 or 2	(1) Describes what he/she is doing with the correct pronouns (2) Describes what you are doing with the correct pronouns (3) Either 1 or 2	**Date Introduced**	**Date Mastered**
1. I/Your/His/Her			
2. You/My/His/Her			
3. Randomize 1 and 2			

▶ *Helpful Hint:* Do this program with peers during circle-time activities.

| Program | **Advanced Possessive Pronouns (He/She)** |

- Program Procedure:
  (1) *He/My/Your/His/Her*—Have the child observe a male person touching a clothing item or a body part on himself, the child, you, or another person. Say "What is ___ (person's name) doing?" Prompt the child to say what the person is doing with the correct pronouns (e.g., "He is touching my nose"). Reinforce the response. Fade prompts over subsequent trials. Differentially reinforce responses demonstrated with the lowest level of prompting. Eventually, only reinforce correct, unprompted responses.
  (2) *She/My/Your/His/Her*—Have the child observe a female person touching a body part or a clothing item on herself, the child, you, or another person. Say "What is ___ (person's name) doing?" Prompt the child to say what the person is doing with the correct pronouns (e.g., "She is touching his nose"). Reinforce the response. Fade prompts over subsequent trials. Differentially reinforce responses demonstrated with the lowest level of prompting. Eventually, only reinforce correct, unprompted responses.
  (3) *Randomize 1 and 2*—Have the child observe 1 and 2 simultaneously. Present either question #1 or question #2. Prompt the correct response. Reinforce the response. Fade prompts over subsequent trials. Differentially reinforce responses demonstrated with the lowest level of prompting. Eventually, only reinforce correct, unprompted responses.

- Suggested Prerequisites: Labels familiar people, action, possession, gender, pronouns (my, your, I, you, he, she); repeats sentences.

- Prompting Suggestions: Model the correct response and use a time-delay procedure.

Question	Response		
(1–3) "What is ___ doing?"	**(1–3) Describes what the person is doing with the correct pronouns**	**Date Introduced**	**Date Mastered**
1. He/My/Your/His/Her			
2. She/My/Your/His/Her			
3. Randomize 1 and 2			
▶ *Helpful Hint:* Do this program with peers during circle-time activities.			

| Program | **Uses Correct Tense** |

- Program Procedure:
  (1) *Future*—Sit in a chair across from the child. Establish attending and ask the child to perform an action (e.g., "Clap your hands"). Before the child performs the action, say "What are you going to do?" Prompt the child to say what he or she is going to do with the correct tense (e.g., "I'm going to clap my hands"). Reinforce the response. Fade prompts over subsequent trials. Differentially reinforce responses demonstrated with the lowest level of prompting. Eventually, only reinforce correct, unprompted responses.
  (2) *Present*—Sit in a chair facing the child. Establish attending and ask the child to perform an action (e.g., "Clap your hands"). While the child is performing the action, say "What are you doing?" Prompt the child to say what he or she is doing with the correct tense (e.g., "I'm clapping my hands"). Reinforce the response. Fade prompts over subsequent trials. Differentially reinforce responses demonstrated with the lowest level of prompting. Eventually, only reinforce correct, unprompted responses.
  (3) *Past*—Sit in a chair facing the child. Establish attending and ask the child to perform an action (e.g., "Clap your hands"). After the child performs the action, say "What did you do?" Prompt the child to say what he or she did with the correct tense (e.g., "I clapped my hands"). Reinforce the response. Fade prompts over subsequent trials. Differentially reinforce responses demonstrated with the lowest level of prompting. Eventually, only reinforce correct, unprompted responses.

- Suggested Prerequisites: Labels actions in self; uses pronouns; repeats sentences.

- Prompting Suggestions: Model the correct response.

Question	Response	Date Introduced	Date Mastered
(1) "What are you going to do?" (2) "What are you doing?" using present tense (3) "What did you do?"	(1) Provides description using future tense (2) Provides description (3) Provides description using past tense		
1. Future			
2. Present			
3. Past			

▶ *Helpful Hint:* Eventually teach more complex descriptions with correct tense (e.g., "I'm going to go to the kitchen to get a cup," "I'm getting a cup from the kitchen," and "I went to the kitchen and got a cup"). Teach responding to pictures (e.g., use the Verb Tensing Cards; see resource list).

Program	Answers Questions About a Conversation

- Program Procedure: Sit in a circle with the child and another person. Have the child observe a simple conversation about a specific topic between you and the other person (e.g., "Mike, what's your favorite thing to eat?" "Pizza. What's your favorite thing to eat?" "I like to eat hamburgers"). After the conversation, ask the child specific questions about the conversation (one at a time) (e.g., "What are we talking about?" "What's Mike's favorite thing to eat?" "What do I like to eat?"). Prompt the child to answer each question (e.g., "You're talking about your fa-vorite thing to eat," "Pizza," "Hamburgers"). Fade prompts over subsequent trials. Differentially reinforce responses demonstrated with the lowest level of prompting. Eventually, only reinforce correct, un-prompted responses.

- Suggested Prerequisites: Retells a story; listens to a story and answers questions about the story; asks questions and retells information; recalls events.

- Prompting Suggestions: Repeat portions of the conversation. Model the response.

A question about a conversation	Response: Child correctly answers question	Date Introduced	Date Mastered
1.			
2.			
3.			

▶ *Helpful Hint:* During the conversation, prompt the child to look at each person as he or she is speaking. Begin with simple conversations and progress to more complex conversations. If your child has trouble answering many questions about a conversation, begin with one question (e.g., teach responding to "What are we talking about?" across a number of conversations before adding additional questions). Videotape conversations.

Program	Describes How

• Program Procedure: Sit in a chair across from the child and establish attending. Ask a "How" question (e.g., "How do you brush your teeth?"). Prompt the child to provide a description (e.g., "First I get my toothbrush and toothpaste. I put the toothpaste on the toothbrush, . . . and then I put the toothbrush away"). Reinforce the response. Fade prompts over subsequent trials. Differentially reinforce responses demonstrated with the lowest level of prompting. Eventually, only reinforce correct, unprompted responses.

• Suggested Prerequisites: Describes sequence of pictures; recalls events; tells stories.

• Prompting Suggestions: Model the response. If your child reads, use written prompts (write out the description for the child to read) and fade the prompts over the teaching sessions.

Examples of a "How" question	Response: Describes how	Date Introduced	Date Mastered
1. . . . do you brush your teeth?			
2. . . . do you make a peanut butter and jelly sandwich?			
3. . . . do you play ___?			
4. . . . do you wash your hands?			
5. . . . do you make a snowman?			
6. . . . do you get dressed?			
7. . . . does this work?			
8. . . . do you make a sand castle?			
9. . . . do you take a bath?			

▶ *Helpful Hint:* When your child is engaging in the activities that he or she will later describe, verbalize the sequence as your child is going through each step (e.g., as your child is brushing his or her teeth, say "First you get your toothbrush and the toothpaste . . ."). Generalize responding about events in which your child participates (e.g., Make waffles with your child. When you're finished, ask your child "How did we make the waffles?").

Program	**Same and Different (Expressive, in View)**

- Program Procedure:
  (1) *Same*—Sit in a chair across from the child. Present two objects that are the same and say "What is the same about these?" or "Why are these the same?" Prompt child to describe the similarities between the objects (e.g., "They're both apples"). Reinforce the response. Fade prompts over subsequent trials. Differentially reinforce responses demonstrated with the lowest level of prompting. Eventually, only reinforce correct, unprompted responses.
  (2) *Different*—Sit in a chair across from the child. Present two objects that are different and say "What is different about these?" Prompt the child to describe what is different about the objects (e.g., "One is an apple and the other is a ball"). Reinforce the response. Fade prompts over subsequent trials. Differentially reinforce responses demonstrated with the lowest level of prompting. Eventually, only reinforce correct, unprompted responses.

  (3) *Randomize Same and Different*—Sit in a chair across from the child. Present two objects that are similar but have different attributes (e.g., two balls, one red and one blue). Say either "What is different about these?" or "What is the same about these?" Prompt the correct response (e.g., "One is blue and the other is red" or "They're both balls"). Reinforce the response. Fade prompts over subsequent trials. Differentially reinforce responses demonstrated with the lowest level of prompting. Eventually, only reinforce correct, unprompted responses.

- Materials: Objects.

- Suggested Prerequisites: Labels objects, attributes, colors, and categories; discriminates *wh*-questions about an object; and identifies objects that are the same/different.

- Prompting Suggestions: Model the correct response.

Question	Response		
(1) "What is the same about these?" (2) "What is different about these?" (3) Either 1 or 2	(1) Describes similarities between the objects (2) Describes differences between the objects (3) Either 1 or 2	**Date Introduced**	**Date Mastered**
1. Same			
2. Different			
3. Randomize Same and Different			

▶ *Helpful Hint:* You can teach expressive responding while you are teaching receptive responding (e.g., after your child hands you the objects that are the same, ask "Why are these the same?"). Eventually, teach your child to describe several things that are similar and/or different about the objects (e.g., "One is red and you eat it, and the other is blue and you color with it"). Be sure to point out similarities and differences in natural contexts (e.g., "Look at those two boys. They both have hats. What's different about their hats?" Response: "One is red and the other is blue").

Program	Same and Different (Expressive, out of View)

- Program Procedure:
  (1) *Same*—Sit in a chair across from the child. Establish attending and say "What is the same about a ___ and a ___?" (e.g., "What is the same about an apple and a banana?"). Prompt the child to describe the similarities between the items (e.g., "They're both fruit"). Reinforce the response. Fade prompts over subsequent trials. Differentially reinforce responses demonstrated with the lowest level of prompting. Eventually, only reinforce correct, unprompted responses.
  (2) *Different*—Sit in a chair across from the child. Establish attending and say "What is different about a ___ and a ___?" (e.g., "What is different about an apple and a banana?"). Prompt the child to describe what is different about the items (e.g., "One is red and the other is yellow"). Reinforce the response. Fade prompts over subsequent trials. Differentially reinforce responses demonstrated with the lowest level of prompting. Eventually, only reinforce correct, unprompted responses.
  (3) *Randomize Same and Different*—Randomize the presentation of question #1 and question #2. Prompt for the correct response. Reinforce the response. Fade prompts over subsequent trials. Differentially reinforce responses demonstrated with the lowest level of prompting. Eventually, only reinforce correct, unprompted responses.

- Suggested Prerequisites: Describes objects out of view; describes similarities and differences between objects in view.

- Prompting Suggestions: Model the correct response.

Question (1) "What is the same about a ___ and a ___?" (2) "What is different about a ___ and a ___?" (3) Either 1 or 2	Response (1) Describes similarities between objects (2) Describes differences between objects (3) Either 1 or 2	Date Introduced	Date Mastered
1. Same			
2. Different			
3. Randomize Same and Different			

▶ *Helpful Hint:* If your child has difficulty with this program, hold the objects in view for the first trial and then repeat the question with the objects out of view on the following trial.

Program	Answers "Which . . .?" Questions

- Program Procedure: Sit in a chair across from the child. Establish attending and ask a "Which . . ." question (e.g., "Which one is big, an elephant or a mouse?"). Prompt child to answer the question (e.g., "an elephant") and reinforce the response. Fade prompts over subsequent trials. Differentially reinforce responses made with the lowest level of prompting. Eventually, only reinforce correct, unprompted responses.

- Suggested Prerequisites: Answers yes/no for objects, answers who, where, and why questions and general knowledge questions.

- Prompting Suggestions: Model the correct response.

Examples of a "Which . . .?" question	Response	Date Introduced	Date Mastered
1. . . . one can swim: a fish or a bird?			
2. . . . toy can you throw: a puzzle or a ball?			
3. . . . food tastes sweet: candy or lemons?			
4. . . . animal says roar: a tiger or a cat?			
5. . . . season does it snow: winter or summer?			
6. . . . one do you wear on your head: a sneaker or a hat?			
7. . . . do you ride in: a car or a chair?			
8. . . . animal is soft and furry: a snake or a cat?			
9. . . . one is little: a mouse or an elephant?			
10. . . . one flies in the sky: a bird or a dog?			

▶ *Helpful Hint:* Begin with objects in view (e.g., place an apple and a banana on the table and ask "Which one is yellow: the apple or the banana?"). Use the MEER 2 book for additional "Which. . ." questions (see resource list).

Program	Asks a *Wh*-question When Provided with Vague Information

- **Program Procedure:** Sit in a chair facing the child. Establish attending and present a vague statement to the child (e.g., "I went somewhere last night"). Prompt child to ask you a question related to the statement (e.g., "Where did you go?"). Reinforce the response and answer the question (e.g., "I went to the movies"). Fade prompts over subsequent trials. Differentially reinforce responses demonstrated with the lowest level of prompting. Eventually, only reinforce correct, unprompted responses.

- **Suggested Prerequisites:** Reciprocates information, answers *wh*-questions about topics, answers when and why questions, asks "Where is . . .", "What is . . .", uses advanced possessive pronoun, and uses correct tense.

- **Prompting Suggestions:** Model the question. Use a time-delay procedure by modeling the question immediately after the vague statement is presented, and then fade the presentation of the model by 2-second increments across trials.

Sample Vague Statements	Response: Asks *wh*-question related to the statement	Date Introduced	Date Mastered
1. "I got a new toy."	"What did you get?"		
2. "I bought something at the store."	"What did you buy?"		
3. "My friend did something funny."	"What did he do?"		
4. "I had something good for lunch."	"What did you have?"		
5. "I went somewhere last night."	"Where did you go?"		
6. "My dad went on a trip."	"Where did he go?"		
7. "I'm going somewhere tomorrow."	"Where are you going?"		
8. "I saw someone today."	"Whom did you see?"		
9. "There's someone here."	"Who is here?"		
10. "Someone bought this for me."	"Who bought it for you?"		
11. "I had to go to the doctor."	"Why?"		
12. "I can't go to the park today."	"Why not?"		
13. "I'm going to Disney World."	"When are you going?"		

▶ *Helpful Hint:* Start with questions related to play activities (e.g. "I'm making something," "I'm drawing something," or "I have something"). Your statements should be ones that would naturally evoke a question (e.g., saying "I went to McDonald's" does not naturally evoke a question, but saying "I found something at the park" may evoke the question "What did you find?"). Present evocative statements in natural contexts (e.g., before going out, say "We're going somewhere." Pause and prompt for "Where are we going?").

Program	Answers "Why . . .?" and "If . . .?" Questions

- Program Procedure:
  (1) *"Why . . .?"*—Sit in a chair facing the child. Establish attending and ask a "Why" question (e.g., "Why do you eat?"). Prompt child to answer the question (e.g., "Because I'm hungry"). Reinforce the response. Fade prompts over subsequent trials. Differentially reinforce responses demonstrated with the lowest level of prompting.
  (2) *"If . . .?"*—Sit in a chair facing the child. Establish attending and ask an "If" question (e.g., "What do you do if you're hungry?"). Prompt child to answer the question (e.g., "I eat something"). Reinforce the response. Fade prompts over subsequent trials. Differentially reinforce responses demonstrated with the lowest level of prompting. Eventually, only reinforce correct, unprompted responses.

- Suggested Prerequisites: Answers who, what, where, questions; labels actions, emotions, and functions.

- Prompting Suggestions: Model the correct answer.

Question (1) "Why do you ___?" (2) "What do you do if (you're) ___?"	Response (1) "Because I'm . . ." (2) "I . . ."	Date Introduced	Date Mastered
1. Eat/Hungry			
2. Drink/Thirsty			
3. Sleep/Tired			
4. Cry/Sad			
5. Smile/Happy			
6. Go to the doctor/Sick			
7. Take a bath/Dirty			
8. Put on coat/Cold			
9. Laugh/Something's funny			
10. Use an umbrella/It's raining			

▶ *Helpful Hint:* Use incidental teaching procedures (e.g., when your child asks for a drink, present the question "Why do you want a drink?" Prompt the answer, "Because I'm thirsty," and then give your child a drink). Teach responding about pictures (e.g., show your child a picture of a boy who has fallen off his bike and is crying. Present the question "Why is the boy crying?" Prompt the answer, "Because he fell off his bike").

| Program | **Completes Sentences Logically** |

- Program Procedure: Sit in a chair across from the child. Establish attending and present a picture relevant to the examples below. State part of a sentence (e.g., "His hands are dirty. He has to . . ."). Prompt the child to complete the sentence (e.g., "Wash them"). Reinforce the response. Fade prompts over subsequent trials. Differentially reinforce responses demonstrated with the lowest level of prompting. Eventually, only reinforce correct, unprompted responses.

- Materials: Pictures.

- Suggested Prerequisites: Describes irregularities; answers "Why . . .?" and "If . . .?" questions.

- Prompting Suggestions: Model the response.

Examples of an unfinished sentence	Response: Completes the sentence	Date Introduced	Date Mastered
1. "He's hungry. He needs to . . ."			
2. "It's raining. She needs a . . ."			
3. "He's thirsty. He needs a . . ."			
4. "The door is locked. She needs a . . ."			
5. "He cut his finger. He needs a . . ."			

▶ *Helpful Hint:* Use the MEER Book I for additional examples (see resource list).

Program	Describes Irregularities in Pictures

- Program Procedure: Sit in a chair across from the child and establish attending. Present a picture that depicts something wrong (e.g., a picture of a car with square tires) and ask "What's wrong in this picture?" Prompt the child to describe what is wrong in the picture (e.g., "The tires are square"). Fade prompts over subsequent trials. Differentially reinforce responses made with the lowest level of prompting. Eventually, only reinforce correct, unprompted responses.

- Materials: Picture cards that depict something wrong (see resource list).

- Suggested Prerequisites: Describes pictures; states similarities and differences between objects; answers "Why?" questions.

- Prompting Suggestions: Model the description for the child to imitate.

Question: "What is wrong in this picture?"	Response: Describes the irregularity in the picture	Date Introduced	Date Mastered
1.			
2.			
3.			
4.			
5.			
6.			
7.			
8.			
9.			
10.			
11.			
12.			
13.			
14.			
15.			
16.			
17.			
18.			
19.			
20.			

▶ *Helpful Hint:* Vary your question (e.g., "What's silly about this picture?"). Eventually, teach your child to say what should be happening in the picture (e.g., "Cars should have round wheels"). Perform irregular events for your child to observe (e.g., look at a book upside down, write with a fork) and teach your child to describe what's wrong.

Program	**Predicts Outcome**

- Program Procedure:
  (1) *To Pictures*—Present a picture to the child depicting an event where an outcome can be predicted (e.g., a boy pouring juice). Present one of the following questions "What do you think the ___ (person, e.g., boy) is going to do next?" "What do you think will happen next?" Prompt the child to say what will happen next (e.g., "The boy's going to drink the juice"). Reinforce the response. Fade prompts over subsequent trials. Differentially reinforce responses demonstrated with the lowest level of prompting.
  (2) *To Story*—Tell the child a short story about an event where an outcome can be predicted (e.g., "One day Bill was hungry. He decided to make a sandwich. When he went to get some bread, it was all gone"). Present one of the following questions: "What do you think ___ (person, e.g., Bill)

is going to do next?" "What do you think will happen next?" Prompt the child to say what will happen next (e.g., "Bill is going to go to the store to buy more bread," or "Bill is going to make something else to eat"). Reinforce the response. Fade prompts over subsequent trials. Differentially reinforce responses demonstrated with the lowest level of prompting. Eventually, only reinforce correct, unprompted responses.

- Materials: Pictures of events where an outcome can be predicted (see resource list, e.g., Verb Tensing Cards).

- Suggested Prerequisites: Describes irregularities; answers "Why?" questions; tells story; recalls events; makes logical completions to sentences.

- Prompting Suggestions: Model the response.

Question	Response		
(1–2) "What do you think will happen next?" or "What do you think ___ will do next?"	(1–2) Child predicts an appropriate outcome	**Date Introduced**	**Date Mastered**
1. To pictures			
2. To stories			

▶ *Helpful Hint:* Use pictures that suggest an obvious outcome to predict.

Program | Provides Explanations

- Program Procedure: Sit in a chair across from the child and establish attending. Present a picture that depicts a scene or an event (e.g., a beach, a picture of a kitchen, a picture of children making a snowman). Ask the child a question about the picture (e.g., "What season is this?"). After the child answers the question (e.g., "winter"), say "How do you know ___?" (e.g., "How do you know it's winter?"). Prompt the child to provide an explanation (e.g., "Because there is snow on the ground"). Reinforce the response. Fade prompts over subsequent trials. Differentially rein- force responses demonstrated with the lowest level of prompting. Eventually, only reinforce correct, un- prompted responses.

- Materials: Pictures of scenes and events (see resource list).

- Suggested Prerequisites: Describes pictures; states similarities and differences between objects; answers why/because questions.

- Prompting Suggestions: Model the explanation for the child to imitate.

Question: "How do you know __?"	Response: Provides an explanation	Date Introduced	Date Mastered
Examples:			
1. A picture of a birthday party. Ask: "What are they doing?"	"Having a birthday party."		
"How do you know they are having a birthday party?"	"Because she's blowing out candles and they have party hats."		
2. A picture of a park. Ask: "What is this place called?"	"It's a park."		
"How do you know it's a park?"	"Because there's a slide and jungle gym."		
3. A picture of a girl smiling. Ask: "How does she feel?"	"She's happy."		
"How do you know she's happy?"	"Because she's smiling."		
4. A picture of a girl wearing a swimsuit. Ask: "Where is she going?"	"Swimming."		
"How do you know she's going swimming?"	"Because she has her bathing suit on."		

▶ *Helpful Hint:* Generalize responding to events observed in natural contexts (e.g., Child observes a boy carrying a bat. Ask "What is that boy going to play?" "Baseball." "How do you know he's going to play baseball?" "Because he has a bat.").

Program	Excludes an Item Based on Attribute and Category

- Program Procedure:
  (1) *Attribute*—Place a group of objects varying according to attribute on the table in front of the child. Present the instruction "Give me something that's not ___ (attribute)" (e.g., "Give me something that's not yellow," "Give me something that is not little," or "Give me something that does not feel soft"). Prompt the child to hand you the correct object. Reinforce the response. Fade prompts over subsequent trials. Differentially reinforce responses demonstrated with the lowest level of prompting. Randomize instruction #1 with the instruction "Give me something that is ___ (attribute)" (e.g., "Give me something that is yellow"). Eventually, only reinforce correct, unprompted responses.
  (2) *Category*—Place a group of objects varying according to the category they belong to on the table in front of the child. Present the instruction "Give me something that's not ___ (a category)" (e.g., "Give me something that's not a food," "Give me something that's not an animal," or "Give me

something that's not a fruit"). Prompt the child to hand you the correct object. Reinforce the response. Fade prompts over subsequent trials. Differentially reinforce responses demonstrated with the lowest level of prompting. Randomize instruction #2 with the instruction "Give me something that is ___ (a category)" (e.g., "Give me something that is a food"). Eventually, only reinforce correct, unprompted responses.

- Materials: Objects in categories and objects similar in attribute.

- Suggested Prerequisites: Identifies objects that are described; answers "Yes" and "No" in response to questions about objects; identifies objects that are the same and different; answers "Which . . . ?" questions; identifies objects that do not belong based on attribute and category.

- Prompting Suggestions: Physically guide the child to hand you the correct object.

Instruction	Response	Date Introduced	Date Mastered
(1–2) "Give me something that's not ___."	(1–2) Child gives the correct object		
1. Attribute			
2. Category			

▶ *Helpful Hint:* Begin with simple exclusion. For example, place four objects, three identical, one different (e.g., three balls and one cup) on the table and present the instruction "Give me something that's not a ball." Eventually vary the instruction (e.g., "Which one isn't ___?").

Program	Defines People, Places, and Things

- Program Procedure:
  (1) *People*—Sit in a chair facing the child. Establish attending, and say "What's a ___(community helper, e.g., librarian)?" Prompt the child to define the function of the community helper (e.g., "*Someone* who works at the library"). Reinforce the response. Fade prompts over subsequent trials. Differentially reinforce responses demonstrated with the lowest level of prompting. Eventually, only reinforce correct, unprompted responses.
  (2) *Places*—Sit in a chair facing the child. Establish attending, and say "What's a ___ (place, e.g., library)?" Prompt the child to define the place (e.g., "It's *a place* where I get books"). Reinforce the response. Fade prompts over subsequent trials. Differentially reinforce responses demonstrated with the lowest level of prompting. Eventually, only reinforce correct, unprompted responses.

  (3) *Things*—Sit in a chair facing the child. Establish attending, and say "What's a ___ (something, e.g., book)?" Prompt the child to define the item (e.g., "It's *something* you read"). Reinforce the response. Fade prompts over subsequent trials. Differentially reinforce responses demonstrated with the lowest level of prompting.
  (4) Randomize the presentation of 1, 2, and 3.

- Suggested Prerequisites: Labels community helpers, functions of objects, and scenes; describes objects out of view; answers *wh*-questions about objects; repeats phrases.

- Prompting Suggestions: Model the definition.

Question	Response	Date Introduced	Date Mastered
(1–4) "What's a ___?"	(1) **Defines community helper** (2) **Defines the place** (3) **Defines the item** (4) **Either 1, 2, or 3**		
Examples 1. Fireman	"*Someone* who puts out fires."		
Fire house	"A *place* where firemen live."		
Fire truck	"It's *something* a fireman drives."		
2. Doctor	"*Someone* who gives me medicine when I'm sick."		
Hospital	"It's *a place* where people go when they are sick."		
Medicine	"It's *something* I take when I am sick."		
3. Teacher	"*Someone* who teaches me."		
School	"It's *a place* I go to learn."		
Blackboard	"It's *something* I write on at school."		

▶ *Helpful Hint:* Use pictures of the community helpers, places, and things.

Program	Imitates Peer

- Program Procedure:
  (1) *Gross Motor Movements*—Sit the child in a chair facing a peer. Prompt the peer to demonstrate a gross motor movement (e.g., whisper in the peer's ear so that the child does not hear the instruction "Clap your hands" or provide pictures as prompts of the actions to model). While the peer is demonstrating the action, present the instruction "Do what ___ (peer's name) is doing" (e.g., "Do what Michael's doing"). Prompt the child to imitate the gross motor movement. Reinforce the response. Fade prompts over subsequent trials. Differentially reinforce responses demonstrated with the lowest level of prompting.
  (2) *Actions*—Sit the child and a peer in chairs next to one another. Prompt the peer to perform an action out of the chair and to return to the chair (e.g., "Go shoot a basket"). Peer should perform the instruction (e.g., peer should get the ball and make a basket). When the peer returns to his or her seat, present the instruction "It's your turn. Do what ___ (peer's name) did" (e.g., "It's your turn. Do what Billy did"). Prompt the child to imitate the action.

Reinforce the response. Fade prompts over subsequent trials. Differentially reinforce responses demonstrated with the lowest level of prompting.
  (3) *Verbal Responses*—Sit in a chair across from the child and a peer. The peer and the child should be seated next to one another. Present a picture to the peer (child should not see the picture) and ask the peer "What is this?" After the peer labels the picture, say "What did ___ (name of peer) see?" Prompt the child to name what the peer saw (e.g., "apple"). Reinforce the response. Fade prompts over subsequent trials. Differentially reinforce responses demonstrated with the lowest level of prompting.

- Suggested Prerequisites: Imitates behavior of adult; repeats phrases; follows one-step instructions.

- Prompting Suggestions:
  (1–2) Physically guide child to demonstrate the response.
  (3) Provide a verbal model or allow the child to see the picture while you are presenting the question.

Instruction	Response		
(1) "Do what ___ is doing." (2) "It's your turn. Do what __ did." (3) "What did __ see?"	(1–2) Imitates peer's demonstration (3) Names what peer saw	**Date Introduced**	**Date Mastered**
1. Gross motor movements			
2. Actions			
3. Verbal responses			

▶ *Helpful Hint:* If your child has trouble with instruction #1, have the peer present the instruction "Do this" while he or she is demonstrating the action. Prompt the peer to perform play-related activities for your child to imitate. Eventually, change instruction #2 to "It's your turn" without saying "Do what ___ did," and do not allow your child to hear the instruction that is presented to the peer. If your child has trouble with #3, have the peer present single words directly to the child for him or her to imitate (e.g., have the peer sit across from the child and say "Say 'book'" etc.), until the child can imitate verbal responses of peer.

Program | Initiates Play Statements to a Peer

- Program Procedure:
  (1) *Verbal Instruction*—During playtime activities with peer, approach the child and state the instruction "Go ask ___ (peer's name) to play ___ (a preferred activity for peer and child)" (e.g., "Go ask Billy if he wants to play with the trains"). Prompt the child to approach the person, gain his or her attention, and initiate the play statement (e.g., "Billy, do you want to play with the trains?"). Reinforce the response. Allow the child and peer to play with the activity. Fade prompts over subsequent trials. Differentially reinforce responses demonstrated with the lowest level of prompting. Eventually, only reinforce correct, unprompted responses.
  (2) *Without Verbal Instruction*—Place a number of highly preferred play activities in the play area. When the peer and the child enter the play area, wait to see which play activity the child goes to. As soon as the child approaches a play activity (e.g., child walks over to the trains), immediately guide the child to approach the peer and prompt the child to initiate a play statement about the activity to the peer (e.g., model the initiation statement or say "Billy, let's play with the trains"). Reinforce the response. Allow the child and peer to play with the activity. Fade prompts over subsequent opportunities. Differentially reinforce responses demonstrated with the lowest level of prompting. Each time the child demonstrates interest in another play activity, repeat the procedure.

- Suggested Prerequisites: Repeats sentences; delivers verbal messages; requests in sentences; follows two-step instructions; plays with toys.

- Prompting Suggestions: Physically guide child from behind to approach the child, and model the initiation for the child to repeat.

Instruction: "Go ask ___ to play ___."	Response: Approaches peer and initiates a play statement to peer	Date Introduced	Date Mastered
1. With verbal instruction			
2. Without verbal instruction			

▶ *Helpful Hint:* Make sure you use compliant peers who will respond positively to your child's initiation. Once your child is reliably initiating, teach your child what to do when the peer declines his or her initiation (e.g., offers another alternative). Use photographs of play activities and written cues to prompt initiations.

Program	**Demonstrate New Responses Through Observation**

- Program Procedure:
  (1) *To Unknown Pictures* —Sit in a chair across from the child and a peer. The peer and the child should be seated next to one another. Present a picture of an unknown object to the child. Ask the child "What is this?"; child should answer "I don't know" (see prerequisites below). Present the same picture to the peer (picture should be one that the peer can successfully label) and ask the peer "What is this?" Peer should correctly label the picture. Reinforce the response of the peer (e.g., "You're right!"). Re-present the same picture to the child and say "What is this?" Child should correctly label the picture (e.g., repeats peer's response). Reinforce the response.
  (2) *To Unknown Questions*—Sit in a chair across from the child and peer. The peer and the child should be seated next to one another. Ask the child a novel question. Child should respond "I don't know" (see prerequisites below). Present the same question to the peer (question should be one that the peer can successfully answer). Peer should correctly answer the question. Reinforce the response of the peer (e.g., "You're right!"). Represent the same question to the child. Child should correctly answer the question (e.g., repeats peer's response). Reinforce the response.

- Materials: Pictures that child cannot identify but peer can identify.

- Suggested Prerequisites: States "I don't know" to unfamiliar question and objects; imitates verbal responses of peer.

- Prompting Suggestions: Have child observe the response again, model the response following the peer's model (e.g., "You're right it's a ___ [label]").

Question	Response		
(1) "What's this?" (2) A novel question	(1) **Correctly labels picture following peer's model** (2) **Correctly answers the question following peer's model**	**Date Introduced**	**Date Mastered**
1. To pictures			
2. To novel questions			

▶ *Helpful Hint:* Make sure the child is attending to the peer when the peer models the response. Generalize responding to other labels (e.g., pictures of novel actions). Increase the latency between the time the peer models the response and when you re-present the picture or the question (e.g., have the peer model the response, ask the child some known questions, and then re-present the novel question).

Program

- Program Procedure:

- Materials:

	Response	Date Introduced	Date Mastered
1.			
2.			
3.			
4.			
5.			
6.			
7.			
8.			
9.			
10.			
11.			
12.			
13.			
14.			
15.			
16.			
17.			
18.			
19.			
20.			

▶ Comments:

Meeting Summary Form

Date

Present

1. _____
2. _____
3. _____
4. _____
5. _____

6. _____
7. _____
8. _____
9. _____
10. _____

Programs Reviewed

1. _____
2. _____
3. _____
4. _____
5. _____

6. _____
7. _____
8. _____
9. _____
10. _____

Program Changes

1. _____
2. _____
3. _____
4. _____
5. _____

Program Additions

1. _____
2. _____
3. _____
4. _____
5. _____

6. _____
7. _____
8. _____
9. _____
10. _____

▶ Date of next meeting:

Data Sheet

- Score (+) if child responds correctly without prompts.

- Score (+wp) if child responds correctly with specified prompting level.

- Score (−) if child does not respond correctly or fails to respond to specified prompting level. Note changes in prompting procedure.

Date:_____

Program:_____

Therapist:_____

1._____ 6._____
2._____ 7._____
3._____ 8._____
4._____ 9._____
5._____ 10._____

_____% Correct

Comments:

Date:_____

Program:_____

Therapist:_____

1._____ 6._____
2._____ 7._____
3._____ 8._____
4._____ 9._____
5._____ 10._____

_____% Correct

Comments:

Date:_____

Program:_____

Therapist:_____

1._____ 6._____
2._____ 7._____
3._____ 8._____
4._____ 9._____
5._____ 10._____

_____% Correct

Comments:

Date:_____

Program:_____

Therapist:_____

1._____ 6._____
2._____ 7._____
3._____ 8._____
4._____ 9._____
5._____ 10._____

_____% Correct

Comments:

Date:_____

Program:_____

Therapist:_____

1._____ 6._____
2._____ 7._____
3._____ 8._____
4._____ 9._____
5._____ 10._____

_____% Correct

Comments:

Date:_____

Program:_____

Therapist:_____

1._____ 6._____
2._____ 7._____
3._____ 8._____
4._____ 9._____
5._____ 10._____

_____% Correct

Comments:

PART FOUR

How to Teach

CHAPTER SIX

Teaching New Skills to Young Children with Autism

Stephen R. Anderson

Marie Taras

Barbara O'Malley Cannon

This chapter recommends educational practices for teaching young children with autism in a home-based training program. It is intended to serve as a practical guide for parents and professionals who have little experience or formal training in the area.

The recommended practices are based largely upon the principles of Applied Behavior Analysis (ABA). Applied Behavior Analysis emphasizes employing instructional technology designed to change behavior in systematic and measurable ways. The key words of this definition are *technology, systematic,* and *measurement.* Any specific strategy can fall under the rubric of ABA as long as it is conceptually consistent with the basic principles of child development, it can be described in detail for others to use, and it can be introduced in a systematic manner that allows for accurate measurement of effectiveness. We are taking the time to make this point because there continues to be considerable misunderstanding of the ABA approach. In this chapter, we have recommended practices that have been demonstrated scientifically to work or that are at least described in sufficient detail to allow evaluation of effectiveness.

It is important to state that home-based training may not be appropriate for every child and every family. The effects on the family system, as well as the lives of its individual members, can be significant. First, it involves considerable sacrifice and commitment from everyone, with no guarantee of significantly favorable outcomes for the child with autism. Second, it may not be easy for some parents to accept the basic philosophical and practical tenets of the ABA approach. According to some, the emphasis on instructional technology, systematic intervention, and ongoing evaluation departs too much from their understanding of typical child development and normal parent-

ing practices. In short, the decision to develop an intensive home-based program is a very personal one. Parents should begin only if they are completely committed to giving the approach an *opportunity* to succeed. You cannot implement part of an ABA approach, then conclude that the entire approach failed. This would be tantamount to providing only half of a prescribed antibiotic to treat a child's ear infection, and then concluding that the medicine did not work when the child's infection did not improve.

Another word of caution: Although professionals and programs who espouse ABA methods may agree on the basic principles and general practices, the specific applications may vary within and across consultants (e.g., curricular items, number of hours, age of the child, amount of teacher-led vs. child-directed instruction). We will present in this chapter what we believe are the best applications of the ABA approach. We also have limited our suggestions to children who are more than 24 months of age and less than 6 years. Important variations in the ABA approach might occur for younger and older children (e.g., selecting more functional goals for an older child). The parents need to work with the home-based consultant to develop the most clinically sound approach for their child and their specific situation.

Finally, home-based training is largely about hope—hope that the child will acquire social and language skills similar to those of her peers, attend kindergarten, participate in normal school activities, and in the final analysis, live a normal and productive life. We can safely say that some children may achieve these goals. We also know that not all will do so, although most children will benefit, to a greater or lesser degree, from intensive home-based intervention. At this time, there is no way to predict accurately which children will achieve the most significant outcome.

Jeffrey

Jeffrey was $2\frac{1}{2}$ years old when his parents first heard the word *autism* used to explain his peculiar behavior. His life appeared to start out so normally. They remembered him to be an affectionate baby who reached each developmental milestone (e.g., smiling, reaching for objects, crawling, and walking) like any other young child. And, like any other family, they had significant hopes and aspirations for their firstborn. Their troubles began when Jeffrey's day care director commented that he seemed passive and isolated in his play. Instead of joining in with the art and play activities, he spent his time lining objects, opening and closing cabinet doors, repeatedly flushing the toilet, or simply sitting passively in a corner. By the time he was 3 years old, he spoke fewer than 50 words and rarely placed words together to form a sentence. On the other hand, his parents expressed that he seemed exceptionally smart in some areas. He could identify most colors when asked, complete complex puzzles, and count to 20. Although they did not fully understand the inconsistencies in his development, they were convinced that they needed to do something extraordinary to help him.

THE ROLE OF PARENTS

The normal process of development seems to unfold almost magically for children without a developmental disability. For their parents, it is reasonably clear that their job is to foster and support their child's development by providing a safe and caring environment, providing appropriate models, and taking advantage of the thousands of natural opportunities for imparting information. This is a job that most parents are reasonably prepared to do. In contrast, a child with autism presents a more daunting task. In the case of Jeffrey (the example provided above), his parents had few experiences to draw upon in their lives that adequately prepared them to face the significant challenges of raising a child with autism.

Most parents assume the role of either educator or advocate for their child with autism. Some are able to accomplish both. In either role, the parents typically provide the best perspective on their child's developmental history, current needs, and learning style. Furthermore, while many professionals will come and go across the child's lifetime, parents remain constant. Parents also form the foundation for learning at home, including the carryover of school programs and the teaching of relevant community skills.

We recommend that parents be empowered by learning to apply the most effective instructional methods for teaching their young child with autism,

as well as by acquiring the skills to manage behavior problems (Anderson, 1989). This requires that parents participate in the initial assessment of the child, assist in establishing specific training objectives, and provide direct instruction. Parents must understand that simply reading and intellectually understanding the recommendations in this chapter may not adequately prepare them for their application (the same can be said about untrained professionals). However, with practice, modeling, and feedback provided by a trained professional (or another trained parent), parents typically become excellent teachers. As the home-based training program develops, the parents assume an increasingly larger role in designing the child's program and monitoring his progress.

Evelyn

Evelyn was nearly $3\frac{1}{2}$ years old when her parents sought home-based services. They were concerned that she had not developed functional speech, nor did she appear to show any interest in playing with other children, including her 6-year-old sister. They were encouraged when she occasionally repeated a word or phrase from a song, but then they would never hear it again. Evelyn communicated most effectively by leading someone by the hand to the desired object or activity. She did not appear to understand what was said to her, although it was sometimes difficult to sort out understanding from her willingness to comply. If given a toy, she would often hold the object to her lips or rub it against her skin rather than play with it appropriately. If someone tried to engage her in an instructional activity, she would become very upset, crying and struggling to leave the area. She was interested in eating only a small variety of foods and refused to remain at the table while the rest of the family ate. She slept only a few hours each night but insisted on taking long naps during the day.

DECIDING WHAT TO TEACH

This topic is addressed in the preceding chapter, so we will make only a few points needed to set the stage for our discussion of how to teach. This is necessary because what you decide to teach may affect how and where the teaching occurs. Let us again refer to Evelyn and Jeffrey to illustrate our point. In the case of Evelyn, the first several months were spent teaching readiness skills (e.g., following simple instructions, imitating motor movements, sitting in a chair). Nearly all training occurred in short sessions under highly structured conditions (e.g., sitting across from each other in chairs). The teacher led all instructional exercises, using direct physical guidance as needed. He systematically faded his guidance across many sessions as Evelyn became more responsive.

Jeffrey, on the other hand, could already sit in a chair, could imitate (although inconsistently), and had labels for common objects; therefore, his educational curriculum was comparably broader, addressing all of the major skill areas from the beginning. His trainer provided some highly structured situations similar to those provided to Evelyn, but she also used natural opportunities to teach throughout the day. For instance, Jeffrey was required to ask for objects that previously were provided to him without the need to use his language. Physical guidance was rarely needed. However, other subtle instructional techniques (e.g., delayed modeling) were used to encourage greater spontaneity. As these different cases show, accurately understanding the child's current level of ability can significantly affect the instructional approach.

The first step in deciding what to teach is to gather information about the child. A variety of formal and informal assessment tools are available to guide you, including (a) an interview or survey of the individuals who know the child best (typically the parents), (b) a direct observation of the child at home, (c) the administration of formal assessment instruments, and (d) the use of commercially available curricula. Some tests and scales are more suited than others for helping to develop specific instructional targets. For example, we have found the Early Learning Accomplishment Profile (ELAP) (Glover, Priminger, & Sanford, 1988) or the Learning Accomplishment Profile (LAP) (Sanford & Zelman, 1981) to be useful. These instruments assess the child's existing skills across a variety of developmental domains and help parents and professionals to identify specific learning objectives. The Individualized Goal Selection Curriculum (IGS) (Romanczyk, Lockshin, & Matey, 1994) and the Carolina Curriculum for Children with Special Needs (Johnson-Martin, Attermeier, & Hacker, 1990) can also be used to assess current functioning, set instructional priorities, and identify specific objectives for learning. We also refer you to Chapter 5 in this book. Once the child has been assessed, identify 15–20 objectives to be targeted over the next 3–6 months. The total number is limited so that significant repetition or instructional trials occur for each objective. Start by addressing 3–5 objectives from this set, then gradually add the others as the child is able to tolerate longer and more frequent sessions.

The training curriculum should be developmentally organized (like the IGS), although common sense should always be used in establishing specific objectives. Avoid teaching skills that have no apparent relevance for enhancing current or future learning. Include the major skill areas of learning readiness, language and cognitive development, fine and gross motor skills, play, socialization, maladaptive behavior, and self-help. The curricular content should move in a linear direction from learning readiness (e.g., orients to teacher, follows instructions, remains seated in a chair, imitates motor movements) to early developing language and cognitive skills. The curriculum typically addresses those areas that immediately impede the child's ability to learn. Eventually, training addresses all skill areas, and trials on related concepts are interspersed (e.g., vocabulary items may be embedded within a play curriculum).

DEVELOPING A PLAN FOR INSTRUCTION

Figure 6.1 provides a lesson plan to teach Evelyn to imitate simple motor movements. To complete the plan, consider the answers to several important questions:

1. When will you know that the child has achieved the skill (the behavioral objective)?

2. How is the target behavior defined?

3. Where and when will training occur?

4. What materials will be needed?

5. What reinforcers will motivate the child to learn?

6. How will you measure the child's progress?

7. What are the steps for teaching the program? How will you know when to move to a new step?

8. How will instructions and materials be presented?

9. What will you do when the child responds incorrectly? How about correctly?

10. How will you encourage generalization and maintenance?

The first step in developing a plan is to specify an objective for each of the skills to be taught. For example: "When instructed ('Do this'), Evelyn will imitate 10 randomly presented motor movements with 80% accuracy across three consecutive sessions." This degree of specificity allows the trainer to objectively determine when a skill has been achieved. Behaviorally stated objectives include three major parts: (a) a statement of the condition in which the behavior will occur (e.g., "When instructed" and "randomly presented"); (b) a statement of the expected behavior (e.g., "imitate 10 motor movements"); and (c) a statement of the criteria for attainment (e.g., "with 80% accuracy across three consecutive sessions").

Child's Name: Evelyn   **Target Behavior:** Motor Imitation

Behavioral Objective: When instructed "Do this," Evelyn will imitate 10 randomly presented motor movements with 80% accuracy across three consecutive sessions.

Definition of Target Behavior: A correct imitation is defined as a response that closely matches the model provided by the trainer and occurs within 5 seconds.

Setting, Time & Activity for Teaching: During direct teaching sessions at a table.

Materials Needed: None

Reinforcer(s) Identified: Reinforcer assessments will be conducted on a daily basis. Praise, potato chips, candy, tickles, and hugs have been identified as potential reinforcers.

Measurement System: The percentage of trials correct.

Task Analysis or Step Analysis

Step	Teacher Presentation	Student Response	Consequence
1	Teacher says, "Do this" while clapping and then physically helps student to clap	Student claps hands with physical guidance	Teacher delivers reinforcer if response is correct
2	Teacher says, "Do this" while clapping and provides a partial prompt for student to clap	Student claps hands with partial prompt	Teacher delivers reinforcer if response is correct If no response, provide full physical guidance, no reinforcement
3	Teacher says, "Do this" while clapping	Student claps hands	Teacher delivers reinforcer for correct responses If no response or incorrect response, teacher provides full physical guidance with no reinforcement
4	Repeat steps 1–3 for the response arms up, while randomizing presentation with clap hands	Student imitates movements	Teacher delivers reinforcer for correct responses If no response or incorrect response, teacher provides full physical guidance with no reinforcement
5	Repeat steps 1–4 for the following motor movements: pat legs, touch head, stomp feet, touch nose, arms out, pat belly, shake head, touch ears	Student imitates movements	Teacher delivers reinforcer for correct responses If no response or incorrect response, teacher provides full physical guidance, no reinforcement

Assessing Generalization

	Cues	Materials	Setting	Persons
1	"You do"	N.A.	Music	Mom
2	"Do the same"		Bedroom	Dad
3	Song w/words & actions		School	Neighbor

Postchecks (Dates):

Week 1	Week 2	Week 3	Week 4	Week 5	Week 6
1/12/95	1/19/95	1/26/95			

Start Date	End Date	Date Closed
9/15/94	1/12/95	1/26/95

Figure 6.1. Sample lesson plan for teaching Evelyn motor imitation.

A lesson plan also provides a definition of the target behavior. Normally this is needed most when the skill is very complex (e.g., positive social interactions) or when targeting the reduction of problem behaviors (e.g., defining tantrums). A clear description of the behavior helps to ensure consistency in the implementation of treatment programs and identifies what responses should result in positive reinforcement. Consistent administration of consequences helps the child learn correct vs. incorrect responses and acceptable vs. unacceptable behavior.

For the next part of the plan, specify where the training will occur and under what conditions. In the case of Jeffrey, the trainer chose naturally occurring opportunities to teach him to request common items using words already in his vocabulary. On the other hand, if the number of natural opportunities had been low, she would have decided to use a combination of natural and contrived activity-based situations for the instructional context (e.g., engaging in a cooking activity and placing many of the needed ingredients out of reach). Again, clearly specifying in writing the instructional context fosters consistency across multiple trainers.

When describing the instructional context, visualize three points along a continuum. We refer to the three points as follows: (a) direct teaching, (b) activity-based instruction, and (c) incidental teaching. We must admit in advance that the distinction gets somewhat blurred at times. In direct teaching, the teacher maintains unusually tight control over the instructional activities. The teacher and student often sit face-to-face, and trials are presented in rapid succession. In activity-based instruction, the instructional trials are embedded within a specific activity. For example, language trials might be embedded within an art activity. The teacher may intentionally fail to provide all the materials and teach the child to ask for them. Both direct teaching and activity-based instruction are typically teacher led (i.e., the teacher controls the materials, asks questions, and so on). In contrast, incidental teaching typically involves child-directed activities. The trainer observes and interacts with the child and uses any naturally occurring opportunities to provide relevant instruction (e.g., the child indicates that he wants a drink by pointing to the refrigerator, and the trainer models the correct language). As you might surmise, direct teaching sessions are more highly structured and allow for more repetition or trials than either activity-based instruction or incidental teaching. On the other hand, activity-based instruction and incidental teaching often result in greater generalization of skills taught. All three strategies are important and should be used at different times depending upon what specific skill is being

taught and the child's ability. For example, it may be necessary to teach vocabulary to a highly distractible child using direct teaching methods. Then, once a small vocabulary has been acquired, activity-based instruction and incidental teaching methods should be used to make the skill functional.

The remaining areas of the lesson plan (selecting reinforcers, measuring progress, completing a list of training steps, and assessing generalization and maintenance) will be discussed later in this chapter. We will conclude this section by simply saying that thoughtful planning will result in greater consistency across trainers and will lead to a more successful outcome for the child.

STRUCTURING THE LEARNING ENVIRONMENT

The physical environment must be properly designed to maximize any intervention efforts. In short, be prepared. For children like Evelyn, the first day of home-based training may be the first time they have been required to sit and attend for more than a minute or two. You can expect that most children will resist your efforts by trying to leave the area, crying, and throwing a tantrum, and they may even exhibit aggression and self-injury. You can minimize or avoid this by following a few simple guidelines.

First, make the sessions fun. Remain highly animated, provide nearly constant praise for staying in the chair, and blend work demands and play activities. Start by making sessions very short (5–10 minutes), with breaks of similar length. Initially, we allow children to do whatever they want during the breaks, but eventually this time also should become a context for instruction. In spite of your best plans, many children will still protest the initial intervention efforts (we will deal with this in a later section).

Choose a quiet room for instruction that is free of distractions. Provide two child-size chairs (one for the trainer and one for the child) and a table for instructional materials and reinforcers. Leave the materials out of the child's reach. Also, remember to bring the lesson plans relevant to the tasks to be taught, as well as data sheets for monitoring progress. We typically put these into a notebook with labeled dividers for each program area (e.g., language, self-help, learning readiness) and tabs for each program.

The initial instructional activities should involve a task the child is already capable of performing. Emphasize skills such as remaining in the chair and following simple instructions. Avoid tasks involving materials that can be easily broken, thrown, or inappropriately used.

In Jeffrey's case, we started with the imitation of simple motor movements (e.g., "Do this": trainer touches her nose), because this was an emerging skill and was easy to prompt.

Avoid using materials or reinforcers that are difficult for you to give and take away. On the one hand, items the child plays with frequently probably are reinforcing to him or her. On the other hand, the child may respond very dramatically if the item is removed and controlled by you. Striking a balance here can sometimes be a little tricky. For instance, Evelyn often carried small Disney characters that she would place in neat rows. When we attempted to withhold them and provide them for appropriate sitting, she became extremely upset and was unable to remain quiet, even for a few seconds. After trying for several days, we decided to put the toys out of sight, and we identified other reinforcers. Fortunately, we were able to reintroduce the toys several weeks later. In the long run, if the reinforcers you have chosen seem to be interfering with the child's attention more than motivating the child to respond, then put the objects away and out of sight (at least during sessions) until a later point in the program.

Begin each direct teaching session by placing the two chairs directly in front of each other with the trainer and child sitting face-to-face. Sit very close to the child with his legs resting between your legs. You may find it necessary to wrap your legs and feet around the legs of the child's chair to prevent him from pushing away. The child should be praised frequently for simply staying in the chair, making eye contact, and following instructions. If the child attempts to leave the chair, physically prompt him back.

As the child becomes more compliant, move the table closer to the chairs. Eventually, you and the child should sit at the table on adjacent sides. Now begin to introduce additional materials and expand the content of the training curriculum. Then begin sometimes to introduce training trials at more natural times, using activity-based instruction and incidental teaching techniques. For example, once Evelyn is imitating motor actions, integrate her new skill into a musical activity or game. In short, all activities of the day become a stage for instruction and learning.

MOTIVATING YOUR CHILD TO LEARN

Learning does not come easily for a child with autism. The things that motivate most children (e.g., receiving praise from their parents, imitating peers, successfully completing a task) do not appear to motivate many children like Jeffrey and Evelyn; therefore, it is necessary to identify and use more extrinsic rewards (we will use the word *reinforcers*) to motivate the child to attend and respond to instruction. The use of a planned reinforcement system may be the most important thing that you do to help your child to learn. It may at times seem unnatural and extraordinary, but it must be done to foster and maintain new skills.

Almost any behavior has an obvious or not-so-obvious payoff for adults and children. For instance, we ask questions to get answers, we work to receive a paycheck, and we complete homework assignments to improve our grades. All of these outcomes represent the use of reinforcement. This principle of ABA states that behavior that is followed by a reinforcing consequence is more likely to happen again. In short, a trainer who wants to increase the future occurrence of desirable behavior should reinforce it.

There are many different kinds of reinforcers. The most important thing to remember is that they must be individualized. What may be a reinforcer for one child may not be for another. Reinforcers are typically perceived as positive objects or activities, such as food, hugs, kisses, praise, or stickers. What defines a reinforcer, however, is not what others perceive as its positive qualities, but whether it increases the occurrence of the behavior it follows. Therefore, a variety of objects and activities, however unusual, may be reinforcing to a particular individual (e.g., access to a fan, a flashlight, a favorite article of clothing).

When teaching a child a new skill, reinforce every correct or desired response. For example, each time that Evelyn correctly imitated the trainer's model, she received tickles, hugs, and a small piece of candy. As her performance improved, the frequency and the amount of reinforcers were reduced or faded to an intermittent schedule (i.e., every second or third response resulted in praise). It has been demonstrated that an intermittent schedule of reinforcement results in more lasting change.

Identify reinforcers by observing the child to see what she chooses to do during free time, asking directly, presenting several choices and asking the child to choose one, and conducting a reinforcer assessment (Dyer, 1987). In a reinforcer assessment, a variety of potentially reinforcing items (e.g., toys, crayons, food) are presented one at a time. The reinforcing value of the object is evaluated by noting whether the child reaches for it, manipulates it, resists when it is taken away, and so on. You should conduct a reinforcer assessment at least daily, but you may need to do so even more frequently if the child is difficult to motivate. Once several reinforcers have been identified, they are held by the trainer and delivered one at a time contingent upon correct responses to specific instructional activities.

Praise is the most natural, convenient, and universal reinforcer that you can use. Unfortunately, praise is not naturally reinforcing to many children with autism. Nevertheless, by providing it simultaneously with the delivery of small portions of food or other reinforcing consequences, it also may gain reinforcement value to the child. Make your praise statement very specific and descriptive of the target behavior (e.g., "Good sitting" vs. "Good boy").

USING GOOD INSTRUCTIONAL METHODS

During the last 20 years we have learned a great deal about how best to instruct children with developmental disabilities, including autism. (See Appendix A for a list of references that discuss teaching techniques in greater detail.) These instructional methods are guided by the core principles of ABA and have been validated by many well-controlled research studies. We will discuss here several methods that increase the likelihood that a child will give the desired response, so that it can be reinforced and ultimately result in learning.

Discrete-Trial Methods

Throughout intervention, employ good, discrete-trial methodology. Although discrete-trial methods are generally associated with direct teaching, they also are important for activity-based instruction and incidental teaching. A good discrete trial consists of four parts: (a) the trainer's presentation, (b) the child's response, (c) the consequence, and (d) a short pause between the consequence and the next instruction (between-trials interval).

Instructions

How you state the instruction may influence whether it is followed. If the child is paying attention, hears the instruction, and it is within his abilities, he is more likely to follow it. Prior to giving the instruction, get the child's attention (e.g., say the child's name, make eye contact, touch the child). The instruction should be clear, concise, phrased as a statement, and given only once. If the instruction contains too many words, the child may not attend to the key words. Here is an example of a poor instruction: "Evelyn, can you stop running around and sit down over here so mommy can put your shoes on?" In contrast, a good instruction would be, "Evelyn, sit down."

When the child is first learning to respond to an instruction, keep the wording the same each time it is given; otherwise, each variation might be perceived by the child as a different instruction. After the child demonstrates initial understanding of the instruction, vary it systematically to enhance generalization (this is discussed further under "Programming Generalization").

Child's Response

In response to the adult's instruction, the child may respond in one of three ways: correctly, incorrectly, or not at all. In general, allow approximately 3–5 seconds for the child to initiate his response. If the child begins to respond incorrectly or engages in inappropriate or competing behaviors (e.g., attempts to leave the seat), immediately provide a consequence.

Consequences

The consequence, or the adult's response, will vary depending upon the child's response. If the child responds correctly, immediately reinforce the response with enthusiastic praise in combination with any other identified reinforcers (e.g., food, hugs, tickles).

If the child responds incorrectly or does not respond at all, provide an effective prompt or guidance. For example, provide mild verbal feedback ("No," or "Wrong," or repeat the instruction) while physically guiding the child to respond (this is called a *correction trial*). Physical guidance may be a touch on the arm or hand, or it can mean hand-over-hand assistance. The most important point is that whatever you choose, it should work the first time. Repeating the direction or repeating the prompt several times may teach the child that he does not need to respond the first time you ask. The physical prompt helps the child learn what your words mean. If he understands but chooses not to respond, the physical guidance teaches that you expect him to comply. Either way the child benefits. Initially, less enthusiastic praise can be given following the correction trial. When it becomes evident that he is beginning to understand what you are asking him to do, reserve reinforcement only for correct responses that occur following the first request (i.e., before the correction trial).

Between-Trials Interval

The period between the consequence (reinforcement or correction) and the next instruction is called the between-trials interval. Include a very discrete pause of 3–5 seconds between the consequence and the next trial. This helps you define for the child that you have ended one request and are now delivering a new one. Begin each new request with a clear and concise instruction and the child's attention. During the be-tween-trial interval, praise the child for appropriate sitting and allow her a few moments to consume or play with the reinforcer. At the same time, record the child's response to the last trial on the data sheet and organize the instructions and materials needed for the next presentation.

Teaching Methods

Sometimes the behavior that you want to teach does not occur or does not occur often enough to be rein-forced. For example, we could not increase Evelyn's verbalizations using reinforcement alone, because we could not reinforce a behavior that never or rarely oc-curred. Fortunately, there are a variety of accepted teaching methods to encourage new behaviors. In this section we discuss the techniques of shaping, prompt-ing, and prompt fading. The method chosen must be appropriate for the child's current level of functioning, her learning style, and the skill to be taught.

Shaping

Shaping is a technique that is used when the child ini-tially does not have the desired skill in her repertoire. This method takes advantage of related responses the child already has, reinforces those, and then only re-inforces closer and closer approximations to the de-sired response. For example, to shape Evelyn's imita-tion of words, the trainer first reinforced imitating the trainer's mouth movements (e.g., opening her mouth, pursing her lips to blow, and so on). Once she was able to consistently imitate mouth movements, Evelyn re-ceived reinforcers for producing any sound, whether it matched the trainer's verbalization or not. Gradually, the trainer required closer and closer approximations of the modeled word. As this example demonstrates, shaping and reinforcement strategies were used in combination to achieve the desired goal. Keep in mind that shaping techniques require a great deal of patience. It often takes weeks or months to achieve the desired results.

Prompting

Some children need extra help to perform the desired skill or behavior so that you can reinforce it. Prompting is an instructional technique that helps the child to make the correct response. You can give prompts at the same time as the instruction (e.g., modeling the desired response), during the child's response to help minimize errors, or after the child's incorrect response to show him the expected answer. One risk of using prompts is that the child may become dependent on

them for correct responding. You can foster indepen-dence by using a technique called *prompt fading*, which is discussed in the next section.

There are several types of prompts: verbal, mod-eling, physical, and gestural and position cues. Verbal prompts provide the child with a verbal instruction, cue, or model for the desired response. For example, the trainer initially taught Jeffrey to label new objects by holding up an object and saying "Cup. What is this?" The label was gradually faded leaving only the ques-tion "What is this?" The trainer also used verbal prompting to teach Jeffrey to take turns. After he com-pleted his turn in a game, she paused briefly and then said "It's my turn," as a prompt for Jeffrey to pass the dice. Again, this verbal prompt was eventually faded.

Modeling consists of actually demonstrating the correct response for the child. For example, when teaching an appropriate greeting skill, the trainer may show the child how to shake another person's hand following an introduction. We must note, however, that a child can only benefit from modeling if he is able to imitate.

Physical prompts consist of physically guiding the child through all or part of the desired response. The degree of physical assistance varies from complete hand-over-hand to a light touch at the shoulder to ini-tiate the response (i.e., partial prompt). Many children with autism need a great deal of physical prompting. For example, the trainer used full physical assistance to teach Evelyn to follow a few simple instructions. She first gave the instruction (e.g., "Stand up"), paused briefly, provided a full physical prompt, and reinforced responding without resistance. Physical prompts were faded gradually until Evelyn was standing up in response to a gesture.

Gestural cues are actions such as pointing to, look-ing at, moving, or touching an item to indicate the cor-rect response (e.g., the trainer may point to the circle while simultaneously giving the instruction "Point to the circle"). Position cues also occur prior to or si-multaneously with the trainer's instruction. When us-ing position cues, you should place the correct item in an advantageous position in relation to the child (e.g., when asking the child to point to the item that is red, place the red item closer to the child than those of other colors).

Prompt Fading

As we have mentioned, the child may become depen-dent on prompts for correct responding. Therefore, use prompts in the initial stages of learning and gradually fade them as progress occurs. There are four methods of fading prompts: graduated guidance, most-to-least prompting, least-to-most prompting, and time delay.

The technique of *graduated guidance* is used to progressively fade physical guidance. One way to accomplish this is gradually to reduce the amount of physical effort that you exert to help the child to respond. For example, Evelyn was taught to point to one of two objects to indicate preference. Initially, a full physical prompt (hand-over-hand) was used to obtain the desired response. Next, the trainer progressively changed from a hand-over-hand prompt to a light touch on top of the hand by applying less and less effort. This occurred very slowly over many sessions. The trainer also could have chosen a slightly different approach. Instead of applying progressively less effort directly to the hand, he could have gradually moved the placement of his physical prompt away from the hand by moving from a prompt given hand-over-hand to a prompt to her wrist, then to her forearm, and so on until the prompt was no longer needed.

The *most-to-least prompting* strategy begins with a full physical prompt for the desired response, then fades to a gesture or model, and ends with the verbal instruction. Let us refer again to our program to teach Evelyn to follow simple instructions. First, the trainer provided the instruction (e.g., "Stand up") followed by a full physical prompt. Next, he provided the instruction with a gesture (e.g., a sweep of his hand and arm upward) as a cue to stand. Finally, the gesture was faded (e.g., a smaller sweep of the hand alone) until the response was controlled by the instruction only.

Least-to-most prompting starts off by giving the child the opportunity to respond independently, then the trainer progressively increases the amount of assistance provided until the child responds. This is a good technique when the goal is to encourage greater spontaneity (e.g., teaching Jeffrey to ask for desired objects during natural times). It is not a good technique for teaching brand-new response, however, because it can allow the child to make too many errors, and it can encourage dependence on prompts. The hierarchy typically begins with a brief delay and progresses to a verbal prompt or model. If that level of prompting is unsuccessful, a physical prompt may be used when it is appropriate. For example, when Jeffrey indicated that he wanted a drink (by pointing to the pitcher of juice), the trainer first used a simple time delay. He looked at Jeffrey and paused to determine if Jeffrey would use his words to ask. *Time delay* fades the use of verbal and physical prompts by inserting gradually longer intervals of time between the instruction and the delivery of the prompt. If he did not respond during the time delay, the trainer next said "What do you want?" If there was still no response, the trainer modeled "Say 'want juice.'" In this particular example, a physical prompt did not apply.

DEVELOPING THE SPECIFIC STEPS FOR INSTRUCTION

In order to teach a complex skill, you need to break it into a series of smaller, more manageable steps. We will refer to the delineation of steps as either a *step analysis* or a *task analysis*. Learning is enhanced because these smaller steps lead to greater success for the child. When writing the steps for your lesson plan, try to view the task from the child's point of view. How would she learn a new task? That is, how can you break the task down into steps that reduce the number of response errors, promote more rapid learning, minimize frustration, and create a more positive atmosphere for the child? The ABA techniques of shaping, prompting, and prompt fading can be used individually and collectively to break the task into a series of steps. Later we will discuss a different technique, called *chaining*, that you can use to enhance the child's learning.

Delineating Steps Using the Technique of Shaping

The steps of a program may be delineated by gradually increasing or decreasing what the child must do before reinforcement is delivered. For example, you could require that the child work or play for progressively longer periods of time, or with fewer prompts from an adult, or with greater productivity. We refer to this kind of program as a *step analysis*. For example, we developed an objective to teach Jeffrey to play more independently (i.e., when presented with three sets of toys and asked to play, Jeffrey will play appropriately for 15 minutes with two or fewer prompts across three consecutive sessions). From our assessment, we concluded that prior to the start of instruction, Jeffrey was able to play only about 4 or 5 minutes, and several prompts were needed to achieve even this level of performance. Thus, if we simply waited for Jeffrey to demonstrate the target response of 15 minutes, few if any responses could be reinforced. We knew that the task would have to be broken down into a step analysis so that some correct responding would occur and could be reinforced. We decided to progressively increase the amount of time Jeffrey needed to play before a reinforcer was delivered. We taught one step at a time until he achieved the predetermined criterion. The steps were as follows:

Step 1: Jeffrey will play for 3 minutes with two or fewer prompts.

Step 2: Jeffrey will play for 5 minutes with two or fewer prompts.

Step 3: Jeffrey will play for 10 minutes with two or fewer prompts.

Step 4: Jeffrey will play for 13 minutes with two or fewer prompts.

Step 5: Jeffrey will play for 15 minutes with two or fewer prompts.

We used a similar step analysis to teach Evelyn to color, with the following objective: When presented with crayons, a picture to color, and the instruction "Color," Evelyn will color the picture with one or fewer prompts across three consecutive sessions. The step analysis for Evelyn was as follows:

Step 1: Evelyn will color ¼ of the picture with one or no prompts.

Step 2: Evelyn will color ½ of the picture with one or no prompts.

Step 3: Evelyn will color ¾ of the picture with one or no prompts.

Step 4: Evelyn will color the entire picture with one or no prompts.

As we mentioned earlier, the exact sequence and number of steps in the step analysis must be individualized. Some children may need many steps to learn a new skill, while others may require far fewer steps to accomplish the same goal. You may need to revise your step analysis if the child does not progress on a particular step or series of steps.

Delineating Steps Using the Techniques of Prompting and Prompt Fading

Let us again refer to our program to teach Evelyn to follow simple instructions to illustrate how the techniques of prompting and prompt fading would be used to develop a step analysis. The objective was as follows: Evelyn will follow four simple instructions given by an adult at least 80% of the time across three consecutive sessions of ten trials each. The results of our assessment showed that Evelyn was unable to follow any of the targeted instructions (i.e., "Come here," "Stand up," "Sit down," and "Give me"). Therefore, we decided to begin with a full physical prompt and to fade our prompts systematically as Evelyn became more independent. We also decided to introduce one instruction at a time to minimize confusion and errors. Within each instruction we used the following step analysis: (a) full physical prompt, (b) touch

prompt behind the arm, (c) touch prompt at the shoulder, (d) gesture near the shoulder, and (e) independent. Here are examples of each of the steps to illustrate the process.

In Step 1, the trainer gave the instruction "Stand up" and immediately provided a full physical prompt by placing his hands on the child's upper arms bringing her to a standing position. Initially Evelyn was reinforced for responding even if she resisted the prompt. Eventually, only cooperative responses were reinforced. The step was considered mastered (i.e., she was ready to move on to the next step) when she met the program criterion of "at least 80% of the time across three consecutive sessions of ten trials each."

In Step 2, the trainer provided a partial prompt by placing his fingers at the back of Evelyn's upper arm and nudging her gently. A correct response was scored if Evelyn stood up within 3–5 seconds. An error was scored if a greater degree of prompting was needed (e.g., full physical prompt). The criterion for movement to the next step was the same as that given for Step 1.

In Step 3, the trainer provided a partial prompt by placing his fingers at the back of Evelyn's shoulder and nudging her gently. The criterion for movement to the next step was consistent with Steps 1 and 2. The trainer continued in this manner until all of the steps were completed.

Delineating Steps Using the Technique of Chaining

Chaining is the linking together of component skills to comprise an entire, more complex skill. A description of the specific steps in the chain is referred to as a *task analysis*. Like the step analyses that we have been discussing, a task analysis is a description of the sequence of behaviors needed to perform a task. It is most often associated with teaching self-help skills, although it is relevant to any task in which steps are performed in a specific order (this is what distinguishes it from a step analysis). To develop the list of steps in a task analysis, look at the skill and write down all the separate steps it takes to complete the entire task. A sample task analysis for washing hands is presented in Table 6.1.

There are two types of chaining methods: forward and backward. *Forward chaining* begins by teaching the first step of the task analysis, while physically guiding the child through the remaining steps. After the child masters the first step, training begins with the second step, while prompting continues for the remaining steps of the chain. This procedure is repeated

Table 6.1.
Task Analysis of Hand Washing

Step	1:	Turns on cold water
Step	2:	Turns on hot water
Step	3:	Places hands under water
Step	4:	Gets soap
Step	5:	Rubs soap between hands
Step	6:	Puts soap down
Step	7:	Rubs front of hands together
Step	8:	Rubs back of right hand
Step	9:	Rubs back of left hand
Step	10:	Places hands under water
Step	11:	Rubs front of hands together
Step	12:	Rubs back of right hand
Step	13:	Rubs back of left hand
Step	14:	Turns off warm water
Step	15:	Turns off cold water

for each step until the child can independently perform all steps of the task analysis. For example, when Evelyn was taught to use a spoon to eat, grasping the spoon was taught first (Step 1 of the task analysis). The trainer gave the instruction "Use your spoon" and then used prompting, prompt fading, and reinforcement techniques to teach the step. The remaining steps of the chain were completed with hand-over-hand guidance. This eliminated any potential errors. When Evelyn had mastered grasping the spoon, then Step 2 (i.e., bringing the spoon to her mouth) was trained in combination with Step 1. Again, the rest of the steps in the task analysis were physically prompted to prevent errors. We continued in this manner until all steps were completed independently and linked together in a single chain.

Backward chaining uses the same principle as forward chaining, but the steps are taught in reverse sequence; that is, training begins with the last step of the task analysis and works toward the first. Using the task analysis provided in Table 6.1, the trainer physically guided Jeffrey through Steps 1–14, preventing any errors. Prior to the last step (turns off cold water), she paused to give Jeffrey an opportunity to complete the step independently. If guidance was needed, the trainer provided a least-to-most prompting sequence to teach the step. When Jeffrey was consistently performing the last step independently, the trainer introduced Step 14 (turns off warm water). The trainer continued in this manner until all steps were trained and the complex skill of hand washing was learned.

PROGRAMMING GENERALIZATION

A common characteristic of children with autism is their inability to generalize newly learned skills to circumstances different than those that were present during training. Although generalization to other times, places, and with new people may occur naturally, it is not always predictable. For example, children may learn to label common objects, but rarely use the words to request the items; they may be toilet trained at home but not at school; they may follow instructions given by their teachers but not their parents; and they may respond to the greeting "Hi" but not "Hello."

During initial teaching situations, the trainer often maintains unusually tight control over the instructions provided, the materials presented, the seating arrangement, and other setting conditions. This level of control is often needed to help children attend to the task and to minimize distractions. On the other hand, training in this restrictive manner may lead to less generalization. Thus, before a skill is considered learned, the trainer must determine whether the skill has generalized across cues, settings, and people. In the lesson plan shown in Figure 6.1, we suggest that you indicate how you plan to assess generalization.

If your assessment indicates that generalization has not occurred, the best way to encourage it is to expand the conditions (e.g., the range of materials, settings, and cues) that were initially a part of training. For example, if Jeffrey is able to label only when working with his trainer, then we should incorporate trials at other times of the day, in different rooms of the house, with different people, and so on. Once you have taught across several different conditions, the target skill is more likely to occur in new situations as well. We often assess and program for generalization after the target skill has been achieved. However, for more capable children (like Jeffrey) it is possible to begin programming for generalization as the skill is emerging. For example, we taught Jeffrey to label common objects under direct teaching conditions but simultaneously used naturally occurring times throughout the day as additional opportunities for instruction (incidental teaching). The reader should refer to Stokes and Osnes (1988) for a complete discussion of this issue.

PROMOTING LASTING CHANGE

Until now, we have recommended that each time the child demonstrates the desired skill, a reinforcer is given. Once a skill has been acquired, maintenance and generalization can be enhanced by gradually fading the frequency and type of reinforcement. This can be accomplished by following some, but not all, correct or appropriate responses with a reinforcer (e.g., every third correct imitation), and by changing to more natural reinforcers (e.g., praise instead of food).

After reinforcers have been faded and the child has generalized the skill, a postcheck (or maintenance phase) is introduced. During this phase, the frequency of training trials is reduced. We typically assess maintenance once a week across a 3- to 6-week period (see Figure 6.1). If data indicate that the child has not maintained the skill, then we repeat the last phase of training and the generalization conditions. If data indicate that the skill has been maintained for at least 3 weeks, we consider it mastered. Ongoing data-collection systems are then eliminated or drastically reduced. Nevertheless, we continue to practice and encourage the use of this skill whenever it is appropriate.

ASSESSING PROGRESS AND REVISING INSTRUCTION

Applied Behavior Analysis stresses direct measurement of the child's performance. Direct evaluation is important because it allows the trainer to determine the child's progress, and it guides objective, clinical decision making. Trainers and parents who do not collect data may continue ineffective intervention programs or discontinue programs prematurely. In addition, it is important to show that the programs actually are producing the skill developments as claimed. We could be stealing valuable time from the child if in fact the gains reported are not occurring.

A variety of recording strategies are available, and only a few will be described here; see Cooper, Heron, and Heward (1987) for additional consideration of recording strategies. The most commonly used measurement method is a frequency count (e.g., number of prompts) and its variations (e.g., percentage correct). A frequency recording simply involves tallying or counting each occurrence of the target behavior. For example, the trainer might record the number of times the child makes eye contact, the number of bites of food eaten, or the number of prompts required to get the child to brush his teeth. Typically, for skill-development programs, the frequency of a response is measured either by recording the number of prompts required to complete the task or the percentage of correct trials (i.e., number of correct responses divided by the number of opportunities, multiplied by 100%). For example, if the child correctly imitates seven times out of ten trials, convert this to a percentage (e.g., $7/10 = .70 \times 100\% = 70\%$). It is not necessary to score the child's response to every trial. You can obtain a sample of trials for each instructional program (e.g., the first 10–20 trials each day) to evaluate progress.

After data are collected, graph it for visual inspection. The reader again is referred to Cooper, Heron, and Heward (1987) for a complete discussion of graphing methods. Graphing provides a meaningful way of monitoring changes in behaviors and skills. It also is an efficient way to organize, store, summarize, interpret, and communicate the results of intervention to other parties.

Use the collected data for treatment planning, decision making, and evaluating the effectiveness of each intervention. Actually, data collection should begin prior to your first day of intervention. We typically obtain a preintervention, or *baseline,* measure of the child's performance. Baseline data provide the "before" picture with which to compare the treatment results (the "after" picture). In addition, a baseline can provide information on the child's current level of functioning. In turn this information can assist you in developing realistic objectives, establishing performance criteria, and developing task and step analyses. Collect baseline data for a minimum of three data points (i.e., sessions) and continue until a stable baseline is achieved.

Once you begin instructional sessions, the data will help you to determine when the child is ready to move to the next step within the step or task analysis that has been developed. We often use a step criterion of 80% accuracy for three consecutive sessions. If you notice that after many sessions the child is not making progress, then you will need to develop smaller intermediate teaching steps. In short, your step or task analysis should be revised. Finally, use the data to determine when the objective has been achieved and when generalization and maintenance have been demonstrated.

DEALING WITH THE RESISTANT CHILD

Initial sessions for a child with autism can be extremely difficult. One of the defining characteristics of many of the children with autism is their resistance to instruction. This becomes most evident during the first minutes of intervention. As soon as you begin to set limits (e.g., containing the child in the chair), the child may verbally and physically resist.

Evelyn was described by her parents as a child on the move. Her typical day was spent moving quickly from one activity to another. She rarely remained seated for more than a few minutes until she fell asleep at night. As soon as the trainer tried to contain her in a chair for instruction, she began to cry, tried to stand up, and physically resisted the trainer's physical prompts to keep her seated. This resistance was a behavior her parents had indicated occurred often throughout the day (e.g., she would not remain seated for meals). They admitted that Evelyn usually would win those battles and was allowed to move, stand, and walk as she wanted; that is, she was allowed to escape from tasks or activities to situations she found more comfortable and possibly less demanding. Because she lacked speech, her only way to communicate her desire to escape was her physical resistance and tantrums.

Her trainer decided to approach this problem in a multidimensional way. First, he tried to select objects as reinforcers that he was reasonably sure Evelyn wanted. Second, he decided to keep the sessions very short and to expand them as Evelyn become more tolerant of the instructional demands. Third, he provided reinforcers contingent upon her remaining in the chair without crying and trying to get up. Initially this meant that he physically guided Evelyn to the chair, sat her down, reinforced following directions, then immediately let her get up. Gradually, the amount of time that Evelyn needed to remain seated before getting up was expanded. If she began to throw a tantrum while in the chair, it was ignored until she was quiet. Simple tasks were gradually introduced into the sessions. At first the tantrums were long and very difficult, in spite of the trainer's preventive measures. However, within and across sessions Evelyn began to throw tantrums less and for shorter periods of time.

This approach to dealing with extreme resistance to instruction has been very successful for many young children with autism. It enables them to learn that crying and other problem behaviors will no longer function to get them out of the session demands. Sometimes, positive results can be enhanced by teaching the child an appropriate alternative skill that replaces the problem behavior (e.g., we taught Evelyn to use a manual sign to indicate that she wanted a break). In other situations, the behavior problems persist, and more complicated intervention strategies may be necessary. Appendix A contains a list of relevant publications.

SUMMARY

In conclusion, we have herein provided a brief summary of educational practices that have been demonstrated to work with children having autism. It is not a comprehensive discussion. Each child with autism brings to the situation unique biology, learning experiences, and skills. The child's disability may affect the course of training as much as training affects the child's course of development. Most instructional programs include many subtleties that were developed and shaped to meet individual needs. We have tried to address potential variations by providing a couple of examples of children with autism, each at a different point along the continuum of abilities. Our aim has been to provide a set of best practices that will enable the reader to begin a successful program for any child. However, along the way most parents and professionals will need the advice of a good ABA-trained consultant in order to maintain an effective program.

USEFUL BOOKS ON APPLIED BEHAVIOR ANALYSIS

Baker, B. L., & Brightman, A. J. (1989). *Steps to independence: A skills training guide for parents and teachers of children with special needs.* Baltimore: Paul H. Brookes.

Cooper, J. O., Heron, T. E., & Heward, W. L. (1987). *Applied behavior analysis.* Columbus, OH: Merrill.

Foxx, R. M. (1982). *Increasing behaviors of severely retarded and autistic persons.* Champaign, IL: Research Press.

Foxx, R. M. (1982). *Decreasing behaviors of persons with severe retardation and autism.* Champaign, IL: Research Press.

Horner, R. H., Dunlap, G., & Koegel, R. L. (1988). *Generalization and maintenance: Life-style changes in applied settings.* Baltimore: Paul H. Brookes.

Koegel, R. L., Rincover, A., & Egel, A. L. (1982). *Educating and understanding autistic children.* Boston: College-Hill Press.

Lovaas, O. I. (1983). *Teaching developmentally disabled children: The ME book.* Austin, TX: PRO-ED.

Snell, M. E., (Ed.). (1993). *Instruction of students with severe disabilities* (4th ed.). New York: Merrill.

Sulzer-Azaroff, B., & Mayer, G. (1991). *Behavior analysis for lasting change.* Orlando, FL: Holt, Rinehart and Winston.

REFERENCES

Anderson, S. R. (1989). Training parents of autistic children. In B. L. Baker (Ed.), *Parent training and developmental disabilities* (Monograph of the American Association on Mental Deficiency, No. 13).

Cooper, J. O., Heron, T. E., & Heward, W. L. (1987). *Applied behavior analysis.* Columbus, OH: Merrill.

Dyer, K. (1987). The competition of autistic stereotyped behavior with usual and specially assessed reinforcers. *Research in Developmental Disabilities, 8,* 606–626.

Glover, M. E., Priminger, J. L., & Sanford, A. R. (1988). *The early learning accomplishment profile.* Winston-Salem, NC: Kaplan Press.

Johnson-Martin, N. M., Attermeier, S. M., & Hacker, B. (1990). *The Carolina curriculum for preschoolers with special needs.* Baltimore: Paul H. Brookes.

Romanczyk, R. G., Lockshin, S., & Matey, L. (1994). *The individualized goal selection curriculum (IGS).* Appalachian, NY: Clinical Behavior Therapy Associates.

Sanford, A. R., & Zelman, J. G. (1981). *The learning accomplishment profile* (Rev. ed.). Lewisville, NC: Kaplan Press.

Stokes, T. F., & Osnes, P. G. (1988). The developing applied technology of generalization and maintenance. In R. H. Horner, G. Dunlap, & R. L. Koegel (Eds.), *Generalization and maintenance: Life-style changes in applied settings* (pp. 5–19). Baltimore: Paul H. Brookes.

CHAPTER SEVEN

Behavioral Analysis and Assessment

The Cornerstone to Effectiveness

Raymond G. Romanczyk

The field of autism is strongly associated with a great number of fads and movements that over the last several decades have promised much but consistently failed to deliver in the light of objective evaluation (Delmolino & Romanczyk, 1995; Romanczyk, 1994). In contrast, however, the behavioral approach, (also known as behavior modification, behavior therapy, or Applied Behavior Analysis), with its roots strongly within a research/academic framework, has often been grossly misunderstood, yet is an effective approach that has only recently received the positive attention it deserves (see Maurice, 1993).

Over the past three decades, consistent and systematic research projects have demonstrated the utility of the behavioral approach, and many recent, larger-scale outcome studies have consistently demonstrated that this approach yields significant benefits for children with autism (Harris & Handleman, 1994). The most important of these outcome studies, which has sparked the enthusiasm that has resulted in the demand for a book such as this one, is the outcome study by Ivar Lovaas (1987). His long-term outcome study clearly demonstrated the magnitude of positive change that is possible and has set a new standard against which to compare existing treatment approaches (McEachin, Smith, & Lovaas, 1993).

THE IMPORTANCE OF INDIVIDUALIZATION

Intervention programs must be tailored for the individual child using the specific information, principles, and strategies of behavioral research. The specifics of programs will be different for different children. Assessment and evaluation of your child as an individual, not simply in a comparison to the "typical" child thus becomes a central task. The rigid adoption of a technique-oriented approach can have severe detrimental effects. Children with autism are often characterized by idiosyncratic learning styles and overly rigid learning styles. Thus one must be very careful in identifying and defining the problem behaviors and behavior deficits, and what measures are to be used to evaluate positive outcome. For example, it is not necessarily true that a child who performs every task item correctly in a teaching lesson is doing better than another child who makes some errors but continues to participate in the lesson; that is, often we are attempting to teach problem solving to children. Some level of trial-and-error learning, particularly persistence in the face of error, is a critical skill that must be learned. A child who is experiencing only success may have great difficulty when faced with novel situations in which the rote response no longer applies. However, this must be balanced by the fact that many children with autism find simple learning experiences very difficult, and rote responding is often a necessary first step.

Thus two issues that we must constantly consider are the balance of teaching items and goals, and how to interpret the data we collect. It is not an easy perspective to acquire as a parent, because you are working only with your child, so that each step is a novel experience both for you and the child. All procedures, all approaches, must be individualized for the child, and this can only take place if you are very sensitive to the child's needs and reactions, and scrupulously *objective* in the measurement and analysis of those reactions. This is perhaps one of the most difficult things for a parent to do: to step back and be truly objective. Thus procedures for quantifying the child's behavior that can be used to create and evaluate intervention strategies are essential.

THE BEHAVIORAL APPROACH

The behavioral approach is a conceptual model of behavior that takes into account at a precise and moment-to-moment level how individuals learn, in the context of their unique physical and social environment, biology, and learning history. Factors include the way in which stimuli are perceived, (that is, their salience, or value), the way in which an individual reacts to those stimuli, the consequences that occur as a function of those specific reactions, and how those consequences influence the future occurrence of behavior. Thus we speak about the characteristics of lesson materials presented, the timing of the task presentation, the distribution over time of the teaching sessions, the behaviors the child is expected to perform at different steps in the presentation of stimuli, and what the consequences for the child will be depending on the response to the stimuli. One must be sensitive to issues of perception, motivation, memory, fatigue, response repertoire, sequences, and a myriad of other variables.

To fully describe behavioral assessment is not possible in a single book chapter. There are many good sources available, however. Two books, one by Gelfand and Hartman (1984), and the other by Powers and Handleman (1984), are highly recommended.

IMPORTANCE OF ANCHOR POINTS

We measure and assess for two basic purposes: to establish absolute points of development and to assess relative change from one point in time to the next. To assist in developing a good teaching program and to place assessments into context, a good curriculum can serve as a map, indicating position, direction, and routes. Thus a curriculum addresses the most frequently raised question: "What should I teach next?" The answer requires assessment of the child and the framework to provide perspective.

More than 20 years ago, starting with long evening meetings with staff and colleagues on the floor of my living room, with papers and charts scattered all about, I began constructing and continually revising a curriculum. In particular, Dr. Stephanie Lockshin and Linda Matey have had a central role in the continuing refinement and expansion of this curriculum, the Individualized Goal Selection Curriculum (Romanczyk, Lockshin, & Matey, 1982, 1995; IGS, current version 8.0). The IGS curriculum is designed to enhance decision making and child evaluation and is structured both by learning and development domains, and in a hierarchical format of area,

level, stage, and task. It contains 18 specific areas of development, with approximately 2,000 specific goals that serve as a road map through these various areas, levels, and stages of development. It cannot be overemphasized that with any curriculum, one cannot focus on all areas of development simultaneously. It is critical to adopt a focused prioritized approach (Romanczyk & Lockshin, 1984; Romanczyk, Lockshin, & Matey, 1994). One of the reasons that children with autism have traditionally made little progress in educational and therapeutic settings is that a balanced curriculum approach is typically utilized, whereby many different service providers provide a little of many different procedures and approaches addressing a multitude of need areas simultaneously. For many children with autism this is a formula for confusion and lack of progress.

BEHAVIORAL ASSESSMENT

It is important to note that individual behaviors can have multiple causes and maintaining factors. Human behavior is very complex, and the behavior of a child with autism can be complex along multiple dimensions (Romanczyk, 1986b; Romanczyk, Lockshin, & O'Connor, 1992; Taylor & Romanczyk, 1994; Taylor, Ekdahl, Romanczyk, & Miller, 1994).

The essential element of behavioral assessment is quantification. For most of us the processes of social, language, and cognitive development proceeded relatively easily throughout our childhood years, and little attention was given either by ourselves or parents and teachers to the specifics of those processes. We learned it "naturally." A great deal of our learning is done through observation, and we are also highly motivated by the social aspects of our environment to continue to participate in various learning and social activities. When this process does not take place easily, as it does not for a child with autism, we need to analyze the situation to understand where the difficulties lie. Behavioral assessment gives us powerful tools to conduct such analysis.

Figure 7.1 presents the basic elements of behavior analysis in pictorial form. The essence of behavior analysis (functional analysis) is that you serve as a detective to closely observe and figure out motivation and sequences of events. There are seven basic steps: (a) define and quantify, (b) observe, (c) record, (d) analyze, (e) evaluate, (f) hypothesize and challenge, and (g) conceptualize.

The figure illustrates the sequence and interrelationship of these components. First, definition and quantification are important, because humans are not

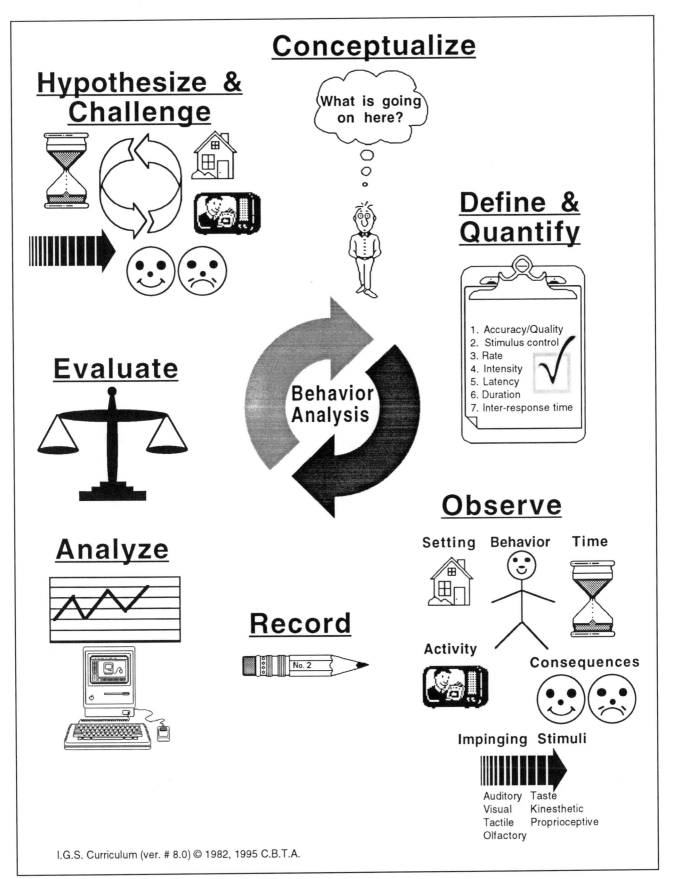

Figure 7.1. Behavior analysis diagram. Reprinted with permission.

very good at being objective. One of the main difficulties with objectivity is that most people believe that they can indeed be objective. But we are actually flawed in our ability to process information, so we set up elaborate systems of rules, regulations, and laws to help mediate social disputes. Thus, for our purposes, we need to be like scientists and detectives.

Defining and quantifying is the first step in making a judgment about the extent of a behavior and its influences. It is important here to measure not just the child's behavior, but also the reactions and events in the child's environment. Next, a schedule is made to precisely observe the child, the settings, the times, and the activities in the environment—that is, to *sample* the range of behavior and events. This should be done on as broad a sample as possible. Most parents are familiar with the phenomenon of a child behaving in a particular way for one family member and a different way for another family member. Often this is just assumed to reflect the child's preferences, and because close observation is not being made, the true factors that are influencing the child's behavior are missed. Observations must be recorded in a format that allows detailed analyses, which can be as simple as looking at numbers in a column, constructing graphs, or organizing sophisticated computer analysis. These data are then evaluated. We must weigh the relative importance and meaning of each source of information and also determine if appropriate amounts and kinds of information have been collected.

Using this evaluation, we begin to form hypotheses as to what might be causing or influencing the behavior and then construct "challenge" situations, that is, we begin to systematically alter the elements in the environment that were observed to produce a pattern. By changing these elements, we are "challenging" the individual with these particular elements. In many ways this is similar to testing the child for an allergy. A physician does an interview to ask questions about the child's reaction, talks about seasonal changes and specific reactions, and then applies small quantities of the hypothesized allergens to the skin to observe possible reactions.

The next step in our assessment is to conceptualize and understand what is going on. It is important to distinguish the very broad type of understanding, such as "What is the meaning of life," from the very specific and focused task that we have: to understand those aspects of the environment and social interactions that are influencing your child's behavior. Thus, this diagram illustrates an ongoing process that can have very different results for different behaviors displayed by the same child; as with most adults, all of a child's behavior is not affected and maintained by only one small set of influences and events.

Figure 7.2 presents diagrams showing possible sources of motivation for behavior, particularly maladaptive (dysfunctional) behavior. In these examples, children are having temper tantrums, but for very different reasons in each instance. In these diagrams, the child's behavior serves as a metaphor for communication.

The first is termed *approach*. In essence, the child is saying "Get over here now." That is, she desires contact or attention for some reason; it may be social, it may be to have you get a glass of juice, or any of a variety of reasons. Be aware that attention can be positive or reinforcing from the child's perspective, even though the adult may intend the interaction to be unpleasant. For instance, a reprimand explaining why the child's aggressive behavior is so hurtful to someone else may be perceived by the child simply as attention. Some children will seek both positive *and* negative attention; the form doesn't matter as long as the adult is interacting with the child.

In the second example, escape, the purpose of the behavior is very different. Here an adult has made a demand, such as "Give me the glass," and the child's behavior serves to remove the demand by having the adult withdraw or stop asking. The message is "Back off." Anyone who doubts the power of such behavior needs only to observe adults with young children in the checkout line in grocery stores, when a child begins a temper tantrum because the parent would not purchase a particular cereal item or candy bar. One can usually observe such confrontations escalate on the child's part until finally the adult gives in and gives the child what he or she wishes. The tantrum then "miraculously" ceases, and the blood pressure of the adult typically falls. In this example, the escape behavior was engaged in by the adult; in order to escape the temper tantrum, she gave in to the child's request and thus made the unpleasant social scene go away. Such interactions can have an extremely powerful influence on behavior, but in this example it is clear that, although the adult may find immediate relief from an embarrassing situation, such escape behavior is neither in the adult's nor child's long-term best interests.

The next mechanism is termed *avoidance* behavior. This is much more complex. It is similar to escape, but the individual is responding to something associated with an unpleasant situation. In this example, the child notices that it is 9:00, and this is when the teacher usually comes to say "It's time to get started," which leads to working on specific tasks. While working on the tasks is actually the unpleasant aspect for the child, having learned the sequence of events, the child responds immediately to those cues in the environment that lead to unpleasant events. Using our metaphor of language, the child is saying "I'm not going to put

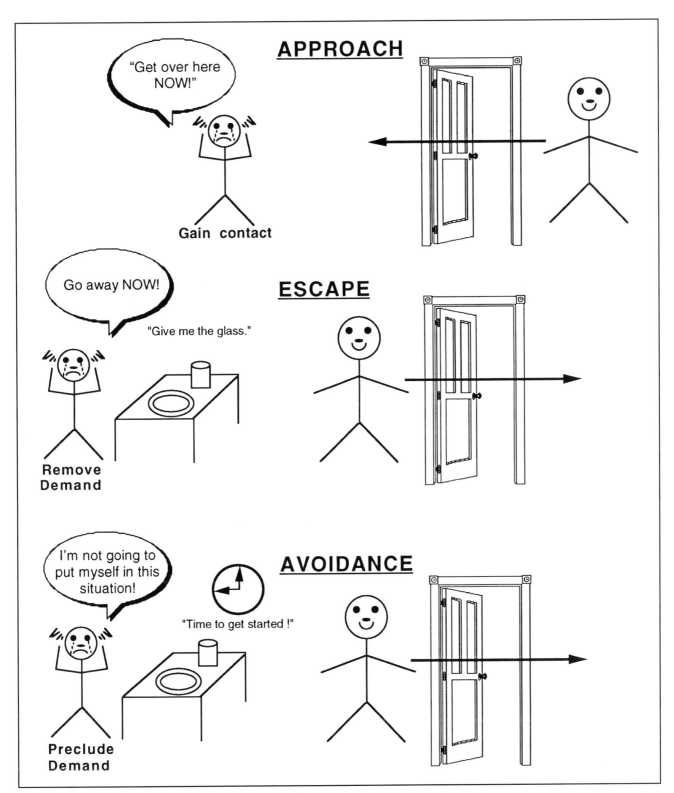

Figure 7.2. Motivation of behavior schematic. Reprinted with permission.

myself in this situation." Avoidance behavior is often very difficult to analyze because, while we are looking for immediate distressing or unpleasant events in the environment, the child is actually reacting well in advance of such unpleasant or distressing events that may be quite idiosyncratic as well.

To ascertain these types of motivation (that is, approach, escape, or avoidance), we use the tools of behavior analysis. A key aspect of quantification is the operational definition, which is a description of a behavior in terms that are limited to *observable* events. A simple example illustrates the point. Often one hears a parent say to a child, "Be good." "Being good" is actually a highly sophisticated concept involving social norms, context, modulation of intensity and quality of behavior, and the motivation to comply with such norms and guidelines. The meaning of "being good" can change. Often the phrase "be good" is simply a translation of "stop doing all this annoying behavior." It thus serves as an unclear signal to the child that something not very specific is annoying to the adult and that it should cease. Another common example would be a request for a child to clean up his room. This could mean simply to pick up the toys that are on the floor, or to pick up the toys that are on the floor and place them in the toy chest, or to pick up the toys and also put dirty laundry in the hamper; or perhaps the command really refers just to the dirty laundry and making the bed. In typical situations this lack of specificity often works itself out by repeated examples, trial and error, and parental feedback. This is a very imprecise way of teaching and transmitting expectations; therefore, for a child who has significant communication difficulty, it is clearly not the preferred method of interaction.

The purpose of precisely defining behavior is to help not only the person taught but also the instructor by maintaining precision and consistency, which are critical components of an effective teaching program. Creating good operational definitions takes practice, feedback, and getting into a particular "mind set." The following are some simple examples of operational definitions:

- **Good sitting.** When placed in a chair in preparation for conducting an individual activity or lesson, the student will remain seated with buttocks on the chair, feet on the floor, and body oriented toward the instructor. Response must be present for a minimum of 15 seconds. The instructor will record the number of times the 15-second criteria is met in each of six 15-minute instruction periods scheduled per day for this goal. Reinforcement is delivered at the end of each correct 15-second period and con-

sists of physical affection, clapping, and stating "Good sitting!"

- **Imitates single action.** Instructor will extend her hand in a random position (e.g., to the right/left, up, down, etc.). The instructor will then give the verbal direction, "(Student), do this." (Student) will extend hand in a mirror image of the teacher's arm position within 5 seconds of the instruction to do so. Record each trial as + or −, and present 10 trials for each of four instruction periods according to schedule. Reinforce correct responding with verbal praise and one cheddar cheese goldfish cracker.

- **Copies shapes.** When presented with one picture of a shape chosen at random from the materials box containing five shapes, the student will copy the shape in the space provided. The shape will contain all aspects of the original (number of sides, angles and arcs) and possess the appropriate proportionality required by its geometric definition (e.g., a square would have four roughly equal-length sides, with four right-angle corners). The student has 1 minute to copy each shape. Provide verbal feedback as to correct and incorrect responses. Put shape aside and draw another from box and repeat until all shapes are used. Record responses as +, A+ (approximately correct), and −. Reinforce both A+ and + with verbal praise, but for + also give a colored sticker on the work sheet.

- **Decrease throwing objects at others.** Throwing is defined as projection of any object in the direction of another person, regardless of accuracy of aim. This does not include playing catch with a willing recipient of the thrown object, indicated either verbally or by having outstretched hands. To be recorded as frequency on a continuous basis by each person supervising/teaching/observing the child. Record the person toward whom object was directed. Do not intervene at this time except if possible to block object's path or grab object before child releases it for projection.

MEASUREMENT

Once behaviors have been operationally defined, we can observe them with greater precision. Observation and measurement are crucial components of our efforts to intervene effectively. These are complex processes involving how often a behavior is observed, under what circumstances, with what units of quantification, and whether the child reacts to being observed. Objective markers provide us with feedback as to when things are going well and, even more important, when programs are not going well.

Adequately monitoring your child's behavior and performance is difficult, but an essential aspect of the behavioral approach is the objective, quantitative analysis of behavior and performance. It is tempting to simply "get a feel for" the child's behavior or performance, but most errors in program development come from inadequate objective analysis and overreliance on memory and impression. Thus, appropriate tools and procedures must be used.

One important concept in measurement is *interobserver agreement,* a technical term that simply means that two people observe the child at exactly the same time, without conferring, and then compare how well their observations agree. This is a good procedure to do at the start of programs and intermittently thereafter. It is often surprising to people to see just how differently they observe behavior even when they think they have clear definitions. These reliability checks on observation should foster discussion in order to resolve the inconsistencies between observers. Never assume that everyone is observing accurately; it is a skill, and individuals require practice and feedback.

There are several basic measurement types: frequency, episode, proportion, duration, latency, intensity, quality, and interresponse time. The choice of which to use depends upon the specific task or behavior being taught. Measurement need not be continuous; we often sample behavior simply because it's not possible to observe every behavior and task of concern every moment. Sampling means setting up an unbiased schedule for observation. For instance, sampling by having mother record aggression and father record self-stimulation (mother usually does most of the speech tasks and father does most of the self-help tasks) would be a biased sample: the observations of specific behaviors would also be specific to people and activities. Good sampling is designed to eliminate such bias. A better approach would be for both mother and father to record aggression and self-stimulation, to conduct speech and self-help programs, and to agree to record for every third teaching session. This would then be an unbiased sample.

In my own work the use of computer technology is invaluable in producing highly detailed analyses of child behavior and performance as well as producing detailed individualized teaching programs (Delmolino, Romanczyk, & Matey, 1994; Romanczyk, 1984, 1986a, 1991, 1993; Romanczyk & Delmolino, 1994). However, as part of the development of the IGS curriculum, which can be used with or without computer resources, a number of data-collection and analysis forms were created as examples of a good basic paper-and-pencil procedure, a few of which will be presented here. All of them are based on the principle that recording data must be an inherent part of the intervention process. Data collection in the context of interacting with your child is a skill, and like any skill it takes practice and organization on your part. With a little perseverance you will find after a time that it becomes almost second nature.

Performance Measurement

The minimum requirements for measurement are that we look at the accuracy of performance, the rate of performance (responses per unit of time), nonresponding versus incorrect responding, and the pattern of responding. This basic system provides us with the minimal information necessary to evaluate progress. It is not sufficient to evaluate learning anomalies or assessment of learning deficits, but for the purpose of conducting a home program and providing feedback to modify the child's learning program, it will serve as a good basic foundation.

Figure 7.3 presents the IGS Performance Record Form, a simple data-recording sheet for discrete-trial, performance-oriented programs. It is very useful when teaching basic skills and assisting a child to reach particularly difficult goals that require concentration, repetition, and mastery. Of course, this format should not be used for all learning tasks, but it is an important component of the child's overall program.

A form such as this permits you to look for a pattern such as increasing or decreasing performance both within a session of 10 trials and across sessions within a day and across days of the week. The task is to understand and promote your child's learning. By looking at patterns you can begin to make hypotheses as to what may be influencing the behavior beyond the task materials themselves. You may also use "permanent product" measures for some tasks, such as number of drawings completed, or worksheet problems correctly completed, or the dinner table set correctly. In these instances a correct response leaves a "product" that you can observe after the child has completed the task or activity.

The information from each session should be summarized and graphed in order to provide an ongoing perspective on your child's performance. It is not sufficient to have simply a "good idea" of where your child is heading or a "feel" for her performance.

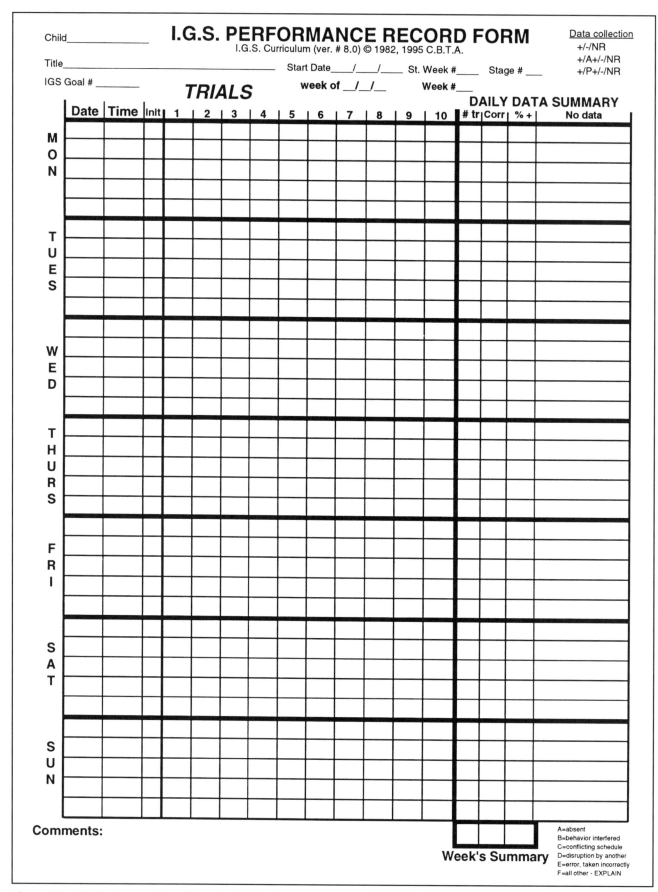

Figure 7.3. IGS Performance Record Form. Reprinted with permission.

Be aware that the parent's or teacher's perception of the child's progress is influenced by many factors other than the child's actual performance, such as fatigue, distraction, stress, expectations, depression, selective memory, systematic and nonsystematic performance variations, the number and type of other goals being simultaneously evaluated, and so on. Your task is to analyze and understand patterns of performance and behavior as objectively as possible.

Figure 7.4 presents the IGS Standard Multiple Data Plotting Form, a simple summary format for evaluating and graphing each performance program (as well as behavior as we'll discuss later). You can use some simple processes to make the evaluation easier. For instance, if you are consistent in placing calendar dates on the *x* (horizontal) axis of the graphs so that they are always synchronized, then it is easy to lay the graphs out on the living room floor, stacking them vertically, and to look at patterns over time for both behavior and performance. That is, if you start your first graph with the first data point on the *x* axis being May 1, and then start your second graph of a different program that started on May 10, do not put May 10 at the first point on the *x* axis of your second graph, but rather at the tenth point. Thus, a vertical line through related graphs will always indicate the same point in time. It is a little wasteful of paper, but the benefits far outweigh this aspect. Interpreting graphs of behavior and performance and analyzing patterns is a difficult task and often takes great expertise. However, the more you can systematize and arrange your information in a logical fashion, the greater the chance that you will be able to put it to good use.

This next important aspect is to note on your graphs any important teaching changes or situational changes. For instance, if you begin to utilize a food reward for certain behavior, and playing with a favorite toy for certain performance goals, you should note the date on which you start these procedures on your graph by drawing a vertical line on the graph and labeling it. This allows you to see patterns in the teaching methods and procedures that are most effective for your child. It also will quickly show you if you are attempting to change too many things too rapidly. Remember that one of the most important tasks you have is to find what methods are more or less effective for your child. If you are trying many things simultaneously, then often you will not be able to discover how they are interacting, whether they are additive in their positive value, or subtractive in their negative value, and you will simply be employing guesswork and relying on your gut feeling rather than utilizing the precision that skilled professionals use in order to make their decisions.

Behavior Measurement

The IGS Behavior Analysis Form shown in Figure 7.5 is used for the initial attempt to quantify your observations. It is very important always to be precise and timely in this endeavor, as memory is faulty and we are all influenced by particular biases and influences. One parent might find a particular behavior more or less troublesome than the other, and their recollection of the frequency and events surrounding the behavior can often bear little resemblance to what is actually going on. One must adopt the view of an objective observer who is collecting detailed diagnostic information. This form thus becomes a diary. Each time you observe the problematic behavior, indicate the start and end time, intensity of the behavior, and any important characteristics such as setting, activity, antecedent, the specific form of the behavior, the consequence, and the comments. The following are just a few examples of possible specific items.

Setting

bedroom	kitchen	transition
bathroom	work area	
living room	outdoors	

Activity

waiting	play	transition
specific task	unstructured	
break	bathroom	
meal/snack		

Antecedent

demand	physical contact	loss of privilege
request		
feedback	instigated	attention to other
denial	no contact	
reprimand	play	removal of attention
reinforce	task difficulty	vicious circle

Consequence

attention	remove demand	restraint
physical contact		response cost
	ignored	overcorrection
distraction	reprimand	relaxation
verbal interaction	time out	
soothing	redirected	

I.G.S. Standard Multiple Data Plotting Form
I.G.S. Curriculum (ver. # 8.0) © 1982, 1995 C.B.T.A.

Child:_____ Month:___ Yr:___

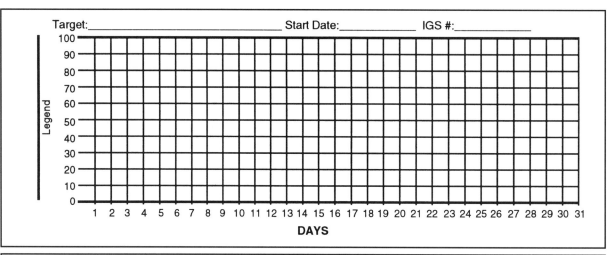

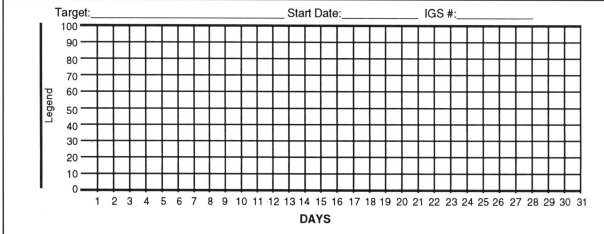

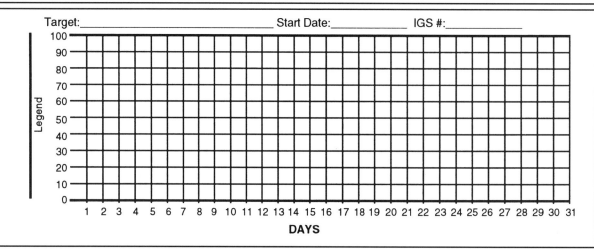

Figure 7.4. IGS Standard Multiple Data Plotting Form. Reprinted with permission.

I.G.S. BEHAVIOR ANALYSIS FORM

I.G.S. Curriculum (ver. # 8.0) © 1982, 1995 C.B.T.A.

Child:_____________ Date:_______

Page __ of __

	SETTING	ACTIVITY	ANTECEDENT	BEHAVIOR	CONSEQUENCE	COMMENTS
Time start:_____ Time end:_____ Intensity: _____ Initials: _____						

	SETTING	ACTIVITY	ANTECEDENT	BEHAVIOR	CONSEQUENCE	COMMENTS
Time start:_____ Time end:_____ Intensity: _____ Initials: _____						

	SETTING	ACTIVITY	ANTECEDENT	BEHAVIOR	CONSEQUENCE	COMMENTS
Time start:_____ Time end:_____ Intensity: _____ Initials: _____						

	SETTING	ACTIVITY	ANTECEDENT	BEHAVIOR	CONSEQUENCE	COMMENTS
Time start:_____ Time end:_____ Intensity: _____ Initials: _____						

	SETTING	ACTIVITY	ANTECEDENT	BEHAVIOR	CONSEQUENCE	COMMENTS
Time start:_____ Time end:_____ Intensity: _____ Initials: _____						

	SETTING	ACTIVITY	ANTECEDENT	BEHAVIOR	CONSEQUENCE	COMMENTS
Time start:_____ Time end:_____ Intensity: _____ Initials: _____						

	SETTING	ACTIVITY	ANTECEDENT	BEHAVIOR	CONSEQUENCE	COMMENTS
Time start:_____ Time end:_____ Intensity: _____ Initials: _____						

	SETTING	ACTIVITY	ANTECEDENT	BEHAVIOR	CONSEQUENCE	COMMENTS
Time start:_____ Time end:_____ Intensity: _____ Initials: _____						

	SETTING	ACTIVITY	ANTECEDENT	BEHAVIOR	CONSEQUENCE	COMMENTS
Time start:_____ Time end:_____ Intensity: _____ Initials: _____						

Figure 7.5. IGS Behavior Analysis Form. Reprinted with permission.

It is very important in using this form to be objective about what you observe. For example, when observing a common form of misbehavior, one might make a notation of a child being reprimanded by his father for jumping on the furniture while the family is watching TV. The specific behaviors are important, not the supposed intent. For instance, it provides no clinically useful information to say that a child was frustrated, began jumping on the furniture, and then was punished. In contrast, an observation that "Father picked up Sammy, carried him to the kitchen, sat him on a chair next to the table, and stated 'I don't want you jumping on the couch'" is much more useful because it is behaviorally descriptive. Next, a description of the child's reaction to this, such as "Sammy smiled and struggled to get away" is necessary. Last, one needs a description of the antecedent events, such as "Sammy was watching TV and Martha (sibling) would not let him change the channel." This series of observations is much more useful and lends itself to useful interpretation of possible causes of Sammy's behavior.

Much of behavior analysis is the process of determining what the reaction of the individual is to antecedents and consequences rather than the intent of those trying to influence the child or the intent of the child to influence the environment. Intent is an elusive and slippery concept, and usually an oversimplification for purposes of behavior analysis. Thus, when a parent says that she "rewards" her child for saying please and thank you but is disappointed because the child rarely says please and thank you without constant reminders, then in fact the behavior is **not** being appropriately reinforced. What is really occurring is that the parents are describing their *efforts* and their good *intent,* rather than objectively observing the effect of their behavior on the child. The reward being used was assumed by the parents to be effective, but it was not a reinforcer; that is, it was not serving to increase the behavior. In order to be effective in conducting good behavior therapy programs, one must constantly evaluate the gap between intent and effect. Good intent is a prerequisite, but not a substitute for precision of analysis.

The IGS Behavior Record Form shown in Figure 7.6 is designed for recording behavior for 6-hour blocks of 15-minute intervals across the days of the week. (This is just one of many different IGS forms that we use.) This form is used for long-term monitoring after clues have been found using the IGS Behavior Analysis Form, and for detecting patterns over longer time periods that may lead to clues as to further possible influences. Certainly for most families the routine on Saturdays and Sundays is quite different from that of weekdays. The influence or lack thereof of this change in schedule and activities can be seen quite readily.

By monitoring several behaviors on one form, we can look for possible important patterns across behavior. This is where the true detective work comes in, not only with respect to analyzing what you have recorded, but also in the choice of what you record. For instance, the basic form provides four choices for the units of measurement: frequency (how many times did the behavior occur?), occurrence (did the behavior occur or not occur in the observation interval?), duration (for how long did the behavior occur during the interval?), and proportion (of the opportunities for the behavior to occur, what percent of the time did it occur? For example, if the child was asked three times to come when called, and did it twice, then 66% would be recorded). This last example is also appropriate for latency measurement; that is, how long does it take the child to respond when the request or situation arises? Sometimes the difficulty is not in the actual responding, but in the speed of responding. The choice of how to record a behavior is as important as which behavior to record. There is no simple answer: it will always depend upon the purpose and context of the behavior or performance goal.

For instance, one might record the times of naps as well as play activities along with frequency of aggression, occurrence of self-stimulation, and proportion of appropriate play that occurs in response to another child trying to initiate play with your child. By looking at the patterns across such behaviors and taking into account normal scheduled activities, you can make deductions about possible influences. You can use the form in a number of ways: for frequency, use little slash marks to indicate when the behavior has occurred; for duration, write in the number of minutes; for proportion, use percentage; and for occurrence, use a + or a −. If you can't observe for a particular interval, be sure to cross it out so you know when you summarize what the correct denominator will be (you don't want to mix or count nonobservation periods in with times when you are actually observing).

For frequency, if you find that there is not enough room in each box because the behavior is occurring too often, simply change the resolution of the matrix. Instead of 15-minute periods, you might use 10-, or 5-, or even 1-minute intervals. The resolution is completely dependent upon the individual characteristics of your child and the behavior being monitored. There is no one correct answer other than to say it is reasonable to start with 15-minute periods and if the patterns remain elusive, then one adopts other time resolutions in an effort to systematically evaluate the behavior. Summary data, such as rate per day, can be plotted on the IGS Standard Multiple Data Plotting Form, as for performance data.

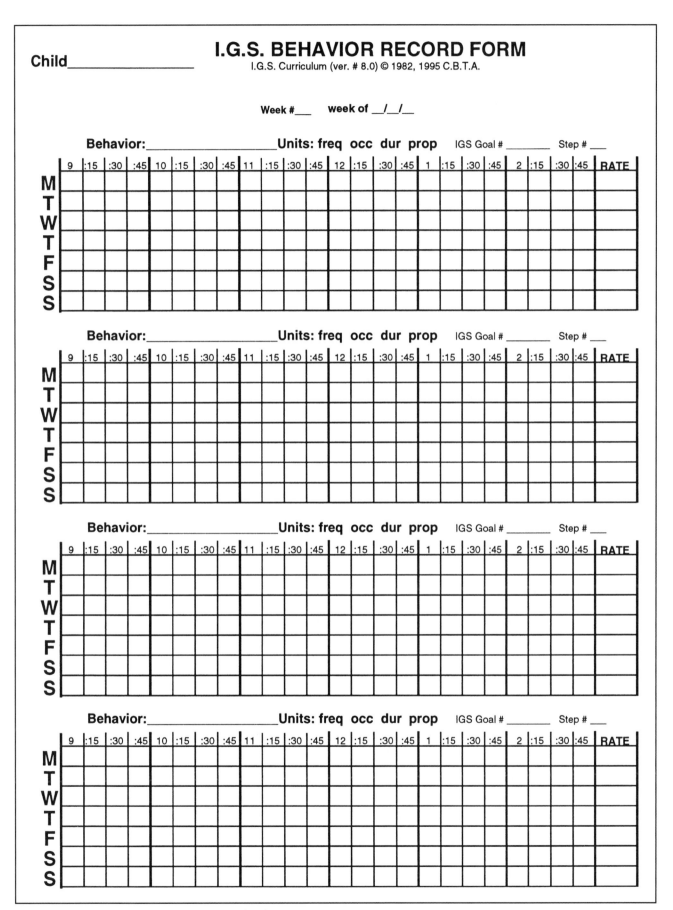

Figure 7.6.   IGS Behavior Record Form. Reprinted with permission.

The IGS Temporal Behavior Analysis Form shown in Figure 7.7 is an example of one of several of this type that is used for very precise analysis of a particular behavior problem. Each sheet records only a single behavior and indicates the precise time at which the behavior occurs for each day the samples are taken. It is very important therefore to indicate within any particular day times when the behavior was not recorded by crossing out the box. Not doing so can generate false patterns that reflect more the parental schedule of being able to monitor the behavior rather than any temporal characteristics of the behavior itself. This form has many permutations, including a 24-hour analysis, analysis for short periods of time, such as an hour, where specific task variables and social variables are manipulated, and also plotting and analysis of long-term trends over many months. However, the basic format is one of recording by time of day when a specific behavior occurs, which allows you to look for patterns across days that are occurring at the same time of day. These patterns are the basis for speculation as to issues concerning fatigue, interaction with specific activities and people, or the sequence of demands and stimulation in the child's day. It is common to see patterns based upon physical distress, meal times, parents leaving or arriving from work, planned family activities, the times of favorite TV shows, and so on.

What is most important in this section is that the purpose is not simply to count behaviors to indicate how "bad" a day it was (what I have referred to in various conference presentations as "the pain index"), but rather to analyze and understand behavior patterns. Doing so enables you to intervene more effectively by altering the specific conditions that lead to, or elicit, the behavior problem. This is a much more useful and effective approach than arbitrarily punishing undesired behavior and hoping that the punishment will decrease the behavior (Romanczyk, 1986b, 1990). The more information and understanding you have about the purpose and function of a behavior and the conditions that tend to elicit and maintain it, the better your chance of developing an effective intervention program that will maximize the child's short-term and long-term success.

Figure 7.8 shows the IGS Language Development Form, which is similar in concept to the IGS Behavior Analysis Form. Language training involves not only the production of specific sounds and words, but also the appropriate use of those words in context. This is often referred to as *spontaneous* speech. In fact, very little speech is truly spontaneous; that is, in a technical sense, the individual who is speaking spontaneously is in fact reacting to subtle social and environmental cues that are appropriate for this speech. Thus, when a child walks into the kitchen in the morning and sees a parent working at preparing breakfast, it is very appropriate to spontaneously ask "What's for breakfast?" In like manner, when a parent arrives home from work, it is quite appropriate for the child to say "Hi, I missed you all day." These are spontaneous statements in the sense that they are not directly prompted by another individual, but as you can see, they are prompted by the particular stimulus conditions that are present.

One of the tasks in helping to develop appropriate language repertoires is to remain aware of the subtle but ever-present cues for appropriate communication. We are so used to them and find them so easy to respond to that we rarely pay direct attention to them. However, the essence of being a good teacher is to analyze these common situations and help the child to develop the skills necessary to respond spontaneously. The IGS Language Development Form permits various family members to share and monitor language use and then to promote its sustained use. This form is particularly useful in the initial stages of language development, when sounds and words may be used only intermittently and involve poor stimulus control. The data may be plotted on the IGS Standard Multiple Data Plotting Form to look at long-term trends.

The IGS Scale Rating Form shown in Figure 7.9 is used in a similar way to record behaviors that occur intermittently for which it is not as important to count the number of times they occur as to note the quality or some other dimension of the behaviors when they do occur. Such behaviors could include showing affection, cleaning up toys after playing with them, cooperating in a joint task, or assessing the degree of independence in self-dressing. A scale rank of 0–10 is perhaps the easiest to use, as it translates most readily to our general concept of 0–100% of accuracy. However, it is important to note that a scale of 0–10 can also be used to rank the intensity or quality of behavior. For instance, in rating temper tantrums, one would use 10 to indicate the most severe temper tantrum that you have ever observed, 5 being the midpoint and 1 being extremely mild. One uses such a scale to look at issues other than frequency. As an example, for most young preschool children, temper tantrums are part of normal development. Thus, the goal of having a young child never display temper tantrums would be both an unreasonable and uninformed expectation as well as an example of a poorly chosen criterion. However, reducing the intensity and duration of temper tantrums to half of what is currently observed may be a quite reasonable and appropriate goal.

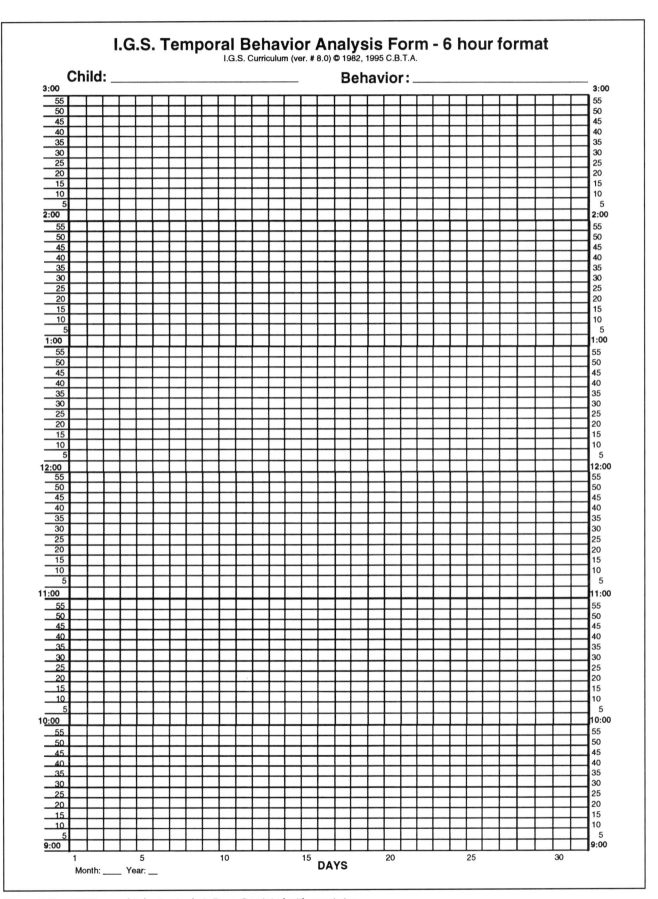

Figure 7.7. IGS Temporal Behavior Analysis Form. Reprinted with permission.

I.G.S. Language Development Form

I.G.S. Curriculum (ver. # 8.0) © 1982, 1995 C.B.T.A.

Child:_____   WEEK of : ___/___/___

Record any new word used. Rate the level of articulation - poor, adequate, good. Indicate time, situation, who child was speaking to, as well as what was being said. Also record if a word child has used, was NOT used when the situation required it. Record any other unusual language event in the same manner. Look for patterns in terms of the development of new words, use of words child has learned, and very importantly, words that disappear or fall into disuse. Note changes, either positive or negative, in articulation and if child begins to substitute gestures or signs for spoken words. Make some entries each day, even if there are no unusual or striking events. At the end of each day, indicate the amount of language used that day - LOW, AVG, HIGH.

	MONDAY	TUESDAY	WEDNESDAY	THURSDAY	FRIDAY	SATURDAY	SUNDAY
1							
2							
3							
4							
5							
6							
7							
8							
9							
10							
Amount of Language	low avg high	low avg high	low avg high	low avg high	low avg high	low avg high	low avg high

Figure 7.8.   IGS Language Development Form. Reprinted with permission.

Child _____	**I.G.S. SCALE RATING FORM**	APPropriate responses

I.G.S. SCALE RATING FORM

Child_____

Week of __/__/__   Week #___

I.G.S. Curriculum (ver. # 8.0) © 1982, 1995 C.B.T.A.

APPropriate responses
INDependence level
QUAlity of response
CONsistency of response
COOperation level
FREquency of response
INTensity of response

All scales are rated 1>10

IGS# ____ Scale ____
Behavior ____

	9:00	9:30	10:00	10:30	11:00	11:30	12:00	12:30	1:00	1:30	2:00	2:30	#	AVG
Monday														
Tuesday														
Wednesday														
Thursday														
Friday														
Saturday														
Sunday														

IGS# ____ Scale ____
Behavior ____

	9:00	9:30	10:00	10:30	11:00	11:30	12:00	12:30	1:00	1:30	2:00	2:30	#	AVG
Monday														
Tuesday														
Wednesday														
Thursday														
Friday														
Saturday														
Sunday														

IGS# ____ Scale ____
Behavior ____

	9:00	9:30	10:00	10:30	11:00	11:30	12:00	12:30	1:00	1:30	2:00	2:30	#	AVG
Monday														
Tuesday														
Wednesday														
Thursday														
Friday														
Saturday														
Sunday														

Figure 7.9. IGS Scale Rating Form. Reprinted with permission.

WHEN THINGS GO WRONG

There are many components to a good teaching program. (In my own work, teaching programs for each goal address more than three dozen specific variables.) We cannot expect that all goals will be taught in the same manner nor that the child will respond in exactly the same way to the same teaching technique in different situations. Thus, in order to create good programs, it is important to recognize that many children with autism share a common set of learning difficulties. Our teaching needs to compensate for these difficulties, which tend to be (a) poor attention, (b) poor motivation, (c) poor stimulus control, (d) poor generalization, (e) poor cause-effect learning, (f) poor observational learning, (g) poor communication, (h) poor perspective taking (walking in another's shoes), (i) poor understanding of social and behavioral expectations.

Sequencing of goals is a very complex issue and concerns the child's overall development, the strength of the child's existing behavioral repertoire, responsivity to the environment, and your skill in constructing the program. We are always confronted with the need for fine balance and careful judgment as to whether a child is not succeeding because insufficient time has been devoted to teaching the particular goal or whether the goal is poorly chosen and poorly taught. Such evaluation and judgment is greatly enhanced by specific training, supervision, and experience. It is not possible to give a magic formula for the answers to these complex questions. Thus, it is important that you be sensitive to the issues and continuously evaluate your child's treatment plan. As with any important decision, this is best done with someone who can serve as a sounding board to challenge and critique what you are doing and to take an objective look at the data you are collecting and the conclusions you are drawing. You do not want someone who is simply being supportive and trying to tell you that everything is okay and that you are doing your best. Such interpersonal support is crucial and very important, but should not be confused with the hardnosed analytical evaluation that you need in order to optimize your child's treatment plan.

Figure 7.10 presents the goal problem flowchart for the process of evaluating program adequacy. Once again there is not enough space to detail each step and the multitude of possible options. However, the logic of the flow of decision making should assist you in how to problem solve. The chart has two basic emphases: Is the problem specific to (a) one goal or (b) do many goals involve problems? If specific to one or a few goals, then you must inspect the teaching program itself to see if it may be contributing to

lack of progress. One must review the materials and their appropriateness, the instructions given to the child (are they perhaps too complex or insufficient to produce clear understanding?). Is the particular response required too complex for the child at this point in time, and should a simpler response be accepted? Is the complexity of the task beyond the child's current abilities? Finally, are the task and goal appropriate for the child's current skill and development level? These are all complex considerations. For instance, we often see in teaching interactions instructions that go far beyond what is required for the task and actually involve points of confusion. Thus, if one wants a child to match a sock to a sock and a cup to a cup in a simple match-to-sample teaching process, it is much better to use verbal instructions such as "Match sock" rather than "OK Johnny, now I'd like you to take the sock and match it to the other sock so you can show me how well you can do it." It is always critical to remember that language can be very difficult for individuals with autism and that your language should be as functional and simple as possible; that is, each word should be used because it contains relevant and important information. The "filler" that we all use in normal conversation can be a source of confusion and frustration. As the child's skills progress, certainly you can expand the verbal interchanges that occur, but in the beginning it is wise to be direct and simple.

When problems are present for many goals, there can be many discrete impediments to progress, often in combination. A good start is with a three-part investigation. First, is there a problem with the child's attention? If so, there could be many possible causes. Certainly factors like physical discomfort, fatigue, too-stimulating a learning environment, and poor reinforcers are some of the possibilities. What is important here, as always, is that these are factors to which the child may be sensitive, but which may not be significant to you or to other children. For instance, the issue of whether the environment is too stimulating is not a question that can be answered on a normative basis, such as whether most people would find it overly stimulating. The answer must be ascertained for your particular child. It could be that the noise level is too high, or there are too many interesting things in the room, such as favorite toys, or perhaps the child's clothing is not comfortable, or the chair the child is sitting on is too high and the feet cannot touch the floor. In like manner you must question whether the reward being utilized is in fact a reinforcer. A child may like a particular food item, or a hug, or a toy to play with, but that does not necessarily mean that it will be an effective reinforcer (that is, act to increase the behavior desired).

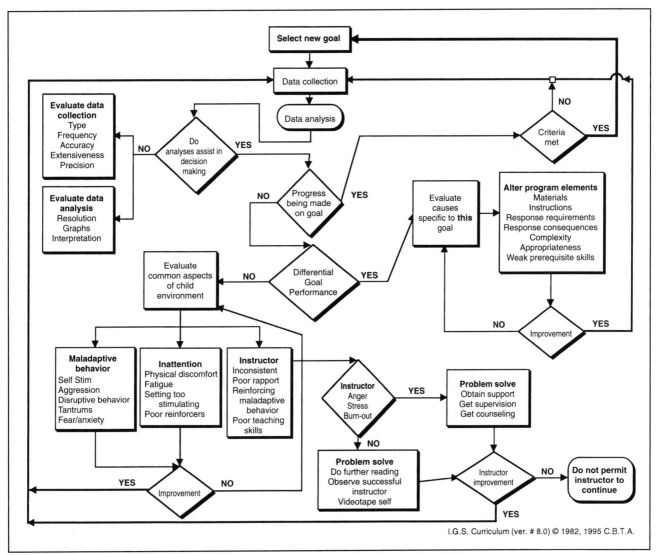

Figure 7.10. Goal problem flowchart. Reprinted with permission.

A second area of possible difficulty would be the presence of problem behaviors. If the child is engaging in a great deal of self-stimulatory behavior or interfering behavior such as aggression or disruption (throwing materials, yelling and screaming, falling to the floor, etc.), then all of these prevent the teaching program from being appropriately implemented. If this is the case, these behaviors need to be dealt with directly. The presence of such behaviors, however, often indicates that there are problems elsewhere. For instance, as just mentioned, if the child is inattentive due to physical discomfort, fatigue, and so on, and therefore is not receiving the reinforcer desired, then becoming aggressive or disruptive may be her response to that situation. It is always important to first analyze the teaching environment before attempting to directly suppress a behavior. Most often the answer lies in the teaching program and interactions rather than in the behavior problem itself.

Third, we must examine the characteristics of the teacher. This is an emotionally difficult task if the teacher is the parent, or one spouse is examining the efforts of the other. Clearly, the teacher is critical to achieving success, and thus the cold light of evaluation must constantly be applied. As stated before, intent to help is not sufficient; skill and proficiency are mandatory. Some characteristics can be easily improved, for example, by videotaping your teaching sessions and reviewing them with someone in a calm setting, where the emphasis is on critiquing skills, not criticizing the person. It does happen at times that a particular person does not have the skill, temperament, or personality at a given point in time to be an effective teacher. Such a person can still assist in all of the logistics of conducting a home program, and perhaps the most valuable contribution may be to help with activities to allow more free time for the more proficient teacher to teach.

Figure 7.11 expands upon the process in Figure 7.10. Intervention for problem behavior is to be undertaken with great caution (Romanczyk, 1990). This flowchart illustrates the process of intervening for a behavior, using many of the procedures described throughout the chapter. Figure 7.12 presents a flowchart that incorporates the investigation of specific motivation for the behavior. These three flowcharts illustrate the process of problem solving. Although they may seem complex and overwhelming, in fact they are simplified illustrations of the process a master clinician uses.

SUMMARY

Taking the task of developing and implementing your child's program upon yourself is a great burden and challenge. Assessment and measurement are essential tools to the process of teaching and helping your child develop. Remember that you will always be learning and improving your skills. Remember also to pace yourself and set a reasonable schedule to learn, prepare, and implement. Do not work in isolation. Seek feedback. Be objective. Remember to devote quality time to yourself, family, and friends. Dedication is wonderful; obsession is not.

You have much hard work ahead of you, and you will enjoy success. But not everyone will achieve the same degree of success, and in the end remember the value of the journey and not just the destination. Expect the best for your child but also accept the limits that may emerge. Experience the joys the journey can bring, and the joys each day can hold. Share your hopes, successes, and disappointments, and obtain guidance and support from those you respect.

ACKNOWLEDGMENTS

The author wishes to thank Dr. Stephanie Lockshin for her support and insightful discussions concerning the development of this manuscript and related materials. This chapter references a small portion of the material and information presented in the IGS Curriculum, © 1982, 1995. It also makes reference to the IGS Computer Information and Data Management System, © 1994. The author also thanks Lara M. Delmolino, B.A., co-developer of the system, for her stimulating and creative discussions and development efforts with the author concerning behavior analysis and information management.

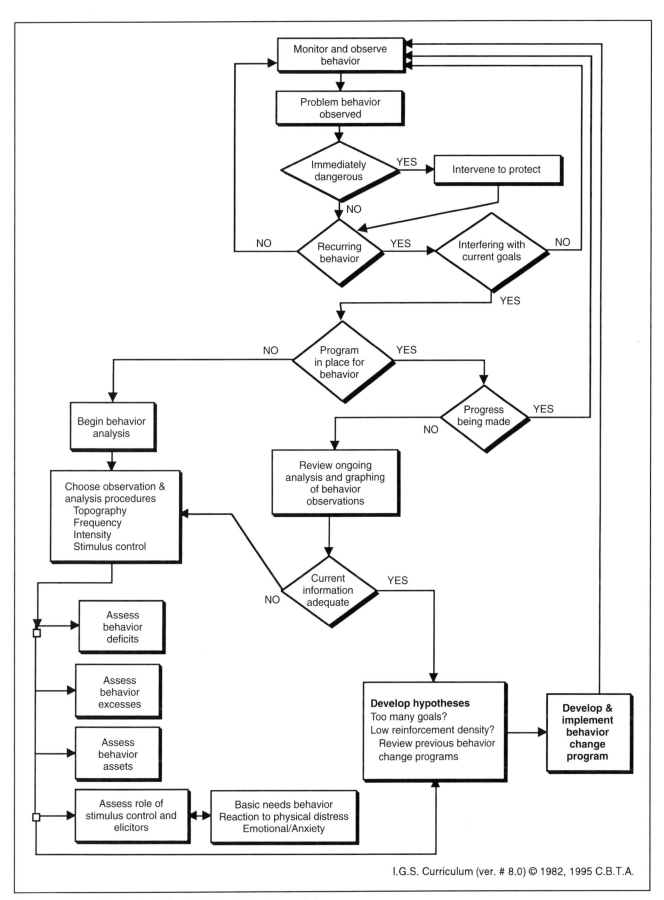

I.G.S. Curriculum (ver. # 8.0) © 1982, 1995 C.B.T.A.

Figure 7.11. Problem behavior flowchart. Reprinted with permission.

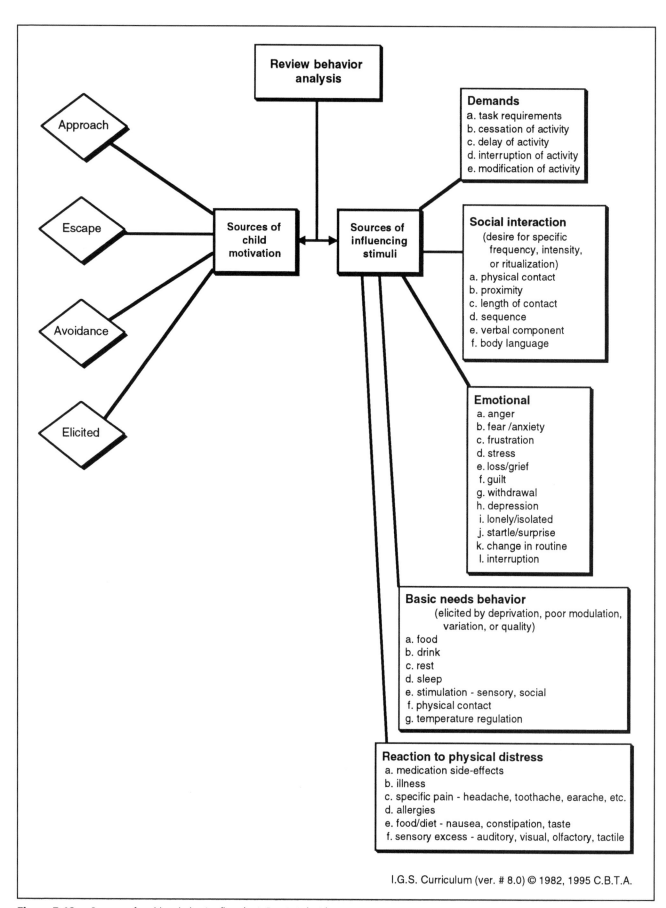

Figure 7.12. Sources of problem behavior flowchart. Reprinted with permission.

REFERENCES

Delmolino, L. M., & Romanczyk, R. G. (1995). Facilitated communication: A critical review. *The Behavior Therapist, 18*(2), 27–30.

Delmolino, L., Romanczyk, R. G., & Matey, L. (1994, May). *Impact and cost-benefit of "off-the-shelf" computer-assisted behavior analysis.* Presented at the 20th Annual Convention of the Association for Behavior Analysis, Atlanta, GA.

Gelfand, D., & Hartman, D. (Eds.). (1984). *Child behavior analysis and therapy.* New York: Pergamon.

Harris, S., & Handleman, J. (Eds.). (1994). *Preschool education programs for children with autism.* Austin, TX: PRO-ED.

Lovaas, O. I. (1987). Behavioral treatment and normal educational and intellectual functioning in young autistic children. *Journal of Consulting and Clinical Psychology, 55*, 3–9.

Maurice, C. (1993). *Let me hear your voice.* New York: Knopf.

McEachin, J. J., Smith, T., & Lovaas, O. I. (1993). Long term outcome for children with autism who received early intensive behavioral treatment. *American Journal on Mental Retardation, 4*, 359–372.

Powers, M., & Handleman, J. (Eds.). (1984). *Behavioral assessment of severe developmental disabilities.* Austin, TX: PRO-ED.

Romanczyk, R. G. (1984). A case study of micro-computer utilization and staff efficiency: A 5-year analysis. *Journal of Organizational Behavior Management, 6*, 141–154.

Romanczyk, R. G. (1986a). *Clinical utilization of microcomputer technology.* New York: Pergamon Press.

Romanczyk, R. G. (1986b). Self-injurious behavior: Conceptualization, assessment and treatment. In K. D. Gadow (Ed.), *Advances in learning and behavioral disabilities,* (Vol. 5, pp. 29–56). Greenwich, CT: JAI Press.

Romanczyk, R. G. (1990). Aversive conditioning as a component of comprehensive treatment: The impact of etiological factors on clinical decision making. In S. L. Harris & J. Handleman (Eds.), *Aversive and non-aversive intervention: Controlling life-threatening behavior of the developmentally disabled.* New York: Springer.

Romanczyk, R. G. (1991). Monitoring and evaluating clinical service delivery: Issues of effectiveness of computer data base management. In A. Ager, (Ed.), *Microcomputers in clinical psychology.* New York: Wiley Press.

Romanczyk, R. G. (1993, May). *The appropriate utilization of computer applications for early intervention.* Presented at the 14th Annual Division TEACCH Conference, Chapel Hill, NC.

Romanczyk, R. G. (1994). Autism. In V. S. Ramachandran (Ed.), *The encyclopedia of human behavior* (Vol. 1, pp. 327–336). San Diego, CA: Academic Press.

Romanczyk, R. G., & Delmolino, L. M. (1994). *IGS Computer Information Management System.* Apalachin, NY: CBTA.

Romanczyk, R. G., & Lockshin, S. L. (1984). Short-term, intensive services: The deficit-oriented, focused model. In W. Christian, J. Hannah, & T. Glahn (Eds.), *Programming effective human services.* New York: Plenum.

Romanczyk, R. G., Lockshin, S., & Matey, L. (1982; 1995). *The Individualized Goal Selection Curriculum.* Apalachin, NY: CBTA.

Romanczyk, R. G., Lockshin, S., & O'Connor, J. (1992). Psychophysiology and issues of anxiety and arousal. In J. Luiselli, J. Matson, & N. Singh (Eds.), *Self-injurious behavior: Analysis, assessment, and treatment.* New York: Springer-Verlag.

Romanczyk, R. G., Lockshin, S., & Matey, L. (1994). Intensive early intervention. In S. Harris & J. Handleman (Eds.), *Preschool education programs for children with autism.* Austin, TX: PRO-ED.

Taylor, J., Ekdahl, M., Romanczyk, R. G., & Miller, M. (1994). Escape behavior in task situations: Task versus social antecedents. *Journal of Autism and Developmental Disorders, 24*(3), 331–344.

Taylor, J., & Romanczyk, R. G. (1994). Generating hypotheses about the function of student problem behavior by observing teacher behavior. *Journal of Applied Behavior Analysis, 27*(2), 251–265.

PART FIVE

Who Should Teach?

CHAPTER EIGHT

Identifying Qualified Professionals in Behavior Analysis

Gerald L. Shook
Judith E. Favell

Parents of individuals with autism often have difficulty finding qualified professional behavior analysts to provide the specialized services needed by their children. Although this problem may extend to other professions such as medicine and dentistry, there are usually a number of these professionals in the community from which to choose, and parents can rely on the license of the particular profession to provide assurance that the individual has the training and experience necessary to give basic treatment. This choice and assurance of quality service, in general, is not available for behavior analysts. Professionals with adequate training and experience in the use of behavior analysis usually are not available in sufficient numbers to provide extensive choice for parents. Furthermore, with the few exceptions discussed later in this chapter, states do not license or credential behavior analysts. This lack of a credential in behavior analysis makes it difficult for parents to identify professionals who are qualified to provide behavior analytic services.

Not all direct behavior analysis services need to be provided by professionals, however. Adequately trained and supervised paraprofessionals are capable of providing many direct behavior analytic services and are, in fact, the providers of choice in many situations (behavior analysis paraprofessionals are discussed in a separate chapter). Still, professionals are needed for many behavior analysis services such as functional analysis, program and staff supervision, and direct implementation in particularly difficult cases.

This chapter addresses some of the questions that parents may have regarding behavior analysis professionals. Parents will learn where to look for qualified behavior analysts and how to identify a qualified behavior analyst. Finally, the chapter provides a description of behavior analysis certification and offers suggestions to parents who are interested in exploring behavior analysis certification in their own states.

WHAT FORMAL TRAINING SHOULD BEHAVIOR ANALYSTS HAVE?

Professionals in behavior analysis should have either a master's or doctorate degree within a human services field. They may receive their training from a variety of university departments. Behavior-analytic training may be offered in psychology, special education, regular education, social work, or other human services disciplines. The coursework taught in a particular department (such as psychology) varies considerably among universities. For example, one psychology department may be oriented toward clinical psychology and may offer few, if any, courses in behavior analysis, while a psychology department in another university may focus on behavior analysis and offer more than a dozen courses in that area. Parents should expect professionals in behavior analysis to have a minimum of three or four graduate courses specifically in behavior analysis.

Because behavior analysts emphasize the acquisition of new skills, their coursework should cover this important area. Material on ethical applications of behavioral principles should be covered as part of a course or as a separate course. If the behavior analyst will be dealing with significant behavior problems, coursework should be directed at that area as well. Generally speaking, the more severe the behavior problems to be addressed, the more extensive the training should be. Programs that treat severe behavior problems should have professionals with doctorate degrees in behavior analysis heading the clinical component and a number of individuals with master's degrees in behavior analysis on staff, the total number depending on the size of the program.

Behavior analysis is a rapidly evolving field with significant new developments occurring every year. The competent behavior analyst will need to keep abreast of these new developments by attending professional conferences and workshops in behavior analysis. Parents should expect this continuing education to be an ongoing activity for behavior-analytic professionals.

WHAT EXPERIENCE SHOULD THE PROFESSIONAL BEHAVIOR ANALYST HAVE?

Formal coursework is not sufficient to ensure that an individual is a competent behavior analyst; he or she also should have supervised experience in working with persons with autism. This experience may have been obtained before graduation in the form of a practicum or internship, or after graduation through on-the-job experience. In either case, it is important that the experience be supervised by individuals who have adequate formal training and experience in behavior analysis themselves. Obviously, the more experience an individual has as a behavior analyst, the more confident the parent can be that the treatment will be provided in the proper fashion. The quality and relevance of the experience obtained is as important as the quantity, with experience being more relevant if it involves individuals who have autism or another pervasive developmental disability rather than those whose needs are quite different.

TO WHICH PROFESSIONAL ORGANIZATIONS ARE BEHAVIOR ANALYSTS LIKELY TO BELONG?

Although behavior analysts may belong to any number of professional organizations, the Association for Behavior Analysis (ABA) is the premiere international professional organization in the field of behavior analysis. Members can belong to the ABA at a number of membership levels, with membership requirements varying with the levels. Professional behavior analysts usually have "full member" status or above. Many ABA members are university professors or other leaders in the field, and the organization is decidedly academic in nature. A membership list may be obtained by contacting the Association for Behavior Analysis at the address provided at the end of this chapter.

The ABA has a number of affiliated chapters that are formed at the state or regional level (for example,

the Northern California Association for Behavior Analysis, the Texas Association for Behavior Analysis, and the Delaware Valley Association for Behavior Analysis). Membership requirements may be more inclusive and less rigorous with affiliated chapters than the membership requirements of the ABA. The focus of these chapters tends to be less academic than that of the ABA, and they usually have a more applied, practitioner-based membership. A behavior analyst may be active at both the international ABA organization and an affiliated chapter, or be active at only the ABA or affiliated-chapter level. Not all areas of the country have affiliated chapters. The address of the local affiliated chapter may be obtained from the Association for Behavior Analysis.

WHAT UNIVERSITIES FEATURE GRADUATE PROGRAMS IN BEHAVIOR ANALYSIS?

Several universities either have excellent programs in behavior analysis or offer several courses in the field. Not all of these programs fall within psychology departments; special education, social work and other similar departments may offer excellent training in behavior analysis that may be relevant to individuals who have autism. The Association for Behavior Analysis compiles a listing of programs that are behavior analytic in nature under the title *Graduate Programs in Behavior Analysis*. This directory may be obtained for a small fee by contacting the ABA office. Although the directory lists many programs, its main function is to provide information on graduate programs for prospective graduate students, and the listings are not complete as a guide for consumers. Some graduate programs that are not listed may offer good training in behavior analysis. Local ABA-affiliated chapters may be able to provide suggestions regarding nearby graduate programs.

ARE ANY GRADUATE PROGRAMS ACCREDITED TO PROVIDE TRAINING IN BEHAVIOR ANALYSIS?

The Association for Behavior Analysis has established an accreditation board to accredit programs of study in behavior analysis at the master's and doctoral level. At the master's level, the course of study must provide instruction in behavior-analytic approaches to research and/or in conceptual issues and behavioral interventions. The program also must include a thesis, review paper, or general examination based on a behavior-analytic approach to problems or issues. At the doctoral level, the course of study must provide instruction in behavior-analytic approaches to research and/or in conceptual issues, and include advanced curriculum topics in a specialized area of nonhuman and/or human basic research literature, research methods, and one or more applied areas. In addition, a dissertation is required in which questions and methods are based on a behavior-analytic approach to issues.

Although this accreditation process makes a significant contribution to standardizing training in the field of behavior analysis, it does not address all of the specific coursework or experience required by behavior analysts working directly with persons with autism and pervasive developmental disabilities. Although the standards may be expanded to include such coursework or experience in the future, the current accreditation process does not guarantee that those who are graduated from accredited programs have the training necessary to work with children who have these conditions.

Parents should also be aware that, because this accreditation process is relatively new, very few graduate programs have had an opportunity to become accredited. The ABA accreditation process will become more valuable to parents and people with autism as the number of accredited programs increases and the course requirements are altered to require more training in clinical issues relating to pervasive developmental disabilities and autism.

ARE INDIVIDUALS WHO HOLD OTHER PROFESSIONAL LICENSES QUALIFIED TO DO BEHAVIOR ANALYSIS?

Individuals who hold licenses in professional areas other than behavior analysis (such as psychology, education, or other human services fields) may be qualified to do behavior analysis, but their licenses do not guarantee that they will be so qualified. None of these professions has sufficient behavior-analytic coursework requirements in the standards for accrediting graduate programs to ensure adequate training in behavior analysis. Neither do their licensing examinations require sufficient content in behavior analysis to ensure that those who pass the examinations have adequate knowledge and skill to practice behavior analysis. Parents may be best served by applying the criteria described above to all individuals who would practice behavior analysis with their children, even those professionals who hold licenses in related areas.

DOES ANY PROFESSIONAL CREDENTIAL OFFER A SPECIALIZATION IN BEHAVIOR ANALYSIS?

The American Board of Behavioral Psychology awards diplomate status to licensed psychologists who demonstrate excellence in the behavioral field. The Diploma in Behavior Therapy offers subspecialization in one of the following areas: behavior analysis, behavior therapy, and cognitive therapy or cognitive-behavior therapy.

Applicants must be licensed psychologists and document that they meet a number of criteria. Prior to taking an examination, the candidate must submit one or more work samples reflecting his typical practice. The work sample is reviewed by diplomate-level committee members who usually are peers of the candidate, selected from the same subspecialty field. The committee then conducts an oral examination in the following areas: realistic assessment of the problem, effectiveness research, and sensitivity to ethical implications of professional practice. Persons who meet all criteria are awarded diplomate status in their particular subspecialty.

Diplomate status, with a subspecialty in behavior analysis, may be helpful to parents in identifying licensed psychologists qualified to practice behavior analysis with their children. Of course, such professionals should have experience in working with persons who have pervasive developmental disabilities or autism and should have specific training in those areas.

Florida offers a credential in behavior analysis through the state's Behavior Analysis Certification Program. This certification is solely in behavior analysis and does not require a credential in another profession. The program has several components, including passing a professionally constructed written examination and completing degree and coursework requirements, experience requirements, and continuing-education requirements. Behavior analysis certification will be discussed in detail later in this chapter.

WHAT KNOWLEDGE, SKILLS, AND ABILITIES SHOULD A QUALIFIED BEHAVIOR ANALYST HAVE?

The Florida Department of Business and Professional Regulation recently conducted a national survey of behavior analysts to determine the content area for a new version of the Florida Behavior analysis Certification Examination. Persons who were surveyed were currently certified behavior analysts in Florida or Oklahoma, or were full members of the Association for Behavior Analysis. A total of 276 individuals from 35 states responded to the survey.

The survey asked the respondents to give opinions as to the importance of each of more than 100 competencies to the practice of behavior analysis. The following items were judged to be the critical and essential skills in behavior analysis and formed the content area in which questions were constructed for the new version of the examination.

Content Area 1: Definition and characteristics of Applied Behavior Analysis

1. State assumptions of behavior analysis that distinguish it from other approaches to studying behavior (e.g., behavior is lawful [conforms to certain predictable patterns], behavior can be studied scientifically, behavior is a function of genetics and environment).

2. Distinguish between behaviorism, the experimental analysis of behavior, and applied behavior analysis.

3. Describe dimensions of Applied Behavior Analysis that, taken together, distinguish it from other treatment approaches (i.e., applied, behavioral, analytic, technological, conceptually systematic, effective, and has generality).

4. Define behavior/response/response class.

5. Define environment.

6. Define stimulus.

7. Define consequence.

8. Define antecedent.

9. Define reinforcement.

10. Define punishment.

11. Define stimulus control.

12. Define establishing operation.

13. Define contingency.

14. Define functional relations.

15. Define extinction.

16. Define generalization and maintenance.

17. Describe the respondent conditioning model.

18. Describe the operant conditioning model.

19. Define contingency-shaped and rule-governed behavior and distinguish between examples of each.

Content Area 2: Legal and ethical considerations

20. Assess behavior within applicable legal and ethical standards.

21. Decide when to intervene within applicable legal and ethical standards.

22. Select target behaviors and goals within applicable legal and ethical standards.

23. Choose intervention procedures within applicable legal and ethical standards.

24. Obtain formal informed consent within applicable legal and ethical standards.

25. Obtain approval from other appropriate entities within applicable legal and ethical standards.

26. Implement behavior-change interventions within applicable legal and ethical standards.

27. Evaluate interventions within applicable legal and ethical standards.

28. Protect confidentiality within applicable legal and ethical standards.

29. Use emergency and crisis interventions within applicable legal and ethical standards.

Content Area 3: Emergency procedures

30. Define an emergency situation.

31. State the role and function of emergency procedures.

32. State the essential components and precautions for managing emergency procedures.

Content Area 4: Behavioral assessment

33. State the reasons for conducting a behavioral assessment.

34. State the benefits and limitations of behavioral assessment.

35. Use various methods to gather assessment information.

36. Use various methods to display, summarize, and interpret data.

Content Area 5: Selection of target behaviors and goals

37. Define and develop goals.
38. Define and develop target behavior.
39. Define and develop objectives.
40. Prioritize goals/objectives.

Content Area 6: Measurement of behavior

41. Define response measures that provide direct, continuous measurement (dimensional quantities) of behavior (e.g., frequency, rate, latency, intensity, duration).
42. Define response measures that provide indirect, discontinuous measurement (dimensionless quantities) of behavior.
43. Define and determine the optimal duration of recording interval.
44. Select the recording apparatus (e.g., data sheet, timer, stopwatch, wrist counter) based on ease of use and potential measurement reactivity (i.e., the change in behavior as a result of the awareness of measurement).
45. Use rate (frequency).
46. Use latency.
47. Use duration.
48. Use interresponse time (IRT).
49. Use celeration.
50. Use percent of occurrence.
51. Use partial-interval recording.
52. Use whole-interval recording.
53. Use momentary time sample recording.

Content Area 7: Data display and interpretation

54. Select the best graphic display to effectively communicate quantitative relations (e.g., cumulative record, linear graph, histogram).
55. Decide when to use equal interval (a.k.a. conventional or plain paper) graphs.
56. Decide when to use standard celeration charts (a.k.a. standard behavior chart or six-cycle precision teaching chart).
57. Label and calibrate the scale of the horizontal and vertical axes of equal-interval graphs.

58. Plot data points on equal-interval graphs.
59. Plot data points on standard celeration charts.
60. Display baseline, intervention changes, major environmental changes, and interruptions in data collection on equal-interval graphs.
61. Display baseline, intervention changes, major environmental changes, and interruptions in data collection on standard celeration charts.
62. Determine and describe the level, trend, and variability of data displayed on equal-interval graphs.
63. Determine and describe the level, trend, and variability of data displayed on standard celeration charts.
64. Interpret data and make decisions using level, trend, variability, and the change in each.
65. Interpret data on a cumulative record consistent with principles of behavior and the behavior-analytic literature.
66. Interpret articles from the behavior-analytic literature.

Content Area 8: Demonstrating functional relations

67. State the primary characteristics of the process of demonstrating functional relations.
68. State the rationale for determining functional relations and for determining the reliability and generality of functional relations.
69. Use various methodologies to demonstrate functional relations and to determine the reliability and generality of functional relations through direct and systematic replication, respectively.
70. Identify factors particular to applied settings that must be managed when attempting to demonstrate functional relations.
71. Complete a component analysis (e.g., determining effective components of a treatment package).
72. Complete a parametric analysis (e.g., determining effective parametric values of consequences such as duration or magnitude).

Content Area 9: Establishing and strengthening behavior

73. Determine reinforcers.
74. Identify potential reinforcers.
75. Select and use appropriate parameters and values of reinforcement (e.g., quantity, duration).

76. Select appropriate schedules of reinforcement.

77. Describe variables affecting reinforcement effectiveness (e.g., establishing operations, effort).

78. Use differential reinforcement.

79. Develop and implement token economy procedures.

80. Develop and implement shaping procedures.

81. Develop and implement chaining procedures.

82. Use stimulus-control strategies.

83. Select appropriate techniques for developing incidental learning.

84. Use contextual variables.

85. Use establishing operations.

Content Area 10: Weakening behavior

86. Develop a behavior-replacement plan using the least restrictive interventions likely to be effective given the function of the behavior.

87. Determine punishers.

88. Identify potential punishers.

89. Select and use appropriate parameters and values of punishment (intensity).

90. Select appropriate punishment procedures based on assessment data.

91. State the possible negative effects and limitations of punishers in changing behavior and their effects on behavior.

92. Address other variables influencing punishment effects (e.g., reinforcement frequency, availability of alternative responses).

93. Use differential reinforcement.

94. Use extinction.

95. Use stimulus control strategies.

96. Use contextual variables.

97. Use establishing operations.

Content Area 11: Maintenance and generalization

98. Select behaviors for acquisition that will contact natural contingencies in the target setting.

99. Select appropriate stimulus and response generalization procedures to the target setting.

100. Select appropriate maintenance procedures.

101. Determine when it is appropriate to use a molar system (e.g., stage, levels) to arrange for the maintenance and generalization of target behaviors.

102. Describe how to arrange for generalization and maintenance of target behaviors through a molar system.

103. List the advantages and disadvantages of a molar system for promoting maintenance and generalization of target behaviors.

104. Develop a self-control repertoire to facilitate maintenance and generalization of the target behavior.

Content Area 12: Performance management, incidental learning, and accountability

105. Establish systems that promote positive interpersonal relations and incidental learning and support behavior-change interventions on the part of persons directly involved with (affected by) behavior analysis services.

106. Establish support for behavior-change interventions from persons (individuals or groups) not directly involved with these interventions (e.g., administration, advocacy groups, consumer groups, lawmakers, other human service providers).

107. Establish competency-based training for persons who will be responsible for carrying out behavior analysis procedures.

108. Establish performance-monitoring systems.

The above competencies, which were selected as a result of the survey process, can help parents to identify essential skills in behavior analysis. Parents should expect professional behavior analysts to be skilled in these areas and may wish to use this information when selecting behavior analysts to provide services for their children.

SUMMARY

The above information can help parents to locate professional behavior analysts or to determine if an individual claiming to be a behavior analyst is qualified to work with their children. However, following these suggestions does not guarantee that a professional will be successful when working with an individual. Although a professional credential in behavior analysis is not a foolproof method either, it offers a systematic and professional approach to making this determination.

BEHAVIOR ANALYST CERTIFICATION

Reasons for Certification in Behavior Analysis

Parents of children needing behavioral services should find that certification in behavior analysis is a helpful credential for a number of reasons. Certification gives parents some assurance that the professional has at least minimal qualifications in behavior analysis. Furthermore, because all persons certified would be meeting the same standards covering the same content, parents would know what to expect from a certified individual and could assume some consistency across certified behavior analysts. In addition, parents would have an easy way to refer to an individual qualified in behavior analysis (certified behavior analyst) when requesting services from state agencies or others.

An Example: The Florida Behavior Analysis Certification Program

The State of Florida's Developmental Services Office has offered a certificate in behavior analysis for more than 10 years. During that period, the state has credentialed more than 1,500 individuals as certified behavior analysts (although not all of them specialize in working with individuals who have autism or pervasive developmental disabilities). Florida recently strengthened its certification program by updating its examination and adding more structure and requirements for certification. A number of states are actively engaged in establishing programs based on the Florida model. Information on the Florida Behavior Analysis Certification Program may be obtained by contacting the Florida Developmental Services Program Office at the address provided at the end of this chapter.

Components of a Behavior Analysis Certification Program

Certification programs in behavior analysis should include all or most of the following components. A prototype for language regulating the certification of behavior analysts may be obtained by contacting the Florida Developmental Services Program Office.

Education and Experience Requirements

Certification should require that the practitioner meet certain educational criteria, such as degree(s) held, coursework or other educational preparation, and/or internship or practicum. The degree requirement may specify that the individual hold a degree of a certain level (e.g., a minimum of a master's degree) and/or in a specific field of study (e.g., psychology, social work, special/regular education, or a health science). Coursework requirements may be general, for example specifying that the primary focus must be in behavior analysis, or specific, perhaps delineating the number of credit hours, specific courses, and/or hours of internship or practicum. Florida offers certification at the master's/doctoral level and at the bachelor's level. Course requirements are specified for each level.

Individuals should be required to have experience as practitioners either before or after the degree requirements are met. This experience should be of a specified duration and completed under the supervision of a qualified individual who is certified in behavior analysis and has practiced for a number of years. The Florida program requires supervised experience at both levels of certification.

Written Examination

A written examination is considered to be the single most objective and powerful means to determine competence. The purpose of the written examination process is to separate those candidates who are qualified to practice within a given field from those who are not. The examination must proceed in accordance with principles developed by the field of test construction and measurement and must be consistent with a substantial body of case law. Both of these specifically address how the test instrument must be developed and how the entire examination process must be conducted. Passing the examination becomes extremely important because it may affect the candidate's ability to practice. The importance of passing the examination virtually guarantees that some of the candidates who do not pass will challenge one or more aspects of the examination process through administrative hearing or in court. Failure to withstand the challenge of a serious aspect of the examination might result in the collapse of the entire certification process. This could have a profound effect on those wishing to be certified and those already certified. Therefore, the test instrument must be developed by professionals in the field of test construction and measurement, and the examination process must be administered by professionals who are specifically trained in that activity.

The current Florida Behavior Analysis Certification Examination was developed in accordance with appropriate professional and legal standards by a professional test construction firm and is updated and administered by the Florida Department of Professional Regulation. This examination contains multiple-choice questions based on the 12 clusters of 108 competency tasks developed during the recent updating.

Definition of Practice

The certification program should contain a definition of behavior analysis and the scope of the behavior analysts' practice. This definition should establish what the behavior analyst does professionally as well as what is not part of the practice of behavior analysis. The Florida certification program contains such a definition.

Code of Ethics

Persons who are to become certified behavior analysts should sign an appropriate professional code of ethics. This code could come from a national organization such as the American Psychological Association, from a state professional organization such as the Florida Association for Behavioral Analysis, or it could be specially constructed for the certification program. An example of a state professional association code of ethics may be obtained by contacting the Florida Association for Behavior Analysis at the address provided at the end of this chapter.

Discipline

A component of certification should include provisions for disciplining certified individuals who overtly violate basic professional, ethical, or legal standards. Penalties for those found guilty of violations should vary from a reprimand for a mild infraction to suspension of license and substantial fines for severe infractions.

Continuing Education

Continuing education should be required in order to maintain a certification in behavior analysis. Certified individuals must attend preapproved educational activities in order to obtain a specified number of training hours over a specified interval of time. The basic purpose of continuing education is to ensure that behavior analysts have contact with current content in their profession to maintain an appropriate level of competence. The Florida Behavior Analysis Certification program contains continuing education requirements.

Developing State Certification Programs in Behavior Analysis

Parents who may be interested in establishing a behavior analyst certification program in their particular state should keep the following in mind. Certification programs are usually operated by state government, generally through a professional board or through a state agency. Parents may find that it is easier to convince a state agency dealing with pervasive developmental disabilities and autism to establish a program than to convince the state legislature to pass laws establishing certification programs.

Florida's certification program is the most developed and can serve as a model for other states. Parents may wish to obtain information on the Florida program to serve as a prototype for their state, although modifications certainly will be needed on a state-by-state basis. The most expensive part of a certification program is the development and maintenance of the written examination. Because the update process for the Florida examination involved a national survey, the examination may be appropriate for use in other states. Florida has been willing to provide testing services for other states for a reasonable charge in the past, thereby substantially reducing the expense of this component.

If parents have a personal relationship with government agency officials or state legislators, they may be able to expedite the establishment of a certification program. Unfortunately, state officials often seem to respond more to tragedy than to be proactive, so it may take an abuse of behavioral procedures to initiate action.

ADDRESSES

Association for Behavior Analysis
Department of Psychology
Western Michigan University
Kalamazoo, Michigan 49008

Florida Association for Behavior Analysis
Department of Psychology
Florida State University
Tallahassee, Florida 32306

Developmental Services Program Office
Department of Health and Rehabilitative Services
Winewood Boulevard
Tallahassee, Florida 32301

SELECTED READINGS

American Board of Behavioral Psychology. (1989). *Procedures and regulations for the creation of the diplomate in behavior therapy.* New York: American Board of Behavioral Psychology.

American Psychological Association. (1992). *Ethics code.* Washington, DC: American Psychological Association.

Department of Business and Professional Regulation and Department of Health and Rehabilitative Services. (1994). *Information and registration booklet for the behavior analysis certification examination.* Tallahassee, FL: Department of Business and Professional Regulation and Department of Health and Rehabilitative Services.

Department of Health and Rehabilitative Services. (1989). *Behavioral programming manual.* Tallahassee, FL: Department of Health and Rehabilitative Services.

Florida Association for Behavior Analysis. (1989). *Code of ethics.* Tallahassee, FL: Florida Association for Behavior Analysis.

Johnston, J. M., & Shook, G. L. (1993). Model for the statewide delivery of programming services. *Mental Retardation, 31,* 127–139.

Lovaas, O. I., & Favell, J. E. (1987). Protection for clients undergoing aversive restrictive interventions. *Education and Treatment of Children, 10,* 311–325.

Shook, G. L. (1993). The professional credential in behavior analysis. *The Behavior Analyst, 16,* 87–101.

Shook, G. L., & Van Houten, R. (1993). Ensuring the competence of behavior analysts. In R. Van Houten & S. Axelrod (Eds.), *Behavior analysis and treatment.* New York: Plenum.

Shook, G. L., Hartsfield, F., & Hemingway, M. (1995). Essential content for training behavior analysis practitioners. *The Behavior Analyst, 18,* 83–92.

CHAPTER NINE

Recruiting, Selecting, and Training Teaching Assistants

Jack Scott

Teaching assistants are the people who do most of the work in intensive behavioral programs. They may be referred to as teachers, teaching assistants, or therapists. Regardless of what we call them, their role is critical in the success of home-based behavioral, early intervention programs. They are, in a very real sense, the backbone of the program. For the purpose of this section, they are called teaching assistants, or simply TAs.

The rationale for choosing this term is simple. Autism, from a behavior-analytic view, constitutes a host of behavioral deficits and excesses. With our intervention efforts we teach new skills or teach so as to reduce problem behaviors. The behavior analyst, whether a parent or someone working with a parent, is not in this sense a therapist treating an illness or disorder but a teacher. As teachers, behavior analysts make the critical instructional decisions, select the skills to be taught, analyze data, and assess progress. The people carrying out the intervention under the guidance of a behavior analyst are assisting in this teaching effort; hence, they are teaching assistants.

Teaching assistants are essential to home-based intensive behavioral programming. Parents are rarely able to do the job alone. The energy required of parents to meet the nonintervention needs of a child with autism (as well as the needs of other children and family members) may leave little or no energy for active teaching. Delivering 25–40 hours per week of intensive programming would leave parents with time for nothing else. Remaining fresh so as to be effective in essential parental roles requires time away from the child. It takes time to coordinate intervention activities and personnel. From a technical perspective, using several TAs allows newly acquired skills to be more readily generalized to different trainers. In some families, there may simply be no one with the time or capacity to provide intensive teaching. For these, and many more reasons, TAs are necessary.

Although they are necessary, you may not welcome these helpers with open arms. Catherine Maurice, in *Let Me Hear Your Voice* (1993), describes her initial attitude toward Bridget Taylor, her first behavioral teacher. "In the beginning I was to think of Bridget as a (barely tolerable) necessary evil" (p. 70). This is not unusual. Parents may feel inadequate because they must rely on other people to help teach their child during a time in a child's life when the teaching is usually done entirely by the parents. These strangers become a fixture in the home and privy to the most carefully guarded information about family strengths and weaknesses. The loss of privacy that accompanies home-based intervention efforts (and the lives of most families with a child with autism) may be most keenly felt when the first TAs start coming. Parents may perceive a loss of decision-making power and be resentful of the TAs. It may be painful when a parent must stay away during initial tantrums by the child confronted with instructional demands. The TA is paired with these stressful situations and likely to be a mixed blessing, at least for a while. Maurice was alert enough to realize that she could not, at first, appreciate the value of Bridget. She writes "I would not have known a gift of gold from a lump of coal." Only later did she see her as a "gift from heaven" (p. 69).

THE TEACHING ASSISTANT'S ROLE

What should you expect these TAs to do? This will depend on the nature of your program, the skills of the TAs, and the specific needs of your child and family. Some parents may think they want someone to provide general child care and do a little specialized teaching on the side. This will probably not work very well. In the absence of a clear mission and a determined and systematic intervention plan, you might as well use this person as a baby-sitter. If you have a clear plan and are determined to make a difference, the role specifications come into focus pretty easily. You will want someone to carry out the intervention activities. This initially means someone to run discrete trials, take data on the response to each trial and reinforce good work according to the established program. Your TA must be able to withhold reinforcement and re-present trials as specified in the program. While you would be happy to get all the additional time you can manage in your program, you want someone who can give you at least 2 hours per week of high-quality time. You must have someone who is dependable. TAs must be capable of understanding the program objectives and should be committed to helping your child make rapid progress. In order to be effective, they must be able to relate to your child and find joy in his or her progress. They must do this while insisting that the child comply with the program and earn reinforcement only for correct (or improved) responses.

In short, you will want someone who is a teacher of your child. This teacher will be expected to carry out a systematic instructional sequence planned by a specialist. He will be expected to act independently, manage your child when necessary, interpret the program in light of your child's progress during the session, and reinforce your child as enthusiastically and effectively as possible, contingent on good performance. You will treat him like a teacher, and he should act like a teacher.

PARENT RESPONSIBILITIES

Parents incur several important responsibilities in this relationship. Among these are maintaining the role expectations for the TA, providing the necessary program supports, and providing feedback and positive reinforcement. Once you have established the teaching and training expectations, you should stick with them. You expect the TA to deliver home-based teaching according to a systematic behavioral plan. Do not expect her to be a nanny. You should not bring your child to a preschool undressed, and you should not bring your child to the home-based teaching setting undressed. You should not expect the TA to dress your child or otherwise prepare the child for the teaching session. To do so on anything other than an emergency basis diminishes her role as a teacher. You may institute dressing or toileting skills in your program and do so on a systematic basis. But you will do this in accordance with the plan, when your child is ready to learn these skills. Do not push these general child-care chores on your TA for your convenience. If you are paying your TA to do the program, you are wasting your money when they provide low-level baby-sitting services. The TA will see this as a loss of status, and you will see a decrease in performance on critical teaching behaviors.

The TA will count on you to coordinate the learning activities and provide the needed materials. Unless you specifically pay TAs to do so, do not expect them to gather the materials for teaching. As parents, you will want to keep these items for the use of all the TAs. It is not appropriate to ask the TA to plan or supervise other TAs in the program. This is the responsibility of a professional with training in behavior analysis who will be working with you to create and guide the program. Parents may decide to become trained and to guide their own program. In either case, responsibility and authority for the program must not be shifted to nonprofessional teaching assistants. This is not their role. The TAs will need skilled support, and parents must either offer this support themselves or see that it is provided.

Parents must provide many forms of support for the TAs. Parents will typically incur the costs of initial training. They pay for the professional consultation and program monitoring essential to keep the program on track, which often includes some direct consultation for the TAs. This consultation should be responsive to any special concerns or questions they may have. Apart from this, parents must provide feedback on session progress and keep the TA appraised of progress achieved by other TAs. Your feedback must be accurate and honest to be useful. If you, as a parent, see that the TA is making an error or is off-track, you must provide corrective feedback in a supportive manner, telling them just what to do to correct the performance deficit. Many parents may initially feel awkward in this role. Don't worry. Concern for your child will make you strong. Mistakes and wrong steps happen, but they must be addressed. You also must address TA effort, enthusiasm, skill, and progress. When you see these behaviors, you will naturally want to provide all the positive reinforcement you can muster. Praise, especially specific praise for successful work, is always welcome. Praise new TAs extensively and as immediately as possible. Refine your praise with your more experienced assistants and direct them to what you saw that was praiseworthy. For example, you may have noticed that they achieved a high percentage of correct responses on a troublesome skill. Point this out when you praise them. Parent praise is one important component of the total package of TA appreciation. Beyond this, you will ask your TAs to share your family's joy in your child's progress. You will invite them to feel a partnership with the other members of the team. At the same time, you will come to respect and value the individual goals of the TAs. Celebrate with them when they have completed their degree requirements or go on to a college. Empathize when they have three finals in one day and a big term paper due the next. Whether they are volunteers or paid, good teaching assistants are worth their weight in gold. Let them know it.

GUIDANCE FROM PROFESSIONAL LITERATURE

Many family programs are guided by *Teaching Developmentally Disabled Children: The ME Book* (1981), by O. Ivar Lovaas. Although strong in teaching procedures, this book does not provide much information on the role of the teaching assistant in the home-based program. It does provide clear information for the use of teaching assistants when the child is being transferred to a regular classroom. Lovaas refers to them as assistant teachers; their role is the same as that of the specialized instructional aide or unique aide. Lovaas recommends the use of volunteers recruited from university, community college, and high school programs. When volunteers participate in a school program under the supervision of a certified teacher, they may be able to use this work as an internship or student teaching. However, when the teaching is in a home-based program, a program not directly supervised by a certified teacher, such teaching will probably not be useful for internships. Apart from this brief section in *The ME Book,* not much has been available to guide parents in working with teaching assistants.

RECRUITING TEACHING ASSISTANTS

Teaching assistants are where you find them. Creative recruiting is essential if you are to staff your home program with talented, energetic, and responsible people. The conditions prevailing in your area will, to a large degree, determine the nature of your search for assistants. If you live near a university, students will obviously be prime candidates. If you live in a rural area, you will need to depend more heavily on high school students, neighbors, relatives, and perhaps church members or retired persons. In any case, parents would love to be able to select from highly motivated, experienced, and well-trained people. In most parts of the country, however, this is just not possible. You must seek out new teaching talent. Family finances dictate other considerations. If you have a tight budget, you must be willing to rely on volunteer help. If you can afford to pay wages, you can be far more particular in the selection and probably more demanding in terms of adherence to the program and less tolerant of no-show days and other lapses in responsibility. A common pattern is for a family to have both paid and volunteer assistants working at the same time. The candidate pool and recruiting strategies are likely to be very similar for both groups.

Recruitment Strategy Development

Before beginning your recruitment effort, establish a strategy. It may be best to consider your recruitment strategy as a behavioral recruitment strategy. You have an array of potential reinforcers, including an excellent training opportunity, a supportive, friendly and nonthreatening teaching-learning environment (in which you will offer coaching and feedback), and you may or may not be offering wages. In many cases you will have other reinforcers available or available in conjunction with faculty at the student's host institution. These factors include grades, positive teaching evaluations, and letters of recommendation. These letters could mention not only strong character and ability, but also dedication, involvement in an innovative family-based program, and the value of services rendered. In addition, the sense of accomplishment that comes from seeing a child progress and the satisfaction that comes from helping a family are powerful reinforcers. Identify other reinforcers available to your family and list them. Just as with a child receiving intensive behavioral intervention, you must determine what is reinforcing for your potential TAs. It may help to recall the functional definition of reinforcement: A reinforcer is not a reinforcer unless it functions to increase the probability of the desired behavior. You must be able and willing to match your reinforcers to your potential teaching assistants. Put another way, you must determine the likely reinforcers for your teaching assistants, determine the reinforcers available to you, and develop your recruitment strategy with these reinforcers in mind.

This may seem obvious, but failure to realistically assess the available reinforcers appears to be at the heart of several otherwise well organized home-based intervention efforts. Parents are usually highly reinforced by anything that helps their child. They are likely to be totally committed to a program offering success and perhaps too enthusiastic to understand clearly that their hopes and objectives for the child are not more widely shared. This requires a dose of realism. Of course, you can appeal to teaching assistants in desperation and get some of them to agree to work in your home-based program. However, maintaining TA involvement and faithful participation in these situations is likely to be far more difficult. Similarly, setting too high a performance expectation may scare away or quickly drive off some otherwise good assistants. This is likely to be a problem if parents insist on rigid adherence to a teaching schedule or exert pressure for TAs to commit to a long-term service obligation.

Recruiting Students as Teaching Assistants

The following strategies for recruiting students have worked successfully in Broward and Palm Beach counties in Florida. This region has large cities and extensive suburban areas with at least four university/college campuses and two large community colleges. Public funding for home-based programs, with one encouraging recent exception (*Drucker vs. Broward County School Board,* 1995), is not available. Parents must rely on their own resources and creativity to recruit assistants and run their program.

Students offer a number of real advantages for the family. They are typically young, energetic, and reasonably free of complicating responsibilities. They are eager and enthusiastic. When they see the changes in a child with autism, changes they made possible, they become committed to the program. Students, if carefully selected, will have good skills and be relatively easy to train and supervise. As people actively engaged in learning, they are open to new ideas. Students, you can hope, will be relatively influenced by the research literature and the data from your home program. With students it is often possible to arrange for academic, credit-bearing participation, which increases motivation and dependability.

The disadvantages must be considered and demand flexibility on the part of the family. Students often have heavy academic demands, and you will need to make allowances for final exam periods and breaks in the academic calendar. If you insist that a student teach as scheduled during final exam or break periods, you may run into problems, especially if your students are volunteers. Your recruitment discussions should recognize the commitment of students to their academic programs. Parents might like to expect that a teaching assistant will work each and every Tuesday and Thursday from 9:00 to 12:00 for the next year, but with students this is just not possible. Rather than attempting to pressure or coerce students, be realistic in terms of their needs and flexible in terms of how you can meet your child's needs. A good way to deal with the final exam or holiday break period would be to use some fill-in assistants. These fill-ins could be relatives or local retired persons who would like to help but cannot do so on a regular basis.

You can recruit students, whether for volunteer service or for pay, in the same manner. Post attractive flyers prominently on campus with clear information about your needs. Some colleges have strict rules about posting nonapproved flyers, which are often flagrantly violated. You may be able to get help in posting approved job notices through the office of student employment. Most universities have such employment offices, which help students to find work. You

can reach a large number of students with such a posting, but be prepared to screen out some naive and hard-to-motivate people. Your flyers can be handwritten or easily done on a computer. Figure 9.1 shows sample flyers. Provide lots of information. An interested student will read the entire flyer and call. This saves you valuable time and energy talking on the phone with people who will not work out. If they decide to call, you can provide additional information, and if they seem capable, you can set a time for them to visit and see your program.

Working with Faculty

Enlist faculty at regional colleges and high schools to help in your recruitment efforts. Many programs require students to complete service hours or deliver specific types of educational or therapeutic activities. Faculty need placement sites, and students want placements in which they can make a difference. Traditionally, students are placed in established schools and agencies. This is changing. In the human services we are finally recognizing the importance of the family in the delivery of services to young children. A great way for professionals to demonstrate this recognition is to send students to assist in parent-directed home programs, although many are afraid to do so. Professors may feel some security in sending a student to a school with certified teachers and a state-approved program, but they may hesitate to commit students to an untried family program.

Parents must be prepared to work with teachers and university professors to demonstrate the mutual benefits of the arrangement. The faculty benefit as students learn innovative techniques for early intervention in a structured, research-guided, data-based program. The program demands quickly sort out the talented from the insincere, while allowing weaker but dedicated students a chance to grow and strengthen their skills. Faculty can more accurately assess the capability of their students in this way. As noted, these efforts allow faculty to bring students into direct and meaningful contact with parents on a more equal footing. We increasingly speak of a parent-professional partnership, and faculty support for a parent-directed program is a clear way to show this commitment. The last advantage makes a sad commentary on the state of educational practice. In many places faculty know the quality of the school or agency placements is deplorable. Students may learn the best practices in the lecture hall and see ongoing disasters in the real world. This is especially true, in many parts of the United States, in programs for preschool-age children with autism. Home-based programs provide faculty with a real alternative to mixed or low-quality placements.

EMPLOYMENT OPPORTUNITY

Students needed to work with our 4-year-old autistic child. We have an intensive home program. This program is based on applied behavior analysis and the skillful use of positive reinforcement.

Professional training will be provided.

FAU academic credit may be available.

Flexible hours: Afternoons and weekends.

We are located in Boca Raton in the Glades Road/ I-95 area close to FAU.

Please call Peter or Prudence Brennan at (407) 555-1244.

Autism teaching assistants (407) 555-1244 | Autism teaching assistants (407) 555-1244 | Autism teaching assistants (407) 555-1244 | Autism teaching assistants (407) 555-1244 | Autism teaching assistants (407) 555-1244 | Autism teaching assistants (407) 555-1244 | Autism teaching assistants (407) 555-1244 | Autism teaching assistants (407) 555-1244 | Autism teaching assistants (407) 555-1244 | Autism teaching assistants (407) 555-1244 | Autism teaching assistants (407) 555-1244 | Autism teaching assistants (407) 555-1244 | Autism teaching assistants (407) 555-1244 | Autism teaching assistants (407) 555-1244 | Autism teaching assistants (407) 555-1244 | Autism teaching assistants (407) 555-1244

Figure 9.1.   Sample fliers for recruiting students on a university campus.

FAU STUDENTS NEEDED TO WORK WITH YOUNG CHILDREN WITH AUTISM

Needed: FAU students interested in working directly with preschool children with autism on a volunteer basis or for independent study (EEX 4905) credit. Students who are dependable, smart, and most importantly caring, are needed to work as teaching assistants with young children. You will receive training, regular supervision, and other assistance as you work in a structured, research-based approach helping a child with autism. The program is based on the work of Dr. O. Ivar Lovaas at UCLA and features positive behavioral techniques carefully sequenced and structured for the child. Lovaas has reported (Lovaas, 1987) that approximately 50% of intensively treated young autistic children have been able to reach normal (non-handicapped) levels of functioning when this training is applied early and intensively. These results would be seen as miraculous if not for the skillful hard work and dedication needed to achieve these gains.

For these efforts to be successful, families need bright, energetic, and dependable people to help them. Several area families are actively seeking the assistance of FAU students. We have a number of parents in Palm Beach and Broward counties who have assembled teams of teacher-therapists, arranged for professional training and routine supervision by certified or licensed professionals, and have instituted this training for their child. The results have been amazing. You may have an opportunity to make a truly profound difference in a young child's life and learn valuable teaching and therapeutic techniques at the same time. You don't have to know anything about autism. What you need is a willingness to learn and a strong desire to help.

If this is of interest to you, contact Dr. Jack Scott in the Department of Exceptional Student Education. My office is in the College of Education Building, Room 431 and my phone is 407-367-3239. If I am not in, please leave a message on my voice mail and I will call you back. Note a good time for me to call you. If you would like to do this but don't need independent study credit, you are also welcome to call and explore options.

If you are interested please plan to attend <u>one</u> of four informal information meetings to be held on Tuesday August 23 , Wednesday August 24, Thursday August 25, or Monday August 29. All meetings will be held in the College of Education, Room 402 from 2:00-3:00 PM.

Figure 9.1. (continued)

Although the advantages are obvious, parents must be prepared to actively develop and cultivate the placement relationship. Parents must seek out the right people at the school and make a strong case. Fortunately, most university and high school teachers will be influenced by the professional literature and scientific research. If your program is based on sound behavior-analytic principles and practices, you can surprise them with the results you can obtain. Provide them with a packet of the key research articles. Gina Green's section of this manual offers the kind of powerful research synthesis that high school and university faculty should appreciate. Seek to determine the nature of service and internship requirements at the school. Then explore ways to make your home program fit these requirements. Many colleges permit professors to offer independent study credits or sections on special topics. These limited involvements can offer a good starting point for both parties. When you approach university professors and especially high school service-activity coordinators, it is best to have a firm plan in hand. Determine ahead of time how many people you can use, how many hours per week you seek to cover, and how and when you will provide professional training and supervision. Provide the name and specify the credentials of the professional support person. A vague plan will not receive a good reception. Parents may feel intimidated in this regard or feel that they should approach these professionals with an open-ended arrangement. This will not work. A carefully crafted plan shows that you have done your homework and will probably be able to offer a good placement experience. Prepare a one-page overview of your plan with a section on the anticipated involvement of students serving as TAs. Many universities require 60–90 hours of direct, on-site work for 3 hours of academic credit. Divide this over a 15-week semester and you have 4–6 hours per week. Have an hours log available and bring a copy of the agenda for the training session.

Be prepared to start small and grow. It may help to point out to the professionals that these students not only earn credit but they also should be able to count on important letters of recommendation (from both faculty and parents), which seem to be increasingly important as students with uniformly high grades compete for prize spots in special programs. Parents may be in a good position to offer talented students paid positions on the team upon completion of the credit-earning experience. In this situation parents have a wonderful screening and selection opportunity.

Parents should creatively explore the potential for working with high school and college faculty. If these professionals are biased against behavioral techniques, it may not matter what you say or do. Be prepared to cut your losses and find a more receptive or more reasonable person at the institution.

Contacting the Behavioral Community as a Recruitment Strategy

In many regions it is easy for parents to feel they are operating in isolation from professionals who share an appreciation for behavioral technology. One way to reduce this is for parents to make contact with their state and/or regional behavioral organizations. The Association for Behavior Analysis (ABA), with offices at Western Michigan University, is the main behavioral professional organization. The ABA has affiliated chapters in many states and regions of the United States as well as international chapters. The ABA phone number is 616-387-8341. Ask for the name and phone number of the state contact person or state president. You may be able to contact local behavior analysts. Such contacts may yield information on approachable university faculty, behavior analysts in private practice, training sessions, and conferences. The Florida Association for Behavior Analysis (FABA), for example, holds an annual conference attended by approximately 600 behavior analysts. ABA members have known for many years that intensive behavioral interventions could dramatically improve the lives of young children with autism and related disabilities.

SCREENING AND SELECTION OF TEACHING ASSISTANTS

Screening

Your recruitment efforts will yield people interested in the program, and you must be confident that these strangers will help and in no way hurt your children. Not all who are interested will be acceptable. Parents should be honest about this. Let your flyers and other promotion materials reflect this fact. For example, in your flyer it may be wise to say something like, "Those eager *to be considered* for this placement or position should call. . . ." You do not want to be in a situation in which you feel you must accept someone. This should also be a factor with faculty-facilitated university or high school student participation. Your children are your very special responsibility. Because you seek to help them as much as possible, you must be tough, when necessary, to protect them from unqualified people. Your situation and values will dictate the final criteria for selection. Parental instincts will guide you on the most critical decisions.

You will be able to assess many things during phone calls. Avoid students who are too willing to commit without having any idea of the nature of the involvement. Someone who seems difficult or cranky on the phone will probably not get any better in person. Your time and access to your home and family is precious, so be prepared to make tough decisions about who you will and will not invite for a visit to your program. You must be prepared to say no to some eager volunteers and to use your selection instincts. If you can't do this, have someone assist in the process. If you still feel uncomfortable, you may not be ready to coordinate a home-based intervention effort. Managing the total program requires a great deal of direct person-to-person contact and strong decision-making skills. Screening and selecting teaching assistants is a real test of these skills.

Before you have candidates visit your home, make sure they understand the nature of the program. If they are familiar with behavioral psychology or the work of Ivar Lovaas, you can expect that they will. If not, consider providing them with some program descriptions and articles. Lovaas (1987) is ideal for this purpose, as are brief selections from *The ME Book,* and Gina Green's section of this manual. Provide selections from your training materials. Tell candidates to call you when they have read the materials. At this point some may decide this is not right for them and others will be more convinced that they want to help. A high school teacher or a university faculty member that you are working with can supply the students with the materials and explain the program and in other ways prescreen your recruits. In all cases the next step is essential.

Invite the candidate to observe your program. Set a time during which a competent TA is working directly with your child. Tell the candidate that you want him to observe. Explain that interruptions would not be appropriate and that you can answer questions and give more information after the observation. Thirty minutes to an hour should be adequate.

Interviewing

With those who remain interested, discuss your expectations and the nature of the supports available. It is best to consider more than one person. Telling each candidate that you are considering several people will give you a graceful way to turn down those you do not wish to accept. Ask candidates to tell you their motivations. Ask about their training, grades, work history, and family history. Explore any area that seems suspect or which appears to make them uncomfortable. Sadly, too many people who have unnatural interests in children and those with other major problems seem eager to work with children. Unless you are prepared to begin intensive treatment for adults with problems, it is best to steer clear of them. As a parent of a child with autism, you have your hands full providing a high-quality, in-home intervention program. Plan to select only the most responsible, talented, and caring individuals you can find.

Take time to make your decision. In a two-parent family it is wise to have both parents meet each candidate. If you have asked for references, take time to check them. If you have lingering concerns, it may be best to say no and provide fewer hours of intervention than to take too much risk. Often you will know right away that certain people are just right; others you will feel will probably be okay. Some families may be in a position to run the candidates through training and then consider making a final hiring or selection decision. In some cases, this will not work out. Taking everything into consideration, you will make your selections. Call these TAs and get the ball rolling. Provide them with the times and dates of training and begin to work on the schedule. Establish communication with them and be sure they know how to make contact with you. Once they say yes, welcome them to the team.

Securing adequate resources for a home-based program presents a tough problem in relation to recruitment and selection. In some parts of the country, public funding may be mandated. Pay arrangements may be influenced or controlled by the nature of the funding policy. Where public funding is not yet provided, churches, synagogues, service groups, civic organizations, or charities may be willing to help fund some of the TA and other program costs. Parents, however, are likely to be picking up most of the cost. Maximizing the use of volunteers and students for academic credit results in a cost savings. Beyond this you will be paying for services. If people do not meet the expectations you have set for them, you must do something. After you have told performance-deficient TAs of your concerns, help them to correct the situation. If they cannot or will not change to meet your expectations, you should let them go. Seek someone new and chalk this up as a learning experience.

TRAINING

A person with professional levels of skill in Applied Behavior Analysis should provide training for your TAs. A few professionals with skills in behavior analysis and training in psychology, special education, speech language pathology, and related fields are beginning to specialize in providing support for home-based programs. In south Florida we are blessed to have several strong professional in-home behavioral interventionists. Some parents have become self-trained and have established themselves as experts in home-based intervention. The competencies featured in Chapter 8 of this manual offer important objective criteria in this regard. Someone competent in behavior analysis and experienced in running a home-based program should provide the TA training.

Teaching assistants must be trained to be effective. In home-based programs, parents must assume the responsibility for training. Although parents may be able to recruit one or two assistants with previous experience and training, they must usually be prepared to arrange for the training of several people. A competent trainer will have his or her own priorities for training. Again, the second half of this chapter provides a good deal of guidance. In home programs, the training tradition has emphasized demonstration of teaching techniques and highly practical skills in managing the trials and teaching sessions. The training should also provide general information about the concepts supporting behavior analysis and the philosophy of behaviorism.

Initial training focuses on task and mission but should also present the basics of applied behavior analysis. Such content will provide a conceptual base, allow the teaching assistants to understand both progress and problems more effectively, and help to develop a shared technical language. Both praise and corrective feedback statements offered to students in this shared language will make for more effective communication.

Basic university courses in behavior analysis typically involve 45 hours of class time and the expectation that the student will spend 2–3 hours of preparation for each hour of class time. Few family-supported training efforts can hope to provide such depth and scope of coverage. Rather, your training should seek to orient the TAs to the field of behavior analysis and highlight key principles and trends. The challenge facing the skilled trainer is to accomplish this in the shortest time possible. Skilled presenters have refined techniques for doing this and an array of textbooks can guide less experienced presenters. The research literature facilitates this effort as well. Consider, for example, what most behavior analysts regard as the classic description of the field by Baer, Wolf, and Risley, published in the first issue of the *Journal of Applied Behavior Analysis* in 1968. These authors present seven defining dimensions of ABA, which can serve as the core of the presentation. In addition, the use of helpful mnemonics can make it easy for students to recall key facts. The phrase "GET A CAB" helps in recalling the key words/phrases for the seven dimensions offered by Baer, Wolf, and

Risley: G = generalization, A = applied to real problems, T = technological, A = analytic, C = conceptually based on principles of behavior, E = effective (well beyond a mere statistical test of significance), and B = behavioral (focus on observable behavior).

Beyond this, the principles of reinforcement—both positive and negative—punishment, and extinction should be considered essential. It would be important to have a brief discussion of the progress made by behavior analysts in advancing the treatment of and quality of life for persons with severe disabilities. Initial training should also feature the recent trend toward positive (nonaversive) technology and the restriction or elimination of aversives. Training can also highlight the communicative functions of what are usually seen as problem behaviors. Presenting these topics in addition to the basic skills necessary to carry out the program will help orient students to this exciting discipline. It will prepare them to refute some of the outdated and inaccurate criticism of behavioral technology that they will almost certainly encounter. Finally, it will provide an appreciation for the essential contribution made by B. F. Skinner, which was to identify the role of consequences in shaping and strengthening behavior.

FUTURE ISSUES

Several important issues remain to be addressed in the future. Parents and professionals will want to consider establishing a system for differentiating TAs based on skills and experience. This will become more important as public funding becomes more widely available for home programs and TA positions become regarded as regular employment options by students and others. In addition, the use of community coordinating agencies to recruit and screen TAs holds great promise. Parents in several areas have joined together to share in training and recruitment efforts, as in the regional SPEC* parent group in South Florida. Finally, we need detailed and systematic information on parent and TA expectations and experiences. This information can result in refinement of training and support efforts and wider sharing of successful techniques.

In the meantime, parents will continue to support each other and, with the help of a dedicated group of progressive educators and behavior analysts, they will recruit, select, train, and support the growing corps of teaching assistants who are taking the teaching of young children with autism to new and wonderful heights.

---

* SPEC Group, Inc., P.O. Box 970161, Boca Raton, FL 33497. Pamela Gorski and Ruth Singer-Strunk, directors.

REFERENCES

Baer, D. M., Wolf, M. M., & Risley, T. R. (1968). Some current dimensions of applied behavior analysis. *Journal of Applied Behavior Analysis, 1*, 91–97.

Drucker vs. Broward County School Board, State of Florida, Division of Administrative Hearings. (1995).

Lovaas, O. I. (1981). *Teaching developmentally disabled children: The ME book.* Austin, TX: PRO-ED.

Lovaas, O. I. (1987). Behavioral treatment and normal intellectual and educational functioning in young autistic children. *Journal of Consulting and Clinical Psychology, 55*, 3–9.

Maurice, C. (1993). *Let me hear your voice: A family's triumph over autism.* New York: Knopf.

CHAPTER TEN

The UCLA Young Autism Model of Service Delivery

O. Ivar Lovaas

Any history documenting progress in the treatment of autism should note that it is the parents of such children who have suffered most due to the ineffective treatments offered to their children. At the same time, they have been the leaders in identifying and promoting effective treatments. The pioneering efforts of parents began as early as the 1960s with the publication of Rimland's (1964) book and continues in the present, with the publication of Maurice (1993) and Johnson and Crowder's (1994) autobiographical accounts. There may be many reasons for the parent's leadership. Parents hurt the most when they observe their children's steady deterioration in settings where they were supposed to be receiving treatment and education. The parents were thus exposed to evidence they could not escape, prompting the search for better treatments.

Unlike parents, most professionals are trained to rely on clinical theory, and few clinicians conduct empirical research. Instead they place their faith in "clinical intuition," which may well override data. Only recently have empirical data regarding treatment outcome been objectively recorded and communicated, so as to better inform everyone about treatment effects, allowing for progress in the design of more effective treatments. Behavioral psychologists have played a leadership role in bringing data to bear on the design of treatments, some of which is summarized below.

DATA FROM RESEARCH

Certain basic findings in behavioral treatment research influence the design of our treatment programs. Seven such findings are described below.

1. There is little or no evidence that by changing one behavior we will concurrently significantly change other behaviors of the same person. For example,

when we help a client to acquire language, we are not likely to observe a concurrent increase in other behaviors, such as emotional attachment, peer play, and self-help skills. Even within an area like language there is little evidence that, for example, mastery of prepositions will facilitate the use of pronouns. In short, data fail to suggest the existence of one pivotal or critical behavior or conflict, which when treated, results in a comprehensive and concurrent improvement in many or most areas of functioning. Instead, effective treatment requires us to address all of the client's behavioral deviations.

2. Perhaps as a corollary to the need for comprehensiveness, we strongly suggest that an intervention encompass a large percentage of a child's waking hours, about 40 hours per week (Lovaas & Smith, 1988). Past studies indicate that 10 hours a week is inadequate (Lovaas & Smith, 1988), as is 20 hours (Anderson, Avery, DiPietro, Edwards, & Christian, 1987). The majority of the 40 hours, at least during the first 6–12 months of intervention, should emphasize the remediation of speech and language deficits (Lovaas, 1977). Later, this time may be divided between promoting peer integration while continuing to remediate speech and language deficits.

3. We have seen little or no evidence that children with autism benefit from group instruction in the initial stages of treatment. On the contrary, findings indicate that these children learn only in one-to-one situations for approximately the first 6 months of treatment (Koegel, Rincover, & Egel, 1982). In our experience, this one-to-one training need not be administered by degreed professionals, but can be effectively delivered by people who have been thoroughly trained to use behavioral treatment techniques, such as undergraduate students or family members (Lovaas & Smith, 1988).

When a child is ready to enter a group situation, data indicate that the group should be as normal or average as possible. Children with autism perform better when integrated with typical children than when placed with other children with the same diagnosis (Strain, 1983). In the presence of other children with autism, any social behavior that they may have developed usually disappears within minutes (Lovaas & Smith, 1988), presumably because it is not reciprocated. Mere exposure to typical children, however, is not sufficient. Children with autism require explicit instruction from trained tutors on how to interact with their peers (Strain, 1983).

4. There is little evidence that behavior change brought about in one environment will generalize to other environments. In contrast, it is best to plan for situation specificity in treatment effects. This implies that treatment gains made in a classroom environment or in a clinical setting may not generalize to the home and the community. Similarly, gains facilitated by one person, such as a particular teacher, may not generalize to another person, such as the child's mother. In short, the client will have to be treated in most or all of his environments, by most or all of the significant persons in that client's life.

5. Behavioral treatment is based on stepwise and cumulative knowledge from scientific research. No single treatment program, and not even a few, are sufficient to optimize treatment outcome; literally hundreds of programs are required. Each program is designed to teach one skill or concept and is taught in conjunction with 4–10 other programs simultaneously. These programs have been generated over the years by a large number of investigators from across the country. As more discoveries are made in Applied Behavior Analysis, new programs and techniques evolve. Practitioners must become familiar with these programs and keep informed about current developments.

6. We have found that substantial individual differences in treatment outcome occur among clients of the same diagnostic category. The same intervention may have widely different effects on the behaviors of the same physical topography (as in the effect of time out on self-injurious behavior). The person overseeing the case explores how to apply a particular intervention in an individual case and attempts to isolate new and effective treatments expected to help. Most programs help some, but not all clients.

7. There is evidence that the longer the treatment lasts, the larger the client's gains. Furthermore, in most instances of treatment of autism and pervasive developmental disorders (PDD), relapse will occur when treatment is terminated. The only exception to that occurs with early and intensive behavioral intervention. A sizable minority of children with autism who started treatment before the age of 4 were success-fully mainstreamed and appear recovered (McEachin, Smith, & Lovaas, 1993).

Many have refrained from recommending behavioral treatment, citing the use of aversives as the reason. It may be helpful to briefly comment on this issue. Most autistic children will object violently to teaching efforts by screaming out loud, hitting, kicking, and biting the attending adult or themselves. This is understandable considering that the children have met continual failure in understanding what reasonable persons have asked them to do. It is my impression that aggression is a healthy sign and one associated with good motivation. The trick is to make it work in favor of the child's growth. In the past, the University of California at Los Angeles (UCLA) and similar young autism programs employed contingent aversives to suppress self-injuries and destructive behaviors. Over the last several years, new and more effective programs for building alternate and socially appropriate behaviors have been developed, circumventing the need for aversives for young children. Instead, therapists and parents work through the tantrum, behaving as if these behaviors were not happening. To prepare for the child's assaults, the therapist may put on a bathing cap (to prevent hair pulling) and extra heavy covers over arms and legs to minimize damage from bites and kicks. It is often difficult for adults to simply observe a child's aggressions and self-injurious behaviors, and easy to give in. Even a brief, anxious glance by an adult to the child while the child is aggressing seems enough to strengthen/reinforce such behavior. If we have learned one lesson over the last 30 years, it is that most children with developmental delays are teachable. The challenge is not to teach them the wrong behaviors. In summary, we find that the use of aversives is unnecessary with most young children with whom we work. We use contingent aversives only with the more serious, life-threatening behaviors exhibited by older individuals with autism, and only if alternatives have been exhausted.

CRITERIA FOR A COMPETENT BEHAVIORAL TREATMENT

Current data indicate that competent behavioral treatment provides the best hope for broad and sustained improvements in the behaviors of people with autism. Also, given the poor generalization experienced from treatment, therapy must be extended into the community, including the family and neighborhood schools. Without the cooperation of parents and teachers, treatment efforts may be to little or no avail. Data also show that the longer the treatment lasts, the greater the gains. These observations parallel those that characterize the learning of typical children, who learn during all waking hours, 7 days a week, vacations included. It would seem reasonable then, that for developmentally delayed children to approximate the learning opportunities of typical children, similarly extensive learning opportunities should be made available to them. In short, the delivery of competent behavioral treatment can become a complex and multifaceted task. The more extensive the treatment becomes, the more effective, generalized, and long-lasting it will also become.

In the remainder of this article, I use the UCLA Early Intervention Project as a model to show how to arrange for optimal treatment. It may be helpful to start by making two observations. First, inferences concerning the effectiveness of the UCLA program will be more adequately secured after replication of this study by other investigators in other geographic areas. Furthermore, even under the best of circumstances, the outcome from the UCLA project shows that fewer than one half (42%) of intensively treated children maintain normal functioning at follow-up (average age: 11.5 years; McEachin et al., 1993). The other half of our group did better than groups of children receiving community services (a combination of special education, speech therapy, psychomotor therapy, and so on, but still needed ongoing services to continue to progress and prevent relapse). It is apparent that these children will need support for the rest of their lives. In short, we recommend that parents approach the task with the belief that their children will show improvement, however small, with intensive behavioral treatment. The following descriptions of staff training and clinic organization are meant as a model or guideline. No one family or facility would be expected to follow these guidelines in every detail.

HOW TO RECRUIT AND TRAIN STAFF

For many parents, recruiting a staff of people to work with their child is one of the most daunting aspects of beginning a home-based program. However, parents are usually surprised to find that the task is not nearly as difficult as they expected. Most families use a combination of the following resources: (a) local undergraduate students who work for course credit, (b) local undergraduate students paid an hourly wage, and (c) family members.

To recruit students to work for course credit, contact faculty members in the psychology, speech therapy, or education departments of your local college or university. One of the best ways to find faculty members is to visit the chairpersons of these departments and ask who in their areas may be of help. When you meet with faculty members, describe your goals in establishing your program, give them copies of relevant research articles, and describe the training that will be provided to students. Interested professors may make announcements in their classes, or may ask you to make such announcements. Many junior colleges require their students to perform hours of community service and are extremely helpful in recruiting staff.

In order to recruit students to work for an hourly wage, place ads in college newspapers and post flyers around the psychology, speech therapy, and education departments of your local university. A sample flyer might read as follows:

> **Position Available** working with a team providing intensive early intervention for a child with developmental disabilities. Experience in behavioral therapy helpful but not necessary. We will provide training. Time commitment: 6–10 hours a week.

Pay for such students should be comparable to that for other positions available on campus or in the community.

Family members, including grandparents, aunts, and uncles can be another valuable source of staff members. When organizing your staff, make sure that no family members have offered to work an unrealistic number of hours per week.

In the course of recruiting staff, you will probably interview individuals who would like to work on a strictly volunteer basis, rather than for course credit or pay. Volunteers can be helpful, but they should not be relied on to work for a significant number of hours per week. Even those with the best intentions tend to be less reliable than other staff members. Limit your team to at most two volunteers, for a combined total of no more than 10 hours per week of work.

WORKSHOPS

In response to the demand for early intervention, individuals throughout the country have begun to provide workshops. To help families make informed decisions when selecting service providers, the UCLA format for providing workshops and consultation support may be used as a model. In the last several years, the clinic has found the following elements to be critical in delivering beneficial services.

First, it is essential that 3-day initial workshops be scheduled in order to help reduce the confusion that parents may experience when being confronted with an altogether new way of handling their children and with a variety of programs. During these 3 days, the family and their staff are taught how to begin their child's treatment, including instructions about the clinic's teaching procedures, what to teach and when to teach it, how to keep records, how to supervise staff, and how to analyze problems in a child's learning. The majority of the time, however, is devoted to working one-to-one with the child. The workshop leader models teaching procedures, and the family and staff copy these procedures and receive feedback.

Second, the clinic recommends that follow-up workshops be conducted on a regular basis, typically 1 month after the first one, and then every 3–4 months. In these follow-ups, the child's overall program is evaluated, new goals are established, problem areas are assessed and rectified, and further therapist training is implemented. These workshops can be from 1 to 3 days in length. Furthermore, elaborate written notes present specific guidance on how to proceed with new programs after the workshop is over.

Third, two types of follow-up services should be provided to parents between workshops. Phone consultations with parents are arranged on a regular or as-needed basis. Parents and workshop leaders should arrange a time during the week when parents will call the clinic to discuss specific problems encountered during the preceding week. These consultations range from 20 minutes to 1 hour and occur weekly.

In addition, the clinic offers videotape consultations, in which a workshop leader views and evaluates a videotape sent by the parents, and conducts a phone consultation after this evaluation. Parents are asked to limit the length of the videotape to 30 minutes, and to include a review of programs, problem areas, or whatever is of concern on the tape.

Finally, the clinic staff meet as a group and share experiences as workshop leaders, discuss problems that arise, and seek consultation from each other; many of them have similar experiences. We recommend that written evaluations be obtained from each family receiving services, regarding the adequacy of anyone's workshop. This feedback is used to help improve upon the services of each workshop leader. Because of the amount of work required to conduct these workshops effectively, no one staff member has more than 15 families in treatment. Even those staff members who have been actively involved in the clinic's treatments for as long as 8 years maintain this limited number of families in treatment.

In order to lead a workshop, senior staff members must have at least 2 years experience and training in directing treatment programs from the UCLA clinic. This experience is considered minimal in order to maximize treatment outcome. Workshop leaders are usually full-time employees who conduct research, do administrative work and teach in the clinic. They hold a bachelor's or more advanced degree in psychology or a related field and have worked their way into clinic supervisor positions or have acted as senior therapists for at least 1 year. As of March 1995, workshop leaders earned an annual salary of between $24,000 and $30,000, depending on experience.

These salaries are obtained through workshop fees. As of March 1995, the fee for an initial 3-day workshop was $2,000 plus airfare, hotel, and expenses. Each workshop leader receives a sufficient portion of the workshop fee as a salary. The clinic allocates the remaining funds from workshop fees to research, administrative costs, and salaries for teaching assistants.

STAFF STRUCTURE

New student therapists should commit themselves to a minimum of 6 months of service, because it will take 3 months of training for them to achieve significant skills. They should initially work in a one-to-one apprenticeship relationship with a student therapist who has already been trained. After 3 months at the clinic, a student therapist has acquired the skills needed to assume some training responsibilities for new therapists. In short, there should be considerable overlap between incoming student therapists and more experienced student therapists.

The importance of supervised practica, as in apprenticeship training, cannot be overestimated. This model parallels developments in modern medicine, which built its practice on scientific research in the area of physiology. Behavioral treatment built its practice on basic scientific research on learning processes. In medicine, the practical application of scientific findings is accomplished through internships in which a newly graduated physician works in a one-to-one apprenticeship with an experienced physician. The more specialized the medical practice, the greater the need for knowledge of basic research in physiology and the greater the requirement for supervised training in medical practice. This rule should also apply to the practical application of basic research in psychology. We are dealing with problems no less serious or damaging than those that face medical personnel.

Each student therapist should provide 6 or more hours per week of one-on-one treatment. Many student therapists will elect to stay for more than 6 months. At the end of 6 months, it is beneficial to identify and invite a particularly talented student therapist to become a senior therapist. A senior therapist supervises the work of the rest of the team, each team comprising several student therapists.

Ideally, there should be more than one family receiving services in any geographic vicinity (within a 40-minute driving radius). If so, it is best to start a clinic site. The informational exchange among therapists greatly enhances the effectiveness of the treatment provided to each child. With additional children and treatment sites, one would want to select a clinic supervisor. A clinic supervisor can oversee the work of 5 senior therapists, a corresponding number of children, and 20–40 student therapists. Clinic supervisors typically have a master's degree and should have been with the project for 2 or more years. Especially in cases where there is not a project director (described below), clinic supervisors may be required to meet licensure standards in the state where the clinic is located. Licensure in psychology or a related field by at least one staff member in the clinic or the supervisor ensures that the clinical practices of the staff will abide by the ethical standards of a clinical practice. Because licensure also requires extensive knowledge of a wide variety of diagnoses, it is helpful in caring for families whose members may have clinical needs in addition to autism. With 3 clinic supervisors, 15 senior therapists, and a student therapist staff of about 60–90, a clinic will be treating 15 children receiving a total of 600 hours of one-on-one treatment per week. An educated guess is that a clinic can only supervise a maximum of 15 children and still provide high-quality treatment. The clinic supervisors and the senior therapists together will be able to maintain almost daily contact with each family as well as each student therapist. Because of the complexity of the treatment, all promotions, from student therapist to senior therapist and on to clinic supervisor, should occur from within. To deliver optimal treatment, the clinic must be a cohesive unit with a maximum of mutual support among therapists and parents.

When a region includes more than 15 children seeking treatment, more than one clinic should be established, at which point it may be wise to hire a project director. A project director should have a doctorate degree and several years of clinical and educational experience and be responsible for supervising all assessments and treatment, helping raise financial support, representing the project to the community, and so on. It may seem overly ambitious to conceive of several clinics operating under the same administrative umbrella at this point in our development. Nevertheless, for larger, metropolitan areas, it seems safer to project such a development, considering the enormous increase in the demand for services over the last 3 or 4 years. This option, of an organization starting a clinical or educational site, gains some urgency when one considers the long time required to develop professional work forces. For example, departments of special education are years away from introducing sufficient numbers of staff qualified to meet the needs of children requiring intensive behavioral support.

Of paramount importance is the creation of a parent advisory group, as documented in Chapter 15 of this manual describing the FEAT organization. The children belong to their parents; informed parents have final control over what kind of treatment their children should receive.

STAFF SUPERVISION

Quality control is essential and requires an ongoing effort. Every week, the programs being run for each child should be reviewed for 1–2 hours in a clinic meeting. This means that one or both parents, the child, the student therapists, the senior therapist, and the clinic supervisor meet to discuss the child's program. At that time, each student therapist works with the child in a one-to-one format in front of everyone. Strengths and weaknesses in a therapist's performance are given for improving upon treatment delivery. All staff are expected to model suggestions for improving upon treatment, and solutions to problems are just as likely to come from student therapists as senior staff. The atmosphere in the staff meetings emphasizes positive consequences and is democratic and respectful of the need for diversity in the continuous demand for creating solutions to unique problems.

Persons who want to participate in this treatment effort are keenly interested in being helpful. Almost all persons want to help the developmentally delayed, given the opportunity to do so. After years of reading about psychological problems, most are eager for the opportunity to practice what they have read. The best way to harness this energy is perhaps by helping to avoid certain problems. We have seen from our experience that parents should refrain from, or at least limit, negative feedback to student therapists, but should emphasize the positives so as to help maximize effort. Student therapists more readily accept negative feedback from the senior therapist and clinic supervisor. Any therapist conduct of which parents disapprove should immediately be brought to the attention of senior staff, and information about how such behaviors were dealt with should immediately be communicated to the parents.

An apparent restriction on most home-based programs is the short number of hours that volunteers and students can work. There is often a high turnover of student therapists. Even if a student therapist could devote full-time to this work, there is a limit to the number of hours per week that any one person can devote to such treatment. An educated guess would place that ceiling at 20 hours of one-to-one treatment per week, because the treatment is so intensive and energy-consuming. There are ways in which one may be able to extend the hours of one-to-one therapy to 30 hours. For example, when a therapist treats two or three different children, the monotony is broken, enabling longer hours of treatment. A full 40 hours of service can be arranged by some combination of supervisory, administration, assessment, and other duties. The fact that no two children are alike requires individualized treatment which, in turn, requires care in the search for the ideal combination of programs, as well as extensive supervision.

WORKING WITH PARENTS

Before any treatment is begun, parents should be informed that they are in charge of the treatment, that no treatment should take place without their consent, and that their participation in the program is critical. Without their collaboration, the child's treatment will not be optimized and may, in fact, deteriorate. Also, treatment takes place in the child's home where the family's privacy must be respected. To help optimize treatment, senior staff should meet with the parents for a closed, private consultation after each weekly staff meeting. This gives parents the opportunity to present problems that may affect their child's treatment and that may be best discussed away from the treatment room. Parents' problems with therapists and treatment should continuously be brought to the attention of supervising staff. Parents are anxious about their child's condition and uncertain about the treatment being delivered, an anxiety that seems to peak during the first days or weeks of treatment.

Several problems in the area of staff-parent interaction may necessitate considerable interpersonal skill on behalf of the staff. Some therapists respond to the parents' anxiety by befriending them in various ways, working extra hours, or by placing fewer demands on them, obligating them or otherwise reducing their contribution. Repeatedly, staff must be reminded not to take over. Some staff may try to handle the parents' anxiety by siding with one parent, for example, with the father against the mother (e.g., describing the mother as too lenient), thereby risking alienating the mother. Responses to the parents may

take such forms as requesting disproportionately high treatment fees in relation to the therapist's academic credentials. Other forms, less obviously exploitive, may include accepting expensive gifts or paid vacations. On the other hand, parents may handle their anxiety by becoming suspicious and questioning every move the therapists make, watching them like hawks. Conversely, some parents may praise a particular therapist for possessing the "highest talents," in contrast to others on the team who are "less talented," which undermines the parents' and the team's efforts.

At the same time, student therapists are taught to behave in a professional manner with parents, which includes complying with the assigned working hours, informing parents when they will be late for their treatment with the child, making up for lost hours and so on. It is easy for anyone to miss an occasional appointment, but it is also easy to inform the parents in advance. Failure to do so could be misinterpreted as not caring for the child. A therapist who fails to inform the parents after one or two warnings should be dismissed. Student therapists are taught to develop constructive friendships without receiving special favors. Parents have come to the clinic to receive services for their child and to develop close working relationships with the staff, not to satisfy anyone's need for friendship. Close emotional relationships may too easily interfere with competent treatment.

The problems mentioned above are examples of extra-therapy variables that must be quickly identified and corrected, otherwise the treatment effort will be sabotaged. The anxious and suspicious parent will not be reassured verbally ("Don't be anxious"). Seeing that therapists are doing a good job and that the child is improving is the best treatment for an anxious parent. If a parent persists in having strong feelings against a particular student therapist, it may be wise to substitute another student therapist, even if the senior staff considers the first therapist to be competent, in order to avoid an unnecessary confrontation.

Some parents, like staff, have problems that are independent of their child or staff behavior. Examples of these are alcohol addiction, severe depression, and/or an unstable marriage, all of which could be accentuated by the birth of an exceptional child. Each problem is a powerful deterrent to the child's treatment and becomes obvious to senior staff through the extensive contact they have in providing therapy and running the therapy review sessions in the clinic. The delivery of effective treatment requires that, at some level, supervising staff be trained to deal with these problems, able to help decrease the problems in a few meetings, or be wise enough to refer the parents to others who may be more competent to deal with the situation. For that reason, access to clinicians whose experience goes beyond children with autism may be needed for some cases. The main point is that every effort should be directed toward enlisting, securing, and maintaining the cooperation of the parents and team members.

WORKING WITH TEACHERS

At some time during the treatment, after achievement of certain behavioral competencies, the child may be proposed for school placement. At that point, the senior therapist or clinic supervisor will work with the parents to help identify a suitable school in the neighborhood. Once the school is identified, the new teacher is approached and asked if she can help integrate a child who is delayed in language and peer play. Initial mention of the diagnosis of autism is avoided because of the bias that may arise from the pessimistic outcome many associate with that diagnosis. If the teacher agrees to include the child, she is asked if a trained staff member (a "shadow") can be present to help the child. If the answer is yes, the teacher is asked if the child can attend for just 1 hour at a time in the beginning, and if the teacher will accept some suggestions about how to best deal with the child. If the teacher agrees to these conditions (and in our experience, 9 out of 10 preschool teachers will), then a most important extension of the child's treatment has begun. At that time, it is appropriate for the staff to facilitate communication between the teacher and the parents, ideally on a daily basis. At the same time, the "shadow" has to help the child to follow the teacher's directions, help establish peer relationships in school, and to develop friendships with children in the neighborhood. Slowly, treatment is handed over to the teacher and the parents, an ideal and essential combination, because even the best-outcome children may continue to experience minor problems, as in first grade. Ideally, the preschool teacher informs the kindergarten teacher of problems and how to deal with them, and the same transfer of information occurs between kindergarten and first grade. At no time are matters left to chance, and the parents see to it that information flows regularly and constructively.

FAILURE IN MAINSTREAMED CLASSES

For the children who do not achieve the best outcome, special treatment has to last for a lifetime. Although professionals come and go, parents can provide for continuity in treatment, hence the importance of their being informed about treatment options. In all treatments, maximal effort is directed to ensuring the child's success and minimizing failure so as to ensure cooperation in the learning process. If a particular program fails, try a new one. In our experience, for example, we are beginning to see that some children appear to be auditory learners, while others are visual learners. (Terms such as *high-functioning* versus *low-functioning* children are derogatory and should be avoided.) We assume that auditory learners do well in the UCLA program, which emphasizes vocal language. The UCLA program has begun developing reading and writing programs for visual learners, and a number of investigators have reported success with the use of pictures to help communication (Bondy & Frost, 1994; Pennington, Lloyd, & Willis, 1991) and sign language (Cipani, 1991).

Although more research is needed, the most constructive approach for any educational program is to consider failure in the child's progress as a reflection of inadequacies in the educational program, rather than failure on the child's part. Children with autism have deviations in their underlying nervous systems that require the development of special environments to help the deviant nervous system acquire knowledge. We can do something about educational environments, but very little about the child's deviant nervous system, at this time.

Progress in optimizing treatment outcome should continue. Two factors are considered essential to ensure future progress. The success of our approach depends upon the creative contributions of the many individuals who care and on objective data that help us to identify which of these contributions may help and which to discard.

SUMMARY

This chapter describes certain critical elements in a treatment program designed to offer the best outcome of early and intensive behavioral treatment for young children with autism. The most important element requires parents to identify treatments based on studies published in peer-reviewed journals where other scientists found the study "believable." The treatment provided should report objective measurements of intellectual, social, and emotional functioning in long-term follow-ups (see the chapters in this manual by Green and Smith). Behavioral treatments reporting the most favorable outcomes show the importance of starting early, addressing most or all of the child's behaviors in most of the child's environments, and involving most of the child's waking hours. The treatment is expected to last for many years. To arrange for such treatment, parents were given some advice about how to select persons who could form a treatment team, and how they could be trained as therapists to work effectively with the child, other therapists, the parents, and teachers in the community.

REFERENCES

Anderson, S. R., Avery, D. L., DiPietro, E., Edwards, G. L., & Christian, W. P. (1987). Intensive home-based early intervention with autistic children. *Education and Treatment of Children, 10*, 352–366.

Bondy, A. S., & Frost, L. A. (1994). The Delaware autistic program. In S. L. Harris & J. S. Handleman (Eds.), *Preschool education programs for children with autism* (pp. 37–54). Austin, TX: PRO-ED.

Cipani, E. (1991). Developing functional sign capabilities in nonverbal children. In E. Cipani (Ed.), *A guide to developing language competence in preschool children with severe and moderate handicaps.* Springfield, IL: Charles C. Thomas.

Johnson, C., & Crowder, J. (1994). *Autism: From tragedy to triumph.* Boston: Branden Book.

Koegel, R. L., Rincover, A., & Egel, A. C. (1982). *Educating and understanding autistic children.* San Diego: College Hill Press.

Lovaas, O. I. (1977). *The autistic child: Language development through behavior modification.* New York: Irvington.

Lovaas, O. I., & Smith, T. (1988). Intensive behavioral treatment for young autistic children. In B. B. Lahey & A. E. Kazdin (Eds.), *Advances in clinical child psychology* (Vol. 11, pp. 285–384). New York: Plenum.

Maurice, C. (1993). *Let me hear your voice.* New York: Knopf.

McEachin, J. J., Smith, T., & Lovaas, O. I. (1993). Long-term outcome for children with autism who received early intensive behavioral treatment. *American Journal on Mental Retardation, 97*(4), 359–372.

Pennington, G., Lloyd, L. L., & Willis, J. (1991). Augmentative and alternative communication: The preschool child with severe disabilities. In E. Cipani (Ed.), *A guide to developing language competence in preschool children with severe and moderate handicaps* (pp. 111–161). Springfield, IL: Charles C. Thomas.

Rimland, B. (1964). *Infantile autism.* New York: Appleton-Century-Crofts.

Strain, P. S. (1983). Generalization of autistic children's social behavior change: Effects of developmentally integrated and segregated settings. *Analysis and Intervention in Developmental Disabilities, 3*, 23–34.

PART SIX

Practical Support

Organizing and Funding

CHAPTER ELEVEN

Community-based Early Intervention for Children with Autism

Ronald C. Huff

In this chapter we describe how parents and professionals in Sacramento, California, developed an organization to deliver support services to families who have chosen to implement and manage in-home early intervention for young children with autism. The purpose of this chapter is to explain why community-based programs are both important and necessary. This chapter outlines organizational concepts, identifies the basic elements necessary to the development of a community-based program, and summarizes what you can do to start a program in your community.

THERE IS HOPE

Realistic hope for the parents of a young autistic child can be found in an early intervention program (Birnbrauer & Leach, 1993; Fenske, Zalenski, Krantz, & McClannahan, 1985; Harris, Handleman, Gordon, Kristoff, & Fuentes, 1991; Lord, Bristol, & Schopler, 1993; Lovaas, 1987; McEachin, Smith, & Lovaas, 1993; Sheinkopf & Siegel, in press; Simeonnson, Olley, & Rosenthal, 1987; Strain, Jamieson, & Hoyson, 1986). The hope offered by early intervention is that the autistic child's innate capacity to learn, and to learn how to learn, will be stimulated to optimal growth. With early intervention, the young autistic child has a chance to acquire critical developmental skills at the level of his personal best. The challenge faced by the parent of a young autistic child is to find the courage, determination, and direction necessary to create an in-home early intervention program.

An encouraging development in the field of early intervention is the increasing availability of a comprehensive teaching technology (Anderson, Avery, DiPietro, & Edwards, 1987; Lovaas & Smith, 1988). Compared to those of 20 years ago, significantly improved and highly effective teaching methods, although complex and demanding, are now accessible (Koegel & Koegel, 1995). Parents, more than ever before, have a better chance to bring intensive[1] early programming directly to their child. Families who resolve to implement an in-home program need to know how to effectively organize a way to pay for and deliver the program.

TAKING CHARGE

Parents are now leading the struggle to gain access to high-quality early intervention programming in their respective communities. Parents of children with autism correctly and logically expect their school districts to provide state-of-the-art teaching. Despite the best intentions of special educators to provide a meaningful learning environment (for example, see Kohler, Strain, Maretsky, & DeCesare, 1990), the impaired learning style of the young autistic child and the lack of opportunity for high-level teacher training have dampened or completely thwarted effective early intervention in most school environments. Parents must therefore take control and bring intensive, cost-effective, high-quality teaching programs into their own homes. Figure 11.1 shows some of the obstacles they face. What is missing is an efficient and practical method of transporting this advanced teaching technology to the optimal learning environment—the child's home and community.

Parents continue to demand increased proficiency from special education programs, but the consensus of families who have successful in-home programs suggests that *only* parents possess the commitment and determination to carry out an intensive intervention. An alternative to the frustration and hopelessness caused by the unavailability of effective teaching is to create a parent-driven, community-based organization that provides early intervention services. Parents are

---

[1] The term *intensive* follows the Lovaas protocol and refers to treatment programming that ranges from 20–40 hours per week for 2 or more years.

beginning to combine their talents and work with dedicated professionals to establish early intervention support organizations. The goal of such an organization is to promote and deliver intensive, cost-effective, in-home early intervention programming (see Figure 11.2). An organization in Sacramento, California, called Families for Early Autism Treatment (FEAT) is an example of such an effort. FEAT is a demonstration project with the goal of finding cost-effective ways of enabling and supporting families who want intensive, in-home early intervention programs.

PARTNERS FOR PROGRESS

Parents by themselves cannot reasonably be expected to organize the components of an intensive early intervention program. Without strictly organized parent–professional collaboration, effective in-home programming is probably not a realistic possi-

---

- Coordination is impossible for a parent to manage alone.

- Time and energy demands are great, burnout is high.

- Access to a comprehensive teaching curriculum is difficult.

- Technical expertise to guide the child's program is rare.

- Training hands-on teachers is expensive and laborious.

- In-home programming is expensive.

Figure 11.1. Obstacles to early intervention.

- Create high-quality, local early intervention resources for in-home programming.

- Bring down the cost of early intervention.

- Raise funds more efficiently for early intervention services.

- Promote public awareness of the need for and benefits of early intervention.

- Gain quicker access to resources for their children.

- Develop support services for the families of young children with autism.

- Control access to early intervention and related support services.

Figure 11.2. Reasons for parents to organize.

---

bility (Moroz, 1989). The combined complexities of the autistic child's developmental needs (Siegel, 1991) and intensive treatment programming (Lovaas & Buch, in press) prevent parents from working effectively on their own. A stable partnership between parents and professionals must therefore be founded on unity and harmony of effort. Parents of children with autism possess an array of talents that they can use to create a stable and self-sustaining community-based organization. The leaders in a parent–professional collaboration must discern who among them is properly motivated and qualified to contribute. As we will see later in this chapter, the success of a community-based organization depends on the same factors that determine success in a small business.

THE FIRST STEP

The first step in a community's effort to deliver early intervention program services is for parent leaders to identify a local group of qualified professionals who have the training, experience, and motivation to work with parents of young autistic children for an extended period. They must be willing to assist parents in establishing an organization to deliver needed services. Agencies that have a federal or state mandate to provide early intervention services to children with developmental disabilities are a good place to recruit dedicated professionals. Among the professionals who can contribute to the establishment of a community-based organization are physicians, psychologists, behavior analysts, administrators of developmental services, special educators, speech and language specialists, university professors, and graduate/undergraduate students in any of the above fields.

WHY TEACH AT HOME?

Experience and research have shown that the home and neighborhood environment can be an ideal treatment setting for young autistic children (Prizant & Wetherby, 1988; Rutter, 1985; Sherman, Barker, Lorimer, Swinson, & Factor, 1988; Simeonsson, Olley, & Rosenthal, 1987). At home, there is greater access to and control of naturally occurring reinforcers, including neighborhood children as models. The child's familiarity with the home environment and neighborhood leads to increased opportunities for teaching communication skills and generalizing newly learned behavior. Additionally, parents and extended family members are likely to be present more often to actively promote learning. Experience has shown that the parent who is given adequate support can achieve a very high-quality, intensive early program at home. Most parents are solidly motivated, and family-centered supports enable them to create and manage an in-home program for their child.

FAMILIES FOR EARLY AUTISM TREATMENT (FEAT)

FEAT has demonstrated that a cost-effective, parent-driven, community-based early intervention program can be achieved by parents and professionals working together. The working premise behind FEAT is that treatment benefits and cost-savings are maximized when families share the same resources and distribute the financial and labor burden equally among themselves, public agencies, and the private sector. In Sacramento, a small group of parents took the challenge to create and deliver a cost-effective early intervention program to any family with a child, between 18 and 60 months,[2] diagnosed with Autistic Disorder, Pervasive Developmental Disorder, Not Otherwise Specified (PDD–NOS), or Asperger's Syndrome (American Psychiatric Association, 1994). The goal of FEAT is to support fund-raising efforts and expedite preparation of families who have chosen to implement intensive in-home programming. For the past 2 years, FEAT has served an average of 15 families a year, with in-home programs that range from 10 to 40 hours a week (see Figure 11.3).

Joining Forces

In the diligent search for a comprehensive curriculum and expert training, FEAT ultimately endorsed Dr. Ivar Lovaas's program at the Clinic for Behavior Treatment of Children (CBTC) on the UCLA campus, Los Angeles, California. Dr. Lovaas and his graduate students have provided consistent, high-quality, professional training to the parents and student therapists of FEAT. FEAT families receive ongoing follow-up consultation from the staff at the CBTC.

What If a Ready-Made Early Intervention Resource Is Not Available?

In nearly every community there are persons who possess the interest, awareness, knowledge, and abil-

- Outreach and identification of families with young autistic children
- Funding for start-up and follow-up early intervention workshops
- Face-to-face counseling on issues of assessment, diagnosis, and treatment of autism
- Recruitment and training of therapists/teachers
- Support and guidance for implementation of intensive in-home programming
- Access to teaching materials
- Parent-to-parent and parent-to-professional networking
- Guidance and support for full community and school inclusion
- Advocacy for school and other public agency services

Figure 11.3. Some of FEAT's services to families.

ity to support an early intervention project. A survey of the community must be conducted to determine which individual or group is best suited to assist in developing an early intervention project. In most communities, there are behavior specialists who work privately to deliver an array of routine intervention services to persons with developmental disabilities. They are usually associated with specific programs for persons with developmental disabilities. Specialists with experience in providing services to developmentally disabled children are usually well informed, practical in their approach to problems, and sympathetic to a parent's needs. Depending on their expertise, these specialists can be invited to participate in an early intervention project. For example, local behavior analysts supervised student therapists in the early months of the FEAT project, before FEAT had access to formally trained senior therapists.

If there is a nearby academic institution, professors in the fields of psychiatry, psychology, special education, speech and language, social work, and child development are likely to have the awareness and consulting ability to assist parents in organizing the building blocks for an early intervention project. A great database of information about behavior programs for young autistic children has been published in professional journals. At least a portion of the basic curriculum appropriate to an early intervention program could be adapted from published articles, books, and training manuals.

---

[2] The age range of 18–60 months reflects an arbitrarily defined age limit used to decide which children to include in FEAT's demonstration grant and is not intended to imply that intervention with older or younger children is unsuitable or in any way less beneficial.

Despite the fact that information is easier than ever to acquire, professionals and academicians often do not understand that an effective teaching technology is available and appropriate for early intervention with autistic children. Parents must educate themselves and conduct positive public relations programs to share information about available technology with the interested professional. The appeal to interested professionals, to capture their attention and get them involved, must be compelling, logical, and based on objective findings. In some communities the special education department of the local school district may be interested in supporting an early intervention program.

The possibility of importing specialized training from neighboring communities should not be overlooked. After parents and interested local professionals have identified themselves in the public's eye as a reliable resource, outside experts with more extensive experience can provide curriculum, training, consultation, and ongoing consultative services to the organization.

A Picture Is Worth . . .

FEAT's success at organizing parents to work together was tied to a graphic demonstration that early intervention can lead to rapid and dramatic changes in a young autistic child's development. Although experts cite a behavioral approach as the most useful approach (Pfeiffer & Nelson, 1992; Waters, 1990), many are skeptical about any improvement. It took the organizers of FEAT only a few weeks to demonstrate and document on videotape that preschool children with autism can learn and, in some cases, learn quite rapidly. Documentation of the possibility for measurable gains in young autistic children motivated additional families to think seriously about organizing a community-based intervention project. For instance, students from local college campuses were invited to receive hands-on training at a demonstration workshop conducted in a parent's home. The experience gained from recruiting those students became an important concept in FEAT's grant design. Documented developmental change in the children that participated in the demonstration workshop convinced local public agency administrators that early intervention, if adequately managed, could be cost-effective and preventative. Thus, a short-term early intervention demonstration set the stage for FEAT's public relations, community support, fundraising, and a demonstration grant.

Within a few weeks after the demonstration workshop, other parents of autistic children began to seek funding for their start-up workshops. As interest in early intervention programs grew, the need for coordinating and organizing parental efforts became more apparent. Little by little, families became more effective at identifying and pursuing potential community resources. Even though parents were told that no treatment resources existed for intensive early intervention, they remained determined to create a meaningful program. Their courage in pursuing the impossible was the beginning of what became a wonderful opportunity for children with autism in Sacramento.

A New Beginning

Eventually, a small group of motivated parents met to discuss coordinating their efforts toward establishing an early intervention program in the greater Sacramento area. Several families, none of whom participated in the demonstration workshop, agreed to meet. During those first few meetings, parents defined the goals and objectives of the project and potential community resources. Later the parents, in concert with local professionals, drafted a grant proposal. During all of these activities, it became more apparent that there was a real need for precise coordination and management of what was now a rapidly growing community project. The solution was to apply for federal and state nonprofit tax status, establish a board of directors, and assign actively participating parents to focused work teams to coordinate key activities.

Benefits

The benefits of organizing parents into an identifiable group of individuals all working toward the same end were numerous. Parents immediately felt a surge in positive support because they were now surrounded by others who were experiencing the same problem and had the same goal. In a matter of weeks, many other parents and professionals began to contact FEAT. Newcomers added more energy to the effort and helped with the growing list of tasks. Within 6–9 months, FEAT parents were able to raise funds more easily because they could refer to their organization as a professionally operated resource for treating young children with autism. As FEAT's organizational structure emerged, needed support services were identified, parents with relevant skills were asked to take responsibility, and a more concerted fund-raising effort began. Equitable distribution of job responsibilities among FEAT participants further reduced stress on parents whose time was now absorbed by the demands of implementing their child's program.

Support Services

Support for families who were managing programs of 10–40 hours per week came in many forms. A valuable emotional support was the opportunity for frequent face-to-face contact with other parents of autistic children who had encountered and solved similar problems. FEAT parents got together on outings and holidays and assisted each other with respite care. A phone tree for passing along program information became another valuable form of support. A parent-generated monthly newsletter, and regular chat sessions on the internet, are now routine forms of information exchange.

FEAT parents hold monthly support meetings. The agenda reflects the current needs of the group. To ensure the meeting's focus, the parent leader of the support group conducts an informal survey and adapts the agenda to the results of the survey. Sometimes the focus is on sharing technical program information or, as the need arises, the meeting is an open discussion of feelings and frustrations. Occasionally, professional counselors from the community donate their time to assist parents in recognizing and managing stress.

Cost-Effectiveness

Because an intensive early intervention program lasts for 2–3 years and can cost as much as $45,000 or more per year, an innovative approach to reducing costs was a high priority for FEAT. It was determined very early that salaried positions, leased office space, and other high operational costs were unnecessary. Hence, FEAT adopted a strategy of taking advantage of every no-cost, or low-cost opportunity. For example, professionals who work for agencies whose mandate is to serve children with autism were asked to get involved with the project as a routine part of their job responsibility, that is, to integrate FEAT's goals into their work objectives. Under this agreement, the agency could take credit for meeting its outcome objectives by serving a larger number of families with minimal added costs. The importance of establishing positive and complementary relations with public agencies cannot be overemphasized as a means of ensuring cost-effectiveness. Another example of cost cutting is the granting of fieldwork credits for hands-on teaching performed by trained college students. The opportunity for high-quality, career-related training and hands-on experience attracted professionally motivated students.

Volunteerism is a hidden resource that can reduce costs. One way to reduce the cost of fund-raising is to ask the vendor who is being paid for a service to donate a portion of the service, labor, or materials. For example, the director of a toy-lending library volunteered her time, knowledge, and equipment to catalogue and distribute developmental teaching materials for the families served by FEAT. When a child in treatment masters a skill, the materials used in the teaching exercises for that skill are given to the library for cataloguing and distribution to another family with a child who needs them. In the spirit of volunteerism, the owner of the toy-lending library went a step further and wrote a small grant to acquire more materials and toys for FEAT's exclusive use. This is a good example of how careful organization, focused public relations, and volunteerism can produce cost-cutting benefits and support for families.

Every Dollar for the Child

A guiding principle for FEAT is that, as much as possible, every dollar raised should go directly to the child's treatment program. Operational costs (e.g., phone bills, transportation, teaching materials, mailings, etc.) are absorbed by parents and/or their extended family. In FEAT's first year, lodging, rental cars, and airfare for CBTC training consultants were donated by local corporations as a result of parent fundraising and spirited public relations work. The printing costs of FEAT's corporate sponsorship packet were donated by a local printer. Advertisement for fund-raisers, including flyers and public announcements on television and radio were donated. Local radio personalities contributed greatly to FEAT's fundraising by attending and personally promoting FEAT's goals.

Teamwork

Focused teams, composed of parents and professionals, can accomplish specific tasks that will make or break a community-based organization. Each team is given a specific assignment with clear lines of responsibility. Parents are assigned to work on specific teams according to their interests, talents, available time, and experience. Each work team reports to the president, who reports to the board of directors. Figure 11.4 shows the activities performed by different teams.

What You Can Do

Ultimately, parents are responsible for their child's program, which means they must take charge and

- Assist families in recruiting student therapists
- Conduct fund-raisers
- Perform financial accounting
- Assist and participate with parents in grant writing
- Produce a monthly newsletter
- Assist families in preparing individual education plan (IEP) objectives
- Conduct support meetings
- Schedule start-up workshops and follow-up consultation
- Orient new parents

Figure 11.4. Activities of parent-driven work teams.

- Identify, screen, and orient two or three families with young autistic children
- Conduct an early intervention demonstration workshop
- Establish a method for outreach and identification of other families with young autistic children
- Announce the project and hold public lectures for parents and professionals
- Procure demonstration grant funding
- Initiate fund-raising activities to start training
- Publicize the opportunity for participation in an early intervention project
- Orient and educate parents to enable them to manage an early intervention program
- Obtain federal and state nonprofit tax status
- Elect a board of directors and select work teams to conduct fund-raising; to recruit students; to schedule workshops, follow-up consultations, and parent support meetings; and to secure relations with entitlement agencies
- Conduct board meetings for long-range planning
- Involve business consultants to resolve organizational issues
- Organize public relations to enhance fund-raising, gain community acceptance, and attract volunteers

Figure 11.5. Steps in establishing a community-based program.

oversee the events that affect the outcome of the program. Parents must decide such things as when to start, number of hours per week of programming, who will be on the team, whether to involve the child in supplemental services, and how to coordinate a complex schedule of events. In addition, parents must understand their child's strengths and needs, along with the pros and cons of a behavioral approach. They must be aware of potential pitfalls and be able to recognize, acknowledge, and correct mistakes in the child's program. Experience among FEAT families suggests that the better-managed in-home programs produce better results. Once a child's program is underway, parents must do whatever is necessary to keep it going. They must know who can help and when to ask for help. Parents differ widely in their ability to recognize and ask for help (Morgan, 1988). A sensitive professional (social worker, teacher, psychologist, physician, etc.) can help parents to understand the need for support services and how to find them.

Figure 11.5 summarizes the major steps in creating a community-based organization. Items roughly reflect the steps taken by parents and professionals who created FEAT.

Recruitment

It is possible to select and train professionally minded college students to work effectively one-on-one with young autistic children (Lovaas & Buch, in press; Sheinkopf & Siegel, in press). Using carefully defined selection criteria and, later, guidelines for professional conduct greatly improves recruitment efficiency. Cost-effectiveness is lost when improperly selected students are trained and then quit shortly thereafter. Written ethical and professional guidelines help parents to better manage team members

and ensure stability of the treatment team. Those guidelines explain the ethical and professional responsibilities of student therapists who work for a family. Those responsibilities include attendance at and active participation in weekly team meetings, understanding and monitoring the extent of their responsibility to parents, accurately documenting work time, maintaining a professional demeanor and appearance, careful data collection, and confidentiality.

The majority of student therapists trained to work for families in FEAT come from local campuses. Psychology, education, child development, and speech and language majors show a strong interest in working with young children with autism. Advertising in the local newspaper, placing posters on campus that announce the opportunity for work with a child with autism, and word-of-mouth reporting are other ways of recruiting student therapists. College and university classroom presentations are an effective way to identify potential student therapists. The classroom presentation should include a general discussion of autism and its impact on the family. A live classroom demonstration of a child's in-home teaching program is a very concrete and illustrative way to demonstrate the need for student therapists. Following a classroom presentation, interested students are interviewed by phone. If a student's response to questions related to her availability and professional interests is positive, she is invited to the child's home on a Saturday morning to meet and interact with the child. At that first meeting, parents discuss the child's treatment goals, expectations for members of the treatment team, how the in-home program works, the child's projected weekly teaching schedule, and the benefits of becoming a student therapist.

As recruited students become familiar with what an early intervention program entails, parents ask them to think about their commitment. Parent and student must arrive at the point of honest and mutual disclosure about the time and effort the student is willing to commit in terms of number of hours per week and number of months of availability. Where there is doubt, it may be best to advise students to wait until their availability is certain. Parents must assess whether a student is mature enough to handle assigned responsibilities, training demands, and issues of confidentiality. Student therapists recruited from campuses are first offered the opportunity for hands-on training in exchange for field credit units. Most colleges and universities offer units of credit to students who train in their field of interest. If circumstances prevent a student from working 3–6 months (one or two quarters/semesters) solely for credit, the parent must decide if payment of an hourly wage is feasible. If so, the student is told that she must work under supervision for a set number of hours before becoming eligible for pay. All student therapists must demonstrate their competence to the satisfaction of the parents for whom they work.

Prepare to Get Started

It is important to hold orientation meetings for families to describe, in concrete terms, how to prepare for start-up (see Figure 11.6). Parents who are already experienced with the curriculum and teaching methodology and who have been successful at implementing in-home programming must attend the meeting. During orientation, experienced parents answer questions and describe the day-to-day realities of running an in-home program. Before the orientation meeting, new parents should have read a list of selected articles or books about early autism intervention and viewed videotapes that cover issues related to treating autism. After the orientation, experienced parents should introduce themselves and invite a new parent to their home to watch the treatment team in action.

In the month or two before the start-up workshop, one or both parents should participate in a be-

- Selected readings about early intervention programs
- In-depth discussion of clinical issues (e.g., impact on marriage, siblings, possible outcomes, etc.)
- View videotape examples of treatment programming
- Visit to a home to observe an early intervention program in progress
- Parent training in behavioral techniques prior to start-up workshop
- Participation in the parent support group

Figure 11.6.   Summary of recommended orientation activities.

haviorally based parent training course. A few weeks of training in the use of behavior analysis followed by at-home attempts to teach self-help skills prepares parents to take greater advantage of the information presented at the start-up workshop. Parents who understand task analysis, effective use of reinforcement, prompting, and so on are better managers of the treatment team. The parent who is familiar with fundamental teaching principles is consistent and effective at incidental teaching.

Starting Up

To ensure cost-effectiveness, it is a good idea to organize start-up workshops for two or three families at once. Start-up workshops, depending on whether two or five families are involved, can run from 2 to 5 days. The workshop begins at 9:00 A.M. and continues until 5:00 P.M., with an hour for lunch. The site for the workshop should be chosen to minimize as much as possible the travel required for each family and treatment team members. The family with the largest (most convenient) home should host the workshop. Space is important because, in addition to family members and the child, many student therapists will be present. During the workshop, as many as 20–25 persons may be present. Consideration for the conveniences (e.g., food, use of bathrooms, child care, parking, foot traffic, etc.) is important. To keep confusion to a minimum, persons interested only in observing should be invited to observe on the first day only.

The workshop begins with a discussion of how learning occurs, along with an explanation of terminology and a description of behavioral techniques. After that, one child is selected to begin the first hour of treatment. See Lovaas and Buch (in press) for a detailed description of the overall treatment process.

The child's treatment program begins the first day of the workshop and continues every day thereafter.

Student therapists come to the house at scheduled times to implement the procedures taught during the start-up workshop. To ensure quality control over student therapists' use of behavioral techniques and their adherence to the procedures described during the workshop, a senior therapist is present to supervise. The senior therapist and parent(s) work collaboratively to supervise the program and maintain training standards between CBTC follow-up consultations. Table 11.1 shows a typical treatment-team schedule. In certain circumstances, but not always, it may be necessary for two team members to be present. One conducts the teaching exercise, while the second manages teaching materials, logs data, and/or assists during the teaching exercise. For this reason, the total number of team members' hours per week may be greater than the total time the child is in treatment.

Training the Treatment Team

Multiple levels of training supervision ensure effective in-home programming. A student therapist begins with the least hands-on experience but is under three levels of supervision. Depending on the number of hours a child is in treatment, a typical intervention team might consist of 4–8 student therapists, a lead therapist, and a senior therapist. The lead therapist is usually present more hours per week than a student therapist and must have more supervised, hands-on experience. Student therapists and their lead therapist are supervised by the senior therapist. Senior therapists in the FEAT project received clinical supervision and training with several different families for 3 months at the CBTC under Dr. Lovaas's supervision. They are expected to demonstrate a higher level of expertise for implementing a child's individualized teaching program. Senior therapists meet with and supervise each child's team from 2 to 4 hours per week. The highest level of supervision is provided by a graduate student or doctorate. from the CBTC. Families in the FEAT project appear to be able to maintain acceptable progress if they receive a 3-hour consultation every other month from a CBTC consultant.

Training of therapists is the essential activity that must continue without interruption as a community-based, early intervention program develops. Table 11.2

Table 11.1.
Hypothetical Schedule for 20 Hours of In-home Early Interventions

	Child's In-home Intervention Schedule					
Therapist	**Mon**	**Tues**	**Wed**	**Thur**	**Fri**	**Total Hrs/Wk**
Senior Therapist		2		2		4
Lead Therapist	2	2	2	2	2	10
Therapist 1	2		2		2	6
Therapist 2		2		2		4
Therapist 3	2		2		2	6
Therapist 4		2		2		4
Therapist 5	2		2		2	6
Total No. Hours	8	8	8	8	8	40

Note: Schedule arbitrarily assumes two therapists are present during each hour of treatment.

Table 11.2.
Levels of Training and Supervision

Degree	**Title**	**Training**
Doctorate or Master's	Clinic Supervisor	Several years at CBTC
Bachelor's	Senior Therapist	Minimum of 3 months
Undergraduate Student	Lead Therapist	240 hours
Undergraduate Student	Student Therapist	40+ hours

shows FEAT's pyramidal training model with four levels of training competency.

In the early phase of development, workshops are an efficient method of training. They allow families to get started quickly, and they provide a convenient format for follow-up consultation and, as needed, more advanced training of therapists. As an early intervention project matures, selecting the more competent teachers for advanced training ensures quality teaching and longevity for the project. After the first year of the FEAT project, 3 student therapists from more than 100 involved with the project were selected for advanced training at the CBTC. FEAT contracted with them to attend a 3-month training program at the CBTC, after which they agreed to return to Sacramento to supervise five children's programs each and train student therapists.

To ensure cost-effectiveness and longevity, a community-based project will eventually need to hire a highly trained person with a graduate degree to fulfill the role of clinic director. The clinic director's responsibilities include supervising all training for the project and designing and conducting research. However, until a community project is stable and self-sufficient, training should probably occur via workshops and periodic individual family consultations.

Managing Expectations

Parents' initial expectations about their child's rate of progress during an early intervention program will, in most cases, develop into a more objective understanding of the child's capacity to learn. As the child's early intervention program continues, parents typically learn to appreciate and value their child's strengths and limitations. Hence, measurement of developmental progress, especially during the first year, becomes a necessary condition of the intervention program. Standardized psychological tests are available for assessing a child's ability in different developmental domains (Wodrich & Kush, 1990). A clinical psychologist or school psychologist trained and experienced in assessing children with autism is qualified to perform the evaluation.

Evaluation in this case refers to the child's overall ability relative to chronological age, not day-to-day acquisition of specific skills. Children with autism learn at different rates within each developmental domain (Siegel, 1991). Parents need to acknowledge the child's rate of learning in each domain. Therefore, it is important to arrange for a preintervention psychological evaluation to establish a baseline. If a preintervention evaluation is not possible, then periodic standardized testing is a good way to establish a baseline for determining rate of progress within each domain. Periodic, serial administration of tests of cognitive and adaptive ability is a reasonable way to monitor progress (Freeman et al., 1991; Volkmar, Sparrow, Goudreau, Cicchetti, & Cohen, 1987). The interval between assessments will depend on the need for specific information about the child's ability and issues associated with school placement. Test scores collected throughout the child's early intervention program provide information for decisions regarding appropriate classroom placement and eligibility for supplementary school services. In addition to standardized psychological tests, videotaping the child periodically in a variety of situations, at home and in the community, is an objective way to get ideas about treatment needs and document growth.

Because a child's progress, or lack of progress, is obvious, you might ask, Why measure it? One reason is to provide an objective basis for deciding if meaningful progress is occurring. Given the investment of time, energy, and money, it is important to know how much progress is occurring, that is, what are the cost benefits? Estimates of rate of developmental change address the question of whether or not an intensive intervention (20–40 hours per week) is justified and whether or not the child is achieving an acceptable level of readiness for school. For children who have experienced a well-designed and well-executed program but show a limited response to treatment, a reduction in the number of hours of treatment per week makes sense. Likewise, for the child who is showing a marked response to intervention, total hours per week may need to be increased. A rule of thumb is to find the optimum level of stimulation, without overstimulating or understimulating the child. The number of hours of treatment for one child is not necessarily suitable for another child. When test scores show little developmental progress and it has been determined that sufficient learning opportunities were provided, the parent has an opportunity to reconcile his or her expectations.

Children who begin early intervention with greater internal resources will probably gain developmentally at a relatively higher rate (Harris et al., 1991; Rutter, 1985). Preintervention assessment data, combined with good clinical consultation, should alert parents to the range of possible treatment outcomes. Assessment data combined with honest clinical discussion of the variables that affect rate of learning in children with autism should enable parents to form a sound impression of their child's progress during the intervention period.

For some children, especially those who have not received any form of early intervention and who present difficult behavior problems, it may not be possible to administer a valid, standardized test of intelligence. Nevertheless, an assessment should be attempted. A patient and experienced test administrator can obtain a working estimate of the autistic child's cognitive ability (Freeman, 1976).

The Role of the Professional

The role of the helping professional is to advise, assist, and consult with parents. Where appropriate, the professional conducts key activities that enable progress in implementing a child's program. Figure 11.7 shows some of these activities required of the helping professional.

BUSINESS PLANNING AND THE FEAT ORGANIZATION

A well-focused organization allows all members to concentrate on achieving their goals. FEAT uses standard business planning techniques to focus on the best means of serving the needs of our children and families.

Two Key Benefits of Business Planning for the FEAT Organization

1. *Business planning contributes to a strong team orientation.* Developing a common vision of the members' needs and collaborating on a set of objectives and strategies results in strong, shared commitments among the leaders of the organization.

2. *Business planning provides the means to choose among alternative strategies for achieving the orga-*

- Setting up a demonstration project (i.e., the groundwork for organization)

- Assisting parents in grant writing

- Assessment and diagnosis of autistic children

- Parent orientation, screening, and consultation for early intervention issues

- Coordination of activities in support of in-home programs

- In-home program monitoring and quality control

- Maintenance of parent-professional collaboration

Figure 11.7. Some activities of the helping professional.

---

nization's goals. When the ability to choose a sound strategy is combined with well-executed implementation, an organization can focus its limited resources and have a better chance of achieving its goals.

The Process Is Critical to the Results

The business planning process collects and creates important information about an organization. An organization gets out of business planning what it puts in; don't expect perfection the first year. When viewed most constructively, business planning becomes a way of looking at meeting members' needs as an ongoing project rather than as a one-time event.

We Started with a Complex Set of Problems

Despite all of Sacramento FEAT's gains, we clearly still have problems. In fact, when we first started the business planning process to determine members' needs, we identified the following concerns:

- Parents can't do both their child's program and fund-raising.

- Schools still don't understand this approach.

- The organization is not functioning properly.

- The organization has unclear lines of authority.

- The organization has unclear accountability.

- Important projects have too many false starts and not enough finishes.

- Need to find dependable students.

- Confusing process, missing information.

- Frustrating for parents who don't have the resources.

- Access to materials is difficult.

- Perceived inequity in distribution of services.

- Inconsistency of funding.

Change a few of the words and you quickly realize that we were confronting the same issues as any business in transition, including resource constraints and misallocation, communication breakdowns, and a variety of organizational inefficiencies. We decided to address these standard business issues with standard business tools.

We Enlisted the Support of a Local Group of Professionals

Sacramento FEAT enlisted the support of a local business school alumni group called Community Partners, which is a volunteer consulting program. It links charitable and civic organizations that need business advice with local Harvard Business School alumni. Projects generally involve 10–15 hours a month for 3–5 months; project teams involve two to four alumni. Such groups are available in almost every community. In our case, Community Partners was looking for a project like FEAT when we found each other.

Break Down Complex Situations

Applied Behavior Analysis breaks down complex situations into manageable, measurable components. Similarly, business planning can break down complex organizational situations into manageable, measurable components.

An organization will never have all of the data it wants, but at some point it is important to cut off debate and make decisions. The plan and its assumptions can be fine-tuned later as more information is gathered.

Elements of Business Planning

The basic elements of the business planning process are as follows:

- Statement of purpose: the fundamental reason for an organization's existence.

- Five-year objectives: the mission—a "finish line" to work toward.

- FEAT service recipients: our "customers."

- Alternative service providers: our "competition"—we don't want to duplicate services.

- Necessary FEAT services: the services that address the needs.

- Service development plan: how to develop and deliver the services.

- Financial analysis: the financial consequences—need to match sources and uses of funds.

- Potential problems analysis: what could go wrong—develop contingency plans.

- Dependencies: state assumptions; for example, FEAT depends on representatives from the CBTC for monitoring the quality of its members' in-home early intervention programs.

- First-year tactical plan: the implementation details—what will you do tomorrow?

Know What Your Starting Line Looks Like

Defining your organization's reason to exist is the starting line. The statement of purpose presents the fundamental reasons for your organization's existence. For example, the following is Sacramento FEAT's statement of purpose:

The *purpose* of FEAT is to deliver training to families with *autistic children*. Specific objectives include the following:

1. Serve families in Sacramento, Yolo, Placer, and El Dorado counties.

2. *Demonstrate* that an intensive early intervention program has the highest *success* rate.

3. Share what we learn beyond Sacramento. No need for families to relocate to the Sacramento area.

Italic terms above are clarified below.

- *Purpose.* FEAT's purpose guides its allocation of resources (money, time, etc.).

- *Autistic.* FEAT includes the following disorders under the heading of autism: Autistic Disorder, Pervasive Developmental Disorder (PDD), Pervasive Developmental Disorder, Not Otherwise Specified (PDD-NOS), and Asperger's Syndrome.

- *Children.* FEAT focuses its limited resources on intensive early childhood intervention rather than on services for other age groups.

- *Demonstrate.* The data from FEAT members' in-home programs should demonstrate the effectiveness of intensive, early intervention and be persuasive to parents, school districts, the scientific community, and funding sources.

- *Success.* Success means that the child reaches his or her maximum potential. Success may mean noninstitutionalization, a normal life, or anything in between.

Know What Your Finish Line Looks Like

As a result of the business planning process, Sacramento FEAT wants an organization with the following characteristics:

- community-based
- sustainable
- financially solvent
- organized
- accountable
- replicable

Communicate the Plan

After the plan is complete, it is imperative to communicate the plan throughout the organization. One of the most potent benefits gained in any business planning exercise is that all members of the organization understand the mission and can personally relate their roles to the goals of the organization. To achieve this, it is crucial for the business planning team to personally communicate the plan to all members and help them understand what it means for their role in the organization.

Keep the Plan Current

Finally, to be a useful, real-time management tool, the plan must be kept current. To accomplish this, some form of tracking mechanisms should be used to keep watch for changes that challenge your ability to meet the plan's objectives and/or invalidate the plan's assumptions. When such a situation occurs, part of the business planning team should reconvene to assess the situation, consider the implications, and recommend appropriate adjustments to the plan.

FUNDING

Funding Goals

During its first year, a community-based organization can survive on grant funding and money raised from fund-raising events. By the end of the first year, the organization must have developed plans and strategies to establish permanent sources of funding. After the organization demonstrates that it can deliver high-quality, cost-effective early intervention ser-

vices, it can ask for funding from institutions whose mandate is to provide early intervention services. As the organization accumulates more knowledge and experience, opportunities to charge fees for training and consultation arise. The organization's ultimate goal is to become financially self-sustaining.

Expenses

At the beginning of a community-based project, the costs of in-home programming result mainly from consulting fees, therapist reimbursement, and teaching materials. Workshop fees, follow-up consultation fees, and the associated costs of airfare, lodging, rental cars, and per diem expenses for meals and parking are the most expensive items. After completion of a mandatory period of voluntary teaching or work for educational credit, reimbursement to student therapists becomes a high-priority budget item. Remuneration encourages consistency and quality of teaching in the child's program. Therapists remain with a family longer when opportunities for increasing responsibility and advancement exist. Rates of reimbursement for student therapists vary according to level of competency. Table 11.3 shows a hypothetical team, composed of five therapists and a senior therapist, for a child in a program for 20 hours per week. Expenses for the start-up workshop and follow-up consultation are not shown and must be added to the cost of early intervention.

The cost of each child's program varies with the number of hours of treatment per week. A large number of variables, some under the family's control and some not, determine the number of hours of treatment per week. Those variables include availability of funding, the family's ability to recruit and manage a treatment team, the child's inherent capacity to learn (Rutter, 1985, p. 197), and the availability of relevant resources and support services. Relevant resources means well-trained therapists, expert consultants, and the availability of desirable alternative early intervention programs. Relevant support services include arrangement for adequate care of siblings, respite care for parents, support from other family members, and cooperation from the school district for planning and carrying out the child's transition into an appropriate classroom placement.

Fund-Raising

Going into the community to raise money for your child's program may sound threatening or, at best, like a huge inconvenience. Perhaps for some individuals fund-raising is not a desirable activity. Actually, obtaining relatively small amounts ($1,000–$5,000)

Table 11.3.
Hypothetical Costs for an Early Intervention Team

Team Member	$/Hour	Hrs/Wk	Amount
Senior Therapist	$20.00	3	$ 60.00
Lead Therapist	8.00	15	120.00
Therapist 1	6.01	6	36.06
Therapist 2	6.01	6	36.06
Therapist 3	6.01	6	36.06
Therapist 4	6.01	6	36.06
Weekly Total			324.24
Monthly Average			1,296.96
Annual Total			15,563.52

Note: Based on 48 weeks of annual programming.

can be quicker and easier than you might imagine. Assisting young children with autism to become more self-sufficient appeals strongly to most individuals. The idea of treating children intensively and at a young age is a logical idea. The key to obtaining contributions for a child's program is to organize a rational, informative, and compelling presentation. Solid assurance that charitable money will go directly to the child's treatment is very important.

There are probably hundreds of ways to raise money. Methods range from very quick methods to those that require a greater investment of time and energy. Figure 11.8 shows several methods used to raise small amounts.

These activities are expeditious and enable a family to get started within a few weeks. A long-range effort should be initiated simultaneously to ensure sub-

stantial and more permanent sources of funding. Grant writing, developing contracts with entitlement agencies, and establishment of the organization as a private, nonprofit preschool that qualifies for Department of Education funding are options available to most communities.

Grants: Public and Private

The first goal of a community-based organization should be to demonstrate that the support services needed for early intervention can be organized and made available in a cost-effective manner. Private health foundations have an inherent interest in lowering health costs and promoting community programs capable of achieving perpetuity. A major selling point for FEAT's first grant, which was funded by a private health foundation, was that quality programming could be achieved for far less than previously thought. The charitable foundation perceived FEAT's proposed reductions in the cost of treating a child with autism as reasonable and feasible. In addition, foundation staff were impressed with the fact that FEAT was organized as a nonprofit corporation, had a board of directors, and was supported by the professional community. From the grantor's point of view, the immediate availability of an early intervention curriculum and the expert training/consulting offered by the CBTC made the project more attractive. Having documented success with several children before approaching the grantor made the grant proposal easier to understand and accept.

Grants can be written by parents and professionals who combine their knowledge to define the goals and priorities of a demonstration project. A small group of parents, with professional assistance, is capable of drafting a successful grant proposal. In communities where experienced parents or professionals are not

- Pledges for a percentage of sales from local fast-food restaurants
- Fund-raising dinners sponsored by local business groups
- Cash grants from corporations
- Donations from the company where a family member works
- Dinner dance with silent auction involving local celebrities
- Donation cans placed in restaurants
- Media interviews about the early intervention program
- Open discussion in the community about the need for financial support

Figure 11.8. Ways to conduct fund-raising quickly.

available to draft a grant, professional grant writers may be asked to contribute their skills. Public seminars and workshops on how to write grants are offered in most communities. Libraries keep published references that identify funding sources for nonprofit organizations.

Sponsorship

In addition to fund-raising events, parents may decide to appeal to the philanthropic interests of corporations. Several FEAT parents made well-organized presentations to local corporations and obtained $2,000–$5,000 simply by asking. Two well-organized parents, working together, can make an effective and persuasive sponsorship team. When community-based organizations have nonprofit status, representatives requesting funding from corporations need to be familiar with nonprofit guidelines, which define the legal and ethical limits of what parents can say to corporate representatives. Visual-graphic materials and clearly written narratives that describe the organization, its goals, and the treatment program, as well as the program's success, are essential tools to be used by a sponsorship team.

Entitlement Funding

Any community interested in developing an early intervention program needs to identify the agencies responsible for providing services to children with autism. Those agencies have an intrinsic interest in participating in resource development for the underserved population of young children with autism. In some states, persons with developmental disabilities are entitled to services including, but not limited to, diagnostic assessment, case management, respite, and behavioral treatment. These services are funded by county, state, or federal tax dollars. Professional staff who work for the local agency responsible for serving your child are familiar with early intervention services and are apt to view the creation of a community-based early intervention program as a valuable resource. In the long run, these agencies benefit from being able to refer families for valuable and cost-effective services.

Private Donations

Local charitable and philanthropic organizations can be approached for contributions. Although the amount of money raised is less, multiple sources of small amounts accumulate to enable funding for new start-up workshops and follow-up consultations. Examples of organizations in Sacramento that conduct ongoing fund-raising events and are willing to share proceeds are the 20–30 Club, Soroptimist,

Lions Club, Rotary, university sororities and fraternities, senior citizens groups, and church youth groups.

Using the media, including newspaper, radio, and television interviews, to tell the story of autism and educate viewers about the need for early intervention is an efficient way to obtain money. Media interviewers sometimes permit giving a phone number for donations.

Spaghetti dinners, silent auctions using objects donated by local merchants, theme dances, and educational scholarships offered by civic groups are other examples of small, but important, fund-raising activities. Banks are often very interested in funding community projects and require relatively little paperwork for amounts up to $5,000. Restaurants will permit placement of donation cans near cash registers. The above activities require more effort for less return, but are valuable for raising money quickly to cover day-to-day operational costs.

School District

School districts have a keen interest in the outcome of a child's in-home program. Representatives from most school districts are willing to discuss the many complex issues that emerge when parents organize a community-based, early intervention program. School districts and parents share the same goals for children. By working together to arrive at a consensual agreement, parents stand to benefit in many ways. School districts have many options for offering assistance to families who demonstrate the need for and determination to run a well-organized in-home program. Well-organized and documented in-home programs are perceived by the local district as evidence of the parent's competence and determination. See Luce's (1987) discussion of educational transition issues.

Schools have an incentive to support the in-home program because the child becomes significantly more teachable and is less likely to present serious behavior problems later (Harris et al., 1991). See Sasso and Reimers's (1988) article for a practical discussion of how behavior analysis in the classroom can ensure a smoother transition between home and the school classroom.

One form of direct support from the school district is active participation of teachers' aides in the child's in-home program. Aides come to the home to become acquainted with a child's program and individual learning style. The teaching aide's familiarity with the child and the details of the in-home program ensure greater consistency when the child reaches the classroom. School districts also have the option of purchasing teaching materials for use in the child's home.

CONCLUSION

Parents cannot afford to wait for institutions or public agencies to understand and deliver the complex programming required to promote the growth of a young child with autism. If not a parent, who else would be responsible for coordinating and managing the thousands of details required by an intensive in-home program? A fundamental premise of this chapter is that with relevant support services and collaboration from caring professionals, a parent can survive and, in almost all cases, expect positive results from an early intervention program (Anderson et al., 1987; Birnbrauer & Leach, 1993; Lovaas, 1987; McEachin et al., 1993; Sheinkopf & Siegel, in press). Parents must work collaboratively with informed professionals to achieve success. Professionals must provide technical advice, support, and occasionally direction. By organizing themselves, parents have it within their power to create high-quality intensive teaching programs in their own homes and the school environment.

Clearly, there are unique and mutual benefits when parents organize to promote early intervention programming. Although there will be stress, which will manifest in many different forms and eventually reach every member of the child's family, including siblings (see Siegel & Silverstein, 1994), evidence shows that the benefits of early intervention outweigh the risks. One of the many challenges faced by parents is finding the patience and determination to continue the child's program when progress does not seem great. As the managers of their child's treatment team and program, parents must come to know what stimulates learning. As team managers, parents must hire and fire team members according to what they feel is best for their child.

For the well-prepared organization, fund-raising will probably be easier than anticipated. Generosity and kindness are familiar emotions in those who understand the opportunity and promise of early intervention. As parents become more organized, others will be attracted to join in and assist in many different and highly spirited ways. Feelings of hopelessness and frustration dissipate as parents gain more control of the variables that determine their child's destiny. Parents who embark upon an in-home program develop a self-reliance and initiative for creative problem solving that they may not have otherwise developed.

ACKNOWLEDGMENTS

The author wishes to acknowledge Dan Strauss for his contribution to the business section of this chapter. Dan's keen business acumen and sense of direction are invaluable assets to this project. Special thanks to Linda Copeland, M.D., whose devotion to children and professional interests in early intervention programs contributed greatly to the success of the project. The author wishes to thank all of the parents in Sacramento, especially Linda Mayhew, Carl and Diane Haynie, Scott and Joni Price, Tina O'Leary, Shari Scott, and all of the FEAT committee members whose tireless efforts and personal sacrifice made it possible to establish the organization and successfully complete the demonstration grant. Special thanks to Dr. Ivar Lovaas and his graduate staff, without whose input, fulfillment of the grant goals would not have been possible. The FEAT board of directors and Dr. Huff wish to thank Jeff Kramer, Tanya Demarest, and Jody Glenn as well as more than 150 other students who volunteered unselfishly for many months to work face-to-face with the children. The staff of Applied Behavior Consultants, especially Brenda Terzich, M.A., and Joe Morrow, Ph.D., empowered the project by providing teaching insights and valuable training for student therapists. The FEAT board of directors wishes to thank Alta California Regional Center staff, who contributed to the project by counseling parents, developing administrative guidelines, and monitoring the in-home programs. Special thanks to Tom Mullaney and John Peters of Community Partners of Sacramento, who contributed significantly to the project by providing business consultation to the organization. The author, on behalf of all the parents in FEAT, extends deep gratitude to the Sierra Health Foundation of Sacramento, California. Sierra Health Foundation recognized the value of early intervention, endorsed the feasibility of a community-based approach, and supported the project with funding for 3 years. Lastly, the author wishes to thank all of the businesses and corporations in Sacramento who donated money and services to FEAT families.

REFERENCES

American Psychiatric Association. (1994). *Diagnostic and statistical manual of mental disorders* (4th ed.). Washington, DC: Author.

Anderson, S. R., Avery, D. L., DiPietro, E. K., & Edwards, G. L. (1987). Intensive home-based early intervention with autistic children. *Education & Treatment of Children, 10,* 352–366.

Birnbrauer, J. S., & Leach, D. J. (1993). The Murdoch Early Intervention Program after two years. *Behaviour Change, 10,* 63–74.

Fenske, E. C., Zalenski, S., Krantz, P. J., & McClannahan, L. E. (1985). Age at intervention and treatment outcome for autistic children in a comprehensive intervention program. *Analysis and Intervention in Developmental Disabilities, 5,* 7–31.

Freeman, B. J. (1976). Evaluating autistic children. *Journal of Pediatric Psychology, 1*, 18–21.

Freeman, B. J., Rahbar, B., Ritvo, E., Bice, T. L., Yokota, A., & Ritvo, R. (1991). The stability of cognitive and behavioral parameters in autism. A twelve-year prospective study. *Journal of the American Academy of Child and Adolescent Psychiatry, 30*, 479–482.

Harris, S., Handleman, J., Gordon, R., Kristoff, B., & Fuentes, F. (1991). Changes in cognitive and language functioning of preschool children with autism. *Journal of Autism and Developmental Disorders, 21*, 281–290.

Koegel, R. L., & Koegel, L. K. (1995). *Teaching children with autism: Strategies for inititating positive interactions and improving learning opportunities.* Baltimore: Paul Brookes.

Koegel, R. L., & Schreibman, L. (1982). *How to teach autistic and other severely handicapped children.* Austin, TX: PRO-ED.

Kohler, F. W., Strain, P. S., Maretsky, S., & DeCesare, L. (1990). Promoting positive and supportive interactions between preschoolers: An analysis of group-oriented contingencies. *Journal of Early Intervention, 14*, 327–341.

Lord, C., Bristol, M. M., & Schopler, E. (1993). Early intervention for children with autism and related developmental disorders. In E. Schopler, M. E. Van Bourgondien, & M. M. Bristol (Eds.), *Preschool issues in autism* (pp. 199–221). New York: Plenum.

Lovaas, O. I. (1987). Behavioral treatment and normal educational and intellectual functioning in young autistic children. *Journal of Consulting and Clinical Psychology, 55*, 3–9.

Lovaas, O. I., & Buch, G. (in press). Intensive behavior intervention with young autistic children. In N. N. Singh (Ed.), *Practical approaches to the treatment of severe behavior disorders.* Pacific Grove, CA: Brooks-Cole.

Lovaas, O. I., & Smith, T. (1988). Intensive behavioral treatment for young autistic children. In B. B. Lahey & A. E. Kazdin (Eds.), *Advances in clinical child psychology* (Vol. 11, pp. 285–324). New York: Plenum Press.

Luce, S. C. (1987). Transitional programming for autistic youth. *Focus on Autistic Behavior, 2*, 1–8.

McEachin, J. J., Smith, T., & Lovaas, O. I. (1993). Long-term outcome for children with autism who received early intensive behavioral interventions. *American Journal of Mental Retardation, 97*, 359–372.

Morgan, S. B. (1988). The autistic child and family functioning: A developmental-family systems perspective. *Journal of Autism and Developmental Disorders, 18*, 163–280.

Moroz, K. J. (1989). Parent-professional partnerships in the education of autistic children. *Children & Youth Services Review, 11*, 265–276.

Olley, J. G., Robbins, F. R., & Marelli-Robbins, M. (1993). Correct practices in early intervention for children for autism. In E. Schopler, M. E. Van Bourgondien, & M. M. Bristol (Eds.), *Preschool issues in autism.* New York: Plenum.

Pfeiffer, S. I., & Nelson, D. D. (1992). The cutting edge in services for people with autism. *Journal of Autism and Developmental Disorders, 22*, 95–105.

Powers, M. D. (1992). Early intervention for children with autism. In D. Berkell (Ed.), *Autism, identification, education and treatment* (pp. 225–252). Hillsdale, NJ: Lawrence Erlbaum.

Prizant, B. M., & Wetherby, A. M. (1988). Providing services to children with autism (ages 0 to 2 years) and their families. *Topics in Language Disorders, 9*, 1–23.

Rutter, M. (1985). The treatment of autistic children. *Journal of Child Psychology & Psychiatry, 26*, 193–214.

Sasso, G. M., & Reimers, T. M. (1988). Assessing the functional properties of behavior: Implications and applications for the classroom. *Focus on Autistic Behavior, 3*, 1–16.

Sherman, J., Barker, P., Lorimer, P., Swinson, R., & Factor, D. (1988). Treatment of autistic children: Relative effectiveness of residential, outpatient, and home-based interventions. *Child Psychiatry and Human Development, 19*, 109–125.

Sheinkopf, S. J., & Siegel, B. (in press). Home-based behavioral treatment of young autistic children. *Journal of Autism and Developmental Disorders.*

Siegel, B. (1991). Toward DSM-IV: A developmental approach to autistic disorder. *Psychiatric Clinics of North America, 14*, 53–68.

Siegel, B., & Silverstein, S. C. (1994). *What about me? Growing up with a developmentally disabled sibling.* New York: Plenum.

Simeonnson, R. J., Olley, J. G., & Rosenthal, S. L. (1987). Early intervention for children with autism. In M. J. Guralnick & F. C. Bennett (Eds.), *The effectiveness of early intervention for at-risk and handicapped children* (pp. 275–296). Orlando, FL: Academic Press.

Strain, P. S. (1987). Parent training with young autistic children. *Zero to Three, 7*(2), 7–12.

Strain, P. S., Jamieson, B., & Hoyson, M. (1986). Learning experiences—An alternative program for preschoolers and parents: A comprehensive service system for the mainstreaming of autistic-like preschoolers. In C. J. Meisel (Ed.), *Mainstreaming handicapped children: Outcomes, controversies and new directions* (pp. 251–269). Hillsdale, NJ: Lawrence Erlbaum.

Volkmar, F. R., Sparrow, S. S., Goudreau, D., Cicchetti, D.V., & Cohen, D. J. (1987). Social deficits in autism: An operational approach using the Vineland Adaptive Behavior Scales. *Journal of the American Academy of Child and Adolescent Psychiatry, 26*, 156–161.

Waters, L. (1990). Reinforcing the empty fortress: An examination of recent research into the treatment of autism. *Educational Studies, 16*, 3–16.

Wodrich, D. L., & Kush, S. A. (1990). *Children's psychological testing: A guide for nonpsychologists.* (2nd ed.). Baltimore: Paul Brookes.

CHAPTER TWELVE

Funding the Behavioral Program

Legal Strategies for Parents

Mark Williamson

There are basically three legal possibilities available to parents attempting to fund a behavioral program: special education, insurance, and the Americans with Disabilities Act (which actually ties back into insurance funding). The outlines that follow attempt to develop legal strategies that will allow you to understand and assert your rights under all three alternatives.

The first outline on special education was developed to help parents involved in a home-based, intensive, behavioral program obtain financial support from their school district. This outline arose out of my own family's successful effort to obtain funding for our son's home-based behavioral program. Because I am both an attorney and a parent of a child in such a program, I have tried to blend the law with the factual setting of the early, intensive behavioral model in a manner other parents could understand. For many families, making the decision to implement an intensive behavioral program is the easy part; trying to finance it is the hard part. After I settled our case, I began to receive many calls from other parents regarding their rights in special education. I developed the outline as an attempt to answer some of these questions. The outline is not a legal treatise and should not be read that way. The key points to keep in mind are to (a) go into the process knowing what your legal rights are, and (b) if you cannot work things out on your own with your school district, hire a good attorney to review your legal situation. If you do both of these, your chances of a successful outcome are good.

The second and third parts of the outline contain a thumbnail sketch on insurance law and a federal statute called the Americans with Disabilities Act (ADA). Space limitations, as well as the enormous variability in insurance policies, preclude any attempt at a more comprehensive discussion of these topics. However, I have tried to make at least a few brief comments on both topics.

Insurance law issues are hard to summarize because policy terms and practices vary widely among insurers. The ADA is a fairly new statute without a lot of case law to interpret how it applies to the field of insurance. I believe ADA has enormous potential to help disabled children get some of the coverage they need and hope that some solid precedents dealing with its applicability in the area of insurance will be established in the future.

A few disclaimers are in order. First, these outlines should not be read as determinative of your own legal rights on these issues and are not intended to give specific legal advice. Your individual rights will depend on a variety of facts and circumstances and the laws applicable in your jurisdiction. Moreover, as the law in this area is just beginning to evolve, new precedents may arise at a rapid pace. You should always consult with an experienced attorney on your own facts and circumstances.

Second, outlines are not designed to be an even-handed dissertation on the relative legal merits of the applicable issues; they are wholly designed to give you legal ammunition to advocate successfully on behalf of your child for the program you feel he needs. It is my hope that if you are properly versed in the legal options, you will be able to use that knowledge to achieve a favorable settlement and get the help you need *without* going to court.

Third, these outlines start with the premise that you have come to the conclusion (like many have, including myself) that in 1995 all credible research points to an early, intensive, behavioral intervention as being the treatment of choice for autism, PDD, and similar neurologically based developmental disorders.

Finally, do not get so tied up in all the legal wranglings that you forget what your real objectives are. An unfunded program that works is far superior to a funded program that fails. You must hold firm for the essential elements of your program.

OUTLINE ONE ••

SPECIAL EDUCATION FUNDING

I. Introduction/Assumptions

    A. You are a parent who has decided that the goals and objectives important to you for your child can best be achieved by a high-intensity, discrete-trial, behavioral program and have established or are in the process of establishing a home-based program.

    B. You would like the school district or other applicable funding body to aid you in funding the program.

    C. The school district believes that its own placement is sufficient—generally, a multihandicapped program or a special school for autistic children. Your child may or may not have already tried (and failed) in this program.

    D. I assume your child has already been referred to the school district and found eligible for special education services. If this is not true, you need to call your school district and begin the referral and eligibility process. In most states children become eligible for special education at age 3. In some states the age of eligibility is 2.

NOTE: This article is not intended to give specific legal advice on individual cases that depend on the facts and circumstances of each individual situation. You should always consult with an experienced attorney on your specific facts. Additionally, each state may have additional laws and regulations to be considered—in fact, some states mandate services above the federal minimum. Finally, the IDEA legislation is soon up for reauthorization, and it is possible that the provisions of the statute may change during this process or that other legal precedents will be established superseding the information contained in this outline.

II. Special Education Generally

    A. In the early and mid-1970s, Congress passed legislation now known as IDEA (Individuals with Disabilities Education Act)[1] requiring local school districts to educate all disabled children regardless of the severity of their handicap. Among others, autistic and PDD (pervasive developmental disorder) children are or should be eligible for services pursuant to the Act.

    B. Prior to this point in time, many if not most school districts had excluded handicapped children from the educational system.

    C. The IDEA legislation and implementing regulations established a somewhat elaborate procedural system requiring local school districts to deal with each child on an individual basis.

    D. Unlike the traditional educational system for the nonhandicapped, the IDEA legislation allows parents to have a very strong say in developing an educational program for their children.

    E. In theory, educational decisions are jointly made by parents and the school division based on the unique needs of the child and without regard to cost or a preconceived notion of service delivery. Put another way, the educational program should conform to the child, not vice versa (as is commonplace).

    F. In practice, the system breaks down considerably, partly because of money and partly because of bureaucratic inertia.

    G. School districts often follow Newton's rule that an object put into motion tends to stay in motion. Thus, once a school district has a program that they believe is designed to deal with a given population (whether it actually does so successfully is another question), it is often difficult to convince them to abandon that system in favor of something more promising, particularly when the something more promising is relatively expensive and involves a one-to-one teaching arrangement in the home. Remember, school administrators have been part of a system all their lives that advocates group teaching in a school setting.

    H. The special education procedures set forth under IDEA establish generally a six-part process for providing services to the child: referral, evaluation, eligibility determination, IEP (individualized education program) development, placement, and subsequent evaluation of the child's progress.

---

[1] IDEA is a separate and distinct federal statute from ADA (the Americans with Disabilities Act). The former sets forth the legal requirements imposed on the school districts and states to educate disabled children; the later generally prohibits discrimination "on the basis of a disability" in a number of settings such as employment or employer-provided benefits.

I. The *substantive* standards of IDEA (as distinct from the *procedural* requirements) are somewhat weaker and certainly more ambiguous and require the school district to provide your child with a free and "appropriate" public education (FAPE). Additionally, the school district must do everything possible to educate your child with nonhandicapped peers. There has been much dispute about what the term *appropriate* means. Generally, the district is not required to "maximize" your child's potential (remember, some states have a higher standard), but to provide your child with an educational program that confers a "meaningful" level of educational benefit.

J. To use an analogy, the school district is not required to provide your child with a Cadillac of an education, but only a Chevy.

K. The good news is that if your school district cannot provide your child with a Chevy, you can go buy the Cadillac and receive reimbursement for the cost.

L. Your job is to convince the decision makers and/or hearing officer that what the school district wants to provide doesn't even have wheels.

M. If your child has not yet been referred to special education, you need to call or write the special education department of your local school district and refer your child. They will then send out a team of specialists to evaluate her and make a recommendation to the eligibility committee. Under federal law (remember individual states may have different standards), there should be a lag of no more than 65 working days between referral and the eligibility hearing. Once your child is found eligible for special education services (this should be a foregone conclusion), a group called the IEP committee (the parents are automatically members of the IEP committee) must write an individualized education program for the child (within 30 calendar days) to address her individual and unique needs, setting *specific and objective* goals for the child (e.g., "Billy will imitate five words by the end of the first semester") in all educational domains. Once the goals and objectives have been decided, *with your participation,* the child is supposed to be placed in a program or "placement" where those goals can best be achieved. This is usually where the controversy begins. Remember that you are an equal member of the IEP committee and have as much right to direct your child's education as the school district. If you and your school district cannot agree upon an educational plan, the matter is decided by a neutral third party ("due process").

N. The intensive, behavioral cases usually fall into two groups. In the first group, the parents have tried the school district's program for some time only to have it fail; in the second, the parents have begun an in-home program without ever enrolling the child in the school district's placement. Usually the debate is not over the basic goals and objectives of the IEP (everybody wants your child to talk and act normally); the issue is how best to achieve these goals. You will feel that your child needs a very intensive, individualized behavioral program to achieve these critical goals. School districts have historically advocated for some sort of low-intensity, group educational program involving placing your children with other autistic children or other handicapped children. As you may know by now, there appears to be little or no data-based research that supports such an approach.

O. At this point, you need to convince your school district through negotiation and persuasion (the nice guy approach) or due process (the hardball approach) that your position is correct. I would try the nice guy approach first but be prepared to switch tactics rather quickly if it becomes apparent that the nice guy approach is going nowhere.

III. Alternative One: Trying to Work with the School System

Working with the school system is your best alternative, because litigating with the school district often entails a lengthy and personally draining process. At the same time, you are trying to run your program, and this is like trying to fight a war on two fronts. If your finances allow, you probably want to get your program up and running for some time before you take on the school district.

A. *Document Your Successes and Their Failures.* The nice guy approach requires you to convince the decision makers at the school district that either (a) what they have is inadequate and what you suggest has the potential to achieve success (what I call giving you the right program for the right reason) or (b) that litigating with you will ultimately prove more costly to them than settlement (what I call giving you the right program for the wrong reason). At the appropriate time, you should provide your district with information in support of your position, such as the following:

1. Documentation (test scores or IEP progress notes) of the child's failure in their program. For example, the child's receptive language age has not changed measurably after 1 year in the district's

program, or a string of "NPs" (no progress) appears on the child's IEP progress notes. If the child was never placed in the district's program, you will not have this documentation and will have to argue that the district's program will fail based strictly on the research (or lack thereof) and your expert's opinion on your child's progress.

2. Copies of the research done by Dr. Ivar Lovaas at UCLA and by others. Please consult Dr. Gina Green's chapter titled "Early Behavioral Intervention for Autism: What Does Research Tell Us?" in this manual for an overview of the relevant research. Be sure to mention the success of the other programs that use intensive behavioral techniques to counter any specific criticisms of the Lovaas/UCLA research.

3. Tape produced by UCLA titled "Behavioral Treatment of Autistic Children."

4. If obtainable, letters of recommendation from professionals in the field. Your ability to get a persuasive letter may depend on the sophistication of experts in your area. The failure of the district to consider the recommendations you offer may give rise to a procedural violation of the Act. Be sure the expert has personally observed your child.

5. Copy of your proposed curriculum.

6. If your child has already begun the program, tapes documenting your child's success in the behavioral program. Where possible, the tapes should paint a distinct contrast between the child's skills at the beginning of the program versus his accomplishments later on. Your tape should also attempt to show your child's generalization of acquired skills. *If you are just starting the program, always tape him from the beginning so that you can paint the contrast later on.* You may not want to tape him at the beginning because his behaviors are so horrible—but this is very important! This tape may be the key piece of evidence if you have to go to due process.

If you are engaged in the initial IEP process, you should probably shy away from discussing placement options until the goals and objectives of the IEP have been agreed upon. If you already have an IEP and want to amend it, request a new IEP meeting in writing; an IEP can be amended at any time for virtually any reason. Offer your documentation at the meeting or in a follow-up letter or presentation. Always document exactly what you want them to provide you. State your position, for instance, that you believe some number (generally 30–40) of hours of discrete-trial behavioral therapy should be provided via an "in-home" placement to achieve the goals and objectives of the IEP,[2] to provide an appropriate education, and to maximize your child's potential to be mainstreamed over time. Always ask for *everything,* even if you may settle for something less later on. This will allow the school district to obtain a psychological victory in backing you off your original position.

B. *Put the School District on the Defensive.* Ask the district to provide their research and documentation showing that what they propose is effective (i.e., that the kids in their program have better outcomes than this population generally). Also, the district's research should show that their program is capable of leading to mainstreaming (ask what percentage of kids that have been through their program have been mainstreamed, without aides, by first grade). Require *hard proof* (e.g., published research articles), not vague testimonials to their system. Remember that some small percentage of this population will make some progress without behavioral intervention, so pointing out one success story (out of many children) represents no adequate representation of effectiveness. It is important to appear willing to consider the school district's options if they have hard data to back up their proposed plan. However, because the only hard data in the field supports an early, intensive, behavioral intervention, they are unlikely to have data to support an alternative approach (see Chapters 2, 3, and 4 of this manual).

C. *Work up the System.* Go up the hierarchy: teacher, supervisor, special education director, assistant superintendent, superintendent, school board. All it takes is one person along the way to be sympathetic to you. Do not be afraid to go over someone's head once you know that person is not supportive of your plan. Everybody has to answer to somebody. Your school board members are elected officials and answer to you, not the bureaucracy. Board members may be particularly cooperative around election time. In some communities, going to the newspaper may bring added pressure. Additionally, each district is supposed to maintain an advisory board comprised of parents of children with special needs. This board is answerable to you as a parent and not to the school district. The board may be able to intercede on your behalf.

---

[2] I assume you do not have access to an adequate center-based program.

D. *Why School Districts Resist.* It is important to understand the perspective of the school district.

1. The program you are proposing is new and would mean that the school district would have to change its system of service delivery.
2. Your program is one-on-one, and the district is afraid that it will set a precedent for other children.
3. Most of the bureaucrats have a vested interest in maintaining the status quo.
4. It is expensive.
5. It is delivered in the home and puts parents in charge. School district officials do not like parents telling them how to run their school.

Fortunately, none of the above reasons are valid under the law, which focuses on the individual needs of the child and not the convenience of the school district. Success of the nice guy approach will depend on finding someone in the chain of command who is willing to buck the system. Try not to criticize their program directly, but point out that you do not see it as suitable for dealing with the complex and unique needs of your child. In the preschool area many school districts are still fumbling around for adequate programs (remember they do not otherwise serve children this early). The school personnel also have to realize that you are fully committed to following through with litigation. Once you file for due process, the school district will have to incur a number of expenses. This is often a strong incentive toward settlement. Without that threat, there is no down side to saying no from the district's standpoint.

IV. Getting Ready for Due Process

A. *What Are Your Rights Generally:*

1. The school district must comply with the *procedural* requirements of the Act, and they often lack a solid grasp of the procedures. Procedural requirements were inserted to provide for, among other items, a complete, knowledgeable, and individualized determination of each child's needs; active participation by the parents in the process; decision making based on the unique needs of the individual child; and accountability on the part of the school district.
2. The school district must offer an *appropriate* education. There is substantial ambiguity as to the level of services required of the school districts. The case law suggests the level of benefit should be "meaningful" but not "best," and appropriateness must always be determined by reference to the individual child. This controversy will often play out as a battle between your expert witnesses versus theirs, so make sure you have good experts.
3. The school district must *mainstream* (educate your child with nonhandicapped peers) to the "maximum" extent appropriate. To date, many programs for children with autism did not (and do not) consider this an obtainable outcome. The intensive behavioral programs are consistent with the law in this area because their end goal is mainstreaming and integration. A school district might offer a placement that otherwise satisfied the "appropriateness" standard of the Act, but the placement would still be deficient because it was not designed to mainstream and integrate. The school district probably has little hard evidence to show that its program is capable of producing real mainstreaming (note that educating handicapped children with less handicapped children *is not mainstreaming*). See if you can get the school district's experts to admit that mainstreaming and integration are not really the goals of their program.

If they do not meet these standards, the general rule is that (at least as to items 1 and 2 above) they should be required to fund your program and reimburse you for what you have paid to date *provided you establish that your program is appropriate.* The appropriateness of a behavioral program should be easily established by the research and the cases cited in Section V.F. below. If you win they also have to pay your legal and expert fees.

B. *Procedural Violations.* Procedural violations are often overlooked but are probably the most common way to win. Some common examples follow.

1. Inadequate evaluations. Remember it is the school district's responsibility, not yours, to adequately evaluate your child within the required time frame.
2. Failure to involve someone knowledgeable about the disorder in the IEP process.

3. Failure to notify and involve parents in the IEP process. The law is clear that parents are to be involved at each step of the IEP process. Look to see if the district is making decisions at meetings where you are not present or otherwise acting to exclude you from the IEP process.

4. Failure to maintain a continuum of placement options. In theory, the school district is supposed to offer a continuum of placement options for a child with a disability ranging from most restrictive to full inclusion.

5. Determining placement prior to the writing of an IEP. Try to find documentation that the school district had already determined that your child would go to a certain school before the IEP was ever agreed upon. All placement decisions are to be based on the IEP goal and objectives, so it is against procedure to make a placement decision before the goals and objectives of the IEP are mutually determined (remember that placement is supposed to be where the child will be best able to accomplish the IEP goals and objectives). Note that parents should also be careful not to appear to be predetermining placement.

6. Accountability requirements. Failure of the district to be able to document and support the rationale for their decisions.

7. Notice requirements. Failure to notify parents of their rights, such as the right to a due process hearing.

C. *Documenting Procedural Violations.* Tape-record meetings or have a third party take notes. I generally prefer the first option. Although bringing an attorney to the IEP meeting may be helpful, I am always concerned that once the district sees an attorney involved, they will become more careful in what they are doing and clean up the procedural stuff, which is often a strong opportunity to prevail. Always correspond in writing and require the school district to state their position in writing. Try to get the school district's position on record *before* they have had an opportunity to hire an expensive lawyer. Often the school district will refuse to correspond with you, and this will make them look bad later on.

D. *Again, Put the School District on the Defensive.* Make them provide research and documentation on the success and mainstreaming results of any alternative they offer you. The lack of objective accountability in special education (at least as to this disability) is troubling. Would a child be treated for cancer with medicine that had never been tested? Would you invest your life savings in a company that had no documentation of its successes? Why should the result be any different for the disabled?

If the procedural violations are apparent, this may give the due process officer a way to get your child the program she needs without getting into a so-called battle of methodologies between the behavioral program and the school district's program. Note that there is some debate as to when procedural violations, in and of themselves, constitute a denial of FAPE (free and appropriate education). Generally, the more frequent and severe the violations, the better off you are. The Supreme Court in the *Rowley* (*Board of Education v. Rowley*, 458 U.S. 176 [1982]) decision clearly attaches great significance to compliance with the procedural aspects of the Act, and I believe it can be fairly argued that *any* violation constitutes the denial of a FAPE. If the hearing officer concludes that the procedures of the Act were violated, you should never reach the issue of whether the educational program of the district is appropriate. If the hearing officer determines that the procedures were correctly followed, the next issue will be whether the program developed by the district was appropriate for your child.

V. Due Process

A. *Obtaining an Attorney.* I recommend against filing for due process until you have obtained or at least consulted with a knowledgeable attorney. Paid attorneys who have established a name for themselves in the area of special education are generally preferable to public or *pro bono* (free) attorneys, if your finances will allow it. Public advocates can run the gamut from very good to horrible, and in fact some are excellent. If you decide to use a public advocate, be sure that person has had substantial previous experience in special education matters. A list of resources to help you find a capable *pro bono* (free) attorney are listed in the appendix to this chapter. Each state should have some sort of protection and advocacy department for the rights of the disabled, and the legal support offered by these groups is often superior to a local *pro bono* outfit.

B. *Get Your Case Prepared and Then File.* When it becomes clear to you that you can make no further progress by working in a cooperative fashion, you should begin to line up your case, particularly your expert witnesses. It is probably a good idea to get your case in order before you file for due process.

C. *Get Your Experts Together.* Solid expert testimony is critical to your case. To back up your position, have your child evaluated by somebody knowledgeable in the field. Ideally, this person should be published in the field, have exposure to other programs, and have testified in a courtroom setting. Additionally, your expert witness will be more credible if he is deemed not to have a vested financial or professional stake in your program; therefore, try to get additional testimony from someone other than the professional who is running your program.

D. *Getting Your Expert to Review Their Program.* Once you get away from procedural matters, the critical part of the case will be convincing the hearing officer of the inadequacy of the district's program. The school district will bring a variety of experts (most of whom are employed by the school district) to tell the officer what a wonderful program they have. But they will go to great lengths to hide their program from your expert (if it's so wonderful, why do they go to such lengths to hide it?), so that you will not be in a position to refute this testimony. Your expert should fully review the district's placement (including the IEP and supporting documents) and agree that it will provide no educational benefit to your child (other than trivial).

E. *When Do School Districts Settle?* They settle if they think there is a possibility or probability that they will lose. It is costly and embarrassing for them to lose. If the claim is for $100,000 and they think they have a 50% chance of losing, $50,000 will be their settlement offer. Remember, the total cost to the school district not only includes the cost of your program but also (a) the cost of their (presumably expensive) lawyers and experts, (b) the cost of your lawyer and experts (if they lose), and (c) the due process officer's time. They have much at risk once you file for due process.

F. *The Successful Cases to Date: Martin K. and B. Smith.* While you may think you have an uphill battle, the only two cases to reach the federal courts as of the time of this writing have been victories for the parents.[3] However, these cases have turned to some degree on procedural issues as opposed to substantive matters.

1. *Martin K.* In the *Martin K.* case out of Pennsylvania, the school district ultimately offered a PDD child a 10-hour-per-week placement in a program modeled after North Carolina's TEACCH program.[4] The parents argued against the TEACCH placement and in favor of a 40-hour Lovaas-based program they had begun at home. After first losing at the due process level, the parents won a complete victory at the administrative appeal level. At this level, the panel ruled that the TEACCH program, even if optimally implemented (i.e., run at the recommended 30-hour-per-week level), could never be appropriate when compared with the Lovaas program because the TEACCH program, *by its own admission,* was not designed or even attempting to achieve the IDEA goals of mainstreaming, integration, and self-sufficiency. Thus, when faced with two programs, one specifically designed to achieve self-sufficiency and integration and another that was not, the appeals panel felt compelled to sanction the first (Lovaas) program. The case then went to the federal court for the Eastern District of Pennsylvania. Although the federal court did not really adopt the mainstreaming rationale of the appeals panel decision, it nonetheless held for the parents on all points, citing somewhat narrower and more technical grounds, including the fact that the school district's program was a substandard imitation of the TEACCH program due to its reduced hours. This case clearly establishes the appropriateness of the intensive behavioral program. The rationale of the appeals panel is particularly strong.

2. *Smith.* The *Smith* case originated out of California and involved parents who rejected the school district's "generic" placement and enrolled their child in UCLA's Young Autism Project (not a home-based program).[5] At the due process level, the hearing officer considered the testimony of the parent's experts (all of whom advocated the UCLA program) to be far more credible than the

---

[3] Note that at the due process level there is now at least one adverse decision (in Virginia) and probably five to ten favorable decisions that I know of. Although these precedents are helpful, they are not necessarily determinative of your case.

[4] *Delaware County Intermediate Unit #25 v. Martin K., et al.,* 831 F. Sup. 206 (Eastern District of Pennsylvania, 1993).

testimony of the school district's experts (most of whom were employed by the school district). The school district had offered the child a placement in a "communication handicapped" (18 hours per week, I believe) preschool. The case was affirmed ultimately by both the federal district court (in an unpublished decision) and by the Federal Court of Appeals for the Ninth Circuit. On appeal, the courts seemed to place some emphasis on the fact that the teacher for the school district's placement had no substandard prior training or experience in dealing with autistic children. The Federal Court of Appeals dealt with more technical aspects of the case, and its decision ultimately resulted in a total victory for the parents. Not only did the parents receive reimbursement for their program, but they were also able to recover the mother's costs and expenses for moving to Los Angeles and commuting back home.

VI. Final Pieces of Advice

A. *Be Prepared for a Battle.* Litigation often becomes quite adversarial. You may be portrayed as a desperate parent or one who wants more than you are legally entitled to. They would love to intimidate you into dropping your case or settling on less than favorable terms. The more the school district perceives a victory for you as meaning they will have to change their entire system, the more they will fight.

B. *Courts and Hearings Deal with Proven or Provable Facts.* Be sure you have documentation to verify each step you make along the way. This is really to your benefit, because the school district will also be required to furnish hard proof of the viability of their system. This may be the first time they have ever had to do this.

C. *Hearing Officers Are Human Too.* Ultimately the case will hinge on your ability to convince the hearing officer that what you are doing is right. There is ample precedent to find in favor of an intensive, behavioral program if the hearing officer is so inclined. Compassion and sympathy are powerful allies in your corner. You must convince the due process officer that what you are doing is right for your child and that without the intervention, your child faces a dismal future. Nobody wants to be the bad guy or be responsible for your child leading a lifetime of handicap. If you are successful in convincing the officer that without this intervention your child is destined for a lifetime of handicap, I doubt you will lose regardless of how good or bad the law is under your specific facts. Do not hesitate to appeal to their sympathies; they are human also.

D. *Do Not Ever Back Down or Be Intimidated.* The more of a thorn in the side you are, the more the district will be willing to do things (like give you all or part of your program) to make you go away. Be persistent. You have the added advantage of being right!

E. *Multiple Programs.* In the strongest cases, the child tries the school district's program for a significant length of time, makes no or minimal progress (as documented by the school district's own records), is pulled out of the school district's program and put into a behavioral program where she makes substantial progress (as documented by videotape and/or independent evaluations). A case is more difficult to argue when the child is in the school district's program and a home behavioral program at the same time. To the extent that the child is making gains, both sides will take credit for them, and the issue of where they are coming from will be murky. Additionally, the school district will be able to argue with some logic that if the child is not obtaining some benefit from the school's programming, then the parents should not be agreeing to keep him there. I think the cases in which the child is in two programs at the same time are hard ones to win.

F. *Trial Placement.* A little-known section of the regulations allows for a temporary, or trial, placement to see if the proposed placement will best allow the child to achieve the goals and objectives of the IEP. You may want to ask for a trial placement to see if your child is one of the many who will respond positively to an intensive, behavioral program.

G. *Additional Reading.* An excellent book on this topic is *Negotiating the Special Education Maze,* by Winifred Anderson et al., published by Woodbine House, 6510 Bells Mill Road, Bethesda, Maryland 20817 (1-800-843-7323). The appendix to this chapter is reproduced from this fine book with the publisher's permission.

---

[5] *Union School District v. B. Smith et al.,* 15 F.3d 1519 (9th Circuit - 1994); *Bernard Smith v. Union Elementary School District,* California Special Education Hearing Officer (Case No. SN404-89H) (1990).

OUTLINE TWO ···

Note: Both the outlines on insurance law and the ADA are merely some comments on those topics. *They are not intended to represent a full discussion of the law in those areas.* As always, you should consult with an attorney on the law with regard to the facts and circumstances of your individual case.

INSURANCE LAW

It is next to impossible to set forth a list of unifying principles dealing with insurance law. This is because insurance law is primarily contract law, and thus the potential coverage provided by an insurance policy is pretty much determined by the terms and conditions of your individual policy. Your first step should be to obtain a copy of your insurance contract and review it quite carefully as to the extent of coverage and whether there are any explicit exclusions from coverage for autism, pervasive developmental disorder, or the like. Many policies do contain such exclusions, and most insurance policies are written in a fairly one-sided way in favor of the company. I would start with the position that unless your child's disability is *explicitly* excluded from coverage, then it is included; and unless the behavioral therapy sought is *explicitly* excluded, it is included. If specific and unambiguous exclusions apply, you should then analyze your rights under the Americans with Disabilities Act (see below).

Additionally, you should also note that the legal requirements of individual states vary considerably. Finally, a very complex federal statute, called the Employment Retirement Income Security Act (ERISA), affects many if not most employer-provided insurance plans. It is impossible within the constraints of this outline to do justice to this statute, but it is generally more difficult to litigate a claim where ERISA applies. With these disclaimers in mind, keep the following points in mind as you review your insurance situation.

1. *Medical versus Psychological.* Autism, PDD, and other developmental disabilities are organic, medical brain dysfunctions as opposed to psychological disorders. There should be no serious dispute over this point. Thus, if your insurance company has refused or limited coverage on the theory that your child's disorder is psychological and not medical, this can easily be refuted. In fact there is a case entitled *Daniel Kunin v. Benefit Trust Life Insurance Company*, 696 F. Supp. 1342 (C.D. Cal, 1988) where a U. S. District Court in California validated this principle. Therefore, your insurance company should not be able to exclude your child from coverage (or limit benefits) on the basis of a psychological or mental condition.

2. *Mandated Benefits.* Many states by statute list certain benefits an insurance plan must provide. For example, the state may have a statute requiring insurance plans to provide benefits for "neurological" or "nervous" disorders. If your state has a similar statute and coverage is excluded for your child, you may be able to argue that the policy violates the terms of the state statute and therefore coverage must be granted. Call the office of your state commissioner of insurance to get more information on mandated benefits in your state.

3. *Ambiguities.* Ambiguities in the insurance policy must generally be interpreted in favor of coverage. Courts recognize that due to the unequal bargaining position between the insurance company and the insured, the company had the upper hand in drafting the actual language of the policy. Thus, if the language is ambiguous, it should be construed *against* the company. If the exclusion the insurance company is relying on does not squarely meet your child's diagnoses, then you can use this rule in your favor to argue that because the disability is not expressly excluded, then it must be included in coverage. Almost any lawyer worth his salt can create an argument that a certain provision in a contract is ambiguous (in large part because many of them are).

4. *Diagnoses.* Many insurance policies have a provision that if the insured suffers from multiple conditions (one of which is covered and one of which is not), that coverage will be provided for the broader of the two diagnoses. I believe (and the *Kunin* case supports) an argument can be made that the "primary" diagnosis for a child otherwise characterized as "autistic" or "PDD" should be something along the lines of "organic brain dysfunction," and that the behavioral expression of the underlying brain dysfunction is "secondary" or a result of the underlying medical condition. Thus, if your policy excludes autism, PDD, or the like, you could argue that this is a secondary or tertiary condition caused by the primary diagnosis, "organic brain dysfunction."

Alternatively, you may want to discuss with your doctor if there is a supportable diagnosis you can utilize that is not expressly excluded from the policy. I don't know whether this will work, but it might be worthwhile to make the argument.

5. *ERISA.* Most employer-provided insurance plans qualify as benefits under an enormously complex federal statute called ERISA. **The ERISA requirements are far too complex to address adequately in this outline and may significantly limit your rights to recovery.** Basically, additional requirements and more difficult standards may apply in an ERISA-qualified plan dealing with, among other issues, the issue of whether the plan administrator was unreasonable, arbitrary, and capricious in his or her treatment of your claim. If you are dealing with an ERISA-qualified plan you should be sure your attorney has experience with this statute.

6. *Jury Trial.* One of the benefits of bringing a breach of contract claim is your right to a jury trial on the issue (however, this right may not apply to ERISA-qualified plans). It is unlikely that an insurance company wants to let you or your enormously sympathetic, young, disabled child be presented in front of a jury. This fear alone may be enough to convince your insurance company to settle its case. A jury will not get bogged down in all the legal minutiae of the insurance contract and will not be too sympathetic to a large insurance company trying to deny benefits to your disabled youngster.

Finally, even if you are able to determine that coverage is available, the question arises as to what benefits you are entitled to. There are a host of issues dealing with certified providers, diagnostic codes, licensed personnel, and so on that are set forth in the individual policy. For example, the policy may not exclude treatment for autism or PDD but may exclude behavioral therapy as a benefit available under the plan. The terms of the insurance plan may present additional obstacles to obtaining reimbursement for a behavioral program. "Managed care" and "HMO" plans may have further obstacles to overcome in obtaining coverage. Again, you must examine the individual policy to determine how much of an obstacle all these considerations are.

OUTLINE THREE ••

THE AMERICANS WITH DISABILITIES ACT

I. Overview

    A. Signed into law in 1990, the Americans with Disabilities Act (ADA) prohibits discrimination based on a disability in employment (including benefits of employment), public services, public accommodations, and related areas.

    B. Effective July 26, 1994, the ADA covers employers with 15 or more employees.

    C. The primary enforcement agent for the employment-related provisions of the ADA is the Equal Employment Opportunity Commission (EEOC).

    D. The ADA statute is notable because it provides for two things that any potential defendant dislikes: (a) trial by jury, and (b) punitive damages (although the extent of the punitive damages is limited by statute).

    E. The ADA statute and subsequent interpretations make it clear that employer-provided insurance is included within the bounds of the ADA.

    F. Because the ADA statute is in its infancy, there is little case law or other interpretive guidance on how ADA will be interpreted in the area of insurance.

    G. If your insurance plan excludes coverage for autism, PDD, or the like, you may be able to utilize the ADA to obtain insurance coverage for your child's condition.

II. The ADA and Insurance

    A. The ADA prohibits discrimination on the basis of a disability in employment and related benefits of employment, *including employer-provided insurance.*

    B. Clearly a child with a neurological disorder such as autism, PDD, or aphasia would meet the statutory definition of disabled. Thus, the attempt to exclude such a child from the benefits of an employer-provided insurance plan *by reason of his disability* should set forth a *prima facie* violation under Title I of the ADA. **However, there is a major exception to this rule, discussed below.**

C. If the insurance is provided by the state or other governmental authorities, there may also be a violation under Title II of the ADA dealing with public services, as well as under § 54 of the Rehabilitation Act of 1973 prohibiting discrimination on the basis of a disability in any program receiving federal aid.

D. There are *strict procedural guidelines* for filing a complaint under the ADA. Without getting into all the technical parameters, you should generally plan on filing a complaint with the EEOC within *180* days of when the act of discrimination occurred. **Failure to file your complaint in a timely fashion may ultimately bar your claim.** The EEOC will then investigate your claim and would either intervene on your behalf to mediate the claim or issue a "right to sue" letter, which will allow you to take the claim to federal court.

E. An articulation of the EEOC regulations in the area of employer-provided health insurance is provided by EEOC release dated June 8, 1993, titled "EEOC Issues Interim Enforcement Guidance on the Application of the ADA to Disability-Based Provisions of Employer-Provided Health Insurance" and related EEOC Notice N-915.002 dated 8 June 1993. Call the EEOC at (202) 663-4900 to get a copy of these publications.

III. The Section 501(c) Exemption

A. Any potential ADA insurance claim must be analyzed in view of the Section 501(c), 42 U.S.C. § 12201(c), exclusion.

B. There is no way within the constraints of this outline to explain adequately all the nuances of the Section 501(c) exclusion. Moreover, as the statute is fairly new, there is limited judicial authority to flesh out Section 501(c). The basic idea of Section 501(c) is that the insurance company *can* engage in disability-based distinction so long as (a) the health insurance plan is a bona fide plan not inconsistent with state law, or it is a bona fide self-insured plan, and (b) the plan is not being used as a "subterfuge" to evade the purposes of the Act. The EEOC guidelines are clear that the employer has the burden of proof to establish that the 501(c) exemption applies. The general idea here is that, to be permissible, the distinction must be based on hard, analytical data applied in a rational, nondiscriminatory, and evenhanded way and not based on prejudices or stereotypes related to the disorder or unfounded assumptions.

C. The employer/insurance company would then probably argue that an exclusion for autism, PDD, or other applicable diagnoses is justified as a business matter because payment of benefits for these conditions are (a) not medical in nature, (b) will unduly financially burden the insurance plan, or (c) will prove of little benefit to the insured.

D. Again, I would remind you that there is not yet a case that definitively resolves some of the ambiguities under Section 501(c); however, in response to the arguments stated above, consider the following points:

1. One of the underlying purposes of the ADA was to stop discrimination based on myths, prejudices, and unsupported stereotypes. I believe the exclusion of disorders like autism, PDD, aphasia, and so on from insurance coverage is often based on two unsubstantiated stereotypes: (a) the disorders are mental and not medical in nature, and (b) there is very little one can do to help. However, the neurological nature of the condition and the effectiveness of early behavioral intervention are clearly established by current research.

2. Determine if similar neurological disorders do receive coverage. The policy probably covers stroke, Parkinson's disease, and the like. Thus, the coverage of some neurological disorders but not others is arbitrary and discriminatory on its face. Also, the fact that the insurance policy covers some conditions listed in DSM IV but not others may violate the antidiscriminatory provisions of the ADA. Generally, sound underwriting principles would require that conditions with comparable actuarial data be treated in the same way.

3. If the employer asserts that the disability-based distinction was necessary to prevent the occurrence of an unacceptable change in coverage or premiums, the evidence presented should include non-disability-based options that were considered and why they were rejected. (See page 2 of the above-cited EEOC guidelines.) Thus, if your policy will provide speech therapy for some children but not your son or daughter, ask why an equal ceiling on speech therapy (without regard to disability) was not considered for all participants.

4. Require the employer/insurance company to produce hard data supporting their conclusions. Because they carry the burden of proof, they are responsible for producing this data, which they may or may not have.

Please note that none of the above theories have been tested in court; they are just some suggestions that appear to have support in the EEOC regulations and guidelines. If a violation of the ADA is determined, you can then request reimbursement for your behavioral program as part of your damages. Remember, just filing the claim may provide the impetus for a favorable settlement.

IV. Conclusion

The impact of the ADA on insurance policies that exclude coverage for certain disorders is unclear at best. With a couple of favorable interpretations limiting the scope of the 501(c) exemption, the potential impact of the statute could be enormous. If your health insurance policy clearly excludes coverage for whatever disability your child has, you may want to consider exploring with a competent attorney your options under the ADA. **If you do this, remember you must act quickly due to the short statute of limitations under ADA.** The availability of both a jury trial and the possibility of punitive damages makes ADA a very attractive statute for plaintiffs. Moreover, your employer/insurer may want to settle as opposed to setting an unfavorable precedent on the 501(c) issue, which could open the floodgates for similar claims. Finally, remember that your state may have similar antidiscrimination statutes that may be even broader than the ADA coverage.

APPENDIX

State Offices

For each state, the following offices are listed:

1. Director of Special Education

2. Protection and Advocacy

3. Vocational Rehabilitation Agency

4. Parent Training and Information Project(s)*

Alabama

Director of Special Education
Student Instructional Services
State Department of Education
1020 Monticello Ct.
Montgomery, AL 36117-1901
(205) 261-5099

Program Director
Alabama Disabilities Advocacy Program
P.O. Drawer 2847
Tuscaloosa, AL 35487-2847
(205) 348-4928

Director
Rehabilitation & Crippled Children
   Service
P.O. Box 11586
Montgomery, AL 36111-0586
(205) 281-8780

Special Education Action Committee
P.O. Box 161274
Mobile, AL 36606
(205) 478-1208

Alaska

Director of Special Education
Office of Special Services
Alaska Department of Education
P.O. Box F
Juneau, AK 99811
(907) 465-2970

Disability Law Center of Alaska
615 E. 82nd St., Ste. 101
Anchorage, AL 99518
(907) 344-1002
(800) 478-1234 (w/in state)

Director
Division of Vocational Rehabilitation
Pouch F, MS 0581
Juneau, AK 99811
(907) 465-2814

American Samoa

Director of Special Education
Special Education
Department of Education
Pago Pago, American Samoa 96799
(684) 633-1323

Client Assistance Program
P.O. Box 3407
Pago Pago, American Samoa 96799
4-011-684-633-2418

Arizona

Director of Special Education
Special Education Section
Department of Education
1535 W. Jefferson
Phoenix, AZ 85007-3280
(602) 255-3183

Protection & Advocacy
Arizona Center for Law in the Public
   Interest
112 N. Central Ave., Suite 400
Phoenix, AZ 85004
(602) 252-4904

Administrator
Rehabilitative Services Administration
1300 W. Washington Street
Phoenix, AZ 85007
(602) 255-3332

Pilot Parents
2005 N. Central Ave., #100
Phoenix, AZ 85004
(602) 271-4012

Arkansas

Director of Special Education
Special Education Section
Arkansas Department of Education
Education Bldg., Room 105-C
#4 Capitol Mall
Little Rock, AR 72201
(501) 371-2161

---

*Not every state has a Parent Training and Information Project, and a few states have several.

Executive Director
Advocacy Services, Inc.
Medical Arts Bldg., Suite 311
12th and Marshall Streets
Little Rock, AR 72202
(501) 371-2171

Commissioner
Arkansas Department of Human
    Services
Rehabilitation Services Division
P.O. Box 3781
Little Rock, AR 72203

Arkansas Coalition for the Handicapped
519 East Fifth Street
Little Rock, AR 72202
(501) 376-3420

FOCUS
2917 King Street, Suite C
Jonesboro, AR 72401
(501) 935-2750

California

Director of Special Education
Specialized Programs Branch
Special Education Division
P.O. Box 844272
Sacramento, CA 94244-2720
(916) 323-4768

Executive Director
Protection & Advocacy, Inc.
2131 Capitol Ave., Suite 100
Sacramento, CA 95816
(916) 447-3327
(213) 481-7431
(415) 839-0811
(800) 952-5746

Director
Department of Rehabilitation
830 K St. Mall
Sacramento, CA 95814
(916) 445-3971

Team of Advocates for Special Kids
    (TASK)
18685 Santa Ynez
Fountain Valley, CA 92708
(714) 962-6332

Parents Helping Parents
3041 Olcott St.
Santa Clara, CA 95054
(408) 727-5775

DREDF
2212 6th Street
Berkeley, CA 94710
(415) 644-2555

Disability Services Matrix
P.O. Box 6541
San Rafael, CA 94903
(415) 499-3877

Colorado

Director of Special Education
Special Education Services Unit
Colorado Department of Education
201 E. Colfax
Denver, CO 90203
(303) 866-6694

Executive Director
The Legal Center
455 Sherman Street, Suite 130
Denver, CO 80203
(303) 722-0300

Director
Division of Rehabilitation
Department of Social Services
1575 Sherman Street, 4th Floor
Denver, CO 80203

Parent Education and Assistance
    for Kids (PEAK)
6055 Lehman Dr., Suite 101
Colorado Springs, CO 80918
(719) 531-9400
(800) 621-8386, Ex. 338 (in Colorado)

Connecticut

Director of Special Education
Bureau of Special Education and Pupil
    Personnel Services
P.O. Box 2219
Hartford, CT 06102-2219
(203) 566-3561

Executive Director
Office of Protection & Advocacy for
    Handicapped & Developmentally
    Disabled Persons
90 Washington Street
Hartford, CT 06106
(203) 566-7616/2102
(800) 842-7303 (in Connecticut)

Associate Commissioner
State Department of Education
Division of Vocational Rehabilitation
600 Asylum Ave.
Hartford, CT 06105
(203) 566-4440

Connecticut Parent Advocacy
   Center, Inc.
P.O. Box 579
East Lyme, CT 06333
(203) 739-3089
(800) 445-CPAL (in Connecticut)

Delaware

Director of Special Education
Exceptional Children/Special Programs
   Division
Department of Public Instruction
P.O. Box 1402
Dover, DE 19903
(302) 736-5471

Administrator
Disabilities Law Program
144 E. Market Street
Georgetown, DE 19947
(302) 856-0038

Director
Division of Vocational Rehabilitation
Department of Labor
State Office Building, 7th Floor
820 N. French Street
Wilmington, DE 19801
(302) 571-2850

Parent Information Center
   of Delaware, Inc.
325 E. Main Street, Suite 203
Newark, NJ 19711
(302) 366-0152

District of Columbia

Director of Special Education
Division of Special Education and Pupil
   Personnel Services
D.C. Public Schools
Webster Administration Bldg.
10th & H Streets, NW
Washington, D.C. 20001
(202) 724-4018

Executive Director
Information, Protection, and Advocacy
   Center for Handicapped
   Individuals, Inc.
300 Eye Street, NE, Suite 202
Washington, D.C. 20002
(202) 547-8081

Administrator
D.C. Rehabilitation Services
   Administration
Commission on Social Services
Department of Human Services
605 G Street, NW, Room 1101
Washington, D.C. 20001
(202) 727-3227

Florida

Director of Special Education
Bureau of Education for Exceptional Students
Florida Department of Education
Knott Building
Tallahassee, FL 32301
(904) 488-1570

Executive Director
Advocacy Center for Persons with
   Disabilities, Inc.
2661 Executive Center Circle, W
209 Clifton Bldg.
Tallahassee, FL 32301
(904) 488-9070
(800) 342-0823 Voice/TDD

Director
Division of Vocational Rehabilitation
1709-A Mahan Dr.
Tallahassee, FL 32399-0696
(904) 488-6210

Parent Education Network
   of Florida, Inc.
2215 East Henry Ave.
Tampa, FL 33610
(813) 238-6100

Georgia

Director of Special Education
Program for Exceptional Children
Georgia Department of Education
1970 Twin Towers East
205 Butler Street
Atlanta, GA 30334-1601
(404) 656-2425

Executive Director
Georgia Advocacy Office, Inc.
1447 Peachtree Street, NE, Suite 811
Atlanta, GA 30309
(404) 885-1447
(800) 282-4538 (in Georgia)

Director
Division of Rehabilitative Services
Department of Human Services
878 Peachtree, Street, NE, Room 706
Atlanta, GA 30309
(404) 894-6670

Parents Educating Parents
Georgia ARC
1851 Ram Runway, Suite 104
College Park, GA 30337
(404) 761-2745

Guam

Director of Special Education
Special Education
Department of Education
P.O. Box DE
Agana, Guam 97910
(671) 472-8901, ex. 375

Administrator
The Advocacy Office
P.O. Box 8830
Tamuning, Guam 96911
(671) 646-9026/27 or 646-6204

Director
Department of Vocational Rehabilitation
414 W. Soledad Ave.
Government of Guam
Agana, Guam 97910
472-8806 (Dial 011671 first)

Hawaii

Director of Special Education
Special Needs Branch
State Department of Education
3430 Leahi Ave.
Honolulu, HI 96815
(808) 737-3720

Executive Director
Protection & Advocacy Agency of Hawaii
1580 Makaloa Street, Suite 1060
Honolulu, HI 96814
(808) 949-2922

Administrator
Division of Vocational Rehabilitation &
    Services for the Blind
Department of Social Services
P.O. Box 339
Honolulu, HI 96809
(808) 548-4769

Idaho

Director of Special Education
Special Education
State Department of Education
650 W. State Street
Boise, ID 83720-0001
(208) 334-3940

Idaho's Coalition of Advocates for the
    Disabled, Inc.
1409 W. Washington
Boise, ID 83702
(208) 336-5353

Administrator
Division of Vocational Rehabilitation
Len B. Jordan Bldg., Room 150
650 West State
Boise, ID 83720
(208) 334-3390

Illinois

Director of Special Education
Illinois State Board of Education
Mail Code E-216
100 North First Street
Springfield, IL 62777-0001
(217) 782-6601

Director
Protection & Advocacy, Inc.
175 W. Jackson, Suite A-2103
Chicago, IL 60604
(312) 341-0022 Voice/TDD

Director
Department of Rehabilitation Services
    (Illinois)
623 E. Adams Street
P.O. Box 19429
Springfield, IL 62794-9429
(217) 785-0218

Coordinating Council for Handicapped
    Children
20 E. Jackson Blvd., Room 900
Chicago, IL 60604
(312) 939-3513

Designs for Change
220 South State Street, Room 1900
Chicago, IL 60604
(312) 922-0317

Indiana

Director of Special Education
Division of Special Education
Indiana Department of Education
229 State House
Indianapolis, IN 46204
(317) 629-9462

Indiana Protection & Advocacy
Service Commission for the
    Developmentally Disabled
850 N. Meridian Street, Suite 2-C
Indianapolis, IN 46204
(317) 232-1150
(800) 622-4845 (in Indiana)

Commissioner
Indiana Department of Human Services
251 N. Illinois Street
P.O Box 7083
Indianapolis, IN 46207-7083
(317) 232-7000

Task Force on Education for the
Handicapped, Inc.
833 Northside Blvd.
South Bend, IN 46617
(219) 234-7101

Iowa

Director of Special Education
Division of Special Education
Iowa Department of Public Instruction
Grimes State Office Bldg.
Des Moines, IA 50319-0146
(515) 281-3176

Director
Iowa Protection & Advocacy
    Services, Inc.
3015 Merle Hay Rd., Suite 6
Des Moines, IA 50310
(515) 278-2502

Administrator
Division of Vocational Rehabilitation
    Services
Department of Education
510 E. 12th Street
Des Moines, IA 50319
(515) 281-4311

Iowa Exceptional Parent Center
33 North 12th Street
P.O. Box 1151
Ft. Dodge, IA 50501
(515) 576-5870

Kansas

Director of Special Education
Kansas Department of Education
120 E. Tenth Street
Topeka, KS 66612
(913) 296-4945

Executive Director
Kansas Advocacy & Protection Services
513 Leavenworth, Suite 2
Manhattan, KS 66502
(913) 776-1541
(800) 432-8276 (in Kansas)

Commissioner of Rehabilitation Services
Department of Social & Rehabilitative
    Services
Biddle Bldg., 2nd Floor
2700 W. 6th
Topeka, KS 66606
(913) 296-3911

Families Together, Inc.
P.O. Box 86153
Topeka, KS 66686
(913) 273-6343

Kentucky

Director of Special Education
Kentucky Department of Education
Office of Education for Exceptional
    Children
Capitol Plaza Tower, Room 820
Frankfort, KY 40601
(501) 564-4970

Director
Department of Public Advocacy
Protection & Advocacy Division
1264 Louisville Rd.
Perimeter Park West
Frankfort, KY 40601
(502) 564-2967
(800) 372-2988 Voice/TDD

Assistant Superintendent of
Rehabilitation
Department of Education
Bureau of Rehabilitative Services
Capital Plaza Office Tower
Frankfort, KY 40601
(502) 564-4440

Kentucky Special Parent Involvement
Network
318 W. Kentucky Street
Louisville, KY 40203
(502) 587-5717 or 584-1104

Louisiana

Director of Special Education
Louisiana Department of Education
Special Education Services
P.O. Box 44064, 9th Floor
Baton Rouge, LA 70804-9064
(504) 342-3633

Executive Director
Advocate Center for the Elderly &
Disabled
1001 Howard Ave., Suite 300-A
New Orleans, LA 70113
(504) 522-2337
(800) 662-7705 (in Louisiana)

Director
Division of Rehabilitation Services
P.O. Box 94371
Baton Rouge, LA 70804
(504) 342-2285

United Cerebral Palsy of Greater
New Orleans
1500 Edwards Ave., Suite O
Harahan, LA 70123
(504) 733-7736

Maine

Director of Special Education
Division of Special Education
Maine Department of Educational and
Cultural Services
Station #23
Augusta, ME 04333
(207) 289-5953

Director
Advocates for the DD
2 Mulliken Ct.
P.O. Box 5341
Hallowell, ME 04347
(207) 289-5755
(800) 452-1948 (in Maine)

Director
Bureau of Rehabilitative Services
Department of Health & Welfare
32 Winthrop Street
Augusta, ME 04330
(207) 289-2266

Special Needs Parent Information
Network (SPIN)
P.O. Box 2067
Augusta, ME 04330
(207) 582-2504
(800) 325-0220 (in Maine)

Maryland

Director of Special Education
Division of Special Education
Maryland State Department
of Education
200 W. Baltimore Street
Baltimore, MD 21201-2595
(301) 333-2489

Director
Maryland Disability Law Center
2510 St. Paul Street
Baltimore, MD 21218
(301) 333-7600

Assistant State Superintendent
Division of Vocational Rehabilitation
State Department of Education
200 W. Baltimore Street
Baltimore, MD 21201
(301) 659-2294

See Parent Educational Advocacy
Training Center under Virginia

Massachusetts

Director of Special Education
Division of Special Education
Massachusetts Department of Education
1385 Hancock Street, 3rd Floor
Quincy, MA 02169-5183
(617) 770-7468

Executive Director
DD Law Center of Massachusetts
11 Beacon Street, Suite 925
Boston, MA 02108
(617) 723-8455

Commissioner
Massachusetts Rehabilitation
Commission
20 Park Plaza, 11th Floor
Boston, MA 02116
(617) 727-2172

Federation for Children with Special
  Needs
312 Stuart Street, 2nd Floor
Boston, MA 02116
(617) 482-2915
(800) 331-0688 (in Massachusetts)

Michigan

Director of Special Education
Special Education Services
Michigan Department of Education
P.O. Box 30008
Lansing, MI 48909-7508
(517) 373-9433

Executive Director
Michigan Protection & Advocacy
  Service, Inc.
109 W. Michigan Ave., Suite 900
Lansing, MI 48933
(517) 487-1755

State Director
Michigan Rehabilitation Services
Michigan Department of Education
P.O. Box 30010
Lansing, MI 48909
(517) 373-0683

United Cerebral Palsy Assn.
  of Metropolitan Detroit
Parents Training Parents Project
17000 West 8 Mile Rd., Suite 380
Southfield, MI 48075
(313) 557-5070

Citizens Alliance to Uphold Special
  Education (CAUSE)
313 South Washington Sq., Suite 040
Lansing, MI 48933
(517) 485-4084
(800) 221-9105 (in Michigan)

Minnesota

Director of Special Education
Special Education Section
Department of Education
812 Capitol Square Bldg.
550 Cedar Street
St. Paul, MN 55101-2233
(612) 359-3490

Managing Attorney
Legal Aid Society of Minneapolis
222 Grain Exchange Bldg.
323 Fourth Ave., S.
Minneapolis, MN 55415
(612) 332-7301

Assistant Commissioner
Division of Rehabilitation Services
Department of Jobs and Training
390 N. Robert Street, 5th Floor
St. Paul, MN 55101
(612) 296-1822

PACER Center, Inc.
4826 Chicago Ave. South
Minneapolis, MN 55417
(612) 827-2966
(800) 53-PACER (in Minnesota)

Mississippi

Director of Special Education
Bureau of Special Services
State Department of Education
P.O. Box 771
Jackson, MS 39205-0771
(601) 359-3498

Executive Director
Mississippi Protection & Advocacy
  System, Inc.
4793B McWillie Dr.
Jackson, MS 39206
(601) 981-8207
(800) 772-4057 (in Mississippi)

Director
Department of Rehabilitation Services
Vocational Rehabilitation Division
932 N. State Street
P.O. Box 1698
Jackson, MS 39215-1698
(601) 354-6825

Association of Developmental
  Organizations of Mississippi
6055 Highway 18 South, Suite A
Jackson, MS 39209
(601) 922-3210
(800) 231-3721 (in Mississippi)

Missouri

Director of Special Education
Special Education
Department of Elementary and
  Secondary Education
P.O. Box 480
Jefferson City, MO 65102
(314) 751-2965

Missouri Protection & Advocacy Services
211-B Metro Dr.
Jefferson City, MO 65101
(314) 893-3333
(800) 392-8667 (in Missouri)

Assistant Commissioner
State Department of Education
Division of Vocational Rehabilitation
2401 E. McCarty
Jefferson City, MO 65101
(314) 751-3251

Missouri Parents Act (MPACT)
P.O. Box 1141 G.S.
Springfield, MO 65808
(417) 882-7434 or 869-6694

Montana

Director of Special Education
Special Education
Office of Public Instruction
State Capitol, Room 106
Helena, MT 59620
(406) 444-4429

Executive Director
Montana Advocacy Program
1410 8th Ave.
Helena, MT 59601
(406) 444-3889
(800) 245-4743 (in Montana)

Administrator
Department of Social & Rehabilitative
   Services
Rehabilitative-Visual Services Division
P.O. Box 4210
Helena, MT 59604
(406) 444-2590

Parents, Let's Unite for Kids (PLUK)
1500 N. 30th Street
Billings, MT 59101
(406) 727-4590
(800) 222-PLUK (In Montana)

Nebraska

Director of Special Education
Special Education
Nebraska Department of Education
Box 94987
Lincoln, NE 68509-4987
(402) 471-2471

Executive Director
Nebraska Advocacy Services, Inc.
522 Lincoln Center Bldg.
215 Centennial Mall South
Lincoln, NE 68508
(402) 474-3183
(800) 422-6691 (in Nebraska)

Associate Commissioner & Director
Division of Rehabilitative Services
State Department of Education
301 Centennial Mall, 6th Floor
Lincoln, NE 68509
(402) 471-2961

Nevada

Director of Special Education
Special Education
Nevada Department of Education
Capitol Complex
400 W. King Street
Carson City, NV 89710-0004
(702) 885-3140

Project Director
Office of Protection & Advocacy
2105 Capurro Way, Suite B
Reno, NV 89431
(702) 789-0233
(800) 992-5715 (in Nevada)

Administrator, Rehabilitation Division
Department of Human Resources
Kinkead Bldg., 5th Floor
505 E. King Street
Carson City, NV 89710
(702) 885-4440

Nevada Association for the Handicapped
6200 W. Oakey Blvd.
Las Vegas, NV 89201-11142
(702) 870-7050

New Hampshire

Director of Special Education
Special Education Bureau
New Hampshire Department
   of Education
101 Pleasant Street
Concord, NH 03301-3860
(603) 271-3741

Executive Director
Disabilities Rights Center, Inc.
94 Washington Street
P.O. Box 19
Concord, NH 03302-0019
(603) 228-0432

Director
State Department of Education
Division of Vocational Rehabilitation
78 Regional Dr., Bldg. JB
Concord, NH 03301
(603) 271-3471

Parent Information Center
155 Manchester Street
P.O. Box 1422
Concord, NH 03302-1422
(603) 224-6299

New Jersey

Director of Special Education
Division of Special Education
New Jersey Department of Education
P.O. Box CN 500
225 W. State Street
Trenton, NJ 08625-0001
(609) 292-0147

Director
Division of Advocacy for the
    Developmentally Disabled
Hughes Justice Complex, CN850
Trenton, NJ 08625
(609) 292-9742
(800) 792-8600 (in New Jersey)

Director, Division of Vocational
    Rehabilitation Services
Labor & Industry Bldg., CN398
John Fitch Plaza, Room 1005
Trenton, NJ 08625
(609) 292-5987

Parents and Children Together
    Organized for Family Learning
    (PACTO)
66 Lakeview Dr.
P.O. Box 114
Allentown, NJ 08501
(201) 324-2451

Statewide Parent Advocacy Network
    (SPAN)
516 North Ave. East
Westfield, NJ 07090
(201) 654-7726

New Mexico

Director of Special Education
Special Education
State Department of Education
State Educational Bldg.
Santa Fe, NM 87501-2786
(505) 827-6541

Protection & Advocacy System
2201 San Pedro, NE
Bldg. 4, Suite 140
Albuquerque, NM 87110
(505) 888-0111
(800) 432-4682 (in New Mexico)

DVR Director
Division of Vocational Rehabilitation
604 W. San Mateo
Santa Fe, NM 87503
(505) 827-3511

Education for Indian Children with
    Special Needs (EPICS)
P.O. Box 788
Bernalillo, NM 87004
(505) 867-3396

New York

Director of Special Education
New York State Department
    of Education
Office of Education of Children with
    Handicapping Conditions
Education Building Annex, Room 1073
Albany, NY 12234-0001
(518) 474-5548

Commissioner
New York Commission on Quality
    of Care for the Mentally Disabled
99 Washington Ave., Suite 1002
Albany, NY 12210
(518) 473-4057

Deputy Director
Office of Vocational Rehabilitation
One Commerce Plaza, Room 1907
Albany, NY 12234
(518) 474-2714

Parent Network Center
1443 Main Street
Buffalo, NY 14209
(716) 885-1004

North Carolina

Director of Special Education
Division of Exceptional Children
North Carolina State Department
    of Public Instruction
Education Bldg., Room 442
116 W. Edenton
Raleigh, NC 27603-1712
(919) 733-3921

Director
Governor's Advocacy Council for
    Persons with Disabilities
1318 Dale Street, Suite 100
Raleigh, NC 27605
(919) 733-9250

Director
Division of Vocational Rehabilitation
  Services
Department of Human Resources
State Office
P.O. Box 26053
Raleigh, NC 27611
(919) 733-3364

Exceptional Children's Advocacy
  Council
P.O. Box 16
Davidson, NC 28036
(704) 892-1321

ARC, North Carolina
Family and Infant Preschool Program
Western Carolina Center
300 Enola Rd.
Morganton, NC 28655
(704) 433-2661

North Dakota

Director of Special Education
Special Education
Department of Public Instruction
State Capitol
Bismarck, ND 58505-0440
(701) 224-2277

Director
Protection & Advocacy Project
State Capitol Judicial Wing, 1st Floor
Bismarck, ND 58505
(701) 224-2972
(800) 472-2670 (in North Dakota)

Division Director
Division of Vocational Rehabilitation
State Capitol Bldg.
Bismarck, ND 58505
(701) 224-2907

Pathfinder Services of North Dakota
RR1 Box 18-A
Maxbass, ND 58760
(701) 268-3390

Ohio

Director of Special Education
Ohio Department of Education
Division of Special Education
933 High Street
Worthington, OH 43085-4017
(614) 466-2650

Executive Director
Ohio Legal Rights Service
8 E. Long Street, 6th Floor
Columbus, OH 43215
(614) 466-7264
(800) 282-9181 (in Ohio)

Administrator
Ohio Rehabilitation Services
  Commission
4656 Heaton Rd.
Columbus, OH 43229
(614) 438-1210

SOC Information Center
106 Wellington Place, Suite LL
Cincinnati, OH 45219
(513) 381-2400

Ohio Coalition for the Education
  of Handicapped Children
933 High Street, Suite 106
Worthington, OH 43085
(614) 431-1307

Oklahoma

Director of Special Education
Special Education Section
State Department of Education
Oliver Hodge Memorial Bldg.
2500 N. Lincoln, Room 215
Oklahoma City, OK 73105-4599
(405) 521-3352

Director
Protection & Advocacy Agency
9726 E. 42nd Street
Osage Bldg., Suite 133
Tulsa, OK 74146
(918) 664-5883

Administrator of Rehabilitation Services
Department of Human Services
23rd & Lincoln, Sequoyah Bldg.
P.O. Box 25352
Oklahoma City, OK 73125
(405) 521-3646

PRO-Oklahoma (Parents Reaching
  Out in Oklahoma)
1917 S. Harvard Ave.
Oklahoma City, OK 73128
(405) 681-9710
(800) PL94-142 (in Oklahoma)

Oregon

Director of Special Education
Special Education and Student Services
    Division
Oregon Department of Education
700 Pringle Parkway, S.E.
Salem, OR 97310-0290
(503) 378-2677

Executive Director
Oregon Developmental Disabilities
    Advocacy Center
400 Board of Trade Bldg.
310 S.W. 4th Ave.
Portland, OR 97204
(503) 243-2081

Administrator
Division of Vocational Rehabilitation
Department of Human Resources
2045 Silverton Rd., NE
Salem, OR 97310
(503) 378-3830

Oregon Coalition for Exceptional
    Children and Young Adults/COPE
Oregon COPE Project
999 Locust Street, NE, #42
Salem, OR 97303
(503) 373-7477

Pennsylvania

Director of Special Education
Bureau of Special Education
Pennsylvania Department of Education
333 Market Street
Harrisburg, PA 17126-0333
(717) 783-6913

Pennsylvania Protection &
    Advocacy, Inc.
116 Pine Street
Harrisburg, PA 17101
(717) 236-8110
(800) 692-7443 (in Pennsylvania)

Executive Director
Office of Vocational Rehabilitation
Labor & Industry Bldg.
Seventh & Forster Streets
Harrisburg, PA 17120
(717) 787-5244

Parents Union for Public Schools
401 North Broad Street, Room 916
Philadelphia, PA 19108
(215) 574-0337

Parent Education Network
240 Haymeadow Dr.
York, PA 17402
(717) 845-9722

Puerto Rico

Director of Special Education
Special Education
Department of Education
G.P.O. Box 759
Hato Rey, PR 00919-0759
(809) 764-8059

Director
Planning Research and Special Projects
Ombudsman for the Disabled
Governor's Office
Chardon Ave., #916
Hato Rey, PR 00936
(809) 766-2333/2388

Assistant Secretary for Vocational
    Rehabilitation
Department of Social Services
P.O. Box 118
Hato Rey, PR 00919
(809) 725-1792

Associacion Padres Pro Bienestar/Ninos
Impedidos de Puerto Rico
P.O. Box 21301
Rio Piedras, PR 00928
(809) 765-0345/763-4665

Rhode Island

Director of Special Education
Special Education Program Services Unit
R.I. Department of Education
Roger Williams Bldg., Room 209
22 Hayes Street
Providence, RI 02908-5025
(401) 277-3505

Executive Director
Rhode Island Protection & Advocacy
    System
55 Bradford Street
Providence, RI 02903
(401) 831-3150 Voice/TDD

Administrator, Vocational Rehabilitation
Division of Community Services
Department of Human Services
40 Fountain Street
Providence, RI 02903
(401) 421-7005 (TDD 421-7016)

South Carolina

Director of Special Education
Office of Programs for Handicapped
South Carolina Department of Education
100 Executive Center Dr., A-24
Columbia, SC 29201
(803) 737-8710

Executive Director
South Carolina Protection & Advocacy
   System for the Handicapped, Inc.
2360-A Two Notch Rd.
Columbia, SC 29204

Commissioner
South Carolina Vocational
   Rehabilitation Department
P.O. Box 15
W. Columbia, SC 29171-0015
(803) 734-4300

South Dakota

Director of Special Education
Section for Special Education
State of South Dakota Department
   of Education
Richard F. Kneip Office Bldg.
700 N. Illinois Street, 3rd Floor
Pierre, SD 57501-2293
(605) 773-3678

Executive Director
South Dakota Advocacy Project, Inc.
221 S. Central Ave.
Pierre, SD 57501
(605) 224-8294
(800) 742-8108 (in South Dakota)

Secretary
Division of Rehabilitative Services
Department of Vocational Rehabilitation
State Office Bldg.
700 Governors Dr.
Pierre, SD 57501
(605) 773-3195

South Dakota Parent Connection
P.O. Box 84813
330 N. Main Ave., Suite 301
Sioux Falls, SD 57118-4813
(605) 335-8844
(800) 422-6893 (in South Dakota)

Tennessee

Director of Special Education
Special Programs
State of Tennessee Department
   of Education
132 Cordell Hull Bldg.
Nashville, TN 37219
(615) 741-2851

Director
E.A.C.H., Inc.
P.O. Box 121257
Nashville, TN 37212
(615) 298-1080
(800) 342-1660 (in Tennessee)
Voice/TTY

Assistant Commissioner
Division of Rehabilitation Services
1808 W. End Bldg., Room 900
Nashville, TN 37203
(615) 741-2095

Texas

Director of Special Education
Special Education Programs
Texas Education Agency
1701 N. Congress Ave., Room 5-120
Austin, TX 78701-2486
(512) 463-9734

Executive Director
Advocacy, Inc.
7700 Chevy Chase Dr., Suite 300
Austin, TX 78752
(512) 454-4816
(800) 252-9108 (in Texas)

Commissioner
Texas Rehabilitation Commission
118 E. Riverside Dr.
Austin, TX 78704
(512) 445-8100

Partnerships for Assisting Texans with
   Handicaps (PATH)
6465 Calder Ave., Suite 202
Beaumont, TX 77707
(409) 866-4762

Utah

Director of Special Education
Utah State Office of Education
250 E. 500 South
Salt Lake City, UT 84111
(801) 533-5982

Executive Director
Legal Center for the Handicapped
254 W. 400 South, Suite 300
Salt Lake City, UT 84101
(801) 363-1347
(800) 662-9080 (in Utah)

Executive Director
Vocational Rehabilitation Agency
250 E. 500 South
Salt Lake City, UT 84111
(801) 533-5991

Utah Parent Center
4984 South 300 West
Murray, UT 84107
(801) 265-9883

Vermont

Director of Special Education
Division of Special and Compensatory
  Education
Vermont Department of Education
State Office Bldg.
120 State Street
Montpelier, VT 05602-3403
(802) 828-3141

Director
Vermont DD Protection
  and Advocacy, Inc.
6 Pine Street
Burlington, VT 05401
(802) 863-2881

Director
Vocational Rehabilitation Division
Osgood Bldg., Waterbury Complex
103 S. Main Street
Waterbury, VT 05676
(802) 241-2189

Vermont Association for Retarded
  Citizens
Information and Training Network
37 Champlain Mill
Winooski, VT 05404
(802) 655-4016

Virgin Islands

Director of Special Education
Department of Education
State Office of Special Education
P.O. Box 6640
Charlotte Amalie, St. Thomas
Virgin Islands 00801
(809) 774-4399

Director
Committee on Advocacy for the
  Developmentally Disabled, Inc.
31-A New Street, Apt. No. 2
Fredericksted, St. Croix
U.S. Virgin Islands 00840
(809) 722-1200

Administrator
Division of Disabilities & Rehabilitation
  Services
Department of Human Services
Barbel Plaza South
St. Thomas, VI 00801
(809) 774-0930

Virginia

Director of Special Education
Office of Special and Compensatory
  Education
Virginia Department of Education
P.O. Box 6Q
Richmond, VA 23216-2060
(804) 225-2402

Director
Department of Rights for the Disabled
James Monroe Bldg.
101 N. 14th Street, 17th Floor
Richmond, VA 23219
(804) 225-2042
(800) 552-3962 (in Virginia)

Commissioner
Department of Rehabilitation Services
Commonwealth of Virginia
P.O. Box 11045
4901 Fitzhugh Ave.
Richmond, VA 23230
(804) 257-0316

Parent Educational Advocacy Training
  Center
228 S. Pitt Street, Suite 300
Alexandria, VA 22314
(703) 836-2953
(Serves Virginia, Maryland, and West
  Virginia)

Washington

Director of Special Education
Special Education Section
Superintendent of Public Instruction
Old Capital Bldg.
Olympia, WA 98502-0001
(206) 753-6733

Washington Protection & Advocacy
    System
1550 W. Armory Way, Suite 204
Seattle, WA 98119
(206) 284-1037
(800) 562-2702 (in Washington)

Director, Division of Vocational
    Rehabilitation
State Office Bldg., No. 2
Department of Social & Health Services
P.O. Box 1788 (MS 21-C)
Olympia, WA 98504
(206) 753-0293

Washington PAVE
6316 South 12th South
Tacoma, WA 98645
(206) 565-2266 Voice/TDD
(800) 5-PARENT (in Washington)

West Virginia

Director of Special Education
Special Education
West Virginia Department of Education
Bldg., #6, Room B-304
Charleston, WV 25305
(304) 348-2696

Executive Director
West Virginia Advocates for the
    Developmentally Disabled, Inc.
1200 Brooks Medical Bldg.
Quarrier Street, Suite 27
Charleston, WV 25301
(304) 346-0847
(800) 642-9205 (in West Virginia)

Director
Division of Rehabilitation Services
West Virginia State Board
    of Rehabilitation
State Capitol Bldg.
Charleston, WV 25305

See Parent Educational Advocacy
    Training Center under Virginia

Wisconsin

Director of Special Education
Division of Handicapped Children and
    Pupil Services
Department of Public Instruction
125 S. Webster
P.O. Box 7841
Madison, WI 53707
(608) 266-1649

Executive Director
Wisconsin Coalition for Advocacy, Inc.
30 W. Mifflin, Suite 508
Madison, WI 53703
(608) 251-9600
(800) 328-1110 (in Wisconsin)

Administrator
Division of Vocational Rehabilitation
Department of Health & Social Services
1 Wilson Street, Room 850
P.O. Box 7852
Madison, WI 53702
(608) 266-5466

Parent Education Project
United Cerebral Palsy of SE Wisconsin
230 W. Wells Street
Milwaukee, WI 53203
(414) 272-4500

Wyoming

Director of Special Education
State Department of Education
Hathaway Bldg.
2300 Capitol Avenue
Cheyenne, WY 82002-0050
(307) 777-7417

Executive Director
Protection & Advocacy System, Inc.
2424 Pioneer Ave., No. 101
Cheyenne, WY 82001
(307) 632-3496
(800) 624-3496 (in Wyoming)

Administrator
Division of Vocational Rehabilitation
Department of Health & Social Services
326 Hathaway Bldg.
Cheyenne, WY 82002
(307) 777-7385

Indian Affairs

Director of Special Education
Bureau of Exceptional Education
Office of Indian Education Programs
Bureau of Indian Affairs
18th & C Streets, NW, Room 4642
Washington, D.C. 20245
(202) 343-6675

PART SEVEN

Working with a Speech-Language Pathologist

CHAPTER THIRTEEN

Incorporating Speech-Language Therapy into an Applied Behavior Analysis Program

Robin Parker

Speech-language therapy can be an important and beneficial addition to an Applied Behavior Analysis program. When combined appropriately, the two disciplines may complement one another to enhance the overall effectiveness of the intervention program. This cohesive approach allows for both structured and naturalistic language learning. Within this approach, the speech-language pathologist (SLP) focuses on the pragmatics of language (i.e., the social use of language), helps develop language goals that follow the normal developmental sequence, incorporates the principles of symbolic and abstract language, and, most important, maximizes overall language and communication skills.

It is important to note, however, that many successful programs have been run with the support of only one discipline (e.g., a group of applied behavior analysts but minimal support from a speech-language therapist). Graduate programs in speech-language pathology train people to do a variety of tasks. For example, some SLPs are needed in the rehabilitation process of older persons who have language problems resulting from an accident or stroke. Others specialize in the evaluation and treatment of individuals with speech impairments such as stuttering or voice disorders. It is understandable, therefore, that some SLPs are not prepared or are unwilling to take on the task of training a nonverbal child to speak or communicate.

Parents who are lucky enough to have both applied behavior analysts and a SLP with the special skills necessary to teach a young child should consider a coordinated program. However, if the child is at an age where therapy should start, it would be wise to initiate a program with only one of the disciplines represented rather than wait for the missing professional.

I hope this chapter will assist SLPs to apply their training to a program for children with autism. It should also be useful for those who are not trained in speech-language pathology to understand how we apply our training to the young child with autism who demonstrates significant language deficits. Some language concepts discussed here are basic and apply to many children with language problems, while others are specific to children with autism.

My perspective, reflected throughout this chapter, comes from working with several children while they were in an intensive program. I typically work with the child 2 or 3 hours a week. A child is usually treated in a behavioral program by behavior therapists and their parents or other teachers for 10–35 hours a week.

COORDINATING SPEECH-LANGUAGE PATHOLOGY WITH AN APPLIED BEHAVIOR ANALYSIS PROGRAM

Coordination between the disciplines is important when adding speech-language therapy to an applied behavioral program. All objectives must reflect a common goal in order to build speech, language, play, and social skills. Specific suggestions for coordinating the two disciplines follow.

1. *The SLP should develop language goals similar to those developed by the behavior program in order to facilitate generalization.* For instance, if the behavioral goal is expressive labels and the child is expected to answer the question "What is this?" then the speech-language goal can use the same vocabulary and have the child *request* those objects in a low-structured play context. Thus, both goals are focused on the same vocabulary.

2. *The SLP should help to make the discrete-trial goals of the behavior program as communicative and functional as possible.* For instance, she can develop

request programs that concentrate on objects of high interest to the child, or focus on a receptive or expressive label program where the child might hold or play with an object for a few seconds after completing the required response.

3. *The SLP can add valuable information about speech-language goals that are being addressed in the behavior program.* For example, he can offer information to the other therapists on how to remediate specific sound errors such as placing a hand at his throat to teach the /k/ sound.

4. *The SLP helps to ensure that all therapists are attempting to use similar vocabulary, commands, and toys in focusing on their goals.* For example, if the child is working on following simple commands, all therapists would focus on those particular commands when playing with toy dolls or animals. If the same child was also working on gestural imitation in the behavioral program, the SLP could also work on imitation tasks, using the same toys and animals employed in the behavioral program. In addition, a child at a beginning level should be playing with basic dolls, cars, and books. The SLP may help therapists stay away from toys such as a complicated doll house or a garage. Note that the need to use similar language and materials across all therapists and sessions will become less crucial as a child's communication and language skills increase.

5. *The SLP can offer information to the behavior team and parents on developmentally appropriate linguistic forms and the developmentally normal communication sequence.* In this context, she can help with the periodic reassessment of linguistic goals as the behavioral programs progress. (See the "Language Development Guidelines" following Chapter 14.)

6. *The SLP can demonstrate how to incorporate specific goals into daily, preexisting activities such as dinner, bath, and bedtime, which will be helpful with generalization and sequencing.* It is beneficial to talk about activities as they occur, relating the "running commentary" to the child's structured language goals. The more a child participates in the activity, the better. A daily activity such as cooking dinner can be used to teach sequencing skills and specific language forms. For example, if the child was working on prepositions the adult could say "First we put the water *in* the pot, then the spaghetti *in*, then the salt *in*," and so on. Such commentary can be modified for all language levels and many different situations.

7. *The SLP should help develop reinforcers—both tangible, such as food, stickers, and toys, and social, such as praise, hugs, and tickles.* The SLP should also try to keep the reinforcers logical and functional. For example, if the child requests a toy figurine, a good reinforcer would be the figurine, not candy.

8. *The SLP should assess the manner in which speech-language skills are used within the classroom or play group in order to ensure maximum benefit from these interactions.* For instance, if the SLP notices that the teaching staff is giving the child a snack or a toy when she yells, the SLP may help the staff recognize and respond to more appropriate communicative cues. He may provide ideas to help the child interact more frequently with peers. He might suggest, for instance, that the classroom teacher give the child a toy that the teacher knows another child likes, and then encourage the two children to play together, or he might show the teacher how to prompt the child to request toys or a snack from a peer. He might also have the classroom teacher set up activities that require a "buddy," and pair the child with a peer who is both a strong language model and a friendly child.

9. *The SLP can also help troubleshoot specific linguistic problems.* If, for instance, the child has difficulty remembering the names of objects, the SLP can develop appropriate categorization and word-knowledge tasks by leading the child through vocabulary exercises involving antonyms or synonyms of certain words. Such exercises often help the child increase his techniques for storing words in memory and retrieving them readily. Focusing on categorization tasks, such as naming 10 barnyard animals or five fruits, can also help children retrieve words more easily.

10. *The SLP can also aid in the diagnosis and treatment of concurrent disorders (e.g., apraxia, which is a motor-sequencing problem, or dysarthria, which involves a weakness or paralysis of the muscles used for speech).*

Overall, whenever we add speech-language therapy to an Applied Behavior Analysis program, we expect to be working towards similar goals but sometimes in different ways.

Planning for a speech-language curriculum should include language-facilitation techniques. These techniques can be taught by the SLP and used by the therapists and parents. Chapter 14 provides an in-depth discussion of these strategies and techniques.

ASPECTS OF COMMUNICATION

When incorporating speech-language therapy into an applied behavior analysis program, we must consider many goals. In determining these goals, the speech-language pathologist needs to assess various aspects of communication.

1. *The SLP attempts to determine the degree of **intentional communication** that the child exhibits.* Speech-language pathologists understand an intentional communication or an intentional communicative act to mean a behavior that is deliberate, goal-directed, and has a preplanned effect on another person. Most of the techniques that an SLP uses to assess intentional communication are more inferential than the techniques of measurement employed in a behavior analysis program. To determine the degree of intentional communication, the SLP can examine if and how the child requests, greets, or comments. This can be done during play on a typical day or through the use of structured situations designed to elicit communication through gestures, vocalizations, and/or words. Such structured situations have been devised by Wetherby and Prutting (1984), who call them "communication temptations." For example, the therapist might put a child's hand in pudding to possibly elicit a protest, or she may blow up a balloon and let it deflate to elicit a request from the child to blow it up again. The SLP attempts to determine if the child uses a behavior to accomplish a desired goal. She asks herself, "Is there awareness of the goal?" and "What is the child's response if the goal is not achieved?" Her answers are based on a variety of factors. She looks at the child's *persistence*. That is, does the child continue to hit the therapist until the balloon is blown up? Does the child hit the balloon on the table until the therapist blows it up? Any change in a child's *proximity* to the therapist or to an object might indicate intentionality; for instance, moving closer to an object or to the therapist might indicate a request. *Eye gaze* is also assessed for evidence of intentionality. If the child vocalizes and looks at an object or looks at the object and then toward the therapist, this behavior might give evidence of intentional communication. *Body language*, such as stiffening or changes in hand position, might be interpreted as intentional communication if it persists until a communication is achieved, or if it is repeated when the "communication temptation" is set up again. Unconventional behaviors such as hitting, screaming, or jumping should be observed for persistence and consistency to determine if they serve as communication. The SLP uses such inferential hypothesizing to determine if intentional communication is present. The goal of intervention would then be to develop increased evidence of intentionality. Any evidence of intentionality may be shaped into more purposeful behaviors such as pointing or signaling "no" with a head shake. These gestures are precursors to verbal language. If intentional communication is not present, the SLP can use means-end toys and games (e.g., pop-up boxes, jack-in-the-box, pull toys, etc.) to facilitate intentional communication. Turn-taking games also facilitate communication. It is important to increase the number of turns progressively in a sequence.

2. *The SLP must also address **communicative functions**.* Communication typically occurs for the following functions or reasons:

a. To regulate another's behavior, including to request an object, to request an action, and to protest.

b. To participate in social interaction, including requesting social routines, showing off, greeting, acknowledging, and calling.

c. To focus joint attention, including commenting, providing information, and requesting information. As an example of commenting, the child may look at the dog in the street and then look at mommy and then back at the dog.

These communication functions may be understood as ranging from the least to most social, with behavioral regulation being least social and focusing joint attention being the most social. The communication of autistic children usually serves to regulate another's behavior (Wetherby, 1986), while the communication of typically developing children encompasses all three of the above functions. The SLP should develop goals to facilitate more social communication, doing so in the following ways:

a. The SLP should incorporate *social routines* such as peek-a-boo, hide-and-seek, creep mouse/crawl mouse, piggy went to market, or any social game the child enjoys into the therapy. The key is to have the child initiate the game.

b. *Showing off* is also important. This can be accomplished through silly faces, jumping, or clapping for oneself.

c. The SLP should also focus on the initiation of greetings with real people, pretend people, animals, and puppets.

d. *Commenting* is a goal that is often difficult, but should be addressed in all phases of the intervention program. From the earliest stages of therapy, the SLP encourages the child to point at objects of interest. Later, if the child learns to talk, the SLP encourages all evidence of verbal commenting in the child.

3. *The SLP must consider **means of communication**, that is, the forms in which the child communicates.* Does a child use gestures, vocalizations, hand manipulations, echolalia, screaming, or words to communicate? Is the means of communication conventional (words or pointing) or unconventional (screaming, throwing, etc.)? The SLP can help formulate goals to make communication conventional. For example, he can teach a child to shake his head "no" instead of screaming or throwing. Once the child shows evidence of using conventional communication, the therapist can facilitate more complex communicative means: for example, by teaching the child to use word approximations ("O" for open) when the child hands the

therapist objects to have them opened; teaching the child to use single words when he has been using word approximations; teaching the child to use two words if he has been using one-word sentences. It is important to consider the means of communication for each communicative function, because such means may be different. For instance, to regulate someone's behavior, a child may request an object through two-word utterances, but he may not yet comment (i.e., participate in social interaction.) Therefore, the child would be taught to use three-word utterances to request, and be taught to gesture for commenting.

4. *The SLP should address **frequency of communication.*** The more a child communicates, the better, because this can decrease the child's communicative frustration and increase rapport with other people. Many opportunities for a child to initiate communication should be designed. For example, the therapist could activate a wind-up toy (if the child enjoyed this) and let the toy stop. When the child hands it back or gives evidence that she wants more, the therapist would model a target word or sound ("more"), as a precursor to activating the toy again. This should be repeated each time the toy stops to elicit the same communicative intent. Waiting expectantly each time before blowing bubbles may encourage use of intentional communication. Another example of an opportunity for communication would be to "accidently" color on the table and say "Uh-oh." Help the child look at the mistake. Repeat the situation and model "Uh-oh" again. Also, children communicate when something in their environment is changed. The therapist might move furniture, or temporarily hide a favorite toy, in order to provide an opportunity for the child to comment. Putting a favorite toy or food on a high shelf out of reach but in sight encourages requesting. *Repeated modeling and waiting will increase the frequency of communication as long as the child is interested in the materials.*

In summary, understanding the diverse aspects of communication will help to clarify and specify discrete communicative goals, such as (a) increasing the evidence and degree of intentional communication; (b) facilitating a wide range of communicative functions, including communication to regulate another's behavior, participating in social interaction, and focusing joint attention; (c) increasing the complexity of means of communication for each communicative function; and (d) facilitating the frequency of communication.

PRAGMATICS

Pragmatics is defined as the social use of language. Pragmatic language skills should be addressed by the speech-language pathologist in conjunction with the behavior analyst. Pragmatics includes the communicative aspects described above (requesting, protesting, and commenting) but also involves many other verbal and nonverbal language skills. The following are goals to consider in all phases of treatment of pragmatics:

1. *The SLP should address eye contact for communication.* Holding a desired object near the eyes of the therapist prior to giving it to the child may facilitate eye contact. Another technique to facilitate eye contact with a child who is more linguistically advanced is to play a game that involves the child looking and asking for an action, before this action is allowed to take place ("Remember the rule of the game is to *look at me* and say 'It's my turn' ").

2. *The SLP should make sure the child can use language equally well whether interacting with the therapist or with anyone else by encouraging requests, comments, and so on with many different people in many different contexts.*

3. *The SLP can also work on turn-taking, which is a form of pragmatic communication.* Nonverbal turn-taking games primarily involve tasks that require turns to complete a sequence (e.g., throwing a ball to another person, rolling a toy car back and forth). In addition, verbal turn-taking tasks can focus on using a "my-turn/your-turn" prompt (e.g., therapist and child can build a tower together, each of them adding one block at a time; they can do a puzzle, with each person adding a piece; they can take turns drawing pictures on a Magna Doodle). A higher level verbal turn-taking skill would be to take a turn in a conversation by commenting or providing new information (e.g., the SLP can focus on a key phrase such as "Let's talk about _____"; then the therapist and child can take turns adding information, using the my-turn/your-turn prompt if necessary.

4. *The SLP should utilize a "nontherapy," or natural, voice and intonation as appropriate.* As a child masters receptive commands through discrete-trial drills, the SLP should begin to use these same commands speaking in a less firm and structured voice.

5. *The SLP can focus on having the child follow commands while engaged in other play tasks.*

6. *The SLP should focus on awareness of unusual situations or disruptions in the environment.* Goals can be developed to encourage the child to comment about these situations. These disruptions may occur incidentally, or they can be contrived (e.g., dropping all materials off a table purposefully). Depending on the child's language level, a one-word sentence can be

paired with the situation, or a full sentence and conversation can occur.

7. *Topic maintenance is an important goal once a child has begun using short three- to six-word sentences.* The SLP can create games to target topic maintenance. For example, each person might choose a card and have to say three things about that card/topic. If the child deviates from the topic, a verbal cue such as "We are talking about _____" can be given. Another example would be to talk about a past event like the weekend (make sure information is known by the therapist) and require the child to tell three different things about the event. A key issue is that both the child and the SLP must add new information to the topic.

8. *Another aspect of topic maintenance is the situation where a child talks about only a few topics or returns to perseverates on the same topic.* Responding at the child's language level may help to decrease this type of communication (e.g., "That's silly, you already talked about the cars" or "No more cars. Look, here's Play-Doh").

9. *Inferencing is a high-level pragmatic language skill that the SLP can begin to address with wh-questions.* As soon as a child begins answering accurate *wh*-questions in discrete trials, the SLP may introduce questions for which a specific answer has not been provided (e.g., show a picture to the child, or read her a page from a storybook, and then ask "What will the boy do next?"). Introducing a carrier phrase such as "I think" can also be used to work on inferencing in a spontaneous manner (e.g., while reading a book that says "Rabbit has to go to bed without dinner," the adult models "I think the rabbit is going to be hungry because he didn't eat"). Another game to facilitate inferencing is a guessing game (e.g., "I am thinking of something that is yellow and is in the sky during the day. Guess what it is"). Remember that both the therapist and the child should always take a turn describing the object and guessing.

10. *The SLP should encourage socially interactive language in a variety of ways.* Age-appropriate toys may be used as materials to facilitate such interaction (e.g., Power Rangers, Barbie dolls, etc.). Vocabulary should be "child-based." Listen to typical children's language for current slang. As soon as appropriate, use peers in therapy sessions. Goals should stress having the children make requests and comments to each other.

SYMBOLIC PLAY

SLPs view symbolic play as an essential part of any language program. Symbolic play is defined as play behavior of young children in which an object or toy is made to represent some other object. For instance, a stick can be used as a sword, or a block can be used as a telephone. There are developmental stages of increasingly complex play behaviors. Play and language are both symbolic behaviors and are interrelated (Westby, 1988). Symbolism is necessary in play in order to maximize creative language. Prerequisites to symbolic play and activities that facilitate the development of symbolism are means-end behaviors (e.g., pushing a button to have a toy pop up), tool use, and imitative behavior. Means-end behavior and tool use can be facilitated through push-button toys and pull toys. Imitation can be taught with games, including banging on drums, playing with toy figurines pretending to eat and sleep, and brushing a doll's hair. Emerging symbolic play begins with single steps that represent familiar activities (e.g., pretending to eat, pretending to wash your hair, etc.). As symbolic play increases in complexity, a number of sequential steps are involved (e.g., the child cooks food, eats the food, and then washes the dishes, or the child puts people in a car, drives them to school, then returns home). More complex play involves pretending about less familiar activities, such as policemen catching robbers, and creating fantasies around such topics as dragons or dinosaurs. For more information of typical symbolic play stages, see Westby's Play Scales in the appendix to this chapter.

ADDITIONAL ISSUES

Several additional issues may need to be addressed, including the following:

1. *Augmentative communication.* If a child is having significant difficulty with articulation or expressive language, the SLP should explore another means of communication. We usually focus on oral expressive language for 6–12 months. If progress is very slow, we consider an augmentative communication strategy. Communication boards, communication books, sign language, and computer devices are among the strategies to consider. Augmentative communication does not refer to Facilitated Communication, and the goal of using an augmentative communication device should be independent communication. As mentioned above, we consider augmentative communication when we have worked for 6 months to 1 year on speech and language skills, and limited or no verbal communication or intelligible speech emerges. The main purpose of adding an augmentative system is to increase communication. An increase in communication has been shown to increase speech and not impede it; therefore, initiating an augmentative system sooner

rather than later will *only* help speech. Remember that the system may be faded if sufficient verbal language is present.

2. *Echolalia.* Immediate echolalia is the repetition of a previously heard utterance. Delayed echolalia is the repetition of a stored utterance from another context or situation. Echolalia often serves a communicative purpose and should not automatically be extinguished. A simpler sentence with the same meaning as the echoed utterance should be modeled for the child, while still acting on the child's intent. For example, if the child echoes "Do you want juice?" the therapist should give the juice to the child and say "Yes, I want juice." A child may use delayed echolalia to initiate new topics. One strategy is to try to relate the delayed echo to a relevant topic. Using concrete objects to do this is beneficial. For example, if a child says a sentence from a book or movie, get the book and add more information to the conversation. Echolalia should be discouraged if it is interfering with the learning process, as in the case where a child repeats before the speaker is finished. If this occurs, a visual cue to wait can be used.

3. *Prosody.* Prosody refers to the intonation of speech. The child's speech may sometimes be monotone, and can be enhanced by modeling an exaggerated intonation in the utterance that follows the child's monotone utterance. This should be done repeatedly and by everyone who interacts with the child. Use reinforcement whenever the child's voice is not monotone (i.e., the therapist could say "Wow, you used a big voice. That was great!").

4. *Vocal intensity.* Vocal intensity is the volume of the voice. Treatment options are similar to those discussed with prosody.

CONCLUSIONS

The SLP and the behavior analyst can forge a compatible relationship in order to optimize the language program for the child. From a practical standpoint it is essential for the speech pathologist to set up measurable linguistic goals. These goals should be known and available to each of the disciplines so that everyone involved can take every opportunity to reinforce them. It is also important to be organized in all facets of the therapy. This includes recording goals and data, and keeping clear and concise notes in a central log. Regular meetings and communication among all individuals involved with the child will ensure that goals are coordinated, and will allow for brainstorming to maximize the effectiveness of the intervention programs.

Intangible qualities also enter into the optimal relationship. Necessary components are mutual respect, an open mind to each other's discipline, and the option to use techniques from both disciplines. This allows for the joint monitoring of progress and smooth adjustments to therapy.

APPENDIX

Symbolic Play Scale Check List

Play	Language

Stage I: 9 to 12 months

_____ Awareness that objects exist when not seen; finds toy hidden under scarf.

_____ Means-end behavior—crawls or walks to get what he wants; pulls string toys.

_____ Does not mouth or bang all toys—some used appropriately.

_____ No true language; may have performative words (words that are associated with actions or the total situation).

Exhibits following communicative functions:

_____ Request (instrumental)

_____ Command (regulatory)

Stage II: 13 to 17 months

_____ Purposeful exploration of toys; discovers operation of toys through trial and error; uses variety of motoric schemas.

_____ Hands toy to adult if unable to operate.

_____ Context-dependent single words; for example, child may use the word "car" when riding in a car, but not when he sees a car; words tend to come and go in child's vocabulary.

Exhibits following communicative functions:

_____ Request	_____ Protesting
_____ Command	_____ Label
_____ Interactional	_____ Responsive
_____ Personal	_____ Greeting

Stage III: 17 to 19 months

_____ Autosymbolic play: for example, child pretends to go to sleep or pretends to drink from cup or eat from spoon.

_____ Uses most common objects and toys appropriately.

_____ Tool use (uses stick to reach toy).

_____ Finds toys invisibly hidden (when placed in box and box emptied under scarf).

Beginning of true verbal communication

Words have following functional and semantic relations:

_____ Recurrence	_____ Agent
_____ Existence	_____ Object
_____ Nonexistence	_____ Action or state
_____ Rejection	_____ Location
_____ Denial	_____ Object or person associated with object or location

Stage IV: 19 to 22 months

Symbolic play extends beyond the child's self:

_____ Plays with dolls: brushes doll's hair, feeds doll a bottle, or covers doll with blanket.

_____ Child performs pretend activities on more than one person or object: for example, feeds self, a doll, mother, and another child.

_____ Combines two toys in pretend play: for example, puts spoon in pan or pours from pot into cup.

_____ Refers to objects and persons not present

Beginning of word combinations with following semantic relations:

_____ Agent-action	_____ Action-locative
_____ Action-object	_____ Object-locative
_____ Agent-object	_____ Possessive
_____ Attribute	_____ Dative

(continues)

Symbolic Play Scale Check List (cont'd)

Play	Language
Stage V: 24 months	
_____ Represents daily experiences; plays house—is the mommy, daddy, or baby; objects used are realistic and close to life-size.	_____ Uses earlier pragmatic functions and semantic relations in phrases and short sentences.
_____ Events short and isolated; no true sequences; some self-limiting sequences—puts food in pan, stirs, and eats.	The following morphological markers appear:
_____ Block play consists of stacking and knocking down.	_____ Present progressive (*ing*) on verbs _____ Plurals _____ Possessives
_____ Sand and water play consist of filling, pouring, and dumping.	

Play	Language
Stage VI: 2½ years	
Represents events less frequently experienced or observed, particularly impressive or traumatic events.	Responds appropriately to the following *wh*-questions in context:
_____ Doctor-nurse-sick child	_____ What?
_____ Teacher-child	_____ Who?
_____ Store-shopping	_____ Whose?
Events still short and isolated. Realistic props still required. Roles shift quickly.	_____ Where?
	_____ What . . . do . . . ?
	_____ Asks *wh*-questions—generally puts *wh*-word at beginning of sentence.
	_____ Responses to *why* questions inappropriately except for well-known routines, such as "Why is the doctor here?" or "Baby sick."
	_____ Asks why, but often inappropriately and does not attend to answer.

Play	Language
Stage VII: 3 years	
_____ Continues pretend activities of Stages V and VI, but now the play has a sequence. Events are not isolated: for example, child mixes cake, bakes it, serves it, washes the dishes; or doctor checks patient, calls ambulance, takes patient to hospital, and operates. Sequence evolves, not planned.	_____ Uses past tense, such as "I ate the cake" or "I walked." _____ Uses future aspect (particularly "gonna") forms, such as "I'm gonna wash dishes."
_____ Compensatory toy; reenactment of experienced events with new outcomes.	
_____ Associative play.	

(continues)

Symbolic Play Scale Check List (cont'd)

Play	Language
Stage VIII: 3 to 3½ years	Descriptive vocabulary expands as child becomes more aware of perceptual attributes. Uses terms for the following concepts (not always correctly):
_____ Carries out play activities of previous stages with a doll house and Fisher-Price toys (barn, garage, airport, village).	
_____ Uses blocks and sandbox for imaginative play. Blocks used primarily as enclosures (fences and houses) for animals and dolls.	_____ Shapes _____ Sizes _____ Colors
_____ Play not totally stimulus-bound. Child uses one object to represent another.	_____ Texture _____ Spatial relationships
_____ Uses doll or puppet as participant in play.	_____ Gives dialogue to puppets and dolls. _____ Metalinguistic language use, such as, "Mommy said. . . ." _____ Uses indirect requests, such as "Mommy lets me have cookies for breakfast." _____ Changes speech depending on listener.
Stage IX: 3½ to 4 years	Verbalizes intentions and possible future events:
_____ Begins to problem-solve events not experienced. Plans ahead. Hypothesizes "what would happen if . . ."	_____ Uses modals (can, may, might, will, would, could).
_____ Uses dolls and puppets to act out scenes.	_____ Uses conjunctions (and, but, if, so, because) Note: Full competence for these modals and conjunctions does not develop until 10–12 years of age.
_____ Builds three-dimensional structures with blocks, which are attempts at reproducing specific structures child had seen.	_____ Begins to respond appropriately to why and how questions that require reasoning about perception.
Stage X: 5 years	
_____ Plans a sequence of pretend events. Organizes what he needs—both objects and other children.	_____ Uses relational terms (then, when, first, next, last, while, before, after) Note: Full competence does not develop until 10–12 years of age.
_____ Coordinates more than one event occurring at a time.	
_____ Highly imaginative. Sets the scene without realistic props.	
_____ Full cooperative play	

Source: Westby, C. E. (1980). "Assessment of cognitive and language abilities through play. *Language, Speech, and Hearing Services in Schools, 11,* 154–168.

REFERENCES

Bloom, L., & Lahey, M. (1978). *Language development and language disorders.* New York: John Wiley and Sons.

Lahey, M. (1988). *Language development and language disorders.* New York: Merrill/Macmillan.

Mirenda, P., & Donnellan, A. (1986). Effects of adult interaction style on conversational behavior in students with severe communication problems. *Language, Speech, and Hearing Services in Schools, 17,* 126–141.

Owens, R. E. (1992). *Language disorders.* Boston: Allyn & Bacon.

Prizant, B., & Wetherby, A. (1988). Providing services to children with autism (ages 0–2 years) and their families. *Topics in Language Disorders, 9*(1),1–23.

Westby, C. E. (1980). Assessment of cognitive and language abilities through play. *Language, Speech, and Hearing Services in Schools, 11,* 154–168.

Westby, C. E. (1988). Children's play: Reflections of social competence. *Seminars in Speech and Language, 9,* 1–14.

Wetherby, A. (1986). Ontogeny of communicative functions in autism. *Journal of Autism and Developmental Disorders, 16,* 295–316.

Wetherby, A., & Prutting, C. (1984). Profiles of communicative and cognitive-social abilities in autistic children. *Journal of Speech and Hearing Research, 27,* 364–377.

CHAPTER FOURTEEN

Strategies for Promoting Language Acquisition in Children with Autism

Margery Rappaport

This chapter offers various strategies as examples of some of the ways in which children with autism have been helped to acquire language. Parents often ask for exercises to use in order to help their children to talk. The following suggestions should not be thought of as isolated exercises to be worked on individually, but as ideas to shape all of your daily communicative interactions with your child. These techniques are meant to be integrated into the context of your child's life as you move through your day together, and they work best when used on a consistent basis. Generalization takes place faster when these strategies are utilized in a variety of contexts and by a variety of adults. This list is by no means exhaustive, nor is it meant to represent everything that a speech-language pathologist (SLP) would do when working with a child with autism, but is meant to communicate to parents some of the ways in which families can work to improve their children's communication skills. Due to limitations of space, the focus of this section is on language; speech/articulation skills are not addressed.

We begin with some general principles that apply to children with autism at all stages of language development. These are followed by recommendations for children at three different stages of language growth: (a) the preverbal child, (b) the child just beginning to use words, and (c) the child who is using creative, multiword utterances.

GENERAL RECOMMENDATIONS

1. *Minimize Direct Questions.* It is important to minimize your use of direct questions. Parents, with the very best of intentions, often believe that they are developing language in their children by asking a lot of questions. Some questions that parents typically overuse when trying to facilitate language follow:

   • What's this?

   • What do you want?

   • What are you doing?

   • What do you call this?

   Avoid such questions as much as possible, although you will not be able to eliminate them completely. Parents can listen to each other as they speak with their child and remind each other to minimize questioning.

2. *Commenting.* Follow your child's lead. Watch what he is doing and *comment* upon it, providing what might be his internal dialogue. Once you have begun to minimize direct questions, you will find that you are commenting more. Questions and commands are constraints upon developing language. Commenting promotes language development.

3. *Wait and Signal.* In a communicative exchange, the adult waits with clear visible anticipation while looking expectantly at the child. The expectation is that after the adult has spoken, the child will take a turn. When she does, the behavior should be rewarded.

   • *How to look expectantly:*

     Establish eye contact

     Lips slightly apart

     Eyebrows raised

     Lean head and body in slightly toward child

4. *Set Up Communicative Situations.* Parents can encourage spontaneous language by being on the lookout for and going out of their way to set up situations that force communication. Do not anticipate your child's every need. Create a little moment wherein he will have to talk to get what he needs.

5. *Use Abundant Gesture and Facial Expression.* Using abundant, exaggerated facial expression and bodily gesture is crucial in fostering language acquisition. Movement and gesture in both you

and your child will encourage speech. Don't be stiff. Ham it up! Capture your child's attention and support the meaning of your words, which may not be clear to her, with a visual illustration of what you mean.

6. *Modeling.* Modeling means presenting an example of what your child should say. Think of modeling appropriate language versus correcting mistakes. It is depressing for anyone to feel as if he is being corrected all day long. Modeling keeps you affirmative, whereas correcting makes it feel as if you are attending more to how your child is communicating than to what he is communicating—something you want to avoid.

7. *Reduction.* When modeling language, commenting on a child's activity, or just speaking to your child, shorten your sentences; that is, reduce the complexity of your language. You will be maximizing comprehension as well as modeling something that you expect her to be able to imitate at her present level of language development. For example, if your child is not yet using words, speak to her in single-word utterances as much as possible. If she is approaching the two-word level, reduce your sentences as much as possible to two words in length.

8. *Use Exaggerated Intonation, Volume, and Rate of Speech.* We need to capture the attention of children who have trouble communicating spontaneously. Using exaggerated intonation, volume, and rate of speech tends to do this. This is why songs and nursery rhymes are good for stimulating early language development; they are repetitive and rhythmical. You might sing a song and leave a space for your child to fill in a response.

9. *Eye Contact.* Looking at the person you are speaking to is a crucial part of communicating with him. Look at your child's eyes and encourage him to look at yours. "Look at me" is the simple directive used.

10. *Reinforcement.* It almost goes without saying, but here it is. To promote and increase spontaneous language, it is paramount that you respond to and thereby reinforce your child's spontaneous productions. Do not ignore her attempts to communicate, be they verbal or nonverbal. Respond in some way, preferably one of the ways described here. Respond verbally or nonverbally, but respond, thereby reinforcing the child's effort to talk and teaching her that there is a payoff for talking.

11. *Make It Fun!* Have fun with this. Talk in a pleasant voice. Smile a lot. Help your child to associate communicating with warmth, affection, and joy. Try to stay relaxed. Why should he want to communicate, if it is not fun? Be playful, imaginative, and creative.

SECTION ONE

These suggestions apply specifically to children who are at the preverbal level of communication.[1]

1. If your child does not appear to be communicating intentionally, that is, she does not vocalize, gesture, or use eye gaze meaningfully, means-end toys and games can be useful. Engage your child with toys such as pop-up boxes (Sesame Street and other characters are available in boxes with five different faces), jack-in-the-box toys, windup toys, and pull toys.

2. *Turn-taking* games promote communication. Examples of activities that encourage turn-taking skills are rolling a ball or a car back and forth, taking turns playing a toy instrument, and taking turns writing on a toy slate. When working on turn-taking, at first the physical space between the adult and child should be small. The adult may have to walk the child through the game by physically prompting his movements (i.e., hand over hand) and reinforcing all evidence of compliance. If your child has demonstrated interest in one of the aforementioned materials, begin with that one; if not, you might choose the ball. When rolling the ball back and forth, sit on the floor with your legs apart and place the child in the same position across from but quite near to you. Count one, two, three-e-e as you roll the ball to your child. Make sure it gently bumps into him. Now place your child's hands on the ball. Then lean over and place your own hands over your child's hands. Count one, two, three-e-e and roll the ball back toward yourself. Reinforce. Over several days try to increase the number of turns in a sequence.

3. To encourage participation in *social interaction,* try games such as peek-a-boo, hide-and-seek, piggy went to market, and this is the way the ladies ride. The key is to have the child *initiate* the game. When playing peek-a-boo, as you cover your face with a blanket or cloth, be sure that your face is very close to your child's, literally

---

[1] The author wishes to thank Robin Parker for her help in developing this section.

"in her face." If your child turns away, be persistent, follow her, and repeat. Call her name from behind the cloth. She may require many demonstrations of peek-a-boo before you see her looking expectantly for your sudden appearance or actually grabbing the cloth when you cover your eyes. Reinforce the smallest increments of compliance. You may wish to use the same cloth, such as a red bandana, whenever you play this game, so that you may get her to initiate the game just by placing the familiar cloth on her lap.

4. *Greetings* can be targeted with a wide variety of real people (all the people in your neighborhood) as well as pretend people, animals, and puppets. Wave bye-bye to the toys as you put them away. Pick up the child's hand and teach him the gesture by shaping it while saying "Bye-bye."

5. Your child may try to take your hand and lead you to a desired object. Resist letting her do this. Pull back your hand and ask "What?" using an exaggerated gesture. Shape her finger into a point for the request. Straighten her elbow and aim the finger toward the desired object. Walk next to her, not pulled by her, toward the object.

6. *Commenting* by your child can be begun at the very earliest stages by encouraging him to point to show an object of interest. Shape his hand into a point when something is, for example, funny (say "Funny!" as you point or "scary," or "big," "broken," and so on).

7. Unconventional means of communication such as screaming or throwing can be changed into more *conventional means.* For example, if the child throws a toy in order to stop a game, teach the more conventional means by shaking your head no. Combine the head shake with the vowel *o* if your child is unable to say no. If she is unable to produce an *o,* try another vowel combined with the shake. A gesture paired with some vocalization is considered a higher-level communicative act than a gesture alone.

8. *Design* opportunities for your child to *initiate communication.*

   - Habitually place favorite toys or food on a high shelf out of reach but in sight.

   - Blow a bubble and then seal the jar and hand it to her. Model *bu* for bubble if she indicates that she wants more.

   - "Accidentally" color on the table and say "Uh-oh." Help your child look at the mistake. Repeat the situation and model "Uh-oh" again.

   - Place a desired object in a clear, tightly sealed plastic container. Hand it to the child.

   - Children communicate when something in their environment is changed. Furniture can be moved, a favorite toy could be missing, and so on.

   - When it is time to leave, pretend that the door is stuck and you cannot get out.

   - Set up a turn-taking routine, perhaps three or four turns, then hand her something or do something unexpected.

9. *Eye contact* must be encouraged at all levels of communication. Holding a desired object near your eyes prior to giving it to the child will facilitate eye contact.

10. The same words should be taught *simultaneously, both receptively and expressively.* Adult: "Where's bottle?" Child looks at or points to it. Adult: "Ba" looking expectantly and waiting for the child to repeat.

11. Talk to your child on his physical level by sitting or bending down so that you are at eye level with each other.

12. *Receptive language skills.*

    - Teach your child to follow commands of increasing length and complexity within the play setting; for example, first "Get the ball," and later, "Get the ball and the shoe."

    - Teach the child to respond to her name while she is playing with a toy.

    - Once understanding is established with a particular command, add variety to the way it is presented (e.g., "Put the paper in the garbage" versus "Throw it away").

    - Give your child sufficient time to understand what you have said.

SECTION TWO

This section applies to the child who has demonstrated that he is able to use words. Now your goals are to help him to increase his language and to initiate language spontaneously, not merely to function as a *responder* to other people's cues and questions. Children will learn to wait for these questions and may not initiate language without them. Try the following suggestions in order to help him to increase verbalization and to use self-initiated language.

Increasing Self-Initiated Language: Requesting Object

Here is an example of how to promote a self-initiated verbal request for an object without direct questioning, which you should eliminate as much as possible. Let us say that the child has demonstrated that he is able to say "More *x*" within a discrete-trial program or in some context, but that he is not saying it consistently and/or spontaneously. Try the following:

Give your child a taste of a desirable dessert (pudding, for example). Your target response will be "More pudding." Then place the dessert out of your child's reach, but within view. When he reaches for more, use your hand to *physically block* his attempt to reach the dessert while looking at him expectantly (see above) as if to say (but do *not* say), "What do you want?" Then wait.

If your child cries, vocalizes, reaches harder, expresses frustration, but does not use words to request, *pick up the dessert* with one hand and *point* to the dessert with the other. Using your child's name as you point to the dessert should help to focus his attention and signal that you expect something from him. Again, wait.

If the child does not use the words, move the dessert closer to him (it is still in your hand), *point* to the dessert, lift your chin up and *close your lips together* as if to make the *mmmm* sound of "More" (but do not), simultaneously looking expectantly as described above.

If, again, the child does not use words, repeat all the above while producing a loud, prolonged *mmmm* sound. If no target response results, continue all the above, each time prompting more heavily by adding the next sound in the phrase "More pudding" until, if necessary, you are forced to model the entire phrase. At whatever point he says "More pudding," you say "Good job" and immediately give him some pudding.

Begin again, each time giving the *lightest prompt* necessary in order to attain your verbal target. It is better to model the entire target and then quickly repeat the task using a much lighter prompt than to ask the direct question "What do you want?" This would only serve to reinforce the child's functioning as a responder, which you do not want to do.

Set Up Communicative Situations: Requesting Action

Here are several ideas for designing situations that will help to develop communication with children who are at the one- or two-word level.

Your child has signaled that she is thirsty and that she wants water. Instead of handing her a glass of water, place a tightly closed bottle of water directly in front of her. Look at her and wait. Say nothing. Wait for a direct request for action from you. You are waiting for her to say something like "Open" or "Help." Again, avoid a direct question, such as "What should you ask me?" If necessary, model the lip position for the first sound of your target word and add sounds as explained above, using the same principle of offering the lightest prompt first. Try the same with candy jars, cookie containers, Play-Doh containers, and so on.

Your child wants to draw. Give her a piece of paper without a crayon or give her a crayon without a piece of paper. Wait, looking expectantly. Resist asking a question. If she says nothing, silently hold the desired object in front of her as a prompt for her to use the word. You may also try the following:

- Give your child dinner without a fork.

- Place your child in the bathtub without turning on the water.

- As your child is dressing, give him (or put on) two shoes and only one sock.

- Stand in front of a door without opening it.

- Hold the picture book you are reading together upside down.

- Give her an empty glass when she signals that she is thirsty.

Promoting Commenting and Protesting

Focus on awareness of unusual situations or disruptions in the environment. These can be used to promote commenting. These disruptions may occur incidentally or can be contrived, for example, dropping materials off the table by accident. A one- or two-word phrase can be paired with the situation: for example, "Fall down."

- Attempt to put his shoe on his hand.

- While your child is watching, put your shoe in the silverware drawer or put a bunch of celery in the clothes hamper, setting up an opportunity for your child to comment "That's wrong!" If he does not, model "That's wrong" while shaking your head "no" and making a funny face to illustrate your ridiculous mistake.

- Put a familiar toy together the wrong way.

- Your child indicates that she wants milk. As she watches, pour just the tiniest drop of milk in her cup and hand her the cup. Then look pointedly into the virtually empty cup. Wait. Model the comment "Not enough!" with an exaggerated facial expression. Add another tiny drop. Wait. Cue with the same facial expression and "That's . . .."

- *All gone* can be cued in many situations: for example, show an empty cereal bowl, water draining out from bathtub, empty bottles, empty cookie boxes, or water draining out of the sink.

- Put a puzzle piece in the wrong slot.

Use Abundant Gesture and Facial Expression

Many bottles, jars, doors, and lids are too tight for a young child to open. Use these to model the comment "Stuck" in the following manner. Place a tightly closed bottle of bubbles in front of the child. He tries but fails to open it and hands it to you. Pick it up and feign an enormous physical attempt to unscrew the cap accompanied by a huge, long grunt that explodes. Then say the word "Stuck!" with a funny face. Kids love this and often learn it quickly. Pass the bottle to him. You accompany his next attempt to open it with the same huge grunt, and if he doesn't follow it with "Stuck!" then you say it. Try the same routine in many different contexts in order to facilitate generalization: for example, a locked closet door, toothpaste tube, knot in a rope, and other lids. Of course, go out of your way to set these situations up.

The appropriate use of the "yes" response is often late to develop in children with autism. An echo for affirmation is frequently presented instead of "yes." Remembering to keep language learning fun, ask your child "Do you want this?" holding up something that you are quite sure she wants. As she starts to echo "Want this," immediately answer for her (that is, cut off her attempt to echo you) by modeling "Ye-e-e-e-e-e-e-e . . .-es". As you say the "Ye-e-e-e-e-e . . ." your head, chin, and eyebrows go up and back, and as you say the "-es" part, snap your head forward quickly. Make sure your hair flops as you snap your head and go for a very big laugh, which you will probably get. Repeat promptly. This time, she should provide the "-es." As soon as possible, fade your vocal cue to only the head gesture and lip posture, and then fade that as well.

Specific gestures have proven helpful in encouraging the acquisition of *difficult to learn words,* for example, pronouns. In teaching the pronouns *me* or *my,* take your child's hand in your hand and place it on your child's own chest as you model "My turn!" As soon as possible, lighten the prompt to putting his hand on his chest, saying only "Mmmmmmm." You can cue the phrase "My turn" with the word "It's. . . ." A second example would be to ask him "Whose hat is this?" as he is about to put it on. Put his own hand on his chest and cue "Mmmmmm" or model "My hat."

In teaching your child to say *you* or *your,* take your child's hand in your hand and place it on *your* chest as you model "Your turn!" Again, as soon as possible, lighten the prompt to his hand on the adult's chest and only the *Y* lip position.

My turn/your turn are best taught with toys that require specific turn-taking. One example might be a toy workbench. Only one person can hold the hammer and bang the bench at a time. Take it from or put it into your child's hand, modeling "My turn" or "Your turn" with the appropriate gesture as you do so.

In teaching the request phrase *Give me,* try modeling the following gesture. Reach your hand, fist open and facing down, in front of you. As you say "Give me," quickly pull your hand into your chest, closing the fist. For example, the child requests "apple." You model "Give me apple" accompanied by the above gesture. After several repetitions, you can then cue "Give me" with the gesture alone whenever she omits it.

Expansion

The principle of expansion is an efficient way to help your child move on to the next level of linguistic complexity. Your child says something; you take his utterance and add one word to advance the grammatical complexity. Then wait and signal, communicating that you expect him to repeat what you have said. You can try a friendly "You say" if necessary to get him to repeat the entire expanded utterance.

CHILD: Notices a cat and says "Cat."

PARENT: *Big* cat (with 'big' gesture).

CHILD: Big cat.

CHILD: Milk.

ADULT: *Want* milk.

CHILD: Door.

ADULT: *Open* door.

CHILD: Mommy come.

ADULT: Mommy come *here*.

CHILD: Baby sitting.

ADULT: Baby *is* sitting.

A last word about using gesture. By *pointing*, one can offer a visual rather than verbal cue. Visual/gestural cues are lighter prompts than actually saying even part of a targeted word. You are always trying to use the lightest prompt possible to achieve the desired verbalization. Point in order to bring the child's attention to a particular object that you want him to talk about. Let us say that the target verbalization is "Need scissors." During an arts and crafts project, you might say "Oh, John, it's too big." Wait for him to infer that something has to be done. If he is silent, you point to the scissors, or if necessary pick them up and point, a heavier cue, for the targeted "Need scissors."

Commenting

Here are examples of a parent using commenting as opposed to questioning or commanding in order to develop language on the one- to two-word level.

- Child is drawing. Parent watches and says "Drawing."

- Child places doll into a cradle. Parent says "Baby sleep."

- Child throws a ball. Parent says "Throw ball."

- Child sits down. Parent says "Sit down."

- Child drops a toy. Parents says "Fall down."

In commenting on what your child is doing, you will be forced to talk about the here and now. This is important because language acquisition begins with talk about the present, not yesterday or next week. Yesterday and tomorrow have little meaning for young children. They live in the here and now and therefore they talk about what is here and now.

Reduction

In reducing the length of sentences and grammatical complexity of your language, the idea is that you will be maximizing comprehension as well as providing a model that your child will actually be able to imitate. So, instead of saying "Your father has come home now,"

say "Daddy home." This is called *telegraphic language* because the function words are omitted. Parents sometimes worry that by modeling telegraphic language they will thereby delay their child's language development. It does not seem to work that way. As soon as your child is able to say "Daddy home" on his own, you will model the next level of complexity.

Use Exaggerated Intonation, Volume, and Rate of Speech

Encourage *greetings*. Use a high-pitched, elongated "Hi!" and accompany it with a long wave, which follows the elongated tempo of your "Hi"; big smile; and eyebrows up. "Bye-bye" can be sung. Try the first *bye* on a pitch beginning, perhaps, five tones higher than the second *bye*. Catch the child's attention with an exaggeratedly slow production.

Children with autism often respond well to music. As first words are emerging, it is helpful to sing a lot. The pitch and rhythm heighten attending and appear to make the words more interesting to the child. (*My turn/your turn* are good phrases to model by singing them.)

All done and *All gone* are ubiquitous childhood expressions and are attended to readily when sung. Model "All done" with a falling melody and cue with the word "We're" while gesturing palms up and arms out to side. Use silent open mouth to prompt for the "all." Pause to give your child time to say "All done" spontaneously; if not, you say the "all" and wait and signal. Say "done" if necessary. Cue "All gone" in the same manner with the word "It's" instead of "We're."

Teach *calling*. Tell your child "Eric, call Daddy. Da-dee." Model six musical notes sliding down the scale from "Da" to "dee" and two hands on either side of your mouth as if you are calling over some very great distance.

It is not uncommon for children with autism to have trouble using appropriate *volume*. Children may actually be using language but remain unintelligible because their voices are extremely low. This may relate to a basic autistic problem of not using language to reach out to another person, that is, of not using language for communicative purposes. When working on volume, the useful educational principle of *contrast* is recommended. Playfully say something very loud and then very soft, being sure to label each so that later, when you use a verbal cue such as "Say it louder," you will be sure your child knows what you are asking her to do. You can say anything at all: "I WANT CANDY!!! SAY IT LOUD!!!!" versus "I want candy . . . say it soft." Children often think this game is a lot of fun.

SECTION THREE

This section contains language goals for the child who is using multiword utterances. As your child acquires more language, the language goals will begin to resemble ones that might be used in treating significant language disorders of any etiology. This is because language in autism can be conceptualized as if on a continuum, with the severe communication disorder of autism on one end, and on the other end, a specific language disorder with little of the characteristic symptomatology of autism. This section addresses three areas of language: form, content, and use. Form refers to grammar and syntax; content refers to vocabulary and what the child talks about; and use refers to the pragmatics of language, that is, conversational rules and language functions. Using language to greet, to comment, and to request are examples of language functions. For our purposes, we discuss these three areas of language separately. Remember, however, that form and function in language use are interrelated and that conversation and structure are functionally inseparable. The following suggestions are offered for helping to develop grammar, vocabulary, and pragmatic skills in the child whose language is beyond the two-word level.

Vocabulary

This section focuses on the words your child knows and the content of his conversation, that is, what he talks about. The following paragraphs present some ideas for improving a child's word knowledge.

New experiences present new vocabulary. Joint activities at home such as cooking, baking, planting, sewing, building, repairing, washing dishes, cleaning, and laundering involve new words. Include your child in chores and think of them as vocabulary-building experiences. It is important to use the new vocabulary repeatedly during the activity and subsequently to ask your child what he wants in order to give him the experience of using the new words. Joint activities outside the home are excellent vocabulary-building experiences. Short excursions to the grocery store, fruit and vegetable market, post office, gas station, library, hardware store, and floral shop, as well as special outings to the zoo, the circus, the museum, a fair, a flea market, or a restaurant are all useful. Point out and comment upon what you see. Again, use a new word several times. Define it several ways. Suggest an association to help your child to remember the word, for example, "Cousin Sara loves coconuts" or "Raspberries grow in back of David's house." Try to get him to be actively involved by asking him to go and get the item with the new word or by asking him what he thinks of it. Here is a four-part strategy for learning new words. Obtain and read books about an anticipated trip to introduce the new vocabulary; then use the same vocabulary when you are there, for example, "Oh, look there's the *acrobat* that we saw in your book at home." Comment on the differences between the two acrobats in order to reinforce his attending: "But the acrobat in your book is wearing a clown costume; this one is just wearing black. Which one do you like better?" Back at home, reread the book in order to generate discussion about what you have seen and reinforce the vocabulary. Later, refer back to these events with new listeners in new contexts, using the new vocabulary.

In a familiar context, the dinner table, for example, purposefully substitute a higher-level vocabulary word for a familiar word. Hold up your child's glass and ask "What *beverage* do you want with your dinner?" As you are sorting the laundry together, feel the flannel, the silk, and the cotton and ask her which *fabric* she likes best. As you fill the bathtub, ask her to "Feel the *temperature* of the water. Is it too hot? Is it too cold? How is the *temperature*?" Again, be sure to use the words repeatedly as you are demonstrating their meaning, and try to get her to use them. Be sure to make this kind of vocabulary enhancement a goal of yours. You might target a certain number of new words per day. You will be rewarded when you hear your child use a new word spontaneously.

Empower your child to learn new words by setting up an ongoing game in which he gets a nickel every time he asks "What does that word mean?" Give him a special jar or bank for collecting the money. Purposely use vocabulary that you are sure he does not know the meaning of and see if he asks for the meaning.

Work on words in categories. Play this game with the whole family, when you are riding in the car, for example, or at the dinner table. One person calls out a category name, and each family member must name something from that category. Mom says "I'll go first. Clothing: Hat. Ann, your turn." Ann says "Coat. Dad your turn."

For a more sophisticated language user, keep in mind that the content of the child's language should reach beyond the here and now to events that are not just immediate. Help her to talk about events that have passed and events that she is anticipating. Photographs of past special events in which the child has participated such as birthday parties, school outings, or family outings are excellent for recall and conversation. Create photo books with these. In discussing future events, use calendars and other visuals to help make phrases like "next Thursday" meaningful. Use concrete words, for example, "after breakfast" rather than "soon" to convey time. Suggest important associations to upcoming events, for example, "We will go swimming there." You might use toys and books depicting similar locales if she is going to spend some time at a relative's house. Associate the house with things that are most relevant to her, perhaps her cousins' names, pets, and so on. Photos can be helpful here as well. Use figurines and toys such as a car, airplane, and doll house to act out her journey and what might take place once she gets there.

Introduce topics such as holidays, watered-down versions of major news events, weather, trips, and family news in order to enrich the content of his language. Your child will learn these things faster if you appeal to his senses: see it, touch it, and so on.

Grammar

In working on grammatical errors and teaching more sophisticated grammatical constructs, the following two-part strategy works well. When a child is using sentences with persistent grammatical errors, it is usually not enough to merely model or correct the production at the moment the error occurs. First create an activity or a game featuring the particular grammatical target. For example, let us say that your child persists in using the pronoun *he* for both male and female persons. Together you might draw a picture of a girl. Add lots of detail such as bracelets, earrings, and ribbons. The girl could be holding a balloon. She might have a dog on a leash or a bird on her shoulder. Her car could be nearby. The more items you include, the better. Now take turns saying what she has. "*She* has a ribbon. Your turn." "*She* has a dog. Your turn." To increase his interest level, if necessary, use a tangible reinforcer each time he remembers to say "she."

Prepared piles of magazine pictures, photos, or drawings can be used to facilitate other grammatical targets. Play a favorite board game with your child. Take turns selecting a picture from the pile, using the appropriate construction to describe it and then taking your turn at the game, which may function as reinforcement.

After engaging in activities like these on several occasions, your child will be ready for the second part of the two-part strategy. Your child should be able to use the new construct correctly in the game. Now you can point out the error in his spontaneous speech in the following manner. During conversation, when the error is presented, merely say "What?" in an altogether nonjudgmental fashion, as if you had been thinking of something else and just needed to have that last sentence repeated. This will give the child the opportunity to give some thought to producing the correct grammatical form, which he has been practicing in the game, and to say it correctly now, in context, with this very slight prompt from you.

Language Use

Language use, also called *pragmatics,* or *language in social contexts,* is a subject that encompasses a wide variety of topics. Pragmatics pertains to the function or use of language. It includes the understanding and application of the rules of conversation as well as addressing the various functions for which language is used. Pragmatics is how language becomes meaningful in context. For example, someone might say "He is smart." This sentence could mean he is intelligent, he is a smart aleck, or he is smart as opposed to the rest who are dumb; it could also be a question or a sarcastic statement depending upon the speaker's intent, communicated by context or tonality.

As children with autism progress in their development of language, what may evolve is primarily a pragmatic language disorder. Well-developed pragmatic language skills, that is, language used in social contexts, may be the last of the language skills to develop fully. Pragmatics addresses the weakness that is an essential feature of autism: social communication. Children whose grammar and word knowledge may be fairly well developed may still have considerably weak conversational skills and may demonstrate only a few language functions in their conversation. An overview of pragmatics follows, including some of the many important issues to look for. Once parents are made aware of what to listen for in this subtle area of language, they can help their children become more effective language users.

Conversational Rules

Rules for conducting a conversation are rarely considered until they are violated. When they are violated, something seems amiss, although it may not be immediately clear what it is. Conversational rules include initiating or terminating a conversation, changing a topic, maintaining a topic, and signaling or repairing a communication breakdown, such as failure to hear or to understand. You would not begin a conversation by saying, for example, "I really liked it." Clearly, you need to give a word of greeting or a topic sentence, taking the listener's perspective into consideration (do you share the same information about the topic?). It would be better to say "Hi, Sally. How are you doing? I was just thinking about a book I finished yesterday. I really liked it." One would not terminate a conversation about a deeply felt issue with an abrupt "Bye now." One would bridge the sensitive topic and the departure with a cohesive element, a connective sentence, for example, "I'm really sorry to hear that, but I must go now." Speech-language pathologists think of conversation as a tennis match in which one player serves and the partners each take a turn volleying the conversational ball back and forth. In a conversation, the idea is to keep the ball in the air over several turns. Young children with pragmatic language disorders depend upon others to control the conversation and do not play their part. They often let the ball drop. They may maintain topics with perseverative statements, inappropriate questions, or off-topic remarks. In the following example the adult helps the child to respond and then steers the child away from an inappropriate response.

ADULT: I saw a great movie last night.

CHILD: (No response)

ADULT: What could you ask me?

CHILD: How many minutes was it?

ADULT: That's a silly question. ask me something else.

By asking these kinds of questions, adults can improve their children's conversational skills. Introduce topics and then help the child to respond by maintaining or extending the topic with an appropriate question or by adding relevant information.

ADULT: I ate too much at Thanksgiving.

CHILD: (No response)

ADULT: What could YOU say?

CHILD: I didn't eat too much.

It is important to keep in mind that children who are able to use multiword utterances are not always proficient language users. For example, the child may use long sentences that are echolalic, off the topic, or irrelevant. Echolalia may be used to take a conversational turn, to respond affirmatively, or for other constructive purposes. A parent could use a word or two or a visual prompt as cues to help the child generate a novel, non-echoed response, or provide a simplified model of what the child intends. Being relevant is an important pragmatic skill. If I tell you that I met my father at the airport, and you respond by telling me that you like peanut butter, you may be speaking in a syntactically correct, multiword utterance, but you are off-topic. If I tell you that I met my best friend at the station, and you ask me how many buttons were on her jacket, that might be an irrelevant question. It is ironic that children who speak this way are sometimes described favorably as being "highly verbal." They may be verbal, but they are not appropriate communicators.

Irrelevant or off-topic responses could be amended by using the "That's silly. What else could you say?" or "That's silly. What else could you ask me?" strategies. If the child cannot think of something appropriate, model an appropriate reply and try again.

Children who speak on the sentence level may perseverate on a topic or purposely resort to jargon at times. Parents have found it helpful to label this "Silly talk" as in, for example, "Oh, that's silly talk," and suggest "Let's talk about something else."

Being clear and unambiguous is another pragmatic skill that can be seen as closely related to semantic and syntactic development. Listen to your child as she converses and judge whether she is clear in making a point or is frequently ambiguous. One way she may be unclear is by using pronouns to refer to people and things without clearly identifying the referent of the pronoun. These are called *unmarked pronouns.* Children who are consistently unclear shift the burden of interpretation upon the listener. Shift it back. It is not helpful to merely take the short route, that is, to figure out what she meant to say and to go on with the conversation. Take the time each time she is ambiguous to request clarification, for example, "Who hit Jake on the playground? Who said that, Ted or the lady?" Feign misunderstanding, even if you are able to figure out what your child means. A simple "What do you mean?" will get her to repeat and rework the sentence for clarity. You may have to model.

When your child looks up at the shelf and says "I want that one," and you say "Which one?" you have signaled a *communication breakdown.* He may have difficulty making a repair, perhaps because his descriptive language is limited. Try saying "Tell me more." Or *scaffold* his language by suggesting a word that he might use in a description. For example, you offer "Red?" Child: "Yes, the red one." Adult: "Box?" Child: "Yes, the red box. I want the red box." Your child must also learn to signal to you when he does not understand what you mean. See the description of barrier games below for a way to work on this skill in a formal manner.

Sometimes children converse without appropriate cohesive elements in their conversation, as in the following example.

CHILD: Blue.

ADULT: Blue?

CHILD: Red.

A cohesive phrase before the child's second response might be "Oh, I meant to say red." Cohesive phrases that clarify the message for the listener are typically absent in the language of children with pragmatic language weakness. Some of these phrases, which help maintain the flow of conversation by linking one message to another, follow: That reminds me; Actually, I meant to say; I'm just kidding; I forgot; What do you mean?; I want to tell you about; Isn't that neat?; Just a minute; I thought, and so on.

Perspective Taking

A speaker must consider the listener's perspective in conversation. A listener needs to know certain facts in order to appreciate and understand what a speaker is saying. If your child does not consider his listener's needs, tell her "I don't know what you are talking about." Another way to work on perspective taking is to ask during story time, for instance, "What do you think the lady might say to him?"

In summation, parents may sense that their children, although they can use longer sentences and may be in certain respects "highly verbal," are actually not efficient language users. Here is a summary of some of the pragmatic aspects discussed above in which your child may be deficient:

- off-topic responses

- ambiguous responses

- irrelevant responses

- unmarked pronouns

- abrupt or repetitive topic introductions, topic shifts, or topic terminations

- lack of or inappropriate topic maintenance

- inability to extend topic

- inability to signal or repair communication breakdown

Parents need to look for these subtleties in their children's language in order to see what makes the language deficient and to help their children become proficient language users.

Language Functions

Children with autism may be speaking in relatively complete sentences, but may use language for a limited number of functions. Requesting, for example, is often an early pragmatic skill, and commenting is often limited at first. More sophisticated pragmatic func-

tions include using language to convince or to negotiate. Other examples of language functions include using language to greet, to respond, to protest, to request, to comment, to narrate, to refer to, to predict, to explain, to compare, and to joke. Many children with significant language disorders who speak in multiword sentences have difficulty with some of these functions.

Descriptive language is often underdeveloped in children with language disorders. Speech-language pathologists call descriptive language *referential communication*. We can work on referential communication with barrier games. In a barrier game one person describes a picture not visible to another person so that the listener can identify or construct the same picture on his side of the barrier. You can play such games at home by drawing pictures, setting up cut-out shapes, or by purchasing two of the same peel-and-stick or Colorform type of game that include various scenes. Use a small briefcase as your wall or barrier so that you cannot see each other's boards and must depend upon words to give and receive messages. This activity helps children to be active listeners and to seek information. They need to be clear in their messages and to seek more information if they do not understand the other person's message. You can help your child use descriptive language in other ways, for example, at the donut shop. Stand at the counter and ask her to describe which donut she would like you to buy for her.

Narratives, or stories, are an important part of language. Games such as Ravensburger's *Tell A Story* are useful in helping young children with the various aspects of narrative: plot, setting, cohesion, and a bit of character development. Remember to model cohesive words like *so, and then,* and *but* while telling stories. Stories also occur in real life (the time we went to the beach, the day we spent in the park, etc.) and should be worked on in the same manner, that is, pictures to aid in recall, modeling use of cohesive words, and attending to plot, locale, character, and episodes.

Practice using language to *problem solve,* for example, to *offer explanations* or to *make predictions.* When you read with your child, watch TV, or watch videos, make these experiences interactive, and practice using language to predict and to explain. Ask, for example, "Why do you think the man said that?"; "Why shouldn't they go?"; or "What do you think the boy will do next?"; or in other contexts, "What should we do about this problem?"

Practice using language to *compare and contrast.* You might do this in the kitchen as your child is helping you prepare dinner. Compare various vegetables, fruits, cooking utensils, or dishes.

Being able to *draw inferences* is an important pragmatic skill. If a child walked into my room and did not shut the door, I might say "The door," expecting him to infer that I want him to close the door. If I said "I sure am thirsty," I would expect the child to infer that I would like some water. Communication Skill Builders (1-800-866-4666), Thinking Publications (1-800-225-GROW), and Linguisystems (1-800-PRO-IDEA) are companies that publish materials for working on inferencing and other pragmatic language skills.

Your child should be using and interpreting facial expressions that convey meaning. Children with pragmatic language disorders often ignore subtle messages that accompany speech, such as *facial expressions, tone of voice,* and *body language.* They therefore interpret messages literally, attending only to the words. Help your child focus on these more subtle ways of conveying messages by pointing them out and asking what they might mean. Be sure she is using them with her own speech.

Using *humor* in language is a pragmatic skill. You can model humor in many different ways. Put on a funny hat and say "I look like a clown." Have your child do this and say what he looks like. You can joke, "Martin, I live in Mexico!" Look at him, smiling. "Nah, I'm just kidding. I live in New York. Where do you live?" Try to get him to joke. Make sure he labels what he is doing, saying, for instance, "I'm just kidding." Clown it up around the house.

As your child gets older and is able to think and talk more abstractly, she will be expected to be able to understand and use *figurative language,* that is, language that employs figures of speech such as metaphors, similes, and hyperbole. A concrete language user will not understand riddles and humor, which require one to understand figurative language or plays on words. Buy joke and riddle books; use the comics from bubble gum and ice cream wrappers.

As children with autism progress beyond the one- or two-word level of language development, we are looking for evidence of socially interactive conversation. When the child is able to display language that relates to the listener by, for example, asking questions such as "Do you understand?" or "What do you think?", we feel he has turned a significant corner in his road to recovery, despite the fact that some problems of form, content, and use may still exist.

SUMMARY

This chapter has presented strategies that parents have found useful in encouraging their children with autism to talk. No parental behavior causes autism, but parents and others can modify a child's environment in order to alter the course of autism. Parents can talk to their child in ways that can stimulate and encourage their child's language acquisition. As discussed earlier, these ideas should not be considered as separate exercises, but are suggested as a way to shape all adult-child communicative interactions throughout the day. Not all children will respond to all of these suggestions. Autism has many degrees of severity, and children will respond to intervention in various ways. Using these suggestions as well as basing ideas of their own on these general principles, parents can become skillful and effective in helping to promote language development in many children with autism.

APPENDIX
Language Development Overview

Age	Language Skill
1–2 months	Cooing, gurgling, smiling in response to stimulation. Startles and looks in response to loud sound.
3–6 months	Babbling appears. Gurgles and laughs. Calls out for attention. Turns toward speaker or ringing bell.
6–9 months	Babbles double syllables: *Mama, Dada.* Imitates some consonants and inflection. Looks at objects and pictures when named.
9–11 months	Babbles more extensively. Imitates sound sequences (echolalia). Preverbal communication gestures appear: points, waves bye-bye, shakes head no, plays peek-a-boo and pat-a-cake. Reaches to be lifted up. Reaches for an object. Understands and responds to his own name. Understands the word *no.*
12–18 months	First true words appear (10–18 months); 3–20 word vocabulary. Words may not be clear. Word type is often noun. Frequently occurring first words are *Mama, Dada, cookie, car, bye-bye, no.* Uses jargon (syllables strung together into well-inflected "sentences"). Babbling and echolalia diminish. Highly communicative via gestures, words, and vocal play. Communicates to request, protest, comment, greet, call, and show off. Follows simple instructions. Points to two or more objects. Identifies one to two body parts.
18–24 months	Two- to three-word phrases appear usually when the child has acquired approximately 20 single words. Examples of typically appearing early phrases are *More milk, Dada, bye-bye, Doggie allgone.* Names five pictures by 24 months. Says own name. Negation (*no bottle*), possession (*Mommy chair*), and verbal turn-taking are used. Questions are indicated by inflection and intonation. Approximately 200-word vocabulary. Likes to listen to stories.
$2–2\frac{1}{2}$ years	Uses three-word phrases such as *My big truck* or *See Daddy car.* Uses at least two pronouns, *-ing* verbs, plurals, articles *a, and, the* and early prepositions (*in* and *on*). Uses 400 words by age $2\frac{1}{2}$. Beginning to use descriptive language. Answering *what* and *where* questions. Listens to 5–10 minute story. Follows two related commands.
$2\frac{1}{2}–3$ years	Asks basic questions. Uses pronouns *I, me, you,* and *mine* with *he, she,* and *it* emerging. Possessive *s, is,* and regular past tense are used. *Not* is emerging. Answers *who, why,* and *where* questions by age three. Points to 10 use-objects (*Show me the one that you eat with*). Comprehends size (big and little) and 3 prepositions (*in, on, under*). Uses 500 words.
$3\frac{1}{2}$ years	Uses most parts of speech in short, correct sentences, combining four to five words. For example, *He's gonna open this* or *I jumped over the sprinkler.* Asking *who, whose, why,* and *how-many* questions and using *and.* Third-person singular and irregular plurals are emerging. Understands commands involving two objects or two actions. Uses polite forms. Maintains topic over several conversational turns.
4 years	More conversational; fewer grammatical errors. Uses many four- to seven-word sentences. Asks *how, when, why* questions. Uses conditionals and *because.* Can sequence a simple story with events but lacking character and theme. Complies with commands involving three actions. Able to complete simple verbal analogies such as *A daddy is big, a baby is. . . .* ($3\frac{1}{2}$–4 years).
5 years	Average sentence is 5–8 words. Asks word meanings. Defines words. Tells long stories. Uses *will* for future ($4\frac{1}{2}$–5). Grammar sounds like that of the rest of the family. Using figurative language.

Note: Individual variability exists. Ages are approximate.

SUGGESTED READINGS

Bloom, L., & Lahey, M. (1978). *Language development and language disorders.* New York: John Wiley & Sons.

Brown, R. (1973). *A first language: The early stages.* Cambridge, MA: Harvard University Press.

Gard, A., Gilman, L., & Gorman, J. (1993). *Speech and language development chart.* Austin, TX: PRO-ED.

Owens, R. E. (1995). *Language disorders: A functional approach to assessment and intervention.* Boston: Allyn & Bacon.

PART EIGHT

Working with the Schools

CHAPTER FIFTEEN

What Parents Can Expect from Public School Programs

Andrew Bondy

The purpose of this chapter is to help parents understand a public school's responsibilities for the education of preschool children with autism, and the potential for providing comprehensive educational services. My point of reference is the Delaware Autistic Program (DAP), which provides educational services for all students classified autistic in the state. As director of DAP, I oversee the programming for children as young as they can be identified and throughout their school years. The comprehensive nature of the services provided within DAP is the direct result of the strong advocacy of parents in the early 1980s who urged the state to ensure quality programming within the public school system. This chapter describes the nature of the services provided within DAP as an indication of what parents should require their local educational agencies to provide for their children. If parents in one state can successfully advocate for the types of services described in this chapter, other parents can probably advocate successfully for similar services. Most importantly, the services provided by DAP are based on the principles of Applied Behavior Analysis. Parts of this book are designed to help parents implement the methods of behavior analysis. This chapter will help parents determine whether school personnel are implementing those methods within a public school program.

The chapter is divided into three primary sections dealing with (a) What should be taught in a school-based program? (b) How should staff teach? and (c) How should staff be trained? By law, parents should have a major say regarding the first issue, that is, what instructional objectives are included in their child's annual individualized education plan (IEP). Parents should be aware of the other two issues because they bear directly on the quality of the education their children receive.

WHAT DOES THE DELAWARE AUTISTIC PROGRAM OFFER?

The services offered by the DAP represent the scope of services that public schools can provide, but not the only way that a public school can arrange to provide services for preschool children with autism. First, DAP serves children from as early as they can be identified through age 21. It provides full-day programming (6 hours per day) on a full-year basis (up to 241 school days per year). High staff–student ratios are provided; classrooms typically have four or five students with one teacher and one paraprofessional. Funding is available for one speech-language pathologist (SLP) for every 12 students and one psychologist for every 24. In the DAP location in northern Delaware, we have two adaptive physical education teachers, so that every student receives 30 minutes of adaptive physical education every day. We contract out for occupational and physical therapy as needed. We have a community training specialist and a part-time music specialist. We also coordinate services with federal- and state-funded programs (known as "Part-H providers") for children less than 3 years old.

Most DAP preschool children receive services through a center-based program, in classrooms that are relatively small by design (about 300 sq. feet). We have no "pull-out" areas, that is, small rooms designated solely for one-on-one instruction. All specialists, especially SLPs, work with the children in the classroom and in the community. The services of the SLP (and other specialists, such as occupational and physical therapists) are provided within a collaborative framework. One of the primary goals of the SLPs is to make sure that all staff implement each child's communication training procedures consistently throughout the day. This collaboration requires a great deal of planning time from the staff.

Transportation to and from school is provided. Parent training is available on a group and individual basis, both at the school and in the family home. DAP provides residential services for some of its students, but we have never needed to do so for a preschooler. As children's skills develop, we are able to arrange for mainstreaming or part-time placements in regular preschool or day care settings (both privately arranged and recently, within the school district itself). Virtually all preschoolers have an IEP objective involving weekly community trips addressing specific skills with associated lesson plans.

DAP also offers a respite program for parents. Guidelines jointly established by parents and staff permit 24 hours of respite per month within a sliding-scale, copayment plan, wherein the program pays the bulk of the respite worker's salary. Respite can be provided within the family home or in another setting. Almost all respite workers are staff members of DAP; however, DAP may train and approve of individuals suggested by parents.

Parents are provided with daily home-school notebooks with comments from staff. They also receive progress reports four times per year. These progress reports include a narrative and detailed, data-based descriptions specifying the current level of performance on all IEP objectives.

WHAT SHOULD BE TAUGHT?

In general, two things strike us first about preschool children with autism. On the one hand, there are noticeable deficits in interacting and communicating with other people. Over the past several years, 80% of all preschoolers entering DAP have not displayed any useful language skills (Bondy & Frost, 1994a). On the other hand, many of these children have exhibited excessive inappropriate behaviors, including tantrums, aggression, self-injury, and other behaviors that draw undue societal attention. There is a strong tendency for parents and teachers to want to stop these problematic behaviors as quickly as possible. However, even if we could stop (or suppress) an action, some other action must fill that void. From the perspective of the DAP, either we help children fill that void with useful, functional actions, or children will be left to devise some replacement of their own choosing—something likely to be equally problematic. Therefore, our first obligation is to decide what functional skills should be taught to preschoolers that they will find immediately useful in their lives at school and at home.

One way to identify functional skills is to review the places, people, and expectations that a child en-

counters throughout the day. The skills that are most important are those that must be completed if the child cannot do so independently, such as eating, getting dressed, and so on (Brown, Nietupski, & Hamre-Nietupski, 1976). These life *domains* can be categorized as follows:

1. Domestic skills (i.e., skills associated with eating, dressing, cleaning oneself and the environment, bedtime routines, play routines, etc.)

2. School-based activities (i.e., staying with a group, staying seated at a table, following directions, transitioning between activities and locations, possible academic activities, group and individual play routines, etc.)

3. Community skills (i.e., going shopping for groceries, eating in fast-food and sit-down restaurants, walking in the neighborhood or the mall, riding in a car, etc.)

Although some skills occur only or mostly in specific locations (e.g., home vs. school), other skills apply across domains and settings. These more general areas include the following:

1. Communication skills (e.g., expressing significant choices and needs, calmly rejecting or saying "No," asking for help, affirming with "Yes," responding to simple instructions, imitating sounds, words, songs, etc.)

2. Social interaction skills (e.g., imitating the actions of adults and peers, responding to greetings, initiating greetings, maintaining social approaches from adults and peers, initiating social approaches to adults and peers, etc.)

3. Alternatives to inappropriate behaviors (e.g., learning to wait, asking for help, learning to play with a toy instead of fingers, etc.)

It is important for parents to work with staff to develop IEPs for their children that address each of the concerns mentioned above. It may not be practical to work on every skill the child needs to learn; therefore, it is often wise for the team to decide not to address a particular issue immediately but to include it once certain other skills are acquired. For example, everyone may agree that there are no significant problems in community settings and thus no need for the IEP to address such objectives. On the other hand, if parents report that their child has serious tantrums while in supermarkets, and thus disrupts weekly family routines, the team might add to the IEP an objective to develop appropriate alternative responses to take the place of tantrums (see Bondy & Battaglini, 1992).

Another important consideration in identifying functional skills is that they should be taught within natural situations, that is, where they will be used (McGee, Daly, & Jacobs, 1994). For example, rather than pulling a child into a small room with only one other person to work on saying "Hello," it would be more effective in the long run to work on teaching the child to say "Hello" in the actual situations where that skill should be demonstrated, such as when entering the classroom or the house. Our experience has shown that even if a child learns to say "Hello" in the small isolated room, she will have to be taught explicitly to use that skill when entering a room or a house.

With regard to communication, we generally think about two broad skill areas. One is using language expressively, and the other is understanding what is said. For children without handicaps, these skills tend to grow in concert with each other; for children with autism, they often must be taught independently, with little expectation for automatic transfer. Recall that 80% of preschoolers entering programs for children with autism in Delaware have nonfunctional communication skills. Obviously, we would like for these children to acquire speech as quickly as possible, but they must learn a number of skills (e.g., imitating sounds and words) before they can use speech functionally to make their choices and needs known. While they work to acquire foundational skills, many children are unable to communicate calmly about important things. Therefore, it may be wise for staff and parents to consider teaching the child some alternative means of communicating until (or while) functional vocal speech is acquired. (For a comprehensive review of augmentative and alternative communication strategies for children with autism and related disabilities, see Reichle, York, & Sigafoos, 1991.)

One system that has been used successfully to enable children with autism to communicate with pictures and symbols is the Picture Exchange Communication System (PECS; see Bondy & Frost, 1994b). The rudiments of this system have been acquired rapidly (often within the first day of training) by many preschool children with autism and other disorders. PECS emphasizes teaching the child to *initiate* asking for desired items. Learning to initiate communicative interactions is very important because the child who learns to do so is not dependent upon adults asking "What do you want?" or similar questions, but can seek out an adult (or later in training, peers) and spontaneously request important items. Of course, during the initial period of PECS training, the child also needs to learn to follow simple instructions and to imitate both actions and vocalizations. We emphasize that the aim of PECS is to enable

children to quickly acquire certain key communication skills—especially initiating communication with spontaneous social approaches—*not* as a primary speech training method.[1] On the other hand, there have been no reports of children stopping vocal productions when PECS is introduced. In fact, the majority of children who learn to use PECS begin to speak (some in complete sentences) within about a year after they start PECS training (Bondy & Frost, 1994b).

When considering priority objectives for communication skills development, parents need to understand the different functions served by certain key communication responses. Requesting is learned and maintained because it helps the child get desired items (snacks, drinks, favorite toys, etc.). Spontaneous commenting is usually learned and maintained because it gains the attention of other people, as when a child says "Look at the bird!" The words used may be the same whether a child answers a question (e.g., "What do you want?" or "What is it?") or imitates what's said (e.g., "Say 'cookie' "), but these two types of communication skills are uniquely important, and often very difficult for children with autism to learn. Therefore, parents should know which types of communication skills the staff is teaching, and should stress the importance of teaching spontaneous communication early on.

A functional emphasis on communication skill development should introduce new vocabulary in ways that are important from the child's perspective. For example, it was difficult to keep one Delaware youngster interested in learning color names for common items such as blocks and toys. He rapidly learned color names, however, when they were linked to obtaining the particular color of M&M candy that he wanted (e.g., "I want *red* M&M"). Whenever new vocabulary words are introduced, parents and staff should be aware of how the child is expected to use the new words in everyday situations and then create opportunities for the child to use them.

Similarly, instructions that children are taught to follow should help them (and surrounding people!) cope successfully with everyday encounters. For example, orienting toward an adult when one's name is called and coming to an adult when called are extremely important skills for a child to learn. Other critical early skills involve imitating actions, both simple body motions (such as clapping hands and standing up) and actions associated with how to use various

---

[1] I would like to stress the difference between PECS and Facilitated Communication (FC). While FC often uses pictures and symbols, there is no evidence that it works. Furthermore, according to its proponents, FC begins with trying to teach the child to respond to facilitator questions, not to be spontaneous, as promoted by PECS training.

objects (such as playing with toys, marking with a crayon or pencil, using a spoon, etc.). Learning to imitate what other people do, including how to manipulate common objects, will bring the child lifelong benefits.

Finally, when aiming to reduce or eliminate problematic behaviors, we must know what we would like the child to do instead. It is not enough to identify what we do not want the child to do; it is equally important to specify what the child should be doing. Furthermore, these replacements must make sense from the child's perspective and not simply be selected to please us. For example, if a boy screams to get attention, we must teach him another way to get attention.[2] Although we might like the child to be quiet instead of screaming, being quiet is not likely to get the child what screaming achieved, namely, the reaction of other people. If a girl threw materials across the room because she didn't want to do that activity, sending her to time out would probably not be effective because it would achieve what the throwing did, namely, avoiding the task. A better long-term solution would be to teach her to ask for help or to stop the current activity (i.e., take a break), thus teaching a new skill that meets the same child-oriented goals.

This orientation to the long-term modification of problematic behavior is the heart of Applied Behavior Analysis. An excellent summary of recent research in the areas of functional analysis and functional communication training can be found in a special issue of the *Journal of Applied Behavior Analysis* (Vol. 27, 1994).

HOW SHOULD STAFF TEACH?

Although it is the responsibility of school staff to describe how they will teach the skills called for in the IEP, parents should understand what elements go into a good lesson plan. Teachers and specialists may use various technical terms to describe what they are doing but there are only so many ways to arrange an effective lesson (see Bondy & Frost, 1995, or Schreibman, 1988, for details about designing appropriate lessons).

All appropriately described lessons define the skills that will be taught in a manner that clearly indicates how the skill will be *measured* or *counted*. If an IEP objective does not specify clearly what child action will be counted (and how), then the objective needs to be clarified. Skill definition should be easily understood by everyone concerned and should not be open to frequent debate. Objectives should not be so broad (e.g., "Billy will learn to respect his peers" or "Mary will learn to talk") that it is difficult for two or more people to agree when the skill is actually demonstrated. Additionally, the circumstances associated with learning the skill should be made clear, including settings in which the skill is to be demonstrated (e.g., the classroom, the supermarket, with a peer), the time(s) of day, and the prompts or cues used in teaching (e.g., questions, demonstrations, gestural or physical assistance, etc.).

The lesson plan should also include a description of what rewards (or reinforcers) will be associated with doing and completing a lesson. The most successful lessons include rewards that are natural to the situation. For example, we could teach a child to get undressed and dressed because it is 10 o'clock and that is the scheduled activity for the class. A better lesson would associate getting undressed and/or dressed with a special activity—for example, putting on sneakers to go outside and run around, or putting on a particular shirt before art or other messy lessons (assuming that these activities are rewarding to the child). Of course, there may be times when it is difficult to arrange for such natural, rewarding consequences. In such cases, lesson plans should specify what children will receive for their efforts.

Children are expected to work in school. Everyone who works should receive compensation that is important to him or her. In the DAP, we play "Let's make a deal" with all our students to start each lesson. We first determine what a child would like to earn, and then we inform her what we would like her to do to earn what she selected. Sometimes we also use a picture or symbol system to help the child remember the deal. Some people disagree with the practice of rewarding child behavior with tangible items, especially snacks or drinks, for which children can work. However, we live in a society in which most adults in their work environments arrange to take breaks every couple of hours and "reward" themselves with snacks or drinks from vending machines or items they bring to work. If that is a normal societal arrangement, then our goal should be to teach our children similar arrangements; that is, by the time they are adults, they should be able to work for 1 or 2 hours at a stretch before taking a brief break for a snack of their choice. Why should we expect more of our children than we do of ourselves? It is not the use of such rewards that may be problematic but the frequency with which they are used. The key is that the use of such rewards in school or at home should be gradually reduced in frequency across each school year and replaced with praise and other social rewards. Until praise and other social re-

---

[2] The process used to determine the function of a behavior is called a *functional analysis*. This analysis involves identifying critical elements in the environment and then changing (i.e., manipulating) particular elements and noting changes in the behavior. In this example, we assume that such an analysis has been performed by staff.

wards are truly important to a student, we must use other types of rewards to maintain motivation to learn the skills that we are teaching. We also should ensure that we express our reactions to children's accomplishments frequently and with great affect.

Lessons should also specify two other elements: *error correction* procedures and strategies for ensuring skill *generalization*. Lessons often do not run as smoothly as they are written (perhaps because the children don't read them!). Even the best teaching procedures cannot guarantee error-free learning; children will still make mistakes. It is important, therefore, to specify error-correction strategies ahead of time and write them into the lesson plan. Such strategies must indicate a complete repetition cycle (i.e., repeating the behavior in reaction to the *initial* cue, not just cues added by the teacher) to ensure that the child performs the task independently and not only in response to a teacher's efforts to "fix" the situation by providing additional prompts.

For example, imagine a child is being taught to brush her teeth, including putting away the toothbrush and toothpaste and shutting off the faucet. Assume that she has completed most of the sequence independently but walks out of the bathroom without closing the faucet. A common reaction would be to tell her to go back to the sink and turn off the water. This solution might "fix" the immediate problem (that is, the running water) but does not teach her anything new. In fact, it may teach some children that such reminders are part of the sequence. An appropriate error-correction strategy would be to determine the last thing the child did correctly and to lead her back to the situation just *before* that error. In this example, the teacher should prompt the girl to go back into the bathroom and then give her the toothbrush that she had correctly put away. With the child now standing at the sink with toothbrush in hand, the teacher would help the child complete the remainder of the sequence while preventing the error, by helping her put away the toothbrush and immediately turn off the water. Over subsequent tooth-brushing opportunities, the teacher should gradually remove (fade) the prompts used in error correction until the child performs the whole sequence correctly without help. Parents should understand what error-correction strategy staff intend to use with each lesson, and each strategy should be specific to the skill(s) being addressed in each lesson.

Generalization strategies focus on teaching the child to use new skills in situations besides the ones in which they were taught originally. There are two broad concerns about generalization: (a) when, where, with whom (etc.) each new skill will be performed, and (b) expanding aspects of each new skill, such as its intensity, duration, or frequency. If a boy were to learn to say "Hello" only to the one person who taught him to do so, that skill would not be very functional for him. He needs to learn to say "Hello" to many people in many different locations. Similarly, although it might be an important accomplishment for a child to learn to use a spoon to eat just one scoop of cereal, the goal is for the child to eat an entire bowl of cereal with a spoon, unassisted. Teaching procedures to address generalization goals like these should be described in lesson plans.

Another issue is whether lessons will be taught individually or in groups. A great deal of the work that needs to be done with very young children with autism requires one-on-one lessons, that is, one staff member working with one child. Some skills (e.g., turn-taking, playing around) must be taught in group situations (see Strain & Cordisco, 1994). Staff should be able to describe to parents which activities will be taught individually and which will be taught in small groups. Staff should also be able to describe the overall proportion of time a child spends in individual lessons, and parents should require this to be a significant portion of the school day.

Finally, with respect to problematic behavior, parents should ask staff how they will teach appropriate, useful alternative skills and exactly how they will respond when the problem behavior occurs. For example, suppose a child needs to learn to ask for help, or calmly get attention instead of tantruming or hitting himself or others. If the situation has progressed to the point that the child is engaged in a tantrum or aggression, it's too late to try to teach the new, alternative skill. Therefore, lessons to teach the new skill must be designed to occur when the child is calm. Initially, these lessons might require two staff members: one to set up the situation and one to assist the child in producing a constructive solution. For example, if a child usually throws tantrums when confronted by various simple problems, then the staff should arrange such problems (e.g., a container that is tightly closed, a toy that doesn't work, a knot in a shoelace, a door that is stuck, etc.) specifically so they can teach the child appropriate solutions. The key is to teach the child to ask for help before he engages in some inappropriate behavior (e.g., a tantrum).

For instance, one teacher might present the child with a problem by attracting his attention to an opportunity to go outside through a door that is too heavy for him to open. As soon as the child has difficulty opening the door, a second teacher assists the child in asking for help (via speech, gesture, or picture, depending upon the child's current skills). Of course, when the child performs the appropriate request, the first teacher opens the door and allows the child to go outside. Over time, the second teacher's assistance is faded out. The first teacher should not prompt the child to ask for help, because the child could simply learn to wait for this cue (i.e., "Ask me for help") rather than to initiate the request without teacher assistance.

Teachers should also be able to tell parents precisely how they will respond when the child engages in some problematic behavior. Will they ignore the action and prompt the child to do something else? Will they say "no" to the child? Will they physically prevent the child from hurting someone (including herself)? Staff should have a plan for responding consistently and systematically to such occurrences: they should not be left to chance, spur-of-the-moment reactions. If staff intend to use a complicated intervention plan, they should be able to tell the parents what support exists in the Applied Behavior Analysis research literature (i.e., books, journals, etc.) regarding the use of the planned intervention in similar situations. Finally, if staff propose an entirely new procedure, especially an experimental procedure, they should ask for parents' written permission and clearly point out the potential risks, as well as the possible benefits, of the intervention.

Educational goals for children with autism should include skills that are useful to the child both in and out of the classroom. Skills learned at school must be demonstrated in the child's home as well as in the community. For such broad-spectrum goals to be accomplished, parents must also be active teachers (Harris, 1983). School staff should be able to inform parents how the school will help them acquire the skills they need in order to teach their children effectively. A number of strategies have been used to train parents and other family members (Egel & Powers, 1989). Some include having parents hear professional presentations about autism and effective teaching approaches. Others involve parents working directly with their children at school under the supervision of staff (Koegel, Schreibman, Britten, Burke, & O'Neill, 1983). Another strategy is for staff to train parents and other family members in the home. In general, simply telling parents what to do is not sufficient to enable them to teach their children effectively. Parents must practice using teaching techniques to become skilled. Finally, when parents have problems with their children in community settings (e.g., shops, restaurants), we have found it helpful to have parents accompany staff and their children during community training times. After watching staff interact with their children, parents then are given an opportunity to practice similar strategies while staff observe. This direct approach often helps parents form new expectations for what their children can do appropriately in the community.

HOW SHOULD STAFF BE TRAINED?

In general, requirements for certifying teachers are determined by state agencies. Most parents are unaware of these specific requirements. Autism is such a low-incidence disability, however, that few teachers and specialists like speech-language pathologists (SLPs) and school psychologists have received special training to work with this population. Most undergraduate programs for teachers of exceptional children focus on the more frequent mild handicapping conditions, such as learning disabilities and mild mental retardation. The spectrum of deficits and excesses displayed by most children with autism means that they can achieve reasonable progress only if very special and detailed attention is given to their education. Therefore, it is sensible for parents to be aware of the type of training received by staff working with their children.

In Delaware, there is unique certification for teachers of autistic/severely handicapped students. This certificate builds upon requirements of more general teacher certification in exceptional children. The more advanced certificate calls for three core courses that cover the topics of assessment, curriculum design, teaching procedures, behavior management, and functional communication training for students with autism. Teachers must also take two courses in elective topics, such as advanced behavior analysis, augmentative communication systems, preschool programming, and transitional and vocational programming. Teachers with a certificate in exceptional children are required to complete these special courses within 3 years to earn the advanced certificate in autism/severe disabilities. Specialists in speech and psychology are required to hold master's degrees in their area of specialization, and each is required to take at least one course in Applied Behavior Analysis. Bachelor-level speech therapists are not recognized by the American Speech-Language-Hearing Association as speech-language pathologists and are not permitted to work in the DAP.

In addition to the college/university instruction its staff receives, the DAP has a commitment to ongoing staff development. The core training for both professional and paraprofessional staff is based on a detailed staff manual designed specifically for the program. This manual, based on the principles of Applied Behavior Analysis, must be read by all staff. All educational strategies and the key behavior-management strategies also must be reviewed in videotaped format. Each staff member must be observed by designated staff and demonstrate competence in specific instructional and behavior-management strategies.

An active mentoring program has been established for all new staff to the program. Each new staff member is coached by a designated mentor (i.e., someone with more than 3 years of experience and demonstrated excellence in teaching skills) as they learn their new job responsibilities, including instructional and behavior-management strategies. Additional training on various topics is provided throughout the school year, as needed.

Although it may be impractical and unnecessary for parents to be aware of all aspects of the training received by staff working with their children, it is reasonable for them to seek assurance that staff training focuses specifically on information and procedures that sound research has found effective for students with autism. Staff training should be continuous and not limited to one-time workshops or similar short-term ventures. Finally, all staff should be thoroughly trained in the principles and methods of Applied Behavior Analysis, regardless of their previous training. Because all instruction and behavior-management procedures should be consistent with the principles of behavior analysis, all staff must be able to understand, write, discuss, and implement such procedures, which requires that all staff use a common language.

WHAT IS FULL INCLUSION?

Many parents who are offered services through the public schools want to know the benefits and risks associated with what is called *full inclusion*. Parents of young children with autism may not know what the term means, although some may be aware that it is a matter of considerable controversy. Before attempting to define the term, I would like to clarify the roots of the issue. The federal law that states that *all* children are entitled to a free and appropriate education (the Individuals with Disabilities Education Act, or IDEA) includes a mandate that all services should be provided in the "least restrictive environment." To the extent appropriate for an individual student, placement and activities should be with regular students in the student's neighborhood school. If special placement or services are deemed necessary, they must be justified because they will benefit the student (or reduce disruptive effects on other students). In other words, restrictions on student placement must be balanced with the provision of an effective education.

The term *full inclusion* has come to be associated with the idea that *all* students with special needs must be placed in their neighborhood school with their age peers, and all services must be provided within the regular classroom setting. Simply stated, the phrase *full inclusion* is not part of the federal mandate. The term *least restrictive environment* implies that a range of educational options must be available, and placement decisions must be based on each student's individual needs. To help clarify the point for parents and staff, I have often used the phrase "least restrictive *effective* environment." Placement cannot be made on the basis of a student's educational classification; that is, no student can be placed in a particular classroom, whether self-contained or regular, solely because he is classified as "autistic." Federal law recognizes that some children may require self-contained classes, classes with part-time mainstreaming and reverse mainstreaming, team-taught classes, fully integrated classes, or home-based instruction. The choice must be based on the individual student's needs.

If a school district recommends a particular type of placement, parents have the right to information concerning the effectiveness of such a placement for students with similar needs. If the district has no particular history with a certain type of placement, then they must present a rationale, based on findings in the current research literature, on the effectiveness of the suggested placement. Placement should not be based on philosophy devoid of sound, objective evidence of real benefits to the child. The techniques and types of services described in this book all have a solid grounding in empirical research. Although parents should not be expected to be experts on this research base, districts are required to provide empirical support for claims that they are offering a student a "free and *appropriate* (emphasis added) education."

SUMMARY

Historically, few public schools have offered services for preschool children with autism. Recently this has begun to change, in part because more effective techniques have been developed for teaching this population. In many parts of the country, however, it may not be possible for a school to develop an appropriate school-based program for a preschool child with autism. If a school district does offer a program, parents have the right to demand that the services be appropriate for their child, that is, based on the best available scientific evidence about effective strategies for teaching children with autism. Knowledgeable, involved parents are perhaps the best assurance that a child will receive necessary and effective services.

REFERENCES

Bondy, A., & Battaglini, K. (1992). A public school for students with autism and severe handicaps. In S. Christenson & J. Conoley (Eds.), *Home school collaboration* (pp. 423–441). Silver Springs, MD: National Association of School Psychologists.

Bondy, A., & Frost, L. (1994a). The Delaware Autistic Program. In S. Harris & J. Handleman (Eds.), *Preschool programs for children with autism* (pp. 37–54). Austin, TX: PRO-ED.

Bondy, A., & Frost, L. (1994b). The Picture-Exchange Communication System. *Focus on Autistic Behavior, 9,* 1–19.

Bondy, A., & Frost, L. (1995). Educational approaches in preschool: Behavioral techniques in a public school setting. In E. Schopler & G. Mesibov (Eds.), *Learning and cognition in autism* (pp. 311–333). New York: Plenum.

Brown, L., Nietupski, J., & Hamre-Nietupski, S. (1976). The criterion of ultimate functioning and public school services for severely handicapped students. In M. A. Thomas (Ed.), *Hey, don't forget about me: Education's investment in the severely, profoundly, and multiply handicapped* (pp. 2–15). Reston, VA: Council for Exceptional Children.

Egel, A., & Powers, M. (1989). Behavioral parent training. In E. Cipani (Ed.), *The treatment on severe behavior disorders* (pp. 153–173). Washington, DC: American Association on Mental Retardation.

Harris, S. (1983). *Families of the developmentally disabled: A guide to behavioral intervention.* Elmsford, NY: Pergamon Press.

Koegel, R., Schreibman, L., Britten, K., Burke, J., & O'Neill, R. (1983). A comparison of parent training to direct child treatment. In R. Koegel, A. Rincover, & A. Egel (Eds.), *Education and understanding autistic children* (pp. 260–279). San Diego, CA: College-Hill Press.

McGee, G., Daly, T., & Jacobs, H. (1994). The Walden Preschool. In S. Harris & J. Handleman (Eds.), *Preschool programs for children with autism* (pp. 127–162). Austin, TX: PRO-ED.

Reichle, J., York, J., & Sigafoos, J. (1991). *Implementing augmentative and alternative communication strategies for learners with severe disabilities.* Baltimore: Paul H. Brookes.

Schreibman, L. (1988). *Autism.* Newbury Park, CA: Sage Publications.

Strain, P., & Cordisco, L. (1994). LEAP preschool. In S. Harris & J. Handleman (Eds.), *Preschool programs for children with autism* (pp. 225–252). Austin, TX: PRO-ED.

CHAPTER SIXTEEN

Supported Inclusion

Susan C. Johnson
Linda Meyer
Bridget Ann Taylor

Over the last two decades in the field of special education, there has been a movement toward including individuals with a variety of disabilities in regular education classrooms. "The IDEA requires states to establish procedures assuring that students with disabilities are educated to the maximum extent appropriate with students without disabilities" (Osborne & Dimattia, 1994, p. 6).

Some professionals in special education state that all children, regardless of disability, should be educated in the mainstream of public school classes (Stainback & Stainback, 1990, p. 6). Other professionals propose that full inclusion should be viewed as one "alternative with select students with autism, when appropriate" (Simpson & Sasso, 1992, p. 10). Simpson and Sasso go on to insist that "full inclusion be subjected to empirical verifications and that data become the basis for making decisions about which children and youth with autism should be integrated full-time with their nondisabled peers in general education classrooms" (p. 10). We agree with this perspective.

In planning for your child's educational program, you may encounter a variety of terms, including *mainstreaming, total inclusion,* and *integration.* Professionals, advocates, and parents vary greatly on their use of terminology, philosophical orientations, and educational practices. We encourage you to aggressively seek out more information on this and all topics related to autism and your child's education. As a parent, you need to be well-informed about your child's needs and strengths as well as the scientific research in determining what setting and services best meet your child's individual needs.

For the purpose of this chapter, supported inclusion is defined as the act of sending a student with autism or pervasive developmental disorder (PDD) into a regular education program accompanied by an aide or instructor trained in the principles of Applied Behavior Analysis. The Alpine Learning Group (ALG) is a small private school for children with autism/PDD that provides instruction based on behavioral principles. We have developed a supported inclusion model in which children with autism who meet certain behavioral criteria are placed in education settings with typically developing, age-matched peers. A trained aide accompanies the student to the setting to help the child participate fully in all classroom activities. A number of objective measures are used to evaluate student performance. This chapter reviews this model, which has been systematically implemented at the Alpine Learning Group.

As you read this chapter, you will review criteria for participation in a supported inclusion program. If you decide to pursue an inclusion program for your child, this chapter will guide you through the systematic planning, implementation, and evaluation of such a program. The authors strongly recommend consultation from an experienced professional in Applied Behavior Analysis and educational programming throughout this process. We realize that not all parents have ready access to such professional help at the current time. With or without the guidance of a consultant, this chapter provides an overview of relevant issues and techniques to assist you in placing your child in an inclusion setting.

WHY CONSIDER SUPPORTED INCLUSION?

The decision to try supported inclusion for a child with autism should include parents, regular education personnel, special education personnel, behavioral/educational consultants, and school administrators. Determining the appropriateness of supported inclusion for a given child should include careful consideration of the objectives to be accomplished, which might include the following:

1. To generalize social skills learned in a structured, one-to-one teaching situation to a setting with typically-developing, age-matched peers

2. To learn new social skills

3. To generalize academic skills learned in a structured (one-to-one) teaching situation to a group instruction setting with typically developing, age-matched peers

4. To learn new academic skills

5. To gradually and systematically increase the student's time in the regular education setting in preparation for a full transition. The time should be increased contingent on the child's achievement of targeted objectives, and support personnel are gradually faded until the child is included for the full school day.

WILL YOUR CHILD BENEFIT FROM AN INCLUSION PLACEMENT?

As your child develops certain skills through one-to-one teaching in highly structured sessions, these skills should be practiced and reinforced in novel situations throughout the day, including various people and settings. As your child begins to generalize skills, you may want to consider if placement for some length of time in a setting with typically developing peers would be helpful. We have developed a list of prerequisite skills for determining a student's readiness for supported inclusion.

The child should demonstrate the prerequisite skills with proficiency not only in the specialized educational setting, but in various other situations with other people before inclusion placement begins. Standards (or *criteria*) for deciding if a skill has been mastered and generalized should be established well in advance. They may be somewhat different for each type of skill. Some questions to ask in establishing specific and appropriate criteria against which to evaluate your child's performance are: What is a functional level of performance; that is, how accurate and consistent does the performance have to be to produce positive outcomes for the child in various "natural" situations? In general, what level of performance is expected of typical children of the same age? What, in particular, is expected of most children in the inclusion setting you are considering? For example, typical 5-year-olds are probably not expected to follow all verbal instructions from adults or recall their experiences with 100% accuracy all the time, but they may be expected to do so on at least 90% of all opportunities across a range of situations. Certainly a range of performance on academic tasks is considered acceptable for any group of first graders; perfect scores on every classroom test is not a realistic criterion for most typical children, nor would it be for a child with autism.

On the other hand, most teachers in typical classrooms have high standards for all children in certain areas, such as independent toileting, remaining quiet while the teacher is talking, and refraining from disruptive behavior such as tantrums and aggression. An occasional error might be tolerated, but frequent errors would likely garner negative consequences for the child. In short, criteria should be stringent enough that you can be sure the skill is well-established in the child's repertoire before she begins inclusion placement, but not so stringent as to be unreasonable or unattainable. Generally, high accuracy and consistency criteria should be set for the acquisition and generalization of high-priority skills (e.g., 90% accuracy for three consecutive sessions, with three different adults or children, in three different settings).

The prerequisite skills follow:

1. Language skills

   a. Follows two-step directions when presented to a group
   b. Communicates needs and desires
   c. Answers simple questions
   d. Asks simple questions
   e. Engages in simple exchanges of conversation
   f. Recalls experiences

2. Social skills

   a. Takes turns during activities
   b. Waits quietly
   c. Reciprocates greetings from peers and adults
   d. Participates in circle activities
   e. Initiates play activities with peers with or without adult prompts
   f. Imitates peer play

3. Academic skills

   a. Learns through observation of others
   b. Completes seat work independently
   c. Raises hand to seek adult assistance
   d. Learns targeted objectives during group instruction
   e. Completes grade-level academic curricula

4. Behavior skills

   a. Responds to delayed contingencies (reinforcement is delivered to child following a period of time rather than immediately after the targeted behavior; e.g., the mother contracts with her child for ice cream after preschool if the child follows directions. The reinforcer is provided after school so as not to draw extra attention to the child during school)
   b. Exhibits disruptive behaviors at near-zero levels in all environments

c. Stereotypic behaviors under stimulus control; that is, the child engages in stereotypic behavior, if at all, only under certain stimulus conditions (e.g., alone; during playtime at home) and not under other conditions (e.g., in public places like the classroom).

To illustrate how these criteria are used, let's look at an example, a child whom we will call John.

• •

John is 4 years old and has participated in discrete-trial teaching both at home and in a specialized school for 14 months. The data show that he makes eye contact spontaneously and on demand. He has developed spoken language to the extent that he can make requests, answer social questions, and reciprocate social information. He follows one-step directions, takes turns in games, and waits quietly during circle activities or in line. John imitates other peers playing with toys such as blocks, cars, or building materials. Although he exhibited stereotypic behavior and noncompliance at the time of entry into the specialized school program, he now follows directions and exhibits stereotypic behaviors at minimal rates. The topography of the stereotypic behavior has changed from flicking of fingers in front of his eyes to infrequent tracking of objects in his environment. In regard to pre-academic skills, he can complete simple worksheets such as mazes, dot-to-dot puzzles, and coloring within a boundary. He has mastered the skills of observational learning and will raise his hand when he needs assistance. John is currently working on matching and expressively labeling all letters and numerals up to 10. He is learning to write his first name. Although immediate, continuous reinforcement was used for teaching these skills, they are currently maintained by delayed reinforcement. For example, using continuous reinforcement, John earned a candy for each correct response when learning to raise his hand when he needed assistance. Currently when John demonstrates this skill, the instructor provides direct verbal praise at the end of the entire lesson.

John's parents, Mr. and Mrs. A., reviewed his home data and reports from their son's school placement and felt that he would benefit from inclusion with support in a preschool program for typically developing children. Mr. and Mrs. A. requested a meeting with the teacher and administrators of the specialized school program to discuss John's progress. At this meeting, they reviewed the criteria described above and discussed progress on his targeted, individualized objectives. As noted

previously, John has learned much expressive and receptive language and many social skills. He is mastering some early academic skills and has made significant progress on the reduction of inappropriate, interfering behaviors. With respect to the criteria enumerated above, the review revealed that John had mastered the skills (met the criteria) signified by bold print:

1. Language skills

   a. **Follows two-step, complex directions**
   b. **Communicates needs and desires**
   c. **Answers simple questions**
   d. **Asks simple questions**
   e. **Engages in simple exchanges of conversation**
   f. Recalls experiences

2. Social skills

   a. **Takes turns during activities**
   b. **Waits quietly**
   c. **Reciprocates greetings**
   d. **Participates in circle games**
   e. Initiates play activities with peers with or without adult prompts
   f. **Imitates peer play**

3. Academic skills

   a. **Learns through observation of others**
   b. Completes seat work independently
   c. **Raises hand to seek adult assistance**
   d. Learns targeted objectives in group instruction
   e. Completes grade level academic curricula

4. Behavior skills

   a. **Responds to delayed contingencies**
   b. **Exhibits disruptive behaviors at near-zero levels in all environments**
   c. **Stereotypic behaviors under stimulus control**

John's parents and specialized school administrators determined that he had gained a sufficient number of important prerequisite skills to begin supported inclusion. Given his age, it was decided that the primary purpose for inclusion was for socialization, specifically, to provide John with opportunities to generalize social skills learned in individualized teaching sessions to the novel, group situation. At this point, a meeting was scheduled with the special education personnel from the local school district to discuss the recommendations for supported inclusion. They discussed the criteria and purpose(s) for inclusion and decided to begin supported inclusion in a preschool classroom for typically developing 4-year-old students.

• •

HOW DO YOU IDENTIFY POTENTIAL INCLUSION SITES?

Ideally, several options will be available to parents and school administrators who are considering sites for supported inclusion. The site must have the characteristics and resources needed to meet the objectives identified for an individual student. Some possibilities follow:

1. Community settings: YMCA, YMHA, gymnastic classes, dance classes (strictly for nonacademic purposes)

2. Preschools (private or public)

3. Kindergarten and primary classes in private or public schools

Placement options should be reviewed by the full team of involved parties. The supported inclusion coordinator and/or parent should then visit each class for at least an hour to observe a variety of aspects of the class.

Although research has not been conducted, our observations at the Alpine Learning Group suggest that several factors are related to successful supported inclusion placement.

1. Age: Consideration should be given to the chronological age of the student and the age of the peers in the proposed inclusion site. In most situations, you should try to place your child in a site with peers who are her age. Is this a classroom or setting you would consider for your child at this age if she were not diagnosed with autism or PDD? You may decide to place a child in a group with slightly younger or older children depending upon the specific strengths and needs of your child. For example, if you have prioritized social skills for your 5-year-old, you may place her in a preschool classroom with 4-year-old peers to allow for additional social opportunities. When placing your child with different-aged peers, consider any legal restrictions on the age range within the class as well as the size of your child compared to her peers.

2. Proximity to home or specialized school: Investigate settings within the home community or in close proximity to the specialized school program. If the student is taken out of the specialized school program to attend an inclusion program, try to spend minimal time transporting the student to decrease time taken out of individual or small-group instruction. If the inclusion setting is close to the student's home, there may be increased opportunities for contact with classmates (e.g., birthday parties, "play dates").

3. Teacher characteristics:

   a. Look for a teacher who adheres to structure by consistently following a daily schedule in his class, expects appropriate behavior (sitting in seat, raising hand, taking turns) from all students, and allows for little off-task behavior in the class. Observe the teacher's reinforcement style with his students. This includes the rate of reinforcement, use of behavior-specific praise (verbal praise that specifies the behavior being praised, for example, "Good sitting in your seats"), and contingent reinforcement (praise or reinforcement that is given to the student upon occurrence of a specifically defined behavior). The teacher's methods for interrupting inappropriate behaviors and correcting errors are also major factors in determining appropriateness. Does the teacher praise other students' appropriate behavior as a means of redirecting one student's inappropriate behavior (preferred method), or does the teacher interrupt the instructional activity to direct a considerable amount of attention to the child who is engaging in an undesirable behavior (nonpreferred method)?

   b. Teachers who are willing to have a support aide in the classroom: Some teachers may resist this at first. Stress that the support staff is there to ensure the student's full participation in the classroom, not to judge the teacher's skills. The teacher should ask questions to learn how to include students with special needs in her classroom and should be cooperative.

4. Classroom schedule: The schedule must include activities that address the primary purpose for inclusion. If the purpose is socialization, the schedule should include time for snack, circle, free-play, activity centers, and so on. If the purpose is academic, the schedule should include instruction in mathematics, reading, writing, and so on.

5. Class size: Depending on the needs of the student to be included, consideration should be given to the size of the class and responsibilities of the teacher. In preschool settings, class sizes of 12–16 students have worked well.

Once an inclusion site is identified, the activities in which the student will participate and the times she will attend must be determined, considering the purpose of inclusion. For example, if the student is there for socialization, then opportunities for social interaction must occur while she is present. In most cases, it is wise to start by having the student spend 1 hour, two or three times per week in the inclusion setting. As objective data show that the student is progressing, the time can be increased either in terms of the number of hours or number of days. Generally, we prefer to increase the number of days the student attends the inclusion program for the same period of time and activities, so that the student gets more practice at these activities. Remember, children with autism learn best with repeated trials.

● ●

Let's illustrate this process by looking again at John, age 4. Because John has mastered objectives in the areas of language, social, and behavioral skills, it would be appropriate to consider a preschool placement with typically developing, age-matched peers to enhance generalization of social skills. A small group setting with 12–16 students would be an appropriate placement. The school should be close to John's home to allow for development of friendships, with possibilities for after school "play dates" with children who live nearby. For most children with autism or PDD, regardless of the specific purpose of inclusion, a teacher who maintains a high level of on-task behavior in all of her students will benefit John the most.

Two preschool classrooms were identified as possible inclusion settings for John. One was located approximately 2 miles from his home, and the other was located close to his specialized school. The supported inclusion coordinator and John's mother visited both classrooms. The first class observed was the one close to the specialized school. The classroom had 14 children with one teacher and an aide. The teacher explained that she didn't follow a set schedule but determined the schedule for each day individually. That particular morning, the class began with a circle period for 30 minutes, followed by a story, then free play. Following free play, the children did an art project and then had "Show and Tell." While the children were engaged in free play activities, the teacher prepared her materials for the art project. The aide assisted the teacher while doing other clerical duties such as taking attendance, photocopying, and so on. The second class observed also had 14 students with the teacher and a parent volunteer. Parents were expected to serve as volunteer aides one day per month. The teacher discussed her daily schedule: She begins each morning with 10

minutes of free play while children arrive, then morning circle, followed by table-top activities, an art project, and free play. The last three activities are run concurrently; children rotate from one activity to the next. After all children complete these activities, they join together for a story or special project. During the observation, the teacher followed the schedule closely and had materials prepared in advance. She used behavior-specific praise, redirected students when they engaged in inappropriate behaviors in a neutral manner, and maintained an appropriate level of activity within the classroom.

Both teachers were willing to have a new student in the class, and expressed no concerns about having support staff in their rooms.

The supported inclusion coordinator and mother shared their observations of the two potential inclusion classrooms with John's current teachers and team members. After some discussion, they decided to place John in the second class. The primary reasons were the teacher's organizational skills, consistent scheduling, and frequency and quality of interactions with the students. Moreover, the opportunity for the parent to serve as an aide would allow John's mother to observe regularly in his inclusion classroom. Next, a meeting was held with the inclusion site teacher to determine the specific plan for John. Initially he attended the inclusion classroom from 9:00 A.M. to 10:00 A.M. for 2 days per week. He participated in circle (including name song, calendar, and weather activities), free play activities, and listening to a story. Over time, John's schedule was increased to 3, then 4 days per week with the duration of attendance increasing to 2, then 3 hours per day.

● ●

WHAT CAN BE TAUGHT IN AN INCLUSION SETTING?

In choosing the specific objectives for inclusion, consider the student's strengths and weaknesses and the primary purpose to be served by inclusion. For example, if the purpose is socialization, pay special attention to the student's strengths and weaknesses in that area. Observing the student carefully in the specialized school setting as well as the inclusion setting during the first 1 to 2 weeks of inclusion may yield ideas for additional objectives. Below is a list of objectives for Alpine Learning Group students participating in supported inclusion. This list is not meant to be exhaustive, but to provide suggestions.

Curricula

Preschool Setting

Purpose	Objectives
Socialization	Responding to peers' interactions Initiating verbal interactions Making play-initiation statements Interactive play
Academic	Participating in calendar/ weather activities Sitting quietly in circle time
Transition preparation	Independent functioning All of the above

Kindergarten

Purpose	Objectives
Socialization	Responding to peers' interactions Initiating verbal interactions Making play-initiation statements Interactive play
Academic	Participating in circle/group time Completing grade-level academic lessons Raising hand when answer is known Following group instructions Following individual instructions
Transition preparation	Independent functioning All of the above

Elementary Grades

Purpose	Objectives
Socialization	Responding to peers' interactions Initiating verbal interactions Making play-initiation statements Interactive play
Academic	Completing grade-level academic lessons independently Raising hand when answer is known Responding correctly to spontaneous questions Following group instructions Following individual instructions On-task behavior Learning new material
Transition preparation	Independent functioning All of the above

Specific skill-acquisition programs are written for each objective.

• •

Let's look back at John. Now that a site has been identified and a schedule developed for John, you must choose specific objectives. In referring to the listed curricula, you might choose the following objectives for John: (a) responding to peers' initiation; (b) initiating verbal interactions; (c) engaging in play behavior with peers; (d) participating in weather/calendar activities; and (e) increasing independent functioning in the inclusion setting. These objectives are further defined and data-collection systems are developed. Teaching strategies such as gestural prompting, modeling, and reinforcement strategies are reviewed to determine the most appropriate teaching interventions for John.

• •

The following is an example of a program to teach independence.

Sample Teaching Program

Target Skill: Independent functioning in inclusion classroom.

Target Response: Student will function independently of the ALG support staff within the inclusion site while participating in all class activities.

Operational Definition: Independent functioning means that student participates independently and appropriately within the inclusion site without support from the ALG support staff.

Teaching Strategy: Support is given to accomplish the following:

1. Stop the student from engaging in inappropriate behavior such as stereotypy.

2. Prompt the student to follow a teacher's verbal instruction within 15 seconds. The support staff should pause for 15 seconds and observe the student's behavior in order to see if the student will respond independently by either observing other students or receiving an additional prompt from the teacher.

3. Prompt the student to begin independent seat work within 15 seconds after the teacher's request.

4. Prompt the student to respond verbally to a peer's social initiations.

5. Prompt the student to sit appropriately during circle or story time.

Procedural Steps: The support person should position himself in the classroom so that he can see and hear the student and the teacher. He should also be able to get to the student easily if support is required. Initially the support staff should shadow the student and fade as appropriate. Proximity to the student may vary from activity to activity. The support staff should follow the classroom teacher's routine and provide support as necessary for the child to function independently. Unless requested by the inclusion teacher, the trainer should intervene following the above teaching strategy. Use *subtle* physical prompts from behind the child when possible, but verbal prompts can be used if needed.

Data Collection: The time in supported inclusion is divided into 5-minute intervals. Data are recorded on the percentage of intervals in which the student functions independently. If the student functions independently throughout the entire interval, record the interval as yes (Y). If support is required at any point during the interval, record as no (N). At the end of the day, calculate the percentage of intervals in which the student was independent.

Criterion: 100% for 9 of 10 consecutive school days.

HOW DO YOU TEACH STUDENTS IN THE INCLUSION SETTING?

Support staff who work directly with students in inclusion settings must be trained in Applied Behavior Analysis. They must be competent in data collection, time delay (Snell & Zirpoli, 1987), prompt fading, and nonintrusive reinforcement procedures.

In addition to the methods of Applied Behavior Analysis, we recommend that support staff employ the following strategies:

1. Shadow student and systematically fade back from the student as soon as possible. Shadow means to sit or stand directly behind the student to provide prompting and reinforcement as necessary. The physical presence of the support staff may serve to control the student's behavior. Systematically fading back shifts that control to the teacher, activity, or setting.

2. Support a student under the following circumstances:
   a. To stop the student from engaging in inappropriate behavior such as stereotypy
   b. To prompt the student to follow a teacher's verbal instruction within 15 seconds (for explanation of time delay, see Teaching Strategy #2 in the Sample Teaching Program)
   c. To prompt the student to begin independent seat work within 15 seconds after an instruction
   d. To prompt the student to respond verbally to a peer's social initiation
   e. To prompt the student to sit appropriately

3. Students are to follow the classroom teacher's instructions. If a student does not follow the instruction, provide a gestural or physical prompt. The teacher's instructions should never be repeated by the support staff.

4. Provide support or prompts only after 15 seconds elapse after the classroom teacher gives a direction.

5. Give subtle physical prompts from behind to get the student to function independently. Fade prompts as rapidly as possible (e.g., provide reinforcers after every correct response, then after every third response on average, then after every six correct response, and so on).

6. Provide intermittent verbal and social reinforcers when appropriate. Thin reinforcement as rapidly as possible.

7. If a student asks a question or makes a statement to the support staff, redirect him to address the classroom teacher.

8. Foster social interactions as often as possible.

9. If a skill has been targeted for instruction, follow the written teaching procedure.

10. Summarize data on targeted skills daily on graphs.

Because we hope that the student will begin to follow naturally occurring prompts in the inclusion setting (i.e., teacher's directions, peers' behaviors, bells ringing), prompts or support are typically provided following a brief time delay. For example, a teacher may present a direction to the class, such as, "Everyone take out your reading book." If the student missed the verbal direction from the teacher, perhaps she will observe the other students taking out their reading books and imitate their behavior. The support staff should wait 15 seconds and observe to see if the student responds. Sometimes the delay needs to be reduced due to the rapid pace in the class. If adherence to the 15-second time delay would prevent the student from following along with an activity, then it should be reduced.

HOW DO YOU KNOW IF YOUR CHILD IS LEARNING IN THE INCLUSION SITE?

Once specific objectives are chosen for your child, procedures for measuring performance on each objective should be selected. The appropriate measure depends on the nature of the skill and the conditions under which it is to be demonstrated by the child. You should become familiar with standard direct behavioral measures such as frequency, per trial or per opportunity, duration, latency, and others (e.g., see Cooper, Heron, & Heward, 1987 and Chapters 6 and 7 in this manual).

Collect baseline data on all programs prior to starting a teaching intervention. Baseline is the phase of data collection in which the targeted behavior is measured prior to applying a specific intervention (Cooper et al., 1987, p. 151). Baseline data indicate the level of a behavior prior to any intervention and are important in planning for effective intervention.

Setting appropriate criteria is often difficult when dealing with a teaching environment that changes from day to day, as in most regular classrooms. The number of instructional opportunities for the student to exhibit the targeted behavior may vary greatly. For example, one day the students may have 30 minutes of free play during which the support aide can work extensively on interactive play skills. On another day, there may only be 10 minutes of free play and therefore fewer opportunities to work with the child on these skills.

Ideally, data are recorded for the same length of time on each occasion they are collected. In the example above, if data are to be collected on how frequently a child asks peers to play during free time, identify a set period of 10 minutes each day. The duration selected should be based upon the minimum length of play time each day, so that data can be collected frequently.

It is also important to record data on the performances of a variety of peers on the same skills as those targeted for the student with autism. For example, if a target objective for John is to ask friends to play during free time, then pick two or three of John's peers (preferably same-sexed) and collect data on them for the same duration as used in John's program. Two or three days of data should be collected each month on the peers to assess changes in behavior due to maturation or other variables not related to the specific intervention applied to your child. Collecting such normative data is important for establishing appropriate criteria. Criteria for your child may be set close to or at 100% of the rate exhibited by his peers.

Data on targeted objectives should be reviewed weekly to monitor progress toward goals. When data are summarized and graphed, you can visually assess the progress. For example, if you are recording the frequency of verbal interactions toward peers and the graph shows that the behavior is increasing, then the current teaching procedure is effective. As criteria are met, any prompts or motivational systems can be systematically faded. If the graph shows that there is no change in the behavior or that the desired behavior is decreasing, then an alternative teaching procedure is necessary. In this situation, look at the types of prompts and motivational systems used by the support staff. If this skill was previously mastered at home or in the specialized school, refer back to the teaching procedure used and replicate it in the inclusion classroom as much as possible.

If you are recording data on a behavior to be reduced, such as stereotypy, the graph should show a decreasing trend; that is, the level of the behavior should decrease over time. If this is not occurring, the intervention procedure needs to be reviewed and modified. A consultant trained in Applied Behavior Analysis and experienced in inclusion can help in this situation.

In regard to academic skills, identify with the teacher any opportunities she uses to evaluate performance for all students (e.g., weekly spelling tests, worksheets, mazes). When comparing weekly samples checks of work completed over a period of time, you can assess progress. For example, if your child is in kindergarten, ask the teacher if she has weekly worksheets for handwriting. This measurement procedure is referred to as *permanent product,* in that a final product is produced from which you can assess progress.

Following this section are three sample data sheets that we have used in inclusion settings (Figures 16.1, 16.2, and 16.3). The first data sheet is for objectives in a preschool program, the second is for objectives in a primary grade, and the third is for social interaction skills.

Now that we have reviewed how to teach your child in an inclusion setting and how to assess progress, let's look back at our example of John.

• •

As mentioned previously, one of John's objectives was to increase his play behavior with peers. Baseline measurement indicated that during a 20-minute play situation, John played with his peers for 5% of the intervals observed. Three same-sexed, typically developing students played with peers for an average of 80% of intervals. In his home program, John had learned specific play behaviors and generalized them to school and friends' homes; therefore, the focus of this teaching program was play interactions with peers. A reinforcement program was developed to

Interval:	Ind. Functioning	Respond to Social	Greetings	Play Initiation	Statements	Verbal	Interactions	Comments
	Y if independent	Opportunities	Correct Responses	Opportunities	Correct Responses	Opportunities	Correct Responses	
	N if support given							
8:30-8:35								
8:35-8:40								
8:40-8:45								
8:45-8:50								
8:50-8:55								
8:55-9:00								
9:00-9:05								
9:05-9:10								
9:10-9:15								
9:15-9:20								
9:20-9:25								
9:25-9:30								
9:30-9:35								
9:35-9:40								
9:40-9:45								
9:45-9:50								
9:50-9:55								
9:55-10:00								
10:00-10:05								
10:05-10:10								
10:10-10:15								
10:15-10:20								
10:20-10:25								
10:25-10:30								
10:30-10:35								
10:35-10:40								
10:40-10:45								
10:45-10:50								
10:50-10:55								
10:55-11:00								
11:00-11:05								
11:05-11:10								
11:10-11:15								

Name: Date:

Figure 16.1.   Sample supported inclusion data sheet—preschool.

©1996 by PRO-ED, Inc.

increase his play behavior with peers. John's parents put together a "surprise box," a decorated shoe box full of John's preferred items. They included coupons for special outings (e.g., pizza, roller-skating, movies), candy, and handheld games. John was told that we wanted him to share toys with friends, talk with friends while playing, and stay close to friends while playing. Those responses were practiced at home with his sibling. John was shown his surprise box and told that if he got two stars for playing with his friends, he could pick out a treat from the surprise box. At the beginning of playtime in school, John was pulled aside and reminded of what he needed to do to earn a surprise and how many stars he needed. Initially every 30 seconds, contingent upon John displaying the targeted behavior, the support staff provided him with behavior-specific praise (whispered quietly to John) and told him he had earned a star. The star chart was kept with the staff so as not to draw inordinate attention to John from his peers. He did not see the star being put on the chart. If John earned two stars, he was able to go to the surprise box after school and pick out a treat. After John met the criterion for 2 consecutive days, the criterion was increased by one star. John continued to earn a star for each interval with play interaction, but now he needed to exhibit play interactions during more intervals (get more stars) in order to earn the treat. This intervention continued until the data showed that John was playing with friends for 80% of intervals for 3 consecutive days. The stars and surprise box were eventually removed completely. John maintained a rate of play behavior consistent with that of his peers, as documented by the ongoing recorded data.

Name: Date:

Interval:	Ind. Functioning Y if independent N if support given	In response Raises hand/ Circle if called	to questions: Gives correct answer 1st time	# of times called upon spontaneous ly by teacher:	# of times stu- dent gives correct answer first time	Following inst.- Group Opportunities Complies	1st time given Individual Opportunities Complies	Comments
8:30-8:35								
8:35-8:40								
8:40-8:45								
8:45-8:50								
8:50-8:55								
8:55-9:00								
9:00-9:05								
9:05-9:10								
9:10-9:15								
9:15-9:20								
9:20-9:25								
9:25-9:30								
9:30-9:35								
9:35-9:40								
9:40-9:45								
9:45-9:50								
9:50-9:55								
9:55-10:00								
10:00-10:05								
10:05-10:10								
10:10-10:15								
10:15-10:20								
10:20-10:25								
10:25-10:30								
10:30-10:35								
10:35-10:40								
10:40-10:45								
10:45-10:50								
10:50-10:55								
10:55-11:00								
11:00-11:05								
11:05-11:10								
11:10-11:15								

Figure 16.2. Sample supported inclusion data sheet—primary.

©1996 by PRO-ED, Inc.

IS IT WORKING?

A student's progress in the inclusion classroom should be evaluated on the basis of objective data, recorded on an ongoing basis, summarized frequently, and reviewed at least weekly. Regular opportunities should be scheduled for review of the student's progress by all members of the team.

Indicators of success include the following:

1. The student is functioning independently of support. For example, initial data measures indicate that the student performs independently of the support staff for 22% of the time during mathematics period. Two months later the independence has increased to 78%. This indicates that the student was functioning independently most of the time, and that procedures for teaching this skill in the inclusion setting were working.

2. The student masters individual goals in the inclusion class as measured by objective data.

3. The student masters inclusion-site academic objectives as measured by classroom tests. If the student is passing the same academic tests as typically developing peers, this indicates that he is learning the material presented in the classroom.

4. Teachers at the inclusion site are asked to fill out a questionnaire on the student with autism. If she rates the student as consistently following class routines, staying on task, and completing assignments independently, this is another indicator that the student is functioning successfully in the setting.

As numbers 1–3 above are met, time spent in inclusion can be increased.

Supported Inclusion Play Initiation/Interaction Statements Data Sheet						
Date:	Activity:	Duration of play time:	Record play initiation statements to peers	Record verbal interactions to peers	Record response to peer's play-initiation statements	Record response to peer's verbal interactions

Name:
Setting:

Figure 16.3. Sample supported inclusion data sheet—social interaction skills.

When the measures discussed previously indicate that the student is not progressing, alternative prompting or reinforcement strategies should be developed. Direct teaching of some skills may be difficult to accomplish in the inclusion setting. In those cases, direct teaching should be done in an environment that simulates the inclusion setting as closely as possible. For example, let's go back to John.

• •

One of John's objectives was to complete independent seat work. Every day the students in the inclusion classroom completed a simple worksheet involving dot-to-dot tasks, mazes, or coloring. John had demonstrated the ability to complete similar worksheets in the specialized educational program. Observations in the inclusion classroom, however, indicated that John needed frequent prompting from the teacher to stay on task when such worksheets were assigned. To simulate the inclusion setting, the group activity was replicated in John's home program with John's siblings and their friends. All children were given worksheets like those used in the inclusion classroom, and reinforcement strate-

gies were implemented to increase John's on-task behavior. Subsequently, data collected in the inclusion classroom showed that John's on-task behavior generalized.

• •

If inappropriate responses such as tantrums, loud vocalizations, aggression, or darting occur in the inclusion setting: it may be wise to suspend the placement until the responses can be brought under stimulus control again in the home or specialized school. This should be considered a temporary modification; as soon as possible, the student should be returned to the inclusion setting.

WHO'S RESPONSIBLE FOR YOUR CHILD IN THE INCLUSION SETTING?

In most situations, the inclusion program administrators will ask parents or guardians to complete the necessary paperwork (e.g., release of liability, emergency information sheet, immunization records, permission slips, etc.) to enroll their child in the program, just as they would for any other student. If the aide who will accompany your child to the inclusion setting does so as part of his employment with another program, the employee should check with his employer regarding insurance and professional liability coverage within the inclusion setting. If you are employing the aide yourself to accompany your child to the inclusion program, it would be wise to check with the administrator of the inclusion program or a lawyer regarding liability issues.

SUMMARY

Supported inclusion is an exciting, viable educational programming option for some children with autism. After reading this chapter, you may determine that your child could benefit from inclusion with age-matched peers. Perhaps you've decided that your child is not yet ready for an inclusion experience, but the information presented here has given you some ideas for your child's individualized or specialized education program that may help make a supported inclusion placement possible in the future. The decision to begin an inclusion program should be based upon evidence that your child has acquired skills that will enable her to generalize learned information to novel settings and to continue learning new information in a group setting with typically developing peers. It is not enough simply to expose a child with autism to typically developing peers in order for her to learn from them.

If you made the decision to begin an inclusion program, this chapter has guided you through the steps of identifying a primary purpose, whether it be for social or academic skills, or to begin a transition. You've read about factors to consider in choosing an appropriate site that will serve that purpose. You've also read about specific goals and objectives to be taught in the inclusion setting, different teaching strategies, and methods of monitoring progress. Our intention has been to provide you with guidelines and ideas for developing an inclusion program for your child.

ACKNOWLEDGMENTS

As students with autism at the Alpine Learning Group made significant progress in their individual teaching programs, it became apparent that we needed to investigate opportunities for including some of our students in settings with typically developing peers. The original model was developed by Bridget Taylor. Her dissertation, titled *An Empirical Model for Including Learners with Autism in Less Restrictive Educational Settings,* in partial fulfillment of her Doctorate of Psychology degree from Rutgers University, is in process at this writing. The model for supported inclusion continually evolves in response to students' needs, as do all individualized teaching programs for children with autism. The information presented in this chapter outlines the model as it is currently implemented at the Alpine Learning Group.

REFERENCES

Cooper, J. O., Heron, T. E., & Heward, W. L. (1987). *Applied behavior analysis.* Columbus, OH: Charles E. Merrill.

Kazdin, A. E. (1984). *Behavior modification in applied settings.* Homewood, IL: The Dorsey Press.

Osborne, A. G., & Dimattia, P. (1994). The IDEA's least restrictive environment mandate: Legal implications. *Exceptional Children, 61*(1),6–14.

Simpson, R. L., & Sasso, G. M. (1992). Full inclusion of students with autism in general education settings: Values versus science. *Focus on Autistic Behavior, 7*(3),1–12.

Snell, M. T., & Zirpoli, T. J. (1987). Intervention strategies. In M. E. Snell (Ed.), *Systematic instruction of persons with severe handicaps* (pp. 110–149). Columbus, OH: Charles E. Merrill.

Stainback, W., & Stainback, S. (1990). *Support networks for inclusive schooling.* Baltimore: Paul H. Brookes.

PART NINE

From the Front Lines

Parents' Questions, Parents' Voices

CHAPTER SEVENTEEN

Answers to Commonly Asked Questions

Stephen C. Luce

Kathleen Dyer

When parents first realize that their child is developing abnormally, they have many questions. While it is not possible to answer all of the questions that parents may have about autism and developmental disabilities, the following represents our best effort to answer the questions we most often hear relating to early intervention with a child. We are both practicing behavior analysts who have served children and adults with autism in a variety of settings across the country for more than 20 years. We are now serving young children with autism in home-based as well as classroom programs and conducting research on a number of clinical and administrative issues related to service delivery of that kind.

WILL BEHAVIORAL INTERVENTION TURN MY CHILD INTO A ROBOT?

It has been our experience that individuals who are unfamiliar with or threatened by behavioral intervention often ask if the training will "create a robot." The origins of this question are curious. In our experience, this has not been an issue. Such response characteristics may appear to occur in the behavior of a child who has just acquired a new skill (deliberately or cautiously responding). Another explanation may relate to characteristics of autism that some view as robotic. For example, some forms of self-stimulatory or stereotypic behavior may appear to be mechanical.

We are aware of no reports that behavioral interventions result in children behaving like robots. To the contrary, some children who have received intensive behavioral intervention have been reported to be indistinguishable from normal children on personality tests and by observers who are not told that the child had received a diagnosis of autism (McEachin, Smith, & Lovaas, 1993; Perry, Cohen, & DeCarlo, 1995). For those children who have received behavioral intervention and

have made substantial gains (but did not achieve normal functioning), there have been no reports of problematic, robotic behavior.

WHAT IS THE OPTIMAL AGE FOR STARTING INTENSIVE BEHAVIORAL THERAPY?

A considerable amount of evidence shows that the greatest gains are made with children who start training prior to their fifth birthday. Many of us suspect that the optimal date for starting most children is between 24 and 42 months, but we do not have sufficient research evidence to confirm that. Behavioral interventions have been shown to be effective for all individuals with autism, regardless of age. The gains made with the children starting at later ages, however, appear to decrease in accordance with age.

There is also a dearth of data related to starting children too early. Autism, compared to other disabilities that are evident at birth or soon after, usually emerges and is identified rather late. Therefore, treatment would be unlikely to start prior to about 20 months.

WHICH IS BETTER, HOME-BASED PROGRAMMING OR SCHOOL-BASED PROGRAMMING?

Children with autism appear to learn differently than children without disabilities. Most children with autism are raised in environments that support normal learning in typical children. That is, normal children learn, without special training, the social and language skills that are absent in children with autism. Currently, there is some evidence that when trained early and intensively using behavioral principles, some children with autism can learn the skills that their peers learn naturally. The best way to provide that intensive program is subject to some debate. Some recommend that programming be provided in a home with considerable family participation. Others suggest that effective programming can occur in classroom settings specially designed to serve children with autism.

Some proponents of home-based programming are concerned that most school- or center-based programs for children with autism create greater opportunities for children to imitate inappropriate behavior because the classrooms are filled with children with autism. As a result, many advocates of home-based programming recommend that training be initiated in the home where distractions are fewer and autistic behaviors are less frequently modeled. As the child acquires the skills to imitate and learn from others, she can be systematically integrated into classroom settings with typical children. We know of no groups that advocate that all programming be conducted in the home throughout a child's school years. We should also note that most proponents of center-based behavioral early intervention advocate extensive in-home parent training in conjunction with the classroom training.

Therefore, the debate among behavior analysts is whether it is better to *start* programming at home or in a school setting. To date there has not been a sufficient amount of research to answer that question conclusively. Examples of encouraging results can be found in programs that are primarily provided in school settings (e.g., Fenske, Zalenski, Krantz, & McClannahan,1985, Harris & Handleman, 1994) and in home settings (e.g., Lovaas, 1987). The latter study has the advantage of being the most carefully run with the most comprehensive follow-up data (McEachin et al., 1993). The decision about which kind of program to advocate for a child with autism may be based on practical considerations like which type of programming is available, funding, family preferences, and so on.

Most school districts are now serving children with significant disabilities in their preschool years (3–5 years old). Although it is well established that intensive behavioral treatment is most successful for the preschool child with autism, very few preschool classrooms offer the kind of early intervention provided in the studies cited above. Research by Lovaas and his colleagues suggests that the amount of therapy may be an important variable (the children in the experimental group received 40 hours of intensive behavior therapy per week while the control children received up to 10 hours of parent training). Few preschool programs offer that amount of instruction at present. Therefore, many parents are seeking home-based therapy for their preschool children to ensure that the most effective program available can be developed for their child, under their supervision. One drawback of that approach is that school districts (or other agencies responsible for educating preschool children with autism) are unaccustomed to home-based education. Such a program is viewed as unusual as well as hard to license, regulate, supervise, and control, and most school district officials avoid their use. However, home-based early intervention is beginning to be approved and licensed throughout the United States, especially in communities where other options are limited.

WHAT ABOUT AVERSIVES?

As late as 1960, there was virtually no hope for substantial improvement in children with autism. No techniques had shown any effectiveness, and books written about the subject simply described the syndrome and speculated about the causes of such a disorder. In that climate, the first examples of behavior modification with children exhibiting autistic behaviors were published. Many of those accounts included descriptions of procedures that focused primarily on reducing the strength of dysfunctional behaviors, such as stereotypic or self-stimulatory and life-threatening, self-injurious behavior. Those studies may be viewed today as negative and suppressive unless the reader notes how little was known about the disorder in those days and how hopeless it seemed for anyone to try to change the behavior of a person with autism. Today, accounts of significant behavior change in people with autism are seen in a variety of places, and Applied Behavior Analysis research contains few examples of punishment. Nonetheless, some critics persist in describing Applied Behavior Analysis in the terms of the earliest research run more than 25 years ago.

The technical behavioral definition of punishment is a functional one. Specifically, punishment is any event that, when presented after a behavior, decreases the strength of that behavior. In other words, if a behavior is met with a consequence that makes it less likely for the behavior to occur again, that consequence, no matter what it is, is a punishment. That is a broad definition of punishment, and much of the scientific literature adheres to that broad definition. Such a definition would include procedures such as simply correcting the child, redirecting her, or even using the word *no* if those procedures resulted in a decrease of inappropriate behavior. It would also include procedures like contingent electric shock,[1] spanking, or the introduction of a noxious sound, smell, or taste if those procedures resulted in a decrease in the behaviors they followed.

The term *aversive* once had a similar functional definition. Today, however, it is often defined in terms of its effects on the *person observing the interaction* rather than the effects it might have on the behavior of the person with autism. For example, Lovaas and Favell (1987) used the term to "refer to events that are noxious, uncomfortable, or painful to an individual" (p. 313). Because these definitions include only a subclass of punishment procedures, they are less useful for our discussions here. We should note, however, that many procedures that meet the behavioral criteria of punishment do not meet the new, more narrow definition of aversive. That is, an event need not appear to be negative or provoke discomfort to function as a punishment. If a child is told "No" when he gives the wrong answer, and then gives that answer less frequently, the "No" acted as punishment. It is hard to envision a teaching interaction that did not include punishment of that kind.

One procedure that was used experimentally in the early days was contingent electric shock. It was chosen because of its painful effects and because it could be carefully applied in such a way that the precise extent of pain administered could be controlled. Corporal punishment such as spanking was more commonly used in those days, and shock had the advantage of being much easier to control and administer without variability across therapists. The behavioral impact was extremely dramatic. In these early experimental cases, the contingent use of shock administered immediately after the dysfunctional behavior functioned very effectively as punishment. For the first time, severe, life-threatening behaviors were being eliminated in children with disabilities.

Those early applications of behavior modification were very important in the development of our knowledge of autistic behavior. However, our understanding has developed dramatically in the last 30 years. *Today, painful procedures like those administered in the early applications of aversive contingencies are no longer needed.* We are aware of no program for young children with autism that promotes the use of painful or noxious stimulation as an aversive consequence. Lovaas (1987) noted that some of the children in their experimental

group were exposed to "physical punishment." It is our view that other procedures are now available. Therefore, the use of punishment of that kind is among the variables that are not included in replication studies that are currently ongoing. These changes from the methods employed by Lovaas (1987) are designed to increase the impact and generality of the treatment results.

It *is* sometimes necessary to use some procedures that are behaviorally defined as punishment. For example, as we discussed above, in some cases a child may be corrected or told "No" after incorrectly responding. Punishment of that kind does not usually provoke concern by observers. There are a number of problems with any form of punishment, some of which are discussed in the next section of this chapter (e.g., poor generalization); however, a full discussion of those technical learning principles is beyond the scope of this chapter. In some cases a child may progress nicely if the therapist ignores an incorrect response and simply waits for the correct response to occur and then delivers a reinforcer. In other cases, however, the use of feedback such as "No" can be very helpful.

When no feedback is given following an incorrect response, it is particularly important to reinforce the correct response when it is made. This method is often called *differential reinforcement of other behaviors* (DRO)[2] and is quite effective in decreasing the occurrence of incorrect or dysfunctional behavior.

HOW SHOULD WE WORK WITH DYSFUNCTIONAL BEHAVIORS?

Autism can be described behaviorally in terms of behavioral deficits, behavioral excesses, and behaviors that develop normally (see Lovaas, Ackerman, &

---

[1] *Contingent* is a term used to communicate a relationship a behavior has with the events that precede or follow it. The preceding events are called *antecedents*. The events that follow a behavior are called *consequences*. In this case, contingent electric shock means that each time a behavior such as self-injury occurred, the therapist would administer a brief, harmless, but painful electric shock as a consequence.

[2] In most cases, behavior analysts are very careful to be consistent with each other when using terms and definitions. In the case of differential reinforcement when it is used to decrease another behavior, our textbooks vary widely in what the operations are called. DRO incorporates many different procedures such as differential reinforcement of alternative behaviors (DRA), differential reinforcement of incompatible behaviors (DRI), alternate response training (Alt-R), and a variety of others. The reader should not be confused if the same procedure is described differently.

[3] Unlike most other sections in this manual, this one is more technical and contains more references to scientific journals. In addition, we suggest throughout this section that parents solicit the support of professionals. We apologize for what may appear to be digressions from the premises of this manual. The language is technical because this is a very complex issue. Also, while we understand that professional consultation is very difficult to obtain, implementation of the procedures we describe involves some risks that may not be obvious to an individual who has not had considerable experience with the learning and Applied Behavior Analysis literature.

Taubman, 1983).[3] The behavioral excesses that are characteristic of children with autism include tantrums, self-injury, aggression, and stereotypic behaviors. As mentioned above, some of the earliest examples of behavior analysis involving people with autism focused on the reduction of the behaviors that were too frequently exhibited. Today our emphasis is primarily on developing new behaviors in young children, because when children become engaged in adaptive behaviors, problem behaviors usually occur less often. For that reason, this manual devotes a considerable amount of attention to building new skills (see Chapters 5, 6, 7, 13, and 16 in this manual).

One advantage of working with young children with autism is that the prevalence of severe, life-threatening behaviors is extremely rare. While a significant number of older individuals with autism engage in more severe behaviors, such as self-injury, aggression, and property destruction, those behaviors when exhibited by young children are not usually as threatening or dangerous. Typically, the dysfunctional behaviors exhibited by young children that concern parents include temper tantrums, stereotypic, self-stimulatory, and aggressive behaviors in a variety of forms.[4] Some children exhibit many of these behaviors; some exhibit none of them.

From a behavior-analytic and learning perspective, suppressing behaviors is a much more controversial and difficult task than simply teaching new behaviors. The founding father of modern behaviorism, B. F. Skinner, advocated the use of reinforcement (its introduction, withholding, or withdrawal) in almost all circumstances when confronted with a behavior that is exhibited in excess. His stance arose less from an ethical concern than from a learning perspective; effectively suppressing behavior is a difficult task. Punishment is particularly difficult to administer effectively because, among other things, it often fails to result in durable changes in all settings. In addition, punishment sometimes elicits additional disruptive behavior, such as an emotional outburst or escape or avoidance behavior (Favell & Greene, 1981, Luce & Christian, 1981).

There are objections to punishment as a training procedure that have little to do with the empirical findings and extend beyond the discussion needed for this manual. However, in rare circumstances punishment procedures appear to be the only alternative, particularly when positive alternatives have not been effective. It may also be necessary in cases where the individual or those around her are at risk of injury. If this occurs, it is clear that some prior experience would be essential for the person monitoring and running the program. If a child's behavior requires active contingencies that utilize punishment procedures, professional supervision is needed (see Shook & Favell in this manual). This supervision would include review by more than one experienced behavior analyst working for an agency that has access to a human rights committee (Favell, Favell, & Risley, 1981; Lovaas & Favell, 1987).[5]

Before reviewing the most prominent procedures that would be considered for the treatment of dysfunctional behaviors in a young child with autism, we should note that the terminology used to describe the procedures may vary among practitioners. As noted earlier, leading textbooks in Applied Behavior Analysis differ in their definitions of some of the procedures described. Understanding the general strategies is the most important skill for parents starting a program for their child. More specific information and adjustments in the procedure that may be appropriate for an individual child should be derived from the professional overseeing the program. In addition to the terminological differences you may encounter, you should note again that the information we are able to provide in such limited space is not sufficient to equip an untrained person to implement the procedures without oversight by a trained and experienced professional. The discussion of the procedures below should enable parents to evaluate potentially effective procedures with their child and implement those procedures with the assistance of a professional.

To fully evaluate the effects of any procedure, the target behavior should be measured before and during the implementation of the procedure. Behavioral assessment and measurement are described in detail by Romanczyk in this manual. Objective measures of this kind enable us to analyze precisely what is happening to the behavior. The careful analysis of behaviors that are being suppressed is particularly important, because measures may indicate very small changes in the behavior that could go undetected without objective data. Decisions that are made without the benefit of data can be misinformed and possibly detrimental to the child.

---

[4] The reader will note that problematic behaviors exhibited in excess are referred to as *dysfunctional* rather than *maladaptive*. That is because we believe that if the factors controlling behaviors can be isolated, we find that the behavior referred to as maladaptive can be, in fact, quite adaptive. For example, the youngster who babbles or laughs out of context at the events going around him may be doing so to escape demands or to get the attention that appears when he exhibits that behavior.

---

[5] Human rights committees are oversight groups that are mandated in most state regulations to minimize the risk of unnecessarily harsh and inappropriate practices. Virtually all university and human service organizations caring for people with severe disabilities utilize committees of this kind. They are typically composed of people from all walks of life and possibly an attorney. When a treatment plan calls for a procedure that meets specified criteria, this committee reviews the plan to ensure that the rights of the individual are being met.

A variety of procedures can be useful if a behavioral excess needs to be reduced. For simplicity, we reduce the procedures to four general categories: (a) reinforcing other behaviors; (b) providing choices; (c) manipulating consequences that maintain a behavior; and (d) introducing a punishing contingency (Dyer, Dunlap, & Winterling, 1990; Luce & Christian, 1981).

Reinforcing Other Behaviors

The most common and acceptable approach used with young children involves *reinforcing other behaviors.* This may be accomplished by (a) reinforcing any behavior except the targeted dysfunctional behavior at the end of an interval (differential reinforcement of other behaviors [DRO]); (b) reinforcing periods of time in which a specified rate of the targeted dysfunctional behavior is exhibited (differential reinforcement of a low rate of behavior [DRL]); or (c) reinforcing specific incompatible behaviors (differential reinforcement of incompatible behavior [DRI]). The most encouraging novel application of differential reinforcement involves communicative responses used to suppress serious disruptive, self-injurious, and aggressive behavior (Carr & Durand, 1985; Carr, Newsom, & Binkoff, 1980). Basically, a child who is taught to seek attention or support or to avoid a task through some form of language may decrease her use of other behaviors, such as aggression, to get the same reaction from her parents. Much of the training of a young child serves secondarily as differential reinforcement of other behaviors. For example, as a child learns to seek the praise of parents by responding to their requests, she will throw tantrums and resist instructions less.

Providing Choices and Preferences

A relatively new procedure that has proven effective in reducing problem behavior involves providing choices to the child and incorporating preferences during training sessions. Providing choices can be as simple as providing a choice of the next task or a reinforcer to be worked towards (Dyer, Dunlap, & Winterling, 1990). To provide choices of tasks, the teacher can show the child two or three tasks and say "Which one do you want to do?" Likewise, when providing a choice of reinforcers, the teacher can give two or three options with the phrase "Choose one!"

Preference is objectively assessed by carefully watching the child when he is given a potential reinforcer such as a toy, food, or other activity. For example, several toys may be presented to a child one at a time. To assess preference, the teacher may watch to see if he played spontaneously with the toy, resisted when it was removed, and reached for it when it was re-presented. If the child exhibited all three of these signs of preference, that toy would be designated a preferred toy. It has been found that incorporating preferences into a training session resulted in reductions of social avoidance behavior (Koegel, Dyer, & Bell, 1987), stereotypic behavior, and a number of other problem behaviors (Dyer, 1987).

Manipulating Reinforcing Consequences

When the consequences maintaining a behavior can be interrupted, we can use extinction. In many cases, it has been found that an adult's attention is maintaining the rate of a child's behavior. If that is the case, extinction would involve ignoring the behavior, which often entails proceeding as though the behavior never occurred. For example, in the early stages of training, crying and resistance to the instructions are ignored, and the therapist goes on with the lesson. Many forms of stereotypic behavior are maintained by sensory reinforcers. The sensory stimulation may be auditory, visual, kinesthetic, or a combination. The interruption of these stimuli (sensory extinction) may be useful with some children; however, it is often hard to isolate the controlling sensory stimulation (Rincover, 1978). Some of the earliest behavioral studies utilized extinction successfully (Wolf, Risley, & Meese, 1964), but there were also dramatic examples of its unsuccessful use (Corte, Wolf, & Locke, 1971; Lovaas & Simmons, 1969).

Time out in therapeutic settings usually involves removing the child from the environment that contains reinforcers. In many cases, this can be accomplished by moving the child only a short distance away from an activity, as in *contingent observation* (Porterfield, Herbert-Jackson, & Risley, 1976) or *activities time out* (Luce & Christian, 1981). Time-out failures often occur because an autistic youth can engage in preferred activities, such as self-stimulatory behavior, during its administration, or the environment from which they are removed is inadequately reinforcing (Solnick, Rincover, & Peterson, 1977). For that reason, many therapists working in intensive programs may use one of the differential reinforcement or extinction procedures.

Punishment

Most other reductive strategies utilize consequences that suppress the rates of the behaviors they follow. As discussed above, this class of procedures is referred to as punishment, or aversives (Sulzer-Azaroff & Mayer, 1991). We have also discussed the problems associated with the use of punishment. These problems in conjunction with the fact that young children can usually be effectively taught with some of the other procedures described above, make it unnecessary to fully review procedures here. More restrictive procedures are usually reserved for older individuals exhibiting hazardous behaviors that are resistant to the less controversial procedures. Procedures that professionals assisting a family in a home-based program might consider include *contingent effort* and social punishment or verbal reprimands. *Contingent effort* comprises a group of procedures that require some effort contingent upon a dysfunctional behavior when the result is a decrease of that behavior (Luce, Christian, Lipsker, & Hall, 1980). Forms of effort that we have found useful with young children include correction, overcorrection, and positive practice (Foxx & Azrin, 1972). These procedures call for the child to engage in a form of effort that serves the purpose of fixing any damage the behavior may have caused. For example, in toilet training, some children need to spend some time cleaning up after accidents before they learn not to void in their pants. In some cases, forms of effort are used that are unrelated to the inappropriate behavior or its appropriate counterpart. For example, a brief period of contingent physical exercise, easily prompted with voice prompts or pointing cues, was used to reduce bizarre verbal and aggressive behavior in autistic and schizophrenic school-aged children (Luce, Delquadri, & Hall, 1980; Luce & Hall, 1981).

Verbal reprimands (Van Houten, 1980), sometimes called social punishment (Doleys, Wells, Hobbs, Roberts, & Cartelli, 1976), have been successfully applied to youth with autism. In its mildest form, it is sometimes referred to as "negative feedback," which simply informs the youth that she has responded incorrectly. If properly implemented, the potentially reinforcing attention that results can be minimized, and the interaction carried out in a manner that is rated as neutral or positive by onlookers (Van Houten, 1980). In cases where a therapist is subjectively evaluated as too emotional or losing control, observers usually evaluate the adult negatively.

We have briefly discussed the use of behaviorally analyzed and validated procedures that may be relevant to families working with young children in a behavioral program. Our intention is simply to introduce the variety of options one might consider when working with young children. We assume that if you use any of the procedures described in this section, you will have the guidance of a professional. For that reason, considerable additional information would be needed in addition to this manual to implement the procedures discussed. An experienced professional with knowledge of the clinical literature would have access to the additional information needed to fully implement programs that are specifically designed to reduce behaviors.

SHOULD I IGNORE STEREOTYPIC BEHAVIOR OR REDIRECT IT?*

Many children with autism exhibit stereotypic behavior such as finger playing, repetitive motor responses, echolalia, or hyperlexia. These behaviors are stigmatizing and often compete with the development of new skills. Further, if left untreated, they persist over the years, usually becoming the dominant behavior that is exhibited by individuals with autism during their later years. Thus, intervention is imperative and crucial.

The research to date indicates that when the child is engaged in other activities in other ways, his stereotypic behavior becomes less evident. Thus, rather than actively punishing the stereotypical behavior, we now attempt to teach appropriate, useful skills. We can do this in several ways, described below.

Continually Engage the Child in Appropriate Behavior

Early studies examining stereotypic behavior found that this behavior often occurs when there is nothing to do. Further, even when there is something to do, the child still does not engage in the appropriate activities without being prompted to do so. Therefore, enriching the environment with toys and activities in conjunction with engaging the child in appropriate behavior is usually recommended first. A family member or therapist can continually redirect the child to participate in many appropriate activities throughout the day by providing the least amount of prompting possible to engage the child in the activity. For example, a child can be prompted to engage in toy play or daily living skills with a verbal prompt; if that is not effective, more intrusive prompting can be provided through modeling, gestures, or physical guidance.

Teach Appropriate Play Skills

In addition to providing continual redirection throughout the day, we can specifically target new skills for instruction. For young children with autism, the acquisition of appropriate toy-play skills often results in decreases in stereotypic behavior. The way to teach this toy play is through behavioral methods such as breaking the play activity down into small steps and teaching

---

* Although readers may have encountered the term "self-stimulatory behaviors" to describe the stereotypic behaviors of autism, the authors prefer to use the term "stereotypic behavior," as research has suggested that these behaviors may serve other functions for the child, in addition to or instead of providing sensory consequences.

the child each step of play by prompting and reinforcing the appropriate play behavior (Lifter, Sulzer-Azaroff, Anderson, & Cowdery, 1993; Santarcangelo, Dyer, & Luce, 1987). This works especially well if the play activity provides the child with the same type of stimulation that he receives through the stereotypic behavior. For example, if the child likes to make sounds in a stereotypic fashion, a music box would provide him with a similar type of auditory stimulation. If he likes to watch things float through the air (like feathers, lint, or particles of dust), a bubble maker would provide him with a similar type of visual stimulation.

Teach Appropriate Communication Skills

Children with autism have been observed to engage in stereotypic behavior when they are confronted with a difficult situation. Durand and Carr (1987) found that if you can teach children to ask for help in these situations (and then provide the help they need), their stereotypic behavior will decrease. This technique, called functional communication training, is described in detail by Durand (1990). Training of that kind provides the child with skills necessary to ask for things without engaging in dysfunctional behaviors. For example, a child may engage in a stereotypic behavior to solicit some kind of attention or to escape a task. When the child is taught to effectively ask for the desired attention (with a statement like "I want help" or "I want to play") or escape a task (with a statement like "I want a break"), there is a decrease in the dysfunctional behavior. The statements serve as functional communication mechanisms to decrease stereotypics.

When Beginning a Teaching Interaction, Make Sure That the Child is Not Engaged in Stereotypic Behavior

When teaching a new skill, the teacher must first get the child's attention. Because it is often difficult for the child to pay attention to the learning task while engaged in stereotypic behavior, it is advisable to begin the task when the child is not so engaged. The teacher can accomplish this by asking the child to "Get ready," or by providing a gentle physical prompt. After the child is attending, teaching begins. We used to require eye contact to indicate that a child is ready to respond. However, especially in the earlier stages of training, we may not emphasize eye contact as much as we used to, preferring that the child simply be oriented to the task and ready to respond.

When Teaching a New Skill, Use Preferred Reinforcers

Research conducted at the University of California at Santa Barbara showed that when reinforcers were "preferred," children engaged in fewer stereotypic behaviors during the learning session (Dyer, 1987). To determine if a reinforcer is preferred, it is best to conduct a preference assessment before the teaching session. To do this, the therapist gets objects and foods that he thinks the child will like. He may ask people who know the child well for ideas about preferred activities, and may sometimes ask the child what she likes. He might also observe the child to determine how she spends her time. For example, if large amounts of time are spent in stereotypic behavior with an object, that object may be a preferred reinforcer. After selecting a few potentially reinforcing objects, the therapist can present them to the child, one by one. Objects that are preferred are:

1. Those that the child plays with for more than 15 seconds without encouragement (or eats readily, if you are using food).

2. Those that the child resists having taken away from her.

3. Those that the child will try to get back when they are placed about a foot away.

Use Quickly Paced Teaching Sessions

Teaching sessions that are quickly paced can result in the child engaging in less stereotypic behavior (Dunlap, Dyer, & Koegel, 1983), probably because there is less "down time" during which the child can turn his attention away from learning. When you are quickly pacing your sessions, make sure that you start a new teaching interaction immediately after the child finishes enjoying the reinforcer received from the last teaching interaction, that is, in less than 3 seconds. Therefore, you must have all your teaching materials organized and available ahead of time so that you don't spend precious seconds between teaching interactions arranging things, allowing the child to lose his focus and return to stereotypic behavior.

Provide the Child with Aerobic Physical Exercise

Research conducted by Kern, Koegel, Dyer, Blew, & Fenton, (1982) found that stereotypic behavior can be reduced by providing aerobic physical activity to the child. Activities that involve increased use of the child's lung capacity, such as jogging, brisk walking, swimming, aerobics, jumping rope, or jumping on a trampoline may result in decreased levels of stereotypic behavior (and increased levels of responsiveness and learning!). When you do this, make sure that the activity is mildly strenuous, as evidenced by the child's increased breathing or a slightly flushed face. Remember, as with any physical activity, not to overdo it!

HOW MUCH DOES HOME-BASED INTENSIVE THERAPY COST?

The cost of therapy varies greatly depending largely on what kind of therapists are used. In some university settings, students receive credit instead of pay for time they spend with children. In other cases, research or demonstration projects support therapists, which makes the cost to parents or other funding agents (e.g., school districts) lower. Rather than review the considerable variety of tuition rates charged for therapy across the country, we will outline the fee structure we have established with school districts in New Jersey as of 1994.

Most services for children with autism (in New Jersey and throughout the United States) who are younger than 5 years old are provided in classroom settings. In many jurisdictions these preschool settings are managed by local educational agencies or public school districts; however, in some states they are managed separately by county or state agencies.

In 1993 Bancroft Rehabilitation Services developed an intensive, in-home behavioral treatment program for young children with autism. Our services created a dilemma for many school district officials. Home programs are unusual, have been abused in the past, and are difficult to manage and provide. Therefore, proposals for in-home programming can meet with significant resistance from school districts or other funders. To secure school district funding for intensive behavioral intervention for young children in New Jersey, we structure the program to meet the requirements of "home-bound instruction." This kind of programming is often used for children who are unable to attend school for other reasons (e.g., an acute illness).

To qualify for school district funding, a home-bound program requires that a teacher certified in the education of students with special needs be present for 10 hours per week spanning at least 3 days of the week. Other therapy time can be provided by uncertified personnel. Rates are set at $35.00 per hour for certified personnel, and $25.00 per hour for uncertified therapists. Employee benefits, travel expenses, clinical supervision, and administrative expenses are

built into those fees. Our therapists are reimbursed at the rate of $8.00 to $12.00 per hour, and liberal fringe benefits are provided to full-time staff. Our clinic supervisors, who oversee up to 10 cases, start at $30,000 per year plus benefits, and several fully credentialed individuals oversee the programs run with the children and administer the clinic's services. Assuming that we are providing 35 hours of therapy per week (parents provide about 5 hours per week) the cost for an extended school year (212 therapy days) runs about $45,000 per year. In some cases, school districts fund a regular school year (180 days), and negotiate the summer-school charges prior to the end of the regular school year. We strongly recommend year-round programming, especially in the early stages of training. The per diem rate for a program running the full 35-hour weeks, with the certified teacher and supervision, team-planning meetings or clinics, and administrative fees is $220.00. By comparison, our 6-hour, center-based preschool per diem is $157.42, which does not include the cost of transporting the child to the school, a service usually provided by the funder.

In some cases, parents are interested in hiring and supervising people to help serve their children. A private arrangement of that kind can often be organized without many of the expensive components required by a licensed program. Although such an arrangement does not have the safeguards built into a licensed and regulated program, some families have managed to provide successful programming in their homes with outside hired help at about half the expense ($20,000 to $25,000).

HOW MANY HOURS SHOULD MY CHILD BE IN THERAPY?

It would appear from the literature that the number of hours of therapy should be between 35 and 40 hours per week. However, some programs that have provided fewer hours of instruction have met with impressive results. It is difficult to compare different studies to answer this question. Some research studies did not specify how many hours were provided; in others the definition of the time considered "therapeutic" was imprecise.

Remember that therapeutic activities need not be confined to table-top tasks or indoor activities. Especially as the child progresses, the training is taken to a variety of environments to afford the child the opportunity to generalize and maintain behaviors learned in other settings. Although further research is needed, support for our recommendation of 35–40 hours per week is based on Lovaas (1987). Verification of that conclusion may be derived from some examples of early intervention that appear to be very similar except along the variable of number of therapeutic hours. For example, Anderson et al. (1987), Birnbrauer and Leach (1993), and Lovaas and Smith (1988) provided fewer hours with less vigorous results.

ARE THERE BEHAVIORAL TECHNIQUES THAT CAN HELP WITH SLEEP DISTURBANCES AND EATING DISORDERS?

Many children with autism never exhibit problems with eating or sleeping. However, for some children, eating and sleeping disorders may pose significant problems. Although we cannot give a complete description of behavioral techniques available for disorders of this kind, there are a number of programs that families can provide to assist the child. Severe eating and sleeping disorders may pose serious medical risks. In those cases, it is imperative that parents seek professional assistance from a qualified physician or psychologist.

In some cases, the structured schedule of the intensive behavioral intervention described in this manual can have positive effects on the sleep and mealtime behaviors of the children. We have seen both sleeping and eating disorders reduced simply by initiating a program. For children who require more than just a structured environment, a number of successful interventions are useful (e.g., Babbitt et al., in press; Piazza & Fisher, 1991a & 1991b).

Consider the Function of the Behavior

With any dysfunctional behavior, an analysis of what function a behavior serves for the child is very useful. Most behaviors are maintained by the events that come after them. For example, many behaviors result in parental attention or an interruption in the ongoing activity. If a child gets up in the middle of the night, he is likely to get parental attention as they try to return him to bed or supervise him while he is awake. This attention may maintain the dysfunctional sleep patterns. To conduct a full functional analysis, one would have to manipulate the contingent attention and determine whether the bedtime behavior changed accordingly.

A child who exhibits disruptive mealtime behavior may be reinforced by avoiding or escaping the meal. If, for example, a child wants to escape the high demands for language, or a nonpreferred food, she may become disruptive to the point that the meal is delayed until she can eat alone or a substitute meal is provided. Again, just as in the bedtime example above, in a full functional analysis of the disruptive mealtime behavior, one would remove and re-present (or otherwise manipulate) the variables suspected to be functionally related to the behavior. Because eating and sleeping are important for the health of the child and the rest of the family, it is difficult to avoid reinforcing some behaviors, and it may be impractical to conduct a full functional analysis. Therefore, we sometimes observe the behavior, hypothesize what function a behavior serves for a child, and then develop procedures accordingly.

Both examples described above focus on consequences, or events that come after a behavior. Often it is tempting to attribute a behavior to an event that precedes it. For example, a child's behavior may vary depending upon who is home at the time. Usually, however, these preceding or antecedent events are paired with a particular consequence for the behavior. When the consequence is manipulated, the behavior will change in strength even if the antecedent events do not change. For example, a child may perform a newly learned skill with his mother but not when his father is home. While it appears that the antecedent (mother's presence) is controlling the behavior, in fact it may be the case that the mother is rewarding the behavior differently than the father. When the father offers the same rewards (consequences) to the child for the new behavior, the behavior will occur.

Once the maintaining events are identified or suspected, we can propose a procedure that influences those events. In some cases, the maintaining or reinforcing events can be eliminated. For example, if attention is maintaining a behavior, attention can be withheld (the behavior is ignored) when the undesirable behavior occurs (e.g., picky eating) and presented when the desired behavior occurs (e.g., "Great eating! What a big boy you are to try that _____").

In some cases, we might have a good idea what the maintaining consequence is, but we may not know how to change it. For example, if attention is maintaining poor sleep patterns, it is hard to determine how to change the amount of attention without raising safety concerns. Seek the advice of a qualified professional if questions of that kind arise.

Eating Disorders

In the case of eating disorders, several prominent patterns are exhibited by children with autism. Some children exhibit highly selective patterns of eating. Many children with eating disorders tend to eat only one or two foods, creating health problems that may be generated by an unbalanced diet. Others may refuse food, creating an obvious concern for parents. Still others exhibit dysfunctional eating such as pica; that is, a child eats inedible substances.

A functional analysis of the eating behavior may suggest that it is controlled by events associated with eating that can be altered. Parental reaction can influence eating disorders. For example, some children's food refusal is met with parental concern, which can act as reinforcement. Prompts to eat actually may increase a child's refusals. In those cases, changes in the attention received for not eating can produce dramatic results. Other factors associated with the mealtime routine may influence the child's eating habits. For example, food refusal may be controlled by the number of people eating with the child; that is, when eating alone, some children behave differently than when they eat with others. The kinesthetic feedback or the feeling of the food may also control the behavior. This is often related to the texture of the food. For example, some children eat only crunchy foods, while others avoid all foods with that kind of texture. A wide variety of selective patterns of eating evolve.

If the function of the behavior can be determined, the behavior may be changed by eliminating its consequences (extinction), desensitizing the behavior, or providing other occasions where the function can be fulfilled or satisfied when the child exhibits the appropriate behavior. We described an example of extinction above where attention was withheld and reserved for behaviors we hoped to see more frequently in the future. Desensitization involves decreasing the effects of a stimulus. For example, if a child consistently avoids foods of certain textures or tastes, the texture of his preferred food can gradually be altered. An eating disorder may present an occasion for a powerful reinforcer that can be used to shape new behaviors. For example, a preferred food can be withheld and presented only when a new food is tasted or ingested. This would involve requiring the child to take only a very small bite before being rewarded, but gradually increasing the variety and quantity of the new food before the preferred food is made available.

Any one or a combination of the above programs can be useful to specific children. We emphasize, however, that professional assistance is often necessary when eating concerns arise.

Sleep Disorders

Some degree of bedtime disruptive behavior is common in children. Compliance problems associated with bedtime and the disruptive behaviors that accompany going to bed can often be dealt with the same way they are treated during the rest of the day. For example, during the day, a child may be prompted to finish a task when she exhibits disruptive behavior. That would be a good technique to try at bedtime also. More pronounced issues related to night waking, frequent daytime sleeping, or dangerous nighttime behaviors represent a serious predicament for families of some children with autism.

One successful method of addressing sleep problems has been presented by Piazza and her colleagues (Piazza & Fisher, 1991a & 1991b; Piazza, Fisher, & Moser, 1991). Briefly, before any intervention was introduced, an initial bedtime was established based on observations of what time the child was reliably asleep each evening. The average time asleep was calculated and 30 minutes were added to that time. When treatment was introduced, the child was not allowed to sleep before the assessed bedtime and was awakened at a predetermined appropriate hour in the morning. The bedtime hour was faded based on the child's behavior each evening. For example, if the child was asleep within 15 minutes of being put to bed, the next evening's bedtime was set 30 minutes earlier. If the child did not fall sleep within 15 minutes of the bedtime, the time she was sent to bed the next night was made 30 minutes later. If the child was still not asleep within the 15-minute period, she was kept up and awake for an hour. This was repeated as necessary until the child initiated sleep within 15 minutes of being placed in bed. The bedtime hour can be adjusted to the earliest possible time. This procedure has been effective with children exhibiting night awakenings and inappropriate daytime sleep.

ARE THERE STRATEGIES I CAN USE TO HELP MY TYPICAL CHILD INTERACT WITH HIS SIBLING?

The typical[6] siblings of children with autism are often very eager to learn ways to interact with their brother or sister and can be incredibly helpful with the therapy. If the child with autism is receiving intensive behavioral intervention, and receiving a great deal of attention from adults as a result, it would seem particularly appropriate to include the sibling(s), because some of them may feel excluded when the treatment sessions are in progress with their brother or sister. The following section describes three ways to enhance interactions between children with autism and their siblings without disabilities. Specifically, we have outlined how siblings can be useful in teaching a child with autism to (a) learn new skills; (b) engage in social interactions; and (c) engage in reciprocal play.

---

[6] *Typical* is a term now used to describe a child who does not have a disability.

Include Sibling as a Model in Discrete-Trial Training Sessions

As mentioned above, siblings can often feel excluded when their brother or sister with autism is learning new skills during intensive, discrete-trial training sessions. One way to include them in the sessions is to seat them next to the therapist (or family member) and provide them with the same instruction that is being provided to their brother or sister. Observations of this type of intervention have revealed that the typical sibling enjoys being in "the center of the action" and responds to the training sessions as a fun game. Allow the typical sibling to participate in this activity on a voluntary basis, and allow them to leave when they want to.

This type of sibling involvement gives the child with autism a model for appropriate responding, and when imitation of their sibling is reinforced, it can result in generalized imitation of appropriate behavior of the sibling outside of training sessions. Thus, the child has the rich opportunity to observe and imitate virtually every type of adaptive behavior, including communication, self-care, and appropriate play interactions that occur naturally throughout the day.

Teaching the Typical Sibling Behavioral Techniques for Teaching A Brother or Sister New Skills

Siblings of children receiving behavioral treatment at centers for autism at University of California at Santa Barbara and Claremont McKenna College learned to successfully implement therapeutic techniques to teach a variety of learning tasks (Schreibman, O'Neill, & Koegel, 1983). The procedures used to teach behavior analysis techniques to the typical siblings included the following steps:

1. The sibling and a trainer reviewed a videotape that presented examples of behavioral intervention used with children with autism.

2. The trainer described how behavioral intervention techniques could be applied to everyday situations involving problem behavior.

3. The trainer modeled the therapy with the typically developing brother or sister.

4. The trainer provided direction and feedback to the sibling while the sibling conducted therapy with his brother or sister.

This training improved the siblings' ability to use behavioral procedures at a high level of proficiency, and the siblings generally reported that they liked the training. Their brothers and sisters with autism learned a variety of tasks, such as money identification and new words for common objects.

Teaching the Typical Sibling to Engage in Social Interactions with A Brother or Sister with Autism

Siblings can also be taught to engage in social interactions with their brother or sister with autism. For example, James and Egel (1986) taught siblings to engage in interactions such as rough play, sharing, and affection. The therapist taught siblings how to begin a social interaction, how to encourage their brother or sister to respond through prompting procedures, and how to provide reinforcers to their brother or sister. These behaviors were taught through modeling of the new behaviors, as well as direction and feedback to the typical siblings while they interacted with their brother or sister.

The therapists specifically taught siblings to initiate social interactions by holding a preferred toy and waiting for their brother or sister to initiate in order to get the toy. In addition, the siblings were taught to prompt an initiation by saying "You have to ask for it first." The parents were also taught to remind the children to play as they had been taught.

Teaching the Typical Sibling to Engage in Child-Preferred Reciprocal Play

Interactions between siblings can also be increased by teaching child-preferred reciprocal play (Dyer & Harris, 1993; Harris, Dyer, & Sulzer-Azaroff, 1992). The following steps are involved in this procedure:

1. The therapist helps the (typical) sibling select a preferred toy with which she will be rewarded after the session.

2. The sibling helps her brother or sister select approximately five favorite toys that are preferred by the child with autism.

3. The sibling sets out the toys that her brother or sister has selected, showing each toy as she sets them out.

4. The sibling tells her brother or sister to pick a toy he or she would like to play with.

5. The sibling engages her brother or sister in the activity using turn-taking procedures:

   a. The sibling models a request when taking a turn.
   b. The turns last 5–10 seconds

6. The sibling follows her brother's or sister's lead. For example, the sibling may tell her brother to pick a new activity if he is bored. That is, if the child with autism frequently looks away from the activity, exhibits flat facial affect, engages in self-stimulation, or stops the activity, the sibling is taught to redirect him.

7. The sibling is taught to narrate her own play behavior.

8. At the end of the session, the sibling is rewarded by the therapist (or parent) with the preferred toy that she selected before the session.

In some cases the turn-taking sequence will need to be taught to the sibling during the sessions with his brother or sister. Modeling, role playing, and corrective feedback can be used with both children during a session if necessary.

SUMMARY

We have attempted to answer several questions that we often hear from families about to embark on a training program for their child with autism. Despite the fact that the topics covered are quite complex, we have tried to answer the questions with as little technical jargon as possible. We hope that our efforts to simplify information have not caused confusion.

As this chapter suggests, it is very common for parents to have questions about Applied Behavior Analysis. Questioning the behavioral approach is normal and appropriate, especially since the implementation of behavioral procedures can be difficult. It is not possible to answer all the questions that parents will have, but we hope our responses will be helpful.

When more questions arise, it is best to get answers from people or sources you trust. To determine whether a person is knowledgeable about the topic and trustworthy, you should seek information about the person you are asking as well (see, for example, the Shook & Favell chapter in this manual). We have found that some of the misinformation that we hear is spread by people who are unfamiliar with the topic but very willing to provide answers to questions that they are not prepared to address. Using some of the knowledge that you have gained from the chapters in this book, you might be able to discover how much a person knows about the topic before seeking his advice.

Additional answers to questions can often be found in publications about the topic. Published research is most valuable when it has been peer-reviewed. Some literature is not peer-reviewed (e.g., the Internet,

brochures, unedited remarks at a conference, and popular press releases), and some is more extensively reviewed for clarity and validity. For example, in this edited manual, material was reviewed by one or more knowledgeable individuals before it was published. Other publication sources such as scientific journals (e.g., *Journal of Applied Behavior Analysis*) undergo a comprehensive critical review by several top researchers in the field. For that reason, articles from peer-reviewed sources seldom express opinions that are not well founded in the research literature.

REFERENCES

Anderson, S. R., Avery, D. L., Di Pietro, E. K., Edwards, G. L., & Christian, W. P. (1987). Intensive home-based early intervention with autistic children. *Education and Treatment of Children, 10,* 352–256.

Babbitt, R. L., Hoch, T. A., Coe, D. A., Cataldo, M. F., Kelly, K., & Perman, J. A. (in press). Behavioral assessment and treatment of pediatric feeding disorders: A review and program description. *Journal of Developmental and Behavioral Pediatrics.*

Birnbrauer, J. S., & Leach, D. J. (1993). The Murdoch early intervention program after two years. *Behaviour Change, 10,* 63–74.

Carr, E. G., & Durand, V. M. (1985). Reducing behavior problems through functional communication training. *Journal of Applied Behavior Analysis, 18,* 111–127.

Carr, E. G., Newsom, C. O., & Binkoff, J. A. (1980). Escape as a factor in the aggressive behavior of two retarded children. *Journal of Applied Behavior Analysis, 13,* 101–118.

Corte, H. E., Wolf, M. M., & Locke, B. J. (1971). A comparison of procedures for eliminating self-injurious behavior of retarded adolescents. *Journal of Applied Behavior Analysis, 4,* 201–213.

Doleys, D., Wells, K. C., Hobbs, S. A., Roberts, M. W., & Cartelli, L. M. (1976). The effects of social punishment upon compliance: A comparison of time out and positive practice. *Journal of Applied Behavior Analysis, 9,* 471–482.

Dunlap, G., Dyer, K., & Koegel, R. L. (1983). Autistic self-stimulation and intertrial interval duration. *American Journal of Mental Deficiency, 88,* 194–202.

Durand, V. M. (1990). *Severe behavior problems: A functional communication training approach.* New York: Guilford Press.

Durand, V. M., & Carr, E. G. (1987). Social influences of self-stimulatory behavior: Analysis and treatment application. *Journal of Applied Behavior Analysis, 20,* 119–132.

Dyer, K. (1987). The competition of autistic stereotyped behavior with usual and specially assessed reinforcers. *Research in Developmental Disabilities, 8,* 607–626.

Dyer, K., & Harris, T. (1993). Teaching child-preferred reciprocal play to children with autism in the preschool setting. *Association for Advancement of Behavior Therapy's Autism Special Interest Group Newsletter, 8,* 1–5.

Dyer, K. D., Dunlap, G., & Winterling, V. (1990). The effects of choice-making on the problem behaviors of students with severe handicaps. *Journal of Applied Behavior Analysis, 23,* 515–524.

Favell, J. E., & Greene, J. W. (1981). *How to treat self-injurious behavior,* Austin, TX: PRO-ED.

Favell, J. E., Favell, J. E., & Risley, T. R. (1981). A quality-assurance system for ensuring client rights in mental retardation facilities. In G. T. Hannah, W. P. Christian, & H. B. Clark (Eds.), *Preservation of client rights.* New York: Macmillan.

Fenske, E. C., Zalenski, S., Krantz, P. J., & McClannahan, L. E. (1985). Age at intervention and treatment outcome for autistic children in a comprehensive intervention program. *Analysis and Intervention in Developmental Disabilities, 5,* 49–58.

Foxx, R. M., & Azrin, N. H. (1972). Restitution: A method of eliminating aggressive-disruptive behavior of retarded and brain-damaged patients. *Behavior Research and Therapy, 10,* 15–27.

Harris, S. L., & Handleman, J. S. (1994). *Preschool programs for children with autism.* Austin, TX: PRO-ED.

Harris, T., Dyer, K., & Sulzer-Azaroff, B. (1992, May). *Training teachers in a preschool classroom to promote reciprocal interactions between typical children and children with autism.* Paper presented at the Annual Convention of the Association for Behavior Analysis, Chicago.

James, S. D., & Egel, A. L. (1986). A direct prompting strategy for increasing reciprocal interactions between handicapped and nonhandicapped siblings. *Journal of Applied Behavior Analysis, 19,* 173–186.

Kern, L., Koegel, R. L., Dyer, K., Blew, P. A., & Fenton, L. R. (1982). The effects of physical exercise on self-stimulation and appropriate responding in autistic children. *Journal of Autism and Developmental Disorders, 12,* 399–419.

Koegel, R. L., Dyer, K., & Bell, L. (1987). The influence of child-preferred activities on autistic children's social behavior. *Journal of Applied Behavior Analysis, 20,* 243–252.

Lifter, K., Sulzer-Azaroff, B., Anderson, S., & Cowdery, G. (1993). Teaching play activities to preschool children with disabilities: The importance of developmental considerations. *Journal of Early Intervention, 17*(2), 139–159.

Lovaas, O. I. (1987). Behavioral treatment and normal educational and intellectual functioning in young autistic children. *Journal of Consulting and Clinical Psychology, 55,* 3–9.

Lovaas, O. I., & Favell, J. E. (1987). Protection for clients undergoing aversive/restrictive interventions. *Education and Treatment of Children, 10*(4), 311–325.

Lovaas, O. I., & Simmons, J. Q. (1969). Manipulation of self-destruction in three retarded children. *Journal of Applied Behavior Analysis, 2,* 143–157.

Lovaas, O. I., & Smith, T. (1988). Intensive behavioral treatment for young autistic children. In B. B. Lahey & A. E. Kazdin (Eds.), *Advances in clinical child psychology* (Vol. 11, pp. 285–324). New York: Plenum.

Lovaas, O. I., Ackerman, A. B., & Taubman, M. T. (1983). An overview of behavioral treatment of autistic persons. In M. Rosenbaum, C. Franks, & Y. Jaffe (Eds.), *Perspectives on behavior therapy in the 1980s.* New York: Springer Publishing.

Luce, S. C., & Christian, W. P. (1981). *How to reduce autistic and severely maladaptive behaviors.* Austin, TX: PRO-ED.

Luce, S. C., & Hall, R. V. (1981). Contingent exercise: A mild but powerful procedure used with differential reinforcement to reduce bizarre verbal behavior. *Education and Treatment of Children, 4,* 309–329.

Luce, S. C., Christian, W. P., Lipsker, L. E., & Hall, R. V. (1980). Response cost: A case for specificity. *The Behavior Analyst, 4,* 78–80.

Luce, S. C., Delquadri, J., & Hall, R. V. (1980). Contingent exercise: A mild but powerful procedure used to reduce inappropriate verbal and aggressive behavior. *Journal of Applied Behavior Analysis, 13,* 583–594.

McEachin, J. J., Smith, T., & Lovaas, O. I. (1993). Long-term outcome for children with autism who received early intensive behavioral treatment. *American Journal on Mental Retardation, 97,* 359–372.

Perry, R., Cohen, I., & DeCarlo, R. (1995). Case study: Deterioration, autism, and recovery in two siblings. *Journal of the American Academy of Child and Adolescent Psychiatry, 34,* 232–237.

Piazza, C. C., & Fisher, W. (1991a). A faded bedtime with response cost protocol for treatment of multiple sleep problems in children. *Journal of Applied Behavior Analysis, 24,* 129–140.

Piazza, C. C., & Fisher, W. (1991b). Bedtime fading in the treatment of pediatric insomnia. *Journal of Behaviour Therapy and Experimental Psychiatry, 22,* 53–56.

Piazza, C. C., Fisher, W., & Moser, H. (1991). Behavioral treatment of sleep dysfunction in patients with Rhett syndrome. *Brain Development, 13,* 232–237.

Porterfield, J. K., Herbert-Jackson, E., & Risley, T. R. (1976). Contingent observation: An effective and acceptable procedure for reducing disruptive behavior of young children in a group setting. *Journal of Applied Behavior Analysis, 9,* 55–64.

Rincover, A. (1978). Sensory extinction: A procedure for elimination of self-stimulatory behavior in psychotic children. *Journal of Abnormal Child Psychology, 6,* 299–301.

Santarcangelo, S., Dyer, K., & Luce, S. C. (1987). Generalized reduction of disruptive behavior through specific toy training. *The Journal of the Association for Persons with Severe Handicaps, 12,* 38–44.

Schreibman, L., O'Neill, R. E., & Koegel, R. L. (1983). Behavioral training for siblings of autistic children. *Journal of Applied Behavior Analysis, 16,* 129–138.

Solnick, J. V., Rincover, A., & Peterson, C. (1977). Some determinants of reinforcing and punishing effects of time-out. *Journal of Applied Behavior Analysis, 10,* 415–424.

Sulzer-Azaroff, B., & Mayer, G. R. (1991). *Behavior analysis for lasting change.* New York: Harcourt Brace Jovanovitch.

Van Houten, R. (1980). Social validation: The evaluation of standards of competency for target behaviors. *Journal of Applied Behavior Analysis, 12,* 581–591.

Wolf, M. M., Risley, T. R., & Meese, H. (1964). Application of operant conditioning procedures to the behavior problems of an autistic child. *Behaviour Research and Therapy, 1,* 305–312.

CHAPTER EIGHTEEN

In Search of Michael

Margaret Harris

Everything about Michael's development was normal for the first 18 months of his life. He was very happy, cuddly, alert, and attentive. Between 18 and 24 months of age, he did not develop much language, and the few words he had acquired were used less often. By age 2, his language skills were lagging in comparison to what his brother's had been at the same age. William, his only sibling, is 22 months older than Michael. We rationalized our concerns, because his brother was very verbose and outgoing and did a lot of the talking for Michael. Michael also relied heavily on a pacifier and spent time with a Spanish-speaking baby-sitter.

Over the next 6 months, he began to lose what little speech he had acquired and slowly developed strange play habits: he tapped sticks, waved string, and spun wheels; he played alone and engaged in what I later learned was inappropriate toy play. The tantrums and frustration level were increasing rapidly, but we attributed these actions to his lack of language. He was becoming less interested in his brother and other friends and spent more time playing alone. The changes were so gradual and subtle that they were not readily apparent to those who saw him every day.

It took visiting my parents and extended family, who had not seen him in at least 6 months, for us to fully recognize that something was wrong. After a week with them, my husband and I were told by my parents that they and other family members were concerned about Michael. My mother even suggested that he might have a hearing problem or autism. How could my family think this? Yes, he was different from other children, but autistic? At the time, I did not know enough about autism to respond rationally to their observations, but I was terrified by their statements. I immediately called Michael's pediatrician at home and told her of my family's concerns. She assured me she did not think there was anything wrong with him, but agreed it would make everyone feel better if a comprehensive speech and developmental evaluation were performed. She referred me to a diagnostic and treatment center for communication disorders affiliated with a local university. I called that day and requested an application.

We returned home from our trip early and found we could not get an appointment for an evaluation at the center for a month. I was anxious to find some answers and began researching autism and speech disorders. Most of the current material I could find was in the local medical school library. I got a copy of *The Diagnostic and Statistical Manual of Mental Disorders* (DSM-III-R) and copied the chapter covering autism. Although all of the symptoms of the disorder were not fully applicable to Michael, some were. He had an unusual combination of subtle characteristics that made me uncomfortable.

At the recommendation of a friend, I contacted the director of another speech and language evaluation clinic and took Michael to see her a few days later. She observed him and told us there was a developmental language delay, but she was reluctant to comment on our concern that he had autism until he was 3 years old. I later heard of this 3-year threshold from several other professionals. She suggested a comprehensive hearing test, but the results were normal. We eliminated deafness from the list of possible explanations for Michael's problems.

The following week was Michael's evaluation at the center for communication disorders. My husband and I had been interviewed at the center for 2 hours the prior week and gave a complete family medical and developmental history. Michael was exactly $2\frac{1}{2}$ years old at this time. The actual evaluation was conducted by a team consisting of a psychologist, an audiologist, and a speech pathologist. Three hours of comprehensive hearing, speech, developmental, and cognitive testing were performed while we waited anxiously behind a one-way mirror. I was sure there would be some reasonable explanation for Michael's behavior and was willing to accept developmental delays, but was not fully prepared for what we were about to be told.

The evaluation results showed Michael's developmental age at approximately half his chronological age and that, according to the Childhood Autism Rating Scale (CARS), he was in the severely autistic range. When we asked about treatment, we were told there was little we could do and that we should prepare for a difficult road ahead. They suggested we contact the local school district and make arrangements for Michael to enter their autism program in 6 months, when he turned 3. Although we asked, no alternative forms of treatment were suggested. The words "Your son is severely autistic" were hammering in my head. I thought that there had to be other people who heard these same words and said "NO. This isn't the end of it!" I was determined to find these people and their solutions and do whatever it took to make Michael better.

We also were told we could enroll Michael in a 10-hour-per-week preschool program for children with developmental language delays at the center for communication disorders. Each of the 10 children in the program was paired with a graduate student of speech pathology who worked one-on-one with a child. No other options were apparent, and we agreed to enroll Michael in the class, which started in 1 month.

I was unwilling to accept that these options were all I could do for Michael and continued researching autism. Second opinions only confused the situation and depleted finances. Another psychologist diagnosed him as having a "developmental delay of unknown origin" and would not discuss the possibility of autism until he was 3 years old. I had heard enough conclusions by this point based on behavior and wanted him to be evaluated by a physician. A pediatric neurologist's diagnosis was Pervasive Developmental Disorder, Not Otherwise Specified (PDD-NOS) and, again, he wanted to wait 6 months before diagnosing him with autism. He ordered a battery of medical tests, but all were normal.

A month after the autism diagnosis, the language school began. We didn't think it would solve the problem, but were glad to be doing something, however inadequate, about the situation. He seemed to be getting worse, but I thought it was because we were painfully aware of his autism and constantly watching him. In fact, he was deteriorating. He was using virtually no language and became even more withdrawn from the family. It seemed as if the joy had gone out of him, and he was usually discontent with whatever we tried to do to make him happy.

On the first day of school, the mother of another child in the class told me about a book titled *Let Me Hear Your Voice,* by Catherine Maurice. She said it outlined behavioral intervention and the incredible results one family had achieved. I bought the book that day and read it nonstop. It seemed so reasonable and effective, and it was the only rational treatment that gave us hope. Why hadn't any of the professionals, from whom we sought advice mentioned this form of treatment? I asked each one of them, as well as the head of the school district's autism program, a developmental pediatrician, other psychologists, and speech pathologists about it and was shocked by their consistent negative responses. "You will ruin your child if you try behavioral intervention." "Don't try it." "It doesn't work." "All the children who were in the UCLA program are now institutionalized despite what you may read." "It's basically child abuse (referring to the use of aversives)." "You'll end up with a trained seal or a robot."

Their criticism of behavioral intervention was not based on current research or studies, but rather on stale information and what they had learned about this modality many years ago. I asked each of them very specific questions about behavioral intervention and found that they had not bothered to keep up with changes in this field. They all seemed content to criticize a treatment about which they knew very little. But after reading *Let Me Hear Your Voice,* I was still convinced that it was our best hope. I found a number of other treatment programs, but most appeared to encourage acceptance of autism as a permanent condition. Other options offered false hope at enormous prices. I contacted Bernard Rimland, Ph.D., director of the Autism Research Institute, who was profiled in the book as a leading researcher of autism. We spoke at length about behavioral intervention. He answered all of my questions, and I ordered volumes of the research papers from the institute. After reading the research and conclusions, I was more convinced than ever about its effectiveness and appropriateness for Michael.

The thought of setting up, maintaining, and funding such a program was initially overwhelming. My husband and I discussed how we would fund the therapy and agreed to use our savings, originally intended to cover college expenses for our two sons. Based on what we had read about autism, there would be no college for Michael if we didn't do something immediately. We had also just found out that my husband's firm was closing its local office. He was offered a transfer to another city, but we decided this was an inappropriate time to move. A move would also have delayed the start of our program. My husband found another job here, and we stayed. Behavioral intervention was our best hope, and we agreed to make whatever sacrifices necessary to diligently pursue it. We kept Michael in the language school while we set up a home-based program.

I sent Michael's evaluation from the center for communication disorders along with a letter requesting a workshop to O. Ivar Lovaas, Ph.D., at The Clinic for the Behavioral Treatment of Children at UCLA (another resource found in *Let Me Hear Your Voice*). I received a response stating that the wait was at least 6 to 8 months. While we waited, I purchased several copies of *The ME Book* by Dr. Lovaas, and searched locally for professionals to help us set up a program. In a guide to local private schools, which listed alternative institutions for special needs, I was pleasantly surprised to find a center that specialized in the treatment of autistic children. Although I knew I did not want to enroll Michael there, I thought it would be the logical place to find the professionals we needed to set up a home-based program. In fact, two of the teachers there had recently teamed with a speech pathologist and formed a consulting group. They were very familiar with behavioral intervention and had educational backgrounds and extensive experience in working with autistic children.

I met with this consulting group immediately, told them of our needs, and hired them on the spot. We agreed to use *The ME Book,* while pursuing a comprehensive program that included behavioral and speech-language intervention. We also agreed not to use any form of aversive and to use only primary reinforcers (goldfish crackers in Michael's case) for about the first 2 weeks. After that, we phased out the primary reinforcers and used only secondary, or social, reinforcers. Praise, tickles, and hugs were very motivating for him. The consultants then came to our home, met Michael, and we discussed their proposed program for him. I had some concerns because this was the first home program they had set up, but was comfortable with their combined experience and backgrounds and recognized that our local options were limited.

I made fliers stating that we were hiring students to work with our autistic son in a home-based behavioral intervention program. I placed the fliers in the psychology, education, and speech pathology departments at local colleges and universities. I also talked to professors in each of these departments and told them of our situation and intent to start a program. I called every physician, pediatrician, psychologist, and teacher I knew and requested their help in locating people to work with Michael. Each person I contacted received an information package of materials on behavioral intervention I had collected from Dr. Rimland and from hours I had spent at the medical school library. This package served two purposes: to educate them on the importance of early behavioral intervention and to validate my convictions of its effectiveness. I was a full-time mother with no background in this field. My 10 years in corporate finance had not prepared me for this role.

I had an excellent response to the fliers and interviewed four students the next week. My prerequisites for working in the program were simple: a willingness to work in a challenging environment, a belief that change is possible, a commitment to Michael and the program, and an unlimited supply of patience. I did not want to glamorize the program or underestimate its importance. I stressed that progress would probably be slow and that the changes would take time. I was very impressed by the quality of each applicant and hired all four. I gave each therapist a copy of *The ME Book, Let Me Hear Your Voice,* Michael's initial program prepared by the consultants, and an information package. I asked them to read everything before our first workshop, scheduled for a week and a half away.

I set up Michael's bedroom as our therapy room, but continued to have him sleep there. I installed vertical shelving around his room and found that placing all items out of his reach at least forced him to point to what he wanted or look at me for help. He had virtually no language or even gestures by this point (2 years, 8 months). His usual means of expressing desire was screaming, crying, or jumping up and down until he got what he wanted. He had also become very resourceful and independent and would secure most items by himself without attempting to seek assistance. Next, I had to figure out exactly what to put on these shelves. I had discussed the drills with the consultants earlier, but was on my own when it came to buying or making what was needed for the program. I went to several retail stores that specialized in educational and developmental material and purchased items that would facilitate each drill: two each of ten basic objects, and pictures of these objects, for matching and giving in receptive language drills; first-word books for expressive labeling drills; Play-Doh, crayons, peg boards, stringing beads, and puzzles for fine motor drills; a mini trampoline and various balls for gross motor drills; a farm with animals, a road map, and a garage with cars for interactive play time, which started each session; and a small, sturdy table and two chairs, at which many drills would be performed. Magazines and newspapers, especially the advertising circulars, were good sources of pictures with which to make picture cards. These cards were subsequently expanded and later used for drills in categories, functions, actions, emotions, phonics, color/shape discrimination, and occupations. At the suggestion of several speech pathologists, I installed a large mirror at ground level in one corner of his room to be used for verbal imitation drills. The room was set up, the initial program was written, the people were hired, the workshop was scheduled, and we couldn't begin soon enough.

The week before the workshop, I was in Indiana and visited the Institute for the Study of Developmental Disabilities at the Indiana Resource Center for Autism in Bloomington. There was a wealth of information there on autism and developmental disabilities. I had called ahead and asked to meet with anyone who might be able to contribute to our program. I met with Kim Davis, an adapted physical education teacher and technical assistance specialist. Kim has devoted an enormous amount of time and effort to teaching physical education to students with autism (and has even written a book on the subject). She told me in 10 minutes how to teach Michael to ride a tricycle. I had tried in vain for the preceding 6 months. She told me to stand in front of him on the tricycle, bend down to his eye level, place my hands on his knees, and alternately push gently on each knee while saying "Push." He rode a tricycle within 3 days and also learned the word *push*. Several of Kim's other suggestions for gross motor skills were incorporated into our program, and I went home with a box of information that proved to be of great value.

During most of the initial workshop, our three consultants outlined and demonstrated each drill at length for our four therapists, my husband, and myself. We discussed the format of each session and tried to anticipate any problems we might encounter. Each of the therapists would work with a different consultant for the first three sessions. They would be on their own the fourth session. This allowed both the therapists to have the assistance they needed and each of the consultants to observe and correct each therapist immediately. I was pleasantly surprised by the therapists' understanding of the program and ability to carry out the objectives effectively. The program had started, and that was a big relief to my husband and me, but Michael was not as thrilled about it. His behavior the first few days vacillated between curiosity and complete defiance. The novelty of the sessions had worn off by the end off the first week. The tantrums increased dramatically, and he became so resistant that I wondered if anything at all was being accomplished. I had read in *The ME Book* that resistance was a good sign of prognosis, but knowing this did not make hearing the continuous screaming any easier.

The initial drills were very basic: verbal imitation (sounds only), nonverbal imitation, gross and fine motor play, matching, and self-help skills. Each session lasted 2 to 3 hours, and we targeted one or two sessions per day depending on the therapists' class schedules. We realized this was not enough and moved rapidly to two sessions of 3 hours each daily. Michael attended the language school in the mornings, and home sessions took place in the afternoon. At first, he tired easily from the long days, and we considered removing him from the school. We discussed the home program with the director of the school and were glad that she agreed with what we were doing. After all, it was one of her colleagues at the center who had told us, "You will ruin your child if you try behavioral intervention." She reviewed the drills and objectives of his home program and incorporated them into Michael's work at school. We decided that for now he would remain in the class, since the director was willing to work with us. We did not consider the time he spent at school as part of his program. Thirty to forty hours of home therapy on top of the ten hours at school was our goal.

There was a decided unevenness to his progress in the program. Receptive commands and gross and fine motor skills were his strengths, while verbal imitation was the most difficult area. He had babbled constantly, almost as if he understood what he was saying, since around the time he turned 2 years old. But no one could understand the gibberish he produced. He did have, however, about 15 appropriately used words at the start of the program. I put a poster on the back of his door listing these words and asked each therapist to add to them, noting the date, as the new words came. The poster remained unchanged for weeks. The therapists would sit in front of the mirror and try to get him to imitate simple sounds. He would watch the movements of their mouths and listen to the associated sounds, but seemed perplexed by the correlation. After about 1 month, he began to imitate sounds, which quickly became words. He started to label objects and was so proud that he could finally put words to items he knew so well. Michael's intrinsic motivation has had a lot to do with his success in the program. It's almost as if the more he knows, the more he realizes he doesn't know. Once the language started coming, the verbal floodgates opened. The empty poster was soon filled and removed from the door. (Every time I get discouraged about his progress, I pull it out as a reminder of how far we have come.)

By the end of the second month, he could appropriately label about 150 objects and had a total vocabulary of approximately 200 words. He was beginning to learn adjectives and verbs, but most of his expressive language still consisted of nouns. He did not call people by names or use much spontaneous language other than labeling. We began to model adjective/noun and noun/verb combinations for him. Three months after the program began, we enrolled him in a mother's day-out program because his social interaction had improved so much. He began to play actively with his brother and became extremely fond of visiting neighborhood children who, until now, had gone unnoticed when in our home. Within 4 months of the start of the program, we decided that our goal for his expressive language was utterances of at least two words and to have him respond to any one-word statement by expanding it. Most of his speech consisted of concrete statements as opposed to abstract thinking. His receptive language outpaced his expressive, and we could tell that he understood almost everything said to him if it was said slowly and clearly. We introduced full sentence structures, and he responded quite well, but they seemed somewhat rote. Within 6 months, he was using some complete sentences, but most of his spontaneous expressions were two- to three-word combinations. He also began repeating much of what was said to him (echolalia), but we modeled appropriate responses and ignored the echoing. It gradually faded, but when something was said to him that he didn't understand, he repeated it. Conversation was difficult for Michael, but improved daily.

Michael initially resisted the self-help drills, especially toilet training. From the start of the program, we were taking him to the bathroom every half hour, but he would not go if unassisted. After 4 months of little progress in training pants, we put him in underwear. During the next 2 weeks, he averaged about five "accidents" a day, but he soon learned that he did not like being wet or dirty and began going to the bathroom spontaneously. We worked on dressing and undressing as part of every session. He also was initially resistant to brushing his teeth and washing his hands, but all of these skills improved and became part of his everyday life. Most of the stereotypic behaviors had faded, but some were replaced by different forms.

There was a direct correlation between his increase in language and acquired skills and decrease in tantrums, frustration level, and stereotypic behaviors. He learned basic pre-academic skills (alphabet, numbers, colors, shapes) very quickly. These skills were used to expand subsequent drills: prepositions, pronouns, actions, emotions, functions, categories, phonics, choices, block imitation, color/shape discrimination, expressive and receptive commands, nonverbal imitation, writing, occupations, pretend, counting, conversation, yes/no, and who is it? Periods of rapid development were often followed by plateaus of limited progress. These leveling-off phases were very frustrating for all of us, but we reminded ourselves of Michael's overall pattern of growth.

Michael was outpacing the revisions made to his program by the consultants, and we were relying less on their input and more on the therapists' input. He had become very fond of each therapist and usually looked forward to his time spent with them. He still had periods of resistance, but overall was gradually becoming more compliant. When he was in the mood to work, we saw incredible results; when he wasn't, it was difficult for everyone. During team meetings every 2 weeks, we reviewed his progress in each drill and made any necessary changes to them. One therapist outlined *The ME Book* and modified the ideas drawn from it to apply to Michael's program. Incidental teaching, or using everyday experiences, was a big part of his learning experience, and we continually searched for new ways to expand and improve on our methods. (When Michael was having trouble making choices, one therapist took him to our refrigerator. She asked him if he wanted to smell chocolate or vinegar. He usually responded with the last option offered and said "Vinegar." She moved on to many other choices and came back to the chocolate/vinegar choice. He stopped, thought about it, and said "Chocolate!"

As we did more programming on our own, I felt we needed another outside professional to review and comment on our program. I heard that Justin Goldman, a senior therapist from a behavioral intervention center in Encino, California, had moved to our city to set up programs for two families. I contacted him, explained the situation, and requested a consultation and evaluation of our program. Justin spent about 2 hours with Michael and reviewed our program and progress. He was pleasantly surprised that we had done so well. Although I tried not to belittle any successes, I continually worried that we weren't "doing it right." After his visit, I realized that whatever worked for Michael was "right," whether it followed any specific behavioral intervention program exactly or not. We hired Justin to revise the format of our drills and data collection and used our own increasing understanding of Michael's particular learning needs to decide which drills should be added, expanded, or eliminated. Our therapists knew their jobs backwards and forwards and could tell me at any given moment what Michael's strengths or weaknesses were. They contributed more and more input and came up with suggested drills and tasks to expand and generalize his acquired knowledge.

It became apparent that one of our three original consultants, Barbie Blizzard, was extremely effective working with Michael. She was the principal and a teacher at the autism school where I had found the consulting group. She had a lot of experience in working with autistic children, had given us excellent practical advice, and was instrumental in redirecting unwanted behaviors. Justin's programming knowledge and her practical experience and understanding of Michael's needs made a great combination. We hired her independently of the consulting group to work with Justin. He was responsible for program modifications, and Barbie was responsible for training and working with our therapists. Seeing them work together made me realize that I could combine the talents of two (or more) people whom I felt worked well with my child, even though they had never met or worked together before. We were a team, and I stressed to everyone that no one person was in charge: we all worked for Michael.

I put our name on the waiting list for a workshop with the UCLA Clinic for the Behavioral Treatment of Children the same week that we started our home program. Ten months later, a consultant called to say that our name had reached the top of the list. We gathered all of the people who had worked with Michael and held the UCLA workshop. At this time our home program was almost a year old and was going very well. We had already made enormous progress.

The consultant helped with issues relating to school, shadowing (sending a therapist to school with Michael), and peer play programs. These were very timely topics. However, she also wanted us to return to an almost exclusively discrete-trial format and to more basic skill levels. But we were already working on the generalization of acquired knowledge and improvement of social skills and we felt that to go back to this format was a step backward for him. The time we really needed discrete-trial training was at the beginning of our home program.

Michael attended the language school for a total of two semesters. Attending the school alone probably would not have achieved the same dramatic results, but when combined with the work we were doing at home it allowed Michael to generalize a lot of the skills acquired. The student clinicians and the director of the school were very helpful in providing insight into his achievements at school and suggestions for areas of improvement. At the encouragement of the director, we removed him from the language school. He needed to be around more verbal children who could be appropriate models for language and behavior. By the time we left the school, Michael had gone from one of the most to one of the least severely impaired students in his class. Encouraged by the progress Michael had made, five additional families had set up home-based behavioral intervention programs.

Michael attended a mother's day-out program for several months before entering a regular preschool. During this time, his language and appropriate play skills increased dramatically. When I began to look for a regular preschool for Michael, I felt as though I were walking on eggshells. If I told the staff of potential schools about the "language delay" (as I referred to Michael's autism), I was usually told that he would be put in a class 1 year younger. That's exactly what he didn't need. He needed age-appropriate social interaction more than anything at this point. If I did not tell them about it, I worried that he would not be able to fit in and we would put Michael in a potentially frustrating situation.

We first decided to send him to a regular preschool without a shadow. However, it became apparent after a few weeks that he was not ready to attend school alone. We removed him from that school and placed him in another regular preschool with a therapist shadow. Neither of these schools knew of his diagnosis or home program. We told the second school that the therapist was a "language tutor" and was there to model appropriate language and play skills.

He has made the transition quite well and now loves school. Meanwhile, our home program has been modified to reflect more school-oriented activities, such as circle time, worksheets, coloring, imitative play, play descriptions, writing, and drawing.

We have come a long way, but still have concerns. It has been 16 months since Michael's diagnosis and 14 months since the beginning of our home program. A total of fifteen therapists (an average of seven at any give time) and three consultants have worked with Michael during nearly 2,000 therapy hours. We have spent thousands of dollars on therapy, workshops, consultations, and materials. Would we do it again? Absolutely. Would we recommend this treatment to other families whose children receive a diagnosis of autism or PDD-NOS? No question. Has the last year and a half been easy? Not at all, but when I think of the alternatives we faced 16 months ago, this has been the most rewarding time of our lives. This form of therapy has been extremely effective for Michael.

We are prepared to continue Michael's home program indefinitely, modifying the pace to his level of progress. Every victory is celebrated with the joy you would imagine and with trepidation before the next hurdle we will encounter. We have so much for which to be grateful. We received an early diagnosis, were fortunate to receive guidance to pursue behavioral intervention, and found good consultants and therapists. The support from our family and friends has been incredible. We also had the advantage of learning from the experiences of those who went before us and refused to believe that there was nothing that could be done for the future of an autistic child.

CHAPTER NINETEEN

Rebecca's Story

Elizabeth Harrington

I am the mother of two daughters, ages four and three. My husband and I live in a small suburb in New Jersey. Our older daughter, Holly, is a blond-haired, blue-eyed chatterbox who has always been a daily joy. Our younger daughter, Rebecca, a playful child with delicate, doll-like features and huge blue eyes, is autistic. We received a diagnosis of her condition 15 months ago when Rebecca was 22 months old (actual diagnosis: Pervasive Developmental Delay). Since January of 1994, we have had a behavioral therapy program in place in our home, and Rebecca has been receiving between 34 and 40 hours per week of instruction. Although I would unequivocally recommend this type of intensive behavioral intervention to any parent of an autistic child, and although my husband and I have seen our daughter make more progress than we ever would have imagined, it is an all-encompassing and exhausting experience.

Rebecca's case was somewhat unusual because she was the product of a very fragile pregnancy (I was a DES daughter) that ended 2 months prematurely with a long labor and a difficult forceps delivery. Rebecca weighed just over 4 pounds and was kept in the neonatal intensive care unit for several weeks, during which time she experienced episodes of apnea (the cessation of breathing) and bradycardia (a slowing of the heart rate). At 5 months of age, we discovered that Rebecca had a condition known as benign external hydrocephalus (water outside of the brain) that we were told required no treatment and would probably resolve itself within a few years. Because of this unusual start in life, the doctors tended to blame her "symptoms" on Rebecca's prematurity, and they kept telling us that she would catch on and catch up. Rebecca never really had any words. Once or twice when she was about 14 months old, we thought we heard approximations of *mama, dada,* and *baba,* but that was all there was in terms of speech, and even those sounds were short-lived. Despite the doctors' reassurances, I could not understand why Rebecca's behavior had become so odd. Although she had caught up physically and was very strong and pretty, I began to notice at about 15 months of age that she had ceased making eye contact, that she did not respond to her name, and that she had begun to engage in weird, perseverative play activities that are all too familiar to parents of autistic children. When my husband would come home from work and enter the kitchen where we would be playing or eating supper, Rebecca would not even look up. This was in such marked contrast to her sister's enthusiastic antics and, to me, could not be explained away by prematurity. At her 18-month check-ups by both her pediatrician (who is assistant head of pediatrics at a major teaching hospital in New York City) and by her pediatric neurologist (who is affiliated with the same hospital and was also the father of a 2-year-old child), I described Rebecca's symptoms and asked if she was autistic. Both physicians immediately said no (although they offered no alternative explanation for her behavior) and advised us to bring her back in 4 months. Four months later, I was a complete basket case and was utterly convinced that Rebecca was autistic. However, I needed a doctor's sacred word before I could get anyone to listen to or help me. I should say here that my husband and both of our families, though becoming a bit more anxious than they had been, were still in denial. We returned to the pediatric neurologist 2 days before Christmas in 1993 and were told at that time that it was "too soon" to make a diagnosis. During the entire time that my husband and I were speaking with the doctor, Rebecca never once made eye contact with any of the three of us and, at the end of our visit, she began walking around in circles in his office. We thanked him, wished him a Merry Christmas, and walked across the hall to the office of the most senior pediatric neurologist at this hospital, whose name I had been given by the mother of an autistic boy who lives in the next town from us. We could not get an appointment until early January, so we left the hospital and tried to make it through the holidays before the inevitable was confirmed and our lives would be changed forever.

This doctor did diagnose Rebecca, and he strongly advised us to set up a home program using the method of Applied Behavior Analysis. He said that he had seen children make enormous gains using this approach. I had already heard quite a bit about Applied Behavior Analysis and about home programming from the mother I mentioned earlier. She had had a home program in place since the preceding summer and her son was talking and, overall, doing extremely well. I had already decided from speaking at length with this mother and from seeing her son and her program that I wanted to try this method with Rebecca. We drove home from the hospital in a snowstorm, and I started to work the phones in order to assemble a team of therapists who could help our daughter. As I write this, it seems as though I am describing someone devoid of emotion, but I had had a long and very lonely grieving process throughout the preceding fall. Despite the fact that I was fully prepared for the diagnosis, it hit hard. I had many tearful days and many sleepless nights. My husband is a very kind and sensitive person, and I know that he was suffering terribly. I could be of no comfort to him because I had nothing left over after soldiering through a day. All my energies in the weeks following the diagnosis were directed to coordinating Rebecca's care and to keeping my older daughter from being frightened to death by having a mother who was totally zoned out half the time and bursting into tears out of nowhere at other times. I can remember several instances when Holly and I would be in the car together and I would realize that she had just asked me the same question for the fifth or sixth time. I can also remember driving through traffic lights and later realizing that I didn't really notice if the light was still green. I was on autopilot. At the end of the day, my husband and I would both collapse. One piece of advice that I would give to parents with a recently diagnosed child: turn on your telephone answering machine and leave it on. I received so many unwanted calls from relatives, friends, and neighbors. I didn't want to educate them (most people don't understand what autism is) and it would take fewer than five fingers to count the people who were of any comfort to me whatsoever. I just wanted to be left alone, and I didn't want to waste a minute talking to anyone who couldn't help my daughter.

Despite my grief, I was desperate to stop wasting Rebecca's time and to get on with the business (and it is a business) of helping her. By doing a lot of networking with other mothers and then with therapists, I was able to assemble a team rather quickly. The initial team consisted of five therapists, my mother-in-law, my husband, and me. This group assembled in my dining room on a Saturday morning in late January, and we were given a 4-hour seminar on Applied Behavior Analysis and discrete-trial teaching by Bridget Taylor, a specialist in this field. It was very difficult to find someone who could train us as there are less than a handful of qualified people in this area.

Rebecca was finally getting help and she responded very quickly. It seemed to me that she almost welcomed this order and structure that was being imposed on her, as though some lights were starting to get turned on. The first order of business was to establish attending behaviors. This was accomplished by the therapist holding a food reinforcer at her eye level while stating "Rebecca." Rebecca wanted that reinforcer (a raisin or a Cheerio) she would look at the therapist who would immediately give her the Cheerio and praise her verbally (Good looking, Rebecca!). Once Rebecca began to attend, she was taught to follow simple gross motor imitations and simple commands (stand up, clap hands, wave bye-bye) within a couple of weeks. She was also developing basic play skills, which had heretofore been completely absent—for example, she could complete simple puzzles (the kind with the wooden pegs), and she learned to manipulate simple cause-and-effect toys like a jack-in-the-box.

By the beginning of week three, we implemented a request program. The therapist would set out three items on the table in front of Rebecca. One would be a positive food item, such as raisins or juice. One would be a negative food item, such as vinegar or mustard. The third item would be a toy, such as a Barney doll. The therapist would ask "What do you want?" and, as Rebecca still made no sounds, she would point to one of the desired items. We taught her how to point during the first week of the program by holding up a desired item, stating "Point," and then physically prompting her to point by manipulating her hand. She also started matching items, that is, a spoon to a spoon, a crayon to a crayon, and so forth. All of this was taking place within the first month of the program. I learned pretty quickly who the good teachers were and which ones she responded to best. It also seemed to me that her parents and her grandmother were better off being her parents and her grandmother, so I sought to replace us as teachers as soon as was practicable. I felt such a sense of relief when Rebecca was having a session with one of the better teachers and such a sense of anxiety when one of the weaker ones was here. There were also too many people involved. For my own peace of mind as well as for Rebecca's sake, I had to weed out the ones that weren't "A" teachers. I stuck with two from the core group, hired another that I had heard was good, and recruited a psychology major from a local college and trained her myself. This group has been with us now for more than a year. They are all excellent teachers, they relate well to Rebecca, are very kind to Holly, and they are all, I believe, committed to Rebecca and to her continued progress. I have a fairly broad range of hourly rates that they are paid. None of these costs are covered by insurance, and it is a staggering amount of money. Rebecca turned 3 years old a few weeks ago, so we are currently negotiating with our school district to shoulder some of these costs.

Although things are now running as smoothly as can be expected, it took a long time for me to work out the major bugs in the program and to preserve some kind of life for my other child, my husband, and myself. I found that I had to set certain guidelines for the teachers and insist that they be adhered to. In the beginning, because I was so grateful to have people show up who were willing to help Rebecca, I put up with things that I shouldn't have. It finally dawned on me that these people worked for me, that I was paying good money for their services, and I was entitled to expect professional and respectful behavior from them. One serious problem that I had involved punctuality. Rebecca's day is divided into three sessions. The first session begins at 9:00 A.M. and ends at 11:30 A.M., the second session runs from 1:00 P.M. to 3:00 P.M., and her last class goes from 4:00 P.M. to 6:00 P.M. When you are running on a schedule like this, it is imperative that teachers show up on time. Even though most of our teachers have always been extremely reliable, there were one or two who would consistently show up 15 or 20 minutes late. This can and does throw off the whole day. If a teacher is late, either your child misses valuable teaching time or, if they stay late on the other end to make it up, the child gets shortchanged out of necessary rest or play time and will not be refreshed for the next session. My older daughter also has a full schedule of activities with preschool, music, ballet, and swimming classes, so I frequently have to be somewhere to drop her off or pick her up. I became wildly stressed out by this and finally told my teachers that I would have to be completely inflexible with respect to punctuality and, if they couldn't come and leave on time, I'd have to pass them by. I agonized over this because I know how hard it is to find talented therapists, but I was tired of feeling as though people had me by the throat. We now run like clockwork around here, and it's much better all around.

Another big problem that I had involved cleanup after sessions. Some teachers are neat and organized, and others are quite a bit less so. I would often come down to the basement where we have our school set up and want to cry. The room would be littered with toys, flashcards, puzzle pieces, and cookie crumbs or pieces of popcorn strewn all over and ground into the carpet. I am sure that no one meant to be evil, but I regarded it as disrespectful and unprofessional. When you are faced with that kind of a cleanup job three times a day, it can and does exhaust and frustrate you. It is also very distracting for a child like Rebecca to concentrate and work in such a chaotic atmosphere. One of her persistent "stims" has been to hold on to as many little toys and objects as she can get her little hands on, so having so much litter at her fingertips was, literally, playing right into her hands. I finally decided to set up the room and the program so that there would be no excuses for anyone not to leave things in good shape for the next teacher without my having to spend 20 or more minutes doing it myself. I bought two large cardfiles—one for current programs and one

for programs that Rebecca had already mastered but that had to be reviewed periodically. I had additional bookshelves and cabinets built and purchased large plastic bins where items for specific programs and play activities should be placed. I then gave everyone a tour of the basement and of my new system and told them that it would be their responsibility to have the basement in decent shape for the next person. This system works about two-thirds of the time, but that is a big improvement.

In addition to setting basic guidelines for Rebecca's therapists, I have also set them for myself, and I seldom stray. For example, I don't do lunch. In the past 15 months, I have gone out to lunch with other women only once. I found it to be such an exhausting and alienating experience that I resolved never to put myself through it again. My luncheon companions were all mothers of normally developing children. The discussion centered around their tennis lessons, the problems with the bus service that ferried their children to and from school, and one woman's kitchen renovations. I could not relate. In fairness to them, I'm sure that they can't relate to me either, so it's best all around for me to regret these types of invitations. I have so little time to allocate to leisure activities that if the activity is not going to relax and renew me, I skip it. I do believe that it's critical to get out of the house and away from it all, if only to take a walk. My husband likens our daughter's treatment to a marathon, and it won't do anyone any good if the mother burns out. For my part, I leave the house at 6:30 every morning and take a 5-mile walk. My children generally wake up between 7:00 and 7:30, my housekeeper gets them dressed, and we all have breakfast together when I get home. Sometimes I don't think I could get through the day without this time to myself.

As I mentioned earlier, when we began our home program Rebecca had no words and her sounds were, at best, limited to very primitive consonant babble. We addressed the expressive language delay very early in the program, beginning with oral motor imitations to strengthen the muscles around Rebecca's mouth and then gradually getting her to imitate specific sounds that her teacher would make. For example, a teacher would say "Do this" and make an exaggerated "p" sound. We went through all the consonant and vowel sounds in this way and then paired them using a sound grid (i.e., baa, caa, daa, etc., then bee, cee, dee, etc.). Our next job was to get Rebecca to pair an item with an approximation of the sound of its corresponding label. For example, we would hold up a juice box and require Rebecca to say "ooo" before she could get the juice. Once she was consistently saying "ooo" for juice, we then required her to say "ooos." It was imperative that we require her to do this outside of sessions also. By the end of the second month of therapy, Rebecca could say approximately 15 words well enough to be understood. During this time, we began to teach her to identify parts of her body, the meaning of "yes" and "no," and we began to teach her to receptively discriminate between objects. We would start out with fun things like placing a Barney doll and a toy duck on the table in front of her and say "Give me Barney." Once she had the idea, we would move on to more functional objects like cup and shoe. Rebecca's repertoire of receptive labels expanded very rapidly and, by mid-spring, she had at least 60 receptive labels that we knew about. Her skills in this area were acquired in part by some of the play activities that we had her do during her breaks. For example, she loved to match things and was good at it, so I bought several of the Ravensburger Lotto games, and teachers would label items as Rebecca matched them. This helped enormously in expanding her fund of receptive and later expressive labels. For example, we have a Things Around the House lotto game, and Rebecca learned to identify and label such things as a stove, sink, telephone, lamp, and so on. Through an Animals Lotto game, Rebecca now knows such relatively obscure wildlife as ostriches, buffaloes, and peacocks. I would highly recommend these games to parents who are trying to assemble materials for a home program.

Things were going along very well during Rebecca's sessions and her progress continued at a rapid pace. She was generally compliant, learning her programs quickly, and getting great scores for her teachers. However, her behavior and affect outside of the classroom still often distinguished her from her normally developing sister and her peers. She still showed very little interest in, or awareness of, other people. This continues to be an area of resistance to this day. If, for example, I enter the kitchen after my morning walk and the children are sitting at the kitchen table eating breakfast, Rebecca might glance up at me for a second and then look away. There is generally no interest in what anyone in the room is saying or doing. I have to walk up to her, get in her face, and force the interaction ("Hi Rebecca." ["Hi Mama."] "How are you?" ["Okay."] "I love you." ["I love you too."]). I have always found the contrast between my two children to be the most obvious and the most painful at mealtimes. Holly is such a talkative and observant child, and Rebecca will be sitting there like a sphinx, unable to participate in the give and take. We find ourselves continually trying to draw her into our conversations. "Rebecca, what are you doing?" ["I'm eating."] "What are you eating?" ["Pasta."] "Good. What's pasta?" ["It's a food."] "Good! Is it delicious?" ["Yes."] "Say 'It's delicious'." ["It's delicious."]. We either have these forced, one-sided discourses with Rebecca, which is unnatural and no fun for anyone, or we let Rebecca sit there in her own world while the rest of us have our own conversation.

One problem that we used to have with Rebecca, which has greatly improved, involved her behavior in outside situations. I used to dread taking her, for example, to drop off or pick up Holly at school. The trip from my car, through the parking lot, into the school, and up the stairs to Holly's classroom was a nightmare. In no way could I rely on her to walk by my side; in fact, the opposite was true. The second I did not have a firm grip on her, she would dart off aimlessly, completely oblivious to other people, to moving cars, or to anything else in her surroundings. I used to have to hold on to her for dear life. Rebecca did not like to hold my hand, so she would try to wriggle free. I would then grasp her harder and she would start screaming and crying and would then make her body go completely limp. So there I would be, either dragging her along by one arm saying "It's time to walk," or I would just carry her. One of my therapists suggested that it was expecting too much of her to complete that entire task. I should instead reinforce her for simply taking two steps compliantly and then two more steps and so on. Once she was consistently compliant using this reinforcement schedule, I could fade back to reinforcing less often. The first time I implemented this plan I brought a plastic bag of M&Ms that I had cut in half. I gave Rebecca a piece of candy for practically just getting out of the car and said "You're walking nicely, Rebecca!" She would take two more steps, and I would say "Great walking, Rebecca, and you're nice and quiet!" and I'd offer her another M&M. Pretty soon, she got the idea. Nowadays, she loves to go to school with Holly, and it only costs me one or two M&Ms, round trip. Yesterday I drove another little friend of Holly's to school. Rebecca got out of the car, took hold of Holly with one hand and of the friend with the other (the thing that thrilled me so much was that she initiated it) and walked happily into school with me walking a step or two behind them. It was, for me, a sight to behold.

By late fall, Rebecca had acquired a great deal of language. However, she did not always use it appropriately. At times, Rebecca's use of language is bizarre. As with her other odd behaviors, we find that the best solution is to ignore the behavior rather than give Rebecca any attention for it. Usually, we find that the behavior is then extinguished within a couple of weeks. One example of an inappropriate use of language occurred shortly after the holidays. Christmas made a major impression on Rebecca this year, so much so that she would frequently launch off with a litany of what could be called Christmasmania: "I want a Santa, I want a Rudolf, I want a Nutcracker, I want a present, I want a Christmas (pronounced Kissmiss) tree," all strung together and repeated time and time again. It used to drive us crazy. Finally, shortly after Christmas and during one such incantation, I said firmly, "Rebecca! Christmas is all gone!" I should have known better. For the next 2 weeks we were treated to continuous outbursts of "Kissmiss all gone!"

I have already mentioned that Rebecca likes to carry things around with her. We are always on the lookout for this, and we take anything that is in her hands and that has no functional reason to be there away from her. This causes shrieks and screams, which we ignore, and we try to redirect her attention to a more appropriate activity. I do let Rebecca hold a stuffed animal in the morning when she's waking up and also at bedtime. However, if she's walking around in the middle of the day with both fists clenched tight with paper clips, Legos, scraps of paper, and the like, we don't permit it. This behavior is definitely lessening, and I have also noticed of late that Rebecca is protesting far less than she used to. Sometimes Rebecca will even give me the item she's holding if I ask her to. Rebecca also has a tendency to have stims in certain locations in the house. For example, she loves to wrap herself in one of the curtains in our family room, gaze out the window, and just laugh. Here again, our strategy has been to engage her in a more appropriate activity rather than to call attention to the undesirable behavior.

Last fall, I decided to enroll Rebecca in a mother and child preschool program sponsored by a local YWCA. She was 2 years 8 months old, but I put her in a group with children who were between 2 and $2\frac{1}{2}$ so that she wouldn't be way behind the other children. Also, instead of being accompanied by me, Rebecca was accompanied by one of her home teachers as an aide. Although I did not reveal Rebecca's diagnosis to the school, I told them that she had several developmental delays as the result of her having been born so prematurely and that we and several professionals had been working very hard with her. They were most accommodating. Rebecca has been going to nursery school once a week for the past 6 months, and for the most part, she blends in just fine with the other children. An interesting coincidence occurred recently. A therapist who has been working closely with Rebecca since the beginning called to say that she had been retained by another family whose son had just been diagnosed with PDD and that this child was in Rebecca's class at the YWCA. She wondered if I would be willing to speak with the child's mother. I agreed, and when the mother called me, she said that she would never have known that Rebecca had the same problem as her son. During our conversation, she described my daughter as "beautiful" and "talkative" (that one really surprised me!) and expressed her amazement several times. I told this mother that 15 months of therapy have brought Rebecca to a point where she can fit in in many situations with other kids. She plays appropriately during free play, sits in circle time, gives simple answers to simple questions ("Who's this?"/"It's Simba."), does her little craft activity (her fine motor skills are still quite delayed, but she can paint and color), sits at the table to eat her snack, throws her cup and napkin away, and goes on her merry

way. The time when one would notice that something is amiss is if one were to try and engage her in any kind of dialogue beyond "Hi, how are you?" and other simple phrases and questions. People don't expect much from children who are 2 and 3 years old, so if they aren't talking or socializing much, it doesn't look too peculiar. As these children get older the gaps become much more noticeable, which is one reason we are trying to make so much headway early on.

By the time we hit the 1-year anniversary of our program 3 months ago, Rebecca had developed a great deal of skills and language. Mary Beth Villani, a skilled behavioral therapist who had developed a wonderful rapport with Rebecca, had been overseeing the program on a week-to-week basis, assisted by Suzanne Jasper, an outstanding teacher who also has innovative ways of motivating Rebecca. Olga Montoya and Lauri Stokley are the teachers who work with Rebecca the most often, and as a result, they have been doing most of the "heavy lifting" in our program. They are dedicated, top-notch professionals, and Rebecca loves them. Ani Nalbandian, a busy graduate student with a wonderfully gentle manner, has come here religiously every weekend from New York City to give Rebecca several sessions. Bridget checks in from time to time to troubleshoot, and her suggestions and support are always invaluable. Rebecca had come farther than we could have imagined, and she had worked endlessly. A sampling of her current skills includes her ability to expressively identify all the letters of the alphabet presented in random sequence. She knows her shapes and colors, she can count up to 12 items, and she has an extensive vocabulary (several hundred words). Additionally, she has become proficient in categorizing items among nine different groupings. I was recently quizzing her in the car and asked "What's a zebra?"/"It's a [*sic*] animal"; "What's a triangle?"/"It's a shape"; "What's nine?"/"It's a number"; "What's a couch?"/"It's furniture"; "Who's William?"/"It's a person"; "What's a *w*?"/"It's a letter"; "What's a helicopter?"/"It's something you ride in"; "What's a bathing suit?"/"It's clothes"; "What's cake?"/"It's a food." I present these examples to illustrate that many of the things that Rebecca knows are quite advanced for a child her age who has no problems. I am convinced that Rebecca is a highly intelligent child. Her teachers tell me this constantly. In a way, that makes her deficits all the more maddening.

One big problem that we have recently been tackling concerns Rebecca's compliance during her sessions. At times Rebecca becomes very silly, or she might become aggressive, pulling her teachers' hair or swiping flashcards off the table. We had decided to completely ignore Rebecca's behavior during these incidents and to revert to a simple command presented over and over until Rebecca would get bored and comply. Unfortunately, this tactic did not succeed in extinguishing the noncompliance (it was going on for well more than a month), so we are now resorting to putting Rebecca in time out, which we have determined is an aversive for her. We just started this procedure a few days ago, but we are already seeing a big improvement. I have noticed that, in general, when Rebecca is motivated and when her teachers keep things fast-paced and interesting for her, she will work. After 15 months of programming, it takes a lot more than a sip of juice or a Cheerio to incite her to work, especially as the programs become more demanding. I am constantly searching the stores for new reinforcers. For example, Rebecca loves books and stickers, so I always have a big variety on hand. She also likes a peek through the viewmaster or a few seconds of a Barney or a Disney song on a cassette player. If Rebecca senses that a teacher is weak in a certain area or is unsure of herself, she will go for the jugular and torment that poor person. Fortunately, my teachers are highly skilled and are generally not thrown by her antics.

In the past few months, we have made a big push in a few key areas. First, we all agreed that Rebecca needed to get out of the house more. She needs more exposure to the real world and to people and places other than her mother, her teachers, and her home therapeutic environment. I might tell the 1:00 P.M. teacher to take Rebecca to a local pizza shop for lunch. It's critical to give children like Rebecca opportunities to generalize the skills that they learn in therapy to other situations. My husband takes our daughters to a coffee shop for breakfast every Sunday morning. Recently, I accompanied them, and when the waitress approached the table, Rebecca told her father that she wanted pancakes. We said, "Tell the lady," and pointed at the waitress. Rebecca looked dead at her and said, "Lady, I want pancakes, please." We were overjoyed.

The second area that we are trying to focus on is having Rebecca be in more situations with children her own age. Besides her preschool program, Rebecca attends an hour-long kindermusik program (with an aide) once a week. This has been a very good find for Rebecca as she absolutely loves music and singing. The program also forces her to cope with transitions—one minute the teacher is doing a slow story/song, perhaps accompanied by a puppet, and the next minute the class is standing, ringing bells, and doing a fast-paced marching sequence. The teacher (who is aware of Rebecca's diagnosis) recently told me that she doesn't think that anyone observing the class would think that Rebecca was different from the others. We have also begun a peer-modeling program using some of Holly's friends. The goal here is first to get Rebecca to notice and attend to other children and, ultimately, to have her play unprompted with other children. This is something we just started, so I can't assess progress yet, but I'm very excited about it.

Bridget recently came by and suggested that we increase the scope of Rebecca's programs to incorporate more expressive language. We hold up an object and say "Tell me about this." Rebecca has to label the object (e.g., horse) and come up with two or three additional attributes (e.g., brown, tail, neigh). We have also begun to explore her capacity for abstract thinking. That program involves putting out four flashcards, for example, a sun, a moon, a star, and a cloud. The teacher would say "I'm thinking of something that's in the sky and it's very hot." Rebecca has to point to the sun and say "Sun." These have been challenging for her, but she's catching on.

The behavior of Rebecca's that I find the most disturbing, particularly as she gets older, is her habit of screaming. Sometimes you can predict what will set her off, and at other times it seems to come from nowhere. We have determined that, in most cases, Rebecca's screaming occurs when she is trying to get out of doing something or trying to get a rise out of you. Because Rebecca knows that this is inappropriate behavior, we have decided to ignore it. It is so important that, when we decide on a strategy, all people who are involved in Rebecca's care be consistent with the follow-through. This includes not only parents and teachers but caregivers and grandparents as well. I find it frustrating to no end when I have been trying to ignore her during these episodes and I hear my husband or my housekeeper say "What's the matter, Rebecca? Why are you crying, baby?" I know they think they are being kind, but it makes all of our jobs so much more difficult. If Rebecca screams her lungs out and gets ignored for it twenty-five times but, on the twenty-sixth time, someone reinforces her by giving her attention for it, she will be willing to scream thirty times on the next go around.

There was one occasion recently when I came close to losing it. It was on Rebecca's third birthday. We were having a little party for her that afternoon, and I had been dashing around all morning, driving the carpool, and picking up balloons and cupcakes. Rebecca's birthday is a hard day for me to get through anyway, and this year it happened to be especially depressing, cold, gray, and rainy. I had both children and my housekeeper in the car. I decided to drop my housekeeper off at home with the bundles while I drove Rebecca around in the car for her nap (this is a part of our daily routine). Unfortunately, Holly wanted to come along for the ride. The minute that my housekeeper got out of the car with the goodies and I started backing down the driveway, Rebecca started to holler. I figured that the crying would last a minute or two, and then she'd tire herself out and fall asleep. The child continued to screech for 35 minutes. During this time, I said and did absolutely nothing except to quietly reassure Holly. I was terribly concerned about the effect that this was having on Holly, but I could not give in and take Rebecca home, as that would be reinforcing this terrorizing behavior. After about 25 minutes of this nerve shattering din, I considered giving in to the sadness and horror that were about to overtake me. However, I feared that if I opened that floodgate, the tears might never stop. How did our lives come to be this way, I thought. There were two things that saved me that day. One was Holly's presence, which has kept me sane and steadfast at my darkest moments. The other thought that kept me driving that car was to pretend, just for a moment or two, that I was watching someone else go through all of this. There have been a few instances since Rebecca's diagnosis when I have had to use this defense mechanism. This was certainly one of them.

The person about whom I most often worry is Holly. She is very concerned about and protective of her sister, and she is acutely aware of the sadness and frustration that often exist in our home. Earlier this week, I put Rebecca in time out for pulling Holly's hair. Holly was upset that her sister was crying and asked me why I did what I did. In trying to explain my logic in terms that a 4-year-old could understand and relate to, I told Holly that we must teach Rebecca that she can't do things like pull people's hair. If Rebecca did not learn to stop doing things like this, I reasoned, then she would never be invited to birthday parties and play dates, and no one would ever want to be her friend. Holly paused for a second and said "No one but her big sister." One area where I made a mistake in the beginning was in not letting Holly come down to the basement while Rebecca was in session. I was so worried that Rebecca would be distracted by Holly's presence that it didn't occur to me that she had no idea of what was being done to her sister by these people who were constantly invading our house and bringing Rebecca downstairs. I finally started letting Holly come down to play and observe for 10 or 15 minutes so as to demystify what was going on down there.

In spite of my concerns about Holly, she seems to be a well-adjusted and delightful little girl. Recently at my parent/teacher conference, Holly's teacher told me that she had never seen a happier child, nor a more caring one. She is extremely popular among her classmates, and she and her friends are frequently dragging Rebecca into their activities. Holly's nursery school is a cooperative, which means that there is always a parent working in the classroom. I am always glad when it is my turn to work because I want Holly to know that, although I spend an enormous amount of time in Rebecca's "school," her school is important to me also.

Since Rebecca's diagnosis, I have found each and every day to be a struggle. On the one hand, I desperately want to restore a measure of equilibrium to my own life and to our lives as a family. Opposing this desire is our commitment to provide Rebecca with the very best care that we possibly can, and our firm belief that an intensive program based on the principles of Applied Behavior Analysis constitutes the best available intervention for our child. As genuinely fond as we all are of Rebecca's teachers, their continuous presence sometimes makes me feel that our home has become an institution. And in a very real sense, it has. The obvious answer would be to enroll Rebecca in a school. However, there are less than a handful of schools within commuting distance from my husband's job that are committed to the same quality of care and instruction that we are, and they all have waiting lists that are 10 miles long.

At the suggestion of the social worker from our local school district, I recently visited two schools for autistic children where, I was told, Rebecca could be placed. During my visits, I observed children engaging in a wide variety of what I found to be upsetting behaviors. I saw a little boy running a toy truck up and down the side of his face for several minutes before I finally called the teacher's attention to the child. I saw a little girl jumping up and down on top of her chair while shrieking (the teacher was trying to teach another child, and this little girl was supposed to be observing). I also saw two children who repeatedly put little counting bears in their mouths, swished them around inside, took them out to gaze at them for a few moments, and then repeated the cycle. This is not the kind of care—billed as state-of-the-art intervention for autistic children but seeming to me more like baby-sitting—that I want for my child. Therefore, we are doing it ourselves at home.

For at least 6 to 8 months preceding Rebecca's diagnosis, I bombarded her with every kind of therapy I could think of in a desperate attempt to revive her obviously lagging development. I took Rebecca to physical, occupational, and speech therapy sessions. We went to gymboree and kindermusik classes. I started a weekly play group for her, and I read to Rebecca religiously for at least an hour each day. All of these interventions and methods of stimulation combined did not animate her and get the results from her that we saw after just 2 or 3 weeks of home programming. Although it frightens me to contemplate my daughter's future, it frightens me more to wonder what she—and we—would be like if we had not chosen to pursue this course of action for Rebecca. For now, we can only hope, continue to work as hard as we can on her behalf, and support, encourage, and protect her and each other.

CHAPTER TWENTY

Brandon's Journey

Cyndy Kleinfield-Hayes

It's late. All three kids are fast asleep. Marni, my oldest, is 7 years old and gifted. Devin is 5 years old and incredibly sensitive. And then there's my little Brandy. He's 4 years old, a beautiful little blonde with bright blue eyes. He loves music, and he loves to swim. He's autistic.

Brandon was a perfect child. He slept through the night at 5 weeks. He smiled, cooed, sat up, walked, waved bye-bye, right on target. I was always amazed at his intensity. He would get so involved in a task, so focused. There was no question—he was very intelligent.

When Brandon was 18 months old, I began to notice changes in him. For example, he was always good at completing puzzles. Now, he would just scatter the pieces. He wouldn't wave bye-bye or respond to his name. He could no longer drink from a cup. He lost the few words that he had acquired.

I immediately consulted the pediatrician. I was told, "Not to worry. He's the baby. He's a boy. His brother talked late." "But, you don't understand, this is not just about language. He won't even look at me!" At my insistence, he referred us to a pediatric neurologist, who indicated that Brandon was developmentally delayed and set up an appointment at the Miami Children's Hospital on November 30, 1992. Brandon was observed and diagnosed by the Neurobiological Evaluation and Treatment Team.

I'll never forget that day. My son was 2 years, 2 months old. His language and academic skills were assessed at a 10-month age equivalence. His behavior was described as atypical, deficient in social relatedness. He engaged in stereotypic play and lacked imitation and awareness of meaningful communication. Diagnosis: Autism.

The month of December was a blur. Fortunately, I have an undergraduate and graduate degree in psychology, so I was comfortable with the research process. Unfortunately, the leftover reference books from those degrees presented the "refrigerator mom" explanation for my son's challenge. This theory, coupled with guilt over my demanding work schedule, was overwhelming; however, overwhelmed was not a comfortable state for me and certainly not productive for my son and the rest of the family.

January 1, 1993: It was time to get busy. We enrolled Brandon in a public preschool program for children with autism. Several county employees and medical professionals told us we were lucky because it was one of the best programs available and that we were doing the very best thing we could for our son. Brandon's class resembled a typical preschool: there were colorful pictures on the wall, seasonal mobiles dangling from the ceiling, and a caring teacher, assistant, and aide. The children were encouraged to participate in structured social and learning activities. I would have given anything for that class to have been appropriate for my son. But Brandon spent most of his day running aimlessly around the room. He was totally uninvolved with the creative class activities and projects. Weeks, months passed. No change.

Well before Brandon's diagnosis, I had begun an intensive review of the literature. There was one issue that everyone agreed on. Early intervention was critical. Time was rushing by. Exhaustive inquiry kept taking me back to research on Applied Behavior Analysis conducted by Dr. Ivar Lovaas and associates. I was particularly encouraged by one of his articles that indicated that early, intensive, one-to-one behavioral therapy resulted in "normal" functioning for almost half of the preschoolers in the experimental group, and that all of the experimental group made significant progress.

It's difficult to describe my excitement about finally discovering some information that didn't suggest that I write off my 2-year-old son and focus on developing coping skills, his and mine. It's also difficult to describe my disappointment after talking to some of the "experts" in our local autism community. "Lovaas. Oh, you mean aversives." This was followed by dramatic stories of vinegar in the eyes and other equally unpleasant tales. I acknowledged that it was my understanding that Dr. Lovaas's prior work was conducted 30 years earlier with seriously self-abusive children. I strongly urged the review of *current* literature. The reaction of these experts was, "Besides, Lovaas used only high-functioning children," and on and on and on. This reaction was so negative, so unyielding that I began to question whether I had missed something in the literature. The person to whom I was talking was an experienced administrator of programs for children with autism and respected in the parent and professional community as an "expert" in the field. I reread the research and talked to parents. There was no question in my mind, an intensive program based on the techniques of Applied Behavior Analysis provided the best opportunity for my son to reach his potential.

Six months later I withdrew my son from his school, contacted Dr. Lovaas, and along with two other families arranged to share the expense of having a person come out to train our children. This arrangement reduced the cost per family to just over $1,600. A graduate student from UCLA was scheduled to fly to Ft. Lauderdale to conduct our training in early August, 1993.

I lost 6 critical months with my son. I still get angry at the thought. Fortunately, I recognized that it was not a good investment to put my energy into anger over the past. There was so much to do. After I scheduled the training with UCLA, I began to make arrangements. I purchased airline tickets, made reservations at a local hotel, and reserved a rental car. One of the other parents found a conference room for the first day of training. The balance of my energy went into finding therapists to work with Brandon in our home.

I contacted the psychology department at a local university and enlisted their support in identifying interested students. I composed a letter that, in addition to describing the job expectations, heavily stressed the benefits to the student. These benefits included the opportunity to receive intense training and to work in a program developed by Dr. Ivar Lovaas and the UCLA staff. The caliber of the students who responded to my letter was exceptionally high. The majority of my initial therapists were completing graduate degrees in psychology. Important to their decision making was the involvement of a Lovaas consultant. To these therapists, Dr. Lovaas was a seminal expert in the behavioral treatment of autism. Less important was their initial salary, $5 an hour.

Day one of the initial training consisted of a review of research, theory, and methodology, conducted by UCLA trainer Jodie Deming. On day two she modeled technique while working with Brandon and provided feedback to me and my therapists as we worked with him. This was a very difficult day for me. Despite the gentle manner of the trainer, Brandon cried for much of the day. He appeared angry over our initial requests to "Look at me," "Sit down," and "Put in" (imitate putting a block in a bucket).

By day three most of the crying had subsided. Brandon would establish eye contact when M&Ms were positioned at the trainer's eyes, sit down with minimal physical prompting, and actually put the block in the bucket. It was so exciting. This was the first time since well before his diagnosis that he had responded to requests from anyone. At the close of

the third day, I worked with Jodie to develop a notebook that identified specific goals and objectives. We created a list of drills to support Brandon's objectives. We also developed a secondary list of drills to provide next steps. This provided us with a sense of direction.

Informed and constructive feedback has always been a critical component of Brandon's program. Initially, that feedback came exclusively from Jodie Deming. Having provided Brandon's initial training, she was in the best position to brainstorm issues, suggest alternatives, and identify next steps.

Two and a half months into the program, I met Jeannie Hays. Jeannie was recommended by the staff at UCLA. Her background was in speech and language, and she was trained by a Lovaas consultant in 1988. She was, at the time, the sole resource for the behavioral treatment of children with autism in South Florida. Jeannie was a major resource.

She works 7 days a week with families in South Florida. She has incredible talent and experience and loves the children. Jeannie assumed a supervisory role in Brandon's therapy. Supervision continues to be critical to our program's success. It's important to have someone with a broad background of experience with very different children. Brandon's development, like that of other children, is unique. And, like many other children with autism, his progress has not followed a typical developmental pattern. He is on, or near, age level in some areas, but severely delayed in other areas. Additionally, he has spurts of development; he reaches plateaus and, I regret to say, sometimes loses ground.

Recruiting, training, and motivating student therapists has probably been our greatest challenge. Out of our four initial therapists, one still works with Brandon. We have had 11 therapists in the year and a half since Brandon began his home program. The therapist who has been with Brandon from the beginning of the program, Patricia Thomas-Shutt, has probably had the greatest impact on his development. Patty's skills and commitment quickly placed her in the lead therapist position. On a day-to-day basis she facilitates the direction established by the program supervisor, Jeannie Hays. She also provides ideas and feedback to the program-planning process. Together Patty and I determined that it was important for her to spend at least 10–15 hours a week with Brandon. Although the majority of the time is spent working directly with him, some of the time has been spent working in consultation with our other therapists.

The lead therapist also acts as the program cheerleader. Behavioral therapy is hard work. It's critical that our team stay highly motivated. Positive attitude is an important lead therapist attribute, and Patty has been terrific at engaging the balance of the team in celebrating our successes. Team meetings have been a critical component. At least once a month the entire training team meets with Jeannie Hays to review progress, conduct skill-building drills, and establish the next month's programming. These meetings ensure consistency and support effective team building.

After Brandon had been receiving 30–35 hours a week for 6 months in our home program, he was enrolled in a pilot preschool program for children with autism. I participated in the development of the program, a behaviorally based intervention. Although the pilot program would not provide the intensity of his home program, it would provide several hours of discrete trial each day, as well as the social experience very important to Brandon's development.

Another positive element of his new preschool program was the involvement of Robin Parker, who was the speech and language consultant for the program. I felt very fortunate to have the speech and language pathologist I read about in *Let Me Hear Your Voice*. We have had the good fortune to have Robin on our team for the past year. She is currently working with Brandon twice a week. I think it's very important to have a speech and language pathologist who understands and believes in behavioral intervention. Robin has been helpful in providing suggestions to our therapists in the area of receptive and expressive language, improved articulation, skill generalization, social relatedness, and appropriate and symbolic play.

When Brandon entered the preschool pilot, his home programming dropped to 20 hours a week. Over the last year I have continued to evaluate Brandon's progress to ensure the most effective use of his time. Recently, I have increased his home programming to 30 hours a week. Clearly the school experience adds significant value, but a review of his progress at home suggests he will benefit from the increase in his home program. We continue to appreciate the importance of taking data in both his home and school programs.

The cost of a more than 30-hour program is substantial. Although I originally paid $5 an hour for student therapists, most of Brandon's current therapists are experienced and are paid $10 an hour. Our 30-hour-a-week program, including training and supervision, represents a $600 unreimbursed expense per month. This is obviously a major financial burden for most families. In addition to aggressively approaching our insurance companies, several families in South Florida have pursued other resource options.

First, Professor Cecilia Campoverde, a sociologist at Florida Atlantic University and grandmother of a child with autism, included as part of the curriculum for a class of 30 advanced sociology students the provision of home therapy for area families at no cost. The program provided behavioral training for the students. Each student worked with a different family and provided 56 hours of home-based behavioral therapy. In most cases the students continued to work for the families for a minimal charge after the completion of the class.

Dr. Jack Scott, also of Florida Atlantic University, has coordinated the placement of countless students in home programs. Additionally, he supervised the placement of education students in the behavioral preschool pilot in which Brandon participated. The student participation provided the resources to support a one-to-one ratio.

Additionally, recognizing the urgent need to support home programs, other parents and therapists and I have created a home-programming network. It was becoming apparent that the shortage of therapists was creating a bidding war. The goal was to eliminate the inequity and to make the best use of scarce human resources. We have established a nonprofit organization, Reaching Potentials, that will assume the responsibility for recruiting and training therapists. Jeannie Hays and Patricia Thomas-Shutt focus on training the therapists. They provide beginning, intermediate, and advanced training. Their focus on training allows them to reach more families in the area. The network includes all of the families Jeannie currently oversees and their therapists. The families agree to follow a pay schedule based on the therapists' experience and skill level. Through their support of the network, they pay for the ongoing training of their therapists on a pro-rated basis.

Additionally, many of the families recognize that it is unreasonable and unfair to expect therapists to make long-term commitments to home programs without the consideration of the therapists' need for immediate and future benefits. These provisions are being addressed. Beginning in January of 1996 we will provide an opportunity for therapists to participate in a group insurance package. Additionally, after 2,500 hours a therapist will be tenured and can thus participate in a modest retirement plan.

Meanwhile as these community efforts unfold, my son's progress has been steady but slow. Familiar with the literature and constantly in touch with other families with home programs, I was aware that some children progress at a fast pace, and for other children each step is a long and difficult process. After about 6 months, I was aware that for Brandon this was going to be a long, difficult journey. That realization was almost like a second diagnosis. I spent several weeks emotionally immobilized. Then I began to review his milestones, which were considerable. As I reviewed his data, I discovered that if I graphed his progress weekly, it appeared that he was at a standstill and sometimes actually regressing. If, however, I compared his performance at 6-week intervals, his progress was significant. More recently I have found that notable progress is achieved monthly. His rate of progress is increasing.

It has been important to think in term of baby steps. Each small step is a challenge. The breakdown of tasks gives him many more opportunities to be successful. Brandon's relatively slow rate of progress does not mean that he does not get bored with a task. Because drills are worked on for a longer period, we must pay close attention to providing new and interesting training materials.

I have also found that data collected on his programs must be examined carefully to evaluate progress accurately and determine next steps. Often a new therapist reports that Brandon has a certain skill and supports her conclusions by providing data at the 90% level. But a closer examination of the data reveals that approximately 50% of the time Brandon makes an error on the first trial. On trials two through ten he provides a correct response. Clearly, he has not mastered the skill. Based on the feedback from the first trial, he has determined which response is correct or incorrect and then continues this pattern.

Language is a major challenge for Brandon. He has a severe language disorder, including auditory comprehension deficits and reduced play skills. In the beginning of his program we worked 50% of the time on expressive language. He was not able to make any sound on request. It appeared that he was trying very hard to make the sound, and when he couldn't, the situation became very stressful to him. We decided to take the pressure out of the drill. We moved away from the table and made the process very personal. We didn't give a command, but instead said the sound. We encouraged him to touch our lips and helped him to put his tongue in the right position. We reinforced heavily for any verbal production. We saw immediate progress.

We have also found the use of visuals to be effective. Once again, it appeared that when we tried to reduce his frustration at not being able to communicate, his progress accelerated in expressive language. We have also used cued speech. In cued speech a hand signal is used to represent the various consonant and vowel combinations. This has been extremely effective. Initially we provided a cue for the first syllable; now we most often provide a cue to elicit word endings.

Currently Brandon can make many vowel and consonant sounds. He has several words that are clear and many other approximations. He is beginning to request objects using "I want" sentences. Although he has been diagnosed with developmental apraxia, his articulation is improving all the time.

Interestingly, improvements in expressive language precede progress in receptive language. He is able to label verbs but continues to struggle with nouns. He learns how to say the name of an object before he understands what it means.

We have also found that Brandon is very competitive. He is very successful in two-on-one drills with his brother, Devin. The therapist asks Devin to say something. After he answers, he is reinforced. Then Brandon is given the same request. He is much more successful at producing difficult sounds when working with his brother. Additionally, his brother and sister do drills with him. He loves the attention, and they enjoy their involvement with his program. It has been a real confidence booster for all of the kids.

Brandon has also made significant progress in other areas. Progress in self-help skills includes dressing and undressing himself with minimal prompting. He is also potty trained. Appropriate play is now emerging, and his social skills now include greeting others when prompted with a wave and a "Hi," as well as waving and saying "Bye-bye" when someone leaves.

Brandon loves gymnastics, loves to swim, ride his bike, and run races. He is very coordinated. We have found that these activities are great equalizers. Again, our focus has been to provide as many opportunities for success as possible. Also, like most people, Brandon enjoys doing those things he does well. These activities are great reinforcers and provide interesting and appropriate activities for his free time.

We are approaching the year and a half anniversary of our home program. It has been hard work, but the rewards are there. Brandon's rate of progress continually increases. He is a very happy and productive young man. We are all very proud of him.

CHAPTER TWENTY-ONE

Peter's Story

Elizabeth Braxton

Peter, our firstborn and only child, was born on October 16, 1990. He was a beautiful, healthy, and robust little guy with blond hair and blue eyes. He loved to nuzzle his soft, little face into our necks, which is to this day the most divine thing in all the world to me.

Peter's early development followed a normal, if not precocious, course. He was a happy, agreeable, and very social baby. He smiled, cooed, sat up, crawled, rolled over, and played with his baby toys just as he should have, at or before the expected age and with joy. I remember thinking at the time about how bright and alert he was; how perfect he was. In those first 6 months, he seldom fussed or cried, and when he did he was easily consoled. At 3 months I brought him to a photographer to have his picture taken. His attention was easy to capture and he looked up, directly at the camera with a great big, toothless smile. It was a smile that lit up a room.

I cannot pinpoint exactly when Peter's behavior began to regress, but I do know that the onset of symptoms was slow and subtle. Between his first birthday and 15 months of age I began to worry. Looking back at videotapes, I saw that it had become increasingly more difficult to get Peter's attention or evoke that killer smile he had as a baby. His eye contact was dropping off. He no longer oriented in response to his name or followed a single direction, and he had begun what seemed like an endless succession of tantrums complete with head banging. His language acquisition was unusual. He would learn a new word, use it for a day or two, and then we wouldn't hear it again for weeks or even months.

I have a doctorate in counseling psychology, and most of my training and professional experience has been spent working with children. I had seen these symptoms before, although rarely. The regression in Peter's behavior was becoming more and more difficult to deny. I had a copy of the *Diagnostic and Statistical Manual of Mental Disorders* (DSM-III-R) of the American Psychiatric Association in our study and I remember stealing upstairs and reading (and rereading) the section on pervasive developmental disorder (PDD), desperately looking for ways to convince myself that Peter did not really qualify for the diagnosis; that he did not really fit the profile.

Although I suspected autism by the time Peter was 15 months old, I could not convince anyone to give him a diagnostic evaluation until he was 22 months old. That first diagnosis was vague and rather useless as were the treatment recommendations that followed. "Get down on the floor on his level to promote eye contact." (I had spent the previous 7 months living on the floor.) "Follow his lead to encourage reciprocal play." (How much time can one spend throwing rocks and pebbles into the sewer grate, lining up toy animals all facing the same direction, or searching for bits of dust and strands of hair in the carpet?) We were also told to "wait 6 months or a year and see what happens, as some children outgrow such symptoms."

Recently, I asked the first doctor who had evaluated Peter why he had been so reluctant to give him a diagnosis when he was 22 months old. He told me that he viewed a diagnosis of autism as a "life sentence" and saw no reason not to give us time to come to terms with the gravity of the situation before throwing such harsh terms at us. Though well-meaning, his professional behavior had been patronizing, and it had cost us valuable and irreplaceable time.

When Peter was 26 months old, he was evaluated by Dr. Margaret Bauman at Massachusetts General Hospital for a second opinion. She diagnosed him with "pervasive developmental disorder/autism spectrum disorder." She also told us that when young children appear to be anywhere on the autistic spectrum, she would prefer to diagnose them accordingly and recommend an intensive program of early intervention. She noted that behavioral treatments are the most effective approach and also strongly recommended sensory integration therapy.

During the following 8 to 10 months, we tried sensory integration, vitamin therapy, DMG, therapeutic horseback-riding lessons, private speech therapy, and nearly a year of the local early intervention program. This program consisted of 1 hour per week of home-based speech therapy, a center-based group, and, toward the end, an additional hour per week of educational consultation. Nothing seemed to have any impact at all on Peter's ability to communicate.

My husband Keith and I had also spent the better part of that year going to conferences, reading books, and sifting through reams of paper. Then in late July, at the suggestion of a colleague and dear friend, I picked up a copy of the just published *Let Me Hear Your Voice.* I began reading the book on a Friday evening. On Monday morning, with nothing but the appendix to *Let Me Hear Your Voice* as a guide, Peter and I began to do drills. With my education and training in behavior therapy, I was at least somewhat prepared to take an initial stab at it, though I was not trained as a behavior analyst, and I had never before done discrete-trial training. What I was altogether unprepared for was the extent to which my son, then 2 years and 10 months old, would resist my attempts to help him. It quickly became apparent that it would take two people to get him used to the drills; one to keep him seated and prompt him from behind and the other to give him the direction and the reinforcement.

On that same day that I began doing drills with Peter, I also called the Lovaas Clinic at UCLA. I put Peter's name on the waiting list and gathered up the necessary evaluations and other materials to send to them. I was told that the wait would be several months, and I asked to speak with a consultant for some pointers on technique so that I would not, in my haste, begin teaching Peter any bad habits that would take extra time and energy to undo later. I was informed that such services were available but only on Wednesdays between specified hours and on a first-come, first-served basis. I ordered *The ME Book* and continued for several weeks to try to reach a Lovaas consultant.

Meanwhile, *The ME Book* arrived quickly, and with that and the appendix to *Let Me Hear Your Voice,* we were on our way. I started taking data that I figured I might eventually need to convince someone to fund this program. We began with nonverbal imitation, matching, block design, receptive labels, toy play, body parts, and receptive commands and soon thereafter added verbal imitation. We also began teaching Peter his colors, shapes, and letters.

One of our early drills was block design, in which Peter was asked to replicate a block structure. We began with two blocks, and he needed only to place one block on top of the other. He was furious. He screamed, cried, and struggled to get away from Keith, who was restraining him and prompting him in a hand-over-hand fashion. Finally, his hand broke loose, he grabbed a block, and threw it squarely at my face. We continued so as not to reinforce that behavior in any way. I thought he would never enjoy playing with blocks—or anything else, for that matter.

Despite his initial resistance, Peter's progress those first few weeks was astonishing. Using discrete-trial training I could teach Peter more in a single day than I had been able to teach him with months of incidental teaching. After 3 weeks I connected with a consultant from the Lovaas Clinic for telephone consultation, who answered many of my questions and was generally very helpful. Peter's acquisition of new skills soared as did his receptive vocabulary. Within 3 weeks of beginning the program, he was doing verbal imitation and had begun to point to and label objects and picture cards.

As exciting as his progress was, however, it was still very difficult and stressful doing this therapy myself. For me, doing drills with Peter has always been problematic. It is simply too difficult for me to remain neutral and impassive with him when the situation calls for it. Even now when I need to fill in here and there I find myself getting anxious and easily frustrated with him, which is not good for either of us. It is a completely different story with someone else's child. No matter how much you are invested in that child's recovery, it is not the same as working with your own child. The autistic behaviors do not strike terror through your very being. At any rate, one thing was clear. We needed a therapist/teacher.

One month into therapy, Peter was still roughly 2 months away from his third birthday. It was our understanding that, with the exception of 2 hours a week of direct services through a local early intervention program, Keith and I would be completely financially responsible for Peter's home program until he turned 3. We had saved a little money for a down payment on a house, which was more than enough to cover the 2 months. However, it was not enough for a full year of 30–40 hours a week of behavior therapy. We would also need to pay for materials and periodic consultation from the Lovaas Clinic, including the consultant's airfare and expenses. Our parents offered to help. Still, according to our estimates, as an out-of-pocket expense, the annual price tag was going to be a bit daunting.

At the time I did not realize it, but the director of special education in our town, John Tully, is one of a kind. For him, money is not the only bottom line, which, I have since learned, is all too often the case. Having been in John's office not quite a month before, lobbying hard for a structured educational approach with a strong emphasis on picture communication systems and other such adaptational approaches, I was a bit apprehensive as I scheduled our second meeting.

Once in John's office Keith and I began by explaining that since our last meeting, we had read an incredible new book that had caused us to reevaluate our choice of educational plan for Peter. I had brought him a copy of *Let Me Hear Your Voice* along with copies of journal articles documenting the relevant research and my charts and graphs documenting Peter's progress.

Initially, John gave us no answer and suggested we visit a local special needs preschool that is part of a collaborative program involving the city we live in and several surrounding towns. We did so, and we were duly unimpressed. We remained convinced that he needed a more intensive behavioral approach. Once more we returned to John's office. We again discussed the proposed home program at length and reviewed the range of possible treatment outcomes under such an approach. We told John that even though we knew there were no guarantees, an intensive behavioral program might actually give Peter a chance for a normal, happy, and productive life. We could not deprive Peter of that chance. John agreed to give it a try.

Two days after our meeting, John called me with a name. A young woman named Suzanne Gaudin had sent him her resume. She was relocating to the area with her husband, who had accepted a temporary position at Holy Cross College. She would be here for only 1 year. I had hoped for someone that could stay with Peter indefinitely, but I wanted to meet her. She had 6 years of experience as a certified special education teacher and had worked most of that time with autistic children.

I interviewed her. Though her experience was relevant and impressive, Sue had not had much experience with discrete-trial training. This was not a serious concern because I knew that between myself and the consultant from UCLA who would eventually be joining our team, we could teach her the techniques. Besides, Sue had something far more valuable than any amount of training in a particular set of skills could provide. She loved this work, and she had a natural ability for teaching that I did not have. She could take virtually anything (toy, game, kitchen utensil) and make a teaching tool out of it.

We hired Sue in August, and the city funded her salary upon Peter's third birthday in mid-October. Within a month of working with Sue, Peter could tolerate up to 30 hours of therapy per week. Keith and I invested almost all of our free time in the task of incidental teaching in an effort to promote generalization of the skills Peter would learn with Sue during the day. In 1 year Sue taught Peter more than I would have ever thought possible.

Peter's therapy hours were designated almost exclusively for language and communication-based skills. Keith and I had decided to teach daily living skills such as dressing, hygene, toileting, and so on ourselves. It was our belief that as Peter learned to imitate increasingly more complex chains of behavior, and understand and follow more complex instructions, teaching him how to dress, for example, would be a much simpler task than using elaborate backward-chaining programs for that purpose. The primary goal of therapy was to give Peter the tools to learn from his environment rather than teaching specific daily living skills one at a time. Furthermore, we were operating under the hypothesis that there is a critical period for certain kinds of language acquisition. Therefore, we wanted to make the most efficient use of his therapy hours. We could always teach him to dress himself later.

In November the long awaited Lovaas consultant arrived. We had assembled a home team with Sue and me at the helm, and we gathered for a 2-day workshop. Our consultant was immensely helpful. The workshop was like a much-needed tune-up. Furthermore he provided us with many programs that we desperately needed.

Some of the drill programs the consultant gave us were either similar or identical to those we were already using. However, he provided additional programs that helped us to teach Peter prepositions, emotions, same and different, yes and no, drawing, simple sentence structure, identifying missing objects or parts of objects, categories, functions, locations, first, last, before and after, verb tense, plurals, attribute/opposite pairs, counting, discrimination of *wh*-questions, rote conversation, chaining and sequencing, why/because, description, story telling and listening comprehension, and beginning reciprocal conversation. Although we were also given a pronoun drill, it was largely ineffective with Peter, who, until very recently, continued to have trouble with pronoun reversal.

Overall, Peter's progress that first year of therapy was continuous. However, it followed a pattern of two steps forward and one step back. It's not that he lost skills that he had learned. It's more that from time to time he would just fall apart. I don't know how else to describe it. It was so pitiful. He would tantrum and cry for so much of his day. We could find nothing environmental that would explain it. And always I would panic.

Sue, however, did not panic, and after a few of these episodes she shared with me her observations. After each of these difficult periods, which could last from 2 or 3 days to the better part of 2 weeks, he would recompensate at a qualitatively higher level of functioning than he had previously achieved. It seemed as if these episodes always occurred just before Peter mastered a difficult or complex new skill. She hypothesized that they signaled some sort of cognitive growth spurt during which he was struggling to integrate a tremendous amount of new information. This hypothesis worked for me.

By April Peter had gone through nearly all of the programs left by the consultant from the Lovaas Clinic. I tried unsuccessfully to reach him for follow-up programs. Because consultation was so scarce, Sue and I began attempting to reinvent the wheel.

For example, shortly after the consultant's visit I thought that Peter was ready for more advanced symbolic play programs. Play in general was an area with which Peter needed help. Earlier that year Keith and I had heard Dr. Sally Rogers speak on the topic of developmental play therapy. Her presentation had been very informative and intriguing. We adapted some of Dr. Roger's material into a discrete-trial format to get Peter started with it, and his play improved considerably.

One of the many play drills that we developed in this manner was to give Peter a block and instruct and prompt him to pretend that the block was a car, a train, an airplane, a sandwich, and a frog. We would also give him a stick and instruct him to pretend that it was a spoon for stirring, a pencil for writing, and so on. Peter picked up on this quickly and now has a very active and inventive 4-year-old imagination. He is especially skilled at the creative use of available materials in his pretend play.

Peter's drill sessions have typically consisted of about 60% of the time at the work table or otherwise engaged in a very structured and directed activity, and about 40% of the time away from the table in a less structured activity. During these less structured times and between drill sessions, we have devoted much time to play activities. In addition to puzzles, Play-Doh, blocks, Tinker toys, Duplo and Lego blocks, and other such construction toys, we have played a great deal with the doll house, baby dolls, and toy kitchen. Most recently, we have begun experimenting with role play and scripted play routines, both with some good initial success.

We have also arranged and closely supervised play dates for Peter—often with children a few years older than he—and this has worked out extremely well. Older children are typically much more persistent with him than other 3- and 4-year-old children. In addition to their innate ability to provide perfect models of play, they can be easily taught to cue, prompt, and reinforce appropriate play behaviors.

Peter also receives 7.5 hours per week of school-based instruction in an integrated 4-year-old preschool classroom through the public school system. He is accompanied to school three afternoons per week by one of the teachers from his home-based team. This person shadows him, cueing and prompting his interactions with classmates as necessary. In addition to providing good models of age-appropriate play, social behavior and language, the school environment provides Peter with many opportunities to work on the practical application and generalization of skills learned in his one-on-one instruction. We have been fortunate in that Peter has a natural tendency to generalize rather quickly and broadly the skills he has learned in drills.

Peter's one-on-one teacher is also responsible for identifying problem areas that require remediation, which are then addressed during his individual instruction. For example, Peter had difficulty participating in show and tell. We also noted that he made few comments to the other children regarding their show-and-tell items. We therefore practiced show and tell at home with Peter, and taught him to make appropriate comments to the other children when it was their turn for show and tell. In addition, we are always listening to the conversation topics and slang of the other children in his class, and we then work with Peter at home using the topics and slang that are most popular with his classmates.

Keith and I had decided at the outset to allow almost no downtime for Peter. Whenever he would engage in perseverative or stereotypic behavior, he was immediately redirected to a highly reinforcing alternative behavior, preferably one that was interactive. Even his independent play was very structured. It's not that we ceased to lead our lives; it's just that we included Peter in almost all of our activities. We arranged our work schedules so that he was usually with one or both of us. When we were not with him, my parents, sisters, and brothers-in-law usually took turns caring for him and keeping him productively engaged.

Trips to the grocery store became opportunities for teaching colors, shapes, one-to-one correspondence, vocabulary, and following directions. He accompanied us on most of our errands and almost all of our trips. While in the car seat, where he was a captive audience, we would review drill programs such as telling him short stories and asking him questions about them, or quizzing him with regard to categories and objects belonging to categories. If he watched a Disney movie, which he dearly loved, we would prompt him to request joint attention and point things out to us, or we would ask him unrelated questions to encourage him to switch his attention from one topic to another and back again. We read to him a great deal, usually choosing books with the simplest language we could find. These are just a few examples, but every day the world was, and continues to be, our classroom. Now, however, Peter can busy himself with all sorts of wonderful and constructive play activities, and we encourage him to do so.

In June of 1994, Sue's husband was offered a position out of state, and she moved away. We covered the summer with three doctoral students in the clinical psychology program at Clark University. They had worked with Peter on weekends during the winter and spring.

Peter's progress slowed considerably over the summer. I'm not quite sure I know why, but I believe it was a combination of things, most notably Sue's departure and too many homemade programs. The major accomplishment of the summer was successful potty training. Using a training program from the May Center, we managed to potty train Peter in a little under 2 weeks' time.

We had been going along as best we could, making use of whatever resources were available to us, when we had the good fortune to contact Stein Lund, through the Autism Consultation Program at Rutgers University. In late October, 2 weeks after Peter's fourth birthday, we had our first workshop with Stein. Since that first workshop, we have had regular follow-up workshops at 6-week intervals. Stein is an excellent behavior analyst, and under his direction Peter is flourishing again.

Prior to Stein's first visit, we hired a new teacher. Shortly after she began, we knew we had made a terrible mistake. She came to us directly out of a bachelor's program in special education. Although she had no related work experience, she refused to accept direction. I will not go into detail except to give a word of caution about termination clauses. This teacher had been hired on contract through the school system, and to avoid a law suit, the town has had to keep her employed elsewhere at her full salary as a rotating classroom aide and substitute teacher. This has been a tremendous waste of scarce resources. No matter how enthusiastic and/or competent someone may seem, write an iron-clad termination clause or go without a contract.

By November, I was once again looking for a new teacher. My youngest sister, Becky, for whom Peter has always had great affection, is an elementary school teacher. I had trained Becky to work with Peter, although because she is his aunt, I had thought it best that she work with him only to do extra hours or fill in when necessary. Becky began working with Peter to help cover therapy hours, and she did a fantastic job. Just her smile is reinforcing to Peter. He would wait by the window for her in the morning and was delighted to see her come. Also, he has continued to be no less delighted by her regular "Auntie visits." In fact, because at these times she usually brings her 15-month-old son, Sam, Peter is twice as happy to see her. For me, it is a total joy to see him with my nephew Sam. Peter is gentle and loving and is always trying to teach and show Sam new things. And Sam is equally smitten with Peter. Their relationship is proof positive of his striking progress.

As of February 1995, we have a mostly new team of teachers working with Peter. Peter's teachers, Niki, Chris, and Karrie, are all talented and dedicated people. Altogether, Peter's program consists of 36 hours per week with a one-on-one teacher/therapist, and 7.5 of those hours are spent in an integrated preschool as described previously.

We have taught Peter all kinds of things that most parents would never dream of having to teach their children. We have taught him things like how to request and engage in joint attention and to have a sense of humor. Something that is very exciting whenever it happens is to see Peter learn a new piece of language or a new skill from the environment without our hav-

ing to teach it to him. This happens more and more all the time. His vocabulary grows by leaps and bounds now, and we have long since stopped drilling vocabulary words specifically. I delight in the fact that he comes home from school, from the neighbors, from family outings, and from visits with family and friends with all sorts of new information.

Peter is now 4 years and 4 months old. It has been almost 18 months since we began an intensive behavioral home program. Academically, Peter is at least age appropriate. He knows his colors, shapes, letters, and numbers to 30. He has a solid grasp of one-to-one correspondence and can count out at least 10 items. He has begun to read and write using phonics. He sounds out simple words and phrases and comprehends what he has read. Peter knows the days of the week and the month in which each of the major holidays falls. He can build Lego and Tinkertoy structures from diagrams at least as well as any other child in his class. Peter can place in order a six-card sequence story and tell the story, although we are still working on the consistent use of third-person pronouns and verb tense. He can make up his own simple stories.

Peter's conversational skills are always improving. His language becomes more nuanced and abstract all the time. Lately he has begun asking all sorts of informational questions including a flood of "Why?" questions, which is a relatively new skill that he is generalizing, and an occasional "How?" question. In addition, as his contextual or relevant language has increased, his noncontextual language, which in his case usually refers to a movie or a story he has heard, has decreased.

Socially Peter has also made great strides. He flies to the window when he hears a car pull into the driveway and waits excitedly for visitors to knock on the door. When they walk in, he aways greets them with direct eye contact, a smile, and a big hello, adding the visitor's name if he happens to know it. When Keith comes home from work, he nearly comes out of his skin with delight as he cries out, "Daddy's home," and runs to greet his father with a big hug and kiss. I work one or two evenings a week, always returning home in time to read him his bedtime story. As I open the door I am mindful not to open it too fast because if he's been anywhere on the first floor, he is usually standing right in front of the door as I enter. He is constantly showing things to us: "Look what I made, Mommy!"

Peter has what I believe to be a very typical 4-year-old sense of humor. Yucky and absurd are funny. He can be very silly and enjoys it immensely when people laugh at his attempts to be funny. At these times his bright, laughing eyes are usually riveted expectantly on those of his audience, his one dimple especially deep in his cheek.

Recently I observed Peter in his classroom. After circle time, when it was his turn to choose the center in which he wanted to play, he chose to play with pattern blocks. His classmate Devon came to the table and the following conversation, initiated by Peter, ensued.

"What are you making, Devon?"

"I'm making an alligator."

"That's a nice alligator."

"Thanks."

"You're welcome."

"What are you making?"

"I'm making an elephant."

"That's a good elephant."

"Thank you."

Often, for no apparent reason, he stops what he is doing, skips happily over to Keith or me, gives a quick hug or kiss, says "I love you," and returns to whatever he was doing.

Two weeks ago my mother called to tell me that a dear family friend had passed away. I began to cry, and immediately Peter dropped what he was doing and ran to me with great concern. Keith picked him up, and he asked "Why is Mommy crying?" Keith explained that our friend Frank had died and that we would not be able to see him any more on our weekend visits to Cape Cod. "That's so sad," Peter said. "No more Frank in the garden." (Frank was always in his garden.) He got me a tissue, hugged and kissed me several times, and told me that he wanted me to be happy.

The following evening Peter was sitting on my bed waiting for his bedtime story and he asked "Where did Frank go when he died?" I told him that Frank went to heaven, and he was quiet for a minute or so. Then he asked "What do people do in heaven?" I groped around for a few moments and then told him that people rested in heaven. "Is Frank happy in heaven?" "Yes," I answered.

While these anecdotes are intended to illustrate Peter's progress, it is important to note that he continues to have some residual symptoms. Peter's conversational skills are limited, and he is still acquiring syntactic structures. As his sentences become longer and more complex, his speech can at times be disorganized, and he often neglects to orient his listener before embarking on a new topic. While much improved, his eye contact during conversation is still diminished. He continues to "tune out" from time to time and occasionally needs to be reminded to answer a question. I suspect that both of these symptoms are secondary to his difficulty attending to things that are not particularly interesting to him and his difficulty screening out extraneous stimuli. For example, at birthday parties (his own or others) where there is a lot going on and all new toys to look at and play with, it is quite a challenge to keep Peter focused. Although Peter's play is very imaginative, he occasionally gets stuck on perseverative reenactments of scenes from movies or story themes from books.

Peter's program, therefore, is still very much a work in progress, and I have been asked on many occasions whether or not I think it is going to work. My answer is always the same: "It has already worked." Peter is happy and he is charming. He is affectionate. He can communicate well. He has friends. He is the greatest joy in our lives. These gifts are too great to disregard. Of course we hope to eliminate any residual symptoms and that as we continue the program, these symptoms will indeed fade away. That would make Peter's life easier. Regardless, our goal as parents is to give Peter every opportunity to be the happiest and healthiest person that he can be. I am confident that we are doing just that.

About the Authors

Stephen R. Anderson received his doctorate in developmental and child psychology from the University of Kansas, at which he now holds an appointment as adjunct assistant professor. He also serves as a clinical assistant professor at Northeastern University, an adjunct professor at the University of Southern Maine, and member of the professional staff at the Developmental Evaluation Clinic at Children's Hospital in Boston. Dr. Anderson currently is the executive director of the Language Development Program near Buffalo, New York. He also serves as a reviewer for a number of professional journals and has published many journal articles and book chapters on the education and treatment of children with developmental disabilities. A licensed psychologist, Dr. Anderson has been a consultant to more than 40 public and private agencies within the United States and abroad.

Andrew S. Bondy received his doctorate from the University of North Carolina at Greensboro in 1975. He is currently the director of the Delaware Autistic Program. This statewide public school program serves more than 190 students and their families. Dr. Bondy has published and presented extensively about DAP, autism, and Applied Behavior Analysis. He is codeveloper of the Picture Exchange Communication System. He also has taught numerous university courses concerning autism and related developmental disabilities, Applied Behavior Analysis, and communication analysis.

Elizabeth Braxton earned a doctorate of education in counseling psychology from Boston University, and currently works with children and families as a behavioral consultant.

Kathleen Dyer received her doctorate from the University of California in 1985. She is currently the director of evaluation, research, and staff development at Bancroft, Inc., and adjunct professor at Temple University and Rowan College. She has prepared more than 30 publications and 110 presentations in areas including enhancing learning and communication for persons with developmental disabilities, staff training, and family intervention. She has been on the faculty at West Virginia University, University of Massachusetts, and Fitchburg State College, and has served on the editorial boards of several professional journals, including *Behavior Modification* and *Journal of the Association for Persons with Severe Handicaps*. She is currently director of the Delaware Valley Association for Behavior Analysis.

Judith E. Favell has served as the clinical director for Au Clair Programs in Florida and Delaware since 1987. Dr. Favell has been active in the fields of developmental disabilities and behavior disorders for more than 25 years. She received her doctorate in developmental and clinical psychology at the University of Kansas. She is a North Carolina licensed practicing psychologist and a Florida certified behavior analyst.

Previously, Dr. Favell served as senior research associate and director of psychology at Western Carolina Center in North Carolina. She has held adjunct faculty appointments at Appalachian State and Southern Illinois Universities. Dr. Favell has been president of the Association for Behavior Analysis and the Society for the Advancement of Behavior Analysis. She is a Fellow of the American Psychological Association and American Psychological Society. She is on several national professional boards, including the board of directors of the Accreditation Council on Services for People with Disabilities and the panel of professional advisors of the Autism Society of America. She has authored numerous books, monographs, and articles dealing with issues related to persons with autism.

During her professional career, Dr. Favell has consulted widely on the analysis and treatment of severe behavior problems. She has also been actively involved in the development and dissemination of standards of behavioral services and professional practice. She has extensive experience in developing and implementing professional and paraprofessional training programs.

Gina Green received a doctorate in psychology (analysis of behavior) from Utah State University following undergraduate and master's degree studies in psychology and educational psychology at Michigan State University. She taught in the behavior analysis and therapy graduate program at Southern Illinois University for 3 years. Presently Dr. Green is director of research at the New England Center for Autism in Southborough, Massachusetts; associate scientist in behavioral sciences at the E. K. Shriver Center for Mental Retardation in Waltham, Massachusetts; and clinical assistant professor in Northeastern University's master's program in Applied Behavior Analysis. She has authored numerous articles, chapters, and abstracts on various topics in the education and treatment of individuals with developmental disabilities and brain injuries, and the experimental analysis of behavior. She serves on the editorial boards of several professional journals in developmental disabilities and behavior analysis, and the Board of Trustees of the Cambridge Center for Behavioral Studies. Dr. Green lectures and consults widely on autism and related disorders, behavioral research, and effective interventions for people with disabilities.

Elizabeth Harrington has a bachelor of arts degree from Wellesley College. She worked at the U.S. Trust Company of New York for 9 years. Elizabeth retired from U.S. Trust as a vice president in the private banking division after the birth of her first child. She is particularly interested in issues concerning the siblings of autistic children.

Margaret Harris holds a bachelor of arts in business administration. She was employed as a bond trader for an investment management firm for 5 years, then as vice president of corporate finance for a finance company for 5 years. Since the arrival of her oldest son, she has stayed at home with her children.

Since her youngest son was diagnosed with autism, she has spent much of her time researching, setting up, and managing her own home program as well as encouraging and assisting other parents with setting up their programs.

Cyndy Kleinfield-Hayes has master's degrees in psychology and business administration. She is currently pursuing her doctorate in business administration. Her background is in sales and marketing. She is the director of prestige markets at a large confectionery manufacturing company.

Cyndy has three children, and her youngest is autistic. For the past 2 years she has been actively advocating for behavioral school options for young children with autism. She is the founder and director of Reaching Potentials, Inc., a nonprofit organization focused on providing information and services to individuals with autism and their families.

Ronald C. Huff is a graduate of Ohio State University, Columbus, Ohio. He taught and conducted research in experimental behavioral psychology at California State University in Los Angeles before beginning applied work at the Regional Center for Developmental Disabilities. He has worked in the field of developmental disabilities with specialization in autism for the past 20 years. Dr. Huff is currently employed by Alta California Regional Center in Sacramento, California, where he consults with parents, community service providers, and regional center staff to develop and implement intervention services and programs. Dr. Huff initiated collaboration with the parents of young autistic children and other professionals to create the Families for Early Autism Treatment (FEAT) project.

Susan C. Johnson is currently the director of support services at the Alpine Learning Group, Inc. Her responsibilities include the development, implementation, and evaluation of the supported inclusion model and family support services. She holds a master's degree in special education from Boston College and has been involved with the education of children and adolescents with autism since 1985.

Ivar Lovaas is a professor in the Department of Psychology at the University of California, Los Angeles, and the director of the Clinic for the Behavioral Treatment of Children in that department. Dr. Lovaas received his undergraduate degree in Norway and at Luther College in Decorah, Iowa, his master's and doctorate at the University of Washington in Seattle in 1958. He joined UCLA in 1961 and began his work in autism and pervasive developmental disabilities in 1963. His treatment research has been supported by grants from the National Institute of Mental Health and Office of Education on an almost continuous basis since 1962. He has received a Guggenheim Fellowship, Honorary Doctor of Letters, Edgar Doll Award from the American Psychological Association, the Research Award from the American Association on Mental Retardation, and other awards. He has published extensively and served on the editorial boards of numerous publications and on the professional advisory boards of a wide range of institutions. His most recent research centers on intensive, early, home-based intervention for children with autism and pervasive developmental disabilities. This treatment program aims to improve the intellectual, academic, social, and emotional behaviors of children who are developmentally delayed.

Stephen C. Luce, vice president of program operations at Bancroft, Inc., in Haddonfield, New Jersey, received his doctorate in developmental and child psychology from the University of Kansas after completing a master's in education at the University of Georgia. Dr. Luce spent much of his career as a teacher and psychologist working with children and adults who have autism and other developmental disabilities, as well as survivors of head trauma. He has been associated with organizational change in agencies serving individuals with developmental disabilities and brain trauma, and his research on staff training and the wide-scale dissemination of improved practices has received international recognition. Dr. Luce consults, writes, and lectures on these topics widely for private, public, and government agencies in the United States, Mexico, and throughout Europe. He holds adjunct faculty appointments at several universities and is an author and editor of several articles, chapters, and monographs for professional journals and books.

Catherine Maurice received a doctorate in French literature and criticism from New York University. She taught French as an instructor and as an adjunct assistant professor until her daughter was born. In late 1987, her daughter was diagnosed with autism, and in early 1990 her youngest son was diagnosed with autism. In 1993, her chronicle of her family's experience was published in *Let Me Hear Your Voice: A Family's Triumph Over Autism* (Knopf, 1993). This book has since been published in several languages throughout the world. Today, she devotes her free time to writing, to advocacy work for individuals with autism, and to serving on the board of Bancroft, Inc., a rehabilitative facility for people of all ages with neurological or developmental disabilities.

Kelly Ann McDonough is a private consultant providing in-home educational programs to children with autism and related developmental disabilities as well as parent training to their families. She serves also as a consultant to public schools in Connecticut, New Jersey, and New York. Previously she served as a special education teacher in an autism program directed by the University of North Carolina School of Medicine and for two private institutions in New York state. She received a master of arts degree in special education from Columbia University.

Linda S. Meyer is currently the executive director of the Alpine Learning Group, Inc. which is a private, nonprofit school serving children with autism in northern New Jersey. She is cofounder of the program. Linda holds a doctorate degree in education from Teachers College, Columbia University, and is currently attending Seton Hall University's Master of Public Administration Program, majoring in nonprofit management.

Barbara O'Malley Cannon received her master of education degree in human development from Northeastern University and her bachelor of arts degree in psychology from the College of the Holy Cross. Director of home-based services for the May Institute since 1988, she has extensive experience in working with children with autism and their families at both the direct service and administrative levels. In her current position, she supervises staff providing up to 30 hours of intensive home-based training, as well as parent education. Ms. Cannon has coauthored several articles and book chapters on the education and treatment of children with autism. She also is active in regional and national professional organizations and has presented many papers and workshops.

Robin Parker, M.S., C.C.C., is currently a clinical supervisor at the LaBonte Institute for Hearing, Language, and Speech at Nova Southeastern University, Fort Lauderdale, Florida. She supervises graduate students in speech-language pathology and teaches classes in diagnostics and language disorders. Ms. Parker serves as a consultant to the Baudhuin Oral School, which serves the preschool autistic population. She has lectured for the Autism Consortium of Broward County, Florida. Prior to coming to Florida, Ms. Parker was at Mount Sinai Hospital and in private practice in New York City specializing in assessment and treatment of children with language disorders secondary to autism. Ms. Parker received her bachelor of science and master of science degrees from Florida State University.

Margery Rappaport, M.A., CCC-SLP, is a speech-language pathologist in private practice in New York City. Having majored in theater at Boston University, she went on to receive a master's degree in speech-language pathology at Columbia University in 1971. After graduating, she worked at Morristown Memorial Hospital, the Morrisania City Hospital, The Montefiore-Morrisania Hospital Affiliation's Center for Child Development, and the

Head Start program before establishing a private practice. In addition, Ms. Rappaport lectures on language to teachers of young children at various independent schools in New York City.

Raymond G. Romanczyk is a professor of psychology at SUNY—Binghamton. He is a licensed clinical psychologist specializing in the problems of young children, and received his undergraduate degree from SUNY at Stony Brook and his doctorate from Rutgers University. Dr. Romanczyk is the founder and director of the Institute for Child Development, which provides clinical and educational services to children and families through the Children's Unit for Learning Disabilities and the Children's Unit for Treatment and Evaluation. The units are part of the continuum of services in the southern tier of New York and have served more than 1,000 families. Dr. Romanczyk has been involved in advocacy, program development, the judicial and legislative process as expert witness, and direct services to children and families for more than 25 years. He is also former director of clinical training and served two terms as chairperson of the Department of Psychology at SUNY—Binghamton. In addition, Dr. Romanczyk is an adjunct professor of psychiatry of the SUNY Health Sciences Center of Syracuse.

He is a Fellow of the American Psychological Association and his extensive professional activities include service as member and officer in numerous professional organizations, serving on the board of directors and board of advisors of several nationally recognized institutes and treatment facilities, consulting for numerous education and treatment programs, reviewing grants for federal agencies, and serving on ethics and quality assurance boards for several organizations. He also serves on editorial boards and as reviewer for numerous professional journals. His work has been published in many professional journals and books, and he has written extensively in the fields of autism and early childhood behavior. Dr. Romanczyk has presented several hundred addresses at regional, national, and international professional conferences regarding his applied and research work at the institute, and has received numerous awards for his clinical and research accomplishments.

Research and clinical interests focus upon developmental, learning, and emotional disorders, with particular emphasis on autism. Specific research areas are functional analysis of maladaptive behavior and the role of arousal; the role of eye contact, emotion recognition, and play in social development; escape and avoidance behavior; impulsivity; stimulus overselectivity; clinical decision-making; and computer-assisted program management.

Jack Scott is an assistant professor in the Department of Exceptional Student Education at Florida Atlantic University. He has a doctorate in special education from the University of Florida with a program focused on behavioral analysis, individualized instruction, and emotional-behavioral disorders. He is a Florida certified behavior analyst (CBA) and serves as a member of the State of Florida HRS Peer Review Committee for Behavioral Services. He teaches courses in behavior management, emotional disorders, and autism and is active in assisting parents in creating home-based programs for their young children with autism. He is codirector of a U.S. Department of Education grant for personnel preparation in autism. His research interests have focused on the application of systematic instructional procedures to mildly handicapped students, data-based instruction, and the status of autism programs at the regional and state level. He is writing an introductory textbook on autism for the Singular Publishing Group.

Gerald L. Shook is director of program development for Au Clair in Tallahassee, Florida. Dr. Shook has more than 25 years of experience in the field of developmental disabilities. He holds a doctorate in psychology from Western Michigan University and is a Florida certified behavior analyst.

Prior to joining Au Clair, Dr. Shook held faculty appointments at the State University of New York College at Buffalo and the Georgetown University Medical School. He also served as senior behavior analyst for the Developmental Services Headquarters Office of the Florida Department of Health and Rehabilitative Services, where he developed and coordinated the state-wide behavioral programming services system.

Dr. Shook is on the board of directors of the Accreditation Council on Services for People with Disabilities and the Society for the Advancement of Behavior Analysis, and is on the executive council of the Association for Behavior Analysis. He does extensive consultation nationally on developmental disabilities issues, credentialing of behavior analysts, and the development of state-wide service systems. Dr. Shook is a member of the Louisiana, Florida, and Alabama Behavior Analysis Peer Review Committees. He holds an adjunct appointment in psychology at Florida State University.

Dr. Shook has published widely on a number of subjects related to the developmental disabilities field, including recent articles in the journals *Mental Retardation* and *Behavior Analyst,* and has contributed to several books.

Tristram Smith has conducted research and treatment with children with autism and other developmental disabilities since 1983. His research has focused on two areas: (a) evaluating outcomes achieved by treatment programs for children with developmental disabilities and (b) applying findings from experimental psychology to difficult clinical problems, such as improving language instruction and promoting the transfer of skills from treatment settings to everyday settings. He did his undergraduate work at Yale University and attended graduate school at the University of California, Los Angeles, where he received his doctorate in clinical psychology in 1990. He stayed for an additional 3 years in order to pursue postdoctoral studies and then took a position as a visiting assistant professor of psychology at Drake University in Des Moines, Iowa. In the fall of 1995 he became an assistant professor of psychology at Washington State University in Pullman, Washington, where he directs a clinic that provides behavioral treatment for children with developmental disabilities. He also serves as the research director for a multisite study evaluating behavioral treatment for preschool-age children with autism.

Marie Taras received her doctorate in clinical psychology from Louisiana State University, specializing in developmental disabilities. Now a licensed psychologist in Massachusetts, Dr. Taras completed her clinical internship in Applied Behavior Analysis, developmental disabilities, and behavioral pediatrics at the Kennedy Institute and Johns Hopkins School of Medicine in Baltimore, Maryland. Dr. Taras currently directs the May Institute's Community Outreach Program, providing consulting and home-based services in Massachusetts and neighboring New England states. She previously served as director of the Autism Support Center, also a program of the May Institute. Dr. Taras has coauthored a half dozen articles and book chapters relevant to teaching self-help and social skills to individuals with developmental disabilities, as well as strategies for managing challenging behaviors. She is active in several professional organizations and regularly presents papers and workshops at regional and national conferences.

Bridget Ann Taylor is cofounder and educational programming director of the Alpine Learning Group, Inc. Bridget holds a master's degree in special education from Teachers College, Columbia University, and is currently completing the requirements for her doctorate in school psychology from the Graduate School of Applied and Professional Psychology, at Rutgers, the State University of New Jersey. She has coauthored several articles related to autism.

Mark D. Williamson graduated in 1981 from the University of Virginia (with high distinction) and in 1984 from the University of Virginia School of Law. Mark is a partner in the Norfolk, Virginia, office of McGuire, Woods, Battle & Boothe, LLP, practicing primarily in the areas of real estate, finance, and commercial law. Mark's second son Brian, age 4, has participated in a behavioral program since November 1993 under the direction of Bancroft, Inc., of Haddonfield Heights, New Jersey. Mr. Williamson has successfully negotiated a settlement providing funding for a behavioral program within his school district, and he regularly counsels other parents seeking funding support.

Index